PSYCHOLOGIES OF 1930

Edited by
CARL MURCHISON

ARNO PRESS
A New York Times Company
New York ★ 1973

Reprint Edition 1973 by Arno Press Inc.

Reprinted from a copy in
The University of Illinois Library

Classics in Psychology
ISBN for complete set: 0-405-05130-1
See last pages of this volume for titles.

Manufactured in the United States of America

———————◆———————

Library of Congress Cataloging in Publication Data

Main entry under title:

Psychologies of 1930.

    (Classics in psychology)
    Reprint of the 1930 ed. published by Clark University Press, Worcester, Mass., in series The International university series in psychology.
    Includes bibliographical references.
    1. Psychology—Addresses, essays, lectures.
I. Murchison, Carl Allanmore, 1887-   ed.
II. Series. [DNLM: BF21 P973 1930F]
BF149.P83 1973   150'.8   73-2980
ISBN 0-405-05152-2

PSYCHOLOGIES OF 1930

THE INTERNATIONAL UNIVERSITY SERIES IN PSYCHOLOGY

PSYCHOLOGIES OF 1930

by

ALFRED ADLER

MADISON BENTLEY

EDWIN G. BORING

G. S. BRETT

HARVEY CARR

JOHN DEWEY

KNIGHT DUNLAP

J. C. FLUGEL

WALTER S. HUNTER

PIERRE JANET

TRUMAN L. KELLEY

K. KOFFKA

WOLFGANG KÖHLER

K. N. KORNILOV

WILLIAM MCDOUGALL

JOHN PAUL NAFE

I. P. PAVLOV

FRIEDRICH SANDER

A. L. SCHNIERMANN

C. SPEARMAN

LEONARD T. TROLAND

MARGARET F. WASHBURN

ALBERT P. WEISS

ROBERT S. WOODWORTH

Edited by
CARL MURCHISON

WORCESTER, MASSACHUSETTS
CLARK UNIVERSITY PRESS
LONDON: HUMPHREY MILFORD: OXFORD UNIVERSITY PRESS
1930

PRINTED IN THE UNITED STATES OF AMERICA

PREFACE

In planning *Psychologies of 1930* we have tried to profit from all the serious criticisms that came to *Psychologies of 1925*. Associationism, Act Psychology, and Functionalism have been included in their historical setting, but the reader should not presume that these three schools are discussed by partisans in the same way as are the other schools. Professors Brett and Carr have acted largely as historians only in bringing these three schools to the convenient attention of students of this book, though Professor Carr himself is certainly in the direct line of descent from Functionalism.

The former category of "Purposive Psychology" is here presented under the rubric "Hormic Psychology" and is expounded by the leading exponent of both rubrics.

The large group of students who have come from Titchener's laboratory are represented by four different points of view. It may be made self-evident whether or not it is appropriate to apply the term "Structuralism" to the doctrines of this group.

The present-day theories of the Leipzig laboratory are added to the Berlin group under the more general title of "Configurational Psychologies," it being definitely understood that this classification is applied by the Editor only.

The three leading Russian schools of psychology are here presented in comparable, theoretical form for the first time in the English language.

The Factor School of Psychology and three Analytical Psychologies appear also as distinct additions to the program of *Psychologies of 1925*. A separate section on some non-sectarian fundamental problems has also been added.

As I can recall the various types of helpful criticisms and comments concerning *Psychologies of 1925* that have come my way during the past five years, I do not believe I have failed to observe a single one. If I have failed to heed any of them, it has been entirely my fault and I hope the suggestions will be repeated.

Now that psychology is rapidly coming of age, it is no longer a symbol of maturity for a psychologist to neglect the theoretical foundations of his science. Those who have suggested that it is futile to examine theoretically the hypotheses on which all experimental work is based have not been obeyed during the preparation of this volume, but are being quietly left to the tender mercies of time.

I acknowledge with gratitude the assistance of Dr. Luberta M. Harden, who has supervised the preparation of the manuscripts for the printer and has made the indices.

Carl Murchison

Clark University
Worcester, Massachusetts
March 25, 1930

TABLE OF CONTENTS

PHOTOGRAPHS OF CONTRIBUTORS

ALFRED ADLER

MADISON BENTLEY

EDWIN G. BORING

G. S. BRETT

HARVEY CARR

JOHN DEWEY

KNIGHT DUNLAP

J. C. FLUGEL

Photograph by Bachrach

WALTER S. HUNTER

PIERRE JANET

TRUMAN L. KELLEY

K. KOFFKA

WOLFGANG KÖHLER

K. N. KORNILOV

WILLIAM McDOUGALL

JOHN PAUL NAFE

I. P. PAVLOV   FRIEDRICH SANDER

ALEXANDER L. SCHNIERMANN   C. SPEARMAN

LEONARD T. TROLAND

MARGARET FLOY WASHBURN

Photograph by Bachrach

ALBERT P. WEISS

ROBERT S. WOODWORTH

PART I
THE HORMIC PSYCHOLOGY

CHAPTER 1

THE HORMIC PSYCHOLOGY

WILLIAM MCDOUGALL

Duke University

In the volume *Psychologies of 1925* I took the field as an exponent of *purposive psychology*. Anticipating a little the course of history, I shall here assume that the purposive nature of human action is no longer in dispute, and in this article shall endeavor to define and to justify that special form of purposive psychology which is now pretty widely known as *hormic psychology*. But first a few words in justification of this assumption.

Fifteen years ago American psychologists displayed almost without exception a complete blindness to the most peculiar, characteristic, and important feature of human and animal activity, namely, its goal-seeking. All bodily actions and all phases of experience were mechanical reactions to stimuli, and all learning was the modification of such reactions by the addition of one reaction to another according to the mechanical principles of association. The laws of learning were the laws of frequency, of recency, and of effect; and, though the law of effect as formulated by Thorndike may have suggested to some few minds that the mechanical principles involved were not so clear as might be wished, the laws of frequency and recency could give rise to no such misgivings. The law of effect, with its uncomfortable suggestion of an effect that somehow causes its cause, was pretty generally regarded as something to be got rid of by the substitution of some less ambiguous and more clearly mechanical formula.

Now, happily, all this is changed; the animal psychologists have begun to realize that any description of animal behavior which ignores its goal-seeking nature is futile, any "explanation" which leaves it out of account, factitious, and any experimentation which ignores motivation, grossly misleading; they are busy with the study of "drives," "sets," and "incentives." It is true that their recognition of goal-seeking is generally partial and grudging; they do not explicitly recognize that a "set" is a set toward an end, that a "drive" is an active striving toward a goal, that an "incentive" is something that provokes such active striving. The terms "striving" and "conation" are still foreign to their vocabularies.

Much the same state of affairs prevails in current American writings on human psychology. Its problems are no longer discussed, experiments are no longer made with total and bland disregard for the purposive nature of human activity. The terms "set," "drive," and "incentive," having been found indispensable in animal psychology, are allowed to appear in discussions of human problems, in spite of their anthropomorphic implica-

[3]

tions; "prepotent reflexes," "motives," "drives," "preponderant propensities," "impulses toward ends," "fundamental urges," and even "purposes" now figure in the texts. In the final chapter on personality of a thoroughly mechanical text (1), in which the word "purpose" has been conspicuous by its absence, a rôle of first importance is assigned to "dominant purposes." Motivation, after being almost ignored, has become a problem of central interest. Yet, as was said above, we are in a transition period; and all this recognition of the purposive nature of human activity is partial and grudging. The author (Dr. H. A. Carr), who tells us on one page that "Man attempts to transform his environment to suit his own purposes," nowhere tells us what he means by the word "purposes" and is careful to tell us on a later page that "We must avoid the naïve assumption that the ulterior consequences of an act either motivate that act or serve as its objective." Almost without exception the authors who make any recognition of the goal-seeking or purposive nature of human and animal activities fall into one of the three following classes: (a) they imply that, if only we knew a little more about the nervous system, we should be able to explain such activities mechanically; or (b) they explicitly make this assertion; (c) more rarely, they proceed to attempt some such explanation.

Partial, half-hearted, reluctant as is still the recognition of purposive activity, it may, I think, fairly be said that only the crude behaviorists now ignore it completely; that, with that exception, American psychology has become purposive, in the sense that it no longer ignores or denies the goal-seeking nature of human and animal action, but accepts it as a problem to be faced.

It would, then, be otiose in this year of grace to defend or advocate purposive psychology in the vague sense of all psychology that recognizes purposiveness, takes account of foresight and of urges, impulses, cravings, desires, as motives of action.

My task is the more difficult one of justifying the far more radically purposive psychology denoted by the adjective "hormic," a psychology which claims to be autonomous; which refuses to be bound to and limited by the principles current in the physical sciences; which asserts that active striving towards a goal is a fundamental category of psychology, and is a process of a type that cannot be mechanistically explained or resolved into mechanistic sequences; which leaves it to the future development of the sciences to decide whether the physical sciences shall continue to be mechanistic or shall find it necessary to adopt hormic interpretations of physical events, and whether we are to have ultimately one science of nature, or two, the mechanistic and the teleological. For hormic psychology is not afraid to use teleological description and explantion. Rather, it insists that those of our activities which we can at all adequately describe are unmistakably and undeniably teleological, are activities which we undertake in the pursuit of some goal, for the sake of some result which we foresee and desire to achieve. And it holds that such activities are the true type of all mental activities and of all truly vital activities, and that, when we

seek to interpret more obscure instances of human activity and when we
observe on the part of animals actions that clearly are goal-seeking, we are
well justified in regarding them as of the same order as our own explicitly
teleological or purposive actions.

While the academic psychologies of the recent past have sought to explain
the higher types of activity from below upward, taking simple physical
and chemical events as their starting-point, hormic psychology begins by
accepting the higher activities, those which are clearly and explicitly purposive and into the nature of which we have the most insight, and seeks to
extend such insight downwards to the simpler but more obscure types of
action.

TELEOLOGY, INTRINSIC AND EXTRINSIC

I introduce the term 'teleological' early in the exposition because I
do not wish to seem to smuggle it in at a later stage after betraying the
innocent reader into acceptance of a position which commits him unwittingly to teleology. Modern science has shown an aversion to all teleology;
one might almost say that it has a 'complex' on that subject. The origin
and development of this unreasoning and unreasonable aversion is intelligible enough. It developed in the course of the conflict of science with
religion. The favorite explanation of all obscure natural processes offered
by the theologians was that they expressed and were governed by the purpose of the Creator, who had designed and constructed the various objects
of the natural world in order that, as parts of one grand system, they might
exhibit and fulfil His purposes. Whether the theologians conceived natural objects as having been once and for all designed and created in such a
way that natural events would run their courses, fulfilling God's purpose
without further intervention on His part, or believed that the finger of
God still actively directs the course of natural events, these teleological
explanations were, in either case, utterly repugnant to the spirit of modern
science; for science had found it possible to explain many events as the
effects of natural causes, and it had become the accepted program of science
to extend such explanations as widely as possible.

It has become usual to speak of the explanations offered by science as
naturalistic, and to oppose them to the supernatural explanations of the
theologians. Now, to explain an event is to assign the causes of it, the
play of antecedent events of which the event in question is the consequence.
Early scientists inclined to interpret many events after the model of our
own experience of causation. We foresee a particular event as a possibility;
we desire to see this possibility realized; we take action in accordance with
our desire, and we seem to guide the course of events in such a way that
the foreseen and desired event results. To explain an event as caused
in this way was to invoke teleological causation, not the extrinsic supernatural teleology of the theologians, but a natural teleological causation, a causal
activity thoroughly familiar to each man through his own repeated experiences of successful action for the attainment of desired goals. Primitive
man applied explanation of this type to many natural events, regarding an-

thropomorphically many natural objects which modern science has taught us to regard as utterly devoid of any such affinity with ourselves. The early students of physical nature did not entirely discard explanations of this type. They regarded natural events more analytically than primitive men had done; but they still inclined to regard the elements into which they analyzed the given natural objects as acting teleologically, as moved by desire, and as striving to achieve the effects they naturally desired. The Newtonian mechanics put an end to explanation of this type in the physical sciences. For it appeared that very many physical events, more especially various astronomical events, could be adequately explained in terms of mass, motion, momentum, attraction, and repulsion, all exactly measurable; and many such events became strictly predictable from such principles of causation. From such causal explanations all reference to foresight of something, to desire for something, to striving for that something, in fact all reference to the future course of events, was wholly excluded. The explanation of any event was given in terms only of other events antecedent to it; all reference to possible or probable consequences proved to be unnecessary; explanation was purged of all taint of teleology. Explanation of this type was so successful in the physical sciences that, although the hope of strictly mechanical explanation of all events of the inanimate world is now seen to have been illusory, such ateleological explanation has become established as the type and model to which naturalistic explanation should conform. Such ateleological explanation is what is meant by mechanistic explanation in the broad sense.[1] The mechanistic or ateleological explanations of science were dubbed naturalistic and were accepted in place of the supernatural teleological explanations of theology. So far all was well; the procedure was entirely justified. But at this point an unfortunate confusion of thought became very general. The confusion consisted in falling victim to the compelling force of words and in regarding as supernatural, not only the external teleological causation of the theologians, but also the internal teleological causation or causal activity of men.

This, I say, was an unfortunate and unwarranted confusion; and it still pervades the thinking of most men of science when they approach the problems of psychology and biology. Any proposal to take seriously the teleological causation which seems to be revealed in human activities, to regard such causation as real and effective, they repudiate as trafficking in supernatural causes; for, in learning to repudiate the external supernatural teleology of theology, they have come to regard as also supernatural the internal teleological causation of the human organism. Yet there is no good ground for so regarding it. To desire, to strive, and to attain our goal is as natural as falling off a log, and with such teleological causa-

---

[1] As I have shown in my *Modern Materialism and Emergent Evolution* (21), there is no other way of defining the meaning of the word "mechanistic," no other way than this negative way which defines it by excluding all trace of teleology, all reference to the future; mechanistic means ateleological.

tion we are entirely familiar; we have more intimate understanding of it than of mechanistic causation.

During the nineteenth century, under the prevalence of the faith that strictly mechanical or Newtonian causation was adequate to the explanation of all events of the inanimate world, it was natural enough to regard such causation as the one and only type of naturalistic causation, and, therefore, to class intrinsic teleological causation with the extrinsic teleological causation of the theologians, as supernatural. But now, when it has become clear that that faith or hope was illusory and that we have no insight into the nature of mechanistic causation, this ground for repudiating internal teleological causation has been taken away—and none remains.

It is probable that the remaining prejudice against it is more than a hang-over from the days of belief in strictly mechanical or Newtonian causation. To accept the teleological causation of human agents is to believe in the causal efficacy of psychical events; and it seems to be widely felt that to do this is necessarily to commit one's self to psychophysical dualism or animism, and thus to offend against the common preference for a monistic world-view and against the theory of continuity of evolution of the organic from the inorganic. But this is an error which a little clear thinking should quickly dispel. Two monistic theories, both implying continuity of evolution, are now enjoying considerable vogue among both philosophers and men of science, namely, psychic monism and the emergent theory.

Psychic monism, as expounded by Paulsen, Morton Prince, C. A. Strong, Durant Drake, and L. T. Troland, has no ground for doubting the causal efficacy of psychic events; for its teaching is that all events are psychic. Morton Prince, with his ever youthful mind, saw this clearly enough and hence did not hesitate to figure as an exponent of purposive psychology in the volume *Psychologies of 1925* (27). Dr. Troland, curiously enough, seems to cast aside in the most gratuitous fashion the opportunity afforded by his espousal of psychic monism to lift psychology above the sterile plane of mechanistic explanation.

The emergent theory[2] is equally compatible with, and in fact asserts, the causal efficacy of psychic events and the continuity of organic with inorganic evolution; and it is a monistic theory. Hence it fulfils all the requirements of the psychologist who cannot blind himself to the reality of goal-seeking behavior and purposive activity, and yet holds fast to monism and continuity of evolution. And it is a theory now in excellent standing, sponsored by such outstanding thinkers as S. Alexander, L. T. Hobhouse, Lloyd Morgan, H. S. Jennings, R. B. Perry, W. M. Wheeler.

With these alternatives open to the choice of the psychologist, he has no valid ground for denying the causal efficacy of psychic activity in the natural world, no ground for continuing to regard internal teleological

---

[2] Cf. Lloyd Morgan's two volumes of Gifford Lectures, *Emergent Evolution* (24) and *Life, Mind and Spirit* (25), also my *Modern Materialism and Emergent Evolution* (21) for exposition of the emergent theory.

causation as supernatural, and therefore no ground for blinding himself to the purposive nature of human activity. One suspects that the prevalent reluctance to recognize fully and freely the purposive nature of human activity and the goal-seeking nature of animal activities is mainly due to the fact that most of us were brought up to believe in epiphenomenalism of psychophysical parallelism, those equally illogical, profoundly unsatisfactory, and now discredited makeshifts of a generation dominated by mechanical materialism and imbued with an ill-founded prejudice in favor of regarding all causation as mechanistic. Or perhaps the common case is simpler: throughout a considerable period the physical sciences have worked very successfully in terms of purely mechanistic or ateleological causation; therefore psychology and all the biological sciences must do likewise. To this contention the answer is obvious: this policy is running psychology and biology in general into a blind alley. Weismannism, the only purely mechanistic theory of biological evolution, has broken down; and vague theories of creative evolution or orthogenesis are the order of the day. There is renewed interest in the possibility of Lamarckian transmission. Physiologists are breaking away from the mechanistic tradition. Dr. K. S. Lashley, in his presidential address to the American Psychological Association, speaking in the light of his own very extensive researches, has thrown all the prevailing views on cerebral action back into the melting-pot without offering a substitute. Three at least of the leaders of biology in America, Lillie, Herrick, and Jennings, are calling aloud for recognition of the causal efficacy in nature of psychical activities.[3] In Great Britain, Drs. J. S. Haldane and E. S. Russell are building up the psychobiological school, which utterly denies the adequacy of mechanistic principles of explantion in biology. (The former bluntly denounces as "claptrap" the claim, so often repeated "parrot-like," that physiology is revealing the mechanism of life.) The German thinkers interested in the various human sciences, impatient of the failure of the "strictly scientific"

---

[3]Dr. R. S. Lillie (11) writes: "What we agree to call the spiritual appears at times to act directly as a transformer of the physical, as in artistic or other creation. Such experiences cannot be accounted for on physical grounds, for one reason because it is in the very nature of physical abstraction to rule out as irrelevant all factors of a volitional or other 'psychic' kind. To trace the course of the physiological processes accompanying an act of intellectual creation would undoubtedly give us curious information, of a kind, but would throw little if any light on the essential nature of the reality underlying."

Dr. C. J. Herrick (5) writes: "No abyss of ignorance of what consciousness really is, no futilities of introspective analysis, no dialectic, destroy the simple datum that I have conscious experience and that this experience is a controlling factor in my behavior. . . . The prevision of possible future consequences of action is a real causative factor in determining which course of action will actually be chosen." Cf. also (6).

H. S. Jennings is no less emphatic. He writes (9) of "that monstrous absurdity that has so long been a reproach to biological science; the doctrine that ideas, ideals, purposes have no effect on behavior. The mental determines what happens as does any other determiner. . . . The desires and aspirations of humanity are determiners in the operation of the universe on the same footing with physical determiners."

psychology taught in the universities to furnish any psychological basis for those sciences, are turning away to construct a psychology of the kind they need, a *geisteswissenschaftliche Psychologie,* which frankly throws aside the mechanistic principles and recognizes the teleological nature of human activity. The Gestalt school of psychology protests against mechanistic interpretations.

Clearly the dominance of biology by the mechanistic ideal of the physical sciences is passing; while physical science itself is giving up strict determinism and exact predictability. Where, then, is to be found any justification for the old-fashioned prejudice against psychical causation, which, if admitted at all, can be only teleological causation? Why should not we psychologists, whose business is with the psychical, boldly claim that here is the indeterminate and creative element in nature, rather than leave it to physicists and physiologists to show the way and force us to recognize the fact? To admit the efficacy of psychical activity in nature is not, as so many seem to imagine, to deny causation.[4] Science must hold fast to causation, if

---

[4]E.g., Professor R. S. Woodworth (33) writes: "Some authors, as especially McDougall, appear to teach that any thorough-going causal interpretation of human behavior and experience implies shutting one's eyes to the facts of purpose and striving. There is certainly some confusion here. There can be no contradiction between the purposiveness of a sequence of action and its being a causal sequence. A purpose is certainly a cause: if it had no effect, it would be without significance." There is confusion here; but I suggest it is Woodworth's thinking, rather than mine, that is confused. Both in this essay and in his *Psychology* (34), Woodworth professes to give full recognition to "purpose" and even says, as in the passage cited, that a purpose is a cause. To me it seems very misleading to speak either of "a purpose" or of "a cause." And the sentence, "a purpose is a cause," is ambiguous and confused; it leaves the reader in doubt of the author's meaning. We go in search of passages which will tell what the author means by "a purpose." We find in the same essay that "Your purpose would be futile if it had no effects, it would be incredible if it had no causes. It is a link in a causal chain, but it is as fine a purpose for all that." Now, in the same essay, Woodworth characteristically refuses to face the question of what he calls "the philosophy of purpose and striving and their place in the world-process as a whole," as also the question of the validity of the mechanistic conception of life. He will not commit himself for or against the mechanistic conception. He seeks to give the impression that his psychology takes full account of the purposive striving of men and animals. He would like to run with the hare and hunt with the hounds; he desires both to eat his cake and to have it. He is too clear-sighted to ignore the facts of goal-seeking; but his thinking is too timid to allow him to see and to say that here is a parting of the ways, a crucial question to which one of two answers is right and the other wrong, the question, namely—Is human mental activity mechanistic or is it teleological? However these two terms be defined (and as I have said, the only satisfactory way of defining "mechanistic process" is the negative one of defining it as the ateleological), they are by common consent mutually exclusive: if a process is mechanistic, it is not teleological; and if it is teleological, it is not mechanistic. But in spite of Woodworth's careful non-committal ambiguity, and in spite of his air of giving full recognition to the causal efficacy of purposive striving, it seems that he remains mechanistic; that he means by cause and causation always and only the mechanistic type, and means to repudiate all teleological causation. This comes to light in one passage: he writes of a "need" as "the controlling factor in the activity"; and immediately adds: "Whether the concept of 'need' is a useful dynamic concept is perhaps open to doubt; it smacks considerably of the sort of teleology that we

not to strict determination.   Psychical events, though teleological, have
their conditions and their causal antecedents; but in them the foreseeing
activity is a real factor which makes, not the future event foreseen, but
the foreseeing of it as possible and as desirable or repugnant a cooperating
factor in the total configuration of the present moment.   To put it in
other words, valuation is a psychical function which is rooted in the past
history of the individual and of the race; and it is an activity that makes a
difference; applied to the foreseen possibility, it inclines our activity this
way or that, to seek or accept, avoid or reject.

Surely, a future age, looking back upon the vagaries of our own, will
record with astonishment the fact that in this early stage of the development of the biological sciences, men of science, while perceiving clearly that
the power of foreseeing, of anticipating the future course of events, has
developed steadily in the race until in man it has become his most striking
characteristic, yet persistently deny that this wonderful capacity is of any
service in our struggle for existence.[5]

---

do well to leave aside." Even here he suggests vaguely that there is teleology
of some sort that he would not leave aside; but that is merely one more expression of his inveterate tendency to sit on the fence.   When we discover finally
his definition of "a purpose," it confirms our suspicion that, in spite of all his
well-sounding camouflage, Woodworth is on the side of the mechanists: "Conscious purpose is an adjustment still in the making or just being tuned up, and
specially an adjustment that is broad and still precise. . . . Purpose is the activity
itself, initiated but not completed. It is an activity in progress." Again: "A
purpose is a set for a certain activity with foresight of the result of that activity."
But does the foresight play any part, or is it merely an accompaniment? Woodworth refuses to commit himself. "How can a conscious purpose have any effect
on the brain and muscles anyway? Thus one of the old puzzles of philosophy is
injected into our peaceful psychological study, muddling our heads and threatening
to wreck our intellectual honesty. We cannot deal with this metaphysical question here" (34). Woodworth would like to explain human action teleologically;
but he sees that to do so would be to admit the causal efficacy of psychical activity,
and, as he cannot bring himself to take that step, his intellectual "honesty" compels him to put the responsibility on the metaphysicians until such time as the
push from his scientific colleagues of the other sciences shall leave him and his
fellow-psychologists no option in the matter.

[5]Many eminent physicists have insisted on the control and direction of energy
transformations by human agency as something that will not fit with the physicists'
scheme of things. Why, then, should psychologists fear to follow them? I cite
a very recent instance. Commenting on Eddington's discussion of the law of
entropy as universally valid in the physical realm, Sir O. Lodge (12) writes:
"This has long been known, but Eddington illustrates it very luminously by what
he calls the operation of 'shuffling.' Given an orderly pack of cards, it may be
hopelessly disorganized by shuffling, and no amount of shuffling will bring it
back into order. [It is pointless to say, as does a recent reviewer of Eddington's
book, that, if you continue to shuffle for an infinite time, the order will be restored; for the order may be restored by human activity many times in a brief
period.] Many of the processes in nature thus result in greater disorganization;
and, according to Eddington, the irreversible disorganization measures the entropy. Entropy is disorganization. It is easy to break an orderly arrangement
down, but not so easy to build it up. Yet it can be built up. Not by random
and unintelligent processes truly: a mob of monkeys playing on a million type-
writers will not compose a volume of poems. The only way to restore order is

Two Forms of Teleological or Purposive Psychology, the Hedonistic and the Hormic

The psychologist who can summon enough courage to follow the lead of physicists and biologists and to accept the causal efficacy of psychical activity, of foresight and desire, is confronted with a choice between two theories of the ground of all desire, of all striving or conation, the hedonistic and the hormic.

Psychological hedonism enjoyed a great vogue in the nineteeth century and is not yet dead; for it embodies some truth. Not every theory of action that assigns a rôle to pleasure and pain is teleological. Two prominent American psychologists, Drs. E. L. Thorndike and L. T. Troland, have elaborated a theory which remains strictly mechanistic, though it assigns a rôle to pleasure and pain. In this theory, pleasure accompanying any form of activity "stamps in" that activity, affects the brain structures in such a way that similar activity is the more likely to recur under similar conditions; and pain has the opposite effect. It is clear that there is nothing teleological in this form of hedonic theory; it is a hedonism of the past. It is a striking evidence of the strength of the prejudice against teleological causation, that Dr. Troland, who believes that all things and events are in reality psychical, should thus choose to elaborate his psychical theory in terms of purely mechanistic causation.[6]

A second form of hedonism may be called "hedonism of the present." It asserts that all action is to be regarded as prompted by the pleasure or the pain of the moment of experience. Its position in relation to mechanism and teleology is ambiguous. It can be held and stated in a mechanistic form: the feeling accompanying present process is a factor of causal efficacy in the total configuration, one that prolongs and modifies the total process. It can be stated in a teleological form: the pleasure of the moment prompts efforts to prolong the pleasurable activity and secure more pleasure; the pain of the present moment prompts an effort to get rid of the pain and secure ease. In this second form the rôle assigned to foresight renders the formulation teleological.

---

to apply the activity of mind. . . . Shuffling, as Eddington luminously says, is 'an absent-minded operation'. . . . Mind is essential to organization, and organization or reorganization is a *natural result of mental activity consciously directed to a present end.*"

[6]Cf. (31). Dr. C. J. Herrick (7) follows the same strange procedure. He stoutly asserts the causal efficacy of psychical events, especially of ideals, but just as decidedly proclaims the all-sufficiency of mechanistic principles in biology and psychology. Like Woodworth (cf. footnote 4), he seems to believe that to admit the teleological causation involved in the working of an ideal would be to give up causation. His unexamined postulate is that the natural is the mechanistic, and any non-mechanistic or teleological causation is *ipso facto* non-natural or supernatural. He accepts emergent evolution and asserts that the human brain is a creative agent; yet asserts also that it works purely mechanistically. He does not see that these two assertions are in flat contradiction, that a strictly mechanistic event cannot be creative of novelties; that to assert it to be so is to make a self-contradictory statement, since "mechanistic" excludes "creation of novelty" in its definition.

This second variety of hedonism embodies truth. But it is false if put forward as a general theory of all action. We do seek to prolong pleasant activities and to get rid of pain. But it is not true that all, or indeed any large proportion, of our activities can be explained in this way. Our seeking of a goal, our pursuit of an end, is an activity that commonly incurs pleasure or pain; but these are incidental consequences. Our striving after food, or a mate, or power, knowledge, revenge, or relief of others' suffering is commonly but little influenced by the hedonic effects incident to our striving. The conation is prior to, and not dependent upon, its hedonic accompaniments, though these may and do modify its course.

The traditional psychological hedonism is thoroughly teleological. It asserts that all human action is performed for the sake of attaining a foreseen pleasure or of avoiding foreseen pain. It is, however, inacceptable, and for two reasons chiefly. First, it is in gross contradiction with clear instances of human action initiated and sustained, not only without anticipation of resulting pleasure or of resulting avoidance of pain, but with clear anticipation of a resulting excess of pain. Secondly, it cannot be applied to the interpretation of animal action (unless, possibly, to some actions of the highest animals); and thus would make between human and animal action a radical difference of principle, inconsistent with the well-founded theory of continuity of human with animal evolution.[7]

The hopeless inadequacy of psychological hedonism appears very clearly when it is attempted to apply it to the explanation of our valuations. J. S. Mill attempted to extricate the doctrine from its predicament in face of the problem of values by recognizing lower and higher pleasures; but it is generally conceded that in so doing he saved his moral theory at the cost of making an indefensible psychological distinction.

It should be sufficient answer to point to that sphere of human experience which the hedonists most commonly adduce in illustration of their theory, namely, the sexual. When we reflect on the profound influence of the sex urge in human life, its vast range, its immeasurable strength that so often drives men to the most reckless adventures and the most tragic disasters or sustains them through immense and prolonged labors, its frenzies of passionate desire, its lofty exaltations and its deep depressions, we must surely conclude that he who would see the ground of all these phenomena in the pleasurable tone of certain cutaneous sensations must lack all personal experience of any but the most trivial manifestations of sex.

THE HORMIC THEORY OF ACTION

We are thus driven to the hormic theory as the only alternative teleologi-

---

[7]The fallacy that hedonism can explain both human and animal actions involves, I suggest, a confusion of teleological hedonism, the theory that we act for the sake of attaining pleasure or of avoiding pain, with mechanistic hedonism, the theory that pleasures and pains leave after-effects which play their parts in the determination of subsequent actions, and with hedonism-of-the-present, the theory that pleasure sustains present action and pain checks or turns it aside. The first is used to explain human action; the second or third, or both, to explain animal action.

cal theory of action. The essence of it may be stated very simply. To the question—Why does a certain animal or man seek this or that goal?—it replies: Because it is his nature to do so. This answer, simple as it may seem, has deep significance.

Observation of animals of any one species shows that all members of the species seek and strive toward a limited number of goals of certain types, certain kinds of food and of shelter, their mates, the company of their fellows, certain geographical areas at certain seasons, escape to cover in presence of certain definable circumstances, dominance over their fellows, the welfare of their young, and so on. For any one species the kinds of goals sought are characteristic and specific; and all members of the species seek these goals independently of example and of prior experience of attainment of them, though the course of action pursued in the course of striving towards the goal may vary much and may be profoundly modified by experience. We are justified, then, in inferring that each member of the species inherits the tendencies of the species to seek goals of these several types.

Man also is a member of an animal species. And this species also has its natural goals, or its inborn tendencies to seek goals of certain types. This fact is not only indicated very clearly by any comparison of human with animal behavior, but it is so obvious a fact that no psychologist of the least intelligence fails to recognize it, however inadequately, not even if he obstinately reduces their number to a minimum of three and dubs them the "prepotent reflexes" of sex, fear, and rage. Others write of "primary desires," or of "dominant urges," or of "unconditioned reflexes," or of appetites, or of cravings, or of congenital drives, or of motor sets, or of inherited tendencies or propensities; lastly, some, bolder than the rest, write of "so-called instincts." For instincts are out of fashion just now with American psychologists; and to write of instincts without some such qualification as "so-called" betrays a reckless indifference to fashion amounting almost to indecency. Yet the word "instinct" is too good to be lost to our science. Better than any other word it points to the facts and the problems with which I am here concerned.

The hormic psychology imperatively requires recognition not only of instinctive action but of instincts. Primarily and traditionally the words "instinct" and "instinctive" point to those types of animal action which are complex activities of the whole organism; which lead the creature to the attainment of one or other of the goals natural to the species; which are in their general nature manifested by all members of the species under appropriate circumstances; which exhibit nice adaptation to circumstances; and which, though often suggesting intelligent appreciation of the end to be gained and the means to be adopted, yet owe little or nothing to the individual's prior experience.[8]

---

[8]Two very different prejudices have cooperated to give currency in recent psychology to a very perverted and misleading view of instinctive action. On the one hand are those observers of animal life (of whom Fabre and Wasmann are the most distinguished) whose religious philosophy forbids them to admit the

The words as thus traditionally used point to a problem. The word "instinctive" describes actions of this type. The word "instinct" implies that unknown something which expresses itself in the train of instinctive action directed towards a particular natural goal. What is the nature of that x to which the word "instinct" points? The problem has provoked much speculation all down the ages; the answers ranging from 'the finger of God' to 'a rigid bit of reflex nervous mechanism.'

It is characteristic of the hormic theory that it does not presume to give a final and complete answer to this question in terms of entities or types of events that enjoy well-established scientific status.

Hormic activity is an energy manifestation; but the hormic theory does not presume to say just what form or forms of energy or transformations of energy are involved. It seems to involve liberation of energy potential or latent in chemical form in the tissues; and hormic theory welcomes any

---

essential and close similarities between human and animal actions. Thus prejudiced, they select and emphasize all their observations and reports of animal, and especially of insect, behavior the stereotyped unvarying instances, those which seem to imply lack of all individual adaptation to unusual situations. Thus they emphasize the quasi-mechanical character of instinctive behavior.

On the other hand, the mechanists, moved by the desire to find instinctive actions mechanically explicable, also select and emphasize these same instances and aspects, neglecting to notice the very numerous and striking evidences of adaptability of instinctive action in ways that can only be called intelligent. Thus both parties are led into regarding instinctive behavior as always a train of action precisely predetermined in the innate constitution of the animal. And this view, of course, readily lends itself to interpretation of all instinctive action as the mechanistic play of chains of reflexes, the touching-off by stimuli of so-called "action-patterns" congenitally formed in the nervous system.

Yet any impartial review of instinctive behavior [an excellent example is Major R. W. G. Hingston's recent book (8)] shows clearly the falsity of this view, shows beyond dispute that instinctive action (even among the insects) does not consist in any rigidly prescribed sequence of movements, and that any particular type of instinctive behavior cannot be characterized by the particular movements and sequences of movements but only by the type of goal towards which the action is directed. Any such review reveals clearly two much neglected facts: (1) that very different instincts of the one animal may express themselves in very similar trains of movement; (2) that one instinct may express itself in a great variety of movements. A dog racing along with utmost concentration of energy in the effort of speedy locomotion may be pursuing his prey; he may be fleeing from a larger pursuing dog or leopard; or he may be rushing to join a concourse of dogs. On the other hand, in either fighting or pursuing and seizing his prey, he may bring into play a very large proportion of his total capacities for coordinated movement, his native motor mechanisms; and many of the motor mechanisms which he brings into play are identical in the two cases. Or consider the male pigeon in the two very different instinctive activities of fighting and courting; the forms of bodily activity he displays are in many respects so similar that an inexperienced observer may be unable to infer which instinct is at work in him. In both, all the motor mechanisms of locomotion and of self-display, of flying, strutting, walking, running, and vocalization, are in turn brought into action; few, if any, of the many motor manifestations are peculiar to the expression of either instinct. These facts are very difficult to interpret in terms of neurology; but that difficulty does not justify us in denying or ignoring them. The tendency to deny or ignore the many facts of behavior that present this difficulty has long been dominant in American psychology and is a bar to progress of the first magnitude.

information about such transformations that physiological chemistry can furnish. But it refuses to go beyond the facts and to be bound by current hypotheses of physical science; and it refuses to be blinded to the essential facts. And the most essential facts are (a) that the energy manifestation is guided into channels such that the organism approaches its goal; (b) that this guidance is effected through a cognitive activity, an awareness, however vague, of the present situation and of the goal; (c) that the activity, once initiated and set on its path through cognitive activity, tends to continue until the goal is attained; (d) that, when the goal is attained, the activity terminates; (e) that progress towards and attainment of the goal are pleasurable experiences, and thwarting and failure are painful or disagreeable experiences.

These statements imply that hormic activity is essentially mental activity, involving always cognition or awareness, striving initiated and governed by such cognition, and accruing satisfaction or dissatisfaction. The theory holds that these are three fundamental aspects of all hormic activity, distinguishable by abstraction, but not separable or capable of occurring in nature as separate events. Thus it necessarily holds that hormic activity can be exhibited only by organisms or natural entities that have a certain complexity of organization, such entities as have been traditionally called monads. And it inclines to the view that the simplest form under which such monads appear to us as sensible phenomena is that of the single living cell. The theory does not seek to explain the genesis of such complex organizations by the coming together of simpler entities. It inclines to regard any attempt at such a genetic account (such, for example, as has been attempted by various exponents of emergent evolution) as inevitably fruitless: for it regards with extreme scepticism the common assumption that every thing and event can in principle be analyzed into some complex of ultimately simple things and events; and it is especially sceptical of the emergentists' assumption that a conjunction of purely mechanistic events can result in the emergence of teleological events.[9]

The theory is ready to welcome and accept any evidence which physical science can furnish of hormic activity, however lowly, in the inorganic sphere, and is ready to use such evidence to build a bridge between the organic and the inorganic realms; but it is content to await the verdict of the physicists, confident that its own facts and formulations will stand fast whether that verdict prove to be positive or negative. In short, the hormic theory holds that where there is life there is mind; and that, if there has been continuity of evolution of the organic from the inorganic, there must have been something of mind, some trace of mental nature and activity in the inorganic from which such emergence took place.

THE ADEQUACY OF THE HORMIC THEORY

The question arises: Is the hormic theory as here stated adequate to the interpretation of all forms of animal and human activity? And the ques-

---

[9]Cf. my *Modern Materialism and Emergent Evolution* (21).

tion takes two forms: First, can the hormic theory be carried over from psychology into physiology? Can it be profitably applied to the interpretation of the activities of the several organs and tissues? This is a very deep question which only the future course of science can answer. But we notice that biologists are becoming increasingly conscious of the inadequacy of mechanistic principles to their problems, especially the problems of evolution, of heredity, of self-regulation, of the maintenance of organic equilibrium, of the restitution of forms and functions after disturbance of the normal state of affairs in the organism, and are seeing that, as Dr. E. S. Russell (29) emphatically insists, "the essential difference between the inorganic unit and the living individual is that the activities of all living things tend toward some end and are not easily diverted from achieving this end . . . . . all goes on in the organic world as if living beings strove actively towards an end . . . . . . what differentiates a living thing from all inorganic objects or units is this persistence of striving, this effort towards the expression of deep-lying distinctive tendencies." We therefore are all well disposed to agree with this physiologist when he writes: "We must interpret all organic activities as in some sense the actions of a psychophysical individual."[10] That is to say, we may reasonably hope that it may become increasingly possible to extend the hormic principle to the elucidation of fundamental problems of physiology and of general biology.

Secondly, are the inborn impulses (*die Triebe*) the only sources of motive power? For this is the thesis of the hormic theory in the pure form as propounded in my *Social Psychology* in 1908 (13). Let me cite a restatement of it by Professor James Drever of Edinburgh (2). "The basis of the developed mind and character of man must be sought in the original and inborn tendencies of his nature. From these all development and education must start, and with these all human control, for the purposes of education and development, as for the purposes of social and community life, must operate. These are more or less truisms, but they are truisms which have been ignored in much of the educational practice

---

[10]Dr. J. S. Haldane (3), distinguished as one of the most exact of experimental physiologists, referring to the notion that life and mind may have emerged from a lifeless and mindless, strictly mechanistic realm, writes: "I must frankly confess that to me it seems that such ideas are not clearly thought out. In fact they convey to me no meaning whatever. It is very different, however, if we conclude that in spite of superficial appearances something of conscious behavior must in reality be present behind what appears to us as the mere blind organic behavior of lower organisms or plants," to which he adds, though on very different grounds—behind also "what appears to be the mere mechanical behaviour of the inorganic world." In the same volume he rightly insists: "The knowledge represented in the psychological or humanistic group of sciences is not only differentiated clearly from other kinds of scientific knowledge, but is the most fundamental variety of scientific knowledge." He adds: "I am thoroughly convinced of the limitations attached to physiological interpretation of human behaviour. At present there is what seems to me an exaggerated idea among the general public, not of the importance of psychological knowledge, for its importance can hardly be overestimated, but of the importance of mere physiological or even physical treatment of human behaviour."

of the past, and in many of the best intentioned efforts at social reorganization and reform. The original human nature, with which the psychologist is concerned, consists, first of all, of capacities, such as the capacity to have sensations, to perceive, to reason, to learn, and the like, and, secondly, of conscious impulses, the driving forces to those activities without which the capacities would be meaningless." And "though control of primitive impulses becomes more and more complex, it is always a control by that which draws its controlling force, ultimately and fundamentally, from primitive impulses, never a control *ab extra.*" Yet again: "Educationally the most important fact to keep in mind with regard to these specific 'emotional' tendencies is that in them we have . . . . . the original, and ultimately the sole important, motive forces determining an individual's behavior, the sole original determinants of the ends he will seek to attain, as of the interests which crave satisfaction."

If my knowledge of contemporary thought is not gravely at fault, four and only four attempts to supplement the pure hormic theory as here concisely stated call for consideration.

First, we have to consider a view maintained by Professor Drever himself, inconsistently as it seems to me, with his statements cited in the foregoing paragraphs. He writes in the same treatise: "It must be granted that, in the human being, in addition to the instinctive springs of action, or motive forces which determine behavior prior to individual experience, pleasure and pain are also motive forces depending upon individual experience" (2, p. 149). To admit this is to combine hedonism with hormism; and in such combination Dr. Drever does not stand alone; he is in the good company of Professor S. Freud and all his many disciples.

I take Dr. Drever's statement to mean that man learns to anticipate pain or pleasure from this or that form of activity and in consequence to turn away from the former and to choose the latter. Now, in so far as we have in view the modes of activity adopted or followed as means to our goals, this is certainly true doctrine. Past experiences of pain and pleasure attending our activities are remembered; they determine our anticipations of pain and pleasure; and we choose our forms of activity, our lines of approach to our goals, in accordance with such anticipations. But more than this is implied in the statement that "pleasure and pain are also motive forces," as also in Freud's "pleasure principle." It is implied that desire of pleasure and the aversion from pain are motive forces which impel us to goals independently of the hormic impulses. It is a mixed theory of action, which supplements the hormic theory with a measure of hedonism. Is this true? Does the hormic theory require this admixture? The answer seems clear in the case of pain. The anticipation of pain from a certain course of action can only deter from that line of activity; it turns us not from the goal of that activity, but only from the form of activity previously followed in pursuit of that goal; and, if we can find no other line of activity that promises attainment, we may in the end cease to strive toward that goal; but the anticipation of the pain is not

in itself a motive to action.   Pain in the proper sense is always the accompaniment or consequence of thwarting of desire, of failure of impulse
or effort; and, if we desire nothing, if we strive after no goals, we shall
suffer no pains.   This is the great truth underlying the Buddhist philosophy of renunciation.

There is one seeming exception that arises from the ambiguity of language; the word "pain" is applied not only to feeling that results from
thwarting and failure but also to a specific quality or qualities of sensation.
And we are accustomed to regard "pain-sensation" as a spur to action, and
also the aversion from anticipated "pain-sensation" as a motive to activity
the goal of which is the avoidance of such "pain."   Here is a grand source
of confusion; which, however, is cleared away forthwith when we recognize the fact that pain-sensation from any part of the body is a specific
excitant of fear, and fear is or involves a powerful hormic impulse.

It is notorious that threats of physical punishment, if they are to spur
the unwilling child or man to activity, must be pushed to the point of
exciting fear in him; short of that they are of no avail.   The case might
be argued at great length; but the citation of this one fact may suffice.
The activity prompted by physical pain is an activity of one of the most
deeply rooted and powerful of the hormic impulses, the impulse of fear.

If the hormic impulse excited by impressions that involve pain-sensation
is not in every case the impulse of the fear instinct, then we can interpret
the facts only by postulating a specific impulse of avoidance or withdrawal
rooted in a correspondingly specific and simple instinct, closely comparable
to the instinct to scratch an itching spot.

The case for desire of pleasure as a motive force is less easily disposed
of, the problem is more subtle (18).

Let us note first that pleasure is an abstraction, not a concrete entity or
situation; it is a feeling qualifying activity.   Hence we find that "pleasures" we are alleged to pursue are pleasurable forms of activity.   In every
case the activity in question is sustained by some impulse or desire of other
nature and origin than a pure desire for pleasure, namely, some hormic
impulse.   Take the simplest instances, most confidently cited by the hedonist—the pleasures of the table and of sex.   A man is said to seek the
pleasures of the table.   What in reality he does is to satisfy his appetite for
food, his hormic urge to eat, in the most pleasurable manner, choosing
those food-substances which, in the light of past experience, he knows will
most effectively stimulate and satisfy this impulse.   But without the appetite, the hormic urge, there is no pleasure.   So also of the man alleged
to pursue the pleasures of sex.   Moved or motivated by the sex urge he
chooses those ways of indulging it which experience has shown him to be
most effective in stimulating and satisfying the urge.   But without the
hormic urge there is no pleasure to be had.

These instances seem to be typical of all the multitude of cases in which
men are said to seek pleasure as their goal.   Take the complex case of the
man who is said to pursue the pleasure of fame or of power.   In pursuit
of fame or power many a man shuns delights and lives laborious days.

But he is moved, his efforts are sustained, by the desire of fame or power, not by the desire of pleasure. If there were not within him the hormic urge to figure in the eyes of the world or to exert power over others, he could find no pleasure in pursuing and in attaining these goals, and he would not in fact pursue them. You may paint the delights of fame or of power in the most glowing colors to the boy or man who is by nature meek and humble; and your eloquence will fail to stir within him any responsive chord, for in his composition the chord is lacking. On the other hand, in the man in whom the self-assertive impulse is naturally strong, this impulse readily becomes the desire of fame or of power; and, under the driving power of such desire, he may sacrifice all "pleasures," perhaps with full recognition that fame can come only after his death, or that the attainment of power will involve him in most burdensome and exacting responsibilities. Without the hormic urge which sets his goal, neither will he pursue those goals nor would he find any pleasure in the possession of fame or power, if these came to him as a free gift of the gods. These surely are simple truths illustrated by countless instances in fiction and in real life.

Take one more instance. Revenge, it is said, is sweet; and men are said to seek the pleasures of revenge. But, if the injured man is a meek and humble creature, if the injury does not evoke in him a burning desire to humble his adversary, to get even with him, to assert his power over him, the statement that revenge is sweet will have no meaning for him, he will have no impulse to avenge his injury, and the imagining of injury to the adversary will neither afford nor promise him pleasure. On the other hand, injury to the proud self-assertive man provokes in him the vengeful impulse, and in planning his revenge he may well gloat upon the prospect of hurting his adversary; and, if he is a peculiarly sophisticated and ruthless person, he may choose such means to that goal as experience leads him to believe will be most gratifying, most pleasurable.

It is needless to multiply alleged instances of pleasure-seeking; all alike fall under this one formula: the pleasure is not an end in itself; it is incidental to the pursuit and attainment of some goal towards which some hormic impulse sets.

Perhaps a word should be added concerning beauty. Surely, it may be urged, we seek to attain the beautiful and we value the beautiful object for the sake of the pleasure it gives us! Here again hedonist aesthetic inverts the true relations. The foundations of all aesthetic theory are here in question. It must suffice to say that the beauty of an object consists not in its power to excite in us a complex of sensations of pleasurable feeling-tone (if it were so, a patchwork quilt should be as beautiful as a Turner landscape); it consists rather in the power of the object to evoke in us a multitude of conations that work together in delicately balanced harmony to attain satisfaction in a rich and full appreciation of the significance of the object.[11]

---

[11]This topic is closely connected with the much neglected problem of the ac-

A second widely accepted supplementation of the hormic theory is that best represented by the thesis of Dr. R. S. Woodworth's little book, *Dynamic Psychology* (32). I have criticized this at length elsewhere (15) and can therefore deal with it briefly.

Woodworth's thesis may be briefly stated by adopting the language of the passage cited above from Dr. Drever, in which he distinguishes between "capacities" for activities, on the one hand, and, on the other, "conscious impulses, the driving forces to those activities without which the capacities would be meaningless."

The "capacities" that are inborn become immensely differentiated and multiplied in the growing child; all these may be divided roughly into two great classes, capacities of thinking (of ideation) and capacities of acting, of skilled movement. Now Woodworth's contention is that every such capacity is intrinsically not only a capacity but also a spring of energy, a source of impulsive or motive power; it is implied that every capacity to think or to act in a certain way is also *ipso facto* a tendency to think or to act in that way. To put it concretely—if I have acquired the capacity to recite the alphabet, I have acquired also a tendency to repeat it; if I have acquired the capacity to solve quadratic equations, I have acquired a tendency to solve them; and so on of all the multitude of specific capacities of thinking and acting which all of us acquire.

This is the modern form of the old intellectualistic doctrine that ideas are forces; and its long sway proves that it has its allure, if no solid foundation. The hormic theory contends that there is no truth, or, if any truth, then but the very smallest modicum in this doctrine. It asks: If each one of the immense array of capacities possessed by a man is also intrinsically a tendency to exercise itself, what determines that at any moment only a certain very small number of them come into action? The old answer was given in the theory of the association of ideas. Its defects, its utter inadequacy, have been expounded again and again. Yet it rears its head again in this disguised modern form. The hormic answer to the question is that the "capacities" are but so much latent machinery, functional units of differentiated structure; and that the hormic impulses,

---

quirement of "tastes," a problem I have dealt with in my *Character and the Conduct of Life* (20).

Since this article was put in print the International Library of Psychology has published a volume (*Pleasure and Instinct: A Study in the Psychology of Human Actions*. London & New York: Harcourt, Brace, 1930.) wholly devoted to the examination of the question discussed in the foregoing section. The author, A. H. Burlton Allen, after carefully examining the question from every point of view and in the light of all available evidence arrives at the conclusion that the pure hormic theory as defined in this article and in my various books is the only tenable theory of human action. The writer says on p. 273: "Thus it is no doubt true that there is in the feelings no original force that leads to action. The source of all movement and action lies in the driving force of the main instincts, that is to say, in the inherent energy of the organism striving towards outlet in the forms prescribed by its inherited structure. The feelings of pleasure and unpleasure are secondary results dependant on the successful or unsuccessful working of these instincts."

working largely through the system of associative links between "capacities," bring into play in turn such capacities as are adapted for service in the pursuit of the natural goals of those impulses. In other words, it maintains that the whole of the machinery of capacities and associative links is dominated by the "interest" of the moment, by conation, by the prevalent desires and active impulses at work in the organism.

It points to "capacities," simple or complex, that remain latent and unused for years, and then, when "the interest" in whose service they were developed is revived, are awakened once more by some change in the man's circumstances, are brought back into action in the service of the renewéd interest; as when a man, having become a parent, recites once more for his children the nursery rhymes and the fairy stories he has learned in childhood.

It may be suggested that the current psychoanalytic treatment of the "complex" is in harmony with Woodworth's principle; that in this special case "ideas" or "capacities" are validly treated as possessing, in their own right, motive power or conative energy.

It is true that much of the language of Professor Freud and other psychoanalysts seems to countenance this interpretation of the facts. But it must be remembered that the energy of the complex is regarded as in some sense derived from some instinct, generally the sex instinct; it is *libido*. And though these authors speak of emotionally charged ideas, or ideas *besetzt* with emotional energy (as though each complex owed its power to a charge of libido imparted once for all to it), yet it is, I think, in line with Freud's general treatment to say that such a "complex" is a "capacity," a structural unit, which has acquired such connections with the sex (or other) instinct that the *libido,* or hormic energy of the instinct, readily flows into it and works through it, and thus is determined to modes of expression recognizable as due to the influence of the complex. Consider a fear complex, say a phobia for running water. There has been acquired a peculiar formation which leads to a paroxysm of fear with great expenditure of energy upon the perception of running water, a reaction which may be repeated at long intervals through many years. Are we to suppose that this formation, the complex, contains as an integral part of itself all the energy and all the complex structural organization which every manifestation of fear implies, that each fear complex involves a duplication of the fear organization peculiar to itself? Surely not! The essence of the new formation is such a functional relation between the perceptual system concerned in the recognition of running water and the whole apparatus of fear, that the perception becomes one of the various afferent channels through which the fear system may be excited. In this connection it is to be remembered that a sufficient mass of evidence points to the thalamic region as the principal seat of the great affective systems or centers of instinctive excitement. In neurological terms, the perception of running water is in the main a cortical event, while the manifestation of fear is in the main a subcortical or thalamic event; and the essential neural ground of the complex manifestation is a special, acquired corticothalamic connection between the two events, or, more strictly, between the two neuron systems concerned in the two events and respectively located in cortex and in thalamus.

The hormist can find no clear instances that support Woodworth's thesis and can point to a multitude of instances which indicate an absence of all driving power in the "capacities" as such. He maintains therefore that the burden of proof lies upon his opponents; and, though he cannot conclusively prove the negative thesis, that no "capacity" has driving power, he sees no ground for accepting this supplement to the hormic theory.

There remain for brief consideration two very modern theories which claim to find the hormic theory in need of supplementation and to supply such supplement.

I refer first to the psychology of Dr. Ludwig Klages and of his able disciple, Dr. Hans Prinzhorn.[12] According to this teaching (I write subject to correction, for it is not easy to grasp), the hormic theory is true of the life of animals and of the lower functions of the human organism, of all the life of instinct and perceptual activity; but the life of man is complicated by the cooperation of two factors of a different order, *Geist* and *Wille*, spirit and will, two aspects of a higher purely spiritual principle which is not only of an order different from that of the hormic impulses but is in many respects antagonistic to them, a disturbing influence that threatens to pervert and even destroy the instinctive basis of human life.

I know not what to say of this doctrine. To me it seems to involve a radical dualism not easily to be accepted. It seems to contain echoes of old ways of thinking, of the old opposition of the instinct of animals to the reason of man, of Hegel's objectified spirit, even of Descartes' dualism, the animal body a machine complicated in man by the intervention of reason, although, it is true, these authors repudiate whole-heartedly the mechanical physiology. I suggest that the *Geist* and *Wille* which, as these authors rightly insist, make human life so widely different from the life of even the highest animals, are to be regarded not as some mysterious principles of a radically different order from any displayed in animal life; that they are rather to be identified with what the Germans call *objective Geist*, objectified spirit of humanity, the system of intellectual process and of cultural values which has been slowly built up as the traditional possession of each civilization and largely fixed in the material forms of art and science, in architecture, in tools, in written and printed words, in enduring institutions of many kinds. Each human being absorbs from his social environment some large part of this objectified spirit; and it is this, working within him, that gives rise to the higher manifestations of human life which in Klages' doctrine are ascribed to *Geist* and *Wille*. Until this interpretation of the facts shall have been shown to be inadequate, there would seem to be no sufficient foundation for the new dualism of Klages and Prinzhorn.

---

[12]Set forth in numerous works of which one only, Klages' *Psychology of Character* (10) has been translated into English. Prinzhorn's *Leib-seele Einheit* (28) gives the best brief approach to this system.

Lastly, I mention an interesting supplement to the hormic theory offered in a recent book by Mr. Olaf Stapledon (30). The author begins by accepting the hormic theory in a thoroughgoing teleological sense. But he goes on to say: "A human being's inheritance would seem to include a capacity for discovering and conating tendencies beyond the inherited nature of his own organism, or his own biological needs." And he chooses, as the clearest illustrations of what he means, instances of love of one person for another. Criticizing my view that in sex love we have a sentiment in which the principal motive powers are the impulses of the sexual and of the parental instincts in reciprocal interplay, he writes: "But this theory ignores an important difference between parental behavior and love, and between the tender emotions and love. Parents do, as a matter of fact, often love their children; but they do also often merely behave parentally toward them, and feel tender emotion toward them. The love of a parent for a child may be said to be 'derived' from the parental tendency, in the sense that this tendency first directed attention to the child, and made possible the subsequent *discovery of the child* as itself a living centre of tendencies. And it may well be that in all love there is something of this instinctive parental behaviour. But genuine love, for whatever kind of object, is very different from the tender emotion and from all strictly instinctive parental behaviour . . . . . . Genuine love . . . . . . entails the espousal of the other's needs in the same direct manner in which one espouses one's own private needs . . . . . . Merely instinctive behaviour is, so to speak, the conation of a tendency or complex of tendencies of the agent's own body or person. Genuine love is the conation of tendencies of another person . . . . . . if love occurs, or in so far as it occurs, the other is regarded, not as a stimulus, but as a centre of tendencies demanding conation in their own right."

Referring to the patriotic sentiment of Joan of Arc, Stapledon writes: "That sentiment certainly did become the ruling factor of her life. And, further, whatever its instinctive sources, her cognition of her social environment turned it into something essentially different from any mere blend of instinctive impulses. The chief weakness of instinct psychology is that it fails, in spite of all efforts to the contrary, to do justice to the part played in behaviour by environment. And this failure is most obvious in human behaviour." He adds that the "instinct psychologists . . . . have left out the really distinctive feature of human behaviour."

What, then, is this distinctive feature? Here is a new challenge to the hormic theory; a denial not of its truth, up to a certain point, but of its adequacy to cover all the facts and especially the facts of distinctively human activity.

The "distinctive feature," this alleged source of conations not derived from native impulses, is defined as follows: "I am suggesting, then, that the essential basis of conation is not that some tendency of the organism, or of a simple inherited mental structure, is the source (direct or indirect) of every conative act, but that *every* cognition of tendency *may* give rise to a conative act. Every tendency which is an element in the mental content suggests a conation, and is the ground of at least incipient conation. If the tendency does not conflict with other and well-established conative ends, its fulfilment will be desired."

Now, obviously, if this doctrine be true, it is very important. For among tendencies the cognition of any one of which gives rise to corresponding conation, the desire of its fulfilment, Mr. Stapledon includes not only all human and animal tendencies, but also all physical tendencies, e.g., the tendency of a stream of water to run downhill, of a stone to fall to the ground, of a needle to fly to the magnet. Of every tendency he asserts: "In the mere act of apprehending *it,* we desire its fulfilment." And "if we ask—'How does the primitive self expand into the developed self?' we find the answer is that the most important way of expanding is by the cognition of a wider field of objective tendencies and the conative espousal of those tendencies"; for "any objective tendency may enter the mental content and influence the will in its own right."

I find this theory very intriguing. But I find also the grounds advanced as its foundation quite unconvincing. They are two: first, the alleged inadequacy of the instinct theory; secondly, the assertion that every cognition of any tendency tends to evoke corresponding or congruent conation. As regards the former ground, I am, no doubt, a prejudiced witness, yet, in Stapledon's chosen instance of love, I cannot admit the inadequacy. I admit that Joan of Arc's patriotic behavior was "different from any mere blend of instinctive impulses." Here Stapledon has failed, I think, to grasp the implication of the theory of the sentiments. In the working of a developed sentiment, whether love of country, love of parent for child, or of man for woman, we have to do not merely with a blending and conflicting of primitive impulses. Such a sentiment is a most complex organization comprising much elaborated cognitive structure as well as instinctive dispositions, and its working can only properly be viewed in the light of the principles of emergence and Gestalt.

Further, Stapledon seems to neglect to take account of the principles of passive and of active sympathy. It is true, I think, that the cognition of a tendency at work in another person tends to evoke or bring into activity the corresponding tendency in the observer; and in very sympathetic personalities this sympathetic induction works strongly and frequently. When we recognize fully these facts, we cover, I suggest, the manifestation of such complex sentiments as love, which Stapledon chooses to illustrate the inadequacy of the hormic principles. As to his essential novelty, his claim that cognition of any tendency, even merely physical tendency, gives rise to conation similarly directed, I remain entirely unconvinced. There are two parts of this thesis, the second depending on the former; and both seem to me highly questionable. First, he assumes that the conation rooted in the instinctive nature arises through cognition of an active tendency at work in oneself. This is to make a two- or three-stage affair of the simplest impulsive action. First, the tendency is aroused into activity, presumably by cognition of some object or situation; secondly, it is cognized; thirdly, this cognition gives rise to conation. Is not this pure mythology? Is it correct to say that we strive only when we "espouse" a tendency which we cognize as at work within us? Is it not rather true that the activity of the tendency primarily aroused by cognition of some object or situation is the conation which proceeds under guidance of further cognition. It seems clear that the instinctive impulse may and often does work subconsciously, that is, without being cognized; and in any case, its working is so obscure to cognition that the majority of psychologists, failing to cognize or recognize it in any form, deny the reality of such experience of active tendency.

Admitting the wide range in human life of the sympathetic principle, admitting that, in virtue of this principle, cognition of desire in others evokes similar desire in ourselves, or a tendency towards the same goal, or a tendency to cooperate with or promote the striving cognized in the other, I cannot find sufficient ground for believing that cognition of tendency in physical objects also directly evokes in us congruent tendency or conation. I would maintain that only when in the mood of poetry or primitive animism we personify natural objects and events, only then do we feel sympathy, or antagonism; and on the whole we are as liable to feel antagonism as sympathy. When I contemplate the flow of a river I murmur with the poet, "Even the weariest river winds somewhere safe to sea," and may feel a sympathetic inclination to glide with the current; but I may equally well (especially if a resident of the lower Mississippi valley) regard the flowing river as a hostile force against which I incline to struggle, or (if I am a thrifty Scot) as a distressing waste of energy; and, if it is a mountain stream, I may even be moved to try to dam its course. Immersed in the water, I am equally ready to enjoy swimming with the current or struggling up-stream, letting myself be rushed along with the breaker or hurling myself against it. If I contemplate the wind gently moving the branches of a tree or caressing my face, I may feel it to be a friendly power and exclaim, "O Wild West Wind, thou breath of autumn's being"; or I may observe with delight the little breezes that "dusk and shiver." But if I apprehend the wind as tearing at a tree, buffeting the ship, or lashing the waves to fury, I am all against it as a fierce and cruel power to be fought and withstood; I sympathize with the straining tree, the laboring ship, or the rock or stout building that stands foursquare to all the winds that blow. In short, my reaction to the wind varies as it seems to whisper, to whistle, to sing, to murmur, to sigh, to moan, to roar, to bluster, to shriek, to rage, to tear, to storm. Such sympathies and antagonisms provoked by the forces of nature are the very breath of nature poetry; but they seem to me to afford no support to Mr. Stapledon's thesis. The primitive animistic tendency is, I submit, an extension of primitive or passive sympathy; an imaginative extension to inanimate nature of the emotional stirrings we directly or intuitively discern in our fellow-creatures, rather than an immediate and fundamental reaction to all cognition of physical agency, as Mr. Stapledon maintains. In gentle, highly sympathetic natures, such as Wordsworth's, it works chiefly in the form of sympathy with natural forces; but more pugnacious and self-assertive natures are more readily stirred to antagonism and opposition than to congruent conation. It would seem that, as is commonly the case when writers on ethics undertake to construct their own psychology, Stapledon's supplementation of the hormic psychology is determined by the needs of his ethical theory rather than by consideration of the observable facts of experience and activity.

I conclude, then, that the hormic theory is adequate and requires no such supplementations as those examined in this section and found to be ill-based and otiose.

The Advantages of the Hormic Theory

One advantage of the hormic theory over all others is that it enables us to sketch in outline an intelligible, consistent, and tenable story of continuous organic evolution, evolution of bodily forms and mental functions in intelligible relation to one another; and this is something which no other theory can achieve. It does not attempt the impossible task of describing the genesis of experience out of the purely physical and of teleological activity out of purely mechanistic events. It does not make the illegitimate assumption that experience can be analyzed into and regarded as compounded out of simple particles or entities. It insists that experience, or each phase of it, is always a unitary whole having aspects that are distinguishable but not separable. It finds good reason to believe that the life of the simplest creature involves such experience, however utterly vague and undifferentiated it may be. It regards the story of organic evolution as one of progressive differentiation and specialization of structure, of experience and of activity from the most rudimentary and simplest forms. It regards the striving capacities, the hormic tendencies, of each species as having been differentiated out of a primal urge to live, to be active, to seek, to assimilate, to build up, to energize, to counteract the forces of dissolution. Such differentiations of striving involve parallel differentiations of the cognitive function subserving the discrimination of goals. And still further differentiation of it for the discernment and adaptation of means results in longer and more varied chains of activity through which remoter and more difficult goals are attained. The theory recognizes that only in the human species does cognitive differentiation attain such a level that detailed foresight of remote goals becomes possible, with such definite hormic fixation on the goal as characterizes action properly called purposive in the fullest sense of the word. But it claims that, though the foresight of even the higher animals is but of short range, envisaging only the result to be attained by the next step of action, and that perhaps very vaguely, the cognitive dispositions of the animal are often linked in such fashion as to lead on the hormic urge from step to step, until finally the biological goal is attained and the train of action terminates in satisfaction. It finds in human activity and experience parallels to all the simpler forms of activity displayed and of experience implied in the animals. It sees in the growing infant signs of development from almost blind striving with very short-range and vague foresight (when its cognitive powers are still but slightly differentiated) to increasingly long-range and more adequate foresight enriched by the growing wealth and variety of memory. It insists that memory is for the sake of foresight, and foresight for the sake of action; and that neither can be validly conceived other than as the working of a forward urge that seeks always something more behind and beyond that which is given in sense presentation, a something more that will satisfy the hormic urge and bring it for the time being to rest, or permit it to be turned by new sense impressions to some new goal.

If we turn from the descriptive account of evolution to the problem of the dynamics of the process, the hormic theory again is the only one that can offer an intelligible and self-consistent scheme. It notes how the human creature, through constant striving with infinitely varied circumstances, carries the differentiation of both cognitive and striving powers far beyond the point to which the hereditary momentum will carry them, the point common to the species, how it develops new discriminations, modified goals of appetition and aversion, modified trains of activity for pursuit or retreat. It notes that these modifications are achieved under the guidance of the pleasure and the pain, the satisfaction and dissatisfaction, that attend success and failure respectively; it inclines to view the evolution or rather the epigenesis of the individual creature's adaptations as the model in the light of which we may interpret the epigenesis of racial adaptations. Such interpretation implies acceptance of Lamarckian transmisson; but, since the only serious ground for rejecting this is the assumption that mechanistic categories are sufficient in biology, an assumption which the hormic psychology rejects, this implication is in its eyes no objection. Rather it points to the increasing weight of evidence of the reality of Lamarckian transmission.[13]

The hormic theory insists that the differentiation of instinctive tendencies has been, throughout the scale of animal evolution, the primary or leading feature of each step. Bodily organs cannot be supposed to have acquired new forms and functional capacities that remained functionless until some congruent variation of instinctive tendency brought them into play. Rather, it is necessary to believe that, in the case of every new development of form or function, the first step was the variation of the instinctive nature of the species toward such activities as required for their efficient exercise the peculiarities of form and function in question. Given such variation, we can understand how natural selection may have brought about the development in the species of the peculiarities of bodily form and function best suited to subserve such modified or new instinctive tendency. Thus the theory overcomes the greatest difficulty of the neo-Darwinian theory, the difficulty, namely, that, if novelties of form and

---

[13]Since 1920 I have conducted an experiment on strictly Lamarckian principles and have found clear-cut evidence of increasing facility in successive generations of animals trained to execute a particular task. This very great increase of facility seems explicable in no other way than by transmission of the modifications acquired by the efforts of the individuals. Cf. two reports in the *British Journal of Psychology* (19, 22).

function are to be established in a species, very many of the members must have varied in the same direction at the same time and in such a wide degree as will give survival value to the variation. For, given some changed environmental conditions of a species (e.g., a growing scarcity of animal food for the carnivorous land ancestor of the seal), the intelligence common to all members might well lead all of them to pursue prey by a new method (the method of swimming and diving). And if this relatively new mode of behavior became fixed, if the tendency to adopt it became stronger through repeated successful efforts to secure prey in this fashion, natural selection might well perpetuate all congruent bodily variations and might eliminate variations of an opposite kind; and thus convert the legs of the species into flippers. This is the principle that has been named "organic selection," rendered effective by the recognition of the causal efficacy of hormic striving and the reality of Lamarckian transmission, a principle which without such recognition remains of very dubious value.[14]

The hormic theory thus renders possible a workable theory of animal evolution, one under which the mind, or the mental function of cognition-conation, is the growing point of the organism and of the species, a theory under which the intelligent striving of the organism is the creative activity to which evolution is due. Surely such a theory is more acceptable than any that pretends to illuminate the mystery of evolution by such utterly vague terms as "orthogenesis" or *"élan vital"* or "the momentum of life."

The hormic theory is radically opposed to intellectualism and all its errors, the errors that have been the chief bane of psychology (and of European culture in general) all down the ages. It does not set out with some analytic description of purely cognitive experience, and then find itself at a loss for any intelligible functional relation between this and bodily activities. It recognizes fully the conative nature of all activity and regards the cognitive power as everywhere the servant and the guide of striving. Thus it is fundamentally dynamic and leads to a psychology well adapted for application to the sciences and practical problems of human life, those of education, of hygiene, of therapy, of social activity, of religion, of mythology, of aesthetics, of economics, of politics and the rest.[15]

Of all forms of psychology the hormic is the only one that can give to philosophy the psychological basis essential to it. Philosophy is properly concerned with values, with evaluation and with standards and scales of

---

[14]As formulated many years ago by the neo-Darwinians, E. B. Poulton, J. M. Baldwin, and Lloyd Morgan.

[15]When a young man I was invited to dine with a distinguished economist and a leading psychologist of that period. It was mentioned that I was taking up psychology. "Ah!" said the economist, "Psychology! Yes, very important, very important! Association of ideas and all that sort of thing. What!" It was obvious to me that he did not attach the slightest importance to psychology and had neither the faintest inkling of any bearing of it on economics, nor any intention of seeking any such relation. From that moment dates my revulsion against the traditional intellectualistic psychology.

value; it seeks to establish the relative values of the goals men seek, of their ideals, of the forms of character and types of conduct. All such valuation is relative to human nature; a scale of values formulated with reference, not to man as he is or may be, but to some creature of radically different constituion would obviously be of little value to men; and philosophy can advance towards a true scale of values only in proportion as it founds itself upon a true account of human nature, its realities and its potentialities. The claim, then, that hormic psychology is the psychology needed by philosophy may seem merely a repetition of the claim that it is true. But it is more than this; for a glance at the history of philosophy shows that the hormic psychology is the only one with which philosophy can work, the only one on which it can establish a scale of values, that does not break to pieces under the slightest examination.

The intellectualist philosophy, adopting an intellectualist psychology of ideas, finds its source and criterion of all values in logical consistency of its system; and surely it is plain that men do not and will not bear the ills they have, still less struggle heroically against them, supported only by the satisfaction of knowing themselves to be part of a perfectly logical system.

The mechanistic psychology can recognize no values; can give no account of the process of valuation. At the best it can but (as in Mr. B. Russell's essay, "A Free Man's Worship") hurl defiance at a universe without meaning and without value which man is powerless to alter.

The hedonist psychology consorts only with a hedonist philosophy, which can save itself from being a philosophy of the pig-trough only by postulating with J. S. Mill, in defiance of clarity and of logic, a profound difference of value between higher and lower pleasures.

The hormic psychology alone offers an intelligible and consistent account of human valuations and at the same time offers to philosophy a scientific foundation in which freedom of the rational will of man, the power of creating real novelties, actual and ideal, and the power of self-development towards the ideal both of the individual and of the race, can find their proper place consistently with its fundamental postulates. It is thus the only foundation for a philosophy of meliorism.

The hormic theory, holding fast to the fact that cognition and conation are inseparable aspects of all mental life, does not elaborate a scheme of the cognitive life, a plan of the structure and functioning of the intellect, and leave to some other discipline (be it called ethology or praxiology or ethics) the task of giving some account of character. For it understands that intellect and character are, as structures, just as inseparable as the functions of cognition and conation, are but two aspects, distinguishable only in abstraction, of the structure of personality.

Recognizing that introspection can seize and fix in verbal report only the elaborated outcome of a vast and complex interplay of psychophysical events, it avoids the common error of setting over against one another two minds, or two parts of one mind or personality, under such heads as "the Conscious" and "the Unconscious," and steadily sets its face against this mystification, which, though it appeals so strongly to the popular taste for the mysterious and the bizarre, is profoundly misleading.

It recognizes that the fundamental nature of the hormic impulse is to work towards its natural goal and to terminate or cease to operate only when and in so far as its natural goal is attained; that the impulse which, in the absence of conflicting impulses, works toward its goal in trains, long or short, of conscious activity (activity, that is, which we can introspectively observe and report with very various degrees of clearness and adequacy) is apt to be driven from the field of conscious activity by conflicting impulses; that, when thus driven from the conscious field, it is not necessarily (perhaps not in any instance) arrested, terminated, brought to zero; that rather, any impulse, if it is driven from the conscious field before its goal is attained, continues to work subterraneously, subconsciously, and, so working, may obtain partial expressions in the conscious field and in action, expressions which often take the form of not easily interpretable distortions of conscious thinking and of bodily action; that such subconscious activity (but presumably not in any strict sense unconscious activity, far removed though it be from the possibility of introspective observation and report) is a normal feature of the complex life of man, in whom so many natural impulses are checked and repressed by those evoked through the demands of society; that in this way we are to interpret the phenomena now attracting the attention of experimental psychologists under the heads of "perseveration" and "secondary function," as well as all the many morbid and quasi-morbid phenomena of dream life, hallucinations, delusions, compulsions, obsessions, and all the multitudinous bodily and mental symptoms of functional disorder.

The principles of the hormic theory are capable of extension downwards from the conscious life of man, not only to the more explicitly teleological actions of animals, but also to the problems of physiology, the problems of the regulation and interaction of the functioning of all the tissues. It is thus the truly physiological psychology, the psychology that can assimilate and apply the findings of physiology, and in turn can illuminate the problems of physiology, and thus lead to a comprehensive science of the organism; a science which will not regard the organism as a machine with conscious processes somehow mysteriously tacked on to it as "epiphenomena," but a science which will regard the organism as a true organic unity all parts of which are in reciprocal interplay with all other parts and with the whole; a whole which is not merely the sum of the parts, but a synthetic unity maintained by the systematic reciprocal interaction of all the parts, a unity of integration, a colonial system of lesser units, whose unity is maintained by the harmonious hormic activity of its members in due subordination to the whole.

The hormic psychology has the advantage that it does not pretend to know the answers to the great unsolved riddles of the universe. It leaves to the future the solution of such problems as the relation of the organic to the inorganic realm, the origin or advent of life in our world, the place and destiny of the individual and of the race in the universe, the possibility of powers and potentialities of the race not yet recognized by science. In short, it does not assume any particular cosmology; it recognizes the littleness of man's present understanding; it makes for the open mind and stimulates the spirit of inquiry, and is hospitable to all empirical evidences and all legitimate speculations.[16]

It is impossible to set forth here the many advantages of the theory in its detailed application to all the special problems of psychology. It must suffice to point out that, unlike the psychologies which begin by accepting such artificial entities of abstraction as reflexes,[17] sensations, ideas, concepts, feelings, in mechanistic interplay according to laws of association, fusion, reproduction, and what-not, it regards all experience as expressive of a total activity that is everywhere hormic, selective, teleological. Thus its recognition of the selective goal-seeking nature of our activity, of all the facts implied by the words "desire," "motivation," "attention," and "will," is not reluctant, grudging, and inadequate, added under compulsion of the facts to a mechanical system into which they refuse to fit. It recognizes these aspects as fundamental, and traces the genesis of desire, attention, and rational volition from their germs in the hormic impulses of primitive organisms.

The hormic theory projects a completely systematic and self-consistent psychology on the basis of its recognition of the whole of the organized mind of the adult as a structure elaborated in the service of the hormic urge to more and fuller life. Every part of this vastly complex structure it regards as serving to differentiate the hormic impulses, and to direct them with ever increasing efficiency towards their natural goals in a world of infinite complexity that offers a multitude of possible routes to any goal, possibilities among which the organism chooses wisely according to the richness of its apparatus of sensory apprehension and its span of synthetic integration of many relations, the effective organization of its memory, the nicety of its discriminatory judgments, and its sagacity in seizing, out of a multitude of possibilities offered by sense-presentation and memory, the possibilities most relevant to its purposes.

Especially clearly appears the advantage of the hormic psychology in that it is able to render intelligible account of the organization of the affective or emotional-conative side of the mental structure, a relatively independent part or aspect of the whole of vast importance which remains a closed book to all psychologies of the intellectualistic mechanistic types. This side of the mental structure, which the latter psychologies ignore

[16]Hence it does not close the mind to the much disputed field of alleged phenomena investigated by the Societies for Psychical Research, but makes for a truly scientific attitude towards them, an attitude so conspicuous by its absence in most men of science and especially in academic psychologists.

[17]It is of interest to note that from the purely physiological side protests against the mechanical atomizing tendency multiply apace. One of the latest and most important of these is a paper read before the International Congress of Psychology in September, 1929, by Dr. G. E. Coghill, who showed good embryological grounds for refusing to regard the spinal reflexes as functional units that first take shape independently and later are brought into some kind of relation with one another. He showed reason to believe that each reflex unit develops by differentiation within the total nervous system of which it never ceases to be a functional part in reciprocal influence with all other parts.

or recognize most inadequately with such words as "attitudes" and "sets," is treated a little less cavalierly by the psychoanalytic school under the all-inclusive term—"the Unconscious," and a little more analytically under the heads of "complexes" and "emotionally toned ideas." But the treatment remains very confused and inadequate, confining itself almost exclusively to the manifestations of conflict and disorder in this part of the mind. The hormic psychology, on the other hand, insists that the elucidation of this part of the mental organization is theoretically no less important, and practically far more important, than that of the intellectual structure and functions, and is an integral part of the task of psychology, not a task to be handed over to some other science, be it called ethics, or characterology, or ethology, or praxiology, or by any other name; for it insists that we cannot understand the intellectual processes without some comprehension of the organization and working of the affective processes whose servants they are.

Towards the elucidation of this part of the problem of psychology it offers the doctrine of the sentiments, the true functional systems of the developed mind, through the development of which in the growing individual the native hormic impulses become further differentiated and directed to a multitude of new and specialized goals, a process which obscurely and profoundly modifies the nature of these native tendencies; for in these new and individually acquired systems, the sentiments, the native tendencies are brought into various cooperations, form new dynamic syntheses in which their individuality is lost and from which true novelties of desire, of emotion, and of action emerge.

Further, it aims to show how these fundamental functional systems, the sentiments, tend to become organized in one comprehensive system, character, which, when it is harmoniously integrated, can override all the crude promptings of instinctive impulse however strong, can repress, redirect, or sublimate them on every occasion, and thus, in intimate cooperation with the intellectual organization, engender that highest manifestation of personality, rational volition.

Lastly, the hormic theory is ready to welcome and is capable of assimilating all that is sound and useful in the newer schools of psychology. Unlike the various psychologies currently taught in the American colleges, it does not find itself indifferent or positively hostile to these newer movements because incapable of assimilating what is of value in them. Rather it finds something of truth and value in the rival psychoanalytic doctrines of Freud, of Jung, and of Adler, in the allied doctrines of Gestalt and Emergence, in the *verstehende* psychology of the *Geisteswissenschaftler*, in the teachings of Spranger, of Erismann, of Jaspers, in the *personalistische* psychology of Stern, in the *Charackterologie* of Klages and Prinzhorn, in the child studies of the Bühlers, in the correlational studies and conclusions of Spearman, and in the quite peculiar system of dynamic interpretation which Dr. Kurt Lewin is developing. This catholicity, this power of comprehensive assimilation of new truth from widely differing systems of psychological thinking is, perhaps, the best proof of the fundamental rightness of the hormic psychology.

ORIGINS OF THE HORMIC PSYCHOLOGY

The psychology of Aristotle is thoroughly teleological; but it can hardly be claimed that it was purely hormic. In his time the distinction between mechanistic and teleological explanations and that between hedonist and hormic explanations had not been sharply defined. As with most of the later authors who approximate a hormic psychology, his hormic theory is infected with hedonism.[18] But it may at least be said that in Greek thought there were already established two broadly contrasting views of the world, the Apollinian and the Dionysian, and that Aristotle was on the Dionysian side.[19]

The Apollinian view was the parent of European intellectualism, of which the keynote has been Socrates' identification of virtue with knowledge. It has generated the allied, though superficially so different, systems of absolute idealism and of Newtonian mechanism; and modern psychology, from Descartes and Locke onward, has reflected in the main the influence of these two systems, with their fundamental postulates of the idea and the atom (or mass-point) in motion.

The inadequacy of the Apollinian view, the misleading nature of its ideal of perfect intelligibility, of complete explanation of all events by deduction from first principles or transparent postulates, has now been manifested in the collapse of pure idealism and of the strictly mechanistic physics; and no less clearly in the culmination of centuries of effort to reconcile the Apollinian ideal with the facts of nature in the doctrine of psychophysical parallelism; a doctrine so unsatisfactory, so obviously a makeshift, so unintelligible, so obstructive to all deeper understanding of nature, that although it was, in one form or another, very widely accepted at the close of the nineteenth century, the century dominated by the Apollinian tradition, it has now been almost universally abandoned, even by those who have nothing to put in its place.

The Dionysian tradition has lived in the main outside the academies. European thought, though it was dominated by Aristotle until the end of the mediaeval period, was more concerned with reason than with action,

---

[18]Professor W. A. Hammond summarizes Aristotle's theory of action as follows: "Desire, as Aristotle employs it, is not a purely pathic or affective element. Feeling as such (theoretically) is completely passive—mere enjoyment of the pleasant or mere suffering of the painful. Aristotle, however, describes desire as an effort towards the attainment of the pleasant; i.e., he includes in it an activity or a conative element. It is feeling with an added quality of impulse (*Trieb*)." Here we see the cloven hoof of hedonism. The hormic theory would say rather that desire is impulse (*Trieb*) with an added quality of feeling.

[19]Nietzsche seems to have been the first to point clearly to these contrasting and rival world-views. I have attempted elsewhere (23) to show how these two currents have been represented in psychology all down the stream of European thought and how the distinction affords the best clue to a useful classification of psychological theories, since it distinguishes them in respect to their most fundamental features, their inclination towards intellectualism or towards voluntarism.

and yielded more and more to Apollinian tradition; and, with the triumph of intellectualism at and after the Renaissance, the Dionysian tradition was represented only by the poets and came near to exclusion from their pages also in the great age of Reason, the eighteenth century. The early years of the nineteenth century saw its revival in the works of the nature poets and of such philosophers as Oken, Schelling, and Fichte. And in the Scottish school of mental philosophy it began to find definite expression in psychology, especially in the works of Hutcheson and Dugald Stewart, a movement which was well nigh extinguished by Bain's capitulation to the intellectualism of the English association school.

On the continent of Europe, Schopenhauer revived it with his doctrine of the primacy of will; and Von Hartmann, his disciple, may be said to have first written psychology on a purely hormic basis,[20] but marred by the extravagance of his speculations on the unconscious. Nietzsche's scattered contributions to psychology are throughly hormic; and Bergson's vague doctrine of the *"élan vital"* can be classed only under the same heading. Freud's psychology would be thoroughly hormic, if he had not spoilt it in his earlier writings by his inclusion of the hedonist fallacy in the shape of his "pleasure principle." My *Introduction to Social Psychology* (13) was, so far as I have learned, the first attempt to construct a foundation for psychology in strict accordance with the hormic principle; and my two *Outlines* (16, 17) represent the first attempt to sketch a complete psychology (normal and abnormal) built on the hormic foundation. It was unfortunate for the hormic theory that my *Social Psychology* was shortly followed by my *Body and Mind* (14). For my defense of animism in that book created in many minds the impression that hormism stands or falls with animism; an impression that has been, I judge, largely responsible for the waning of the influence of the former book in American academic psychology. But the two theories do not necessarily hang together, as is clearly shown by Sir P. T. Nunn, that wisest of professors of education, distinguished as mathematician, philosopher, and psychologist, who founds his educational theory on a thoroughly hormic psychology, while repudiating animism. In his *Education, its Data and First Principles* (26), he has given the most lucid and persuasive statement of the hormic principles. In this statement he makes what is, I believe, the first definite proposal to use the terms *horme* and *hormic* in the sense in which they are used in this essay.

It is fitting, then, that this essay should conclude with citations from Dr. Nunn's book, citations that may serve further to clarify and fix the meaning of the terms *horme* and *hormic* and the implications of the theory.

"We need a name," writes Dr. Nunn, "for the fundamental property expressed in the incessant adjustments and adventures that make up the tissue of life. We are directly aware of that property in our conscious activities as an element of "drive," "urge," or felt tendency towards an end. Psychologists call it *conation* and give the name *conative process* to

---

[20]Cf. his *Die Moderne Psychologie* (4).

any train of conscious activity which is dominated by such a drive and receives from it the character of unity in diversity." Referring then to instances of the many subconscious activities that find expression in action, he writes: "None of these purposive processes may be called conative, for they lie below, and even far below, the conscious level; yet a super-human spectator, who could watch our mental behavior in the same direct way as we can observe physical events, would see them all as instances of the same class, variant in detail but alike (as we have said) in general plan. In other words, he would see that they all differ from purely mechanical processes by the presence of an internal "drive," and differ from one another only in the material in which the drive works and the character of the ends towards which it is directed. To this element of drive or urge, whether it occurs in the conscious life of man and the higher animals, or in the unconscious activities of their bodies and the (presumably) unconscious behavior of lower animals, we propose to give a single name—horme (ὁρμη). In accordance with this proposal all the purposive processes of the organism are hormic processes, conative processes being the subclass whose members have the special mark of being conscious . . . Horme . . . is the basis of the activities that differentiate the living animal from dead matter, and, therefore, of what we have described as the animal's characteristic attitude of independence towards its world."

Accepting this admirable statement, I will add only one comment. In my recent *Modern Materialism and Emergent Evolution* (21), I have argued that we can interpret the subconscious hormic processes (which Dr. Nunn agrees to regard as purposive or teleological), we can begin to gain some understanding of them, however vague, only if we regard them not as entirely blind but rather as involving, however dimly, something of that foresight (however vague and short-ranging) which is of the essence of our most clearly purposive activities; that therefore we must regard every hormic process as of the same fundamental nature as our mental activity, even if that interpretation involves us in a provisional dualism, held as a working hypothesis the final verdict upon which can come only with the progress of both the biological and the physical sciences.

REFERENCES

1. CARR, H. A. Psychology. New York: Longmans, Green, 1925. Pp. 226.
2. DREVER, J. Instinct in man. Cambridge: Cambridge Univ. Press, 1917. Pp. x+293.
3. HALDANE, J. S. The sciences and philosophy. London: Hodder, 1929. Pp. 344.
4. HARTMANN, E. v. Die moderne Psychologie. Leipzig: Haacke, 1901. Pp. vii+474.
5. HERRICK, C. J. The natural history of purpose. *Psychol. Rev.,* 1925, **32,** 417-430.
6. ————. Biological determinism and human freedom. *Int. J. Ethics,* 1926, **37,** 36-52.
7. ————. Behavior and mechanism. *Soc. Forces,* 1928, **7,** 1-11.
8. HINGSTON, R. W. G. Problems of instinct and intelligence. London: Arnold, 1928. Pp. viii+296.

9. JENNINGS, H. S. Diverse doctrines of evolution, their relation to the practice of science and of life. *Science,* 1927, **65**, 19-25.

10. KLAGES, L. The science of character. (Trans. by W. H. Johnson.) London: Allen & Unwin, 1929. Pp. 308.

11. LILLIE, R. S. The nature of the vitalistic dilemma. *J. Phil.,* 1926, **23**, 673-682.

12. LODGE, O. Beyond physics. *J. Phil. Stud.,* 1929, **4**, 516-546.

13. McDOUGALL, W. An introduction to social psychology. London: Methuen, 1908. Pp. x+355.

14. ————. Body and mind. New York: Macmillan; London: Methuen, 1911. Pp. xix+384.

15. ————. Motives in the light of recent discussion. *Mind,* 1920, **29**, 277-293.

16. ————. Outline of psychology. New York: Scribner's, 1923. Pp. xvi+456.

17. ————. Outline of abnormal psychology. New York: Scribner's, 1926. Pp. xiii+566. .

18. ————. Pleasure, pain and conation. *Brit. J. Psychol.,* 1926, **17**, 171-180.

19. ————. An experiment for the testing of the hypothesis of Lamarck. *Brit. J. Psychol.,* 1927, **17**, 267-304.

20. ————. Character and the conduct of life. London: Methuen, 1927. Pp. xiii+287.

21. ————. Modern materialism and emergent evolution. New York: Van Nostrand, 1929. Pp. viii+249.

22. ————. Second report on a Lamarckian experiment. *Brit. J. Psychol., J. Phil. Stud.,* 1930, **4**, No. 17.

23. ————. The present chaos in psychology and the way out. *J. Phil. Stud.*

24. MORGAN, C. L. Emergent evolution. London: Williams & Norgate, 1923. Pp. xii+313.

25. ————. Life, mind, and spirit. London: Williams & Norgate, 1926. Pp. 356.

26. NUNN, P. T. Education, its data and first principles. London: Arnold, 1920. Pp. 224.

27. PRINCE, M. Three fundamental errors of the behaviorists and the reconciliation of the purposive and mechanistic concepts. Chap. 9 in Psychologies of 1925. Worcester, Mass.: Clark Univ. Press, 1926. Pp. 199-220.

28. PRINZHORN, H. Leib-seele Einheit. Potsdam: Müller & Kripenhauer, 1927. Pp. 201.

29. RUSSELL, E. S. The study of living things. London: Methuen, 1924. Pp. 294.

30. STAPLEDON, W. O. A modern theory of ethics: a study of the relations of ethics and psychology. London: Methuen, 1929. Pp. 278.

31. TROLAND, L. T. The fundamentals of human motivation. New York: Van Nostrand, 1928. Pp. xiv+521.

32. WOODWORTH, R. S. Dynamic psychology. New York: Columbia Univ. Press, 1918. Pp. 210.

33. ————. Dynamic psychology. Chap. 5 in Psychologies of 1925. Worcester, Mass.: Clark Univ. Press, 1926. Pp. 111-126.

34. ————. Psychology. (Rev. ed.) New York: Holt, 1929. Pp. 590.

PART II

"ACT" OR "INTENTIONAL" PSYCHOLOGY
AND ASSOCIATIONISM

CHAPTER 2

ASSOCIATIONISM AND "ACT" PSYCHOLOGY
A HISTORICAL RETROSPECT

G. S. BRETT
University of Toronto

I.

In the language which is at present fashionable we may say that a cross-section of modern psychology shows a number of rudimentary organs or "vestiges of creation" which need valuation. The task to be performed in these paragraphs is defined by the editor as mainly historical, not wholly archaeological but concerned with topics that are rooted in the past, have lost their bloom and now exhibit the "sere and yellow leaf." The reader must therefore be content to find only well-seasoned truths, devoid of paradox and disappointingly lacking in sensational details.

II

Associationism of some kind is probably the oldest factor in psychological theory which has persisted to the present day. It was known to Plato; and the so-called "laws of association" were formulated precisely by Aristotle in language that has survived with no serious variation to the latest textbooks. At the beginning there was no conscious specialization of theories, and consequently none of that hard bifurcation which later schools exploited so dogmatically and so ruinously. It was natural at first to hold together the two fundamental aspects of life, namely, form and matter or (in the special case of psychology) act and content. The reasons for the persistence and the alterations of emphasis in the case of "act" and "association" are found in the equal persistence of two different ideals of method. For one party it seems axiomatic that the most important point is the growth and activity of the mind. The very datum of psychology is the unique kind of activity which constitutes a psychic event. For such events there can be no real causality: the physiological antecedents are not better known than the mental experience, and we can say only that the bodily changes are closely correlated with the data of introspection. For the other party it is equally axiomatic that nothing is innate. The human being thinks, if at all, about what has been given in the temporal sequences of daily life. The order of thought and the connection of ideas is a copy of the order and connection of objective events. Neither axiom is open to refutation, and the course of history shows a perpetual oscillation between affirmation and negation of either doctrine.

Another point needs to be mentioned before the individual topics can be elaborated. This point is the significant fact that neither party has ever been able to keep strictly inside its own boundaries. The bifurcation has always been largely a matter of degree; and the parallel lines, when produced ever so far, showed a dangerous tendency to converge and contradict their definition. A large part of the interest in the exposition consists in watching the slow exhaustion of the methods, the coming of the inevitable crisis when neither of them can be further prolonged, and the only possible conclusion is unity and cooperation. To abbreviate the subject and to give it some coherence, this central idea will be followed in the treatment of the two methods.

The Aristotelians, from the days of the master to the close of the Middle Ages, rarely or never found any difficulty in holding both views of the mind. The active and the passive intellect were both needed, one to produce the unity and organization of thought, the other to account for the presence and the variations of content. The principles of association originally stated were generously ambiguous. They were called similarity (or difference) and contiguity. That these two principles are wholly different was not a cause of perplexity to our forefathers. They took for granted the necessity of explaining both why we recall things having like qualities and why we recall events which came together. They also found no cause for worry in the problem whether the operation was the work of the mind or due to actual spatial closeness of the motions set up in each case. When the modern period began, with its prejudice in favor of mechanics as the type of scientific description, the emphasis was placed chiefly on modes of motion. The influence of theology had been the other way: the soul, like its Maker, "moved in a mysterious way its wonders to perform." The new sciences were pledged to annihilate obscurantism and took no account of the really miraculous powers which they were bestowing on the new deity called motion. So Hobbes, precise and stubborn and pseudo-scientific, copied out the Aristotelian phrases with his own underlining of the points. The "trayne of imaginations" was an excellent name for association; it was supplemented with a promising distinction between free and controlled association, and a vivid example served to make the whole statement a classical passage. After Hobbes the next great contribution was furnished by Hume. In this case the argument was made complete by the combination of an exact recital of the laws with an explicit theory of mental action. Hume included contiguity, similarity, and the cause-effect relation under association. The critics who have failed to see why Hume included cause and effect owe their blindness to the fact that they fail to appreciate Hume's concept of habit. The philosophy implied by Hume's doctrine is the theory that all connections of content are simply the result of the corresponding order of events. Since he proposed to account for all mental products (in spite of some inconsistency) by the relation of events and the consequent relation of ideas, causation was reduced from a special act or insight to the dead level of associated impressions.

It is significant that Hume was skeptical of any physiological basis, but he was prepared to use metaphors and assert that the principle of association does for the mental world what gravitation does for the physical world. This metaphor becomes a dogma in the hands of Hartley. As a doctor Hartley was more accustomed to think in terms of neural motion. Though somewhat ambiguous and curiously attached to theological conclusions, Hartley was a genuine associationist. Adapting his language to the formulae of Newtonian mechanics, Hartley provided "vibrations" as the inner organic effects and "vibratiuncles" as the particular bearers of conscious states. In this scheme, motion and the irradiations of motions are really the agents in association. In spite of his own efforts to support religion, Hartley became a prophet of materialism and was edited by Priestley as a supporter of that doctrine.

By this time the doctrine of association had got about all the exposition it could carry. It tended to show signs of being inadequate and, though it remained a cardinal point in the creed of the empiricists, its wooden simplicity was disliked and criticized. The Scottish school in the days of Thomas Brown were loyal to the principles, but "faith unfaithful kept them falsely true." It was not the mechanistic concept of association that attracted Brown, but the more subtle and ambiguous notion of mental suggestion. Moreover, Brown took the matter very seriously and evolved a distinction between primary and secondary laws of suggestion. The primary laws are the old traditional group, but the secondary are less familiar. They include duration, liveliness, frequency, recency, and some others; even "diversities of state" are to be considered, such as delirium or intoxication. Though James Mill became the accepted oracle of associationism, he added little to the earlier descriptions, and the classical age of associationism ended with the passage from the eighteenth century.

But the story was far from ended. Sir William Hamilton, replete with historical learning and acute enough to know that the German philosophers had another line of goods, proposed to settle the old dispute by accepting "total redintegration." In other words, anything can recall anything, provided the caller and the called have ever been united in one experience. This was good common sense, but a rather drastic reduction of mental life to one comprehensive formula. Hamilton was more a logician than a psychologist, a quality which he shared with the earlier British writers. But Alexander Bain stands out as a genuine psychologist, and his dectrine may be considered the last whole-hearted defense of associationism. The modernism of Bain is shown in his effort to avoid such words as memory, and to give a complete analysis of such concepts as intellect. Intellect is a sort of generic term for memory, imagination, judgment, and reasoning. Discrimination and retentiveness are the two essential functions, and of these retentiveness is more fundamental. So, in fact, the basis of all cognition is retentiveness, and retention is either a physiological characteristic or an empirical psychological fact. Here association is used partly for connected muscular movements, where one acts as a cue for another, and partly for connected experiences. Not satisfied with contiguity and similarity, Bain introduces compound association and constructive imagination. If it is demonstrably true that association will do all these things, it may be necessary to admit that no other hypothesis is required; all cognition will be resolved into associations. For it should be noted that Bain goes on to the uttermost limit. His theory of association reaches the "creative" acts of mind; he not only accepts the problem which made J. S. Mill furtively introduce "mental chemistry," but boldly proceeds to subordinate it to the dogma of associationism. The account is hardly satisfactory, but Bain asserts positively that the mind makes wholly different combinations out of the material as given. In other words, the associationist has swallowed the whole crux of his doctrine with no outward signs of discomfort.

The progress of associationism and its later history depend largely on the character of Herbart's work. The rather fantastic symbolism and the wholly unnecessary mathematical formalism of Herbart did not completely hide the value of his work. For half a century Herbart provided the magic formulae of education. True to the British tradition, in spite of German nationality and mentality, Herbart made the complex products of mental activity no more than collective groups of distinct impressions. This attitude encouraged investigation; what can be taken apart does at least admit some manipulation and invite analysis. But Herbart was never completely empirical; he was theoretically pragmatic. His influence was strong with many later writers who believed in analysis but were not enthusiasts in the field of experimental work. Among these the most significant has been Professor G. F. Stout, who has inclined to emphasize the persistent unity of consciousness and make associations instrumental in a continuous process of "redintegration." A similar modification is seen in James. Precluded from atomism by his doctrine of the stream of consciousness, James was none the less quite sure that the mechanism of association was inescapable. He made a significant contribution by insisting that the mind associates objects, not ideas. But with this amendment he is quite prepared to let the descendants of the Pilgrim Fathers keep their faith in eighteenth-century beliefs. His words are so much to the point, whether referred to 1898 or 1928, that no excuse need be offered for quoting them.

"In the last chapter we already invoked association to account for the effects of use in improving discrimination. In later chapters we shall see abundant proof of the immense part which it plays in other processes, and shall then readily admit that few principles of analysis, in any science, have proved more fertile than this one, however vaguely formulated it often may have been. Our own attempt to formulate it more definitely, and to escape the usual confusion between causal agencies and relations merely known, must not blind us to the immense services of those by whom the confusion was unfelt. From this practical point of view it would be a true *ignoratio elenchi* to flatter oneself that one has dealt a heavy blow at the psychology of association, when one has exploded the theory of atomistic ideas, or shown that contiguity and similarity between ideas can

only be there after association is done. The whole body of the associationist psychology remains standing after you have translated 'ideas' into
'objects,' on the one hand and 'brain-processes' on the other; and the analysis of faculties and operations is as conclusive in these terms as in those
traditionally used."

These are brave words but time has done something to tarnish their
splendor. Two aspects of the question remain to be considered. One is
the experimental treatment of associations; the other is the significance
of association for abnormal psychology. Neither of these can be regarded
as parts of the original outlook; they are the later forms of its evolution.

The experimental approach to questions of association seems to have
begun with the work of Galton. With his peculiarly original and un-
conventional attitude to accepted theories, Galton tested the traditional
views of association in two ways. In part he was concerned with an investigation of the kinds of association afforded by his own experiences,
attempting a qualitative analysis of free association. He had no theory
on which to base an explanation of the associations thus discovered, and
found the proceeding unfruitful. Then he turned to the quantitative side,
the question of the time required for associative reproduction. Incidentally
he came upon the characteristic now known as "perseveration," the tendency for the same associations to repeat themselves: but this also led him
to no further general conclusions. The year of Galton's publication
(1879) is almost the birth-date of experimental psychology. Wundt was
organizing experimental research, and the problems of reaction-time were
among the first investigations undertaken by his school. The work of
Trautscholdt, testing and refining the conclusions reached by Galton, was
the first serious attempt to settle the question of reaction-time in the
matter of association. Then came the classical work of Ebbinghaus. Here
there was a definite attempt to get rid of the qualitative factors: the use
of nonsense syllables was a device intended to make the experiments conform to the requirement that the elements used should be exact and unvarying. It may be doubted whether these ideal factors could be obtained,
whether variations of interest and non-voluntary forms of "meaning"
could be excluded, but at any rate we have the authority of Titchener to
support the assertion that "the recourse to nonsense syllables, as means to
the study of association, marks the most considerable advance in this
chapter of psychology, since the time of Aristotle." Moreover, Ebbinghaus
took a new view of the problem to be investigated. He did not limit
himself to the associations resulting from general experiences, but concentrated on the processes by which mental acts were organized into series.
In other words, he went through the acts which establish memory sequences and studied the characteristics of those acts. We pass over the
well-known results of this work to comment on two special points. It
is evident that the question now broadens out to become the general question of the empirical study of memory. This involved the possibility of a
diffused effect, such that several factors in a series were being associated
in varying degrees of strength at one time. The simple connection of a

series (*a, b, c*) might be complicated in such a way that the recall of *b* was in part also the recall of *c*, and, in fact, a second series (*a, c, e*) was found to be created by the act of forming the first series. The extent of the association was then shown to be larger than had been suspected, and elements in the series separated by considerable intervals acquired a linkage through the fact that the whole series had once been established. Further tests showed that the latent effects of association were demonstrable, for after the acquired associations seemed to have faded away, the time required to reinstate them was less than the normal time for acquiring new material.

Continuation of this topic would involve a complete inventory of all the researches on memory, a task which might well appall the stoutest heart and could by no efforts be compressed into the limits of this essay. The work of G. E. Müller, alone and also in collaboration with Pilzecker (1900), was one of the earliest and most weighty contributions. Complicating factors, such as interference, were introduced by some experimenters (e.g., Bergstrom, 1894). Significant variations were introduced by Cattell (1887) in using variable logical relations, such as class to member and whole to part. Other variations were the consideration of feeling-tone and the age or sex differences of the persons studied.

It will be noted that the work so far discussed is predominantly in the field of cognition. In spite of some restlessness and a general discontent with the dominating tendency to make psychology a study of sensation and thought, the association of ideas exerted its own magic of suggestion and drew the investigators perennially back into the charmed circle of cognitive acts. But this was not inescapable, and with the exhaustion of the possible lines of research there came a tendency to make more prominent the field of muscular or kinaesthetic sequences. The acquisition of skill is a very obvious type of association and may be, physiologically, the most fundamental element in all association. As facility is the term which expresses the fact underlying the observable reduction of time of recall, so it also indicates the establishment of the successive cues which serve to make rapid the series of movements required for skill. So far as association is concerned, there is no difference of principle but only a shift of reference from one group of neural connections to another. The centers involved may be wholly or partly subcortical, but the tendency to limit questions of association to cortical centers is a prejudice which may be legitimately quoted as a remnant of the "intellectualism" from which we are now so strongly urged to emancipate ourselves. Let us then give honor to whom honor is due and not forget to mention the fact that types of skill have been studied, notably in the case of Bryan and Harter, who investigated the acquisition of skill in receiving and sending telegraphic messages; or in the case of Book, whose field was typewriting. In work of this kind the original principles of association are fundamental, except that the emphasis on "ideas" can be partly eliminated. Also there is a close parallel between the methods and results in this field and those of Ebbinghaus. The increase in skill is equivalent to the increase of facility in recall, the persistence of facility during a latent period is found in both kinds of "memory," and the unsolved problems are generically alike. The so-called "plateau" is an ambiguous factor which may point to a process of integration which simplifies the grouping of responses, and it is equally possible that piecemeal learning of words tends in fact to establish groups of responses which act by the principle of "redintegration" and bring into play more rapidly the competent elements.

Consideration of skill and the general field of organized motor responses leads in the direction of behaviorism. Intellectualism in psychology has often met with rebukes and kindly remonstrances, but the treatment accorded to it by behaviorists (meaning the "extreme" behaviorists) may be called castigation. For the present we are not concerned with the quarrel but with the doctrine which has been developed as the basis of a behavioristic interpretation. As we have noted, from time to time there have frequently been attempts to justify associationism by reference to the physiological processes supposed to sustain the psychological relations. The empirical trend of all associationism, though not necessarily physiological in its terms, does consistently make physiological explanation a desirable goal and at least a pious aspiration. Whenever the resistance is weakened, the temptation is triumphant. The word "contiguity" always suggests proximity of the places where the events occur. The progressive facility derived from established associations makes us benevolent toward theories of neural currents and drainage and words that reconstruct, picturesquely, a not impossible alliance between "this too, too solid flesh" and the elusive transactions of the mind. But the vain groping after the required explanation, the disappointing snares of "vibrations" and "brain paths" and other obvious metaphors, faded into oblivion when the course of events put the conditioned reflex into the hands of the distracted seekers after truth. Here, at last, was the long-expected solution. The reflex was accepted already as the indisputable (though painfully abstract) unit which by continual complication in chain reflexes and compound reflexes could be built up into habits; and habit maketh man, in the newer schools of thought. The difficulty which remained was to get the kind of interrelation which was needed between the actual reflex mechanism and the new stimuli provided by a changing environment. Here the conditioned reflex came in to supply the missing link. Accepting Pavlov's results, it was possible to touch the bedrock of experience. Deep down in the recesses of the physiological mechanism (so it seems) there were being formed relations between stimuli and responses from which could be built up an imposing structure that looked very much like the totality of experience. Whether this is a sound psychological doctrine or one more exercise in deductive logic may be left for the future to decide. Our present business is to point out that it is the latest form of associationism. Discarding the unnecessary phrase "of ideas," and broadening both thought and language to suit the new outlook, it is correct to say that the use of conditioned reflexes represents the most significant way in which the central positions of associationism are active today. It may be necessary to add that the theory has been transfigured and that nothing now remains of traditional associationism, but the transfiguration has been a gradual change of the picture in harmony with the total change of outlook produced, no less gradually, by the evolution of the physiological and biological sciences with which psychology has more and more allied itself in some directions.

As an empirical method with some degree of utility, association became a factor in the field of abnormal psychology. This involved no special change of theory but introduced some new aspects dependent on the character of the cases examined. It is of some interest to recall the fact that John Locke, pioneer of the British school and a man with medical training, had taken it for granted that association was found only in cases where the person was not normal. Logical connections were, of course, accepted as rational: but Locke's discussion (*Essay, Book II, Chap.* 33) begins with the heading "Something unreasonable in most men," and the idea of association is employed to explain irrational or illogical connections dependent on peculiar facts. Locke's story of the man who learned dancing in a room where a trunk stood on the floor and afterwards could never dance unless the trunk was present is as good an example of "conditioning" as one could desire. Locke felt that "if this story shall be suspected to be dressed up with some comical circumstances, a little beyond precise nature," it would be desirable to produce evidence: but psychologists are much less tender-minded in this century. Another accepted cause of association was "prejudice," a good old word which covered a multitude of sins. In this respect it has its counterpart in the words "sentiment" (as used by Mr. Shand) and "complex." Locke says: "There are rooms convenient enough, that some men cannot study in, and fashions of vessels, which, though ever so clean and commodious, they cannot drink out of, and that by reason of some accidental ideas which are annexed to them, and make them offensive: and who is there that hath not observed some man to flag at the appearance, or in the company of some certain person not otherwise superior to him, but because, having once on some occasion got the ascendant, the idea of authority and distance goes along with that of the person, and he that has been thus subjected, is not able to separate them?" This seems as much as one need say about complexes, and the last sentence even suggests the exact notion of an "inferiority complex."

But Locke, in common with the men of his day, was content to observe and describe. The new element in modern "association tests" is the reversion of the process and the development of a technique to discover which contents of the mind have significant bonds of union. The so-called diagnostic value was thus added, and it proved to have significance, to a limited extent, partly in defining types of mind and partly in detecting special states of mind, such as the guilty conscience. Whether the latter affords good legal evidence or not is irrelevant to the present discussion; the only point at issue is that some kind of connection, indicated by inhibition, variation of reaction-time, or peculiar forms of association (e.g., water, death), can be discovered by this use of tests. Kraepelin seems to have begun this sort of work in 1883 as a part of the diagnosis of mental diseases, and since that date many investigators have used it in different ways. The tests seem to show a working correlation between degrees of mental activity and range of association, a result which appears to be less a discovery than a proof of a definition. Many interesting details have emerged which throw light on the way in which ideas may be subordinated or superordinated; but general conclusions about such entities as the "criminal mind" will remain precarious until we know more exactly the difference between a criminal and a victim of unwise legislation! The method as such does not stand or fall by the truth of such conclusions, and its judicious use in the way which is now chiefly attributed to Jung may be described in the words of Bernard Hart as "of great service in the preliminary investigation of a case" and able to furnish "valuable indications of the directions along which a subsequent detailed analysis may most profitably be conducted."

The reader may feel that he has now been led away from what he has been accustomed to regard as the distinctive teaching of associationism. The suspicion is justified, but it is necessary to offer the defense that the result is not an act of deception but the inevitable effect of launching out on the stream of history and following the current as it flows. When associationism takes on the forms describable by such words as sentiments and complexes, it becomes doubtful whether it has not changed its fundamental postulates and become merely an instrument in the hands of men whose creed has very little resemblance to the articles of faith accepted by their predecessors. To speak plainly, the later history of associationism reveals a change of front which makes the older antagonism between content and act almost obsolete. We may now turn the coin over and look at the reverse to discover what characters have been stamped on it.

III

Though associationism came into prominence by the impetus derived from experimental science, the opponents were never entirely eclipsed. The deep-seated belief that quantity is not applicable to "the soul" remained unshaken, and the "pure act" of the mind was, in reality, more vigorously supported than the new views about its composition and decomposition. Leibniz uttered the challenge of his school in the most emphatic language: the mind is innate to itself and it is more concerned with expression than impression. Though useful in many ways, associationism had a tendency to run to seed and end in such artificial contrivances as the "statue" of Condillac. The pietist, the mystic, and the mathematician never agreed with the exponents of mechanism; for different reasons they all clung to some formula of insight, spontaneous activity, or creative power. When the British method of empirical analysis was spreading through Germany and the country was being nourished on translations of Locke and Hume, the movement was checked by the impact of Kant's critical doctrine. The persistent and unfailing influence of

Kant down to the present day is not due to peculiar phrases like the "synthetic unity of apperception" nor to any very effective program of work. It is due to the fact that he actually achieved what he claimed to have done: he made materialism and spiritualism equally impossible. The new basis was experience, the raw material of life with no antecedent divisions between soul and body which could justify the necessity to choose one or the other as an exclusive principle of explanation. From this point of view the "given" is the elementary act, the simplest form of self-expression, the "act" as understood by Fichte and interpreted by his many disciples down to and including Münsterberg. It is probably foolish to suppose that national characteristics play any part in the history of theories, though psychologists might be expected to favor psychological explanations of these phenomena. It is also foolish to speak of a French or German or English psychology, when exceptions are as numerous as examples. But in spite of all these warnings, it is difficult not to envisage the long warfare of psychological theories as a struggle between Anglo-Saxon and Teutonic attitudes, with the French to mediate between them at intervals. If something is needed to point the moral, let the reader consider the relation between the main part of Gardner Murphy's *Historical Introduction to Modern Psychology* and Klüver's *Supplement on Contemporary German Psychology*. Whatever the reason may be, Kant has remained the monument that casts its shadow on the whole nineteenth century, and his doctrine was activism. After Kant we come to Lotze, Johannes Müller, and Fechner, all in their diverse ways true to the fundamental tenets; even Herbart was no exception, though he might be claimed as a product of cross-fertilization. If modern psychology really begins with Wundt, we are straightway confronted by his use of the traditional German doctrine of apperception and his obvious desire to transform all associations into synthetic acts (fusions, assimilations, complications), supplemented by equally active forms of analysis. Incidently Wundt showed that this attitude of mind neither cramps nor excludes a zeal for experimental investigation.

For the historian there is hardly any figure in modern psychology more interesting than Brentano. Appearing in 1874 his work was curiously paradoxical. Its title, *Psychologie vom empirischen Standpunkte,* was in itself a challenge, for it ignored the monopoly which the word empirical had already established as a name for sense empiricism, went straight back to the Greek use of the term and (with explicit revival of an Aristotelian tradition) asserted the fundamental importance of activity. Brentano's book might almost be counted a Roman Catholic manifesto if it were not true that what is important in the doctrines of that church has always been equally the possession of pre-Christian and post-Christian Aristotelians. At the same time, in spite of its appearance of being reactionary, Brentano's work really fell in line with the movement from Leibniz through Kant; it was "empirical" in the sense that it was based on the claim that it reached a pure experience and analyzed it. The keyword is activity and the genuine material for psychology is the act.

To expand this further it is necessary to understand that the unit of activity (which is also the actual unit of psychology) is some degree of judgment, not a sensation. This point is really the core of the whole matter, though it is usually difficult to make it intelligible, and almost impossible when the tendency toward physiology is dominant. To make sensation the beginning of psychic activity would be absurd to a psychologist of Brentano's type; it would be like telling the anthropologist that in the beginning was the grammar, not speech. And this postulate of method, though it might shock the followers of Hume or even some of the less critical disciples of Wundt, really forced psychologists to reconsider their position. Wundt was philosophically a Kantian, and, as such, a supporter of activity. But the methods emphasized by his experimental program were the methods of Müller, the physiologist, and Helmholtz, the physicist. As such, they carried in them the seeds of dissension. Wundt himself might hold together the opposing tendencies, for it is not certain that a belief in activity either can or does vitally affect the kind of problem which is solved in the laboratory. But it was equally inevitable that some disciples, either less interested in the physiological approach or feeling that it was for the moment exhausted and lacking promise, should turn to new fields and attempt to find new material. This was the situation which produced the so-called Würzburg school, a legitimate development of part of the Wundtian program which need not have caused any hostility between Leipzig and Würzburg if it had been handled diplomatically or submitted to arbitration. As it was, the difference was more emphasized than the agreement, and the movement became the first stage in the quarrel between the structural and the functional attitudes in psychology. The difference of formulae was further complicated by the shift of emphasis from sensation to thought. What Titchener called "the experimental psychology of the thought processes" was a phenomenon with a double significance. In part it challenged the adequacy of existing methods to solve problems above the level of sensation and motor responses; in part it raised the question whether the accepted "elements" were functions of the organism at all, or merely artificial factors useful for making a mechanical picture of the mind. The first point could be settled only by more experiments, and to these the supporters of Külpe particularly applied themselves. The second point was much more significant and was destined to involve the whole field of psychological theory.

In some respects it might be said that the chief object of the new movement was to escape from the situation which made the "glue of association" either necessary or useful. One way of doing this was shown by Münsterberg. The first requisite was to abandon the kind of unit which had been assumed by previous theorists, the atomic sensation. Münsterberg (who, like most Germans, had definite philosophical leanings and was influenced by Fichte) formulated his concept of the unit in terms of action. The primary psychological act was, therefore, found neither in the sensation as datum nor in the action as response but in the transition itself, the sensorimotor process. The indivisible mental act was then equivalent to the change of mental content, while at the same time the act retained a psychophysical value because it was (or should have been) equivalent to a measurable reaction-time. With this aspect of the subject (the experimental records) we are not concerned in detail. The point of interest is that Münsterberg's approach led him to experiment with a stimulus-response method which took the form of question and answer, thereby introducing the problems of selection, judgment, and decision. How much was proved by the experiments is not easy to say, but it may be inferred that they indicated a difference between simple habits of motor reaction (acquired by previous training) and the selective activity required for complex judgments of new material. From the way in which the experiments were graded, it would be possible to infer that all conscious reactions are dependent on apperception of meaning and vary in rapidity according to the degree to which the motor path is open: in other words, the signal operates most rapidly when the movement is expected and anticipated. On the higher planes of judgment this occurs when the elements have a kind of relation under which they can be easily subsumed. For example, right-left is a relation of this kind; but the question (used by Münsterberg), "Which is of greater importance to man, the most important application of electricity or the most important use of gunpowder," might well cause the most nimble intellect some considerable delay!

Münsterberg's work really created more problems than it solved; and this may be called one of its chief merits. The method seems to have "summoned from the vasty deep" more spirits than it could control, and the most obvious conclusion would be that it is possible to evoke mental acts which defy any kind of measurement or explanation. At any rate the numerical values seem to have become meaningless at this stage, and it became apparent that neither association nor Wundt's formula of apperception was the required solution.

The conspicuous part played by the motor reaction in Münsterberg's experiments has rather obscured other implications of his work. For this reason emphasis has here been laid on a different point, namely, the kind of summation which his question-answer material involves. Somewhere in Münsterberg's results there were concealed two factors: one was the actual kind of synthesis which held together question and answer; the other was the individual differences of the persons employed for the experiments. Either of these factors was enough to destroy the mechanical conception of association, and in fact Münsterberg never seems to have doubted that he was tapping some kind of synthetic process of judgment. For this reason he comes very close to another group of psychologists who never attempted to embellish their procedure with any physiological ornaments. Among these must be reckoned James Ward, a powerful influence in the movement which was to carry British psychology far away from the simple-minded associationism in which it had so long found peace and happiness. Ward was not so insular as his predecessors. Berlin, Göttingen, and Leipzig all contributed to the composition of his mind, and the most decisive influence was Lotze. It was the idealistic rather than the physiological trend in Lotze which appealed to Ward, who was himself struggling to reconcile his outworn creed with the new science of his day. The result was a kind of spiritual biology which was new enough to seem revolutionary and old enough to leave undisturbed the bedrock of tradition. Ward's achievement was impressive. With great diligence and extraordinary grasp of his material, he succeeded in translating the facts of mental life into a language which was free from the metaphors of Newtonian mechanics and flavored with suggestions of the new biological interests. Life and activity and the self as subject were the categories of his psychology. The whole attitude of associationism faded away as the new ideas spread through England, and the isolated figure of Ward at Cambridge became an unsuspected ally of the German idealism which Green and Bradley and Bosanquet were making triumphant at Oxford. At least they had in common an opposition to associationism and a more or less complete tendency to pay no attention to experimental laboratories and their output.

As space will not permit us to deal extensively with these different writers, Ward will be taken for granted as the background of the work of G. F. Stout. More than anyone else Stout has been a faithful disciple of Ward, not as a slavish imitator of the words but as an independent thinker capable of carrying on the work in the spirit of the master. Times have changed since Ward first wrote his famous article for the *Encyclopaedia Britannica* and with the times there have come changes in the restatement of psychological doctrine by Ward's followers. But, on the whole, the pattern has been well preserved. The one unchanging point of agreement is the emphasis on activity. From Brentano onwards we find among these writers the ruling principle that in psychology it is possible to classify activities, but it is not possible to discover inert fragments. They all learned very thoroughly the lesson taught by Lotze, that the mind is not like a wall composed of ready-made bricks but is like the plant, built up of cells that are made as the plant makes itself. There could be no reconciliation between this doctrine and the associationists; in fact, none was needed; for no champion came forward to carry the banner of Hume and James Mill and Bain. Only the "neural shock" of Herbert Spencer was left to remind his countrymen of their lost leaders! The new school took activity as their keyword. It was indisputably true that the word had no very exact meaning; as Bradley said, it was liable to become a public scandal. But Stout at least gave it a meaning by force of the use made of it, and with that we may be content. Its first meaning can be taken from the physiologists, from the primary irritability which all living matter must possess. It can then be elevated to the Spinozistic level, and we may assume that every creature strives to persist in its own existence. This, as the Latinists had been saying from the time of Cicero, is conation. With this basic term to support the structure, we may go on to consider classes of activity, which are knowing, feeling, and willing. These are all conative in their way, but we must guard against thinking about the wrong things; the object at which we strive is always the next state of mind: if I want to turn out the light, my real aim is the experience of darkness which I thus establish. Mental life is a continuity, without break or division; like time itself, it flows without interruption. By the same argument it can be shown that it flows over from one focal center to another: "in the moment of interruption, the interruption itself constitutes a sort of conative continuity between the old process and the new." With such fluent material it is clear that no method is possible except analysis: our author provides us with an "analytic psychology" which is essentially observational and introspective, or, as Mr. Broad would prefer to say, "inspective."

The center of interest is once more the problem of mental connections. In a sense there is nothing but connection, because we have unbroken continuity and inescapable relativity. But these universals are not quite to the point; we still want a closer treatment of the particular experiences. Here we come to two problems. Are we to go back to the old hard-and-fast distinction of images and ideas? Are we to fall back on associations? The answer is provided by the well-established practice of transforming values. Images are not denied, but they are not the isolated mental fragments which rejoiced the atomistic psychologists of earlier days. They are subordinate instruments; they subserve meaning without making up its essence; they "are attended to only so far and so long as they connect themselves with the general direction of mental activity"; they are often only loosely connected with the recognized content of meaning, as when the idea of liberty is accompanied by the fleeting image of the Statue of Liberty; finally, there are some apprehended contents which are not "imaged" at all, the "imageless thoughts" of the later controversy. If we want to hear more about images, we must wander away into illusions, hallucinations, and dreams.

When we come to the question of "trains of ideas" the strategy is very similar but more subtle. Association of ideas is accepted as a formula with some utility; it plays a subordinate part in the process by which one experience leads into another and thereby forms the basis for possible reproduction of mental states. But the conditions of reproduction are so formulated as to remove any suspicion that the doctrine of associationism is retained. We are told that "ultimately all depends on continuity of interest," and "contiguity" is actually translated into "continuity of interest." The space or time relations of mental events are now discarded; the link is between meanings which owe all the connection they have to the interest which sustains them. The problem of selective attention ceases to trouble us, for all attention is selective, and there is no association which is not selective. The exceptions would be pathological. Our terms are now changed to suit the new point of view: there are "dominant interests" and "dominant ideas" which function as organizing agents in the total experiences and, like a magnet in a field of electricity, each central idea holds together all that comes within its range of influence. In so far as ideas can be called "parts" of anything, it is held that there must be some "whole" of which they are parts; and the whole is prior to the parts, because otherwise there could never be more than aggregates or bundles. It is the "total mental state" that really counts in "determining what ideas shall be revived," and by this concept of a total mental state the standpoint is adequately defined.

Stout's point of view is part of a movement which appears in other writers with more or less significant variations. The theory of dominant interests which act as regulative agencies is closely related to the hormic doctrine of P. T. Nunn and the purposive psychology of McDougall. In a special field it has served to support the theory of sentiments used by A. F. Shand to explain the organic relatedness of emotions, and in principle it is not far removed from "complexes," if we limit that term to normal apperceptive processes. But the peaceful penetration achieved by the theory has been masked by the more striking tactics of the German school. When we quoted the phrase "total mental state" from Stout's work, we might have paused to inquire what is included by that set of terms. When is a mental state "total"? Is the reference to the cognitive states only or to complex units of knowing, willing, and feeling? Stout would presumably accept any dominant state: when he speaks of a man being "in the mood for making puns," he introduces a word (mood) which calls for more explanation; but on the whole he seems indifferent to the further possibilities of the problem. But it was exactly these possibilities which stimulated the Würzburg school to make their experimental researches on the thought processes. The details of these are so far familiar that it would be a waste of energy to recount them. We may limit ourselves to a statement of the theoretical significance of what was supposed to be proved.

The first and most comprehensive result was the declaration that all piecemeal "composition of the mind" was a radically unsound view. In the beginning is the act, the undefinable "thinking" itself. But this is not a "pure" act. It is itself the emergence into conceptual form of a tendency, disposition, or attitude. Though emphasis was put on the rejection of images, because that happened to be the precise point in dispute, the real significance of the whole theory was its attempt to grasp once more the concrete flow of life, to observe the flux of thought without arresting it or enclosing it in artificial compartments. The group that acquired fame during this controversy (Ach, Bühler, Messer, Watt, et al.) was never exactly a school; they were a band of workers united by the common hope of finding a way out of the intolerable position created by traditional formulae and unverified dogmas. The results were as various as the workers and tended to be more destructive than constructive. The truth of the position is probably indisputable. Every thought is a ripple in the deep waters of life: the past and the future, the height and the depth, are all summed up in it; as a movement it must have direction as well as speed; as an event it must have relations, and, when it is thought, it will probably have logical or systematic relations. These claims need not be disputed, but the opponent will ask what it all means. Science cannot study the universe; it must abstract and isolate and make artificial in order to attain precision. It must assume points that have no magnitude, motion that involves no friction, cells that might exist alone in no continuous tissue. We know these things are fictions, but they are the price that is paid for the kind of results we want. If we insist on attitudes, dispositions, tendencies, "intention," and the like, can we go on with the psychology of the psychologists? The plain answer is no. This road leads to another goal and that is the study of persons in the totality of their existence. Not merely the whole mind but the whole personality will have to be the starting-point of the new science.

Some have already accepted this and declared for personal psychology. A few continue in the more theoretical ground of a self psychology, determined not to accept Hume and his ways at any price. The German school has been challenged to establish its priority by the "Paris school," in other words, by Binet. As a consequence of other researches, Binet came to the conclusion that it was futile to probe the secrets of thought by the study of images. He, too, found refuge in imageless thoughts and in the "intention" of the mind. When we say "triangle" we *know* what we mean; the word "triangle" signifies the intention, the direction, the sphere of consciousness. We can say, "At any rate *that* is not a triangle," while admitting that we do not know what the datum is. We reject with unsophisticated scorn the assertion that if we say "triangle" we must mean either the scalene, or the equilateral, or the isosceles; the nominalism of Berkeley is as dead as his theistic metaphysics for most psychologists. Even Bain had his moments of weakness (or strength?) and spoke of "attitudes." In fact, if we go on probing much longer, we may find that no serious psychologist ever really denied either a self or a mind or a state of consciousness; all the sceptics really meant to say was that these things are true without being useful, and though we can always *have* them we can rarely or never *use* them. That is perhaps the root of the trouble and it means the parting of the ways. One way will lead to a psychology which is scientific but artificial; the other will lead to a psychology which is natural but cannot be scientific, remaining to the end an art.

We shall perhaps be trespassing on forbidden ground if we take into account another contribution, the writings of Bergson. Whether Bergson would venture to join a company of "real psychologists" or prefer peace with honor among the philosophers, may be left undecided. The *Traité de Psychologie* of Dumas accords him a distinct place, and takes him to be the spokesman of the method called "intuition." Certainly he enters the procession with good right after Maine de Biran, Charcot, Janet, and Binet. From their work he has drawn the conclusions, only exciting because they upset ingrained habits, that we live before we study life, think before we analyze thoughts, and, in general, act before we reflect. That is old enough to need no comment, except that nothing would be more discussed than a man who rose from the dead. The eighteenth century buried the living man; children it ignored altogether, until Tiedemann remembered them; and the result was that it forgot what spontaneity and immediacy could mean. Bergson advanced by going back; he went back behind mechanism to the living man, and behind reflective man to the creature that lived indivisibly before anyone undertook the "anatomy of the mind." Bergson's work, in effect, was a commentary on the brief but despairing phrase, "We murder to dissect." In reply it might be said that we have progressed far enough now to dissect before we kill (such is the ambiguous nature of progress), and in any case dissection is quite useful even if the object is dead. We come back to the original point, which is: Do these attacks on traditional associationism really imply that all psychology is open to condemnation, that mental life cannot really be reduced to the kind of formulae which science requires, that the variables are too many and too diverse for the human mind to control? If so, the future lies with literary descriptions, with art, education, characterology, individual differences, and all the other profitable enterprises which can perhaps be reconciled with any theoretical position, provided it is not associationism or pure structuralism.

Driesch has said that "association psychology is really *dead* now," and the statement expresses something between a fact and a hope. To justify it would require a discussion of topics excluded from this article, particularly the problems of relations and the evidence for the Gestalt doctrine. Having no commission to discuss those extensive topics, we may conclude with a brief summary of the older teaching as defined for the purpose of this section. The disruption which separated behaviorists from introspectionists is a recent event which can now be traced back to the minor breach between those who chose to consider first the empirical content and those who preferred to take their stand on the indivisible act. The evolution which has been sketched here seemed to be most successfully formulated in the terms of that antithesis, which corresponded for practical purposes with the division between empirical and rational psychology. Through various mutations the conflict of interest went its way. The final balance of advantage has seemed to lie with the opponents of empiricism and associationism. The outcome, however, is not simple. The abandonment of faculties for types of activity is one item of progress, but it may prove to be more a change of name than of facts. The corresponding movement from structure to function seems to support the preference for action and totality over content and composition. But on examination the practical value of the associationist principles seems to be very slightly damaged or reduced. A newer and wider significance may accrue to the old terminology from advances in physiology or biology or even sociology; the concept of growth, in particular, may have rendered us dissatisfied with anything that seems rigid and fixed and not perpetually "in the making"; but in the detailed consideration of this and that particular habit, in the positive connections established between one event and another, in the more subtle but not otherwise different concept of conditioning which we now use for association, there seem to survive so many earlier conceptions that we may hesitate to say too confidently that the older points of view have lost all their vitality.

PART III
FUNCTIONAL PSYCHOLOGY

CHAPTER 3

FUNCTIONALISM

HARVEY CARR
University of Chicago

What is a functional type of psychology, and who were the functional psychologists? According to Boring (4), functionalism was a revolt of colonial psychologists against Germany. (Perhaps American would have been the better term to use.) The controversy between Titchener and Baldwin was a phase of the whole. Germany was the more philosophical and America the more practical. Chicago functionalism was the explicit movement, but I think it was symptomatic of what was quietly going on all over the country except at Cornell.

Titchener (11, 12) groups the various psychologies into two classes: (a) the structural or what is now termed the existential type of psychology represented by Wundt, Külpe, Ebbinghaus, and Titchener, and (b) the empirical type which attempts to portray mind as it is, i.e., as it works in dealing with the world about it. This empirical type of psychology goes back to Aristotle and Aquinas, and it forms the staple contents of most psychologies down to and including our twentieth-century textbooks.

Titchener further subdivides the empirical group into two sub-classes —the act and the functional types of psychology. Brentano, Lipps, Witasek, Stumpf, Meinong, Messer, and Stout are referred to as act psychologists, while Ladd, Judd, Angell, James, Baldwin, and Dewey are referred to as functionalists. Titchener states that functionalism was primarily an American psychology, which traces its descent from Aristotle, but which was born of the enthusiasm of the post-Darwinian days when evolution seemed to answer all the riddles of the universe. Functionalism is further described as the dominant psychology of America which suddenly became conscious of itself, and which attempted to justify itself as a system with the introduction of existentialism.

According to Angell (2), functionalism was a movement that embraced a large number of psychologists who had certain principles in common, but who differed considerably in many other respects. He specifically states that functionalism is not to be identified with the Chicago type of psychology. Functionalism found its roots in Aristotle; its modern origin is traced to Spencer and Darwin, while the movement became self-conscious and first attempted to define and formulate itself as a protest and defense against the inroads and threatened dominance of

[59]

the existentialism of Titchener and his disciples.   Angell gives no list of functional psychologists as does Titchener.

These three writers agree that functionalism refers primarily to the dominant modern American type of psychology as contrasted with the structuralism or existentialism of Wundt and Titchener.   I doubt if Angell would limit the term exclusively to American psychologists.   I am inclined to think that he would classify Stout, for example, as a functionalist, while Titchener refers to him as an act psychologist.   Perhaps the distinction between a functional and an act psychology is not as clear-cut and definite as Titchener assumes, or perhaps the two psychologies are not mutually exclusive and the same person may legitimately be assigned to both classes.

These minor differences will be ignored, and, for the present, we shall use the term functionalism to refer to the American empirical movement that rebelled against the proposed limitations of the structural or existential school of Titchener and his disciples.   I shall adopt the caution of Angell and refrain from adding to Titchener's list of functional psychologists, as I fear that some might be rudely surprised, if not insulted, at being labelled a functionalist.   Functional psychology is not to be identified with that of Angell or the Chicago group of psychologists.   There is no functional psychology; rather there are many functional psychologies. In speaking of functionalism, we are dealing with a group of psychologies which differ from each other in many particulars, but which exhibit certain common characteristics in virtue of which they are labelled functionalistic.

What are these common characteristics, and in what respects do the functional psychologies differ from the existentialism of Titchener?   In answering these questions, we shall again refer to the writings of Titchener and Angell—the chief antagonists in this structural-functional controversy.

Before doing so, it may be well to note some points of agreement.   At the time of which we write—roughly the period from 1890 to 1910—practically all psychologists professed to be engaged in the study of consciousness.   Structuralists and functionalists were alike then in that they defined their science as the study of the conscious processes as distinct from their organic conditions and correlates.   The two schools differed somewhat as to the meaning of the term consciousness, and they might differ considerably as to the metaphysical implications of the dualistic distinction involved.   Again, introspection was regarded as the chief, if not the only, method of psychological observation, although the two schools did not agree as to the connotation of this term.

Functionalism, according to Angell (2), differs from structuralism in three respects.

1)   Structuralism deals with the whats or contents of consciousness, and it attempts to describe these in terms of their analytical elements. Functionalism does the same thing, but it refuses to confine itself to this limited program.   It proposes to deal also with the whys and hows of

these contents, and to study them in their relation to the context of which they are a part.

2) This context in its widest and most inclusive sense is the biological process of adjustment. Functionalism regards mental processes as means by which the organism adapts itself to its environment so as to satisfy its biological needs. Mental events are thus studied from the standpoint of their relation to the environmental world and to the ensuing reaction of the organism to that world. Functional psychology is thus practical and utilitarian in spirit and interest. Functionalism studies the uses and utilities of conscious processes, and it is naturally interested in developing the various applied fields—educational psychology, industrial psychology, abnormal psychology, mental hygiene, etc.

3) Functional psychology insistently attempts to translate mental process into physiological process and, conversely, it is interested in discovering and stating the organic concomitants and correlates of the conscious processes. Such a program is obviously incumbent upon any dualistic psychology which regards mental processes as means of adjustment to the environmental world. A functionalist can accept any one of the various conceptions of nature of the mind-body dualism with the single exception of that of epiphenomenalism.

Titchener (11) lists four characteristics of a functional type of psychology.

1) Functional psychologies distinguish between the activity or function of consciousness and its content or structure. They emphasize the study of function in preference to that of content.

2) Consciousness, especially in its active phase, has a value for organic survival. Consciousness is regarded as a solver of problems.

3) A functional psychology is teleological. The whole course of mental life is regarded teleologically.

4) Functional psychologies are written as a preface to philosophy or to some practical discipline. They psychologize as a means to some foreign end and not as an end per se. Their spirit is primarily that of an applied science rather than that of a pure science. Presumably existentialism is a representative of the pure scientific attitude.

These two writers agree that functionalism differs from existentialism in that it refuses to confine itself to the limitations of the existential program, but insists upon doing something more, viz., study functions. Both agree that this program will include a study of the uses or utilities of mind in practical situations, and of its biological or survival value. The reader is left in some doubt as to the extent of agreement in other details, and one still feels the need for a more precise and comprehensive definition of the term function.

Ruckmick (6) canvassed fifteen modern American and English texts, and carefully studied the meaning of the term function whenever used: He found that all usages of the word could be grouped in two classes, and that the same author might use the term in both senses.

1) In the first usage the term function is equivalent to mental ac-

tivity. All mental activities such as seeing, hearing, perceiving, conceiving, imagining, recalling, etc., are termed functions. Mental functions and mental acts are thus synonomous expressions.

2) The term function was also employed to denote service or use for some end, as when an author speaks of the function of a word when it is used as a symbol for an object.

Psychology, according to Titchener, borrowed the term from physiology, and psychologists use it, in my opinion, in the same way. Physiologists refer to breathing as a function, and they also speak of its function or use in furnishing oxygen to the blood and in the elimination of waste products. There is nothing peculiar in the psychological use of the term.

Critics of functionalism have frequently commented on this dual usage of the term. They point out that with such a dual usage it is possible to speak of the "function of a function," or to say that a "function has a function." These writers apparently attempt to discredit the functionalistic movement by suggestive innuendo. Their remarks seem to suggest that such phrases are ridiculous, illogical, or absurd, and that the term function is evidently being used in two inconsistent ways. At least this has been my interpretation of their comments.

Without being contumacious in the matter, the writer is willing to defend the three following propositions:

1) The two usages mentioned by Ruckmick are not inconsistent.

2) They do not, in fact, represent two different meanings. The term function is used in exactly the same sense in both cases.

3) Finally, it is neither illogical nor absurd to speak of the function of a function.

With both usages mentioned by Ruckmick, the term function, in my opinion, is used in the same way as it is in mathematics. When a mathematician says that X is a function of Y, he is asserting that the term X stands in a contingent relation to Y without specifying as to the further nature of that relation. Psychologists, in my opinion, use the term function whenever they are dealing with a contingent relation irrespective of whether that relation is also one of act and structure, cause and effect, or means and end. A contingent relation and a functional relation are synonomous expressions.

The statement that the oxygenation of the blood is a function of breathing merely asserts that this end result is contingent upon the act of breathing. Likewise, when psychologists state that one of the functions of a vocal process is that of symbolizing objects, they are merely stating that the object of thought in this particular case is contingent upon the vocal process. Again the statements that breathing is a function of the lungs and that seeing is a function of the eyes obviously mean that these acts as acts are each contingent upon those respective structures.

Both physiologists and psychologists frequently refer to activities like breathing and seeing as functions without specifying the structures with which they are correlated even when they are known. In other words, they refer to these activities as functions without stating what they are functions of. The nature of the correlated term—some structure in this case—is implied or taken for granted.

Psychologists also refer to various mental acts as functions when their organic correlates are somewhat hypothetical, or inadequately known. Reasoning, conceiving, feeling, and willing are cases in point. In labelling these activities functions, psychologists are asserting that these acts are not disembodied activities, but that each is contingent upon some distinctive set of organic conditions even though the exact nature of these may be largely unknown.

Whenever mental acts are referred to as functions, the term is invariably used, in my opinion, to indicate that these acts are not disembodied acts but are acts of an organism and that each is contingent upon some distinctive organic factor. Sometimes this organic correlate is specifically stated at the time, sometimes it is not stated though known, and often it is not stated because its nature is inadequately known.

In dealing with contingent or functional relations, we may define either term on the basis of its relation to the other. For example, one function of a vocal act is that of representing an object, or we may say that the representation of an object is a function of the vocal activity. One of the functions of breathing is that of the oxygenation of the blood, and this latter may also be characterized as a function of breathing.

We may also note that a series of phenomena may be contingently related to each other as when A is a function of B, and B is a function C, and so on. To keep to our stock example, we may state that the oxygenation of the blood is a function of breathing which is itself a function of the lungs. In this case it is perfectly legitimate to speak of the function of a function, or to say that the function of breathing has a function, viz., the oxygenation of the blood.

Contingent or functional relations frequently exhibit a considerable degree of complexity. A given term may be contingent upon or a function of a number of factors. For example, the color of a negative after-image may at the same time be a function of the color and intensity of the stimulating object, the duration of exposure, the part of the retina affected, and the color of the background upon which the after-image is projected. Breathing may be said to subserve two functions—the oxygenation of the blood, and the elimination of carbon dioxide. Laryngeal activities may likewise be used as a means of communication or as a device for thinking.

Contingent or functional relations constitute a general class that is capable of further specification or particularization. As already noted, functional relations include the relation of activity to structure, and that of use or means to end. It also includes the relation of stimulus and response, cause and effect, the relation between two correlates that are both effects of a common cause, and the relation of present experience to the past experience of the subject. I am not concerned here with the problem of logical classification, but I merely wish to give the reader some sort of a preliminary notion of the wide variety of specific sorts of relation with which a functional psychology is concerned.

With this conception of the term function, we may now return to the distinction between the programs of an existential psychology and a psychology of function, and we shall contrast them on the basis of their treatment of a specific behavior situation.

I leave my laboratory to go home to lunch, come out of the building and encounter a cold and drizzly rain, spy on the other side of the street the parked automobile of a friend with whose habits I am acquainted, wait until he appears, and secure a ride home.

As we have noted, both an existential psychology and the functional psychologies of the period under consideration are couched in dualistic terms and will deal with the above situation in terms of the subject's experience with it.

In this experiential situation it is possible to distinguish between (a) the fact of awareness, (b) the various sensory contents, i.e., the sensory attributes of the objective situation, of the organism, and of the actions of the organism to that situation, (c) the various meanings of these contents, and (d) their intrinsic and extrinsic relations. For the sake of simplicity we shall ignore the possible presence of affective and imaginal contents and confine our treatment to the sensory aspects of the experience.

The program of existentialism may be stated as follows:

1) It proposes to limit itself to the study of these contents as bare existences, i.e., as abstracted from the fact of awareness, from their values and meanings, and from their functional relations.

2) Its problem is that of the description of these contents.

3) It assumes that these contents are to be described only in terms of their constituent elemental contents. It follows then that the existential psychologist first attempts to analyze the various contents into their elements, and these elements, be it noted, are themselves contents. With the descriptive technique thus obtained by analysis, the psychologist then describes these complex contents as a combination of the elemental contents involved.

As previously noted, the functional psychologist has no quarrel with the positive features of this program. Most functional psychologists are accustomed to incorporate a considerable amount of such material in their texts. They object to the proposed limitations of this program, and insist upon the inclusion of other data.

1) Functional psychology chooses mental acts, such as seeing, tasting, conceiving, and willing, as its objects of study, rather than bare contents.

2) It thus includes the phenomena of meaning and of functional relationships within its subject-matter.

3) Some functional psychologists, I am inclined to think, would object to limiting their scientific task to that of mere description.

4) Functional psychologists, in so far as they do describe, insist upon the necessity as well as upon the right of describing an object—be it a content or a mental act—in terms of its relations to other objects, as well as in terms of its analytical components.

5) They have also continually insisted that a description even of contents in terms of their analytical constituents must embrace other components than elemental contents if the description is to be adequate and complete.

I have heard that this latter proposition has been lately rediscovered by the configurationists, and hence I shall add by way of illustration a quotation from an article (7) published in 1909.

"Is the nature of a mental compound accurately seized, after all, when we have told off its constituents, even in their right proportion? . . . And yet nothing, it seems to me, could well be farther from the truth. For the original mental fact which we would describe has, in most instances, what we might call architectural features, and its nature and quality consists not only in the character of its materials but in the manner of their union or arrangement.

"Any analysis that names merely the ingredients may therefore miss the full truth; it may note no difference in compounds that actually are different. The safe and reliable description of the more complex mental facts accordingly requires that our idea of analysis be revised to include an attention to the architectural features of such phenomena, including of course their manner of change. Or if we prefer to let analysis mean what it has ordinarily meant, then only when analysis is supplemented by an account of the form of the process or object is there any guarantee that the description will be faithful to all the fulness of the reality."

A science must first break up its world into convenient units or objects for separate study. As indicated, mental acts are the objects with which a functional psychology is concerned. In experiential terms, an act is a group or pattern of contents exhibiting a unity from the standpoint of its meaningful implications as to end result. An act thus involves the awareness of the adaptive meaning or significance of a pattern of contents, and different acts are to be distinguished on the basis of their end results as well as in terms of their constituent components. The first act in the above illustration is not merely a given pattern of visual and somaesthetic contents, but a pattern exhibiting various meanings. For one thing it is a leg activity, it is also an act of walking, and it is also an act of walking home to lunch. As an act, it cannot be adequately defined except in terms of its actual or potential end result. The act of perceiving the cold and drizzly rain is more than a spatial and temporal pattern of visual contents. These contents also exhibit a meaning and they involve a reaction on the part of the percipient subject. The act of perception involves an interpretation of these contents as to their particular objective significance that is relevant to the preceding act of walking home. Thus a functional psychology in the very choice of its objects necessarily deals with meanings and functional relations as well as with contents. It is also obvious that a study of meanings involves that of functional relations and vice versa, for there can be no meanings without such relations.

A functional psychology studies these acts in various ways. It is willing to analyze these acts into their simpler components of meaning, contents, and the relations involved in a pattern of contents. It is also willing to analyze these contents into their elemental contents. It is also interested in studying the various contingent relations between the several components of an act, such as the contingent relation of meaning to content, the stimulus and response relations of the alternate leg motions in walking, the effect of the adjustive reaction on the sensory contents in perception, etc. It also studies the contingent relations between the various acts of the series, such as the contingency of the perception of the rain to the act of walking home, the effect of this perceptual activity on the act of walking, the effect of the resulting dilemma upon the discovery of the parked automobile, etc. It will also call attention to the contingency of this series of acts upon the preceding fact of hunger, and to the further fact that this series of acts was instrumental in allaying that condition. A functional psychology is also willing to note incidentally that this satiation of hunger entailed consequences of a physiological and biological character. A functional psychology will also study these acts from the standpoint of their genetic history and note the various features of these acts that are contingent upon the previous activity of the organism. Finally, it will correlate these acts with the structure and physiological features of the organism so far as it is possible to do so. A functional psychology is thus primarily interested in correlating these acts in all possible ways. It suffers from no taboos in this respect. It will attempt to correlate the various features of these acts with anything, provided that the correlations are of an observable and demonstrable character.

Functional psychology studies acts whose unity is a matter of reference. Existentialism studies complex contents; it speaks of blends, fusions, combinations, and patterns of contents. What is the basis of the distinction between one complex or pattern and two? The same question may well be asked concerning gestalts and configurations. Are the somaesthetic contents involved in each leg movement separate patterns, or is the whole series of contents involved in walking home just one pattern? Are the unitary complexes qualitatively homogeneous spatial and temporal units? What is the criterion of unity involved? Is there any unity except in terms of meaning or reference? Titchener in his texts first develops his descriptive technique of elemental contents, and then proceeds to describe the group of contents involved in perception, ideas, emotions, moods, memory, imagination, and action, and yet Titchener (13) has taken Wundt somewhat petulantly to task for his lack of insight in retaining a whole array of empirical terms such as perception, emotion, memory, and imagination. Are not the objects of existentialism indirectly differentiated on much the same basis as those of functional psychology, i. e., on the basis of meaning and reference?

Existentialism, as a matter of fact, does not discard all meanings and relations. The contents are named, compared, classified, analyzed into their constituent elements, and described in terms of these elements. Obviously these contents must have some meaning in order to be objects of a science, and obviously these objects are being manipulated on the basis of their relations of similarity and of part and whole, to say the least. The intent of these remarks is not critical. I merely wish to note by way of contrast that existentialism merely discards certain meanings and relations and retains others, for it studies these contents on the basis of certain meanings and relations which they bear to one another.

Existentialism does not even discard all contingent relations. Existentialists frequently study the psychophysical relation. Titchener in his *Primer of Psychology* (8) states that a science must explain, and that mental processes are explained by a statement of their bodily conditions, i. e., in terms of their bodily correlates. Weld (15, p. 65) asserts that the task of the psychologist includes also the correlation of mental and neural processes, but he adds that this correlation implies no causal connection. The writer has always been at a loss to decide whether these relations are studied in their own right, or whether they are utilized merely as a means of analyzing and classifying contents as in the distinction of visual, auditory, and gustatory sensations. If these two relations are studied in their own right, the question naturally arises whether their inclusion is inconsistent with the existential program of analytical description. If their inclusion is not inconsistent with this program, what is the distinctive principle that differentiates the two programs? The author will not attempt to answer these questions.

So far we have been primarily concerned with contrasting the two rival programs, without attempting to evaluate them. We shall now briefly review some of the more important arguments as to the legitimacy of the functional program.

It has been charged that the very term function has been used in a loose, vague, and perhaps inconsistent manner. Certainly the functionalists did not attempt to define the term in any precise way. Perhaps they assumed that the meaning of the term would be evident from the context. Ruckmick has shown that the functionalists did use the term in some consistent way inasmuch as all usages can be grouped under two well-defined categories, while I have indicated that the term as used is capable of a precise and definite formulation.

It has been said that meanings, values, and relations are not introspectable items of experience; only contents can be introspected. Inasmuch as it was generally admitted at this time that introspection is the only observational method of psychology, it follows that meanings, values, and relations are non-psychological data. One cannot introspect a mental act; one can only introspectively apprehend the contents involved in such acts. Much of the functionalistic program is thus non-psychological in character. Meanings, for example, are said to belong to the realm of logic. Functionalism is thus not a true psychology, or rather it is a psychology mixed with logic and other things, with psychology constituting but a small part of the conglomerate mixture.

Titchener (9) has developed his conception of the nature of introspection in a couple of articles. He asserts that we cannot introspect causal relations, physiological dependence, and genetic relations. Causation, dependence, and development are matters of inference and not data of introspection. Introspection, we are told, cannot itself be introspected. Perceiving is an act or function, and acts and functions cannot be introspected;

they are logical abstractions, and we cannot (introspectively) observe any product of logical abstraction. We cannot (introspectively) observe relations, but we can observe content processes in relation. We cannot observe change, though we can observe changing content processes. We cannot observe causation, though we can observe content processes that are causally related. Introspection approaches mind from the special standpoint of descriptive psychology; it gives data with which to describe objects. The introspectively observable items of experience are content processes. Consciousness as a describable object is that which can be described in terms of elemental contents and their attributes. Mental data exhibit a host of real relations, and a competent experimenter will note these relations, but he will not use them for purposes of psychological description. Verbal statements of meaning are informative, but they are not psychologically descriptive. Differences of import or value also transcend description, and psychology must limit itself to description.

Titchener is here engaged in the task of expounding and defining the term introspection as he is accustomed to use it, and it is well to note that all usages of terms are to some extent arbitrary. He defines introspection in both negative and positive terms. On the negative side, introspection cannot itself be introspected, i. e., it cannot be psychologically described on the basis of its analytical constituents. On the positive side, introspection is one of those mental acts or functions that is to be defined in terms of its object, and these objects of introspection are invariably contents and their attributes as abstracted from the context of relations, meanings, and values in which they always appear.

All this is quite clear and simple. If one assumes that introspection is the only psychological method of observation, and also accepts the Titchenerian definition of this term, it requires no great feat of logic to conclude that psychology is concerned only with contents, and that meanings, values, and relations are data of a non-psychological character.

Inasmuch as functionalists do concern themselves with these features of mental life, one must assume that their use of the term introspection differs somewhat from that of Titchener. The question at issue then is a matter of terminology and not one of fact.

There can be no dispute concerning the factual question whether one can give a valid observational report about meanings, values, and relations. According to Titchener, a competent experimenter will note and report these meanings and relations; he is merely forbidden to use them for purpose of psychological description. It is also obvious that if one cannot go beyond these contents and report what these contents mean or represent there can be no science of physics, chemistry, or biology. In fact, the only possible science would be that of existentialism. Questions of terminology should never be allowed to obscure questions of fact, and certainly the phenomena of meaning, value, and relations cannot be excluded from the realm of psychology on the grounds of their non-observability. According to Bentley (3, p. 401), structuralism has never justified its dogmatic assertion that first-hand observation of human experience was synonymous with structural observation.

Several psychologists with functionalistic inclinations have proposed the addition of relational elements to the conventional list of sensory, imaginal, and affective elements, and a few have suggested the inclusion of a meaning element. The writer has sympathized with Titchener in this controversy. Certainly meanings and relations are not contents, and neither are they elements in the same sense of the term as are the conventional elements of existentialism. To refer to meanings and relations as elements that are to be classified as coordinate with the sensory and affective elements is not only illegitimate but confusing. But this fact does not entail their exclusion from all psychological consideration.

One of the most serious charges against functionalism, and in fact against the whole empirical movement, is that it lacks somewhat in respect to its scientific character. Sometimes we are led to infer that functionalism is not a true science, but rather a pseudo-science or a scientific pretender. Empirical psychologies—functional and act psychologies—belong to the realm of the applied sciences as contrasted with the purity of existentialism. Existentialism is a critical science, and empirical psychologies are non-critical or pre-scientific, and, finally, existentialism is referred to as the experimental type of psychology as contrasted with those that presumably are not experimental.

A few excerpts (12, pp. 79-81) may here be quoted to illustrate the general tenor of these criticisms.

"Functional psychology is a parasite, and the parasite of an organism doomed to extinction, whereas intentionalism is as durable as common sense."

"We have found that in both cases (functionalism and intentionalism) they are empirical, that is, technological: they begin and end with 'mind in use.' They represent what we may call an art of living as distinguished from a science of mental life—a general 'applied psychology' that is logically prior to the special 'applied psychologies' of education, vocation, law, medicine, industry."

"It (intentionalism) is thus, like common sense, an applied logic, though unlike common sense its interest lies more in the logic and less in the results of application."

"The one complete and positive reply to intentionalism is the existential system, the system that is partially and confusedly set forth in the works of Wundt and Külpe and Ebbinghaus. If we can build psychology upon a definition that is scientific as the word 'science' is to be understood in the light of the whole history of human thought; and if we can follow methods and achieve results that are not unique and apart but, on the contrary, of the same order as the methods and results of physics and biology; then, by sheer shock of difference, the act-systems will appear as exercises in applied logic, stamped with the personality of their authors. They will not, on that account, languish and die, because 'mind in use' will always have its fascination, but they will no longer venture to offer themselves as science."

It would seem from these and other comments that empiricism (functionalism and intentionalism) transgresses the spirit of a pure science in three respects: (a) It brazenly studies the uses or utilities of mental acts singly and as a whole. (b) It has been avidly instrumental in exploring and developing the various special fields such as testing and educational, industrial, legal, and abnormal psychology. (c) And, finally, it has exhibited some pride in the social utility of its labors.

There is no doubt that functionalism has done these three things, but the charge that its so doing is a violation of the spirit of a pure science is another question, and one concerning which there may be a legitimate difference of opinion.

What is the difference between a pure and an applied science, and why do we regard a pure science as the more valuable?

1) The two cannot be differentiated on the basis of the situation or the locality in which the work is done. Pure scientific research may be conducted in an industrial laboratory as well as in a university laboratory or in a secluded cloister. In fact, many exhibitions of pure scientific research are being furnished yearly by some of our better industrial laboratories and by some of our psychological clinics as well.

2) Neither can they be differentiated on the basis of the field or phenomenon investigated. In the field of educational psychology most of the studies on memory and learning have been conducted in the spirit of pure science. I know of some studies of the perceptual activities involved in reading that are models of a pure scientific attitude. A few of the studies in the field of mental tests are exhibitions of pure scientific procedure, and many studies of aberrant behavior have been conducted in the same spirit.

3) We are sometimes told that a pure science is one that has no concern for values, but it is concerned at least with scientific values. Not all facts or attributes of a phenomenon are equally significant or valuable from the standpoint of science any more than they are from the standpoint of everyday behavior. One might study and compare and classify rocks on the basis of such superficial qualities as color or size and conduct the investigation in a pure scientific attitude, but such a study would hardly be considered a legitimate scientific undertaking. Such facts would lack any scientific value. Many of the early botanical classifications were scientifically futile, and we may refer to James's comment upon the status of the early studies of emotion. Science does not study anything and everything even within its own field. Not all scientific facts are equally valuable even from the standpoint of science. Science does have some sort of a concern for values. What is the criterion of the scientific value of a fact? I raise the question, but shall not attempt to answer it.

4) According to one definition, a pure science is one that is solely interested in an adequate understanding of the phenomena under consideration, but one that has no concern for the social or practical value of its findings. A pure science merely wants to know and is wholly unconcerned as to whether the knowledge it obtains can or cannot be usefully applied to the guidance of conduct.

This unconcern as to the utility of scientific knowledge needs a word of comment. A pure scientist can exhibit no aversion to the discovery of useful knowledge. He will neither intentionally nor inadvertently arrange his investigations so as to avoid the possibility of obtaining useful data. Neither will he refrain from studying certain problems and investigating certain fields for fear he may discover something useful. A pure scientist will welcome both useful and useless knowledge with equal gusto. It is related that a noted mathematician concluded his demonstration of a new mathematical formula with the statement that he was specially proud of the fact that the formula could never be turned to any practical use. Such an attitude is not consonant with that of pure science.

5) Finally, there is the pragmatic point of view that science must *ultimately* justify itself on the basis of the social value of its findings, but that the pure-science attitude of seeking to understand without any concern as to *immediate* values is the best method of ultimately achieving socially useful knowledge. A scientist thus hopes and expects that his labors will ultimately be socially fruitful, but he recognizes that the best way to achieve this result is to adopt an attitude of unconcern as to the immediate value of his experiments. With this attitude of mind, a scientist may deliberately choose, if he wishes, to enter those fields where the probabilities are greatest of discovering socially significant results. This point of view is, perhaps, a reflection of our national temperament.

We may now return to the three charges lodged against functionalism and empiricism in general. The fact that functionalism exhibits some pride in the social value of its achievements is no violation of the spirit of pure science. A pure scientist welcomes both useful and useless knowledge with equal acclaim. We may note that chemistry, physics, geology, and even mathematics are also accustomed to point with considerable pride. As already indicated, the development of the various special fields does not necessarily involve a transgression of the strict letter of the law, for a pure science is not to be characterized on the basis of what it studies. What better exhibition of the pure scientific attitude can be found than that of Spearman in the field of mental tests? Finally, the uses or utilities of mind can be studied with purity of scientific attitude. There is considerable difference between being concerned *with studying the uses of* mind and being concerned *with the uses* of what we find out from that study. Theoretically it is possible to secure wholly useless knowledge about the uses of mind.

We may now raise the question whether existentialism is entirely free from taint in this respect. Do the existentialists exhibit an attitude of strict unconcern and indifference? Do they not show some slight concern lest they find something useful? Why all this aversion to anything that is tinged with use? Why the emotional complex against the special fields? Why the fear of contamination? Why the horror against the useful? Is this the proper attitude of a pure and critical science, or is their attitude somewhat hypercritical? I suspect that the existentialists, like the mathematician referred to, have been leaning over backwards in their attempt to preserve a spotless purity.

Functional psychologies, according to Titchener (11), are teleological, and teleology is essentially non-scientific. Functional psychology was born of the enthusiasm of the post-Darwinian days, when evolution seemed to answer all the riddles of the universe; it has been nourished on analogies drawn from a loose and popular biology. Not only psychology but biology is suffering from an unbridled license of teleological interpretation. Teleology came down to the functional psychologist from the older empiricism. It is guaranteed by philosophy and technology, and it is justified by biological example. Small wonder then that he should step easily, even heedlessly, into the teleological attitude.

Titchener's charge that teleological interpretations have been overdone in both the fields of psychology and biology, in my opinion, is true. Starting with the doctrine that the direction of evolution is a result of natural selection and that natural conditions operate by eliminating the most unfit and selecting those that are fit, many early writers assumed that each and every evolutionary product must have a survival value. If no value is apparent, they must discover and assign one irrespective of the facts. Since emotional reactions, for example, are presumed to be evolutionary products, each emotion and each characteristic of these emotions must have a survival value, and it is the business of the psychologist to assign these even though he can do little better than make a wild guess as to their nature. This attitude is the resultant of several illicit assumptions as to the logical implications of the theory of natural selection.

As careful thinkers early pointed out, evolutionary products need have a survival value only under those circumstances in which they were selected. After they have been selected, they may be perpetuated and continue to exist when the conditions have so changed that they have no survival value. In other words, biologically useful characters may become useless with a pronounced change in the conditions of life.

An organism may be regarded as a unitary group of hereditary characters—structural and behavioristic. It is often tacitly assumed that natural selection operates directly upon the individual characters themselves, and that it eliminates and preserves these characters each according to its own individual merit. Natural selection, however, operates upon the organism, i. e., it selects a complex group of characters. It is the organism that either survives or goes to the wall in the struggle for existence. Not all of the characters of the surviving organisms thus need to be useful. Characters may appear and persist that are neither useful nor detrimental to survival. Organisms with a number of biologically neutral or indifferent traits may survive if they have a sufficient number of useful ones. As a matter of sheer theory, organisms with a detrimental characteristic may continue to exist if this defect is sufficiently compensated for by useful traits. There is thus no need to assume that each and every biological character has a survival value.

The very term natural selection erroneously suggests that natural forces directly select the fit organisms. The natural forces, however, operate to eliminate the unfit, and the selection of the fit is incidental to the process of elimination. Moreover, the degree or extent to which the unfit are eliminated is a function of the degree of competition in the struggle for life, and this latter varies with circumstances. Only the *most unfit* are eliminated, and the *least unfit* survive. Again not all of the characters of the surviving organisms need be useful, and furthermore the organisms that survive do not need to be perfectly adapted to their environment, i. e.,

100% fit. According to the theory of natural selection, they need only to be more fit than those that were eliminated.

It may be well at this point to note the distinction between biological utility and other modes of usefulness. Trees are useful to man for their lumber, but this is not a biological utility. The theory of natural selection does not pretend to account for the evolution of this characteristic of trees on the basis of such a use. The theory accounts for the evolutionary development of a character only on the basis of its utility to the organism that possesses it, viz., the tree, and not on the basis of its usefulness to some other organism like man. Again some characters of an organism may be selected and preserved because of their survival value, and then be utilized for other purposes at a later time. A person might employ his toes for purposes of writing, but this use in no way accounts for the evolutionary development of these organs. Society is accustomed to use the fear reaction to attain certain social ends, but this does not necessarily represent its biological or survival value; in fact, this social value does not even justify the assumption of a biological value for this trait.

In respect to teleological explanations, we may note that the process of natural selection on the basis of survival value accounts merely for the preservation of traits and not for their origin. The process of natural selection does not purport to explain the origin of mutants, but given mutants it accounts for the direction of evolutionary development. Biological needs and utilities select but do not create. The existence of a need does not guarantee the development of an organ to supply that need.

We have admitted that psychologists have been guilty of some weird teleological interpretations, but psychologists have not been the only sinners. Even Titchener is not entirely free from guilt in this respect, for some of his criticisms involve certain of the erroneous assumptions that have just been mentioned.

He takes the functionalist to task for his inconsistency in not giving a teleological interpretation to every mental item. The psychologist may answer any number of whys, but he is still faced by unanswerable why-nots that throw doubt upon his positive explanations. How has the development of red-green vision aided man in the struggle for existence, or what has man gained by the "unique compromise process" which gives rise to the purple sensation? These and like questions are not touched, we are told. Is not Titchener here assuming that all evolutionary products must have a survival value?

He refers to Judd's statement concerning the lack of an electric sense in man and the utility of such a sense-organ equipment, and then makes the following comment:

"Granted that the facts are as stated and granted that this furtherance of knowledge is useful, why have we not the special organ?—for it is surely evident that biological conditions, which have produced the 'electric fishes,' are also competent to produce an electrical sense-organ in man" (11, p. 539).

Does Titchener assume that the theory of evolution by natural selection involves the doctrine that biological needs create the means of their attainment?

As a part of his criticisms, he caustically comments upon the fact that the human eye is far from perfect inasmuch as its native usefulness has been immeasurably improved by the microscope and the telescope. Does this criticism not involve the assumption that the theory of evolution implies a 100% fitness?

While teleological interpretations have been overdone, it does not follow that teleology is essentially non-scientific and that all teleological interpretations should therefore be discarded. One might as well argue that science should cease theorizing and making hypotheses and conclusions because it has made so many mistakes in these respects in times past.

We must recognize that the place of teleology in science is a moot question concerning which there are differences of opinion among biologists, psychologists, and philosophers. Titchener's attitude that teleology is non-scientific finds its supporters among biologists, but it is also well to note that many biologists as well as psychologists have not discarded all telic conceptions.

What is teleology, and in what respects is it legitimate and when is it illegitimate? I would say that telic conceptions are involved in all statements concerning use, utility, adaptation, purpose, and means and ends, and all of these terms imply a certain kind of contingent relationship.

I see no objection to noting and stating these relations in so far as their factual character is observable and demonstrable. Such statements as the sense-organs are the means whereby we gain knowledge of the objective world, the muscles are devices for reacting to that world so as to satisfy organic needs, vocal activities are used in thinking, etc., are unobjectionable as mere statements of fact. One difficulty arises when one of the terms of the relation is supplied by a process of speculative inference, and these speculations masquerade under the guise of fact. But this type of difficulty is not peculiar to the study of telic relations.

The usual objection to such statements of telic relations—even factual ones—is that they imply an illegitimate type of explanation. It is sometimes charged that such statements imply the existence of some design, purpose, insight, or intelligence—some prior existential factor that is causally responsible for these telic relations. Again it is said that such statements tacitly assume that the end result operates as the cause of the prior process by which it was attained—an assumption which violates the temporal requirements of a cause-and-effect relation.

Can one make a statement concerning any of these telic relations as mere statements of fact without any explanatory implications whatever? The author is disposed to believe that these statements can be and are often made without such implications on the part of either the writer or the reader.

When implications are involved, the statements may not imply any particular kind of explanation—let alone an illegitimate one, such as that of design. The purposive psychologist does assume more or less explicitly the existence of innate conscious purposes to explain the origin of adaptive behavior, but in my opinion the great majority of functional psychologists

do not do so either implicitly or explicitly.   With those functionalists
with whom I am well acquainted, implications of design are foreign to their
intent and to their unconscious biases as well.   If design is suggested, is
the fault to be found in the mode of statement or in the interpretative reaction of the reader?

However, there can be no objection to statements that are explanator-
ily suggestive, if these telic relations can be legitimately explained.   The
usual explanation of the adaptive character of our acquired reactions is
that of the law of effect, which accounts for the selection and elimination
of acts on the basis of their consequents.   The law does not attempt to
explain the origin of these acts, any more than does the theory of natural selection purport to account for the origin of mutants.   The law
merely accounts for the fixation of the adaptive acts and the elimination
of the non-adaptive ones, and thus accounts for the direction of mental development.   Neither does the law of effect violate the temporal requirements of a cause-and-effect relation, for many of the effective consequents
occur during the performance of the act, and besides the law assumes that
these consequents merely affect the subsequent performance of that act
(5, pp. 95-96).

We would thus conclude that telic concepts can be legitimately retained
in a science so long as it confines itself to factual statements of these relations and explains these facts in a legitimate manner.

Titchener's statements that science is concerned only with description
and that objects can be described only in terms of their constituent elements deserves a few words of comment.   What is description and why
does science describe?   Scientists necessarily report their findings, and in
this sense of the term they "describe" not only their objects of study but
their methods, procedures, hypotheses, and the knowledge they obtain of
these objects as well.   Description in this sense is only the *final step* of
science, for obviously this description presupposes a considerable variety of
prior activities.   Moreover, this type of description cannot be limited to
statements of the analytical composition of that which is described, for
procedures, hypotheses, and analytical elements, as well as the objects
analyzed are described.   What, then, does Titchener mean by description?
Perhaps the question may be clarified by ignoring the term description and
defining Titchener's program in terms of the type of knowledge sought.
In effect, the Titchener doctrine merely asserts that any legitimate scientific
knowledge of psychological objects is limited to a knowledge of their constituent elements and the laws governing their combinations in those objects.   Titchener's appeal to physics and physiology in support of this doctrine is hardly appropriate.   The analogous program among the natural
sciences is that of chemistry and histology, while the program of physics,
physiology, geology, and biology is more akin to that of functionalism.
Analytical knowledge of the constituent elements of objects is not the only
scientific goal, and in this connection we may quote from Bentley (3, pp.
401-402) :

"Neither has it (structuralism) justified its contention that the main method of science was analysis. It is, as I think, not much less than a caricature of the sciences of nature to say that the physicist, the chemist, and the zoölogist are always and only analyzing. . . . . it has, for some time, been generally conceived to be a formal and logical—not a realistic—view of science which has brought into relief the typical chemist or physicist as forever breaking down his substances into constituent elements. Analysis, surely, but not simply analysis: and, for many problems, not analysis at all."

I would add to this quotation the further statement that there are other modes of analysis than that of the existential type.

The main defects of the functional psychologies of the period under consideration are, in my opinion, those that arose from their adoption of a dualistic position. Dualism involves no difficulties to an existentialist because he stays strictly within the confines of consciousness. When conscious activities, however, are conceived as a separate but effective part of the total biological process, the question of the mutual relations of these dual parts to each other immediately comes to the fore.

The existentialists have been caustic and trenchant in their criticisms. We may here refer to the much criticized and widely quoted statement of Angell (1, p. 59):

"Let it be understood once and for all that wherever we speak, as occasionally we do, as though the mind might in a wholly unique manner step in and bring about changes in the action of the nervous system, we are employing a convenient abbreviation of expression . . ."

Titchener has also voiced his objections to statements as to the origin of consciousness, when and where consciousness comes in, and its function as a solver of problems.

When the functionalist treats of the observed uses of particular acts like perception, he is on safe ground. When he deals with the biological origin of consciousness as a whole and its function in the biological process, he is entering the field of speculation where there is an opportunity for a legitimate difference of opinion. Moreover, speculative opinions are likely to be expressed as statements of fact. Neither should an empirical science of fact adopt a position which forces it to substitute circumlocutions for straightforward statements of fact.

What happened to this functionalistic movement? Did it evolve and disappear in the process of development, or does it still persist in a modified form? In my opinion, American empiricism has undergone two major developments since the time of which we write.

Dynamic psychology represents a further development of the implications of the biological point of view. Functionalism had assumed that mental acts grow out of and minister to the biological needs and impulses of the organism. According to this conception, the organic background of needs and desires operates to motivate and direct the whole course of mental development, but this fact was more or less taken for granted, or at least the influence of these factors was not sufficiently emphasized. In their emphasis upon drives and motivation, dynamic psychologists have been attempting to portray these factors in a manner that is more commensurate with their importance.

Behaviorism, to a considerable extent at least, was an attempt to avoid the difficulties inherent in a dualistic position. The radical behaviorists solved the problem by either denying or ignoring the fact of consciousness, while the moderate behaviorists are prone to talk in monistic terms of the behavior of a psychophysical or a psychobiological organism.

The above fact has been well developed by Weiss (14). He notes that the functionalistic assumption that conscious activities influence behavior is inconsistent with its dualistic position. The further assumption of parallelism the functionalist fails to explain. The functionalist to be consistent must accept interactionism, and he is then confronted with the task of rationally conceiving of this process. The further possibilities are to study consciousness alone and omit its influence upon behavior, i. e., discard a large part of the functionalistic program, or to study behavior alone and neglect or disregard the fact of consciousness. Weiss then proceeds to develop and justify his particular program in which consciousness is disregarded.

Weiss apparently assumes that the dualism of the functionalist is necessarily ontological in character. Given this assumption, there is no escaping his conclusions. I doubt the truth of his assumption, however. Angell has said that a functionalist can accept any one of the various conceptions as to the nature of the mind-body dualism with the single exception of that of epiphenomenalism. I do not pretend to know the philosophical inclinations of most functionalists, but it has always been my impression that Angell's dualism was of the methodological variety. It has also been my opinion that dualism is a poor methodological device for a functionalism with strong biological leanings. I agree with Weiss that a functionalist is bound to adopt some sort of a monistic conception, but I think that there are other monistic positions possible than the two alternatives that he mentions.

The functionalistic movement has thus undergone considerable development. Did functionalism disappear with this development, or are these later developments functionalistic in character? The answer depends upon the definition of functionalism adopted. Functionalism and existentialism represent two opposing points of view toward the subject-matter of psychology, and this subject-matter, at the time of this controversy, was conscious processes dualistically conceived. If functionalism is to be defined in terms of point of view as well as in terms of subject-matter, i. e., as a study of the functions of conscious activities, then functionalism per se is on the wane. If functionalism, however, is to be defined solely in terms of its point of view without any regard to *what it studies,* then the various behaviorisms are functional psychologies. For example, one can study behavior in two ways: (a) One can assert that the object of psychology is to describe behavior, and that it can be described only in terms of its constituent elements, viz., reflexes. It is thus the business of psychology to analyze the various complex forms of behavior into their simplest reflex elements, and to study the laws governing the combinations of these elemental reflexes in behavior patterns. We have here a program essentially like that of the existentialist with simple reflexes substituted for his sensation elements. (*b*) On the other hand, one can adopt the functionalistic program of studying functional interrelations of the temporal parts of a complex act, its functional relation to organic needs, its dependence upon previous behavior, and its relation to the structural and physiological characteristics of the organism. How one shall answer the question thus depends upon the definition adopted. I shall let the reader answer the question as he sees fit.

What has been the outcome of this controversy? Some of the existentialists still maintain the faith, some have developed functionalistic inclinations, and a few have given signs of seeking refuge in configurationism. I know of no whole-hearted conversions to existentialism from the functionalistic ranks. The American empirical movement has maintained itself against attack and has gone on developing in accordance with its own particular genius. The controversy in acute form did not persist for long. A working truce of mutual respect was soon attained—a truce that has not been violated except for an occasional outburst on the part of some irrepressible spirit.

REFERENCES

1. ANGELL, J. R. Psychology. New York: Holt, 1904. Pp. vii+402.
2. —————. The province of functional psychology. *Psychol. Rev.*, 1907, **14**, 61-91.
3. BENTLEY, M. The work of the structuralists. Chap. 18 in Psychologies of 1925. Worcester, Mass.: Clark Univ. Press, 1926. Pp. 395-404.
4. BORING, E. G. The psychology of controversy. *Psychol. Rev.*, 1929, **36**, 97-121.
5. CARR, H. A. Psychology. New York: Longmans, Green, 1925. Pp. 226.
6. RUCKMICK, C. A. The use of the term *function* in English textbooks of psychology. *Amer. J. Psychol.*, 1913, **24**, 99-123.
7. STRATTON, G. M. Toward the correction of some rival methods in psychology. *Psychol. Rev.*, 1909, **16**, 67-84.
8. TITCHENER, E. B. A primer of psychology. New York: Macmillan, 1898. Pp. xvi+314.
9. —————. Prolegomena to a study of introspection. *Amer. J. Psychol.*, 1912, **23**, 427-448.
10. —————. The schema of introspection. *Amer. J. Psychol.*, 1912, **23**, 485-508.
11. —————. Functional psychology and the psychology of act, I. *Amer. J. Psychol.*, 1921, **32**, 519-542.
12. —————. Functional psychology and the psychology of act, II. *Amer. J. Psychol.*, 1922, **33**, 43-83.
13. —————. Experimental psychology: a retrospect. *Amer. J. Psychol.*, 1925, **36**, 313-323.
14. WEISS, A. P. Relation between functional and behavior psychology. *Psychol. Rev.*, 1917, **24**, 301-317.
15. WELD, H. P. Psychology as science. New York: Holt, 1928. Pp. vii+297.

PART IV

PSYCHOLOGICAL THEORIES OF THOSE
WHOSE TRAINING BACKGROUND
WAS THE STRUCTURALISM
OF E. B. TITCHENER

CHAPTER 4

A SYSTEM OF MOTOR PSYCHOLOGY

MARGARET FLOY WASHBURN
Vassar College

I. METAPHYSICAL BACKGROUND

Underlying the suppositions which this system makes are certain convictions regarding the nature of the world and the limitations of human knowledge.

First, dualism. So far as we can comprehend it, the world involves two types of processes: (*a*) material processes, which are qualitatively uniform and can be treated only quantitatively, and (*b*) mental processes. The material world reduces itself, science tells us, to discontinuous quantity, but the world of consciousness is a world of continuity which involves qualities as well as quantity. The material world is a sum of movements, but no sensation quality can ever be identified with a movement. Blue may be caused by movement of a certain frequency, but it is not itself a movement. Hence the world of the behaviorist is a world lacking all qualities: it has neither colors nor tones nor smells nor even feelings of muscular strain (11). Every metaphysical system that attempts to reduce qualities to movements begs this question at some point (10).

Secondly, mechanism. The world of qualities or conscious processes never affects the world of movements or material processes causally. Conscious processes are epiphenomena; merely the invariable accompaniment of certain types of material processes. It is only a movement or material process that can cause or in any way influence another material process.

The evidence for this assertion is as follows:

1) The great fertility of such a supposition in explaining and especially in predicting events in physical science.

2) The proofs furnished, for example by the chemistry of nutrition, that a large body of vital phenomena also can be explained and predicted by the same hypothesis.

3) The danger that if we assume the direct causal action of non-material agents on matter we shall revert to mystical and primitive habits of thinking from which humanity has had a long struggle to free itself even imperfectly. If, for example, we cannot yet explain all the phenomena of growth and regeneration in living beings as due to new combinations of known physicochemical laws, it is more scientific to make further efforts along the lines that have already yielded so much than to assume the existence of a totally new causal agent. Anybody can make such assumptions; it needs no more trouble than primitive man took when he said there was a devil in the thing (15).

The system of psychology which will be here presented rejects the materialism of the behaviorists, on the one hand, and the interactionism of the functional psychologists and vitalists, on the other hand. It will not have recourse to any mysterious agents or indwelling purposes which by hypothesis cannot belong in a mechanistic system. Thus it is as much opposed to McDougall as to Watson.

II. PSYCHOLOGICAL METHODS AND AIMS

Both the observation of behavior and the observation of conscious processes furnish legitimate material for psychology.

Behaviorism itself does not reject introspection, although calling it language behavior instead of the observation of conscious processes. The difference between behavioristic and non-behavioristic psychologies is not in their methods (the early work in the Leipzig laboratory was purely objective) but in their metaphysics (behaviorism denies the *existence* of conscious processes). Objective methods need to be supplemented by introspection; for example, while the galvanometric reflex may reveal an emotional disturbance of which the observer is not conscious, we should hardly be able to make such an inference if no observer had ever reported from introspection the presence of emotion accompanying the reflex.

The aim of psychology should be both to describe and to explain behavior and conscious processes.

If our drives or motives are only those generally called practical, our ultimate aim will always be to control and, as a means of controlling, to explain. Practically, it may be said, all that matters is overt behavior; if we could be sure that a person's bad opinion of us would never be accompanied by hostile behavior, the opinion would be negligible. But if, as becomes the lords of creation, we have the peculiarly human drive to know for the sake of knowing, we shall wish both to describe and to explain both behavior and conscious states, not merely that we may control them but that we may realize more fully the variety of phenomena to be found in the universe. From this point of view it is well worth while, for example, to form a conception of the pattern of consciousness in the lower animals, just to widen one's own horizon; and there are plenty of data on which to base such a conception (12, chap. 13).

Thus structural psychology and its more modern representative, configurationism, have a legitimate task. But no science can rest satisfied with description; it must push on to explanation.

III. THE NERVOUS BASIS OF CONSCIOUSNESS

There is reason for conjecturing that consciousness accompanies a certain ratio between the excitation and the inhibition of a motor discharge (9, chap. 2).

The functional psychologists pointed out that consciousness accompanies *delayed* reaction. When stimulation passes over at once into movement, there is little if any conscious accompaniment. It is a fact of experience that consciousness tends to lapse when reactions are smoothly performed, and becomes intense at an interruption.

On the other hand, Münsterberg (8, pp. 530 ff.) held that the degree of consciousness varies directly with the *freedom* of the motor discharge. If motor discharge is wholly blocked, there is no consciousness. Take the phenomena of attention, which of course means the highest degree of consciousness; when we attend to one thing our reactions to other things often cease altogether. We certainly are not highly conscious of those stimuli to which we make no reaction; for instance, of the telephone bell to which we failed to respond because we were absorbed in reading.

The facts of habit argue that consciousness accompanies interruption of response; the facts of attention argue that it is absent when interruption is complete. The hypothesis which reconciles this conflict is that consciousness accompanies a certain ratio between excitation and inhibition.

IV. The Cause of Inhibition: Incompatible Movements

A motor response is inhibited when an incompatible movement of greater prepotency than itself is simultaneously excited. By incompatible movements are meant movements in opposite directions.

The evidence for this hypothesis cannot be fully presented until we have discussed the function of drives, on which prepotency largely depends. Some of it will appear from a consideration of the nature of incompatible movements. Certain muscles are antagonistic in their effects, that is, they would, if contracting alone, bring about movements in directions opposite to each other: one would raise a limb, the other lower it. They can, however, be simultaneously contracted under either of two conditions: (a) when they maintain a fixed posture of the limb, and (b) when, although one is more strongly excited than the other, the latter exerts a certain amount of drag on the former, so that movement is slow and controlled. But, of course, no part of the body can be simultaneously moved in opposite directions; movements of this sort are what we shall call incompatible movements (9, chap. 2).

V. The Nature of Drives

An important cause of the prepotency of one movement over another lies in internal states of unrest called drives. A drive is often due to the lack or excess of some substance of physiological importance, as in the case of hunger, the sex drive, and fatigue; other conditions which disturb physiological equilibrium may produce drives. It is characteristic of a drive that it tends to set in "readiness," or incipient and tentative performance, the "consummatory reaction" that puts an end to it. This was first pointed out by Wallace Craig (4) in careful observations of the instinctive behavior of birds. An example is hunger: this is uneasiness due to lack of food, but the specific sensations of hunger result from the stomach's making the same contractions that it performs when food is put into it; that is, it anticipates the consummatory reactions of the drive.

When there is a conflict between incompatible movements, ordinary observation will often indicate that the victory goes to that movement which is connected with the stronger drive. A strange dog encounters a man who holds a bone. If the dog has been ill-treated and is not very hungry, he will run away; fear is stronger than hunger. If he is starving, he may seize the bone, hunger being stronger than fear.

VI. The Relation of Drives to Emotions

An emotion may occur either (a) when the energy of a drive is prevented from discharging into movements which lead towards a restoration of the physiological balance (adaptive movements); such prevention may be due either to the absence of some necessary external factor, for example, food in the case of hunger, or to the prepotence of an incompatible movement. Or (b) joyful emotion may occur when an excess of energy is released at the end of a period of unsatisfied drive. In an emotion the energy of the drive, instead of passing into adaptive movements, either discharges into non-adaptive movements or remains dammed up in visceral regions.

Ordinary observation supports these statements. A drive that can be satisfied by adaptive movements without delay gives rise to little or no emotion. The motor processes in emotion are for the most part of no use to the satisfaction of the drive. They consist, of course, partly of contractions of the striped muscles and partly of visceral changes. The striped muscle contractions include some which on the Darwinian principle were useful under more primitive conditions (the frown, for example, no longer directly useful since anger does not mean actual physical combat with the need to keep light out of the eyes) and some that have no use except to drain excess energy from the viscera; these are the non-adaptive movements that constitute a motor explosion, such as swearing and knocking furniture about. The visceral changes have been shown by Cannon to relate to needs. Increased blood-pressure and pulse-rate, shortened blood-coagulation time, and the other effects of sympathetic nervous activity and adrenin, are useful in *combat*. But are they useful in *anger,* which, on the suppositions we are making, results from interference with the fighting drive? They are not useful *in themselves* even in combat; only so far as they aid the performance of adaptive movements. If the increased energy of the drive remains at the visceral level, Cannon (3, p. 196, note) says, "It is conceivable that the excessive adrenin and sugar in the blood may have pathological effects." Tradition holds it to be safer, physiologically, for a person to work off this energy even in a nonadaptive motor explosion, however unfortunate the social consequences may be (14).

VII. The Physiological Basis of Motor Learning

It is convenient to divide motor learning into two classes, substitutive learning (the conditioned reflex) and system-forming learning. The distinction is not absolute; system-forming learning is a special type of substitutive learning. In substitutive learning a stimulus loses the response which originally belonged to it and acquires the response that originally belonged to another stimulus reacted to at the same time with itself. The dog originally gave the fear reaction, running away, to the sight of the man. When the man carries a bone, the hunger reaction, that of coming forward, incompatible with the withdrawal due to fear, is set up and may be prepotent; thereafter the sight of the man even without the bone may cause the dog to move towards him. Thus a stimulus acquires a new response, and a response acquires a new stimulus. This type of learning involves the suppression or dropping out of non-prepotent responses. System-forming learning on the other hand involves not the dropping-out of movements but the dropping-out of external stimuli. In system-forming learning new combinations of movements are formed; no movement is dropped out, but the stimulus for each movement in the system is furnished by the kinaesthetic excitations produced by the performance of another movement in the system. Thus the original stimulus of a movement is replaced by kinaesthetic excitations—a special case of substitutive learning (9, chap. 1).

The existence of substitutive learning is obvious, and the explanation here given for it seems plausible. That in movement systems kinaesthetic excitations are substituted for the original stimuli is strongly suggested by observation of our experience in learning of this type: when we begin to memorize music each movement needs the stimulus of the notes on the page; later these visual stimuli become unnecessary, and if we break down in performing the series of movements we can recover best by repeating the movements that preceded the stoppage. It certainly seems to us in such a case that the *feel* of the earlier movements sets off the later ones.

VIII. Types of Movement Systems

Such systems may be either *static,* involving prolonged states of contraction and relaxation of muscles, that is, attitudes; or *phasic,* involving actual change of position in space, that is, movements in the ordinary sense of the term. In a static system the muscular contractions are simultaneous, and the kinaesthetic theory would suppose that each contraction furnishes an essential part of the stimulus for all the other contractions. Phasic systems may be either simultaneous or successive; in the first case the actual movements must be carried out together, as in swimming or bicycle-riding, and the kinaesthetic theory would again suppose that each contraction depends on stimuli from the others; in the second case the movements form a series, as in reciting a list of nonsense syllables (9, pp. 10-16).

There can be little doubt that successive movement systems of short duration and frequent performance may come to be innervated as if they were simultaneous. As will be pointed out in the next section, the action of the drive tends to set them all in some degree of readiness, greatest for the final or consummatory movement. Some recent experiments of Lashley's (6), indicating that a rat with any portion of the afferent pathways in the spinal cord cut can run a maze from memory, lead him to reject the kinaesthetic theory of learning. But the sequence of turnings in the simple maze path he used must have been performed many times in a rat's ordinary experience and may well have become so organized as to be innervated simultaneously by the stimuli from the external surroundings together with those from the drive.

IX. The Relation of Drives to Motor Learning

a) To substitutive learning. This type of learning obviously depends on the greater prepotence of one movement over another. Prepotence commonly though by no means invariably depends upon the existence of the inner state of unrest termed a drive. There are certain movements which seem to be regularly in a certain degree of readiness; especially the movements connected with withdrawal from injury. Punishment thus produces very rapid substitutive learning and does not need to be aided by a pre-existent drive; whereas food will not produce substitutive learning unless the animal is hungry. The evidence for these statements is found in observations on animal behavior.

b) To system-forming learning. The formation of simultaneous and successive movement systems regularly needs the presence of a drive. An animal will not learn a maze path or acquire any other complex system unless it is, during the learning, under the influence of a drive, say hunger, which is satisfied and put an end to by the final movements of the system; this statement has experimental confirmation.

How does a drive operate to produce the learning of a series of movements, such as the running of a maze, which at their end abolish the drive? This process has been felt to be mysterious because it has seemed as though the end of the series, the reward, for example, food, must have an effect on something that preceded it in time, namely, the animal's movements, which would mean a violation of the law of cause and effect.

In order to solve the puzzle, we must bear in mind several facts. (*a*) The drive itself is not something that happens at the end of the series, but a state that persists throughout the series of movements and their learning. (*b*) A drive sets into incipient performance the final movement necessary to relieve it, the consummatory reaction. (*c*) The tendency of one movement to excite another, while exerted most strongly towards a following movement, exists also, though to a less degree, towards a movement immediately preceding; of this we have evidence from experiments on animals. Thus when a drive has set in readiness its consummatory reaction, this readiness may be communicated to the reaction just preceding. There would then exist on this hypothesis a "gradient" of readiness to be excited, decreasing with the distance of a movement from the consummatory movement. (*d*) The dropping-out of errors during the learning of a successive movement system would be a case of substitutive learning, the right movements having prepotence through their greater nearness to the consummatory reaction (12, pp. 329-337).

Evidently on this theory the latter half of the maze path would be learned first. Borovski (2), in the only investigation which adequately guards against sources of error, has shown that such is actually the case.

The motor theory would explain the formation of simultaneous movement systems also through the influence of the drive. In cases like the combination of leg and arm movements in swimming, the two sets of movements get equal readiness through being equally distant from the consummatory response, forward translation through the water, which will occur only when they are performed together.

X. The Motor Basis of Ideas: Tentative Movements

The "association of ideas" is fundamentally the association of movements; the movements in this case, however, are not full but incipient muscular contractions.

The most important evidence for this statement is perhaps the fact that two conscious processes do not become associated, so that one of them will later recall the idea of another, unless they have been not merely experienced together but attended to together. If we wish to associate a person's name with his face, we react to the two impressions simultaneously; we repeat the name and scan the face. At the outset of this paper it was assumed on good evidence that consciousness accompanies a partial but not total checking of motor response. Attentive consciousness is the highest degree of consciousness. The delay due to the partial inhibition of response is filled, on the one hand, by adjustments of the sense-organ so that the stimulus will be better received, and, on the other hand, by slight, "tentative" contractions, or at least alterations in the physiological state of the muscles whose full action is being checked. These incipient contractions may quite conceivably give rise to kinaesthetic excitations; they may have varying degrees of readiness or prepotency, giving rise to substitutive learning, and they may form static systems and simultaneous and successive phasic systems. Such, at least, is the hypothesis involved in motor psychology. Spinoza said, "The order and connection of things is the order and connection of ideas"; we may paraphrase this by asserting that the order and connection of ideas is the order and connection of movements. The nervous basis of an idea, a "centrally excited" conscious process, is a tentative movement, which originally occurred during attention to an external stimulus, and is revived through the occurrence of other tentative movements that became organized with it into a system (9, chaps. 3, 4).

XI. The Motor Basis of Perception

The theory we are developing means, obviously, that when two stimuli are consciously discriminated from each other, it is because a different reaction is made, fully or tentatively, to each. Up to this point the theory has seemed like a synthetic one, in which systems are built up out of units. But such is not the case. Our discriminations are analyses. In the author's *Movement and Mental Imagery*, the theory of perception is stated in a passage that may be quoted here: "In first making acquaintance with an object we respond to it as an undifferentiated whole: later we come to make specialized responses to various parts and aspects of it; but it is the fact that it can be still responded to as a whole that keeps these specialized movements together in a single system, and thus gives the object its unity. An orange, or a chair, or a tree, is a single object, and not a mere aggregate of qualities and parts, because it can be reacted to as a whole, and because every one of the movements involved in attending to its parts is associated with the movement of reacting to the whole object" (9, pp. 130-131). Upon the nature of the motor response depends the analysis of our total conscious state into perceptions of objects. Thus upon the possession of a movable sense-organ depends to a considerable extent an animal's power of space perception; a movable sense-organ can analyze a situation into a reversible series of sensations, which is the essential characteristic of a spatial pattern. A movable grasping organ, which can detach "things" from their surroundings and move them about independently of one another, aids analysis into a world of objects rather than flat patterns. Motor psychology can explain the facts of perception which the configurationist merely describes. Take, for instance, the phenomena of ambiguous figures, such as the outline cube, which may be perceived either as lying on the ground or suspended in the air; what the configurationists would call the more natural configuration is the former, but surely it is more natural because the reaction of sitting down on cubes occurs oftener than that of looking up at them. One part of a visual field becomes "figure" and the rest "ground" if it seems easier to pick up than the rest; thus a small pattern becomes "figure" on a large background. In illusions, the principle of assimilation, whereby a circle appears larger when it is concentric with a larger circle and smaller when it is concentric with a smaller circle, seems to conflict with the principle of contrast, whereby a circle when surrounded by larger circles looks smaller than when surrounded by smaller circles. Motor psychology can explain this conflict by pointing out that assimilation will occur when the design suggests reaction to the whole of it at once: one circle inside or outside of another looks like a plate, a single object, all parts of which tend to take on the character of the whole. Contrast, on the other hand, will occur when the parts of the design are so arranged in space as to suggest reacting to them separately; when, for instance, a circle is surrounded by other circles. Again, the configurationists describe the ways in which configurations may interfere with and modify one another: the motor theory would explain this interference as due to the presence of incompatible reaction movements and the modifications as due to the elimination of such movements. We cannot, for example, perceive the cube at once as resting on the ground and as suspended in the air, because we cannot at once look down and up (13).

XII. RELATIONAL PROCESSES

The configurationist or Gestalt school of psychology grew out of a structural study of thought, and one of its chief claims is that it gives proper recognition to those conscious processes which arise out of the "togetherness" of others, that is, the Gestalt or form qualities, which may remain the same even though the contexts from which they arise differ. It is probably true that in many such cases the actual stimulus is a process of change rather than a persisting force. The writer once trained a rabbit which had shown in previous experiments that it saw red as very dark gray to push at a red door instead of at a light gray door; this training resulted in its pushing the gray door only 24% of the time. When the same gray was shown on one door and white on the other, the rabbit pushed at the gray door 73% of the time; thus the same gray produced opposite responses in the two settings. The actual stimulus was probably not "gray," but "darkening" (12, pp. 241-242).

Other "relational" processes, however, which occur in thinking may be explained as kinaesthetic, due to movements or attitudes that are common to different situations. For example, the relational feeling of difference might be due to a kinaesthetic excitation accompanying any sudden shift of motor response; that of unfamiliarity to an attitude accompanying suspension of the motor processes accompanying associative activity; that of recognition to the relaxation of the unfamiliarity attitude; that of opposition (the feeling of "but," as James termed it) to suspended reaction when there exist tendencies of equal strength towards incompatible movements. What Ebbinghaus called the "common properties" of sensations, for instance, intensity and duration, would on this theory have a kinaesthetic basis. If the loudness of a sound has something in common with the hardness of a pressure, the basis of this common element is likely to be kinaesthetic. To quote from *Movement and Mental Imagery* (9, pp. 205-206): "Our absolute judgments of high degrees of intensity are probably based on the degree of diffusion of the stimulus energy through the motor pathways of the body. We can by introspection describe the attitude characteristic of high intensity as a kind of general muscular shrinking, which is at the same time a withdrawal and a summons of the muscular forces of the body to endurance, and we can more or less localize the kinaesthetic and organic excitations thus produced. In the case of absolute judgments of very slight intensity, another attitude is apt to be the basis of the judgment: a generalized muscular response, namely, which is not the result of the overflow of stimulus energy, but rather due to the strain that accompanies the effort to attend and to prevent distraction which will cause the stimulus to lose its effectiveness." Judgments of duration Wundt based on feelings of strain and relaxation, which are obviously kinaesthetic, and all spatial judgments can plausibly be referred to a kinaesthetic basis.

Two considerations strengthen the case for kinaesthesis as the source of those relational processes which are essentially the same no matter what the quality of the sensations they accompany, and which arise out of the "configuration" itself. First, when they occur in the course of perception and thinking, we need not be surprised that ordinary introspection does not identify them as coming from muscles; kinaesthetic processes ordinarily go unanalyzed and unlocalized because there is no such necessity to analyze them as to analyze sensory processes originating in the outside world. Secondly, it is obvious that kinaesthetic excitations are constantly present, a continuous common factor in all our experience (9, chap. 10).

XIII. The Motor Basis of Thinking

The processes involved in thinking are: (*a*) simultaneous and successive systems of tentative movements, and (*b*) an inner muscular tension on which is based the persistent influence of the problem idea or purpose.

(*a*) We have already made the assumption that ideas accompany incipient or tentative muscular contractions, and that such tentative movements form systems, static and phasic, simultaneous and successive. The function of simultaneous systems of tentative movements in thinking needs a little further attention, because the objection is sometimes made against a motor theory that the rapid and complex processes of thought would on such a theory demand an impossibly great complication of muscular action. But a simultaneous movement system, as we have just seen in discussing the perception of objects, is usually one that involved at first a single undifferentiated motor response, and it is these responses to the experience as a whole that help to preserve its unity even after analysis has taken place. The idea of a complex thing or system of things could not be dealt with in thinking unless a "symbol" of it could be used, that is, a relatively simple representative; on any theory of the nature of thought it is necessary that a relatively simple symbol should be capable of calling up the associations that belong to complex systems of ideas. This, of course, is why language is essential to thought. If we consider how comparatively few are the component movements involved in speech, and yet how adequately they represent the immense complexities of thinking, we see that "there is almost no limit to the complexity of the system combinations which can be formed through having a single motor outlet for an entire combination" (9, p. 132).

(*b*) What is the difference between reverie and thinking with a purpose? Introspectively, the chief difference between an ordinary idea and a purpose is that an ordinary idea has only a temporary relation to the ideas that follow it (in reverie one idea "suggests" the next, and there its influence ends), while an idea that constitutes a purpose seems to dominate many succeeding ideas until the purpose is executed. One and the same idea may either make a fleeting appearance, as when we say idly to ourselves that we might do so and so, or it may become a purpose held to for years, as when we resolve to do so and so and follow through a complicated series of actions before the resolve can be carried into full performance.

Under what circumstances will an ordinary idea become a purpose?

The facts of purposive thought and behavior have for some thinkers given strong support to vitalism, or the doctrine that there are forces in living beings which cannot be reduced, whatever the progress of physical science, to combinations of those laws which work in the field of inanimate nature. Wherever an animal's action is adapted to an end, according to this school of purposive, vitalistic psychology, foreknowledge of the end operates to cause the action by a type of causality differing from that of the physical world. The system of motor psychology which the present paper defends is opposed to such a view for several reasons. First, because of the general advantage of a mechanistic position, as set forth at the beginning of our discussion. Secondly, because the sharp distinction drawn, for example, by Professor McDougall (7, pp. 51ff.) between reflex and instinctive action, the former being purely mechanical and the latter involving the mysterious power of purpose, is untenable. Thirdly, because the irregularities in the way animals perform instinctive actions look much more like machinery out of order than like errors in carrying out a conscious purpose. Fourthly, because the only way one can explain the first performance of a complex instinctive action such as nest-building, on the purposive hypothesis, is to suppose that the bird inherits a mental image of the nest, a supposition that contradicts what we know of inheritance (15).

A mechanistic explanation of purposive thought and action therefore is needed. The physiological basis of a purpose must be a relatively permanent state rather than a fleeting movement, since the difference between a purpose and an ordinary idea lies in the persistent influence of the former (to be mechanistically accurate, of its physiological basis). Among our bodily processes there are two types of relatively permanent states: drives or conditions of inner unrest, and attitudes or static movement systems.

Evidently, if an idea is to become a purpose, the tentative movement that is the basis of the idea must be connected with a drive. Purposes rest on motives. There must be a drive, and it must be prevented from reaching its consummatory movement at once. Now when a drive is checked, we have seen that its energy may be expended in several ways. It may produce an emotion, in which case the energy either passes off in non-adaptive movements of the striped muscles, that is, in a motor explosion, pacing the floor, abusing the furniture, and making language reactions of a type ordinarily inhibited, or expends itself in visceral disturbances. On the other hand, the drive may produce ordered, purposeful thought and action, leading to its consummatory movements.

"If we watch a man who, when he cannot get relief from a drive by immediate action, begins to think the matter out, we observe that he becomes quiet. If we are that man, introspection tells us that our quiet is not the quiet of relaxation but that of bodily tenseness, especially in the trunk muscles. Whenever this attitude relaxes, the energy of the drive begins again to escape in random movements; we stop thinking and become restless. For all purposive action there must be a persistent inner state of imbalance, the drive. For purposive *thinking,* we may conjecture that this state must discharge its energy not into immediate action, whether useful movements or merely random restlessness, but into a quiet, tense bodily attitude. And any idea may become a purpose if, being first associated with a drive, it becomes associated with this peculiar, persistent attitude of tense quietness" (15).

The evidence in favor of this "attitude" theory of the physiological basis of purposive thinking is as follows: (*a*) the persistent influence of a purpose demands a persistent bodily process as its foundation; (*b*) introspection shows that this process involves muscular tension; (c) the experiments of Jacobson and Bills (5, 1) show that thought is impossible in a state of complete muscular relaxation. As regards (b), it should be noted that a blocking of the thought process often increases the intensity of this tension so that it overflows like emotion into useless muscular contractions, frowning, setting the teeth, and so forth; thus the proper function of the thought attitude is lost.

Incidentally, the motor theory explains how emotion interferes with thought, by using the principle that explains all interferences in behavior and consciousness, that of incompatible movements. Emotion interferes with thought when its energy passes into diffused random movements, the "motor explosion"; such movements are likely to be incompatible both with the tentative movements demanded in thinking and with the thought attitude (14).

It is interesting to speculate about the ancestry of the thought attitude. An important factor in animal learning seems to be the capacity to maintain a general bodily orientation towards the goal, for example, both in maze running and in the delayed-reaction type of experiment. In the maze there is a tendency to check errors made away from the general direction of the goal sooner than those in its direction, though the actual delay in reaching the goal is the same for both types. A striking analogy exists between this orientation and the "activity" or thought attitude; the essential function of both is to check movements either of one type or of an antagonistic type if they deviate too far. In an address before the psychological section of the American Association for the Advancement of Science I suggested a conceivable relation between them in the following words. "In the beginning, while the reflex and tropism were adequate modes of behavior, the drive discharged in a definite direction. As the environment became more complex, the drive discharged into random movements of which those associated with the drive in its last and most intense stages tended to survive and become organized into systems. In this process the drive secured the persistence needed for purposive action, but the definite direction of the tropism was lost. Often, however, in animals, part of the energy of the drive goes into the tendency to maintain and restore a bodily orientation toward the goal; while in man, for whose varied activities general bodily orientation is too confining, directed thinking is sustained by a vestige of this bodily orientation, the tense quietness of the trunk muscles that may persist even when we turn from one position to another" (15).

The problem of orientation in space, that is, of learning the way to a goal, is perhaps the earliest problem in learning that animals encountered in the course of evolution. Other complex systems of movement necessary to animal existence, such as those of attacking food, of mating, and nest-building, are largely innate; finding the way back to food or the nest must be learned. Some general mechanism to assist this learning process may well have been early developed, and may in some degree survive as the basis of our path-finding to a thought goal (16).

SUMMARY OF THE RELATION OF MOTOR PSYCHOLOGY TO OTHER PSYCHOLOGIES

1) *Behaviorism.* The system of psychology here presented agrees with behaviorism in being mechanistic, and its explanatory principles are all in harmony with behaviorism. It differs from behaviorism in being based on a dualistic metaphysics instead of on materialistic monism, which is indefensible, and in therefore regarding the descriptive study of mental processes as possible and worth while.

2) *Structural Psychology.* The system agrees with structural psychology in being dualistic, and with both structural and behavioristic psychology in being mechanistic, that is, in holding that there is no causal action of mental processes upon bodily processes, the causal action being that of the nervous processes underlying the mental processes. It differs from structural psychology in using the laws of bodily movement as its central explanatory principles, and in being less interested in the minute and detailed description of mental processes and more interested in the description and explanation of behavior, since in behavior it finds the explanation of conscious experience.

3) *Functional Psychology.* The system agrees with functional psychology in its motor principles of explanation, but differs from it in rejecting the interactionism which the functional psychologists have often implied. In general, it is closer to functional psychology than to any other school, but attempts to carry functional explanations further.

4) *Gestalt Psychology.* The system agrees with the configurationists as with the structuralists in holding the description and analysis of mental processes to be legitimate and desirable; it differs from the configurationists in presenting a far more adequate principle of explanation.

5) *Purposive Psychology.* The system is fundamentally and totally opposed to the non-mechanistic type of psychology which regards conscious purposes as causal forces acting upon bodily movements and representing a type of causality wholly different from that which prevails in the physical world.

Our knowledge of the working of the central nervous system is still very imperfect indeed, and any physiological hypothesis undertaking to explain the complexities of consciousness and behavior is likely to suffer drastic modifications, if not to be wholly abandoned, with the progress of such knowledge. The strongest element in the system here presented seems to me *the principle of incompatible movements.* Every theory needs most of all a way of demonstrating the *impossibility* of certain occurrences. There is only one surely impossible phenomenon in the universe, if we except merely logical inconsistencies, and that is the movement of a body in opposite directions at the same time with reference to the same points. If we can base our explanation of psychological phenomena on this principle, we have given psychology a sure foundation and placed it on a par with the physical sciences. The soundness of a motor theory is further suggested by the evidence that the evolution of the nervous system in animals began with the effector organs.

REFERENCES

1. BILLS, A. G. The influence of muscular tension on the efficiency of mental work. *Amer. J. Psychol.*, 1927, **38**, 227-251.

2. BOROVSKI, V. M. Experimentelle Untersuchungen über den Lernprozess. *Zsch. f. verg. Physiol.*, 1927, **6**, 489-529.

3. CANNON, W. B. Bodily changes in pain, hunger, fear, and rage. New York: Appleton, 1915. Pp. xiii+311.

4. CRAIG, W. Appetites and aversions as constituents of instincts. *Proc. Nat. Acad. Sci.*, 1917, **3**, 685-688.

5. JACOBSON, E. Progressive relaxation. *Amer. J. Psychol.*, 1925, **36**, 73-87.

6. LASHLEY, K. S., & BALL, J. Spinal conduction and kinaesthetic sensitivity in the maze habit. *J. Comp. Psychol.*, 1929, **9**, 71-106.

7. McDOUGALL, W. Outline of psychology. New York: Scribner's, 1923. Pp. xvi+456.

8. MÜNSTERBERG, H. Grundzüge der Psychologie. I. Allgemeiner Teil: Die Principien der Psychologie. Leipzig: Barth, 1900. Pp. xii+565.

9. WASHBURN, M. F. Movement and mental imagery. Boston: Houghton Mifflin, 1916. Pp. xv+252.

10. ——————. Dr. Strong and qualitative differences. *Phil. Rev.*, 1919, **28**, 613-619.

11. ——————. Introspection as an objective method. *Psychol. Rev.*, 1922, **29**, 89-112.

12. ——————. The animal mind. (3rd. ed.) New York: Macmillan, 1926. Pp. xiii+431.

13. ——————. *Gestalt* psychology and motor psychology. *Amer. J. Psychol.*, 1926, **37**, 516-520.

14. ——————. Emotion and thought: a motor theory of their relations. Chap. 7 in Feelings and Emotions. Worcester, Mass.: Clark Univ. Press, 1928. Pp. 104-115.

15. ——————. Purposive action. *Science,* 1928, **67**, 24-28.

16. ——————. Orientation and purpose. Read before Ninth International Congress of Psychology, Yale University, Sept. 3, 1929.

CHAPTER 5

A PSYCHOLOGY FOR PSYCHOLOGISTS

MADISON BENTLEY

Cornell University

Many are the directions from which the Psychologies of 1930 may be approached; but the most obvious ways are two. One would reveal the general state of progress in psychology's major undertakings, and the other would set forth the individual writer's particular point of view. The first, which appears most attractive, would present a cross-section of the entire subject with references to the past and to the future, omitting bias, systematic differences, and the rivalry of schools. But this mode of approach is practically impossible for any single psychologist within the assigned limits and, moreover, it appears to be the second mode which accords with the design of the present series. So we add one more photographic presentation of our common array of psychological facts and objects, leaving the unfortunate reader to create his own clear perspective out of many limited and divergent views.

Our main and underlying contention will be that the present confusion of tongues, now widely deplored, is chiefly due to the fact that outside concerns and foreign interests have played too great a part in shaping and defining our field. The result is that we tend artificially to maintain our identity by virtue of the common label "psychology." Really psychological points of view and interests have been made secondary to evolutionism, the doctrine of heredity, zoölogical classifications, animal hierarchies, physiological and neurological hypotheses, clinical medicine, psychiatry, theory of knowledge, the training of infants, educational doctrines, sociology, anthropology, propaganda for "efficiency," and amateurish conceits about "human nature." Were you to hold to the light any one of the many proposals for a "new psychology" and to look steadily through it, you would almost certainly see the obscuring shadow of one or another of the extra-psychological subjects named in this long list. And the main reason why so many persons are now ambitious to wear the badge and to speak a dialect of psychology is that practically all men can thereby serve some extraneous interest. A few terms borrowed from one of these outside sources—such terms as conditioning, instinct and habit, mental evolution, original nature, reflexes, learning, the unconscious, introversion, inferiority, intelligence, social responses, primitive man, and achievement test—are enough to give an air of scientific sophistication and to suggest the epithet "psychologist." But practically all such terms are imports from without. In so far as they are assimilated at all they are assimilated not to psychology but to that particular brand of the subject which has derived from, and

[95]

has been fashioned to serve, the context which the given term implies. It is inevitable, therefore, that we should now possess multiple psychologies reducible to no common denominator; psychologies pluralized not in the sense of many envisagements of one and the same universe of facts and principles but in the sense of a common name for many diverse and divergent undertakings.

Now the present *chief* determiners of psychology from the outside are three. They are biology, medicine, and education. Determination from biology is readily understood from the prestige and success of that subject since Darwin and Johannes Müller, as well as from the natural association of psychological facts with the "organism" of the biologist. Medicine comes in directly from our romantic and humanistic concern for the sick and indirectly from that large branch of sociology which treats of the study and care of the aberrant, the abnormal, and the defective. The medical psychology of the French and the Austrians must also be considered. The deep impress of such cults and practices as Freudism suggests the weight of medical sanctions, though the natural allurements of sex and advertising have likewise played their part. Education, finally, has now come to be one of the primary responsibilities and diversions of America and Europe. Interest there has tended toward doctrine, means, and measurement. America at least extols great theorists (not always waiting to understand them), grasps eagerly at new methods, builds and equips lavishly, and diligently applies its measuring stick. The problem of producing wise, intelligent, and cultivated teachers and parents still awaits solution. Meanwhile the educational men and means have been advertised as highly "psychological." Theorists and doctrines are psychological, methods are chosen for their psychological flavor, and educational measurements are phrased in terms of "intelligence" and other alleged psychological faculties.

Of these three great determining influences (philosophy has definitely fallen into the background), one is mainly from the sciences and two come from the arts of practice, the first art designed to keep men sane and well and the second to see them through their first two or immature decades. Biology has mainly injected physical, physiological, and speculative matters into psychology; medicine has warped it toward the abnormal; and education has substituted both the pedagogist's notion of an imperfect childhood and the moralist's notion of responsibility for an independent and disinterested account of psychological development.

Is it possible, now, to restore psychology to a better balance to make it more fundamentally psychological and less accessory to other things?

My general proposal, which was briefly and imperfectly sketched in the *Psychologies of 1925* (1), may be restated in a word. The sciences which *deal with living things as living* comprise two coordinate groups, the biological and the psychological. Neither is logically subordinate to the other; though each presents facts which exhibit a functional (possibly a causal) dependence upon facts in the other group. Living beings are also treated in physics, chemistry, and geology, but not there characteristically as *living*.[1]

The equitable partition of work as between biology (taken here as a brief designation for all the subjects in the group comprising anatomy, physiology, ecology, morphology, genetics, and the like) and psychology is our first concern. It has been made very difficult by the temporal priority and development of the biological group, which long regarded itself as the totality of the sciences of life. When, finally, psychology came into its field of regard, biology assumed a paternal attitude and (not without a scowl of annoyance) adopted the newcomer into the great biological family. This accident of time and priority should suggest to us, however, an attitude of utter neutrality, devoid of tradition and prepossession. Under such an attitude the general delegation of labors and problems will be simple in principle, whatever difficulties we may later encounter in drawing exact lines of demarcation.

To begin with, then, both coordinate groups treat of the living organism. If we take seriously this primary fact, we shall escape at the beginning endless discussions about two ultimately unlike substances, the physical and the mental, about ultimate relations as caused or uncaused, about pre-established harmonies and interacting disparates. All our traditions persuade us toward these terrible distinctions; but let us not be persuaded.[2] Let us rather consider the living organism first of all in its integrity. Before we have allotted it for treatment by the sciences, let us steadfastly disregard our philosophical and scientific traditions and take it quite neutrally as the living being which each of us actually is and of the sort that we actually and constantly live with and communicate with in our fellowmen. This entire and pre-allotted being we may designate as the T-system, to denote its *total character* before its description has been assigned in the two directions. We might also call it the neutral organism (O_n) to denote its *neutrality* so far as future work upon it by the sciences is concerned. Our view of it at the moment is then quite unsophisticated, inasmuch as it has not yet been referred for scrutiny and judgment either to the sciences or to the philosophical disciplines. If we are able to forget the biological limitations set upon the word *organism,* we may say quite freely that the T-system is the organism. But we must not here substitute for our "organism" the anatomist's abstraction of a bodily structure, the taxonomist's abstraction of a kind or class, or the psychologist's abstraction of a "mental" or "conscious" being. It is, instead, the total system or the neutral organism, neither biologized nor psychologized, with

---

[1] Some biologists prefer to be called physicists and chemists, and a few psychologists contend that their materials are likewise reducible to physical ultimates; but no complete and adequate account has been so written upon either side.

[2] Readers who are still troubled by these ancient dichotomies may profitably read candid treatments of them in B. H. Bode (2, Chaps. 1-7) and in G. T. W. Patrick (3, Chaps. 1-4). For his own educational purposes Bode modifies behaviorism in the direction of a "pragmatic psychology" and Patrick stresses "self-adjustment." Both retain the biological pattern of treatment but compound it with the philosophical.

which we begin and to which we shall have often to return. It eats, sleeps, works, worries, and digests. It wears our clothes, is a member of the family, has a savings account, and tries to obey the laws of the state. We are now ready to make our first deflection toward the two types of inquiry, as we approach with our T-system. It is to be a *functional* deflection. That is to say, instead of cleaving our T-system straight through the middle and handing a physical half to the one science and a mental half to the other, we keep our organism (O_n) intact; but we invite biology (B-science) to inspect certain of its functions and psychology (P-science) certain others. Our primary separation, therefore, refers to a way of regarding, a point of view, and not to a partition of the object regarded. Thus our primary category of life becomes *function,* not substrate or material. The primary task of the sciences of life will then be directed toward description in terms of operation or activity.

The next critical problem is to discover modes of operation which are sufficiently diverse and sufficiently characteristic to sanction the proposed coordination. These we shall discuss as the B-functions and the P-functions, according as they fall to the one or to the other science. The B-functions concern metabolism and the relations of metabolism to outside energies and events. They also include the dependence of internal operations upon such accessory means as enzymes and regulators, as well as an account of devices for aerating, circulating, conducting, and eliminating. The P-functions include those operations by way of which the living organism apprehends its surroundings, recognizes and acts upon its varied relations to other organisms, to objects and to events, constructs a present, past, and future, deals with objects and occurrences as absent, supposed, or unreal, discerns its own ends, and devises means for their satisfaction. These functions also include those operations through which it wishes, desires, plans, and executes, is thrown into doubt, perplexity, and predicament, creates and uses language and other symbols, organizes systems of belief and of knowledge, and formulates canons of taste and of conduct. All of these things the living organism (at least the adult, human organism) actually and inevitably does, and with no one of them is biology prepared to treat either in fact or in theory.

At this point the reader is ready to interpose a difficult question. "Can you not"—he will ask—"positively qualify the two sorts of operation so that they may be logically partitioned to the two sciences?" He is probably thinking of "bodily" and "conscious." If he is, we shall have to ignore for the present the natural query because such a division would precipitate us at once into our old disturbing difficulty. There are at least three separate reasons why the P-functions should not be qualified as "conscious." The first is that the term is substantive and so divides the organism itself and not its activities; the second is that it adds nothing but a dubious theory to our designation; and the third is that these functions are not properly described as non-bodily (i.e., conscious) since the body is implied in them quite as much and quite as fundamentally as it is in the B-functions. Let us then rest for the present with our functional distinction and with our gross indication of the kind of operation falling under each of the two varieties.

Here we face our second principal difficulty. Function always implies a medium. Operations do not proceed in a vacuum. The common phrase is that "function implies structure." It thus appears necessary to add means and agencies. The old temptation to dichotomize again assails us, to speak of vital (or physical) forces and of mental faculties or agents. But this solution is as sterile as the distinction of substances.

The difficulty is very real. It raises the acute problem of a distinctive subject-matter for psychology. That biology has a like problem is apparent from the ancient contentions of vitalist and mechanist and from the more modern version of the problem in the alleged reducibility of the sciences of life to physicochemistry. But we may well limit ourselves to our own difficulties. Were we content to adopt the easy and obvious device of the behaviorist we should simply declare that the whole problem is one of adaptive response. Then we should be right back in the old speculative biology of adaptation. But that is not the most serious issue of such an acquiescence. We should have to admit either that the P-functions just enumerated do not exist or that we propose to ignore them. The more consistent behaviorists have taken the second course and have come out with a partial and inadequate account of the organism. The others have retained their old "consciousness" or its equivalent and have simply echoed the phraseology of adaptation. Neither removes the difficulties which beset us and at the same time leaves to us the means for solving, or so much as stating, the main problems of psychology.

The "conscious" psychologists have here a distinct advantage. They have only to declare that they deal with conscious stuff which they observe by the special method of introspection. History has made it apparent that it is very difficult to dislodge a psychologist from this position. Scorn, irony, and boycott have all been used by the dissenters, who have proceeded either to ignore this alleged aspect of the organism or to deny its existence. The result has been a complete lapse into biology, whence the dissenters themselves ultimately came. But the positive limitations of this lapse are very great, as a rough list of the gaps and omissions of the behavioristic books and researches will readily persuade the candid reader.

The structuralist avoids the difficulty by an analogy with anatomical matters. The psychological equivalents of the cells are—for him—sensations, feelings, thought elements, and conations, and the equivalents of the tissues are assimilations, fusions, colligations, perceptions, associations, etc. This figure of speech went as far as the "elements" and very greatly helped to derive psychological parallels for the receptor functions; it also helped to indicate a certain qualitative range and variety in our experiences. Here the analogy stuck. By many it has been abandoned or at least modified in its perspective.

Still another way out was the way of the fluidist, who used the Heraklitean analogy of the stream. We think of James first and of Wundt secondly. This analogy served to break up the rigider and more barren types of associationism. In James the stream ultimately evaporated into a vague directional drift through a certain *locus* in the restless world of existence. Wundt's fluid "immediate experience" led on to the later structuralism and also, in another direction, toward the developmental currents of *Völkerpsychologie*.

The fourth great proposal of a way out of conscious stuff has been offered by *Gestalttheorie*. Here substance becomes a shadow to be so far as possible ignored, and form becomes the psychological substitute for it. This is the psychology of the twilight where figured shadows are fascinating and solid things unreal. The words "consciousness" and "mental" still linger; but they are little more than a *façon de parler*. Form moves upon matter as a sort of unifying faculty, notes fall into their pre-destined places, and the Gestalt proceeds to perfect itself. The best fruits of this conception, thus far obtained, have ripened in the laboratory. The doctrine sometimes enlightens the experimental results, which are, how-ever, easily restated under other and less mystical captions. Once again, shape and configuration are *partial* categories, which have entered from physics, aesthetics, and ontology, and which scarcely seem adapted to the *general* needs of psychology. Much of their momentum has been derived from protest against the imaginary devotion of all the other psychological parties to atomistic realities. Like all protestant movements, it tends to weaken as it exaggerates its own negative virtues in contrast to its oppo-nents' positive vices.

We return unsatisfied from all these proposals to the difficult *medium* of the P-functions. For a positive answer let us go again to our original and undisturbed T-system, our living creature, our neutral organism. And let us observe that whereas this O_n is double-faced when we attempt to functionalize it, it is *singly determined* when we look at it as medium or ground of operation. As seen from any point of view it displays but one *stuff*. We call it "body." This body must then be used as *vehicle*. The B-functions and the P-functions are both referable (wherever refer-ence is necessary) to the body. Only biology, then, has an anatomy and only biology has a morphology, and in so far as embryology is strictly morphological and structural it is to be found in the biological group of sciences alone. Psychology stands in need of no separate doctrine of "structures."

For the common coloring of all the B-functions we have the fortunate qualifier "physiological." On the psychological side we are not so fortu-nate. Were we careful to eliminate all reference to an existential mind, we might say that the P-functions are all alike "experiential." In order to take away the bad flavor of "experience," suppose that we provisionally refer to the common ("experiential") qualification of all matters of desir-ing, thrilling, perceiving, remembering, discovering, and the like, by the symbol C_e. Then we can say for the present that all P-functions have the coloring C_e, as we should say that all B-functions have the common physiological coloring C_p.

We are not yet out of the woods. "It is all very well," you may object, "to eliminate the conscious as a form of existence. But what are you go-ing to do about images and creative thinking and feelings of effort and of pain, about love and hate, imagination, seeing and hearing and all the rest—things which are, as everybody knows, *mental*?" At this point it is difficult not to envy the behaviorist who can expunge all these cobwebs of fancy by a fiat and declare that nothing exists but responses to the environment.

Now there is a very good reason why men have stuck so tenaciously to existential terms in their psychology. The matters which we have enumerated as P-functions do happen; and we neither describe, understand, nor get rid of them when we attach the label "response." We must be more candid.

Let us scrutinize some of these things that are said necessarily to imply a kind of existence which is not of the bodily kind and which certainly is not illuminated by the biological category of environment. In the first place, many of the things are just terms descriptive of performance. I see the car passing the window and I hear the whistle of the distant locomotive; but that is not to say that the hearing and the seeing are fabricated from something conscious. The plain facts are "car," "whistle," and some kind of functional relation to an organism. In our terms, the T-system has been active in the form of a P-function. The old theory of conscious doubles or copies need no longer be discussed. To be sure, we cannot exhaust the matter of seeing and hearing by a reference to the car and the distant locomotive alone; but that is not to say that we must assume in addition to these things a mind which sees and hears or so much as a seeing and hearing consciousness. Neither does the biologist exhaust the matter by referring to certain B-functions in ear and eye, nerve and brain, nor by an interpretation in terms of response to stimulus. The central fact of seeing and hearing, or, stated more generally, of perceiving, is a psychological fact; but it is essentially a functional fact. Car and whistle are, so to say, being *announced* to the T-system.

A special difficulty seems to arise in perception when some state or condition of the T-system itself replaces the perceived "object." But in principle and so far as the operative side of the system is concerned, no difference exists between the apprehension of extended objects, of the slow passage of time, of flashing movement, of melody, or of the substance and condition of the body. Some objects are apprehended as existing by themselves (trees, buildings, chemical compounds), some as existing only for the T-system (rhythms and musical objects), and some again as the apprehending system itself.

The final resort of the mentalist is sheer pain. There we have—so the argument runs—something ultimately different from all "objects." But the underlying logic here reads, "Not physical, therefore mental." And that logic is not inevitable. It is a relic of the dogmatic ontologies of the dualist. We may reasonably challenge the inference.

As a matter of hard fact, when man was added to the world the world was notably changed. We need not go so far as the brilliant Bishop of Cloyne in the exaltation of a single P-function and say that the *esse* of the world resides in *percipi*. We need not resort to any idealistic faith with regard to being or knowing. We simply observe that many things change their characters when they are related to the human T-system. The fact that I see the car, hear the whistle, desire the food, plan to prepare dinner, or discover an enemy in Neighbor X, is not exhaustively and adequately treated by describing car, whistle, the empty stomach, dinner, and neighbor. In plain terms, the P-functions have consequences quite as definitely as the B-functions of breathing, digesting, and secreting. And these consequences have to be taken into account. Regarded in a gross way we may say that cities and railroads are such consequences; laws, customs, and beliefs are others, and organized states still others. Even to the galactic universe, as we imperfectly comprehend it, clings the aroma of that peculiar and unique creature for which alone, of all living creatures, the universe "exists." It is certain that we cannot derive these things from the B-functions, even when we include in the latter such spatial results as flow from the movement of parts and members of the body in the form of "reactions."

The sciences have without question progressed in their descriptions of nature by regarding the organism (O_b) as actively related to an environment (a phase of B-function); but this logical addition is not sufficient. The P-functions and their consequences carry us far beyond the environmental concept. A very simple instance should make this fact apparent. By night I lie quietly in the darkness and "see" the book shelves of a study which was destroyed yesterday by fire. Here the biological relation of organism and environment breaks down. The organism has somehow absorbed the environment so that the latter exists only, so to phrase it, at the organism, i.e., not at all. It is a crude makeshift which puts such things in a mental or social or inner environment. The object is not *in* the organism and it is not outside, either in a spatial or a biological sense. The biologist's relation as of an interaction between a B-system and an environing E-system has simply disappeared. In its present form, the observation cited belongs only to psychology, and psychology shifts its responsibility when it lazily labels such objects "mental."

We must go further. *The concept of the environment has no place in psychology.* It is the biologist's way of conceiving a functional relation between his B-system and certain non-organic systems and agencies. The P-functions transcend it in the sense that they obliterate the line of division at the spatial limits of the body which the environmental concept requires. The equivalent expression in psychology is that objects and events are *announced* by way of certain P-functions. This sort of announcement comes through the *apprehensive* functions, and it appears in perception (objects and events are announced as present), in recollection (announced as past), and in imagination (as future, possible, ideal, or supposed). Events, agencies, forms, and performances are announced quite as much as are those "objects" which the biologist calls "environment" and the physicist "nature." Long ago Mach stumbled upon this fact while he was trying to reduce nature and mind to common "sensations"; and he then found that he had to include in sensations much more than the spatial detail of objects. In order to keep these things "in consciousness" Ehrenfels called them *Gestaltqualitäten;* and more recent configurationists, discerning that bare movement is apprehended quite as directly as colors, sounds, and tastes are, have gone to the opposite extreme and proclaimed that *only* the formal side of things, the shape or unitary whole, is primary in the organism's announcement. That is a natural but exaggerated reaction from the older fashion of filling consciousness with the qualitative or "thing" side of existence. When we free ourselves from the physicist's nature and from the biologist's environment, we find no more difficulty in the announcement of mere movement, bare spatial plans, melodic arrangements, and rhythmical forms than in the organism's involvement (by way of the "sensations") in colors, tones, pressures, and the like. Remember, however, that we must either abandon or revise the conception of discrete conscious existences.

In order to settle the difficulties raised by those "sensations" which refer to the body and to what is going on there, let us observe again that certain P-functions announce these matters quite as regularly and naturally as they do outside "objects." Such "purely mental" things as pain, pleasantness, and comfort stand on quite the same footing as bare movement and rhythm. They are no more and no less "in consciousness." Once we break down, for psychology, the distinctions of inner and outer, of B-system and environment, we see that the alleged difficulty has vanished.

Now when we have provided for all those alleged mental objects which are themselves P-functions and for all those consequences of function which are announced as in nature or as in the body, we have gone a long way. Sensations should no longer vex us: neither should feelings; neither should images, which are either the sheer *quality* side of the announcement or else the announcement itself taken in a less abstractive way. In either case the image is always to be taken in reference to the T-system and not, as it would appear to the biologist (in an "ideational" environment), or to the physically disposed person (as an illusory or "unreal" object).

But more remains. The T-system modifies the world in more ways than by *announcements*. What of striving, desiring, and doing? If we subtract these things from the world (as all biologists, including the consistent behaviorists, do), we certainly annihilate important modes of actuality. We also ignore thereby a very great deal that is of primary importance to the psychologist. These matters plainly exhibit what we provisionally call the experiential coloring (C_e). They belong in some fashion to the T-system, and they do not (in principle) involve the biologist's correlation of body and environment. In order to discover just where these things do lie in psychology, we must venture an observation which has been reserved for this context. When we make a general and catholic survey of the P-functions, we seem to find that they touch the foundations of life (more concretely stated, of *living* in the active sense) in two ultimate ways. They are determined, first, by *local interrelations* within and between bodily and physical systems and, secondly, by the *general tenor* of bodily states and conditions in the T-system. We must consider both forms of determination.

1) *Local Interrelations.* Here fall the neural integrations within the brain, between the brain and the cord, the central nervous system and the

several nerves, the nervous system and the accessory receptor and effector devices, and ultimately between these terminal organs and certain forms of energy which have their primary locus without the T-system, affecting the latter either in the form of stimulus or as the result of bodily movement. The extra-bodily relations are not to be regarded in the biologist's terms of environment and adaptation lest we encroach upon the provinces of ecology and of descent. Since the central neural system is always the primary term in these relationships, we may find in it the *text* of our determination, and in any other part or member involved the *context*. Thus the text may be (e.g.) a limited occipital field and the context a neighboring central field in an unlike chemical or electrical state. Again, the context may be the general functional trend in the brain at a given moment, a conducting pathway, visual receptor, radiant energy, a glandular secretion or muscular contraction. It must be clearly understood that in this first sort of determination of function the distinction between text and context is set by the observational needs of the moment and not by any such fixed and existential coupling as that of organism and environment.

2) *The General Determination.* Most of our psychological consideration of the body has for many years fallen under the local conditions just now discussed. This fact is probably due in part to the ease with which we deal with relatively simple factors and in part to traditional conceptions of the neural system as made up of parallel strings (neuronal bundles) which functionate by end-to-end connections (synaptic arcs). Thus have we dealt locally and piecemeal with our bodily structures and functions. Of late, useful checks upon this analytical point of view have been offered by the neurologist, the configurationist, the functional embryologist, the animal experimenter, the organismal biologist, the pathologist, the biological chemist, and the philosopher of "emergence." All of these checks bear upon the *functional integrity* of the T-system. Individuals, wholes, unities, and consensual part-functions are stressed. We shall presently see that the old functional atomisms went much too far and were much too one-sided. They are adequate neither to the biological and psychological functions nor to the genetic derivation of these functions.

Our present interest lies, however, in the psychological aspects of the general determinations. The search for simple feelings and for simple strivings and conations led, as inevitably as the doctrine of sensations led, to simple bodily correlates. Failure here has been more complete than in the case of sensation, where we have discovered that the qualitative variety does rest *in part* upon differences in stimulus, local differences in reception and conduction, and, very likely, local areas of emphasis in the brain. But the search for local habitations and local operations to determine the P-functions taken at large has always met with limited success. The grossest attempt passed with the passing of phrenology; but advocates of "central localization" have never since been wanting. Attention, speech, thinking, and emotion have all been battlefields of theory.

But the more we know of general trends which sweep lesser systems, of large areal interactions, of the chemical unities of the body, of neural networks of potential and capacity, of gradual genetic differentiation of the specific from the general, and of the constant reorganization of functional wholes, the more we shall look beneath our P-functions for *general* determinations from the B-system as involved at large. Indeed, we may freely pass beyond the limits of the body and discover integral resultants— as L. J. Henderson has well taught us—from large physical systems which play upon the body from without.

Now we should scarcely look for general factors of the sort which we have been considering to determine wholly and separately *any* single class of the P-functions. We might rather expect variable weightings of the general and the local. And what we do seem to find is that local determination is maximal in those perceptual functions where complex patterns of energy play upon delicately attuned receptors and run their course under the general direction of intricately interwoven central and motor systems. What we grossly call visual and auditory perceptions are here conspicuous. At the opposite extreme of determination we find the colored moods and the more general and inclusive stirs to activity. In both of these cases the body is implicated at large. When we neglect in the mood whatever betrays its local origin (e.g., dull aches about the eyes, dragging legs, or lightness in the thorax), we seem to have what the analysts have generally described as the simpler feelings; and it may be that here we come closest to an unmixed determination from a general and inclusive trend of life. In the primary stirs of activity we again detect local influences (e.g., contractions in the forehead, respiratory pulls, and other high local tonicities), and when we abstract from these we find an alert forward-tending which reflects once more the general bodily factor. It suggests the British "conation," and it certainly bears a resemblance to the Wundtian *Trieb*. As regards their difference, we can safely say that the general bodily pattern is, in the case of the activity, richer in strong muscular tonicity and, in the case of the feelings, richer in dermal and visceral moments.

In our emotions the "feeling side" stands for the general component, that is to say, for the momentary trend of things in the body; while the apprehension of the predicament-to-be-resolved stands for the more specific contributions to function. At the stage of resolution, the specific pattern tends to lapse, and we have only to wait for the trend-component to subside. The wide variety of emotions rests in part upon variety in apprehended predicament, in part upon the varied coloring of the general "organic" background, and, in part, finally, upon varied course and outcome.

Within the extensive range of action, reaching from deliberative and reflective performances to immediate and unforeseen movements upon a brief signal, the local and the general determinations unite in varying degrees. The general factor is indicated in alertness or sluggishness, in delicacy or awkwardness, in concurrent and inhibitive trends, and in a general "priming" for the occasion. Frequent repetition, which commonly leads to habituation, results both in a general active temper of the body and in selective preparation for a local function of definite form and end. But the most obvious tendency among the functions of this executive class is progressively to lose *pattern* under habituation and to increase that aspect of action which represents the general thrusts and turns of bodily activity. The local preparation for defined and coordinated movement, which is here on the increase, might well be expected to augment the patterned side of the operation; but usually it does not. It does not because it slips out of the P-function, leaving it bare, uncolored, and, as we say, automatic. For we must remember that, when the *executive* aspect of doing disappears, the P-function either lapses or changes to perception (as in holding up a picture for scrutiny), to recollection (as when the cocked eye and wrinkled brow denote recall), to understanding (as in turning the pages and reading the open book), or to some other, non-executive kind of performance.

In the various forms of understanding and thinking, the specific and the patterned appear in the symbols used and in the concrete progress from stage to stage of comprehending and elaborating; the general and unpatterned in glimpses of insight, of conviction, doubt, hope, belief, and the like. The main uses of the body-at-large and of the inclusive trends therefore punctuate, comment upon, and note the advance and issue of thinking, while the local and patterned determinants supply the concrete means and materials. The two main historical methods in the psychology of thinking have both overlooked this double determination; the one has treated thought as logical meanings, thus neglecting bodily determination altogether; while the other, seeking to analyze thoughts into sensations and other "elements," has found only the specific and patterned and has overlooked the general and unpatterned—whence the futile debate over imaged and imageless thinking.

May we not now write in more general terms these two interwoven modes of bodily performance which cooperately determine the P-functions?

I think that we shall find the patterned sort prominent wherever the functions primarily and immediately depend upon (*a*) *articulated spatial and temporal orders* outside the T-system (as in visual, aural, or tactual apprehension and in those actions, emotions, and understandings which rest upon those orders), and upon (*b*) the *chemical detail of objects and processes which are contributory to life* (as in the taste-smell patterns of food and local disturbances of digestion). Out of these articulated conditions and out of the functions which arise from them, does the T-system build its gigantic space-time structure of the world and establish the active relations of its apprehended self to that changing but abiding structure. The fundamental and typical pattern is the perceptive; but if we leave out of account the executive and the comprehending forms we distort our psychology in the direction of the sensationalist and the intellectualist.

On the other hand, wherever the bodily and physical emphasis rests either upon (*a*) *change of a spatial-temporal kind* or upon (*b*) *internal modification within the B-system,* there the *undifferentiated* factor becomes pronounced. Our apprehension of movement is a case in point. There qualitative variety and articulation count for relatively little. They are usually very meager. The apprehensions of time are similar. And here we discover the main reason why the analyst of the "sense of movement" and of the "time sense" has never succeeded. His "sensational" patterns have never been adequate. The same is true of the emotions. The tremble,

stir, and ebullition of these thwarted executions are only vaguely or second-
arily membered. They rather represent gross forms of seizure upon the
general processes of life within the T-system. Hence the variegated and
inconstant coloring of the emotion and hence the impossibility of complete
analysis. To be sure, we shall go just as far wrong when we neglect the
articulated aspect of the emotion, which produces the "scene" and the predicament, and so also shall we by a one-sided view of thinking, planning,
and deciding. In fact, all P-functions are—as we must repeat—doubly
determined by the body. We shall properly describe and understand them
only when we have discovered for each type and for each higher integration
of the several kinds the precise way in which the bodily and extra-bodily
resources are in each case fused and compounded. This description is
designed to replace alleged "mental" conditions and the organization of
alleged "conscious compounds."

The distinction just now drawn should be useful in our genetic and
developmental accounts. Only a hint of this use can here be given. First
we must sweep away the artificial boundary of birth. Instead of the
landmark which birth properly is, this incident in the course of life has
generally been made the fixed line of division between "original nature"
and "educated nature," between natural man and learned man, between
instinctive heritages and acquisitions, between gifts of nature and gifts of
environment. All of these distinctions are misleading and vicious. Even
the line drawn at the assumed instant of fertilization is more or less arbitrary. In every state and at every moment the living organism (like the
living cell) is functionally determined (a) by a factor which we may provisionally call *stock*, (b) by physicochemical interchange with the outside,
(c) by internal changes (as from new materials), exercise of function and
growth. In addition, many organisms are, at certain eras in their life-
history, functionally determined (d) by the presence of other T-systems,
(e) by active association with other T-systems, and (f) by products of
this active association which appear in the form of beliefs, rules, customs,
traditions, and the like. In our case, life taken in the large is the *constantly
reorganized product* of all these factors. We cannot summate the factors
and we cannot safely dichotomize them into a fictitious nature and nurture,
heredity and environment, artificially conjoined at the moment of birth.
Once we have the general terms of psychological function, with its double
determination by the body and with the six conditions which make the
individual that which observation actually shows it at any time to be, we
have at hand all the necessary materials, as well as the guiding principles,
for a genetic account of the P-functions and of their issues and outcomes.

For a considerable time we may expect to find no evidence of these
functions, just as the physiologist expects to find no evidence of pulmonary
respiration in the embryo. But if we examine the T-system with care
when the symptoms of P-function begin to appear, we shall observe that
this system mainly supplies the general unpatterned conditions, and supplies
these during the physiological episodes of feeding, digesting, and moving of
trunk and members. Here we shall look less hopefully for perception and
for "insight" into character, mood, and intent of the gentle mother or

stern nurse than for a primitive and undifferentiated function which varies its shading from thrust and impulse to gross feeling, and from gross feeling to active and undirected search. Upon these primitive functions—not analyzable in terms of sensations, desires, and the like—play the articulations of receptor, brain, muscle, tendon, and gland. Thereupon gradually appear the grosser perception-actions. Observation finds no warrant at this stage for the separate and independent appearance of perceptions and actions, but only for the inception of a more primitive performance out of which these functions gradually emerge. In the one direction develop the apprehensions of present things and events, and in another direction the active struggle toward objects and states of being by the more and more skilful inclusion of motor resources supported by digestive and metabolic conditions. Only with the advent of the "predicament" comes the real emotion, and only with the apprehension of "desirable" objects comes desire. Before this day arrives, the prolonged concurrent play of our factors, a, b, and c, upon the growing organism would seem to make inappropriate any hypothesis of "innate" emotions and desires. The more elaborate actions and the more socialized emotions further await a fairly long period of preparation. The germs of comprehension would seem to appear to be present as a perceived object or event (e.g., increasing footsteps or an opening door) comes to stand for something beyond the thing perceived and to convey an implication (as of food, bath, or entertainment). The whole term of development is, of course, the entire life-span and not merely the two decades during which parental solicitude and public responsibility for the immature last. Change in the P-functions continues as long as the varying product of our six factors, and that is up to death, however tardily death comes for the individual. An adequate description will therefore include the thirties and the fifties quite as naturally as, and much more thoroughly than, it has heretofore dwelt upon the years of infancy and of adolescence.

Since we insist upon opening our psychology with distinctive functions and decline either to call these functions conscious or to extract them from conscious antecedents, the reader may reproach us for straining out all the essences of the "mentalist" without replacing them by a substitute. Our answer would be, in such a case, that nothing has been lost and nothing annihilated. Whatever there was of actual existence and of actual organic resource must therefore appear in some other form or in another context.

Since our study is pivoted upon certain functional activities which, like the physiological functions, have behind them the anatomical structures and the organized unity of the body, we shall have to look to their products and issues to replace our "conscious" deficits.

What then, we must ask, comes out of our psychological functions? A variety of products. Let us make a rough list of them.

1) Physical objects and occurrences
2) Supposed, assumed, and anticipated objects and occurrences
3) Musical, geometrical, and equated objects, and the like
4) Apprehended state, condition, and change of the body and of the T-system

5) Plural T-systems in communication
6) Motor changes and their immediate consequences
7) Strivings, plans, prophecies, and endeavors
8) Predicamentive situations (sometimes between T-systems)
9) General and conceptual objects
10) Opinions, beliefs, rules, and canons
11) Organized systems of 1 (the cosmos), 2 (imaginary existences), 3 (the world of spaceless things), 4 (the self), 5 (social groups), 6 and 7 (the phenomena of work and will), 8 (baffled endeavors), 9 (logic and mathematics), and 10 (the social life of man).

· If we are to make sense of this ragged and illogical-looking list, two precautionary observations will be necessary. In the first place, the only status of the things named is their status as functional products of the organism. When the T-system operates in the ways which we have designated as "psychological," these things appear. Nothing is here attempted with regard to their interpretation or valuation. If they are looked upon as raw materials for a doctrine of objects, they can be thus considered only in so far as they are dependent upon the system which we assumed at the beginning, namely, the T-system.

Once we separate these objects from their functional origin, canons go to ethics and aesthetics, plural T-systems to sociology, physical objects and occurrences to physics, imaged and supposed objects to fiction and poetry, and so on with the others. But while they are *still attached to their organic origin,* the physical, imaginary, mathematical, and musical objects and events refer to apprehending, and so primarily do the experienced state, condition, and change of the body; predicaments, motor exhibitions, stirrings, and endeavors are chiefly accounted for by the executive functions, which include the actions and the emotions. These functions also play their part in manufacturing the plural and intercommunicating T-systems. Finally, general objects, beliefs, and other "social" products, as well as organized systems, all demand insight, comprehension, and thinking of the elaborative and creative sort. If all these functional *termini* are to be called "objects," we must distinguish them from *Gegenstände* set out against a conscious *Subjekt,* and we must not confuse them either with the value-objects of *Werttheorie* or with ultimate forms of existence or being.

In the second place, we should not fall into the error of the intellectualist or the perceptualist and so limit the organism (or consciousness) to the production of knowledge and the identification of a "given" physical world. Let us remember rather that man is a facile and versatile creature who can turn his hand, as the above list suggests, to a great variety of performances and accomplishments. So firmly is established the opposition between subject and object and between the subjective and the objective that mind and solid object or mind and knowledge have seemed to be foreordained to divide the whole wide world between them.

Were it possible, it would be wise to avoid entirely the term "object," which suggests either a physical thing or the epistemological relation of the knower to the intellectively known. Let us keep the immediate functional flavor, which directs us to the operative modes of the T-system. We may then recall our word *announcement,* which seems moderately apt for the apprehensive modes (classes 1, 2, 3, 4, above) and add to it the terms *initiation, participation, resolution,* and *interpretation.*

The T-system obviously *initiates* in those executive functions which we know as actions. Here, to be sure, announced objects and occurrences play their part; but the primary business of the organism is to release and set going, to play its part (classes 6 and 7) by the use of motor mechanisms. Where the action initiated is shared by other T-systems or by changing physical systems, the mode of activity changes to *participation.* The T-system is also engaged thus in the emotion (class 8), where the predicament depends upon the fact that the organism is caught up with and therefore seized by the dramatic scene or situation; and in class 5, where communication of a social sort likewise involves a participative activity. In those more complicated activities which we call moral and aesthetic, participation is a main resource of the T-system. It compasses both sympathy and empathy (*Einfühlung*) by drawing upon the visceral and tonic resources of the body. We "feel for" our distressed fellows, we struggle with Laocoön, and we stretch upward with the aspiring column of stone. *Resolving* appears in certain later stages of action and it appears in thwarted forms in the emotional predicament.

The second main use made of sensations has been connected with the description of consciousness or of experience in terms of constituent elements. But if we reject the concept of the conscious, we shall here be greatly relieved. What we may do, instead, is to see that the dependence of objects (still using the term as any product of a P-function) is not always a gross and general dependence, but that many of these objects exhibit a qualitative variety which helps us to understand both the organism and its operations. The wall yonder is variegated; and when I observe it at this moment as dependent upon a T-system I discover details of dependence which I can bring, in an orderly way, under the rubrics of hue, tint, and chroma. So likewise I find that musical complexes, speech-sounds, sapiences, and a resisted push reveal analytic dependences which then appear as tones, noises, tastes, smells, and strains. But I discover no reason either for placing these things "in consciousness" or for resolving my entire apprehension into them. The reproach of "stimulus error," "confusion of process and meaning," of "mind and its object" will inevitably be brought; but those reproaches invariably beg the question because they rest upon the assumption of a consciousness which knows. It is wiser here to allow a careful choice of problems and exactness of experimental method to take precedence over doubtful concepts which involve the observer in epistemological tangles. Along with our modified use of "sensation" we may also describe the configurational aspect of our objects, without the exaggerated regard for "shape" and "wholeness" which some enthusiastic theorists maintain.

The problems of *attention* point to certain significant differences in various kinds of object which refer us to a peculiarity in the P-functions. The functions are, e.g., always limited in *range* or capacity, in their courses they sometimes *fluctuate* or shift, the *clarity* or obscurity of parts of objects de-

pends upon functional properties, objects called *figures* are more highly
organized than others called *grounds,* and finally the functions take time to
begin and to change (*inertia* of attention).

The key to the *feelings* lies—as we have intimated—in the general direction of bodily process (digestive, metabolic, and tonic) which indicates the
trend of living at large and which leads functionally to unpatterned and
unarticulated objects. These objects are not of the physical class; although
they may (as in a black mood) deeply color and dye our familiar surroundings. A simple and easy way of interpreting these general trends has been
proposed in the biologist's notion of *equilibrium;* but it is doubtful whether
so complex and so instable a system as the body can legitimately be regarded
as generally falling out of and into equilibrium.

Let us see where the *main problems* of the *behaviorist* fall. So far as
they rest upon the correlatives "organism" and "environment" they formally pass, of course, to biology, and just now biology is very hospitable to the
modes and the manners of the person who deals in adaptive responses.
Under our own conception of psychology, the environment does not there
exist. Once admit it to psychology and it destroys that aspect of the living
organism which is *agent,* and so, of course, the P-functions drop out. They
all drop out save action; and, since agency is removed from action, only
muscular movement and its environmental consequences remain. It is
worth noting that neither stimulus nor response is of any consequence to
the behaving organism itself but only to the observing behaviorist, who
interprets what he sees under the fixed obsession that environment is the
sole determiner of the motor functions of the body.

As for such topics as *habit, instinct, practice, fatigue, learning,* and *conditioning*—all of which are of vast interest to the behaviorist—they may be
claimed by all psychologists alike. They have their biological uses as well.
In fact they all spring from biological contexts. For us they chiefly
appear as conditions and antecedents *before* the functions. That is to say
that the bodily structures are charged through preceding exercise of function, under which the bodily substrate has been reorganized (habituation);
the factor of *stock* has played a part in the functional preparation (instinct); immediately preceding exercise has favorably disposed the function
(practice) or unfavorably disposed it (fatigue); earlier and later segments
of function show characteristic condensations, extensions, and celerities
(learning); new factors admitted in course may come in time to touch off,
even to govern, the function (conditioning). Since we may always understand the performances of the T-system better than we know conditions
and history, these subjects are matters pressing for research. Nevertheless,
the thoughtful psychologist will hesitate to accept terms simply because they
are the battle-cries of schools or because it is easier to borrow from biology,
medicine, or education than to design for his own special purposes.

The mode of activity most outstanding in the more abstractive actions
and emotions and everywhere in comprehension and elaborative thinking
is *interpretation.* In its simplest form interpretation penetrates or passes
beyond the apprehended object or event. The dinner-gong, distant thunder, and the broken bridge-railing are samples. The T-system transcends

these objects, interpreting them as "come," "hurry," and "danger." This simple transcendence we share with many other animals. It is a fashion of the moment to regard a similar mode as explained by the phrase "conditioned reflex" and as understood by demonstrations with dogs and guineapigs. "Reflex" is ill-chosen as an explanatory term and "conditioning" often covers our ignorance of somatic factors. The primary fact is that the object is reorganized and given a new relation to the *interpreting* T-system. It is obvious that no sharp line sets off this "transcending" operation from plain perception; though it is clear that the T-system is here setting out upon a new and very important functional extension.

There are four distinctive forms of interpretation which are distinguishable as sub-classes.

1) An object or occurrence announces itself as an *instrument.* Its usefulness (in pounding, reaching, defending, cutting, etc.) is announced. Those who discover neither accident nor "habit" behind such an interpretation call it *insight;* but it seems (in its simplest form) to be little more than a slight extension of the perceptive form of apprehension.

2) *Symbolization* is the second sub-class. Here the object is not at all its "physical" self. It is something else. This form of the penetration or transcendence of the object perceived has led on, among men, to words, numbers, and mathematical symbols.

3) In the third sub-form, objects are *refashioned.* "Those persons are arguing," "The glare is from a glass roof on the hill," "This mud is from a spring," "Pheasants have roosted here." These are familiar instances. The T-system has "done something" to apprehended objects.

4) In the fourth sub-class, the *refashioning is progressive.* There is advance toward a natural termination. The friends of Gestalt use the word "closure." The T-system, so to say, makes the object go on toward some end. Simple cases are the completion of partial geometrical forms and the establishment of a rhythm only hinted at. But the more involved cases take us into the elaborative forms of thinking, which lead to new beliefs, new information, new problems, new solutions, and the like. Perhaps we may safely say that progressive refashioning is the transitional form of interpretation which leads over from plain comprehension to elaboration or hard thinking.

If our crude survey of the psychological activities of the organism is to be trusted, we detect in announcing, initiating, participating, resolving, and interpreting the key to the world, in so far as the world is actively dependent upon those functions of the organism which we have collectively called psychological.[3]

Having looked ahead to observe the outcome and issue of our psychological performances and having looked behind to discover the organized body as the locus of all the immediate conditions of these performances, let us see how this point of view, which is pivoted upon function, will approach certain of the typical and outstanding problems of the psychologist.

---

[3]All the engaging details of functional combination and interplay, of short-cutting and economy, and of functional development and learning remain for other occasions.

We consider first the focal problems of those psychologists who analyze in terms of process. Their *sensations* would here appear as those aspects of produced objects which refer backward to the specific offices of the receptors. The primary use of sensations in the early researches of J. Müller, Helmholtz, Lotze, and Wundt was to define the function of certain of the sense-organs, visual, auditory, tactual, and kinaesthetic. That supplied the base for physiological psychology. Accepting the philosophical category of consciousness, Wundt imbedded the sensations in it, only providing that they be not confused with the fixed "ideas" and "impressions" of the associationists. But there is no necessity for bringing in this category as a place of deposit for the sensations. When we are interested in these functional details, it is only necessary that we so safeguard our experimental procedure as actually to identify that part of the functional product which refers us back cleanly and unequivocally to the individual receptor and to the hypothetical, chemical, and electrical changes which are there released; thus: red, sweet, bitter, stab, strain, pressure, tone, and so on. These are the sensations of physiological psychology, and when we quantify them and their derivatives, *sensitivity* and *sensibility,* by way of the metric methods, they become the sensations of the older psychophysics.

Since the *facts and principles of association* have played a prominent part in the history of our subject, it will be well to come to terms with them. Regarded from the point of view here proposed, association suggests those means (still little known) by which the T-system sustains its P-functions without direction from receptor and wanting the patterns of outside energies—conditions of the first importance in the ordinary course of perceiving. In memory and imagination, as well as in action, emotion, and thinking, the T-system is observed to functionate as an almost entirely independent system. In part this is because the efficacies of the "environment" have been absorbed within it and in part because the T-system is able by constant reorganization to initiate and to govern what at first required a constant interplay with outside agencies of a physical sort. "Association" is certain to be an unpopular term among the behaviorists (save for the educational hybrids among them). Most behaviorists dislike to see their environment driven from the center of the stage. At the same time this functional independence is not to be ignored. It has grown steadily from sponge and oyster to bee and ant, from amphioxus to man. The dubious side of associationism, upon which the champions of Gestalt have harped, is annoying but adventitious. It comes from a bad use of elements and from the imperfect neurology of the reflex arc.

The point of view here suggested would find the descriptive and explanatory account of the P-functions to be the initial task of general psychology. This account would refer the functions to somatic conditions, on the one hand, and to the functional products, upon the other. As it is of the nature of these functions to suffer constant change and reorganization, the factors which affect growth, development, habituation, and learning would of necessity occupy an important place. Here the direct comparison of earlier and later stages in the same T-system, among various systems, as between the child and the adult, between man and other animals, and upon unlike cultural levels suggests an experimental procedure combined with every other methodical aid. The descriptive account should be supplemented by a quantitative investigation of functional capacity as determined under various conditions. The quantitative or mensural treatment would use both the metric and the correlational methods; but it shall seek to define and to depict the functional mode involved and not merely to state the amount of output or accomplishment, as is the aim and intent of most of the present methods of test. Once carried through, the central description and derivation of the psychological functions should supply a sound basis for all the special psychologies, notably for the various forms of genetic and historical psychology, for social and ethnic psychology, and for the psychological disorders and defects. When complete, we should have for the first time in the experimental era a psychology based upon adequate facts and sound principles, which was applicable, as our present special psychologies are not, to every relevant problem and to every segment and division of the entire field.

A few years ago the present writer (1) tried to indicate how a psychology which possessed its own way of viewing life might set about its several tasks with men and other animals, with children and primitives, with the disordered and the socialized. The present envisagement may be regarded as much more radical, and it certainly departs more boldly from the mentalistic and the behavioristic traditions. At the same time, it can scarcely be accused of encouraging alliances with those current versions of our subject which—as this article has contended—draw their inspiration from, and hastily turn their products into, the other sciences and the arts of practice. The primary contention of the present article has been that any psychology that is to stand upon the level of the older sciences should squarely face all the relevant facts at hand and should deal with them in a distinctive *psychological* way and not as merely accessory to other subjects and to the arts. Special treatments may find their specific applications in the direction of biology, medicine, education, or some other neighboring discipline; but the general usefulness of psychology would seem to require an independent account of the facts which is at once thorough and authentic.

REFERENCES

1. BENTLEY, M. The psychological organism. Chap. 19 in Psychologies of 1925. Worcester, Mass.: Clark Univ. Press, 1926. Pp. 405-412.

2. BODE, B. H. Conflicting psychologies of learning. New York: Heath, 1929. Pp. vi+305.

3. PATRICK, G. T. W. What is the mind? New York: Macmillan, 1929. Pp. xii+185.

CHAPTER 6

PSYCHOLOGY FOR ECLECTICS

EDWIN G. BORING

Harvard University

There are psychologists who belong consciously to schools, and there are psychologists who are not aware of belonging to any school, the scholastics and the eclectics, as it were. The former are conscious of some systematic principle or dogma, which predetermines the nature of psychology for them and evaluates the data which claim to be part of psychology. Logically the content of the psychologies of these men is determined a priori by certain premises, a "point of view." Psychologically the attitude of these men tends to be dynamic and positive; they are quick to attack or to defend, they are possessed of a productive intolerance,[1] and they are conscious of relevant epistemological issues, although they are not always philosophically sophisticated. In fact, an understanding of the schools lies more in the psychological than in the logical approach. However, these psychologists of the schools are not alike in the degree with which they accept labels nor in the degree with which they subordinate themselves to a group mind. Gestalt psychologists seem glad to wear the badge of the school and to confront the public as a unit.[2] Behaviorists seem to find satisfaction in the badge, but have no hesitation about differing with each other in public;[3] each is, perhaps, his own school. There are still other psychologists, who object to a class name for themselves, but who exhibit the same positive systematic orientation as the men of the schools;[4] each of them is, presumably, also a school unto himself. Scholasticism' does not, therefore, interfere with individualism; it is the systematic and a priori manner of approach to psychology.

On the other hand, there are eclectics. They are really very numerous and probably constitute the majority of psychologists. Their presence, however, often goes unrecognized because they have no class name and no group consciousness, no intolerance, and, therefore, no urge to controversy. Occasionally one hears mention of 'the eclectic point of view,' but this phrase seems to involve a contradiction of terms. Mere eclecticism has no single point of view. It is a 'choosing of the best,' and, since there

---

[1] On the function of intolerance in scientific productivity, see (3).
[2] E.g., Wertheimer, Köhler, and Koffka.
[3] E.g., Watson, Lashley, Hunter, and Tolman.
[4] E.g., Bentley, and perhaps even Titchener. Of course, none of these individualists objects to being followed; he objects only to following. Thus Titchener had, in a sense, a school because of his great influence; but he eschewed a label for himself, and his followers likewise have eschewed labels, even the designation, "Titchenerist."

can be established no absolute 'good' with the schools in such sharp disagreement, the 'best' must remain individual and personal. Nevertheless, for all this formal argument against a unitary eclecticism, there seems to be a considerable amount of positive agreement among the eclectics, an agreement which is something more than the mere absence of intolerance. For instance, American psychology, especially as contrasted with the German, seems to be eclectically minded, and, if against this view someone cites the personal quarrels of the American psychologists of the nineties, it is possible, on the other hand, to exhibit the relative harmony, the reciprocal interest, and the incomplete synthesis of the younger generations.[5] The philosophy of the American trend was explicit in the functional school of Dewey and Angell, centered largely at Chicago, although Cattell, Thorndike, and Woodworth—to mention only the Columbia group —belong in this same picture and yet have no label. They are eclectics, but they must be something more or they would all be off the main track. What is the main track?

My thesis is that these 'eclectics' are not really mere eclectics, picking and choosing according to the adventitious operation of personal idiosyncrasies, but that they are *historically* determined. The majority of psychologists, so I firmly believe, define psychology, not in an apriori fashion as the 'scholastics' do, but a posteriori as they find it given to them. They do not attempt to deduce the chapters and data of psychology from some first principles, but they endeavor to induce a definition of psychology, when they engage in this undertaking at all, from the materials given them as psychology. Such an attitude does not mean that anything that pretends to be psychology must be accepted, on its own representations, into the body psychological. History has its warrants and its sanctions. Even the eclectic must choose, and in this case he chooses what has proved its worth. At bottom the test is, of course, pragmatic: those conceptions and methods belong in psychology which have been most fruitful, that is to say, which have placed the resultant data in relationship to the greatest number of other data and have thus enlarged and knit together the systematic structure that psychology eventually must be.

There is no name for this psychology that is thus defined a posteriori by induction from history, nor do I wish to coin one. My point is that psychology in 1930 exists. The task of the psychologist is not to rule out this part or to emphasize that, to say what it should be or what it should not be, but rather to interpret it in the light of its history, and to say what it is. It is a task that should appeal to the empirically minded scientist, for it is like the task of science, to attempt the description of a structure that is given. Of course, individuals will differ in their descriptions, for evaluation of the past is also involved, and the situation is not entirely objective. However, I wish to attempt here a statement of what psychology in 1930, an evolutionary product of the past, would seem to me to

---

[5] On the thesis that there is a unitary American psychology, which all fits together, see the discussion in my recent book (4, Chaps. XX and XXI).

be; and the test of my objectivity will have to be the assent which this article commands.

DETERMINATION VS. FREEDOM

Logically the first choice which the psychologist seeking a system would have to make concerns the definition of science in relation to determinism. It seems hardly necessary to labor this point. The eclectically minded psychologist, who takes as psychology what history provides for him in 1930, is going to choose determinism, for psychology has come to be scientific—in the physical deterministic sense of science. If the psychologist wants freedom, he will not be the historically determined eclectic.

However, the reader must not misunderstand me. Determinism is far from being the 'truth.' The problem of freedom and determinism is the great unresolved problem of philosophy, and the psychologist is quite free to make his choice. I have, for instance, no quarrel with McDougall. McDougall hopes, I think, that there will always be some freedom left to the mind; on no other grounds can I understand the significance of his seven marks of "behavior" (14, pp. 43-57). I hope that mind is really completely determined. Yet we both have the same respect for scientific fact. No causal relationship is ever so precisely established that the determinist does not still believe in the persistence of a probable error; and a probable error measures the persistence of ignorance. Perhaps it leaves room for freedom. The problem is one of limits. Probable errors get less and less as precision of research increases. Is the limit zero or is it a finite value? If we could establish the latter case, we should have measured the range of freedom without, of course, determining freedom. I cannot however, feel that this point of view is profitable in 1930, although I can quite happily leave McDougall free for freedom, because its occurrence cannot be empirically disproved.

If the eclectic refuses to admit freedom into his psychology, it is because he thinks of psychology as scientific and is holding to complete determinism as a fundamental postulate of science. It seems to me that needless argument would be avoided if McDougall would claim that his psychology is, in part, not scientific. He would be accepting the verdict of the majority and bravely surrendering the protection of the majority. However, none of these matters is worth fussing about so long as the issue is clear. We should find ourselves quarreling over nothing more than the use of words.

EXPERIMENTALISM VS. EMPIRICISM

There is no method for dealing with freedom, but, after the eclectic has decided to stick to determinism, he is faced at once with a choice between the experimental and the empirical methods.[6] He has also the third possibility of rationalism.

---

[6] I am using the word 'empiricism' for all systems that originate in experience. The adjective from this noun is 'empirical.' I do not mean the word in the sense of 'English empiricism,' which ought, as Titchener has pointed out, to

Of course, there is no such thing as a mere fixation of the phenomenal world for the purposes of science. The simplest observation in physics or in psychology has in it the essence of a judgment or an interpretation. In this sense all science is essentially rational in method. 'Rationalism,' however, means that the fundamental data as well as the observational processes are given independently of experience. Pure mathematics can be thoroughly rationalistic in method, a fact that appears most clearly in non-Euclidean geometries. For psychology this thoroughgoing rationalism can, I think, be rejected without argument. The verdict of history is too clear for the point to be labored. Even the philosopher who rejects the experimental method accepts the empirical.

The empirical method includes the experimental method, but it is not the same. Empiricism finds its data in experience and interprets them. Experimentalism also finds its data in experience, but it controls its interpretations by definite canons. The fear of the experimentalist is that unconscious prejudice will enter into free interpretation, and psychologists have reason to know the reality of this danger. The experiment repeats observations, because repetition is necessary for inductive generalization. The experiment is analytical, because it isolates factors for independent observation, often by way of artificial control with apparatus. Isolation represents a mistrust by the scientist of selective attention: if the range of observation is too broad, an artifact of attention may enter in. In general, the experimental method is the method of concomitant variations, used to establish, inductively, causal relationships.

The philosopher who is working with psychological problems most often uses the empirical, but not the experimental, method. The man who styles himself a psychologist and explicitly refuses to call himself a philosopher tries to use only the experimental method. There are also, it is true, philosopher-psychologists who lie between these extremes. Now what shall the eclectic choose? In 1930 he will choose, I think, the experimental method and eschew the empirical method that is not experimental. In making his choice he will examine the productivity of the two methods during the last seventy years, and will conclude that the fear of unrestrained empiricism is justified.

We must remember that the experimental method is not immediately adequate to every psychological problem. The history of experimental psychology is a history of the extension of the experimental method to new fields, and the end of the process is not yet. The philosopher dislikes to be limited to the experimental method in psychology, because its shuts him off from problems of his fundamental interests, which, on the other hand, give him courage to risk the dangers of uncontrolled empiricism. However, I do think that the eclectic psychologist will not wish to choose

---

have the adjective "empiristic." Cf. the German: *Empirismus, empirisch, empiristisch.* A genetic theory of space is 'empiristic,' but Brentano's psychology was 'empirical.' The two adjectives help, but it would be better if there were two good nouns. (Cf. 5, 2, and esp. 19.)

the empirical method of the philosopher for psychology. We face again the question of the convenience of terms. Hocking (8) has called experimental psychology, as it exists today, "near-psychology," and left the name "psychology" for the broader, less accurate empiricism. However, he will not in his generation prevail against historical inertia in establishing these terms. Understanding by the largest number of persons would be aided if he would reverse the meaning of "near-psychology" and "psychology." Of course, if he thinks that "near-psychology" is a term of opprobrium, we must leave him free to use words as he wishes, so long as we understand his meaning so that we can re-evaluate them.

BEHAVIORISM VS. PHENOMENALISM

The eclectic of 1930 will accept both behavior and phenomena as the data of his psychology. By 'phenomena' he will mean, of course, the data of "immediate experience," of "experience regarded as dependent upon the experiencing individual," of 'consciousness' if the word be shorn of too explicit a meaning of immanent objectivity, of 'introspection' if that word be divested of its meaning of analysis into fixed elements. But how can he accept both?

He will succeed by rejecting dualism. The Cartesian dichotomy of mind and body has dominated psychology for nearly three centuries, but there is nothing inevitable about it. Empiricism is the method of all science, and the phenomena, as the positivists have said and Mach has made clear to psychologists, are the first data of every science. The behaviorist does not get along without consciousness; he simply substitutes the consciousness of the experimenter for the consciousness of the subject, and erects a system of realities where the basal data are all of visual space. This last statement may surprise the reader, because the behaviorist adopts an epistemology without making his assumptions clear. Let me, therefore, elaborate it.

Behaviorism is sometimes identified with 'objective' psychology. Behaviorists sometimes claim that their method is 'objective.' Hence one asks how any scientific method can be objective when its essence is subjective observation? It appears that the term, 'objective method,' is used in psychology for the method of physics, and it is plain that physics is as subjective as any science, but that the nature of its subjective materials is usually lost sight of because it is nearly always the same: the phenomena of physics are visual-spatial phenomena. Visual space perception is the most accurate perceptual capacity that human beings have. In the case of the perception of the straight extension of a line past a critical point, the case of the vernier, it appears that visual acuity may be accurate for a visual angle as little as seven seconds of arc. Hence the physicist attempts to reduce all his immediate observations to the observation of a permanent visual record or the observation of a seen point upon a scale. 'Objectivity' of method thus means literally the limitation of subjectivity to the most accurate kind of perception. The behaviorist, it appears, avoids consciousness no more than the physicist or the introspectionist.

This subjectification of behaviorism does not, however, provide the eclectic with a positive point of view in combining both behavior and phenomena. Let me approach the matter in two ways, and let me take the more naïve view first. Perhaps it is also the more useful view for the psychologist who dislikes epistemology.

The experimental method yields facts, which are always induced relationships between variable terms. They are, strictly speaking, correlations got by the method of concomitant variations, which experimentation is. A relationship cannot involve less than two terms, and most facts are causal in the sense that one term is logically and temporally prior to the other, that is to say, it is the condition of the other. This is essentially the view of David Hume, Ernst Mach, and Karl Pearson.

Now the psychologist has—if we keep the gross outlines without refinement—three classes of terms with which to work: (a) stimulus, (b) phenomenon, and (c) response. They are related in a fact, temporally and logically, to each other as shown in Figure 1. The simplest psychological

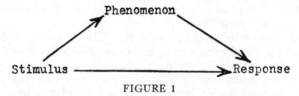

FIGURE 1

fact represents a correlation between two of these variables. The older introspective psychology, which hoped to find causal relations between phenomena, failed. That, I think, is the historical verdict. Even the law of association is not a law of pure consciousness, and no other law comes nearly so close to the ideal of the old 'descriptive' psychology.

The older introspective psychology (of Wundt and Titchener, for example) emphasized primarily the first relation of the diagram, the relation of stimulus and phenomenon. All the chapters on sensation and perception dealt almost exclusively with this kind of fact. There was no assumption of a "constancy hypothesis," as Gestalt psychology would now have us believe, for then there would have been no law to state. From Fechner to the present the laws of sensation and perception have stated the nature of the functional correlation between stimulus and phenomenon, because a simple one-to-one correlation ("constancy hypothesis") did not hold. In the same manner but less obviously, the stimulus, or its equivalent in a less clearly defined situation, appeared in the laws of feeling, attention, memory, action, emotion, and thought. I shall return to the 'situation' in a moment.

Behaviorism has tried to limit itself to the second class of relations, the relation of stimulus to response. I do not need to enlarge upon this point, because the notion has been explicit in behaviorism, whereas the stimulus slipped into introspective psychology unannounced by the backdoor. And we all know the sort of fact that behaviorism yields.

The third kind of relation, the relation of phenomenon to response, has been considered least in psychology, and yet it is not entirely missing. The correlation of a type of reaction consciousness with the reaction-time belongs in this class. So does the relation of imaginal type to accuracy of recall as the topic is usually investigated. In a large measure, psychiatry is interested in this relation wherever behavioral maladjustments are referred to conscious phenomena. Of course, psychotherapeutics uses one of the other relations, because it has to control a cause and the stimulus or 'situation' is the only prior term accessible for direct control.

Now we can turn to the 'situation.' The diagram of the three terms represents the scientific ideal. In it the stimulus and response are what we might call physical values, taken always in relation to another term to establish a fact. Experientially they generally derive most immediately from visual-spatial perception, but we are justified in regarding them simply as physical realities. While the observational methods for the two seem to be alike, they are always discrete in the experimental setting, for one is the prior condition and the other the subsequent effect. However, there are many first terms that do not admit of precise physical definitions. Green light of 505 millimicrons wave-length may be a stimulus, but my grandmother is not a stimulus; she is a 'situation.' The *Aufgabe* is a situation. The *raison d'être* of an *Einstellung* or a determining tendency is a situation. The cat that produces rage in a dog is a situation and not a stimulus in the precise sense of the term. To call these ill-defined, effective objects and events stimuli is to pervert a term from its precise meaning. One can call them 'determinants' if one likes, and then a 'determinant' is a term in a psychological fact which is prior to response or phenomenon, as the case may be, which plays the rôle of the stimulus, but which is still vaguely defined by its meaning to the organism which it affects. The ideal of scientific psychology is, of course, to get rid of the 'determinants' and to learn to translate them into the precisely defined stimuli, and I should recommend the use of the word 'determinant' in this sense, if I were sure that everyone would remember that its use is always a confession of scientific weakness. Unfortunately the adoption of a new word is apt to carry with it the illusion of definiteness.

However, the diagram must finally be modified by its complete denial! The analysis that it represents is "differential" (Köhler's term, 11, pp. 163-168), that is to say, it is like the differential analysis of calculus which is made with the intention of undoing it after it has served its purpose. We want in psychology, by the multiplication of observed correlations between terms, to get rid of the terms and to interpolate continúa. For instance, we may ask: Is the stimulus in the apparatus, in the receptor, or at some one of the successive points along which excitation in the nervous system is propagated? Any determined reality at any one of these points can form the first term of that correlation into which stimulus enters, and ultimately the intercorrelations give us a continuum in which the terms have disappeared. Nevertheless it is necessary to have the terms while the experimentation is in progress; continuity comes later.

If we stop at the naïve level, the phenomena simply appear as middle terms. They may act as consequents with stimuli (or 'determinants') or as antecedents with responses. They do not appear in the simple relation of stimulus and response, but they enter into very many complex relations. Scientific psychology does not stop with relations of two terms; it builds up more and more elaborate systematic structures. Here all three kinds of terms enter, and the phenomena are truly middle terms. The reaction experiment is an example, for in its laws the nature of the stimulus, the conscious pattern, and the reaction-time are all interrelated.

So much for naïveté. What I have said is enough for the eclectic to tell his elementary class in order to avoid the troublesome epistemology of the various schools. He gives the diagram, explains how a fact is a relation of two or more of its terms, shows which are antecedents and which consequents, points out that we have to get along with 'determinants' instead of stimuli in so young a science as psychology, and mentions the ultimate continuity which is the ideal. If he wishes to add that introspection is a method of getting at middle terms, of observing the brain directly, as it were, he will not be telling the exact truth, but he will probably bring his class nearer the truth than by anything else he can expound in ten minutes.

There is not space here for us to go fully into the more sophisticated epistemology of this question, but I wish to indicate where the valid point of view for the eclectic lies. We must distinguish carefully between the *real* and the *actual*. The real is forever unattainable by any direct means. It is inferred from the actual. The actual depends upon the immediately given of experience. In science one proceeds always from the actual toward the real. In behaviorism the actualities are nearly always the data of visual space, but the realities are what these data mean, this stimulus and that response. In the case of phenomena this dichotomy still persists, and the failure to recognize it is a constant source of confusion. Visual space enters in, but so do all the other phenomenal actualities. However, they come to mean other realities, mental objects, as it were. When Külpe called the attribute a conscious actuality and the sensation a psychic real, he meant just this thing, and ultimately Titchener came over to the same view (13, 17, but cf. 16). There has, however, never been formulated on the basis of psychological experimentation a real system of 'mental objects,' like sensation, image, idea, feeling, thought, and conation. Always the stimulus, or behavior, or something of the nervous system has had to be brought in. Hence the emphasis has persistently tended toward the nervous system. Sometimes the total psychological real is said to be the psychophysical organization, but the word 'psychophysical' here implies a dualism that has little significance. Sometimes the real is said to be the nervous system. Such a view holds that introspection is a method for observing brain processes, and that the 'unconscious' is nervous. It is a sound view if one can but think of the brain and the nervous system as being only realities, that is to say, constructs, or even theories and hypotheses. The trouble is that there is also an actual brain given in experience more directly, and the two are apt to be confused. The 'unconscious' is also an unsatisfactory reality because it is apt to be confused with the real brain of the physiologists or the phenomenal actuality. That there is a real 'psyche' which psychologists study by both behavioral and introspective methods, the eclectic will wish to affirm, and, as he will seldom try to press the epistemological question further, we need not seek to name it.

We have dealt at considerable length with the question of the inclusion of both behavioral and introspective data within psychology, because it is at this point that the schools are most divergent, and it is here that the eclectic most needs justification. That the trend of history is toward this synthesis is abundantly evident. Purely introspective psychology failed. Behaviorism got most of its problems from introspective psychology, and ever since Watson formulated radical behaviorism other behaviorists have been busy modifying it in the direction of the older psychology. On the other hand, Gestalt psychology, which began in experimental phenomenalism, has come in Köhler's hands to include behaviorism, or at least the behavioral data (12, Chaps. I and VII). Most psychologists want the synthesis because psychology has always implied it. The eclectic can have his way, if he will but accept this formulation.

ATOMISM VS. ORGANIZATION

Here the eclectic will certainly wish to take the view of Gestalt psychology. Any fixed, predetermined elements of analysis impose upon him too great constraints. He will reject sensationism, because a strict adherence to sensory elements leads him to ignore other phenomenal data of which he wants to take account. He will reject 'reflexism' for the same reason. Wherever total structures appear in his reals, he will accept them gladly. He will remain an atomist in his experimentation, because the variables to be correlated in an experiment are essentially discrete. But he will seek to avoid bundles of correlated terms in constructing his realities, and will there interpolate continuity, structure, and organization.

We must not fail to note, however, that in accepting the doctrine of Gestalt psychology the eclectic is still being guided by history. James (10, Vol. II, pp. 224-290) made the argument against sensationism in 1890. Dewey (6) made the argument against 'reflexism' in 1896.[7] The virtue of Gestalt psychology is that it is simply psychology and as old as experimental psychology. I doubt if any psychologist has seriously held to the "bundle hypothesis" since James Mill in 1829.[8] Certainly Wundt

---

[7] I have just reread this classic article, and it sounds to me exactly like Köhler's discussion of the same matter, a third of a century later.

[8] I have in mind here Max Wertheimer's paper (21). This is the paper that begins with the hypothetical case of the perception of a house, trees, and the sky from a window. Wertheimer asks whether there might be said to be 327 brightnesses and color-tones, 120 in the house, 90 in the trees, and 117 in the sky. He then demolishes such a "bundle hypothesis." When I first read this passage I was shocked, not at the sin of the "bundle hypothesis," but at the assumption that any psychologist, who is worth refuting at the present day, should seriously be

did not. The eclectic who waits upon the course of history need not fear Gestalt psychology because it is new; the new thing about it is that it has made explicit much that often remained only implicit before.

FUNCTIONALISM VS. STRUCTURALISM

The old controversy in America was between functional and structural psychology, as focused respectively in Angell at Chicago and Titchener at Cornell. The eclectic of 1930 will choose neither of these American psychologies of the first decade of the present century, for psychology has outgrown both. However, the old issue still exists as applied to the modern psychologies.

We have already seen that the eclectic will choose modern structuralism, that is to say, he will choose a psychology that deals with structured wholes built upon both behavioral and phenomenal terms. This new structuralism differs from the old structuralism in that it includes behaviorism and in that it does not attempt formal analysis into fixed sensory elements. But can the eclectic accept functionalism, too, without giving up this structuralism?

The four marks of a functional psychology are these: (a) It studies "mental operations" or activities; it is thus dynamic and not satatic. (b) It deals with "the fundamental utilities" of mind and the ways in which the mind is "engaged in mediating between the environment and the needs of the organism"; it is biological in the adaptive sense. (c) For this reason it considers the total organism, and gives attention both to behavior and to phenomena. (d) For the same reason it lends itself readily to technology or practice, for the practical problems of applied psychology always center in the relation of the organism to its environment.[9] These were the characteristics of functionalism twenty-five years ago and they still are its marks.

With respect to the first and third of these marks of a functional psychology we have already had the eclectic make a choice. He has rejected activity as an immediate datum and has included it as one kind of organization in the psychic realities toward which he works. The psychology of *Akt* or *Funktion* in the tradition of Brentano he rejects only as he rejects empiricism that is not experimentalism. Since his psychic reals are

---

supposed to hold such a view. Wertheimer most successfully, however, refutes James Mill's *Analysis of the Human Mind* (15, cf. esp. chap. iii). Similarly Köhler in his latest book (12) triumphantly charges some windmills of his own erection, without a hint, by way of explicit footnote to the unsophisticated reader, that the windmills exist today chiefly in the author's mind.

[9]J. R. Angell (1) enumerated the first three of these marks when he summed up the case for functional psychology in his presidential address before the American Psychological Association. The fourth point about practice is clear on the face of the matter. It was the thesis of John Dewey in "Psychology and Social Practice" (7), and Dewey started the Chicago school by his paper on the reflex arc (6). Titchener (18) made practically the same analysis of G. T. Ladd's functional psychology. Titchener's four points were: (a) the self; (b) activity; (c) teleology or adaptive value; (d) practicality. Here the self is the only new item. The quotations in the text are from Angell (1).

stripped of any reference to the dualism of mind and body, he is dealing with the total psychophysical organism, except that he does not like to use the word 'psychophysical' for the reason that it implies the pernicious Cartesian dichotomy. The crux of the matter must, therefore, lie in his interest in the utilities of mind and in practice.

It has been said that a scientific psychology cannot be functional because we cannot experimentally observe uses or values, and because the whole range of scientific possibilities for psychology is already stated in the triangular diagram which we have already considered. Such a statement is, however, true only in a limited way, for it takes the matter epistemologically and not psychologically. Let us consider both points of view.

Epistemologically it is plain that a fact is a relation and that a relation is a function. Phenomenon is a function of stimulus, and response a function of stimulus or of phenomenon. The psychological *use* of a stimulus is to condition a response or a phenomenon. The psychic real is a functional structure.

This conclusion leads to the rather surprising dictum that psychology deals only with meanings, for a meaning is just such a relation as we have considered a fact to be. I am not here being led by the subtleties of philosophical method into an absurdity. This statement is simply the general form of Titchener's context theory of meaning. The context theory held that meaning is a relation in which a consequent term accrues to an antecedent. The behavioral theory of meaning holds that a response is the context of a stimulus.[10] However, we can go further and say that for most meanings of the older introspective psychology the phenomenon is logically the response to a stimulus (or 'determinant'). Even Titchener came close to behaviorism in his psychology of meaning, because he recognized that most meaning is not present at all except as there is discriminative behavioral response to indicate its presence. An organism 'knows' this or that when it responds selectively, in a phenomenal or motor manner, to a stimulus (or 'determinant').

It is now clear that, in establishing psychological facts by the experimental method of correlation, we are arriving at functional statements of relations, at meanings, at statements of the capacities of an organism. Some of these capacities are important in life. The psychologist does not have to consider this importance, but he can take it into account, if he wishes, without giving up his scientific attitude. The applied psychology that deals with the utilities of mind for living can be nothing more than a selection of the facts of scientific psychology.

It is this question of selection that leads us from epistemological to psychological discussion. The points of view and the motives of psychologists come in. Many psychologists select their problems from the multiplicity of relations which our three-cornered diagram implies, because they

---

[10]That behaviorism has in the past offered the best approach to the problem of meaning and cognition is not generally recognized. I find this belief, however, in the well-known paper of E. B. Holt (9), and in the writings of E. C. Tolman (esp. 20).

hope that some of the relationships will be useful. If they shut their eyes to the practical utility of certain psychological facts, they are for the time being 'pure' psychologists; and then they can open them again and become technologists. The answer to the question as to whether the structuralist can also be a functionalist is Yes. He can work with the same method and be concerned with the same kind of facts, but his interest is broader as against utility and narrower as against the range of facts.

This whole matter is so overlaid with emotion that it is hard to keep thought clear. In part the 'pure' scientist condemns the technologist as a matter of defense, for he wants to be let alone to study apparently impractical facts. He resents the technologist's lack of interest in many of his findings. He deplores the technologist's lack of precision, for a practical urge often leads to gross methods where refinement is impossible, and to a wholesale substitution of 'determinants' for stimuli. But this quarrel is only a psychological matter and quite irrelevant to the logic of the problem. The structuralist may be also a functionalist if he chooses.

And so, I think, the eclectic will choose formally to include the functional interest in his psychology, although he may often not care to cultivate this interest in himself.

The Eclectic's Psychology

What, then, is the eclectic's psychology in 1930 and how does he come by it?

He goes to all the psychologies and examines them genetically as historical developments. He accepts whatever has shown vitality and fertility over a long period of time, and rejects the rest. Thus he accepts determinism and rejects freedom, he embraces experimentalism and avoids other empiricism. His choice is not based upon decisions as to truth and falsity, but upon the pragmatic test of fertility.

When he comes to the choice between phenomenalism and behaviorism, he wishes to accept both, because both have been productive and because both interest him. Here, however, he meets a difficulty. Can he, even as an eclectic, bring under the single name, psychology, the subject-matters of supposedly incompatible schools? He can if he wishes, but, if he is epistemologically and psychologically minded about the matter, he will say to himself: The fact that these schools both claim to be psychology, and the fact that I and many other psychologists find a unitary interest in them both, means that there must be some unitary account of them both which underlies the apparent incompatibility. So he seeks this principle in epistemology, and he finds it, very properly for an experimental psychology, in the notion of what an experiment is, what it yields, and the relation of all scientific experiment to experience. He sees that behaviorism and physics are just as much and just as little 'mentalistic' as 'introspective' psychology, that phenomena are not separated from the other data of science by the gulf of a dualism, and that they are not, as data, the psychic realities which are his objective. He may go as far as he likes in this development, but most psychological eclectics will be satisfied with very little epistemology.

Finally, the eclectic faces the problem of function, use, and practicality in psychology, and he discovers that he can extend his interest in these directions without surrendering any of the principles which he has already accepted. He sees that science and technology ordinarily go hand in hand, and he allows these aims to psychologists and indulges in them himself if he be so inclined.[11]

Is it too hopeful a picture to say that he then, with mind at rest on these epistemological questions, hurries back to his laboratory to start new research and never bothers about such systematic issues again?

REFERENCES

1. ANGELL, J. R. The province of functional psychology. *Psychol. Rev.,* 1907, **14,** 61-91.
2. BORING, E. G. Empirical psychology. *Amer. J. Psychol.,* 1927, **38,** 475-477.
3. ———. The psychology of controversy. *Psychol. Rev.,* 1929, **36,** 97-121.
4. ———. A history of experimental psychology. New York: Century, 1929. Pp. xvi+699.
5. CARMICHAEL, L. What is empirical psychology? *Amer. J. Psychol.,* 1926, **37,** 521-527.
6. DEWEY, J. The reflex arc concept in psychology. *Psychol. Rev.,* 1896, **3,** 357-370.
7. ———. Psychology and social practice. *Psychol. Rev.,* 1900, **7,** 105-124.
8. HOCKING, W. E. Mind and near-mind. *Proc. 6th Int. Cong. Phil.,* 1927, 203-215.
9. HOLT, E. B. Response and cognition. *J. Phil., Psychol., etc.,* 1915, **12,** 365-373, 393-404. Reprinted in: The Freudian wish and its place in ethics. New York: Holt, 1915. Pp. 153-208.
10. JAMES, W. Principles of psychology. (2 vols.) New York: Holt, 1890. Pp. xii+689; vi+704.
11. KÖHLER, W. An aspect of Gestalt psychology. Chap. 8 in Psychologies of 1925. Worcester, Mass.: Clark Univ. Press, 1926. Pp. 163-195.
12. ———. Gestalt psychology. New York: Liveright, 1929. Pp. xii+403.
13. KÜLPE, O. Versuche über Abstraktion. *Ber. u. d. I. Kong. f. exper. Psychol.,* 1904, 56-68.
14. McDOUGALL, W. Outline of psychology. New York: Scribner's, 1923. Pp. xvi+456.
15. MILL, J. Analysis of the human mind. London, 1829.
16. RAHN, C. Relation of sensation to other categories in contemporary psychology. *Psychol. Monog.,* 1913, **16,** No. 67. Pp. 131.
17. TITCHENER, E. B. Sensation and system. *Amer. J. Psychol.,* 1915, **26,** 258-267.
18. ———. Functional psychology and the psychology of act: I. *Amer. J. Psychol.,* 1921, **32,** 519-542.
19. ———. Empirical and experimental psychology. *J. Gen. Psychol.,* 1928, **1,** 176-177.
20. TOLMAN, E. C. A behaviorist's definition of consciousness. *Psychol. Rev.,* 1927, **34,** 433-439.
21. WERTHEIMER, M. Untersuchungen zur Lehre von der Gestalt. *Psychol. Forsch.,* 1923, **4,** 301-350.

---

[11]It seems odd that I should feel that the view of psychology which I have presented in this paper is very close to the underlying view of Köhler, the polemicist, in his *Gestalt Psychology* (12), a book which is supposed to defend an extreme and a new view, and not merely to sum up the work of the last seventy years in the psychological laboratories. Yet I have this impression, and in stating it I epitomize my keen admiration for Gestalt psychology, an admiration which is founded upon my belief that Gestalt psychology is not what it claims to be.

CHAPTER 7

STRUCTURAL PSYCHOLOGY

JOHN PAUL NAFE

Clark University

"Structural" psychology, strictly speaking, applies only to the opposition of the Wundtian influence, as expressed in the work of E. B. Titchener and others, to functional concepts. It has accomplished its sole purpose, and the origin of the name and history of the movement have been adequately treated (1, 2). "Experimental" psychology was the designation of the broader movement, but with the more general acceptance of experimental methods the term lost its earlier obvious significance. Many of the logical and metaphysical questions so important to another generation of psychologists have faded,[1] unanswered, from the picture, and the present generation, impatient of such matters, prefers the risk of untenable positions and temporary confusions to the certainty of time lost in attempts to take positions upon questions of fact before the facts are known. The present chapter treats of the *experimental* psychologies of today, regardless of the philosophical positions of individual psychologists, and the old term, experimental psychology,[2] is used to designate them.

Experimental psychology is an attempt to describe the facts upon which our conception of a mental life is based and to find the conditions or laws under which instances are realized. Determination of purpose and explanation by purpose are excluded. Practically, experimental psychology usually includes a study of (*a*) stimulus conditions, (*b*) nervous processes, (*c*) psychological experience, and (*d*) reaction or response. Besides our general statement of problem and our experimental method, we inherit from an earlier generation a subdivision of the field into three specific problems, those of (*a*) sensation, (*b*) perception, and (*c*) conception or memory (the higher mental processes). In the earlier days these were

---

[1] Faded as a topic of interest. I believe the "fading" has in reality consisted of a tacit assumption by experimental psychologists as a group of a mechanistic hypothesis. Purposive conceptions still find expression in both psychological and behavioristic systems, but their authors lose caste quickly among all psychologists, interesting as such systems may be to other groups. The distinction, however, is not always clear. The influence of a stimulating situation upon a body with unlimited degrees of freedom may be expressed in terms objectionable to some but meaning nothing more "purposive" than physical "force" applied to an electromagnetic field where the determination of reaction is not as obvious as it is in machine systems with a single degree of freedom but mechanically just as effective. Such differences may be classed with language difficulties.

[2] It may be found a bit confusing to use "experimental psychology" as the more general term and "psychology" as a branch, but the words seem to be used more and more in that way.

known as the problems of (*a*) sensation, (*b*) simultaneous association, and (*c*) successive association. With the introduction of the experimental method most, if not all, of the specific theories of the associationists were abandoned, but the revolt did not go to the three problems as there formulated or as stated by Aristotle. Almost unaltered they remain with us to this day as the problems of general psychology although, as it works out, individuals who are active in one of these fields are likely to neglect or even disclaim the others. With the shift of emphasis from systematic considerations to experimentally observed facts, the distinctions between schools of psychology have tended to disappear, and the practical barrier of subject-matter or problem ceases to separate completely our interests. Many collateral branches of psychology have developed, but these usually include a general psychology in some form and will not be separately discussed.

In the development of experimental psychology there have been, within fairly recent years, two major revolts resulting in the schools or movements known as behaviorism and *Gestalttheorie*. Though sharply distinguished from psychology proper by their proponents, there is no doubt that both belong within the field of experimental psychology, and in the present paper I shall attempt in a general way to set forth my own understanding of what psychology, in the narrower sense, is and how these two schools differ systematically from the parent body. All three branches of experimental psychology are adequately defined, in a general way, by their method, that of direct observation, and by their problems, the description of the facts and discovery of laws. Among these problems we may include explanation if by that we mean correlation with the facts of physiology and neurology, and we may include prediction if by that we mean the application of laws to future events. At present all three schools are engaged in problems which expressly or by inference admit the division of the field into the three problems outlined by the associationists, but these problems are at all times subject to reinterpretation in the light of past progress. There are no beliefs which are characteristic of experimental psychology nor any doctrines, other than the restrictions mentioned, to which one must subscribe. In considering stimulus conditions we infringe upon the physical sciences, in our study of the nervous processes we duplicate much of the field of neurology, and in our work upon reaction there is much that is also of interest to physiology, but our problems, as they appear today, are different from those of any one of these other sciences. In our work we also must make assumptions which are not acceptable to all psychologists, but these assumptions are always dependent for verification upon the facts as these are developed, and in themselves form no part of a system. It is the thesis of the present paper that there are no *fundamental* differences between the "schools" of experimental psychology, and that the workers in this field, with all their minor differences, form a homogeneous group comprising almost all psychologists.

PSYCHOLOGY

Sensory Processes. Psychological experience comes to us in patterns closely woven in their spatial and temporal aspects, but from one experience to another certain aspects vary. A study of vision shows a series of such variables, e.g., size, form, hue, location, brightness, contrast effects, degrees of adaptation, etc. Auditory experiences vary in intensity, pitch, timbre, volume, localization, etc. Other sense departments furnish experiences which also have such variable aspects, and it is the problem of "sense psychology" to determine (a) what variable aspects of experience there are in each department of sense and (b) what variables in the stimulus situations and in the neural processes are correlated with them.

The variable aspects of experience are often considered to be of different orders, i.e., quality, intensity, extensity, duration, and sometimes others are given a position of fundamental importance in the sense that they are essential to all experience and that their correlates are presumably to be discovered in essential variables of the sense-organ and neural impulses, while such aspects as form, bidimensional and tridimensional localization, size, timbre, and others are accepted as mere complications of such processes. Such distinctions are made upon bases unsatisfactory to many psychologists and wholly repudiated by others. It is of no practical importance for us here because, regardless of preconceived ideas as to what category a particular variable aspect belongs in, the facts, when determined, are complete in themselves and are unaltered by any classification adopted. One example must suffice: The volume of auditory experiences has been held by some to be a variable aspect which is to be "explained" by finding a correlate in the functions of the sense-organ. By others it has been held to be a complication of experience of the order of partials and entirely explainable upon a basis of the spread or deflections of the sound waves and as a complexity in the neural impulses. A determination of the facts will show the true relation. The problem of determining this relation is the same whether or not, in advance, we recognize a difference in kind between variables.

The concept of "sensation" is built primarily upon the basis of independent variables, a sensation being a collocation of such aspects. Among those who use this concept, the variables are spoken of as "attributes" of the sensation. It is highly doubtful whether any psychologist has ever maintained that experience occurs in such simplified forms, but it has been reasoned that our ordinary meaningful experiences result from a building up of such collocations into definite patterns which make up the experiences. Such a type of analysis or synthesis needs much to justify itself, it having no obvious justification and comprising a possible source of error. Inasmuch as this attempt purports to portray any real existence for such sensations we may say that it has definitely failed because we are unable to find such units either on the stimulus–neural-response side or on the side of psychological experience. The treatment of sensory data under the concept of sensation necessarily involves an assumption of the conventional division of the subject between the existence of such collocations and the principles of organization or association (perception, memory) working between them. The surrender of the concept presumes the occurrence of psychological experience already organized and hence exposing a fallacy in the three-fold division of the field. Recently the tendency among psychologists has been to accept the second position and consequently to assume that any principles of spatial or temporal organization involved will appear in the final determination of the sensory processes themselves.

It is true that in the study of sense psychology we have not as yet evolved a theory that is generally satisfactory for a single one of the sense departments, yet the facts are accumulating steadily and as long as this is the case we are entitled to continue to believe it quite possible that the true relations between stimulus conditions, neural activity, and psychological experience will become known. More remote, perhaps, is the hope that with the solution of these problems we shall receive some indication as to the essential nature of the principles of organization by which such processes, as psychological experiences, are bound into unitary wholes, spatially and temporally, but such a hope is not necessarily more remote than that which prompts us to the study of nonsense syllables and other conditions under which the effects of such organization become patent.

It is not necessary to assume, although some individuals have made the assumption, that psychology ends here. It is true that the interest of many individuals does end with sensory psychology, but also it has been demonstrated that experimental methods may be applied to the studies of perception and the higher mental processes. Such studies will doubtless grow in number, and there is room for only the most friendly cooperation between fields in which the results obtained may be of great importance to the other. Many of us have been led to believe that the theories, when formulated, would be simple, and many of us now think in terms of theories that others of us believe to be greatly oversimplified. These expectations, however, form no part of a system nor are they adhered to with any great degree of tenacity. Every new fact discovered affects our expectations in some degree and to some extent limits the possibilities.

The Higher Mental Processes. It has often been said that in approaching the problems of psychology one should take a naïve attitude toward experience and with that opinion I am in thorough agreement, but the ability to assume such a naïve attitude requires much training and a background that is anything but naïve. Every student of psychology goes through a period of training upon the work which has gone on before him and which, at the time, constitutes the body of the science. The things he learns as the facts and problems of psychology are prejudicial, and his future work must include a critical revaluation of these tenets as well as attempts to carry the science ahead. Without any means at present of relating the two or more problems of sensory processes and their organization in space and time, psychology must include the different interests even though we realize that the separation may prove to be real and even though the interest of individuals engaged in the problems of these fields is not all-inclusive.

If we now assume such a naïve attitude toward experience, it appears that throughout life we have, except possibly during our hours of sleeping, a continuous stream of experiences. These experiences appear to organize themselves or become organized, by principles of abstraction and generalization, into what we call concepts and perceptions. In memory such previous experiences recur and in their reappearance seem to be reassembled according to some principle of association or organization which makes of them related units or wholes. Such memories or concepts are likely to be represented in a word or other symbol, the relationship between the two (concept and word) being also a matter of association. The most remarkable thing about such concepts is their paucity of psychological experience in relation to their great potentiality for associations. Our ideas of independently variable aspects of experience depend altogether upon such conceptualizing, otherwise we could not experience one blue as related to another, etc. Studies of such concepts and symbols tend to verify our naïve opinion as to the unity of experience in general but, so far, have not clarified the laws by which we learn. Studies of related phenomena, such as the conditioned reflex, also verify without clarifying the basic principles.

Perception. There has been a well-defined tendency among many psychologists to exclude from the subject-matter of the science all phenomena which are affected by or are dependent upon memory. Helmholtz, Wundt, and, to some extent, Titchener are identified with this tendency. It is very difficult to denote a class of experiences which are independent of memory. The sensation (Helmholtz' *Perzeption*) was invented for this purpose, and, while sensations, so far, seem to be comparatively harmless in a study of correlations between variable aspects of experience and their physical and physiological conditions, the acceptance of sensation as an analyzable element of experience cannot be carried into the study of the higher mental processes without serious implications. If we conceive of the higher mental processes or of perceptions as being formed by adding sensations together, a concept common to this group, we are at a loss for experimental evidence with which to bolster our view, and there is much evidence to confute it, e.g., after-image, adaptation, movement, etc.

If, in a given experience, we attempt to determine what aspects are independent of memory, we are again at a loss. Spatial and temporal aspects are obviously so affected. Intensities, if the studies of lifted weights are to be accepted as evidence, and even qualities, according to the studies upon memory color, may also be so affected. Titchener has gone to some length to demonstrate that "psychological process" is separable from any particular "meaning" (memory), but no one has shown that any experience at all comes to us entirely free from meaning. Titchener has also attempted to clear the temporal and spatial aspects of experience of the taint of obvious meaning by reducing them to "mere" duration and extensity, but it must be objected that if he has, by introducing such terms, made these aspects less than temporal and spatial he has not met the situation, and if he has only simplified the particular cases, acknowledging, as he does, that our concepts of time and space are essentially meaningful, he has only made them apparently clear of meaning by such simplification.

The theoretical implications of these considerations are far reaching. Even the merest speck upon a neutral field, of undefined extensity and undetermined duration, cannot be regarded as "simple" for, if another speck appears within certain temporal and spatial limits, the first spot will demonstrate one of its potentialities by itself *moving into the second position.*

At this point it becomes apparent that our three inherited problems of sensation, perception, and memory must be modified. We do not yet know the nature of the principles of association or how many such principles there may be, but it becomes obvious that there will be no solution of sensory problems without a solution of one or more of the others.

The term perception, when used in a sense not applicable to the foregoing discussion, is usually conceived of as a cross-section of experience in time. As such it is an analyzed unit similar, except in complexity, to the sensation, and if we attempt a synthesis of experience by adding such perceptions we must meet the same objections that are raised against the similar treatment of sensations.

The type of neural theory accepted by most psychologists as a working hypothesis involves specialized receptor-organs, none of which has as yet been adequately described. These organs, however, are presumed to initiate series of impulses over the individual fibers, which are considered to be insulated from each other, and the fibers are supposed to carry these series of impulses to the central nervous system. At this point most theories lose whatever specific character they have so far maintained. The nature of the functional activity of the cortex and central nervous system generally is so little known that only vague possibilities have, for the most part, even been outlined. Analytical theories have created a well-defined tendency to speak of such activity as though there were a one-to-one correlation between individual fibers and points within the central nervous system and as though, within this central station, there were an additive process of some nature which (almost pictorially) represents the stimulus situation. The tendency to theorize within this field, however, is not great, the more general tendency being to await the discovery of sufficient facts upon which to base a theory that may prove to be a workable hypothesis.

The amount of work that has been done upon perception and the higher mental processes does not at all reflect the importance of these subjects. The phenomenological descriptions of experience that have been made for the purpose of determining the more general principles are few, and much of the work, such as that done upon illusions, has not yet been related to the subject-matter of the rest of the science. The work upon memory and learning has been much greater in amount than the work upon perception, but here again the lack of agreement between statements of fundamental principles is very noticeable.

The greatest present need of psychology is a restatement of specific problems in terms more consistent with the known facts than the present separation into sensory processes and principles of unification, such a restatement as will give direction to experimental work and create more enthusiasm for it.

BEHAVIORISM

Behaviorism, in spite of numerous other definitions, constitutes an attempt to describe the facts and laws underlying our concept of "mental life" in terms which do not involve "mind" or "consciousness." Hence the divergence between the behaviorists and the psychologists runs to the terms of description, not to the problem itself.

Although the study of stimulus-response apparently leaves little room for the separation of subject-matter into sensation, perception, and learning, yet in their formulation of specific problems such a separation is tacitly admitted. Thus we see in the general problems of discrimination a parallel to the psychological study of sensory processes, in form discrimination a parallel to the problems of perception, and in the work on the learning process a parallel to our third problem. The essential sameness of problem is brought out again in their acceptance and enthusiastic prosecution of the work upon conditioning responses where the methods used and the results so far attained are a continuation of the pre-existing work upon association and learning. It is just because of the fundamental identity of the two schools in the matter of problems that behaviorism remains a branch of experimental psychology rather than being identified with the biological sciences.

Watson, in his textbook published in 1919 (8, pp. 38ff.), made introspection a special case of behavior, i.e., a verbal response. The enunciation of this position, which is generally accepted by behaviorists, completed the identification of the two branches by making the facts of the psychologists, if properly reworded, acceptable to the behaviorist, and his results in turn acceptable to the psychologist although they may, for the psychologist, carry inferences as to conscious processes not admitted by the behaviorist himself. For the behaviorist, then, the study of stimulus–nervous-process–experience–reaction is modified by the elimination of experience, but the problems studied are the same and results of the two types of workers are interchangeable.

Some behaviorists may go so far as to deny the existence of consciousness, even for themselves. Whether or not this is the case is unimportant because (a) it is a negative hypothesis and (b) such a position is not essential to the movement nor characteristic of it. A theoretical perfection of the behavioristic position would not so much as raise the issue. Much more often is the belief expressed, as an objection to the method of the psychologists, that a study of consciousness does not admit of objective observation.[3]

Practically the movement has had and continues to have a very great influence. The tendency of the psychologists to limit themselves to the field of sensation and the tendency of the behaviorists to enter the field

---

[3]This objection was answered for another generation by E. Mach (6). It has recently been fully met by W. Köhler and will not be presented again here (5). I am fully in accord with the views the two authors express upon this subject and am of the opinion that logically Köhler has disposed of the matter.

of learning, etc., where the existence of consciousness is, for the present, almost an academic question, has avoided much of the useless conflict which at one time seemed possible. The practical effect of the movement, however, is not our present concern. Polemics on both sides have often been more confusing than enlightening, systematically, because they come from many individuals and stress the matters that seem of importance to them rather than the essentials of systematic position. When two "schools" can use each other's data, the separation is not great. The answer to the behaviorists is, of course, "go ahead." It might be quite worth while if we should all turn behaviorist, now and then, for a time. If such a system can be worked out, it would be an accomplishment of the first order.

Up to the present time the systematic position of the behaviorists has weakened, although in influence, as judged by the numbers interested, it has rapidly gained ground. Köhler, in his work upon apes, found that the behavior of these animals could not be adequately described in terms of the S-R formula (4), Hunter, working with raccoons in the double-alternation maze, found a similar situation (3). Köhler hypothecates "insight" as an x in the formula S-(x)-R, which resembles the formula often written for the psychologists, S-(C)-R where C represents consciousness, and Köhler shows no reluctance in inferring the essential similarity of his x and the C of the other formula. Hunter posits "symbolic processes" as an x in the formula of the behaviorists, but he does not suggest the identity of his x with consciousness and resists Köhler's "insight" as an explanatory concept.

In the reaction against the work of Romanes and the dilettantes with animals, Lloyd Morgan enunciated his now well-known "law of parsimony." The law requires, in the promotion of a theory, the simplest hypothesis necessary to contain the facts. Under the influence of the reaction against dilettanteism, this law was interpreted to forbid the inference of consciousnses in animals, and, inasmuch as such an interpretation fell in with the program of the behaviorists, i.e., to describe our mental concepts without introducing consciousness, little protest was raised. Protests have been heard since and these often to the effect that it is greater economy to assume that animals are alike in kind, varying only in degree, than it is to posit one principle to govern for human adults and another to govern for all other animals. This point seems to be well taken. In regard to the more recent matter, there is no obvious reason why we should assume that Köhler's "insight" and Hunter's "symbolic processes" are not of the same nature; and the lack of economy in assuming that either is different from the one such element we know in ourselves, i.e., consciousness, becomes apparent.

GESTALTTHEORIE

In the development of *Gestalttheorie* we find no such startling difference as in behaviorism. Upon the constructive side of the theory, upon its growth, etc., there is much that might be said, but here again we are principally interested in differences in system. To clarify this issue we shall consider some of the objections which have been offered in this connection against psychology proper. For the sake of specificity we may take Köhler as representative of the group, and, if the following comments seem to constitute an adverse criticism, we must bear in mind the very limited nature of the discussion. The particular points urged by Köhler do not all, I believe, go to a difference in system but to matters of fact and the manner in which our accepted hypotheses affect the formulation of problems for the future. Specifically, among others, Köhler objects to the following matters:

1) The attempt to analyze experience into elements (sensations).

2) The specific theories of sense with which psychologists are now dealing. He offers a substitute.

3) The overemphasis given the doctrine of meaning.

4) The elimination of the problems of "organization" because of the doctrine of meaning.

5) Associationism as a "special and theoretical concept."

1) The first point has been discussed at length under a previous heading. It seems hardly to be an issue *between the two schools* because of the tendency on the part of so many psychologists to deal directly with variable aspects of experience without recourse to fictional elements. It is rather an issue between groups of psychologists where the adherents of *Gestalttheorie* are all on one side of the argument and other psychologists are divided in their opinions. The substitute offered by Köhler appears in the discussion of the next three points and, like all hypotheses, it must stand or fall on its own merits.

2) The current specific theories of the psychologists have much to be said for them, the neurological facts, as we know them, giving more support to the current theories than to *Gestalttheorie,* although there are not a sufficient number of these facts now known to force opinion to either theory. *Gestalttheorie* pictures an uninsulated system of nerve-fibers, and these, with the stimulating situation, form a single system. For the nervous system, the result of stimulation is a redistribution of electrical potentials within the system toward a new point of equilibrium. This rearrangement or the rearranging of the system (not aggregates) is the correlate of consciousness and the determiner of other responses. Current theory, on the other hand, assumes small units within the sensory receptor-organ which are, in practice, functional units as well. Such units connect with fibers which conduct separate impulses to the central nervous system. From here on such theories are very indefinite but usually involve the conception of a one-to-one correlation between the fibers and points within the central nervous system. Inadequacies of the current theories are apparent to all. Köhler cites the visual and tactual perceptions of movement against current theory, and the citation constitutes a telling blow regardless of other questions of fact that have entered into these problems, e.g., Dimmick's gray flash. Yet graphic records of the impulses traveling over nerve-fibers show independent rhythms in the series of impulses, and

there are possibilities of motor responses and other phenomena which tell against the Gestalt hypothesis. Alternatives are obvious, but the difficulties which they may bring are not fully worked out. Even with an insulated system of fibers, however, Köhler's electrical brain-field may be possible.

The acceptance of Köhler's theory as a working hypothesis is a matter of personal evaluation. The acceptance of the theory as the ultimate facts of the case is premature, and I should not accuse the most ardent supporter of *Gestalttheorie* of having gone as far as that. It is a theory in only a very general sense, much more it is a suggestion of the type of theory that is required. It may or may not be a shrewd guess but it requires something other than acquiescence; it must be verified and demonstrated to be the fact.

3) The objection to the concept of meaning follows from the above discussion and returns us to the matter of perception and the higher mental processes. Köhler does not repudiate the problem but objects to the manner in which it is treated. The distinction between meaning and process has varied in presentation with different individuals, and in order to deal concretely we may select one person whose views are typical. I choose Titchener because he is more explicit than many of the others.

For Titchener, then, in a perceptual experience we have given, experientially, a group of sensory experiences (an object). About this sensory data are grouped, so as to form a distinctive pattern, secondary sensations (eye-movements, bodily attitudes, etc.) and images (previous experience, memory). Added to or sometimes supplanting this fringe of added data are certain "mental habits" (involving symbols such as words, musical notes, etc.) which may supplant or supplement the secondary sensations or images or both. All such occurrences are distinguished from the sensory core of the experience and are designated "context." "Meaning, psychologically, is always context" (7). Meanings are often conscious but are not necessarily so; they may be "carried in purely physiological terms." Although Titchener denies at the outset that perception is an additive process in the sense that the nature of the perception depends upon the added elements entirely, yet his treatment of the subject stresses that part of it almost to the exclusion of "arrangement," and it seems always to be an additive process in that the meaning of any particular thing depends upon what accrues or is added to the sheer experience by way of context.[4]

Meaning itself is a matter of logic, not psychology, and as such is legitimately debarred from psychology although it has a representation in consciousness (or out of it) which is subject-matter for psychology. The position is difficult to clarify. There is a difference to be noted between experience actually presented and what that experience means. The ex-

_____

[4]Under his discussion of association Titchener deliberately selects the additive hypothesis. He contrasts the theories by analogy, "electric magnet" (organization?) *vs.* "string of beads," and chooses the latter.

perience itself is core and is purely sensory, but the examples he cites are not of a purely sensory nature, e.g., lines, moving branches, etc. They are already patterned complexes, perceptions. The fringe of secondary sensations and images is obviously a restatement of associationism, and the "mental habits" or their neurological counterparts, "brain habits," are given to account for the fact that our meaningful reactions are not always, or perhaps not even usually, represented in consciousness.

Titchener accepts the implications for psychology, i.e., (a) that consciousness is always a temporal affair and must receive a longitudinal as well as a transverse treatment; (b) we must, as part of our problem, find the physiological correlates for these experiences; and (c) we can never lose sight of the effect of previous experience upon the present consciousness (or reaction).

Köhler does not make clear his precise objections, but one may suppose that they go to the matter of positing sensory data *plus* context to give us our perceptual experiences and that rather we should think of our experience of the present as itself modified by such previous experiences and with possibilities of its own for the future. Facts are cited in support of such a view, e.g., visual and tactual perception of movement, but he helps us little further.

It is not easy to see just how present experience and past experience are so closely woven, and the fact that particular meanings may so easily be added to or disjoined from a given experience has inclined many to an additive hypothesis. *Gestalttheorie* offers no solution and we are left with the problem exactly as it was.

4) In treating the matter of elimination of the problems of organization because of the doctrine of meaning we cannot use Titchener as an example because in this matter he takes a position similar to that of Köhler. We may cite Helmholtz as an example of those who would reject the problem of memory in connection with a study of sensory data.

If we picture a system simple enough, where a given stimulus (object, not situation) produces a given effect upon an organism and if, psychologically, such effects consist of sensations which are added to form perceptions and as perceptions are continued in time to form experience, then we might designate the experience as psychological and the principle by which the organization occurs as something outside or beyond psychology. This is, essentially, the position of certain groups and is the position which attempts to force the problems of learning (organization) outside of psychology. To such an outline we can, at present, say only that we are unconvinced as to the existence of such a system and cite those facts now available against it. The position is unsatisfactory to many psychologists, but the differences of opinion are objected to, not as matters of system, but as matters of fact and oversimplified hypotheses. The position is not peculiar to *Gestalttheorie* as the great amount of work upon perception, learning, memory, etc., testifies.

5) *Gestalttheorie* gives up associationism "as a special and theoretical concept," but the specific complaint seems to stress the attempt to make

the laws, as at present outlined, a sufficient explanation and especially the tendency to offer spatial and temporal contiguity alone for such a purpose. Köhler suggests, with emphasis, "that neighborhood in space and time influences association only insofar as it determines organization," and he concludes that "association depends upon organization because association is just an after-effect of organized processes." This implies that association is the fact, and organization is the process or principle. While such a redefinition may be justifiable or even necessary because of the connotation that has grown around association, for many psychologists association refers to the effective process or principle of unification regardless of what that process may prove to be. Association, so regarded, may be identical with Köhler's "organization." It seems, from the treatment accorded it, that organization may be successive or simultaneous, is affected by temporal and spatial contiguity, etc. The parallel with association seems to be too close to require two names.

Let it not be supposed that in the preceding paragraphs I have attempted to dispose of any of the questions treated. In each case we find a question upon which all experimental psychologists may have, and many do have, opinions. They are not questions peculiar to *Gestalttheorie* nor answered under some general formula held by any single school. The issues raised are the live issues of psychology and, however much we may owe *Gestalttheorie* for forcing these problems to the fore, in no instance do we find the suggestion of a basis for a separate *Gestalt Psychologie*. Much or little as the Gestalt hypothesis has advanced the treatment of the subject of psychology, it has in no sense fundamentally altered it.

RÉSUMÉ

Between experimental psychologists we find a difference of opinion as to the possibility and advisability of describing our concepts of mental life without involving consciousness and we find a division of opinion upon the type of theory which, in the light of known facts, is most valuable as a working hypothesis. If we had dug deeper, we might have found many other differences but none of them of a kind which divides the field in any real sense.

Among the individuals who call themselves psychologists we might find some whose primary interest is in quite other problems, the description of function and the discovery of purpose. Some investigators with such interests use experimental methods to some extent and some, whose interests are more scientific, unfortunately obscure the nature of their work in failing to state it in clear and unequivocal terms. In actual numbers these exceptional cases are few, but psychologists have not only given the outside world to understand, but many are themselves convinced, that systematic differences divide psychologists into factions which are not able to work together. This is far from being the true state of affairs, for with few exceptions psychologists form a homogeneous group whose interests, problems, and methods are similar. There are no fundamental differences between the experimental groups. Polemics directed against systematic positions or imagined systematic differences, if not an excuse for not working, serve effectively to prevent our principal efforts from being directed to that end and comprise by far too large a part of our literature.

REFERENCES

1. BENTLEY, M. The psychologies called "structural." Part VI in Psychologies of 1925. Worcester, Mass.: Clark Univ. Press, 1926. Pp. 383-412.

2. BORING, E. G. A history of experimental psychology. New York: Century, 1929. Pp. xvi+699.

3. HUNTER, W. S. The behavior of raccoons in a double alternation temporal maze. J. Genet. Psychol., 1928, 35, 374-388.

4. KÖHLER, W. The mentality of apes. New York: Harcourt, Brace, 1925. Pp. 342.

5. ————. Gestalt psychology. New York: Liveright, 1929. Pp. x+403.

6. MACH, E. Beiträge zur Analyse der Empfindungen. 1886. (Trans. 1897.)

7. TITCHENER, E. B. A text-book of psychology. New York: Macmillan, 1921. Pp. 552.

8. WATSON, J. B. Psychology from the standpoint of a behaviorist. Philadelphia: Lippincott, 1919. Pp. 429.

PART V
CONFIGURATIONAL PSYCHOLOGIES

CHAPTER 8

SOME TASKS OF GESTALT PSYCHOLOGY

WOLFGANG KÖHLER

University of Berlin

In one of his papers Wertheimer (9) has described observations of the following type:

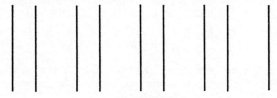

FIGURE 1

1) You look on a series of spots (Figure 1) the distances of which are alternately of a certain larger and smaller width. If I say that these spots appear spontaneously in groups of two (which "belong together") so that the smaller of the two distances is always in the interior of one group, and that beyond the larger distance a new group begins, etc., this statement of the phenomenon is perhaps not very impressive.

I therefore introduce a change, substituting straight parallel lines for the spots (Figure 2), at the same time increasing the difference of the two

FIGURE 2

distances a little. The phenomenon of group formation is now a little more striking. How "real" it is one feels when trying to form other groups in the series, namely, so that any two lines with the larger distance between them form one group and the shorter distance is the space between two consecutive groups. You see that this requires a special effort. To form *one* of the new groups may be rather easy; but to make the change for all of them, i.e., for the whole series simultaneously, is more than I, for instance, can achieve. Most people never will get this other grouping as clear, stable, and optically real as the former one; and in the first moment of relaxation or fatigue, one instantly sees again the spontaneously existing groups as before. It is as if some forces were holding the pairs of nearer lines together.

Is distance in itself the decisive factor? Two spots or two parallel lines may be regarded as rather poor boundaries, enclosing space between them. In our figures they do so better when nearer together, so that we might perhaps formulate our principle in the statement that the members of a series better enclosing space between them tend to form groups. This new principle seems to work because it covers the fact that the parallel straight lines form more striking and stable groups than the spots. Evidently they enclose space between them better than do the spots. And again, we can change our last figure by adding some short horizontal lines so that the larger space between the more distant parallels begins to be better enclosed (Figure 3). The result is that it becomes easy to see

FIGURE 3

the pairs of more distant lines with their annexes as groups, even before the open distance between those annexes is made smaller than the distances of the parallels nearer to each other. But let us be cautious. Perhaps we have two different principles, that of distance and that of "enclosing."

2) In the next figure all members of the series follow each other at equal distances, but there is a regular change in the properties of those members (Figure 4). It does not matter whether the difference is of

FIGURE 4

this type or a difference between yellow and black, for instance. Even in a case like this (Figure 5) the same phenomenon is observed, namely,

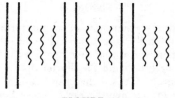

FIGURE 5

that the members of the same "quality" (whatever it may be) form groups, and that a new group begins where we have a change in the quality of members. Again, one may convince himself of the reality of this observation by trying to see the series in another grouping. Most people are not able to see the series as solidly organized throughout when trying to enforce any of the other mathematically possible formations of groups.

3) The description of our observations is not yet complete. If we look back upon the series of parallels, we see that the formation of groups is not an affair of those parallels only. The whole area *in* a group, half

enclosed between the parallels nearer to each other, white like the surrounding paper, still looks different from it and also different from the area between two consecutive groups. In a group there is a certain aspect of "solidity," or we might even say: "there *is* something"; whereas between the groups and around the whole series we have "emptiness" or "there is nothing." This difference, described and discussed very carefully by Rubin (7), who calls it the difference between the characters of "figure" and "ground," becomes the more remarkable since the whole group, including its half enclosed white area, appears to "stand out" in space from the surrounding ground. At the same time we may remark that the parallels, which, as it were, solidify the enclosed area and lift it a little from the ground, "belong to this area" in one more meaning: They are the edges of this enclosed area, but are not in the same manner edges of the indifferent ground outside the group.[1]

There is more to describe in the aspect of even such a simple field of vision. I hasten, however, to carry our observations on into a new direction.

4) The groups formed in the series of parallels included pairs of them. We add third parallels in the midst of each group and find, as one may have expected beforehand, that these three lines so close together still form groups and that the grouping is even much more striking now than before (Figure 6). We may add two more parallels in each group between the three already drawn. Not much of white is left now in the group and

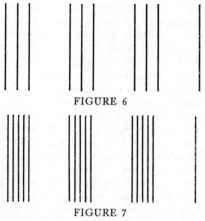

FIGURE 6

FIGURE 7

the stability of group formation is still increased (Figure 7). A few steps more, and the areas of our groups are uniform black rectangles. There would be three of them; everybody looking upon the page would see these "three dark forms." And our gradual procedure has taught us that to see the black content of each of those areas as "one thing" united in itself,

---

[1] Similar laws are found to apply to the formation of units in temporal series [Wertheimer (9), Koffka (1)].

outstanding as one from the ground, may be regarded as a very extreme case of the formation of group units which we first observed. It is not a geometrical truism—it has nothing to do with pure geometry—that continuous uniformly colored areas or spots in differently colored homogeneous surroundings appear as wholes or units; it is a primitive experience in vision. Where neighbors of equal properties are given, groups are formed as a rule. This principle was seen to work with increased effect as the density of the area of the group is increased. It cannot stop working when the group becomes a continuum. (I hardly have to mention that our uniformly colored wholes might have thousands of different forms, usual ones like the rectangle, to which we are accustomed, or quite unusual ones like some spot of ink on the paper or a little cloud in the sky.)

We began our discussion with the observation of groups because it is easier to acknowledge the problem there *as* a problem. To be sure, the unit of our black rectangles is much more stable than that of our first spots and parallels; but we are so used to the fact that uniformly colored areas surrounded by other color appear as segregated wholes that the problem here is not grasped so easily. Most of the observations of Gestalt psychology are of this kind: They touch facts of such general occurrence in our everyday life, that we have difficulty in seeing anything remarkable in them.

Again the progress of our observations obliges us to look back. We formed series of spots or straight lines and observed their grouping. Now we have learned that these members of our series themselves contain the same problem or phenomenon in so far as they already are extended and uniformly colored units. The consequence is that we find formation of units in different "orders" or "ranks," e. g., straight lines (lowest order) and groups of them (higher order). If a unit exists it may still become part of a larger unit or group of a higher rank.

5) With its "being one," the continuous unit has retained another property of the discontinuous group: It still has the "figure" character as something solid, outstanding from the empty ground. Imagine now that we substitute for the rectangle, printed in black, a black rectangular paper, covering the same area and carefully pressed against the page. Evidently nothing of importance is changed; this paper is "one" and has the same character of something solid. Imagine further that this paper begins to grow in the direction at right angles to its surface and the surface of the page. It becomes thicker and is soon a black block or "thing" in space. Again nothing functionally important is changed. But we see that the application of our observations has become much larger. Wherever "a thing" is visible as "one" and as something solid, the same principles are concerned which we first became acquainted with in the formation of groups. There are still other influences working in our appreciation of things as units and as solid, but we have no reason to think that those principles of primitive group formation we were considering (and

others I could not mention here) lose their force when we have to do with things in three dimensions instead of with spots or rectangles.[2]

Our observations have followed a line which leads away from familiar ideas. One of the fundamental methods of natural sciences is *analysis*. The psychologist, therefore, confronted with a complex field of vision, for example, feels naturally inclined to analyze this field into smaller and simpler entities whose properties he may study with more ease and with more hope of clear results than an immediate consideration of the whole field would yield. Generally he does not ask himself what this procedure purports and if, perhaps, the term analysis is rather ambiguous. He simply analyzes down to very small parts of the sensory field—let us call them the "sensations"—which do not contain differences, which show a minimum of area, and so seem to constitute the simplest parts of the field.

Somehow, it is true, our observations also meant an analysis of the field. In our analysis, however, we have followed the natural and evident structure of the field instead of dissolving it theoretically and arbitrarily into minute local things which nobody ever sees. It is not arbitrary and abstract thinking that makes those groups or spots or rectangles or things in my visual field. I find them there as optical realities not less real than their color, black, or white, or red, etc. As long as my visual field remains the same (is not changed by internal or external influences), there is little doubt about what belongs in one of those units and what does not so belong. And if we have found that in the visual field there are units of different rank, a group, for instance, containing several spots, the larger unit containing smaller ones of still stronger unitedness, exactly the same occurs in physics where the molecule, as one larger objective unit (defined by a comparative break of interconnection at its limits), contains smaller objective units, the atoms, the interior of which is again very much more strongly united than is the molecule. There is no contradiction and no vagueness in objective units containing smaller units. And as it remains an objective fact in the physical material, where the boundaries of its units and perhaps of sub-units are, so in the visual field no arbitrary analyzing thought should interfere with observation: Experience is spoiled if we begin to introduce artificial sub-divisions where real units and boundaries of one or the other rank are open and clear before us. This is the principal reason why I think that a concept like sensation is almost a danger. It tends to absorb our attention, obscuring the fact that there are observable units and sub-units in the field. Because the very moment we give up our naïveté in description and theory and think of the field in terms of unreal elements, these unreal little things appear to our thought side by side, indifferently filling space, some of one, some of another color or brightness, etc., and the observable units with their observable boundaries do not occur in this pseudo-description.

---

[2]"Things" again may become members of groups of a higher order. Instead of spots we might have a series of men and still observe the formation of groups. In architecture one knows enough about that (compare the grouping of pillars, windows, statues, etc.).

The most dangerous property of a concept like "sensation" consists in the fact that such local elements are very easily regarded as depending upon local processes in the nervous system, each of which would be determined by one local stimulus, in principle. Our observations are in complete disagreement with this "mosaic theory" of the field. How can local processes which are independent of and indifferent to each other be at the same time organized into larger units of well-observable extent in some areas? How, again, can relative break of continuity at the well-observable limits of those areas be understood, since these limits are not limits everywhere between little pieces of a mosaic, but appear only where one group or unit ends? The hypothesis of independent little parts is unable to give an explanation. All the concepts we found necessary above for the description of the field have no relation whatever to the conception of independent local elements. And more concretely: Where our groups or units are formed can certainly not be deduced by considering the conditions in one point, then independently in the next, etc. Only a consideration which takes account of how the local conditions for the whole field *relate to each other* begins to approach an understanding of those facts. Not the local white along a white line drawn on a black field makes this line a real optical unit in the field; there is no specific unit and no line before the surroundings have a *different* color or brightness. This difference of stimulation around as against equality of stimulation within the line must, in the given arrangement, be the fact which produces a specific unit. And in the same manner for units of higher order: Not the independent or absolute conditions in one of our parallels, then the conditions in the next one, make them form one group, but that these lines are *equal, different from the ground,* and so *near* to each other—three prerequisites which again show the decisive rôle of *relations* of local conditions. And let us be careful not to forget the ground. Because, if a certain group is formed, say two parallels, being half a centimeter from each other, I have only to draw two more parallels on the outside of this group and much nearer to the first parallels than these are to each other, and the first group is destroyed, two other groups being formed by the parallels

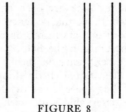

FIGURE 8

which are now nearest to each other (Figure 8). Only so long as we had uniform white in the neighborhood of our first group did this group exist. I change conditions in this neighborhood and what was the interior of a unit now becomes a gap between two others. One more consequence follows immediately: The characters of "figure" and "ground" are so absolutely dependent upon the formation of units in the field that, since these units cannot be deduced from an aggregate of independent local states, neither can the appearance of an area as "figure" or "ground" be so deduced. And still another fact as argument: We draw two parallels and produce a group; we draw another congruent pair, but considerably more distant from the first than the distance between the first lines is, and go on increasing the length of our series. The result is that *all* the groups in the series become more solid than each of them would be when given alone. Even over distances of such an extent the conditions in one place have an influence on what happens in another place, and vice versa.

The fact that it is not the local properties of given stimuli but the relations of these properties to each other (the total constellation of stimuli, to use a better word) that are decisive in the formation of units suggests at once the idea that dynamic intercourse in the field decides about what becomes a unit, what is excluded from it, what is "figure," and what falls back as mere "ground." Indeed, at the present time not many psychologists will deny that, acknowledging those real units, etc., in the visual field, we have at once to draw the adequate consequences for that part of the brain the processes of which are corresponding to our field of vision. The units, sub-units, boundaries, the difference of "figure" and "ground" must exist there as physiological realities (8, 10, 2). Remarking, now, that relative distance and relation of qualitative properties are the main factors determining the formation of units, we remember that exactly such factors ought to be decisive for it if it were the effect of dynamic intercourse in the physiological process throughout the field. Most physical and chemical interaction we know of depends upon the relation of properties and on mutual distance between the material in space. Now, differences of stimulation produce points, lines, areas, of different chemical reaction and in certain spatial relations to each other on the retina. If there is transverse connection between the longitudinal conductors of the optic nerve somewhere in the optic sector of the nervous system, mutually dynamic intercourse ought to depend upon the qualitative, spatial, and other relations of qualitative properties and space which, at a given time, exist in the total optic process, streaming up to or through the brain. No wonder, if we find that the phenomena of grouping, etc., show direct dependence upon those relations.

Intimately related to the existence of real units and boundaries in the field of vision we find the fact that there are *"forms"* in this field. It was practically impossible to exclude them from the foregoing discussion because, wherever we see those units they have forms,[3] this being the reason why in the German terminology those units are called "Gestalten." Again, the reality of forms in visual space is a fact which cannot be understood from the standpoint that the visual field consists of independent local ele-

---

[3] I do not think that the term "configuration" is quite adequate as a translation of the German word "Gestalt." The word configuration seems to mean elements put together in a certain manner, and this is a functional idea which we must carefully avoid.

ments. If there were elements of this kind forming a dense and perhaps continuous mosaic as the "stuff" of the visual field, then we should have no real forms in this field. Mathematically, of course, some aggregates of them might be considered together, but that would not correspond to the reality in which at a given time some concrete forms *are simply there* in vision, not less than colors and brightnesses. And first of all, mathematically, *all* imaginable patterns might be considered in such a field of independent elements, whereas in vision quite *individual* forms are always before us under given conditions (4). If, now, we examine these conditions upon which the real forms depend, we naturally find again the qualitative and spatial relations of stimulation. Naturally, because the now well-known *units* appear in the individual forms we are seeing, and we had to realize previously that these units are somehow a function of those relations. I remember from my own slow development in this respect how difficult it is to make a sharp distinction between an aggregate of stimuli, i.e., geometrically existent patterns of them, and visual forms as realities. On this page there are certainly some black points as parts of letters which, considered together, would be a large group of this real

FIGURE 9

form (Figure 9). Do we therefore *see* such a form as a visual reality? Certainly not so long as so many other black spots are given between and around them. But let those points be *red* and all people who are not color-blind or half blind for forms by brain lesion would instantly see this group as a form.

All this is not only true for forms in a plane or on the paper; it is as much the truth for the things or objects in our surroundings. And so I wish to warn against the misunderstanding that these problems of real units and their forms might perhaps have some importance for aesthetics or for other considerations of a supposedly higher level only, whereas they were foreign to the practical stuff of everyday life. There is no object, no man you have to deal with, whose visual reality is not a concrete demonstration of the same scientific situation.

We draw a physiological consequence: If there is dynamic intercourse between the local processes in a system, they will influence and change each other until equilibrium is reached in a stationary distribution. We were treating visual fields in the state of rest. They must be the psychological picture of a stationary equilibrium distribution in the corresponding processes of the brain. There are enough cases in physics where a process originating in a system under a certain set of conditions develops its stationary distribution in extremely short time. The time in which the equilibrium of a visual process is developed must also be rather short. Because, if we give a set of stimuli suddenly, say by projection, the phase of "something happening," which we observe, has an extremely rapid appearance, and in a moment we see the field, its units and their forms at rest.

In a state of stationary equilibrium, the field is by no means "dead." The mutual stresses in the phase of field formation (which, of course, are themselves interdependent) do not disappear when the stationary distribution is accomplished. They have now (together with the processes) only those intensities and directions everywhere in which they balance each other. The total process in stationary distribution is still a *store of energy*, distributed in the field.

Physiological theory has to solve two different problems with regard to the described properties of the field of vision. These properties, as they really are, involving dependence of the local state on *relative* properties of stimulation in a wider range, including, further, the formation of units, their forms, etc., have appeared almost marvelous, so that they often were considered as the outcome of supernatural mental forces. The first task, then, must be to show that, in the general functional aspect, properties of this kind are far from unusual in physics. So the more general difficulty is removed, by demonstrating a corresponding type of processes in exact science, particularly if we can show that, under the circumstances given in the optic sector of the nervous system, processes of this general type are very likely to occur. When this is done, the second task will consist in finding that *individual* kind of physical (or, if one prefers, physiological) process which may be assumed to be the physiological reality underlying a field of vision. This second task is by far the more difficult, given our lack of physiological knowledge. We have hardly begun to seek our way towards a solution of it, but at least one remark may be allowed even now. In consequence of unequal stimulation in different areas of the retina, different areas of a cross section of the optic sector contain unequal chemical reactions and so contain unequal chemical material in crystalloid and colloid form. If these unequal areas are in functional contact, they certainly are not in equilibrium. There is "energy able to work" in the system wherever areas of unequal properties have common borders. Here in the contours must be the main source of energy for dynamical intercourse. It would be so in physics or physical chemistry under corresponding circumstances (2, pp. 1 ff., 185, 195 ff.).

Our assumption gives a physiological correlate for form as a visual reality. From the standpoint of independent elementary processes such a correlate could not be found. Their indifferent mosaic would contain no real forms or, if you prefer, all imaginable but not real forms in each case, namely, for a mind who would pick them out of the mosaic. Evidently only a kind of process which cannot be split up into independent local elements would be acceptable as a correlate of real form. Now, the stationary equilibrium of the process which we assume to underlie the field of vision is a distribution of stress and process in space[4] which only

---

[4]The concept of space requires a special consideration here since in the brain it cannot simply be measured in cm., cm.^{2}, and cm.^{3} (2, pp. 232 ff.).

maintains itself as this whole. Therefore we make it our working hypothesis that in all cases this distribution is the physiological correlate of the space properties of vision and especially of form. Since our conception of a physiological unit is necessarily relative in so far as any sharp decrease in the intimacy of dynamic intercourse at the boundaries of an area shows its interior to be a real unit, we can without contradiction treat the whole visual process as one for a given time, and still assert the formation of specific (*more* intimately connected) units with their forms in it, depending on the spatial constellation of stimuli.

It will help us to understand the intrinsic tendencies of Gestalt psychology if we discuss a few of the tasks which it will have to solve in the future. For example, we have evidence for believing that the coordination of certain simple motor reactions to a visual field depends directly on our principles. If, in the stereoscope, one vertical line is exposed to one eye and a second to the other eye so that with a given degree of convergence of the two eyes the lines appear nearly parallel and at a rather short distance from each other, we find them uniting into one line almost at once. It is well known that in this case our eyes turn without our intention into that degree of convergence which brings the two lines upon two corresponding verticals of the two retinas, the two physiological *processes* becoming more intimately united under these circumstances than with the previous degree of convergence. But we have already seen that parallel lines near to each other (seen in a monocular field of vision, or both of them with both eyes) form a group. It looks as if, under the conditions given in our stereoscopic observation, the forces which keep two lines together in a group were accomplishing the same thing more thoroughly by really uniting the parallels. An examination of the situation from the standpoint of physics seems to show that such a thing might really occur. We saw that in the equilibrium distribution of process the field is still full of stresses which are for the moment in balance, but represent a store of energy. So, in vision, there seems to be stress tending to bring the two parallels together. In physics, if such a field is functionally connected with movable parts, among whose movements some definite form of motion would release the still existing stresses of the field, this movement will immediately occur, produced by the energy of those stresses. These only *"waited,"* as it were, for an opportunity to let their energy work, for instance, influencing movable parts in the direction of a better equilibrium. The better equilibrium in physics lies always in the direction of those stresses which tend to produce some change, but which in our physiological case *cannot do it directly in the field* because the distance is too great. If possible, then, they will do it by an innervation of the muscles of the eyes as movable parts in the direction of release of their energy. There is nothing supernatural in such an orderly physical process, no process with or without detour can ever produce changes which are not directed toward a more stable equilibrium of the whole system. We have only to adopt this view in the case of the optical part of the brain and its nervous connection with the muscles of the eyeballs in order to find a new explanation of fixation movements which is founded on principles of Gestalt theory and physics (3). Of course the hypothesis needs a careful working out for the concrete conditions given in the nervous system and in the muscles of the eyes.

Without any muscular reactions, two lines which are given separately on the two retinas will fuse in the common field, if their distance in this field is small enough. This may be an effect of the same forces which, according to our hypothesis, produce the fusion movement as well as the grouping of such lines. In another paper I have tried to show how the principle underlying these applications may also explain the phenomenon of stroboscopic or "apparent" movement of two similar figures which are given near to each other in appropriate succession.

So much for the visual field and the processes depending most directly upon it. At present another extension of Gestalt psychology is developing in the field of *memory*. It has been shown that the existence of a geometrical pattern of stimuli on the retina does not at all determine whether I see certain forms or not, because, if we change the surrounding pattern or even our attitude only, the outcome may consist of quite different units and forms. Therefore *"recognizing,"* which in the majority of cases is not a recognizing of color or brightness but rather of the form of a unit, of an object, for instance, will one time occur, another time not, depending upon the principles we were discussing, i.e., upon the reality of units and forms. Rubin has shown this in very impressive experiments.

The same thing occurs with *"meaning"* and with *"reproduction."* Certain stimuli and groups of stimuli will not produce anything at all before the right unit or form, which acquired in previous experience a meaning or a reproductive force, becomes a physiological and psychological reality. Our conclusion will be that the traces of earlier experiences underlying recognition and reproduction are organized in a manner which is quite similar to the organization of those earlier experiences themselves. Otherwise it would be difficult to understand why actual processes must be organized correspondingly, if recognition and reproduction are to be started by them.

We cannot stop at this point, however. In a recent book (6) I have given some reasons for assuming, as all Gestalt psychologists do, that the concepts of association and reproduction themselves have to be reinterpreted from the same point of view. Indeed, even Thorndike, whose attitude regarding association is more conservative, seems to transform the concept in such a manner that a certain "belonging together" is an absolute prerequisite, if an association is to be formed between two parts of our experience.

The application which our principles may find in the case of reproduction is much less known. A few words will suffice, however, to elucidate this point. The problem is this: Whatever the nature of an existing association (AB) may be, there will not be a corresponding reproduction, before a process A', sufficiently similar to A, has found its way to the trace of A. But why should A' come in functional contact with the trace of A rather than with the traces of hundreds of other processes? If A' were

necessarily conducted by the same neurons which have been the ways of
A before, the explanation would be simple enough. We know, however,
that this is by no means a necessary condition and that A' will reproduce
B via A even if it enters the nervous system on different nerve paths.
Therefore a "machine theory" of reproduction becomes impossible and
reproduction must occur on a more dynamic basis which would tend to
bring A' in functional relation with a trace sufficiently *similar* to A' rather
than with other traces. But how may this selection of a corresponding
trace be effected? I do not pretend to know a full explanation. But
sometimes it may help in a science if we can at least unite one problem
with another. This seems to be possible here. Suppose that, in a visual
field, we have one figure in one place and a very similar figure in a second
place. If the space between and around the two figures is homogeneous
or filled by figures of a very different type, the pair of similar figures will
probably be seen as one group. This is nothing more than one of the
simplest observations about organization in the visual field. Furthermore,
in this case we are all confident that some more knowledge of the nervous
system will make it quite clear why similarity, as against surrounding
regions of other properties, makes two processes cooperate in one *Ges-
amtgestalt,* even though their distance be considerable. If this is not too
difficult a problem, the selection of the right trace, which may be called
the starting event in reproduction, will not remain an unsolved paradox
either. Because both problems seem to be but one in principle. The
only satisfactory idea about traces in the nervous system is the assumption that processes leave behind sediments the structural properties of which
are more or less similar to those of the processes which they represent.
In the course of time these minute strata of earlier experience will be accumulated one upon the other; but some, and even a great many of them,
will survive the disturbances exerted upon them by all the following sed-
imentation and other influences. Our hypothesis, then, is simply that the
relation between a well-balanced trace A and an actual process A', similar
to it, may be comparable with the relation between two similar processes in
the actual field of vision. The same reasons which bring about the functional coöperation between these processes, excluding others of a different
character, would also tend to produce functional coherence between an actual process and a trace which is similar to it. This would be the
basis of recognition and, under favorable conditions, the beginning of
reproduction. If, thus, the selective properties of recognition and reproduction represent the same problem as is contained in the selective properties which we find in the formation of groups, a definite consequence
becomes obvious at once. The rules of grouping in perception will necessarily be rules of recognition and reproduction, too. For instance,
precisely as the properties of the field between and around two similar
figures are essential for their forming a group, so the properties of the
traces which have been deposited after the trace A of a definite structure, and before the time of an actual process A', similar to this trace, will
be decisive for the functional coherence of A and A', i.e., for recognition and
reproduction. We have begun to examine this hypothesis experimentally.

About one other extension of Gestalt psychology only some brief remarks are possible here. We dealt with forms or groups of very different degrees of solidity. There are cases in which all attempts to destroy, in actual analysis, a given form in favor of a certain other form
are in vain. But distribute the furniture of a room in an irregular
manner through this room: you will have rather solid and stable units,
the single objects, but no equally stable and firm *groups* will be formed
spontaneously with those objects as members. You observe that one group
formation is easily displaced by another, depending on slight changes of
conditions, probably in yourself. It is evident that, under such circumstances, the influence of changes in the subjective attitude towards the
field will be much higher than in the case of the solid units or stable
groups. Even forces of no peculiar intensity will now be strong enough
to produce new groups in a field which—with the exception of the objects in it—does not resist very much because its interior tendencies of
group formation are too weak.

This consideration will now be applied to the problem of learning. We
remember one of the usual forms of experimentation with animals. The
subject is confronted with two or more objects and learns to choose one
of them, depending upon its position in space, or its color, or some other
discriminating quality. This effect is produced by rewarding the animal
each time it chooses the right object and perhaps punishing it whenever it
chooses the wrong one. Learning of this kind is usually a slow process
without any indication of higher processes being involved. The curve of
learning which shows how the number of wrong choices decreases with
time has an irregular but gradually descending form. One might expect
an ape to solve simple tasks of this type in shorter time. But that is
not always the case. Often the period of learning in anthropoids is at
least as long as with lower animals. However, the *form* of learning is
sometimes quite different from what is found in the case of lower vertebrates.

When Yerkes (11) made experiments of the general type described[5] with
an orang-utan, this ape did not make any real progress at all for a long
time. But finally, when the experimenter had almost lost hope of making the orang solve his task, the ape after one right choice suddenly
mastered the problem completely, i.e., never again made a mistake. He
had solved the problem in one lucky moment, his curve of learning showing an altogether abrupt descent. Some of my experiences on the learning process in chimpanzees are very similar to this observation of Yerkes.
Sometimes the same surprising fact is found in children, and one can
hardly avoid the impression that this ape behaves like a man under
similar circumstances who, after a while, in a certain individual experiment, would grasp the principle of the problem and say to himself,
"Oh, that's the point! Always the dark object!"; of course with the consequence that he, too, would never make a mistake again.

---

[5]It does not matter for our present discussion that the experiments were dealing
with "multiple choice" instead of the simpler sensory discrimination.

We do not well describe experiments of this type by saying, as we usually do, that an animal in such a situation learns to connect certain stimuli with certain reactions and that this connection is "stamped in." This formulation of the process gives too much importance to the memory or association side of the problem, and it neglects another side of it which may be even more important and more difficult.

Although so much has been said against "anthropomorphism" in animal psychology, we have here a persisting case of this error, committed not by dilettants but by very eminent men of science. The experimenter is interested in a problem of sensory discrimination and builds an appropriate apparatus which shall present "the stimuli" to the animal in question. When he looks upon the situation which he has created himself, this situation is completely organized for him, "the stimuli" being the outstanding features of it, and all the rest forming an unimportant background. Consequently he formulates the animal's task as one of connecting "these stimuli" with certain reactions, reward and punishment enforcing this connection. But he is not aware of the fact that now he has credited the animal with the same organized situation which exists for himself, the experimenter, in consequence of his scientific aim and problem. Certainly the experimenter sees the stimuli as dominating the situation whenever he looks upon it. But why should the same organization exist in the sensory situation of the innocent animal? As we have remarked, objective situations may appear in very different organizations. Under the influence of interests, of previous experiences, etc., an original organization tends to change into new ones. It is altogether improbable, however, that an animal when confronted with a new situation of discrimination experiments, should at the outset have the same organization of the field which exists in the experimenter's thought and perception.

Perhaps in this respect the animal's perception of the field is much more different from that of the experimenter than a young student's first perception of brain tissue in the microscope is different from that of the trained neurologist. This student cannot react immediately, and in a definite way, to the differences in the structure of tissues which dominate in the professor's microscopic field, because the student does not yet *see* the field in this organization. Even so, the student at least knows that in this situation his actual experiences of temperature, touch, muscular sense, noises, smells, and the optical world outside of the microscopic field shall be without any importance. Nothing of this eliminating knowledge is given to the animal, who is put in an apparatus and there shall learn "to connect the stimuli with the reactions," but who really is subjected to a world of sensory data in the surroundings and in himself. Whatever the first organization of these data may be, it cannot possibly correspond to the very special organization which the experimenter sees. Therefore the question arises as one of the greatest importance: What rôle does the actual manner in which the situation appears to the animal play in his reactions and in the learning process? And further, is learning going on independently of this factor and of possible changes in the organization of the field? Or is reorganization, which would make "the stimuli" outstanding features in the field, perhaps an important part of the problem? In this case, does the animal need so many trials as it really receives for the building up of a connection of stimuli and reaction, or does he need those trials for the right organization of the field, so that eventually there *is* the right thing to undergo the right connection? Finally, does the stress of reward and punishment exert any influence in the direction of such a reorganization? If not, how else is the reorganization produced?

As yet we cannot answer these questions, so far as the lower vertebrates are concerned. But the observations of Yerkes and my own make it rather probable that in anthropoid apes at least the same thing may occur under favorable conditions that is so common in man: After some experience in a new situation he has to deal with, a sudden change into an organization appropriate to the task, with the accents on the right places. We may even suspect that afterwards not very much time is needed for a connection between the now outstanding stimuli and the reaction, if ever there was a real separation of the two tasks. Animals often learn so surprisingly fast under the natural conditions of their life, when an object *they are already attending to* shows "good" or "bad" properties.

If there is anything in these remarks, we may be compelled to make a revision of our theories of learning. The concept of a reorganization occurring under the stress of the total situation would become altogether essential for learning in animals and in man.

More than one psychologist would say that an animal who (like Yerkes' orang) suddenly "grasps" the principle of a situation in learning experiments thereby shows a genuine type of intelligent behavior. If this is true, another form of experiment may well be more appropriate to the facts in question.

An example frequently to be observed in the classroom will show what I mean.

I try to explain to my students a somewhat difficult demonstration of a mathematical theory, putting all my sentences together with the utmost care in the right sequence and with all possible clearness. I shall probably not have much success in my first performance. Something remains dull in the faces of my audience. So I repeat what I have said, and perhaps in the course of the third repetition one face here, another there, will suddenly undergo a marked change toward "brightness." Soon afterwards I may call the owner of one of those changed faces to the blackboard, and he will be able to give the demonstration himself—we might say, to imitate what I performed before. Something has happened between the sentences of the demonstration in this clever student's mind, something important enough to become immediately visible in the change of his outer aspect and to make a new performance possible.

If we try to apply this experience to experimentation with apes, for instance, we cannot, of course, make use of speech, in giving the model, and instead of mathematics, too, we have to choose another kind of problem. What is the effect on an ape if he sees another ape or a human being perform a certain action which, if imitated by the ape, would be of the greatest advantage for him?

Imitation of new performances is by no means an easy task for an ape. Certain conditions must be fulfilled before imitation becomes possible. One of the chimpanzees whom I have observed in Teneriffe was almost stupid, at least when compared with other apes. He had been present a great many times when other chimpanzees had used the box as a tool for reaching objects in high places. So, eventually, I expected this animal to be able to do the same thing when left alone in such a situation, i.e., with a banana somewhere on the ceiling, a box some yards away on the ground. The ape went to the box; but instead of moving it in the direction of the food, he either climbed up on the box and jumped from there vertically in the air, though the food was elsewhere, or he tried to jump from the ground and to reach the banana. The others showed him the simple performance a number of times, but he could not imitate them and copied only parts of their behavior which, without the right connection in the whole act, did not help him at all. He climbed up on the box, ran from there under the banana, and jumped again from the ground. Decidedly the right connection of box and food in this situation was not yet apparent to our chimpanzee. Sometimes he moved the box a little from its place, but as often as not away from the food. Only after many more demonstrations of the simple act did he finally learn to do it in a manner which I cannot describe briefly. One sees there is a serious task in learning by imitation even for a less intelligent *ape*. An *intelligent* chimpanzee, observing another in this little performance, will, for instance, soon become aware that moving the box means, from the first moment, moving it to a place underneath the food, the movement will be grasped as one with this essential orientation, whereas a stupid animal sees first the movement of the box, not relating it instantly to the place of the food. He will observe single phases of the whole performance, but he will not perceive them as parts related to the essential structure of the situation, in which alone they are parts of the solution. Of course, this correct organization is not simply given in the sequence of retinal images which the action of the imitatee produces. It is with imitation as with teaching. When teaching children we can give only some favorable conditions or "marks" for the new things which the child has "to learn," and the child has always to furnish something from his side which we may call "understanding" and which sometimes seems to arise suddenly, corresponding to the marks given by us. Nobody can simply pour it into the child.

If apes in some cases are able to "see" the necessary connection between the parts of a performance which they observe and the essentials of the situation, the question naturally arises whether or not the same apes sometimes *invent* similar performances as solutions in a new situation. An ape who sees a box obliquely underneath some fruits hanging down from the ceiling will soon try to reach these fruits from the top of the box. Since the box is not quite correctly situated and, therefore, the ape perhaps cannot reach the food immediately, does he "understand the situation" and move the box a little until it is more or less exactly below the food? I have described elsewhere how chimpanzees really solve simple problems of this type without the help of teaching or the model performance of another. Since this description is translated into the English language, there is no need of repeating it (5).

But let me mention one side of the ape's behavior because of its importance in many of these experiments. An ape who has often used a stick as an instrument when he found his food on the ground beyond the bars of his cage finds it there again beyond the reach of his arms. But no stick is in his room, only a little tree is there, a stem dividing into two or three branches. For a long time the ape does not find a solution. He knows about sticks and their use, and now there is a tree. But he does not see parts of the tree as possible sticks. Later on, he suddenly finds the solution, goes to the tree, breaks off one of the branches, and uses it as a stick. But it appears to me important that for quite a while the tree does not seem to have any connection with the problem. Human beings, accustomed to analyzing and reorganizing the structure of their surroundings with relation to a problem, would see the branches as possible sticks from the first moment. In order to understand the ape's behavior from the human standpoint, we must take a somewhat more difficult structure than the simple tree with its branches. Let us suppose that for some reason or other you want a wooden frame of the following

form: ⅄ In your room there is not such a thing. Some other wooden

frames, namely,

do not look in the first moment as if they would be of any use in your situation, even if you apply the saw, which may be the only instrument available. To be sure, after I made the preceding remarks about the ape, you begin to analyze these forms because you must suspect now that there I have "hidden" the frame you want. And so you find it very soon in the

R . But wouldn't you give up, perhaps, in the case that such a sus-

picion were not aroused beforehand, those forms looking like casual parts of your surroundings? For the mental level of the chimpanzee, the tree seems to be, with regard to the stick (the branch), what the group of

forms and especially the R is for us with regard to that frame: The

part which we might use is not a visual reality *as a part* in the whole which is given originally. It may become such a reality by a transformation. Reorganization of the surroundings under the stress of a given situation would then again be an essential side of the task and at the same time its main difficulty.

REFERENCES

1. KOFFA, K. Perception: an introduction to the *Gestalt-Theorie*. *Psychol. Bull.*, 1922, **19**, 531-585.

2. KÖHLER, W. Die physischen Gestalten in Ruhe und im stationären Zustand. Erfurt: W. Benary, 1912.

3. ————. Gestaltprobleme und Anfänge einer Gestalttheorie. *Jahrb. d. ges. Physiol.*, 1922.

4. ————. Komplextheorie und Gestalttheorie. *Psychol. Forsch.*, 1925, **6**, 358-416.

5. ————. The mentality of apes. (Trans. by E. Winter.) London: Kegan, Paul, 1924. New York: Harcourt, Brace, 1925. Pp. viii+342.

6. ————. Gestalt psychology. New York: Liveright, 1929. Pp. x+402.

7. RUBIN, E. Visuellwahrgenommene Figuren. Copenhagen, Christiana, Berlin, London: Gyldendal, 1921. Pp. xii+244.

8. WERTHEIMER, M. Experimentelle Studien über das Sehen von Bewegung. *Zsch. f. Psychol.*, 1912, **61**, 161-265.

9. ————. Untersuchungen zur Lehre von der Gestalt. *Psychol. Forsch.*, 1923, **4**, 301-350.

10. ————. Drei Abhandlungen zur Gestalttheorie. Erfurt: W. Benary, 1925. Pp. 184.

11. YERKES, R. M. The mental life of monkeys and apes. A study of ideational behavior. *Behav. Monog.*, 1916, **3**. Pp. iv+145.

CHAPTER 9

SOME PROBLEMS OF SPACE PERCEPTION

K. KOFFKA

Smith College

The following pages intend to give an application of a method of thought and research to a group of problems which once held the interest of a number of the leading psychologists and sense physiologists, but which of late have receded somewhat into the background of scientific attention. Experimental investigations of space perception in general and of the perception of depth in particular have been carried out by some of the ablest men in our field with great ingenuity and technical skill; they have served as touchstones for general theories, expressing fundamental convictions about the nature of our perceptive processes. And a stupendous amount of facts very little known to the younger generation of psychologists has thus been brought to light. The reason for this change of attitude seems fairly clear. Although most of the space investigations were carried out in order to decide theoretical issues, it soon became apparent that no theory so far advanced had been able to account for all of them. The number of theories grew steadily, but the scientific situation became more and more involved instead of being clarified. And so experimentalists turned to fields that promised a quicker and richer harvest. Much as this relative neglect of our subject is to be deplored, it is the manifestation of a fundamental and scientific tendency; mere collection of facts will not establish a science. As soon as the facts lose their theoretical setting they lose their scientific interest.

The development which the psychology of perception has undergone in Gestalt psychology makes it possible and compulsory to return to these old problems. How do they present themselves from the point of view which has been so fruitful in other fields of perception? This is the question to which this article wants to give an answer in part. The reader must not turn to the following pages as though they pretended to reveal ultimate truths. They are intended as tentative approaches, hypotheses which demand verification, attempts at proving these hypotheses by experimental facts. To understand Gestalt psychology one must understand its procedure, *how* its hypotheses are made, how they are translated into experiments which decide for or against them. If the reader will compare the views presented here with the traditional teachings of the subject, he will be forced to admit the difference between them whether he is willing to accept the new hypotheses or not. In either case, I hope, he will feel that our subject is in need of extensive and intensive experimental work and that it is worth while for the psychologist to devote his energies to such investigations.

I

"It is, I think, agreed by all that Distance, of itself and immediately, cannot be seen. For, distance being a line directed endwise to the eye, it projects only one point in the fund of the eye, which point remains invariably the same, whether the distance be longer or shorter."

This well-known quotation from Berkeley's *Theory of Vision* (5, p. 127) will serve to introduce my topic. The view tersely expressed in his few lines has influenced physiological and psychological optics up to our time. When I studied psychology, not a few of the leading psychologists, like Ebbinghaus and Cornelius, although accepting an innate sensory basis of bidimensional space, were in full harmony with Berkeley in that they rejected *vision* of depth in the proper meaning of the term. Today this view no longer seems to find any explicit expression, but less, I believe, because psychologists have been fully convinced of its falsity than because of the fact that the whole problem has lost in general interest. And even today we find the distinction between original, direct, physiological, and acquired, indirect, psychological factors of the perception of depth very much in the same sense in which it occurs in Berkeley's classical treatise. Thus in the revised edition which has just appeared of one of the most popular American textbooks, the author enumerates the various "signs of distance" which "are utilized together in the visual perception of three-dimensional space" and deems it "quite possible that some sign of distance, probably the binocular sign, does not have to be learned" (40, p. 400).

To Gestalt theory the problem of space perception in all its aspects is of fundamental importance. The reader who is familiar with Köhler's *Gestalt Psychology* (24) knows the rôle which is played in his system by the *total field* and its spatial characteristics. Our organized behavior takes place within an organized spatial field. Consequently to understand the organization of this field is a main task of the Gestalt psychologist. Parenthetically, in our opinion it should be a chief task for every psychologist. My choice of the word "task" is intentional. For I do not concur in the belief, which has been expressed quite recently, that the problem of visual perception of depth or, for that matter, any of the problems of spatial organization, has been carried to a satisfactory solution. Some aspects of this large problem are discussed in Köhler's contribution to the preceding volume in this series (23). I shall take up a few others which are centered around the problem of tridimensionality.

Let us then return to Berkeley. Distance cannot be seen because two points on the same line are projected on the same retinal point. This argument rests on two implicit assumptions: (*a*) The property of the receptor organ, in this case its bidimensionality, determines the properties of the result of stimulation of this organ. Because the retina is a surface, therefore visual perception should be a surface also. (*b*) We can study the properties of our visual field by studying individual points in it. Both assumptions have guided psychological theory for a long time, the second having exerted even greater influence than the first. But both

K. KOFFKA   163

assumptions are far from self-evident. The first takes no account of the
fact that the retina is only a "boundary surface" of the brain, which is a
tridimensional structure. Consequently, a priori it seems quite possible
that the processes which are aroused by stimulation of the retina may result in processes which do affect the brain in all three dimensions. The
second assumption has lost ground so rapidly during the last decade that
it is not necessary to point out its weakness. Furthermore, Köhler's contribution just mentioned shows irrefutably how inapplicable it is to the
theory of the visual field. Thus Berkeley's argument loses its stringency.
And we should try to see whether we cannot build a theory that is more
consistent with appearances, for the naïve person surely is convinced that he
sees depth no less than length and breadth. Such a theory would have to
explain why we see depth and which are the factors that produce tridimensional rather than bidimensional organizations of our visual experiences; it will rest on the psycho-physical axioms as formulated by Köhler
(24, pp. 61-67). The one especially applicable to our problems reads:
"All experienced order in space is a true representation of a corresponding
order in the underlying dynamical context of physiological processes." Consequently, when in the future we speak about the spatial field and its organization, we shall mean at the same time the visual experiences and the
underlying somatic processes.

I shall begin by discussing an example that figures in most textbooks
without receiving a very elaborate treatment, namely, the Necker cube
(see Figure 1). This drawing appears to everyone as a cube, i.e., as a

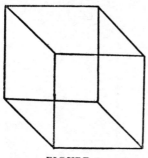

FIGURE 1

tridimensional shape notwithstanding the fact that in reality it possesses
only two dimensions. Surely this would be considered a paradoxical fact
in need of thorough elucidation, were it not that most psychologists have
this explanation ready: because of experience we perceive this drawing not
as what it really is but as something which we have seen frequently before and which as a stimulus had something in common with the present
stimulus (40, p. 414). Now such an explanation is still ambiguous inasmuch as it allows two different interpretations.

1) The cube as a tridimensional shape is acknowledged as a fact of

sensory experience, and therefore also of physiological process. The theory
maintains merely that this particular stimulus, our drawing, could not give
rise to this perception unless the observer had previously seen real cubes,
with the implicit assumption that a real cube as a stimulus would be able
to produce a cube experience.

2) We do not really *see* a cube in Figure 1 but only lines in a certain distribution. But these lines have, through previous experience, acquired the "meaning" cube. Although, according to my judgment, the
second interpretation is the more widely accepted, I shall neglect it in my
further argument since Köhler has devoted a long section of his book to the
discussion of the "meaning theory."

The first interpretation has the great advantage over the second that it
is specific and concrete. It is a statement which it will be very difficult to
disprove, but, I am afraid, still more difficult to prove. Indeed the influence of experience, whether in the form of the first or the second interpretation, although almost universally accepted, has never been put to the
test except in the experiments by Gottschaldt (11, 12), which gave extremely negative results.

Consequently we must consider the traditional explanation of the Necker
cube figure as but one of many possible hypotheses, and we can feel free
to advance another, that will be more amenable to experimental proof.
This more radical hypothesis explains the tridimensional shape of our
figure as the result of spontaneous organization in the visual field. Our
arguments in support of this hypothesis will be indirect. We shall investigate conditions under which bidimensional and tridimensional organizations
are more natural, i.e., when either of them occurs more easily and spontaneously.

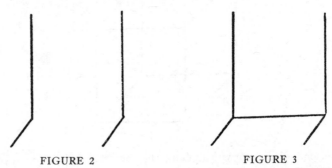

FIGURE 2   FIGURE 3

Figure 2 will appear at first sight as two broken lines in the plane of
the page, i.e., as two bidimensional shapes. In Figure 3 we have added
only one line, but now the experienced shape is tridimensional: the two
oblique lines will lead out of the plane of the page, either backwards or
forwards. Finally, Figure 4 which has been produced from Figure 1 by
the addition of two lines will again appear as bidimensional.

None of these appearances is absolutely compulsory, but doubtless they

are the spontaneous ones.   Furthermore, it is fairly easy to see Figure 2
in three dimensions, but more difficult to see Figure 4 so.   About the same
difficulty exists in seeing Figure 1 as a plane shape, and it seems most difficult of all for me to see Figure 3 as bidimensional.   What can be the cause
of these facts?

Let us begin with Figure 4.   It consists of three main parts: the pattern
of Figure 5 as the center and two isosceles triangles on either side.[1]   These

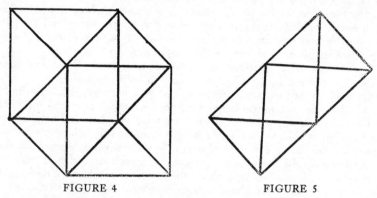

FIGURE 4   FIGURE 5

three parts are easily joined together in a plane, as a matter of fact they
yield a fairly simple and aesthetically not unpleasant form.   In Figure 1,
as long as we see it as a cube, the lines are very differently grouped.   We
see the two square planes, the front and the back ones.   Alone (Figure 6)
they yield a simple plane figure.   But there is a remainder which by itself
also produces a plane shape (Figure 7).   I do not know whether the

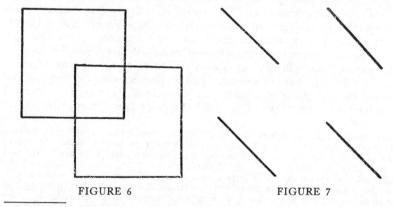

FIGURE 6   FIGURE 7

[1] Almost twenty years ago Benussi (3) pointed out that in a pattern like
Figure 1, particularly when it stands on one of its corners, a similar shape may
be seen, with the result that this figure will appear bidimensional; his whole
method of treatment is, up to a point, similar to the one carried out in this

reader will find it possible to *see* simultaneously the two plane patterns of Figures 6 and 7 when he looks at Figure 1. I certainly have not succeeded in doing so in spite of many efforts, and, if some readers are more successful, they will surely find this mode of perceiving Figure 1 very difficult, because there is nothing in the pattern that tends to break it up into these two parts; these parts are not, to use Wertheimer's terms, good parts of the total patterns. But, if they are to be united into a total pattern, this can be done only if the two squares of Figure 6 appear in different planes and the four lines of Figure 7 connect these planes with each other. This organization produces a particularly strong cohesion among all its parts since now perfect symmetry is achieved: we see six square planes and eight edges between them, each one of them equivalent to every other.

Thus far we have remained on the descriptive level. But this description suggests of itself an explanation: since in both cases, Figures 4 and 1, the actually favored pattern is characterized by symmetry, although the one is a bi- the other a tridimensional form, are we not tempted to infer that the kind of symmetry achieved is the reason for the plane and solid experience? That would mean: when simple symmetry is achievable in two dimensions, we shall see a plane figure; if it requires three dimensions, then we shall see a solid. But always the organization of the field resulting from retinal stimulation will show the greatest possible symmetry. In other words, we have explained the appearances of the Necker cube not by experience but on the ground of principles of organization.

I need not repeat my argument for Figures 2 and 3. The reader will be able to supply it himself, and he will also be able to draw a number of other figures which exemplify the same facts.

Perhaps the reader will admit that the explanation proposed in the preceding paragraph is possible. But far from being inclined to consider it also as the most probable, he will want to know why it is any better than his old empiristic explanation. This I shall start out to demonstrate by discussing some more details of our figures from the point of view of the experience and the organization hypotheses. If the reader admits that Figure 1 appears spontaneously as three-dimensional and Figure 4 as two-dimensional, he would have to explain this by pointing out that Figure 1 as a stimulus has more in common with a stimulus which in the past has aroused the experience of a cube than the second. Can such a statement be validated?[2] First, we might raise the point that the readers are not

---

text. But whereas we attempt to show that such forms have a direct organizing effect upon the total form, Benussi considers them as starting-points of *reproductions*. He is thus representative of the first empiristic hypothesis discussed above. And the same is true of Witasek (39, p. 380), who has enforced the bidimensional appearance of Figure 1 by coloring different parts of it differently. He also believed that this modification affected the reproductive properties of the drawing. Since these two men were more interested in perception of form and knew more about it than any other contemporary psychologists, this historical retrospect shows how much more powerful a tool for theoretical treatment the Gestalt concept has become since then.

[2] In very careful and extensive experiments Gottschaldt has proved the falsity of this general statement (11).

likely to have been exposed frequently to a real cube that projected an image like that of our Figure 1 on their retinas. For only a wire or glass cube would fulfil this condition, and as far as I am aware they do not abound in our environment. But I shall lay no stress on this point. Let us then compare our two drawings, Figures 1 and 4. All the lines of 1 are present in 4; two more lines are present in 4 than in 1. Therefore the addition of these two lines must make our stimulus less similar to a past stimulus that has aroused the cube experience. But why have these two lines this effect? If we succeed in seeing Figure 4 as a cube, we find that these two added lines are perfectly integrated. Then they are diagonals across the front and back. Must we assume that we have never seen such a cube? Perhaps, but then we surely have never seen one with such strange lines added to it as that of Figure 8, and yet we see this figure spontaneously as a cube. Consider that Figure 8 is quantitatively more different from Figure 1 than Figure 4, four lines having been added instead of only two. Lastly, look at Figure 9 which has a slight tendency to become confused, but which will be much more readily seen as a cube with diagonals across its back and front planes than Figure 4. From the point of view of the experience explanation, then, Figure 9 and Figure 4 should be equal, and both superior to Figure 8 in arousing the cube experience. In reality they are not equal, and both are inferior to Figure 8 in this respect.

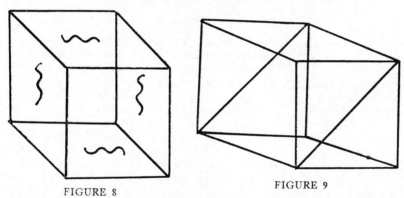

FIGURE 8   FIGURE 9

What should we expect from the organization hypothesis? The extra lines in Figure 8, being totally unconnected geometrically and formally with the general pattern, will not interfere with its organization. In Figure 4 each of the two added lines passes through a significant point of the cube pattern. Thereby at each of these points new line combinations become possible and gain dominance because these two points, heretofore equivalent to the six other corners are now differentiated from them. I need not elaborate the structural factors in further detail, since I have already demonstrated that in Figure 4 the two new lines will tend to change the whole organization, because they serve as boundary lines to a number of single plane figures which fit into each other within the plane. In

Figure 9 the "same lines" by avoiding these corners also avoid this effect. It is true they complicate the conditions somewhat since they are capable of functioning as boundary lines of other plane figures, but these new figures do not fit together so well and therefore our drawing, even when it is not seen as a cube, still appears in three dimensions. Thus we find that the organization theory explains our facts; this is no post factum explanation since, starting from the organization hypothesis, I drew my figures so as to obtain the required effect.

It is not very difficult to see Figure 1 as a plane pattern, whereas Figure 10 offers great resistance to such organization.[3] From the experience

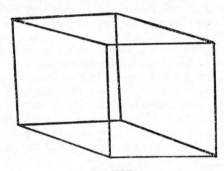

FIGURE 10

hypothesis there should be no difference between them, but from the organization hypothesis the difference is easily deduced. As a plane geometrical pattern Figure 1 is much the more symmetrical of the two, and this symmetry of the plane aspect is enhanced when the figure is turned so that the pattern represented in Figure 5 stands vertical, while the interrupted diagonal of the hexagon lies horizontal.[4] As a matter of fact, in this position the plane effect is more easily obtained. On the other hand, both figures, as cubes, are equally symmetrical and therefore the cube organization is more stable in 10 than in 1. The reader will have no difficulty in applying similar arguments to Figures 2 and 3.[5]

Thus it seems that the organization hypothesis is better adapted to the facts than the experience hypothesis. This has the consequence that we have to abandon our conception that for monocular vision depth is not a primary fact. For in all our examples the specific contribution of binocular vision, the binocular parallax, has been excluded. All our experiments succeed as well or better[6] when we use one eye only. Monocular vision will result in three-dimensional forms whenever the stimulus constellation is such that the processes aroused by it can reach the most stable or-

---

[3]This has already been mentioned by Witasek (39, p. 380).
[4]This has been experimentally proved by Benussi (3).
[5]For an explanation of the fact that Figure 2 can be seen as tridimensional without difficulty, I refer the reader to Wertheimer (38) and my paper (20).
[6]As Ebbinghaus pointed out long ago (6, p. 476).

ganization if they distribute themselves not in a plane of the somatic field but in all its three dimensions. Organization means dynamical interaction, not mere geometrical correlation (24, pp. 103 ff.). And we experience the forces that are at work whenever we succeed in seeing a less stable organization. Then we have to exert our "will" in order to hold the form against the spontaneous distribution of the forces.

Since the organization hypothesis is applicable to every kind of spatial organization, the foundations on which we based it may seem too slender. After all, such simple drawings form a negligible part of the number of objects seen. Therefore I shall adduce some supplementary evidence.

1) A very simple way to enforce tridimensional organization of the field by stimulation in a frontal-parallel plane is the ϕ experiment. In the simple manner first described by Wertheimer one exposes successively two parallel lines in such a way that the experience of optimal movement is achieved; the observer sees one line moving, say from left to right. If one now introduces between the others a third parallel line which remains permanently visible, then the optimal movement will persist, but the original line will now, in its motion across the field, pass *behind* the permanent line. The movement, instead of being interrupted, is *seen* to pass through a tunnel (37, p. 224). In this case the permanent line excludes the ϕ process from its own area without being capable of breaking it up. Thus the process is forced into the third dimension.[7]

2) A change from bi- into a tridimensional movement is described by Benussi under even simpler conditions. He exposed two dots 10 cm. apart in periodic succession. After a certain time the observer, who originally saw the dot running backwards and forwards, saw it moving on a circular track within a plane which forms an angle of approximately 90 degrees with the frontal parallel (4, pp. 111f.). The periodicity of the process tends again to make it more symmetrical, but the stimulus conditions prevent a circular movement in the vertical plane, there being no vectors upwards or downwards. Thus this circular movement develops in the depth dimension.

3) But two-dimensional movement is not always the first to occur in ϕ experiments. As Higginson (15) and Steinig (33) emphasize, certain plane figures will move in tridimensional tracks. Thus the stimulus pattern reproduced in Figure 11,[8] in which *a* and *b* are alternately exposed,

---

[7]Analogous facts in stationary spatial arrangements are practically universal. Thus Fuchs (7, pp. 150 f.), who performed many experiments on such problems (see below), points out that if we look at a vertical black rod standing in front of a white background and at some distance from it, it does not interrupt in our perception the uniform field of the ground; rather will the part of the background which is concealed by the rod persist in some way or other; and, although it is very difficult to find words for the description of this way, it can be demonstrated by contrasting it with another possibility of perceiving the same situation (facilitated by monocular vision); then the rod appears within the plane of the background, which now has three parts, two white ones and a black one between them. In this case the white surface is actually interrupted by the black stripe and no longer lies behind it.
[8]Taken from Steinig.

produces, when the time conditions are such that optimal movement is seen, a rotation around a horizontal axis of symmetry, i.e., through space. In this case a plane down-upward movement would necessitate strong distortions of form; a rotation within the plane of the drawing would mean

FIGURE 11

a longer track for the whole figure than the actually perceived movement. Thus the principle of the shortest track, again a principle of organization, explains the perceived depth.

4) We shall take a last group of facts from the perception of stationary objects. It is impossible to see two different forms in the same place, but it is not impossible to see such forms in the same direction. In such cases, therefore, the forms will organize themselves so that one appears behind the other. This is true of every figure-ground arrangement as Rubin has pointed out (31, p. 59).[9] In most of Rubin's well-known figures the depth between figure and ground is not very great, although in some of his patterns it may reach considerable amounts (up to 1 m.). But

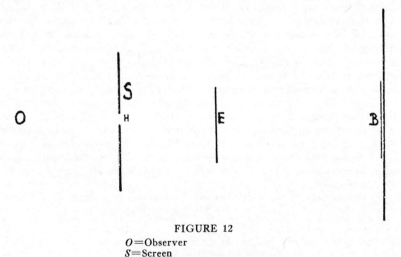

FIGURE 12

O=Observer
S=Screen
E=Episcotister (blue sector-disc)
B=Yellow disc on black ground

[9] Our first ϕ example and the rod in front of the background illustrate the same point.

under other conditions such marked depth effects are easily obtainable. I am thinking of the cases of transparency which have been most systematically investigated by Fuchs (7, 8) after Katz (19) had brought them to the attention of psychologists. Katz's original experiments, described in a simplified form, will bring out my point. Arrange a vertical gray cardboard screen S, (see Figure 12) with a small hole H about 1 cm. in diameter and a black background with a yellow disc B on it, say 1.5 m. behind the screen. Put between the two, about 50 cm. from the screen, a colorwheel with a blue sector of the same diameter as the yellow disc; the rest being open in such a way that the observer's eye at O sees the little hole in the screen filled with yellow or blue according to the position of the sector-disc on the color-wheel. If you then rotate the color-wheel, the little hole will be filled with a yellow-blue mixture, and it is possible to vary the size of the blue sector until the hole appears neutral gray. Now remove your screen, and at once you will see the dark background with a yellow disc through a transparent blue circular disc, though the retinal stimulation has remained unaltered within the area that corresponded to the hole in the screen. And although the yellow of the stationary disc behind the transparent disc is not so saturated as when seen directly, and the blue of the sector-disc is less saturated than the blue of the paper from which it is made, nevertheless both the blue and the yellow are impressive colors.[10] Perhaps no experiment proves more strikingly the inadequacy of the Berkeleyan axioms.[11]

Let us, in accordance with our previous analysis of Berkeley, consider the retinal stimulation point for point. We have to distinguish three different areas. Outside the sector-disc the retina is stimulated by very weak light, within but outside the yellow disc by blue light and, lastly, within the area of the stationary disc by a substitute for white (or gray) light (yellow-blue mixture). Of course, for any separate retinal point a stimulus for transparency, i.e., for duality of color, can exist as little as one for depth. But in our case there are contours on the retina, i.e., the dividing lines between different parts of the field. An outer contour separates the black background as seen outside and inside the area of the rotating sector, and an inner one segregates the stationary disc from its ground. Each of these contours produces and bounds a figure, one corresponding to the rotating sector, the other to the stationary disc. Consequently we have two different organizations in the same direction, since each contour affects one area only and not the other.[12] This results in the splitting-up of the critical field both as regards color and depth. The two aspects are conjoined in every experiment on transparency. And, since the laws which have been discovered for the appearance of transparency are

---

[10]For quantitative values see Katz (19, pp. 341 f.). The effect depends upon a number of conditions which I cannot discuss here. Cf. (7, 8).

[11]Since the phenomenon of transparency appears under these conditions in monocular vision also, we can in our argument neglect the factor of retinal disparity.

[12]This one-sided effect of contours was first described by Rubin (31).

laws of organization (7, and 36, pp. 277f.), it is proved that in these cases depth is also a matter of organization. This explanation of the transparency effect by a splitting-up of the color processes is, needless to say, a hypothesis which requires experimental evidence and therefore indicates new experimental problems. We are beginning such investigations in my laboratory.

II

Few psychologists seem to have seen a problem in the fact that a frontal parallel plane (or a surface lying in the horopter) appears as a plane. But, if we accept the proposition that our visual space in its totality is the product of organization, we can no longer be satisfied with an acceptance of the fact from a purely geometrical point of view, the remnant of the first assumption implicit in Berkeley's argument (see above). Rather must we consider the fact that we are able to see plane surfaces as an indication of a particular kind of organization. And we possess some evidence that such an organization, far from being the most primitive, is a high-grade achievement. On the other hand, we have, in the first section of this article, become familiar with cases where retinal stimulation without retinal disparity tends to tridimensional organization in the somatic field. But if this possibility exists, why do bidimensional organizations occur at all? Why, in other words, are certain processes in the visual cortex confined to a surface instead of spreading out in all directions? This question gives us the proper perspective, for it makes it manifest that bidimensional organization is a very special case, which probably requires very special conditions.

From this point of view I shall now discuss the description of two cases of agnosia caused by brain lesions, reported by Gelb (9).[13] The fundamental cause of the symptoms of agnosia or mental blindness is a defect of organization (10, p. 129, and 24, p. 169). The greater the disturbance, the less articulate are the organizations which the injured system can produce. In the two cases reported by Gelb this defect had a form which throws light from a new angle on this process of organization. Organization has a double aspect. On the one hand, areas or volumes of space must be held together; on the other hand, these units must be segregated from the rest of the field. This fact has, for a long time, been accepted as a matter of course because the traditional thinking in matters of space perception has been geometrical. The fact that we see a blue circle on a gray background seemed in need of no further explanation, since the retinal image of the blue circle was different from the retinal image of the background. "Form is given by arrangement on the retina of colored patches, just as in an oil painting" (40, p. 357). But a simple experiment which has been performed within the last five years proves that pure geometry is inadequate to account even for such simple facts. We need only choose a shade of gray for our background that is equal in brightness to our blue circle, and the

---

[13]Although I owe the ideas presented in the following pages to Gelb's exemplary investigation, he should not be held responsible for the hypothesis here advanced.

blue circle will lose its definition, will become blurred and shapeless, and may even, provided we are not too near to it, disappear completely for short moments (28). At the same time a gray circle, but little brighter or darker than the background, will be clearly visible, although the two grays look much more similar to each other than the gray and the blue.

From this we must conclude that the organization of our field into a circle on a background is a dynamic process, aroused by retinal stimulation, but not a mere geometrical projection of such stimulation. A boundary line must be formed which shapes the circular area and segregates it from the background. And we learn from Liebmann's experiment that such boundary lines are formed very readily by brightness differences and only very poorly by mere color differences. When the color approaches the brightness of the gray background, the cohesive force of the boundary line decreases, the organization becomes weaker and weaker.

Therefore we might expect that defects in the organization processes produced by brain injuries have similar results. Boundary lines will lose some of their integrating and segregating force, and the same should be true of boundary surfaces, if we remember that our space is not bi- but tridimensional.

This expectation is fulfilled when we read about the symptoms of the two patients which have been so excellently investigated by Gelb. For these patients would not see our blue circle on a gray ground,[14] that is, a bidimensional structure with a sharp rim. Instead they would see it projecting from the ground about 10 cm., if they stand less than a meter's distance from it. This does not mean, however, that the blue circle appears in a plane that much nearer, but that the blue *begins* here. For the circle is for our patients not a surface but a space-filling color, into which they have to dip their fingers when they want to touch it. As a matter of fact, the blue stretches also farther back than the light background, as has been proved in very ingenious experiments. Furthermore, the circle has for these patients a larger diameter than it has for us. If they are asked to indicate its rim with a sharp pencil, they will indicate a point a few millimeters outside of its area. Had we chosen a light circle on a dark ground, the ground would have stood out and the circle would have appeared embedded between the walls of a dark funnel. For the thickness and spread (in length and breadth) of the colors was a function of their brightness! The darker the color, the greater its depth. Consequently black was the thickest, and white the thinnest color. Quantitatively expressed, when the black surfaces seemed to project about 15 cm., the white ones stood out only 2-3 cm. It is significant that the images of these patients were essentially similar to their percepts in this respect. All objects which they could visually imagine looked "thick" and "spongy."

Thus the observed phenomena seem to fit our predictions of phenomena of decreased organization so well that we should have little doubt in ac-

---

[14] I disregard the fact that one of the patients was totally, the other partially color-blind, both color anomalies forming part of the general syndrome.

cepting our explanation as the correct one. Several further details strength-
en my conviction. During the course of time both patients recovered more
or less completely, and the process of restitution was carefully observed.
And it was discovered that the change towards normality proceeded from
the center towards the periphery of the field of vision. During a certain
period of this recovery these patients, when fixating the center of a colored
cardboard, saw not a plane but a concave surface, the center being flat
while towards all sides it became progressively thicker. Now we know
that the center of our field of vision is distinguished from the rest by the
degree of its organizing power. What we want to see clearly we fixate,
i.e., we transfer it into the center of our field of vision. The correlation,
then, between degree of recovery and central position serves as a further
proof that the defect was a defect of organization.

We have not yet explained why the different brightnesses possessed different thicknesses. A discussion of this fact will adduce new evidence in
favor of our hypothesis.

We shall again start by citing some facts from normal vision.

1) When we look at a scale of different shades of gray from white to
black, we find a difference that is more than qualitative. A dark gray is
not only a different shade from a pure white but it is also less brilliant,
less "insistent." Titchener, who uses this word as a translation of a German word (*Eindringlichkeit*) describes the same property also by the words
"self-assertive" and "aggressive" (34, p. 55), and all three terms seem
equally good to describe the difference I have in mind. Hering has proposed a physiological explanation for this insistence. Whereas, in his
theory, the brightness of a gray depends upon the relation of two antagonistic processes, independently of the total reaction, this total amount of metabolism is the cause of insistence (14, pp. 108 ff.). I mention Hering's
hypothesis not because my argument relies on his color theory, but because
I believe he was right in looking for some property of the somatic color
process that correlates with "insistence." Without any special hypothesis I
should suppose that some energy or intensity aspect of the process will be
the hypothetical correlate.

2) The same hypothesis is supported by the following fact: when we
try to color a part of a larger gray surface, we need more color the brighter
the area. Ackermann (1), repeating older experiments, added color to a
neutral ring surrounded on both sides by neutral discs of the same brightness and varied consecutively his shades from black to white. He found
the difference between the color threshold for black on black and white on
white enormous, the latter, depending upon the color used, being between
five to twenty times greater than the former. This fact is most easily explained[15] if we ascribe a greater intensity to the white than to the black
process. It might be objected to this argument that under special conditions a black may appear more insistent than white, as, for instance, the
letters on this page. But in accordance with this, Ackermann has found

---

[15] As G. E. Müller did long ago (29, pp. 32 f.).

that a black ring surrounded by white has a higher color threshold (for blue, yellow, and green) than a white ring in the same surroundings. For yellow, where this difference was most marked, the values were 15 degrees for the black ring and 5 for the white. And, of course, under these conditions this black ring is more insistent than the white. However, as experiments just started in my laboratory indicate, this connection between insistence and threshold is not so simple as it may appear, since under other conditions an increase in the insistence does not seem to be accompanied by a rise of the threshold. The total articulation of the field must be a decisive factor. When we now return to Gelb's investigation, we find that he reaches the same conclusion with regard to the colors seen by his patients. He also attributes prime importance to the mutual relations (*Zueinander*) of the colors in order to explain observations which, though slightly different in aim, give us some indication as to the relative color depths. Investigating the transparency of these colors, he made, among others, the following experiment. "When the patient wrote, a part of the nib was 'within this bright' (i.e., of the white paper) although the pen was darker than the paper. The patient said that 'he had to dip into the bright' with his pen in order to reach the writing paper" (9, p. 226). Thus it seems that under these conditions, where the black was the more insistent, it possessed a smaller thickness than the white.

3)   Finally, I shall take a few facts from Tudor-Hart's investigations of transparency (36), which point in the same direction. She found that, if a disc with an open sector (episcotister) rotates in front of a background, then the transparency of the episcotister will depend among other factors, upon its own brightness as well as that of the background. The darker the episcotister and the brighter the background, the greater the degree of transparency.

Having established this connection between brightness and intensity or energy of the somatic process, we can now return to the defect in organization characteristic of Gelb's two patients. I think we can now understand why ordinarily the depth of a color varied with its darkness. Already we have seen that organization in a plane surface with sharp boundary lines is a special case—a case, we might add, which requires strong forces for its realization. Indeed, the formation of quasi-membranes requires very great forces, and such forces presuppose a high degree of stability in the system, otherwise the frame will yield. We can interpret the defects of our patients by assuming that sufficiently strong forces to produce quasi-membranes could not arise, owing to the reduced stability of their system. However, the fact that these patients were able to perceive simple forms, albeit in altered conditions, proves that this incapability had a very definite limit. Segregation was still possible, the "frame" did not yield completely to every pull or push. But then the strength of the forces will also depend upon the intensity of the processes aroused by stimulation. The greater this intensity, the greater the strength. And since we have correlated the surface experience with a high force, we understand that the bright colors, possessing a relatively high intensity, will be more "surfacy," less deep, than the dark colors with their low intensity. This hypothesis, however, has still a weak point. Gelb himself has pointed it out in arguing against an explanation, which, though essentially different from the one here proposed, also connects the depth of the colors with their insistence (9, pp. 220 ff.). Gelb's patients, though they could not see surface colors, still showed the phenomena of color constancy in about the same degree as normal people. In other words, a black surface in the light and a white in the shadow, so arranged that they reflected the same amount of light per unit area, looked as different to them as to us (9, p. 241). That is, white surfaces looked much brighter than black ones, but also, and this is characteristic for the two patients, much thinner. Now Katz (19, pp. 136ff.) has proved that two such surfaces have the same brightness threshold. There is, then, as Gelb has pointed out, an apparent contradiction between the depth of the colors as seen by his patients and their insistence as measured by these threshold experiments.

Experiments, however, which are being carried out in my laboratory at the moment have yielded results which take the edge off this argument. We repeated the Ackermann type of experiment, measuring the color threshold of a ring on a neutral ground of equal brightness. Now this neutral ground is in the one case a dark gray well illuminated, in the other a light gray in the shade—care being taken that the two when viewed through holes in a screen look exactly alike, i.e., reflect the same amount of light per unit area. Under these conditions a small but consistent difference appeared in the color thresholds, the light ring in the shade requiring a greater amount of color than the dark one in the light.

This result would be in opposition to Katz's findings, if the two methods of investigation were comparable, which they are not. It remains as a task for our experiments, which we hope to publish before long, to show the relation between the two methods. This task has a rather general aspect; it means an investigation of the relation existing between thresholds and insistence.

However, our results remove the obstacle in the way of our explanation of the different depth which the different brightnesses possessed for Gelb's patients. For now there is harmony between depth and threshold; the brighter-looking color is thinner and has a higher color limen than the darker even if the two colors result from the same retinal stimulation.

Since the facts of the case, however, are not yet clearly established, it might seem as though I should have done better not to mention them at all. But this would have been against the purpose of this paper which, as I said at the beginning, wants to show Gestalt psychology at work. Besides, I hope, these discussions have made it plain that the color and the space aspect of our perception cannot be treated independently of each other.

Let us summarize: the discussion of this second section has corroborated the conclusion reached in the first. But whereas we treated there of cases of relatively high organization, we have now considered cases with reduced organizing power. Not only is tridimensional vision, as a result of organization, possible without binocular parallax and experience, but inasmuch as less articulate organization seems prior to more articulate organization, tridimensional vision must be the earlier form, in which bidimensional, plane surfaces arise only with progressive capacity of the organic systems for organization.[16]

III

Let us now turn to the other extreme, to cases of highly articulated depth perception such as we find most pronounced in binocular vision. Is there any connection between the efficacy of binocular parallax and the effects we have so far described? Of course, we must confine ourselves to a few aspects of this problem. This field abounds in both experimental investigations and theoretical discussion, which cannot possibly find place in this article. But it is justified to include our problem in this account of the *Psychologies of 1930* since a few investigations have appeared during this last five years which may inaugurate a new epoch of experimenting and theorizing. However, before we take up these new contributions, it will be useful to state some of the problems involved in the theory of parallactic depth perception.

Human binocular vision[17] is the result of the combination of the processes started in the two single eyes. Even the simplest facts of binocular vision reveal that this combination is ruled by certain laws which state the correspondence between the two members of this paired organ. In the classical investigations the discovery of this correspondence *point for point* has been a task of great importance. There we find the definitions of corresponding and disparate points, and for the latter the distinction between cross and longitudinal disparate ones (*quer- und längs-disparat*). Also it is generally conceded that cross disparation is one of the most important factors for the perception of depth, provided it does not exceed a certain amount. If it does, we see two objects instead of one. "Tridimensional vision, the vision of the object as solid, is a halfway house between single and double vision; to see a thing solid is a compromise between seeing it as spatially one and seeing it as spatially two" (34, p. 310).

Let us discuss this seemingly so simple statement of facts.

1) How does retinal disparity produce perception of depth? According to the nativistic theory, which was most clearly and thoroughly elaborated by E. Hering and his followers, retinal disparity is the stimulus for depth just as location on the single retina is the stimulus for direction: "The localization of a point relative to the nuclear plane has to be conceived as a physiological function of a definite pair of retinal points. In this sense we may ascribe to a definite pair of retinal points a space value, and may

---

[16]In this connection I want to quote a passage from Bentley's *Field of Psychology:* "The surface may be mathematically simpler than the solid, but it does not denote either a simpler function of the organism or a more ancient achievement of the race" (2, p. 216).
[17]According to Köhler's experiments the same seems to be true for the anthropoids (21).

contend that this space value is stable, i.e., independent of the localization of the nuclear plane" (16, p. 54). In other words, the relation between the perception of a certain depth and the excitation of two disparate points is perfectly analogous to the relation between the perception of a certain color and the stimulation by light of a certain composition. In the most recent American presentation of the subject such a clear-cut view is replaced by statements that the disparity is "utilized by the brain to see the object in three dimensions" or that the tendency towards diplopia, which always exists with disparate stimulation, "is normally *transformed* into a depth impression." But the terms "utilization" and "transformation" seem to me rather inane as long as we are not told what concrete processes they are meant to denote. I shall mention only that Jaensch proposed a theory of disparation according to which its effect is not direct but mediated by a certain behavior of attention and of the convergence mechanism concomitant with it (17, p. 102). None of these three answers, viz., the stimulus-sensation, the utilization-transformation, or the attention theory seems satisfactory—the second because of its vagueness, the first, as chiefly Jaensch has shown, because it is in disagreement with many facts and also because it puts an end to further questions, the last because the tendency in psychology has been to eliminate the ill-defined term of attention more and more from its explanations (32) and because it puts the cart before the horse.

2) The theory, as usually transmitted, contains the alternative of either double images or depth effect, leaving the depth localization of the double images in the dark, whereas this localization has played an important part in many and some of the ablest experiments on double images and their theoretical interpretation. Helmholtz already knew perfectly well that double images may have a depth localization with regard to the nuclear plan (13, pp. 362ff.). This fact destroys the apparent simplicity of the theory completely, it is incompatible with the two first interpretations mentioned under 1 above.

3) These same interpretations, and as I believe also the third, are open to a last criticism which will give us the first indication of the true solution. I may ask: What right have we to speak of disparate stimulation? This may seem a foolish question, since it can be geometrically shown that certain points will always be so projected that they do not fall on corresponding points, i.e., that they will be disparate. This is, of course, incontestably true, but it is geometry and not psychophysics. For, purely geometrically speaking, as long as we see with both eyes, pairs of corresponding points are always simultaneously stimulated. If Figure 13 represents two stereoscopic pictures A and A', falling on the left and right foveas, then the point on the right retina corresponding to B, though it would not be stimulated by a black point, is stimulated by the white of the paper, and, *mutatis mutandis,* the same is true for C'. Why then do we correlate B and C' and not B with a point B' on the white ground of the right picture and C' with a C on the white ground of the left? Geometrically

there exists not the slightest reason for the true coordination. One cannot even answer that it is the quality of the stimulation, the blackness versus the whiteness, which justifies us in coordinating B and C. For one reason this means that we leave the ground of pure geometry and enter the realm of existing properties or processes and then we should be obliged to explain physiologically why equal processes correspond to each other instead

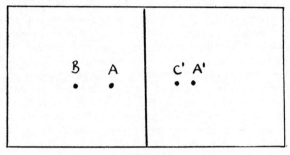

FIGURE 13

of mere locations. And as a matter of fact this is the kind of theory we shall have to make. But before we do this we must turn to the other reason which makes it impossible for the traditional view to fall back on equality. Already Helmholtz has shown that we get the stereoscopic effect from two drawings of which the one is black on white, the other white on black. If we apply this to our simple case, we should have to change one part of our Figure 13, say the right, by making its background black and the two dots white. Then the point which corresponds to point B on the right retina would also be stimulated by black, and the point that corresponds on the left retina to C' also by white, and we should have no reason whatever to correlate the black point B with the disparate and white point C'.

It appears, therefore, that we have been somewhat too naïve in our definition of disparity and correspondence. Obviously we have committed what Köhler calls the experience error (24, pp. 176f.). And yet the fact remains that disparity is a factor of the greatest power in producing depth. This means that our concept of disparate images can no longer be taken geometrically. Instead we must accept it as a *dynamic* fact and try to explain it by the interaction of real processes.[18]

If we see any object binocularly as one, it means that the two processes started in the retinas and proceeding along the optical tracts become united into one process in that part of the brain where the two optical tracts are brought together, which I shall call the combination zone. This holds as well for points that are projected on corresponding as for those that are projected on disparate places. The fact that corresponding points exist

---

[18]The following remarks are largely influenced by experiments performed and hypotheses proposed by Lewin and Sakuma (27). It is impossible to report the details of this work and to indicate the points where my explanation differs from theirs.

indicates a certain anatomic-physiological structure of the optic sector. The sector is so constituted that, normally, excitation starting from corresponding points will form one process in the combination zone. Since the structure of the organ must be considered as a systemic condition of the processes that occur within it, it is clear that exceptions to our rule are possible. They will occur if the properties of the processes, occuring under these systemic conditions, are such that a unification is impossible. Then we should expect them to stay apart with a stress towards unification.

But for the moment we are concerned with the normal case. Applied to disparate points, it would mean that here the systemic conditions are opposed to a unification of the two processes producing diplopia as the natural result. Therefore we see that many psychologists and physiologists try to save diplopia, even in the case of clear depth perception without double images, by reverting to special hypotheses which explain why in these cases we do not become aware of double images. This is another case where the psychologist introduces into experience data which, though not actually experienced, should, according to his theory, be experienced.[19] We accept double images only where they are really seen. But in these cases which we are discussing now, perception of a single object or point in spite of its disparate projection, we stand by our original proposition: if *one* point is seen, then the two processes from the two eyes must have united. As the systemic conditions as such would prevent such a combination, we must look out for special forces which bring it about. These forces must be forces of attraction between the monocular processes.

Of course, if this whole approach to our problem is right, we ought to be able to demonstrate the existence of these forces. Fortunately we possess this proof: lines close together in the visual field attract each other; if each is given to one eye, this attraction will result in an eye movement of fusion which unites the lines by bringing them on corresponding sections of the two retinas. In his contribution to the *Psychologies of 1925,* Köhler has explained this sufficiently (23, p. 192, and 22, pp. 536f.).[20] Disparate points[21] will then attract each other and tend to produce movements of fusion. But in those cases where we see *single* in spite of disparity there are always other points which we see single *without* disparity. Consequently eye-movements which would fuse our disparate points would separate our fused ones, and the total stress in the system would not be diminished. Thus under these conditions the motor system would be in an unstable equilibrium, which is in harmony with the facts as observed by Jaensch.[22] In single vision with disparate points we have then a unification of processes in the sensory field itself without eye movements. This unification has to overcome the constraints of the systemic conditions. This

---

[19]Bentley has sharply criticized this procedure and its application to our case (2).
[20]Other proofs for the attraction of the two monocular processes in (27).
[21]This is an illicit abbreviation for: processes in the combination zone aroused from disparate points.
[22]Consequently Jaensch's theory, which we have criticized above, becomes superfluous. Of course, the details cannot be elaborated here.

apparently it can do if the disparity is not too great and if no other forces are in the way.

At least certain experiments of Jaensch's seem to warrant such an assumption (17, pp. 90 ff.). In these experiments the subjects were presented with incandescent filaments vertically suspended and seen through a screen with an opening 10 x 40 cm. The two lateral threads were in a plane parallel to the frontal plane of the observer while the middle one projected from the plane of the others towards the observer by 6, 8, and 12 cm. Under these conditions not all of the luminous lines can be projected on corresponding retinal lines, and, accordingly, if the room was light, the observers saw the arrangement of this prism very clearly. But when the room was totally darkened so that nothing was visible but the three luminous threads,—they were enclosed within a dark box to prevent their light from illumining the rest of the room—the prism appeared flat, occasionally even as a plane surface. This may be interpreted in the following way: let us, for simplicity's sake, assume that the fixation is on the middle line; then projection of the two side lines would be disparate. But in the combination zone the two disparate line processes would be united without any other change if the room is dark. If the room is not dark, unification takes place also, but it can no longer occur in the plane, because each of these disparate line processes now has a well-defined distance from other objects, and this distance would be distorted by the simple fusion that occurs in the dark. Otherwise expressed, the other objects in the visual field prevent a mere lateral displacement of any of the disparate lines. The attraction between these two processes has to overcome not only the constraints of the system but also forces existing between them and other processes. In such a case the union of the lines takes place in the third dimension. How this takes place we are at present unable to say. In that respect our theory is no better off than the older ones, except for the fact that we make an actual force responsible for this effect and that this force cannot produce the union within the plane. But our theory has the great advantage over the older ones that it conceives of binocular depth perception as a process of organization produced by stresses existing between the visual processes themselves. Thus it connects binocular depth perception both with monocular depth perception and with eye movements, and it opens our field for new experimentation. Thus it should not to be too difficult to test whether my explanation of Jaensch's results is right or not.

To show the applicability of this hypothesis, I will discuss a few more facts. We have postulated a force of attraction between the two double images as the cause of their union. If we now increase the amount of the disparity so as just to make the union impossible, have we thereby also excluded those forces of attraction? Such a view would be unwarranted. For although we have to assume that the strength of these forces is an inverse function of distance, we cannot believe that passing from a point where these forces manifest themselves in union and stereoscopic effect to a point in its close proximity, we all of a sudden change the force from a considerable value to zero. Therefore we must assume that these forces will persist between double images even when they are not capable of achieving their union. But then the same stresses are operative which we have discussed before, and consequently we ought to expect the same kind of depth effect. Furthermore, if the disparity is small, a slight amount of displacement will accomplish the unification, producing a relatively low degree of stress in the system. If the disparity is greater, the stress in the system may be relatively great in spite of the fact that no union occurs. Again the facts are in good agreement with this expectation. Thus Helmholtz already reports a good stereoscopic effect under conditions where the disparity is so great that double images appear (13, pp. 362f.). Pfeifer (30, pp. 130ff.),[23] who made a quantitative study of the depth localization of double images, has found that uncrossed double images are seen farther away than the object if seen single.[24]

If the disparity is increased further, the forces between the two double images will eventually grow so small that they cannot overcome the constraints of the system, no displacement will take place, no effective stress will arise, and consequently the double images will appear in the same plane as the fixation point. How great the disparity must be for this effect to appear depends upon the total organization. If one fixates a point on a thread extending sagittally one will see two threads crossing one another X-like at the fixation point and extending forward and backward. This experiment is interesting from two points of view. On the one hand, the double images of the parts of the threads far away from the fixation point will be widely separated from each other without losing their depth localization, whereas double images of isolated points of the same disparity would be seen without any depth effect. On the other hand, the parts

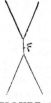

FIGURE 14

near the fixation point have a disparity which remains below the threshold for double vision for isolated lines or points. In other words, if the threshold were independent of the field organization, we should expect to see not an X but a figure like Figure 14, where F signifies the fixation point.[25]

---

[23]Cf. also Kaila (18), who describes elegant and simple experiments which demonstrate the localization of double images. The two articles mentioned contain many references to other publications on the same subject.

[24]This is easily seen by taking one's foot as the object, and fixating one's finger to produce the double images of the foot. Then it will be seen that the double images appear to be farther away than one's foot when fixated and seen single.

[25]This fact has been employed by Trendelenburg and Drescher (35), who have systematically investigated this case.

Here the organization into two straight lines prevents the union of the double images near the fixation point and maintains the depth effect between the far disparate double images at the ends. As Trendelenburg and Drescher have pointed out, a slight modification in the stresses obtaining in the field can change the perception of the lines so that they are seen in the shape of Figure 14.[26] This last experiment has shifted our discussion. We see now that our presentation so far has been too simple, inasmuch as it has dealt with the forces existing between double images as though they were independent of the organization existing in the rest of the field. Instead, the forces which have formed the topic of our discussion must be considered as parts of the total field organization. Wherever we experiment with so-called simple stimulus constellations, the organization of the different parts of the field is unstable and may shift from moment to moment. Therefore we must be prepared to get changing results if we make our double-image experiments with such simple constellations. This fact has been shown by Lewin and Sakuma (27, pp. 352f.), and is also confirmed by Pfeifer's results.

This influence of the organization of the field leads to another question: Where does this organization take place? Is it a matter exclusively of the combination zone or does it already occur within the monocular processes? We possess overwhelming evidence that the latter is the case, thanks particularly to Lau's experiments (25, 26) which he arranged to prove this proposition. He produced a stereoscopic effect by uniting two lines which were projected on corresponding retinal lines, but which through slightly different illusion patterns were distorted to a different degree.[27] In other words, when the two eyes give rise to line processes, which in spite of corresponding stimulation are as different from each other as line processes which would be produced by disparate stimulation, then the same depth effect appears. This shows that each part process before the combination in the combination zone must have had its own organization, because only when organized in their respective fields will these lines be shaped in such a way that their union results in depth. And the same fact is proved, as Lau has also pointed out, by that experiment of Helmholtz' which we have discussed before, in which a drawing in black on white is united with a drawing in white on black and produces the stereoscopic effect (see above, p. 179).

A last proof, which at the same time throws light on the organization involved, is furnished by an experiment which I have recently performed. Figure 15 illustrates again a stereoscopic slide. Each eye is presented with a full and a dotted line, drawn with India ink on transparent mica. The two full lines are united by fixation. The two dotted lines are so arranged that, when they are equidistant from the two full lines, the dots of the one fall into the interstices between the dots of the other, resulting in a broken

---

[26]The explanation of these authors seems to me quite unsatisfactory. It is of the type criticized on p. 180.
[27]He used both the Zöllner and the Höfler illusions.

line with small interstices and lying in the same plane as the full line. If now the right dotted line is moved a little to the right, the combined dotted line recedes behind the plane of the fixated line; if moved towards the left, it protrudes from it. Now no dot of either line has a counterpart dot of the other line in the same cross-section with which it could form a disparate pair. There are no cross disparate pairs of points. But the lines as wholes are cross disparate and therefore show the depth effect, and this organization must be an organization in the monocular processes.

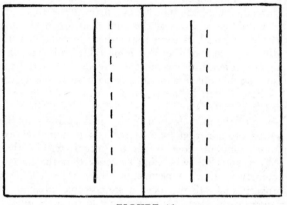

FIGURE 15

We give one last application. At the end of our second section we showed that forces producing the formation of surfaces presuppose a great stability of the system. The same idea must be applied to the stresses which form the basis of our explanation of depth perception. If the stability of the system is reduced, the double images will be united without a stress sufficient to create a depth effect. Consequently we should suppose that Gelb's two patients, whom we have discussed in the second section, should provide us with evidence for this conclusion, if we remember that everything they saw, quite apart from stereoscopic effect, had depth. Of course, one could not make stereoscopic experiments with patients whose perceptive faculties were so greatly impaired. But a simpler and cruder experiment gives us the desired confirmation. "If the patients observed a circular or square colored plate presented in a frontal parallel plane which was turned around a vertical axis through a certain angle, the patient saw now a frontal parallel color in elliptical or oblong form" (9, p. 210). However, the patients would see objects in other than frontal parallel orientation if the angle through which the plates were turned exceeded a certain amount. Just as the thickness of the object, so would this angle depend upon the brightness of the color; the brighter the color the smaller the angle, the darker the greater. This shows that disparate lines can be united without effective stress if the disparity is not too great. And the stress will appear the sooner the brighter and, that means according to our previous discussion, the more stable the separate images are.

It seems, then, that our hypotheses are able to explain a number of facts, but I am fully aware that there are far more facts which I have not attempted to explain and among them many which I could not explain at the present moment. My conclusion is not that therefore my hypothesis is premature, but that it should be applied to an experimental treatment of the inexplicable facts. Then it will be proved how much truth it contains.

The general significance of this hypothesis is that our space perception in all three dimensions is the result of organized brain activity and that we can understand our space perception only in terms of organization, i.e., in terms of actual dynamic processes, and not in terms of mere geometrical stimulus-sensation correlations. From this point of view the third dimension does not offer a special problem accruing to the problem of the perception of length and breadth; rather is bidimensional perception a special case of tridimensional perception. Psychology of "sensation" and perception has lost the position it held in the beginning of the new era of our science just because it was so dead a subject. The distribution of space values on the retinas is indeed a question which will not arouse the enthusiasm of psychologists for a long time. But if we treat perception as the result of ever-changing stresses producing new and ever new organizations, we shall find in our subject something of the drama of life, the interest in which has attracted most of us to psychology.

REFERENCES

1. ACKERMANN, A. Farbschwelle und Feldstruktur. *Psychol. Forsch.*, 1924, **5**, 44-84.

2. BENTLEY, M. The field of psychology. New York: Appleton, 1924. Pp. xvi+545.

3. BENUSSI, V. Über die Motive der Scheinkörperlichkeit bei umkehrbaren Zeichnungen. *Arch. f. d. ges. Psychol.*, 1911, **20**, 363-396.

4. ————. Versuche zur Analyse taktil erweckter Scheinbewegungen. *Arch. f. d. ges. Psychol.*, 1916, **36**, 59-135.

5. BERKELEY, G. An essay towards a new theory of vision. (First published in 1709.) In: The works of George Berkeley, D.D., former Bishop of Cloyne. Vol. I. (Ed. by A. C. Fraser.) Oxford, 1901.

6. EBBINGHAUS, H. Grundzüge der Psychologie. Vol. I. (1st ed., 1879) 4th ed. Leipzig: Veit, 1919. Pp. 320.

7. FUCHS, W. Untersuchungen über das simultane Hintereinandersehen auf derselben Sehrichtung. *Zsch. f. Psychol.*, 1923, **91**, 145-235.

8. ————. Experimentelle Untersuchungen über die Änderung von Farben unter dem Einfluss von Gestalten. *Zsch. f. Psychol.*, 1923, **92**, 249-325.

9. GELB, A. Über den Wegfall der Wahrnehmung von Oberflächenfarben. *Zsch. f. Psychol.*, 1920, **84**, 66-257. (Reprinted in Psychologische Analysen hirnpathologischer Fälle. [Ed. by A. Gelb & K. Goldstein.] Leipzig, 1920.)

10. GELB, A., & GOLDSTEIN, K. Zur Psychologie des optischen Wahrnehmungs— und Erkennungsvorgangs. *Zsch. f. d. ges. Neur. & Psychiat.*, 1918, **41**, 1-142. (Reprinted in the volume listed under the preceding number. The page reference in the text refers this time to this publication.)

11. GOTTSCHALDT, K. Über den Einfluss der Erfahrung auf die Wahrnehmung von Figuren. I. *Psychol. Forsch.*, 1926, **8**, 261-318.

12. ————. Über den Einfluss der Erfahrung auf die Wahrnehmung. II. *Psychol. Forsch.*, 1929, **12**, 1-87.

13. HELMHOLTZ, H. v. Handbuch der physiologischen Optik. Vol. III. (Ed. by A. Gullstrand, J. von Kries, & W. Nagel.) (1st ed., 1866) 3rd ed. Hamburg & Leipzig: Voss, 1910. Pp. viii+564. (The American translation of this 3rd edition contains the German paging so that the reader may turn to it as easily as to the original.)

14. HERING, E. Grundzüge der Lehre vom Lichtsinn. Berlin, 1920. (Also in Handbuch der Augenheilkunde. Part I, Chap. 12.)

15. HIGGINSON, G. D. Apparent visual movement and the *Gestalt*. *J. Exper. Psychol.*, 1926, **9**, 228-252.

16. HILLEBRAND, F. Die Stabilität der Raumwerte auf der Netzhaut. *Zsch. f. Psychol.*, 1893, **5**.

17. JAENSCH, E. R. Über die Wahrnehmung des Raumes. *Zsch. f. Psychol.*, 1911, Erg. 6. Pp. xvi+488.

18. KAILA, E. Versuch einer empiristischen Erklärung der Tiefenlokalisation von Doppelbildern. *Zsch. f. Psychol.*, 1919, **82**, 129-197.

19. KATZ, D. Die Erscheinungsweisen der Farben und ihre Beeinflussung durch die individuelle Erfahrung. *Zsch. f. Psychol.*, 1911, Erg. 7. Pp. xviii+425.

20. KOFFKA, K. Perception, an introduction to the *Gestalttheorie*. *Psychol. Bull.*, 1922, **19**, 531-585.

21. KÖHLER, W. Optische Untersuchungen am Schimpansen und am Haushuhn. *Abh. d. Preuss. Akad. d. Wiss., Phys.-math. Kl.*, 1915, No. 3.

22. ————. Gestaltprobleme und Anfänge einer Gestalttheorie. *Jahresber. ü. d. ges. Physiol.*, 1922.

23. ————. An aspect of Gestalt psychology. Chap. 8 in Psychologies of 1925. Worcester, Mass.: Clark Univ. Press, 1926. Pp. 163-195.

24. ————. Gestalt psychology. New York: Liveright, 1929. Pp. xii+403.

25. LAU, E. Versuche über das stereoskopische Sehen. *Psychol. Forsch.*, 1922, **2**, 1-4.

26. ————. Über das stereokopische Sehen. *Psychol. Forsch.*, 1925, **6**, 121-126.

27. LEWIN, K., & SAKUMA, K. Die Sehrichtung mónokularer und binokularer Objekte bei Bewegung und das Zustandekommen des Tiefeneffektes. *Psychol. Forsch.*, 1925 **6**, 298-357.

28. LIEBMANN, S. Über das Verhalten farbiger Formen bei Helligkeitsgleichheit von Figur und Grund. *Psychol. Forsch.*, 1927, **9**, 300-353.

29. MÜLLER, G. E. Zur Psychophysik der Gesichtsempfindungen. *Zsch. f. Psychol.*, 1896, **10**, 1-82, 321-412.

30. PFEIFER, R. A. Über Tiefenlokalisation von Doppelbildern. *Psychol. Stud.*, 1907, **2**.

31. RUBIN, E. Visuell wahrgenommene Figuren. Copenhagen: Gyldendal, 1915. Berlin, 1921.

32. ————. Die Nichtexistenz der Aufmerksamkeit. *Ber. ü. d. IX. Kong. f. exper. Psychol.*, 1926.

33. STEINIG, K. Zur Frage der Wahrnehmung von Zwischenstadien bei stroboskopisch dargebotenen Bewegungen. *Zsch. f. Psychol.*, 1929, **109**.

34. TITCHENER, E. B. A text-book of psychology. New York: Macmillan, 1910. Pp. vii+565.

35. TRENDELENBURG, W., & DRESCHER, K. Ueber die Grenzen der beidäugigen Tiefenwahrnehmung und Doppelbildwahrnehmung. *Zsch. f. Biol.*, 1926, **84**, 427-435.

36. TUDOR-HART, B. Studies in transparency, form and colour. *Psychol. Forsch.* 1928, **10**, 255-298.

37. WERTHEIMER, M. Experimentelle Studien über das Sehen von Bewegung. *Zsch. f. Psychol.*, 1912, **61**, 161-265. (Reprinted in: Wertheimer, M. Drei Abhandlungen zur Gestalttheorie. Erlangen: Verlag der philosophischen Akademie, 1925. Pp. iv+184.)

38. ——————. Untersuchungen zur Lehre von der Gestalt. II. *Psychol. Forsch.*, 1923, **4**, 301-350.

39. WITASEK, S. Psychologie der Raumwahrnehmung des Auges. Heidelberg: Winter, 1910. Pp. vi+454.

40. WOODWORTH, R. S. Psychology. (Rev. ed.) New York: Holt, 1929. Pp. xiv+590.

CHAPTER 10

STRUCTURE, TOTALITY OF EXPERIENCE, AND GESTALT*

FRIEDRICH SANDER

University of Giessen

The demand upon psychology, the science of psychical reality in all its phases, to dwell no longer in the narrow confines of conscious phenomena, has become more and more insistent the more we have succeeded in determining, completely and systematically, the conditions or conditional relations of actual experiences and attitudes. An analysis of all relevant conditions has necessarily compelled a recognition of some real and active agency, besides the total complex of external conditions or "stimuli," on the one hand, and the physiological conditions, on the other—a psychical principle beyond the bounds of the mere phenomenal given. Regarding the nature and magnitude of this transphenomenal, psychically active reality, opinions have been extremely divergent. The least removed from the standpoint of mere-consciousness psychology is the doctrine of traces of former experiences, which regards past sense impressions as operative in the present conscious manifold in the form of "residua," that lead some sort of mysterious existence and occasionally pop up in the realm of actual consciousness. The extreme opposite is the view that some mere-conscious mental principle is the true reality, and the world of consciousness mere illusion, in fact a concealing mask. Both extremes seem to commit fundamental error in opposite directions. In the former case, i.e., the recognition of some residual component in present experience, everything that exceeds the limits of the immediate stimulus pattern is referred to dispositional aftereffects of previous experiences, i.e., previous contents of consciousness, and thus the sphere of consciousness is not really transcended. In the latter, on the other hand, the world of consciousness is degraded at the outset to mere illusion by the assumption of an unconscious hiding behind the actual phenomena, so that all data of scientific research are ruled out from the very start and speculative theories regarding the nature and intentions of the unconscious introduced in their stead. In dealing with either of these points of view, we must bear in mind that scientific psychology should take the totality of experience for its point of departure, and not thoughtlessly sacrifice that empirical material which is the very basis of its procedure in favor of a one-sided theory that does violence to the facts; but that, none the less, it should muster courage to look beyond, or rather behind, immediate experience, and critically, cautiously approach the non-conscious realms in search of that process, now tempestuously, now calmly unfolding, which is the symphony of living experience.

*Submitted in German and translated into English for the Clark University Press by Susanne Langer.

That epoch of psychology which dealt with consciousness alone, expressed, for instance, in the soul-concept of a Wilhelm Wundt, for whom the actuality of the soul was exhaustively given with that of immediate consciousness, may have been a necessary stage, but has certainly been transcended. A pure consciousness-psychology became impossible as soon as psychological research went beyond the mere analysis of elementary sense data. Coincident with the advent of new problems—problems which were new to this scientific epoch, but had always held an important position in prescientific psychology—was another factor which helped to overcome the one-sided phenomenalistic standpoint, and that was the change in the basic views and principal concepts of our science. This change was first apparent in a negative way, in the repudiation of the traditional ideal of the exact natural sciences, especially physics and its hypothetical constructions. The phenomenalistic prejudice of the previous epoch, the limitation of all researches to the content of consciousness, is closely related to the theoretical primacy of notion of elements, and the assumption of a thoroughgoing and unequivocal dependence of such "elements" on specific stimuli. This limitation to consciousness-phenomena and their fictitious separation into ultimate elements and their corresponding stimuli simply admitted of no problems that did not fit into the conceptual frame of this psychology.

Thus from the phenomenalistic reduction of the psychological sphere there followed other prejudices. I merely make mention of three such neglected fields: the problem of mental development, the problem of emotional life, and of personality. Elements do not develop. They may aggregate in varying numbers, and according to the frequency of their associations arrange themselves in variously complex patterns—but real development, in the full sense of the word, means something more than this. Hence the non-genetic character of the old phenomenalistic element-psychology, which was based almost exclusively on description of the consciousness of adult subjects without any inquiry into genetic and social conditions. And furthermore, this psychology, whose chief tendency was toward an analytic division of the content of consciousness into elementary sensations, by its sensualistic prejudice ruled out the fundamentally important realm of emotional life. Feelings, in the sense of indivisible qualities of consciousness as a whole,[1] are destroyed by analysis. And one central problem of all mental science does not exist at all for a mere-consciousness psychology, namely, the problem of personality. A psychology based exclusively on consciousness phenomena has no access to the problem of personality. For here we are not dealing with an actual phenomenon of consciousness nor sequence of such phenomena, but with a structural principle which endures beyond the immediate moment, with psychodispositional continuous forms, which take part in determining each separate experience as well as each action, and assert themselves again and again in all vital expression despite any changes that may occur in the environmental conditions. It is through

---

[1] For this conception, outlined by Cornelius (1) and developed by Krueger, cf. Krueger (6).

this transphenomenal psychical principle that all our single acts derive their meaning and interconnection. This necessity of crossing over the narrow confines of consciousness into the transphenomenal sphere of this psychical principle which conditions the actual events of experience applies not only to the problem of personality, where it is most evident, but also to the above-mentioned cases of emotional life and of mental development. In this developmental process there seem to be unconscious formative causes at work, which let phase upon phase evolve with internal necessity and ever-increasing complexity; in emotional life the subject becomes directly aware of his own "essence," his tendencies and valuations above and beyond the present moment, through the form wherein his feelings present themselves, the emotive totality-value of his consciousness as a whole.

The following pages contain an attempt to justify the assumption of a transphenomenal effective psychic reality, a complex of psychodispositional conditions, even in a field of research which the past era of psychology proposed to master from the mere-consciousness point of view—the field of perception-theory. Sense perception seems more dependent on the external conditions of the physical environment than any other department of mental life. The assumption of a constant coordination of stimulus and sensation, a dogma of the older school, did not seem to admit any participation of spiritual influences and unconscious forces that might be postulated as transphenomenal reasons for the actual events in experience, with possibly the exception of after-effects or residua of such former events. Thus the demonstration of psychodispositional conditioning in the realm of sensory contents of consciousness must be rated as particularly important, especially as this realm is the most accessible to exact scientific observation.

That the older sort of psychology expected to get along with its purely phenomenalistic outfit is undoubtedly due in part to the fact that its disciples considered certain experiences and aspects of life not worthy of scientific investigation, or failed entirely to observe those things which pointed with peculiar insistence to transphenomenal conditioning factors. These things are the facts of the wholeness of all living experience (*Erlebnisganzheit*), and the structural organization of part-wholes (*Gestaltetheit von Teilganzen*) in the stream of experience at any moment. These facts were rediscovered in the nineties of the last century, but it was only in the last decades that they were brought within the bounds of exact research. Among these totality-factors, it is again the emotional aspects of experience that necessitate a resort to transexperiential, constant tendencies of the soul. The reason why these holistic aspects, which shall be forthwith described in more detail, were so completely overlooked by the previous psychological epoch, lies in the essentially analytic attitude of that time. That which our psychological researches under the watchword of totality have been able to prove in detail—that qualities which belong to a complex as a whole are obscured, even destroyed by an extreme analytic attitude, an exceedingly detailed dissection into component parts—that applies exactly to the analytic attitude of psychology toward its object. The kind of psychology that is directed toward the discovery of ultimate elements has "failed to see the woods for the trees."

The study of totalistic aspects and the structural organization of the actual content of consciousness, which were introduced by such transitional conceptions as Wundt's "creative synthesis," Christian v. Ehrenfel's' "form-qualities" (*Gestaltqualitäten*), or Dilthey's demand for a descriptive psychology that should take the relational structure of experience for its object, has demonstrated in every way the more than synthetic character of the conscious manifold, especially through genetic researches, and thereby upset the doctrine of the primacy of "simple" sensory elements. Gradually the stark abstract concept of the psychological element has been overcome. At first the character of an experiential whole, which is always more than the sum of its parts, was treated as a datum of a secondary sort. Even in the treatment of such simple facts as the wholeness of a melody, a spatial figure, a volition, or a thought process, attempts were made to explain its constitution out of parts. Whoever clung to the primacy of elements was obliged somehow to account for this "qualitative more" that transcended any mere combination of elements. So this period is characterized by the theoretical introduction of conglutinative factors, such as creative syntheses, production processes, collective attention processes, and other such hypotheses all of a compromising nature, which on the one hand take account of the special character and the independence of totality-properties (*Ganzquälitäten*), and on the other retain the supposed primacy of the old fictitious elements. It took an unprejudiced course of observations and comparisons, especially in the genetic field, under well-planned systematically varied conditions, to disclose the factual and theoretical importance of totality-properties.

The content of experience at any time cannot be given through the exhibition of a manifold of elements, some of which cohere as groups or complexes, but it is always a whole containing subordinate wholes that appear more or less distinct from each other and from the general system. Only a further and further dissection, and a destructive analysis, can ever arrive at those disconnected pieces which the old psychology designated as elements. The partial or subordinate wholes are distinguished among themselves by their various kinds and degrees of structural organization, they are heterogeneous wholes, "externally" limited, internally variously membered and possessing a significant connectedness of all their members with one another and with the greater totality. Such configurations may be experienced simultaneously or as continua in time. They may be conceived as standing between two poles, nearer now to the one, now to the other—between unorganized, unarticulated wholeness at the one extreme, and mere discrete togetherness and sequence of elementary data, mere particularity at the other—as closed, self-contained, self-determined structures with mutually distinguishable, structurally limited members. But as subordinate units these configurations (*Gestalten*) always remain imbedded in more comprehensive experiential totalities, finally in the emotive totality-aspect of the realm of consciousness itself at any time. The more comprehensive and the less distinct and internally organized a subordinate totality is, the nearer it approaches to the pole of emotive unity.

Therefore the study of configurations should never be content to regard in isolation the structure that happens at the moment to be most evident, but should proceed systematically to pass beyond the construct under observation and include the totality of the conscious field. Just as the construct in question, as a subordinate whole, exhibits certain totality-properties, so does the inclusive whole of the field of consciousness itself. The totality-properties of the whole content of consciousness are experienced as "states of mind," as feeling-tones which belong to the experience *in toto*. The "state of mind" (*Zumutesein*) in its qualitative particularity is determined in one sense through all the subordinate wholes that are to be found in the experiential content and their experienced relationships, which in turn may possess different degrees of self-sufficiency; in another sense, we find in its peculiarly dynamic traits of internal tendency just that which we recognize as the transphenomenal psychic principle, which is the conditional constant underlying all subordinate wholes with their varieties of kind and degree. In these dynamic qualities, which play a dominant rôle in the realm of emotions, there comes to expression the dynamics of the functional unity of mental life or, as we may roughly say, the soul itself and whither it is directed or "what it desires."

Under special conditions, as we have remarked, the dynamic qualities of the total content of consciousness are experienced with particular force, namely, at times when the configurations which sensory experience presents are quite different from what the dispositional conditions are adjusted to meet. These dispositional features of the soul, with their dynamic which strives for actualization, being themselves a totality, an organic system of unconsciously active forces and impulsive tendencies, may—according to Dilthey's precedent—be called *structure*. Thus structure in our sense is not, as so often in present-day psychology, used synonymously with Gestalt. Structure denotes the set of psychodispositional constants conditioning the *Gestalten* of experience (5). How much of this conditioning complex which is called structure is to be regarded as psychical, and how much as physical, is a matter of indifference; in the personal identity of the experiencing subject these operate inseparably together. The structural constants of the body-soul totality are an independent set of conditions, in relation to the external environment, for the forms of actual experience as well as beyond these for the character of human activity and its result, the work, since the somatic side of this psychophysical totality, by reason of its physico-motor faculties, is able to exert an influence upon the external world. The form of this performance and of the actual content of experience indicates the dynamic function of psychical structure to create configurations out of a totality.

In certain totality-properties of the entire consciousness, in the emotionally tinged "state of mind," this structural dynamic becomes more definitely apparent in its proclivities. From this it follows that any description of Gestalt experiences, just because it is designed to prepare an analysis of the relevant conditions, cannot afford to neglect these emotive total-ity-properties, which are not themselves configurations (*Gestalten*).

If it is true that our perceptions are not determined solely by physical causes, as the old psychology, with its dogma of the unequivocal dependence of sensations on specific stimuli firmly maintained, but are furthermore determined in regard to their configuration by this other scheme of struc-tural conditions, then it ought to be possible to create artificial conditions which would yield effects of a structural dynamic principle in a particularly obvious form. Such instances may be found abundantly in researches wherein the part of the stimulus has been reduced to a minimum—to that minimum which is just able to give rise to a Gestalt experience (9, 10, 11, 14, 3). Experiments of this sort are particularly successful in the field of optics. The presentation of figures by a very brief exposure in the tachis-toscope, in twilight vision or indirect vision, or in extreme miniature, all have this trait in common, that a constellation of stimuli operates under unfavorable conditions, too briefly, etc. The less the perception is de-cisively influenced by the physical condition, the stimuli, the more freely will the dynamic structure come into play and mould the phenomenal con-tent in its own interest. The transition from maximally unfavorable to normal circumstances gives rise to a whole series of sense experiences, whereby the evolution of configurations is exhibited in logical order. [For this process of gradual configuration I have suggested the term "genetic realization" (*Aktualgenese*)]. In this configurative process the emergent perceptual constructs are by no means mere imperfect or vague versions of the final figure which appears under maximally favorable conditions, but characteristic metamorphoses with qualitative individuality, "prefor-mulations" (*Vorgestalten*). These properties, which certainly are not de-termined by the constellation of stimuli, may be traced back to structural causes, and let us deduce the direction toward which they tend in forming the objects of experience. If, for instance, an observer is presented with an irregular, interrupted linear figure, lighted up on a dark surface, in ex-treme miniature, but gradually growing to "normal" size, the observer will experience—often with intense emotional participation—a process of *form-emergence,* as out of a continuous light nebula, originally circular as a rule, figures arise, which in comparison with the end-figure are distinguished by greater wholeness, compactness, and regularity, and approach the irregu-lar final figure only step by step. From these "transformations" with reference to the final form which is "adequate" to the stimuli, we may gather the trend of the psychophysical sub-structure which we are con-sidering; that trend is toward closed contours, toward compactness, in short, toward geometrical regularity, symmetry, softening of all curva-tures, parallelity, toward general as well as detailed conformity to the primary spatial axes, the vertical and the horizontal, finally toward an optimum of configuration on the level of geometrically primitive, non-connotative, purely aesthetic significance; an ideal of meaning expressible terms of lines and planes alone. It is only with an increasing power of the stimulating influence that these homogeneous, progressively differentiating, over-symmetrical preformations are debarred in favor of the claims of the stimulus pattern. These figurations have one property which plainly shows the interplay of structural subjective tendencies and the dictates of the external stimuli, and that is the fluidity and mobility of these constructs. The formation of the successive stages, which usually emanate one from the other by sudden jerks, has a certain shading of non-finality; the intermediaries lack the relative stability and composure of the final forms; they are restless, agitated, and full of tensions, as though in a plastic state of becoming. Their total mobility may in certain parts or regions be heightened to the point of actually perceived motion of particular lines, despite an objective condition of perfect rest, namely, in those parts or regions where the stimulus pattern tends in a different direction from the structural forces. Thus a contour which according to the actual stimulus is interrupted, but whose early appearance is closed due to the structural tendencies, is finally broken for the experiencing subject at the points of interruption, with the increasing preponderance of the stimulus pattern, but tends to close again at the next moment, only to open once more. This opening and closing of the outline, caused by the interplay and antagonistic tendencies of the conditioning factors, is experienced as violent motion. In this apparent "eidogenic" motion under conditions of perfectly static stimulation, we can trace directly the dynamic character of dispositional structures, which tend toward greatest possible symmetry. This structural dynamic, which may be inferred from the phenomenal peculiarities of such percepts to be one of the determining factors in the process of perception itself, enters our immediate experience in the form of certain dynamic qualities of the total "state of mind," in emotive qualitative totalities. The peculiar mode of presentation of these prefigurations that are simplified relative to some final form is in no wise comparable to that of final forms of similar outline; it is considerably richer in quality. Their regular formation is only one trait of these closed self-sufficient constructs, which unfold with well-ordered regularity, without exhausting themselves in these characteristics. The evolution of these unitary, still unmembered constructs into significant forms with increasing membral differentiation is not something that the observer follows with cool objectivity, but all metamorphoses are engulfed in a maximally emotional process of pronouncedly impulsive and tensor nature, and take place through an intense participation of the whole human organism. Every formation is experienced as a satisfactory fulfilment of some inner urge, possessing the whole consciousness with dull compressed feelings, an urge for formation of the formless, significance of the meaningless. What passes here in the sphere of perception is repeated in exaggerated measure in the higher realm of artistic or intellectual formulation. Forms, as we said above, being articulated wholes with members relative to the whole, are ranked between two antipodes, both of which can be approximated only in experience—undifferentiated diffuse wholeness on the one hand, and unrelated, fragmentary heterogeneity on the other. Not only descriptively do they stand between these two opposites, but as the ultimate goal of the tendencies of both. Out of the snarled, dull-feeling, original modes of experience, the structural tendencies of the soul strive for organic differentiation with preservation of the psychic totality, and likewise from the other end seek to bring together that which is fragmentary owing to external determinants, and to subject all parts and aspects to a superior whole. Thus the starry heaven is not experienced as a collection of separate stars, but in constellations in which each star receives its special place. Or from a perfectly even sequence of strokes or impacts a rhythm emerges, which subordinates every sound to a definite temporal series. This incorporation of all items in an all-supporting rhythm occurs quite by itself, often with irresistible constraint, like a work of unconsciously operative forces of the soul. In these experiential membered forms the internal dynamic of the structural architectonic tendencies finds expression again in the changing accentuation of elements in the series, in the rhythmic repetition of subordinate totalities. The fulfilment of the rhythm in turn lends to the total experience that emotive quality of adequacy, living volatility, final orderliness (8). It is different if the external stimulus will serve, indeed, to realize the structural dynamic, but not to let it unfold in entire accord with its inherent tendencies—for instance, if in our last example of so-called "subjective rhythmification" the sounds follow each other too slowly or without any sort of regularity. Under such conditions dissatisfactions, torturing tensions, and inner repudiation are experienced, and again in qualitative emotional wholes, which prove to be symptoms of non-fulfilment or violation of structural tendencies.

Whether the soul's interest in form lets diffuse totalities take organic shape, or smelts fragmentary experiences together into a whole, the structural forces are always tending to coerce the experienced construction into the best possible shape, despite opposed physical stimulatory influences. Concerning what is meant by the best possible shape (optimale Gestaltetheit), something remains to be said. The above-mentioned experiments in the actuo-genesis of forms under conditions of reduced stimuli have thrown some light on the direction wherein we may seek the form-ideal for this level of configuration. Another source of insight is the study of the peculiar feeling-tone with which formulations of this sort are experienced. The formulation of an experiential whole possesses now a satisfying tone, balanced, matured, articulate, characteristic, now an unsatisfied air, weak, tortured, impure, unattuned, spineless. Forms have different values in direct experience; some have an experiential advantage over others, are distinguished from the others. In these distinctions, which are expressed in multifarious feelings, value-accents are experienced, which cannot be explained through any analysis of the stimulus pattern, but point to structural tendencies. To an evenly graded series of stimuli there corresponds not a series of perceived figures of corresponding values, but some of the psychological products are distinguished by a marked qualitative individuality, whereas others display such individuality only vaguely, or appear as indistinct transitional forms between two independent geometric characters. To cite a simple example:[2] if the width of a rectangle is varied

---

[2]Compare the researches by C. Schneider (12), carried on at my suggestion.

by small but even degrees from plus ∞ to minus ∞, keeping the height constant, an objectively even series of rectangles is generated. But psychologically the whole series arranges itself into separate zones of definitely differentiated peculiarities of form. At certain points, which are thereby specially distinguished from all others, the formal character of a zone, let us call it the zone's "eidos," is particularly pronounced. In our series of rectangles the most definite zone, that which is most clearly distinguished, is the zone of the perfect square. The character of "squareness" covers a variable but always small number of gradations, which approximate to the location of the ratio 1-1. At one point within this zone the "squareness" appears most clearly, neighboring forms are still interpreted as "squares," howbeit not perfect, correct, accurate squares, but "bad" squares.[3] These bad squares may immediately be experienced as "good" ones again, if the insistence of the stimulus is reduced, as for instance through tachistoscopic presentation. With increasing departure from the region of best expression of the square, the form-property "square" changes abruptly to that of "rectangle." It is at this point in the objective series where the "assimilation" of height and width, which occurs in the interest of the persistent square with its balance of height and width, suddenly gives place to an inevitable exaggeration of the difference between height and width, again with the intention of expressing a typical rectangle. Figures which stand in the series just between two zones seem, so to speak, to hang in the balance perceptually; a small alteration of the stimuli in one direction or the other lets them incline to one side or the other, expressing the character of either one or the other zone. For this reason the threshold of variability for these transitional structures is very low, whereas in the regions of most pronounced formal character, that of the square for instance, considerable objective alteration is required to bring about a perceptual change, to transport the form out of the squareness zone. This accounts for the oft observed high threshold of variation of the square. A similar condition holds for tonal configurations. There among the innumerable possible vibration ratios we recognize a small number of favored, outstanding intervals. Small deviations from the pure vibration ratio represent tone-forms, which, although they are still experienced as belonging quite unequivocally to a definite zone, that of the octave or the fifth for instance, are none the less heard to be out of tune, somehow impure. Forms of this sort, which certainly enough belong to the region of a certain "eidos," but do not express this "eidos" in its purity, resemble preformations in their general character of non-finality; they are unstable, almost mobile, and give to our experience a certain trend toward the ideal form. A picture hanging crooked on the wall can become unbearable; it fairly shrieks to be ranged along the dominant axes of the visual field, the vertical and horizontal. Here we can recognize in dynamic, emotionally tinged qualities of the experienced totality, clearly oriented forces of the psychophysical structure, which require a configuration of the perceptual field

---

[3]For the concept of "good" and "bad" patterns cf. Köhler (4).

along structurally determined lines. Non-fulfilment of these structural demands is expressed in emotional tensions: "It disturbs me, I cannot stand it." In most cases, however, expression is not limited to these internal repudiations, our experience of the dynamic nature of our consciousness affects not only the sensory field, but sets the motor system of the psychophysical totality into sympathetic activity. These diffuse, tensive, keenly adjusted motor complexes in their turn lend a decisive coloring to the whole field of consciousness. These directed tensions aim to put the motor system at the disposal of the structural tendencies, and to bring the physical conditions perforce into harmony with the structural premises, thus achieving a formulation of the perceptual experience in conformity to the structural demands. Thereby the fluidity and impurity of form are obviated; to return to our trivial example of the crooked picture, the directed dynamic principle of the total experience tends to take possession of the motor system, to put the picture straight.

These structures that incline toward the optimal forms in any given level of meaning, and which are merely organic parts of the total structure of the personality, not only determine the experiential form-properties of the perceptive field *beside* the physical influences, but strive for alterations of the physical stimuli themselves, tending to make them converge with the structural ideal of optimal configuration. This product of this transphenomenal active and real principle of psychic structure is the work which, through its formative characteristics expresses the direction of the dynamic structural principle. The dynamic system of structural interests is not only realized under certain external conditions which allow it to mould the experience, is not only in readiness, expecting outer occasions, so to speak, but strives from within, creative in its own right, strives for the formulation of the physical environment toward a realization and fulfilment of its own immanent orientation.

With respect to our isolated field of perceptual constructs without objective significance, and their ideal formulation, the creative urge can be demonstrated through many human performances. One needs but remember certain childish games of building and moulding. There we see even young children creating out of formless clay, or out of heterogeneous pieces of building material, not only forms which are supposed to represent objective things but also works of primitive but often very beautiful form (13). These form-products of the creatively fashioning child show a high degree of homogeneity and definite articulation at the same time; now they are serially rhythmized, now symmetrically membered, often surprising in the regularity of their construction. In the form-properties of these constructs, which are not supposed to copy or symbolize any natural object, but are without objective content, the aim of the constructive forces of these subordinate structures is evident again. The child's joy in his playfully productive activity, the complete absorption of the youthful soul in the work from its first conception to its completion, lets us see in the profound emotional possession of the whole process the agency of original interests of human nature. In adult persons these structural forces still come easily into play, when the fulfilment of important purposes is deferred through external circumstances and leaves room for playful activity. In the various cases when a man of this age and generation is obliged to wait, or is condemned by external influences to boredom, a pencil just naturally comes to hand and goes to work on some piece of paper. Telephone booths and committee rooms bear plentiful witness to this instinctive urge of creativeness, which ordinarily is sentenced to inactivity by the exigencies of the day's work. Ornamental scribblings of such origin, without objective meaning, and often of remarkable geometric complexity, remind one of certain entoptic phenomena, at whose regularity Goethe has marvelled, as well as of the scribblings of the insane, in which these ornamental form-tendencies often overshadow everything else. In the activity of these insane subjects, a sub-structure dominates in the pattern of the total structure of the personality, which under normal conditions is relatively unimportant.

The playful creations of childhood are early forms of the artistic activity of the adult. The childish products have their analogues in the non-representative, formal ornamentation of savages, and the architecture of civilized man. Architecture, being free from the task of representing anything, though it is partially determined by utilitarian factors, still allows the configurative tendencies which are under consideration here plenty of scope to participate in forming the work. The Gestalt properties of architectonic products let us infer the formative tendencies, the individual as well as epochal modifications of the subordinate structure which is here under consideration. The goal of Renaissance building is the complete, fully finished work, the realization, without any loose ends, of the structural interests, through the building material. The high articulateness of the architectonic products of the Renaissance, their closed and unified character, their regularity and symmetry, the harmonic balance of masses among the several members of the edifice, and in detail the dominance of distinctive forms such as the circle, square, oblong with the golden mean—all these Gestalt aspects produce the emotional effects which indicate the realization without residuum of structural formative tendencies, the resolution of their dynamic element. Hence the repose and liberating beauty of the architectural masterpieces of this epoch. Quite different it is with the baroque architecture, which does not, like the Renaissance, aim at the articulate ideal, but stands still, so to speak, before the last metamorphosis of the material, in order to immortalize in stone the dynamics of becoming, to let it be experienced. Lack of finality together with very apparent, sometimes unorganized unity, slight irregularity, and asymmetry, a distribution of masses in the total edifice which overaccentuates some details and subordinates others, a preference for geometric forms which deviate slightly from a standard figure, such as rectangles which are almost squares, ellipses which are near-circles, and so forth, are all peculiarities of shape which cause the whole product to be ruled by a pronouncedly dynamic quality. The incondite strives for perfection, the unorganized for organization, the belittled detail for recognition, the near-square for genuine squareness. Hence the tremendous motivity, restlessness, excitement in baroque architecture, with its strain, stress, and swing in the total pattern, which draws the spectator into the giddy state of Gestalt-evolution. Herein is sought not the satisfaction of the Gestalt tendencies through the remainderless articulation of the work, but the experience of the formative impulse itself, in that the structural tendencies are realized but not carried to the logical conclusion of their inclinations in the building material. In both cases the analysis of Gestalt properties must fall back upon the structural presuppositions of Gestalt experience.

The foregoing discussion was intended to determine the participation of dispositional interests of the soul which transcend the immediate present, to determine their dynamic structure, anent certain holistic properties of experienced perceptual forms and productions in a general way. Formulation in accordance with structure is not only the goal toward which the structural dynamic is directed, whose attainment is immediately expressed in consciousness by an emotive sense of conclusion and completeness, but is also a means of capacitating the soul to its highest achievements. For instance, the task of impressing something on one's memory is easy in proportion to the articulation of the material that is to be remembered. Whoever has performed memory tests with the piecemeal, senseless materials which traditional memory psychology held in highest esteem, knows what difficulties attend the memorization of such structural inconcinnities, and how at every possible point formulations of one sort or another present themselves automatically as aids in the solution of the proposed anti-structural task. Melodifying, rhythmifying, optical organization of all sorts, all these are means of bringing the senseless fragments into a relational pattern in order to facilitate the task. To these sensuous forms may be added objectively significant relations, through which the separate items, being made to stand for something, receive their meaning and are easily reproducible with the totality. But we shall not speak further of these symbolic constructions, important though they undoubtedly are. Thus in every achievement of memory there is some such structural formulation of the material that is to be retained, some organization of the learning-material and the learning-process, to make the solution possible. Structural formulation not only satisfies us directly but also leads to higher accomplishments. Wherever structurally appropriate form is violated by external conditions, the level of accomplishment sinks concomitantly. Here is an instance from the realm of motor systematization: human motions are essentially organized and sucessive, i.e., patterned. Whenever a normal human being moves freely or dances, his motions appear in unbroken continuity, rhythmic organization, and swing. Even when his motions are harnessed to definite purposes, as for instance the occupational gestures (7), which are determined through outer circumstances by the nature of tools and tasks, there still is room for symmetrical motor totalities, motor melodies to develop. As long as implements and work tempo are, or can be, adapted to the psychophysical structure of the working man, the unity and ordonnance of the occupational movements are preserved and tend to arrange themselves in characteristic labor rhythms, which find audible expression in acoustic labor noises and songs, labor songs which retroactively support and form the labor motions themselves. The pleasure attendant upon rhythmically organized labor motions, which are practiced by savages for their own sake, far beyond the demands of the work, is another indication of the fulfilment of a participating psychophysical structure complex. Quite different is the case, when the external conditions of work do not permit a structurally appropriate patterning of motions to develop. With the rhythm peculiar to the machine, the worker may have movements imposed upon him which do not swing out in appropriate articulation, but are exacted in an ever-repeating fragmentary, disconnected sequence, beginning again and again. Or the machine may cause an acoustic counter-rhythm which moves outside the limits of psychophysical designs. Here the structural interests are not only unsatisfied by the external conditions but actually violated. The result is a torturing dissatisfaction, exhaustion, and inner revolt against the foreign demands that are made again and again with racking monotony. And as for the output, it presents a considerable deficit as compared with accomplishment under structurally appropriate conditions. Many endeavors of industrial psychotechnics are concerned with the problem of adjusting the conditions of work in such a way that they shall not only oppose the structural interests, but shall develop and induce a natural unfolding of the human work impulses in conformity with the immanent laws of structure. Occupational motions of optimal formation, i.e., structurally appropriate motions, not only entail satisfaction on the part of the worker, but permit his whole body-soul complex to exhibit its highest working capacity, in quality as well as quantity. The superiority of well-constructed work movements lies chiefly in their constancy, which guarantees a high degree of precision. Constancy is possible only where the structural interests of the psychophysical totality are completely dominant.

Even more powerfully than in cases where the environmental conditions do not allow an optimally structural articulation to appear, inner dissatisfaction and revolt are produced if an experiential totality is shaken by variations of the physical element, when a structurally acceptable constellation of stimuli is experimentally varied in such a way that it leads not to a change of configuration, but to a destruction of the form as such. For instance (2), if one of the pictures in a stereoscope is turned, with the line of vision for its axis, out of the position which is best for binocular unification, i.e., out of the focus of parallelism of all homologous distances, the unified whole will not immediately divide into double images, but will be seen in single vision through several degrees of deviation. The field of integration within which a totality is experienced, that is to say, one image is seen, varies in size directly with the degree of organization of the experienced whole. The more highly integrated whole is more capable than one of low integration to preserve its unity, because it is more deeply rooted structurally; and it has more elasticity in adapting and asserting itself under external conditions which are far from optimal. Toward the limits of the integration zone, near the line of division into double images, peculiar

changes occur in the experiential manifold, which are intimately connected
with a highly characteristic coloring of the mental state, with an alteration
of the emotive sense of wholeness of the total consciousness. The totality,
which heretofore was stable, grows restless, flickering, tremulous, full of
tension and mobility. The observers report "a veritable fear of dissolution," "a mood that seems to presage disaster." And together with this
torturing fear of the violent destruction of the unity of the optical field,
the total experience is characterized by an emotional directedness, a hankering after the preservation of the optical content in its entirety, as though
the form were defending itself against its annihilation and commanding
the sincerest sympathy of the experiencing subject for the assertion of its
being. In these tense experiences the structural tendencies, aiming at the
preservation of homogeneous totalities, are again evident in emotive aspects
of the experience as a whole. As the limit of integration is passed, the
optical figure vanishes into chaos, a transition which is the more overwhelming, the more Gestalt was possessed by the previous unit. The forces
directed toward preservation of unity and optimal configuration are over-
whelmed by alteration of the external conditions. The tension between the
structural capacities and the demands of the stimulus pattern has become
unbearable, the structural tendencies can no longer prevail. Unrest, nervous excitement, fear, and despair are the emotive states of mind in which
the unfulfilment as well as the violation of structural interests, failure
to attain the goal, find expression.

The sensible configuration of the perceptual field, all the peculiarities of
Gestalt which have so far been mentioned, are subject to other unit properties. In the first place, there are contexts of meaning. Sense patterns
of perception are not exhausted by their formal properties, but are objects
of variegated significance; they belong to a concretely membered world
of facts and relations among facts. Although the peculiarities of form of
our sensible units, their distinctness and organization, are actually presuppositions of any objective organization of our perceptual field into relatively stable "things," that which we have referred to above as optimal non-
connotative formulation may yet become relatively insignificant compared
to the objective relations of meaning and factual contexts which reign as
dominant wholes over all subordinate constellations. On the other hand,
certain units of meaning occur which cut clear across the multiplicity of
"things," gather some aspects of this multiplicity together under the head
of "concepts," and leave others completely out of account. A "thing" may
now figure as an item in a coherent group of material facts, now it may
become a link in the serial pattern of an activity, for instance, as a means to
an end. "The same" thing presents itself differently, has various totality-
properties, according to whether we regard it as a member of a whole
thought process or experience it within a unit of action. Each of these organic total contexts has its peculiarities of form, different degrees of articulation, and its optimal configuration, the attainment of which fills the
thinking or acting subject with a satisfaction which is as profound as the
forms in question are important to his general orientation. Just as, despite

all non-connotational perceptual wholes and all changes of the physical environment, the articulated unity, self-sufficiency, and coherence of organization which ever asserts itself and expresses itself in feelings, points to the presupposition of psychodispositional conditioning principles, the participation of structural forces, so the logical properties of other presentational wholes, of experienced facts, organized thought sequences, processes of volitional activity point to other conditioned systems, other sub-structures of the integrated personality. Wherever in a connotative unit we meet with a member which does not conform to the unit character of the whole, appears gratuitous therein, or jeopardizes its unity, or whenever a member is missing in such a context, these facts are experienced as totalities, and the entire consciousness has the emotive coloring of something ill-attuned, contradictory, and insufficient, unfinished, and open. And wherever the dissonance is not removed, the gap not closed up, there occurs that torturing, highstrung unrest, that peculiar impatience to overcome this condition through structurally appropriate organization and completion according to the experienced orientation. The nervous strain experienced in the face of the task of formulating an intellectual context which is imperfectly presented, stands in direct functional relation with the dynamic and differentiation of the sub-structure which is being realized, which pushes the problem into the center of consciousness again and again, until it finds its structurally adequate solution. In a similar way, the incompleteness of an intended action which for external or internal reasons has not been carried out, remains constantly and emotively in the background of consciousness, as a steady reminder, and in order to break forth at the next opportunity, perchance in the stillness of a sleepless night, threatening in its unsettledness, crying to be settled. In these dynamic, often torturing qualities, which color the whole of consciousness with a characteristic tone, the once-realized structural tendencies press again and again for a satisfactory conclusion. To this tormenting inconclusiveness is opposed the deliverance of conclusion, of finality, when the whole content of an organic activity rounds and completes itself. Or when a long-sought and suspected connection suddenly flashes into mind in perfectly consistent formulation, when fragmentary items suddenly acquire meaning, or a tormenting chaos falls into visible order, then the emotive general condition of consciousness changes at one stroke. The confusions of feeling that accompanied the emergence of the Gestalt resolve themselves in a liberating sense of correctness and definitiveness, states in which the soul and its structural affairs have attained peace.

These things which have been established in a general way above, for a few levels of experience and their formation, ought to be extended over the whole realm of psychical reality, from the biological sub-structures of sexual impulsive tendencies to the sublimest value tendencies of moral and religious forms of experience and attitude. A few words now concerning the structural totality, the personality as the sum-total of sub-structures. All subordinate structures are organically incorporated in the total structure of the personality; from them, as members relative to the whole, shines forth the lawfulness of the whole—*omnibus in partibus relucet totum*. What has been demonstrated as law in one sub-structure applies respectively to any other, and to the totality that supports them all. Furthermore, as in experienced configurations the organic parts may be more or less distinct, more or less contributory to the total, more or less interconnected, so may be the parts of the transphenomenal structural totality. From the point of view of the personality, the subordinate structures (to remain on this one theme) have different degrees of importance in the total pattern of the personality, some of them bear with more intense dynamic toward actualization, determine the actual course of events more potently, than others. The specific directions of the separate sub-structures almost never chime together in an organic unity, though they are always borne within a whole, but usually in a high-strung whole, in which now the one, now the other, determines the actual process of experience, attitude and action, though always in conformity to the immanent plan of the whole. The general state of mind at any time, a sort of indicator for the subordinate structures that happen to be dominant in the total pattern, shows plainly, in the peculiar duality of contrary dynamic qualities, the opposed tensions of separate structural tendencies. Naturally, the more of the total personality is "contained" in an experience, the tenser is the experienced contradictoriness of emotional life, and the more profoundly, in the depth of such experiences, the subject will become directly aware of his "essence," of the active psychical reality within him. If the balance of structural parts, the transfinite form of the soul is temporarily or chronically disturbed by the fact that some sub-structure, say the sexual impulse, gains dominion over the rest, and asserts itself at the expense of other widely diffused structural ambitions, then the soul, the total structure, reacts to this disturbance of the pattern in an enduring fashion with a feeling of "remorse," a typical structural feeling. Or the consequences which ensue from the constant defeat of a sub-structure in process of its actualization, be it through conflicting inner aims or through external hindrances, may be typical general conditions of nervous excitement, fear and despair. And again, when the sub-structures, creatively asserting themselves in harmony with the whole, and finding their redemption, articulate the total structure step by step, there follows the volant sensation of profoundest joy, in which all experience rounds itself into a complete whole and rests in the living and active center, the soul.

REFERENCES

1. CORNELIUS, H. Psychologie als Erfahrungswissenschaft. Leipzig: Teubner, 1897.
2. JINUMA, R. Die Grenzen der binokularen Verschmelzung in ihrer Abhängigkeit von der Gestalthöhe der Doppelbilder. (Sander, F. Beiträge zur Psychologie des Stereoskopischen Sehens, I.) *Arch. f. d. ges. Psychol.*, 1928, **65**, 191-206.
3. KOFFKA, K. Psychologie. In Die Philosophie in ihren Einzelgebieten. (Ed. by M. Dessoir.) Berlin, 1925.
4. KÖHLER, W. Die physischen Gestalten in Ruhe und im stationärem Zustand. Erlangen: Weltkreisverlag, 1920.

5. KRUEGER, F. Ueber den Strukturbegriff in der Psychologie. *Ber. ü. d. Kong. f. exper. Psychol.*, 1924, **8**, 31-56.

6. ————. The essence of feelings: outline of a systematic theory. Chap. 5 in Feelings and emotions: the Wittenberg symposium. Worcester, Mass.: Clark Univ. Press, 1928. Pp. 58-86.

7. SANDER, F. Arbeitsbewegungen. In Arbeitskunde. (Ed. by H. Riedel.) Leipzig: Teubner, 1924.

8. ————. Ueber räumliche Rhythmik. *Neue Psychol. Stud.*, 1926, **1**, 123-159.

9. ————. Ueber Gestaltqualitäten. *Ber. ü d. VIII. Int. Kong. Psychol.*, Groningen, 1927.

10. ————. Experimentelle Ergebnisse der Gestaltpsychologie. Jena: Fischer, 1928.

11. ————. Ueber Vorgestalten. *Neue Psychol. Stud.*, 1930, **4**.

12. SCHNEIDER, C. Ueber die Unterschiedsempfindlichkeit verschieden gegliederter optischer Gestalten. *Neue Psychol. Stud.*, 1928, **4**, 85-157.

13. VOLKELT, H. Neue Untersuchungen über die kindliche Auffassung und Wiedergabe von Formen. *Ber. u. d. IV. Kong. Heilpäd.*, Leipzig, 1929.

14. WOHLFAHRT, E. Der Auffassungsvorgang an kleinsten Gestalten. *Neue Psychol. Stud.*, 1930, **4**.

PART VI
RUSSIAN PSYCHOLOGIES

CHAPTER 11

A BRIEF OUTLINE OF THE HIGHER NERVOUS ACTIVITY*

I. P. Pavlov

State Institute of Experimental Medicine, Leningrad

At the present moment, on the basis of thirty years of experimentation carried out by me together with my numerous co-workers, I feel fully justified in asserting that the total external as well as internal activity of a higher animal, such as a dog, can be studied with complete success from a purely physiological angle, i.e., by the physiological method and in terms of the physiology of the nervous system. The general factual material given below must serve as a proof of this assertion.

The activity of the nervous system is directed, on the one hand, towards unification, integrating the work of all the parts of the organism, and, on the other, towards connecting the organism with the surrounding milieu, towards an equilibrium between the system of the organism and the external conditions. The former part of nervous activity may be called *lower* nervous activity in contradistinction to the latter part, which, because of its complexity and delicacy, may justly take the name of *higher* nervous activity, which is usually called animal or human behavior.

The chief manifestation of higher animal behavior, i.e., its visible reaction to the outside world, is motion—a result of its skeleto-muscular activity accompanied to some extent by secretion due to the activity of glandular tissues. The skeleto-muscular movement, beginning on the lower level with the activity of separate muscles and of small groups of muscles on the upper, reaches a higher integration in the form of locomotor acts, in the equilibration of a number of separate parts, or of the whole organism in motion, with the force of gravity. Moreover, the organism, in its surrounding milieu, with all its objects and influences, performs special movements in accordance with the preservation of the organism and of its species. These constitute reactions to food, defense, sex, and other motor and, partly, secretory reactions. These special acts of motion and secretion are performed, on the one hand, with a complete synthesis of the internal activity of the organism, i.e., with a corresponding activity of internal organs for the realization of a given external motor activity; on the other hand, they are excited in a stereotyped way by definite and not numerous external and internal stimuli. We call these acts *unconditioned,* special, complex *reflexes.* Others attribute to them various names: instincts, tendencies, inclinations, etc. The stimuli of these acts we shall call correspondingly *unconditioned stimuli.*

---

*Submitted in Russian and translated into English for the Clark University Press by D. L. Zyve.

The anatomical substratum of these activities is to be found in the sub-cortical centers, the basal ganglia nearest to the cerebral hemispheres. These unconditioned, special reflexes constitute the most essential basis of the external behavior of the animal. However, alone these responses of the higher animal, without any additional activities, are not sufficient for the preservation of the individual and the species. A dog with extirpated cerebral hemispheres may manifest all these responses and yet, abandoned, it unavoidably perishes in a very short time. In order that the individual and the species be preserved, a supplementary apparatus must, of necessity, be added to the basal ganglia—the cerebral hemispheres. This apparatus makes a thorough analysis and synthesis of the external milieu, i.e., it either differentiates or combines its separate elements in order to make of them or their combinations numberless signals of basic and necessary conditions of the external milieu, towards which is directed and set the activity of subcortical ganglia. In this manner the ganglia have the opportunity to adjust, with fine precision, their activity to external conditions—finding food where it may be found, avoiding danger with certainty, etc. More-over, a further important detail to be considered is that these numberless external agents, now isolated and now combined, are not permanent but only temporary stimuli of subcortical ganglia, in accordance with the in-cessant fluctuations of the environment, i.e., only when they signal cor-rectly the fundamental and necessary conditions for the existence of the animal, which conditions serve as unconditioned stimuli of these ganglia.

The detailed analysis and synthesis produced by the hemispheres, how-ever, is not limited to the external world. The internal world of the organism with its organic transformations is also subjected to similar analy-sis and synthesis. To this analysis and synthesis are especially subjected—and to a very high degree—phenomena taking place in the skeleto-muscu-lar system, such as muscular tension of separate muscles and of their numberless groupings. And some of these most delicate elements and moments of the skeleto-muscular activity become stimuli in the same way as do those coming from external receptors, i.e., they may temporarily be-come connected with the activity of the skeleto-muscular system itself as well as with any other activity of the organism. In this manner, by means of special unconditioned reflexes, the skeleto-muscular activity realizes a multiform and subtle adaptation to continually changing environmental conditions. It is by means of such a mechanism that we realize our most minute, acquired through practice, motions such as those of our hands, for example. Here also belong movements of speech.

The cerebral hemispheres, due to their exceptional reactivity and flexi-bility, make it possible for the strong, although naturally inert, subcorti-cal centers, through a mechanism as yet not well known, to react by appropriate responses to extremely weak fluctuations of the environment.

Consequently, in the higher nervous activity of the animal, in its be-havior, three fundamental topics must be studied: (a) unconditioned com-plex special reflexes, the activity of the basal ganglia, as a foundation for the external behavior of the organism; (*b*) the activity of the cortex; (*c*) the method of connection and interaction of these ganglia and the cortex.

At the present moment, it is the second topic that is being studied by us most thoroughly and in fullest detail. For this reason, the material treated in this outline will be mostly related to it, and then we shall add our first attempts at studying the third topic.

The greater part of unconditioned special complex reflexes is more or less known (I am referring to the behavior of the dog). Among these are, first, individual reflexes such as those related to food, pugnacity, active and passive defense, freedom, investigation, and play; secondly, species reflexes such as sex and parental reflexes. But are these all? Furthermore, we know little or nothing about the methods of their direct excitation and inhibition, their relative strength and interaction. Obviously, one of the important problems of the physiology of the higher nervous activity is procuring higher animals (such as dogs) with extirpated hemispheres, but with intact basal ganglia, in good health, and having a sufficiently long span of life, to enable us to answer the above-stated problems. As for their connection with the hemispheres, all we know is that it is a fact, but we do not satisfactorily visualize its mechanism. Let us take the habitual special food reflex. It consists in a motion towards an external object, serving as food for a given animal, in its introduction into the opening of the digestive tract, and its moistening by digestive juices. What the initial stimulus of this reflex is, we do not know definitely. All that we know is that an animal (such as a dog) with extirpated cerebral hemispheres, a few hours after it has been fed, emerges from its state of drowsiness, begins to move and ramble about until it is fed again. Then it falls asleep again. Obviously, here we are in the presence of motion related to food, but entirely indefinite, not reaching any goal. Moreover, there is a secretion of saliva while the animal is in motion. Nothing definite in the external world provokes either this food motion or this secretion. It is an internal excitation.

With an animal with intact hemispheres, the matter presents itself very differently. A mass of external stimuli may definitely provoke a food reaction, and direct the animal to the food with precision. How does this take place? Obviously, a mass of natural phenomena serve as food signals, and this can be proved very easily. Let us take any natural phenomenon that has never had any relation either to food motion or to food secretion. If this phenomenon precedes the act of eating, once or several times, it will later on provoke a food reaction; it will become, so to speak, a surrogate for food—the animal moves toward it and may even take it into its mouth, if the object is tangible. Therefore, when the subcortical center of the food reflex is excited, all other stimuli reaching simultaneously the finest receptors of the hemispheres seem to be directed toward that center (whether directly or indirectly) and may become firmly connected with it. Then takes place what we have called a *conditioned reflex,* i.e., the organism responds with a definite complex activity to an external excitation to which it did not respond previously. This excitation originates, no doubt, in the hemispheres, for the fact just described no longer occurs in animals after they have been deprived of the cerebral hemispheres. What more can be said about this fact? Since such a temporary connection, under the same conditions, may be formed with every one of the special centers of the nearest subcortical ganglia, one must admit, as a general phenomenon on the higher level of the central nervous system, that every strongly excited center in some manner attracts towards itself every other weaker excitation reaching the system simultaneously. In this manner, the point of application of this excitation for a definite time under definite conditions becomes more or less firmly connected with that center (the rule of the closing of nervous paths—association). An essential detail of this process is that a certain precedence in time on the part of the weaker stimulus in regard to the stronger one is necessary for the formation of the connection. If, while a dog is being fed, a neutral stimulus is added, there is no formation of any measurable and secure conditioned food reflex.

The conditioned reflex may serve as an excellent object for the study of the nature of individual cortical cells as well as of the processes taking place in the whole cortical cellular mass, since the excitation of the cells of the cortex of the cerebral hemispheres serves as an initial stimulus for the conditioned reflex. This study made us acquainted with a considerable number of rules concerning the activity of the cerebral hemispheres.

If in conditioned food reflexes we should start consistently from a food stimulus of definite strength (18-22 hours after the usual satisfying feeding), the fact of a definite relationship between the effect of the conditioned stimulus and the physical strength of that stimulus becomes clear. The stronger the conditioned stimulus, the greater the energy simultaneously entering the hemispheres, the stronger is the effect of the conditioned reflex, other things being equal, i.e., the more energetic is the motor food reaction and the more abundant the flow of saliva, which we consistently utilize in measuring the effect. As one may judge from certain experiments, this relationship between the effect and the intensity of the stimulus must be quite definite (the rule of the relationship between the magnitude of the effect and the strength of the stimulus). There is always, however, a limit beyond which a stronger stimulus not only does not increase but tends to decrease the effect.

The summation of conditioned reflexes may be also clearly observed. Here again we reach a similar limit. In combining a number of weak conditioned stimuli, one may often observe their exact arithmetical sum. In combining a weak stimulus with a strong one, one observes a certain increase in the resulting effect, within a certain limit; whereas in combining two strong stimuli the effect, passing the limit, becomes less than that of each of the components (the rule of the summation of conditioned stimuli).

Besides the process of stimulation, the same external conditioned stimulus may elicit in cortical cells an opposite process—a process of inhibition. If a conditioned positive stimulus, i.e., producing a corresponding conditioned reaction, is continued alone for a certain length of time (minutes), without being accompanied any longer by an unconditioned stimulus, then the cortical cell corresponding to this stimulus necessarily passes into a state of inhibition. And this stimulus, as soon as it is systematically applied alone, conditions in the cortex not a process of stimulation but a process of inhibition; it becomes a conditioned inhibitive negative stimulus (the rule of transition of the cortical cells into a state of inhibition).

From this property of the cell are derived extremely important consequences for the physiological rôle of the cortex. Thanks to it, a working relationship is established between the conditioned and the corresponding unconditioned stimuli, in which the former serve as a signal for the latter. As soon as the conditioned stimulus is no longer accompanied by an unconditional stimulus, i.e., signals incorrectly, it loses its stimulating effect, although only temporarily, spontaneously reappearing sometime later. Also, in other cases when the conditioned stimulus is not accompanied by an unconditioned stimulus, either under constant definite conditions or some considerable time after the beginning of its action, such a stimulus proves to be consistently inhibitive in the former case, and in the latter case inhibitive during the first period of the action of the conditioned stimulus. In this manner, due to the developed inhibition, the conditioned stimulus as a signal conforms to the minute conditions of its physiological rôle, without producing unnecessary work. Moreover, on the basis of the developing inhibition, an important process takes place in the cortex, resulting in a very minute analysis of external excitations. At the beginning, every conditioned stimulus has but a general character. If, for example, a conditioned stimulus is made of a definite tone, several of the neighboring tones will elicit the same effect without any preliminary training. This applies to any other conditioned stimuli. However, if the original stimulus is consistently accompanied by the corresponding unconditioned stimulus, whereas the stimuli related to the original stimulus are repeated alone, then in the latter case a process of inhibition takes place. They become inhibitive stimuli.

Thus, we may reach the limit of analysis of which a given animal may be capable, i.e., most discrete natural phenomena may become special stimuli for a definite activity of the organism. We may think that by the same process by which connections are formed between cortical cells and subcortical centers connections are also formed between the cortical cells themselves. The excitations produced by phenomena taking place simultaneously in the outside world are thus complex. These complex excitations may become, under corresponding conditions, conditioned stimuli, and be differentiated by means of the just-indicated process of inhibition from other closely related complex stimuli.

The processes of excitation and inhibition, originated at definite points of the cortex under the influence of corresponding stimuli, necessarily spread through irradiation over a large or smaller area of the cortex, and then again concentrate in a limited space (the rule of irradiation and concentration of nervous processes).

Above, we have just mentioned the initial generalization of every conditioned stimulus—a result of irradiation of the excitations reaching the hemispheres. The same thing takes place, at first, in the case of inhibitory processes. When an inhibitory stimulus is applied and stopped, inhibition may be observed for some time in other and usually very distant centers of the cortex. This irradiated inhibition, as well as excitation, becomes more and more concentrated, especially under the influence of juxtaposition with an opposite process, i.e., the applied processes have a limiting effect upon each other. There is even an indication of the existence in the space between them of a neutral point.

In the case of a thoroughly worked-out inhibitory stimulus, one may notice in many dogs a strict concentration of inhibition at the point of excitation, since, simultaneously with the inhibitory stimulus, the tried-out positive stimuli produce a full, and often even a greater, effect, whereas the irradiation of inhibition begins only after the inhibitory stimulus was stopped.

Parallel with the phenomena of irradiation and concentration of excitation and inhibition occur, interwoven with these, phenomena of mutual induction of opposite processes, i.e., intensification of one process by another taking place either in succession at the same point or simultaneously at two neighboring points (the rule of mutual induction of nervous processes). The matter, probably a temporary phase, appears very complicated. When either a positive or an inhibitory stimulus (especially the latter) disturbs a given equilibrium in the cortex, there seems to pass over it something like a wave with a crest, the positive process, and with a trough, the inhibitory process, a wave that gradually flattens out, i.e., what takes place is an irradiation of processes with the necessary participation of their mutual induction.

Of course, it is not always possible to give an account of the physiological rôle of the just-described phenomena. For example, the initial irradiation of every new conditioned stimulus, may be interrupted as though every external agent which became a conditioned stimulus, in reality, under the varying conditions of the environment, were subjected to fluctuations not only with respect to its intensity but to its quality. Mutual induction must lead towards the intensification and fixation of the physiological significance of every single stimulus, whether positive or negative, which indeed has been observed in our experiments. However, the spreading of inhibition all over the hemisphere, lasting for a considerable length of time, when it is produced by a definite agent at a definite point, still remains incomprehensible. Is it due to a defect, or the inertia of the apparatus, or is it a definite phenomenon, the biological meaning of which still escapes us (which, of course, is quite possible)?

As a result of the indicated work, the cortex presents a grandiose mosaic, upon which are distributed, at a given moment, a huge number of points of application of external excitations, either stimulating or inhibiting the various activities of the organism. Since, however, these points are in a definite mutual functional relationship, the cerebral hemispheres are at the same time, every single moment, a system in a state of dynamic equilibrium, which one might call a stereotype. Fluctuations within the determined limits of this system are a relatively easy matter. But the inclusion of new stimuli, especially all at once and in large numbers, or even replacing a large number of old stimuli, represents a considerable nervous process, a task which is beyond the strength of many nervous systems, ending in the bankruptcy of the system, expressing itself in a refusal for some time to accomplish normal work. However, every living working system, as well as its separate elements, must rest and recuperate. Rest periods of such highly responsive elements as the cortical cells must be especially taken care of. In the cortex, the regulation of work and rest is realized to the highest degree. The work of every element is regulated with respect to its intensity and its duration. We have seen already how an excitation of the same cell, lasting only a few minutes, leads towards the development in it of a process of inhibition, which decreases its work and finally stops it altogether. There is another, no less striking case of preservation of the cell—the case of a strong external stimulus. For every one of our animals (dogs) there is a maximum stimulus, a limit of harmless functional strain, beyond which begins the intervention of inhibition (the rule of the limit of intensity of excitation). A stimulus, the intensity of which is beyond that maximum, instantly elicits inhibition, thus distorting the usual rule of the relationship between the magnitude of the effect and the intensity of excitation; a strong stimulus may produce an equal and even a smaller effect than a weak one (the so-called equating and paradoxical phases).

Inhibition, as already stated, has a tendency to spread, unless it meets with a counteraction in the conditions of a given environment. It expresses itself in phenomena of either partial or total sleep. Partial sleep is, obviously, what is being called hypnosis. We were enabled to study upon dogs the various degrees of extensiveness as well as of intensiveness of hypnosis, which ultimately passed into complete sleep, when stimulating influences were insufficient.

The delicate apparatus of the cerebral hemispheres was found, as one might expect, very different in various specimens of the same species (our dogs). We had good reasons to distinguish four different types of cerebral hemispheres: two extreme ones, the excitable and the inhibitable; and two central, balanced ones, the calm and the lively. In the former two, one is dominated by the process of excitation, and the other by the process of inhibition. In the latter two, the two processes are more or less balanced. Moreover, we are considering here the amount and the intensity of work which can be furnished by the cells. The cells of the excitable type are very strong and capable of developing, without too much labor, conditioned reflexes to very strong sitmuli. For the inhibitable type, this is impossible. The central types probably (this still remains to be established) are endowed with cells of moderate strength. One must think that this difference determines that an excitable type is not endowed with a correspondingly sufficient inhibitory process, whereas the inhibitable type lacks in sufficient stimulating processes. In the central types, both processes are almost equally strong.

Such is the work of the large hemispheres in a normal healthy condition. However, its work being of extreme delicacy, it may very easily pass into a morbid, pathological state, especially in cases of extreme unbalanced types. The conditions for the transition into a morbid state are sufficiently definite. Two of these are perfectly well known. These are: very strong external stimuli and the collision of the excitatory and inhibitory processes.

Strong stimuli are especially apt to become harmful agents for a weak inhibitable type, which under their influence, passes into a state of complete inhibition. The collision of opposite processes, on the other hand, results in all sorts of disorders in both the strong and weak types. The former loses altogether the ability of inhibition, whereas in the latter the excitatory process is considerably weakened.

Among the pathological phenomena an especially interesting one is that the disorder may be limited to a single, very small spot of the cerebral hemispheres, which undoubtedly proves its mosaic structure. Recently, it was possible, to a certain degree, to reproduce in the laboratory the analogue of the usual war neurosis, when the patient with corresponding cries and movements lives through terrible war scenes while falling asleep or in a state of hypnosis.

After we have become acquainted with the activity of the cortex of the cerebral hemispheres, let us turn to the subcortical centers in order to make a fuller estimate of what they receive from the cortex and in order to see of what significance they are, in turn, to the cortex.

Subcortical centers are inert to the highest degree. It is a well-known fact that a dog with extirpated hemispheres does not respond to a very large number of stimuli from the external world to which a normal animal reacts consistently and quickly. This refers to both the quality and the intensity of external stimuli. In other words, both the external and internal world are extremely limited for dogs with extirpated cerebral hemispheres. Similarly, subcortical centers are deprived of their reactive and movable inhibitions. Whereas, during the activity of the hemispheres, inhibition arises frequently and quickly, the subcortical centers, being very strong and resistant, are very little inclined towards it. Here are a few examples. The investigation reflex to stimuli, of either weak or medium intensity, in the case of a normal dog disappears through inhibition after three to five repetitions, and sometimes sooner. With dogs with extirpated hemispheres, there is no end to it when sufficiently strong stimuli are repeated. In the case of a hungry dog, the conditioned food reflex, originating in the hemispheres, is usually extinguished in a few minutes, even to the extent of refusing food; with an equally hungry dog, the unconditioned food reflex (eating after the dog has had its oesophagus isolated from the stomach, i.e., when food does not reach the stomach) continues from three to five hours and stops because of the probable exhaustion of the masticating and swallowing muscles. The same applies to the reflex to freedom, i.e., to the fighting reaction when the movements of the animals are hampered. Whereas a normal dog can easily and almost consistently inhibit such a reflex, with a dog with extirpated hemispheres such inhibition cannot be achieved. The latter, while taken out from its cage for feeding, manifested daily for months and even years a furious aggressive reaction.

Cerebral hemispheres, in some manner, overcome the described inertia of the subcortical centers with respect both to excitation and inhibition, since in a large number of cases the hemispheres must stimulate the organism to activity or to stop one or another of its activities through the intermediary of subcortical centers. In what manner do weak external and internal stimuli, insufficient for the direct excitation of these centers, excite them through the intermediary of the hemispheres? To this, physiology gives no definite answer. Perhaps a summation of a new excitation with the traces of an old one takes place in the cerebral hemispheres, an accumulation of excitations; perhaps a certain rôle is also played by the usual irradiation of the excitation over the cortical tissue, etc. No clearer is the rapid inhibition of the subcortical centers by the hemispheres when the latter are weakly stimulated. Of course, the simplest case is when the hemispheres gradually accumulate inhibitions, which become strong enough to overcome the direct strong excitation of the subcortical centers. Indeed, we saw in our experiments more than once that long applied and intensive inhibition in the hemispheres may strongly hold back the effect of the unconditioned stimulus. Thus, food which is already in the mouth may not provoke salivation for a long while; thus, also, was it frequently observed that chronic excitation of the cortex, following an operation, totally inhibits the activity of the subcortical centers for a considerable period of time: the animals become entirely blind and deaf, whereas animals totally deprived of the hemispheres react, although in a limited way, to a strong luminous stimulus and especially distinctly to a sound stimulus. One may also easily imagine that the cerebral hemispheres excited to a certain tonus throughout its whole mass, under the influence of a number of excitations reaching them, exert an inhibiting action upon the subcortical centers, according to the rule of negative induction, and thus lighten for themselves every special additional inhibition of these centers. In this manner, the cerebral hemispheres not only analyze and synthesize very subtly the external and the internal world of the animal, for the benefit, so to speak, of the subcortical centers, but continually correct their inertia. Only then does the activity of the subcortical centers, so important for the organism, find itself in the right relationship to the environment of the animal.

However, the reciprocal influence of subcortical centers upon the hemispheres is no less essential. The active state of the hemispheres is being continually maintained by excitations coming from subcortical centers. This point is now being thoroughly studied in laboratories under my direction, and especial significance ought to be attributed to experiments, which are being carried out by Dr. V. V. Rikman, which I shall now describe in detail.

If we start from the habitual sufficient feeding of the dog, during which the rule of the relationship between the magnitude of the effect and the intensity of excitation manifests itself, and if we increase the animal's excitability to food, either by decreasing the daily ration or by lengthening the interval between the last feeding and the beginning of the experiment, or merely by making the food more tasty, we shall surely observe very interesting modifications in the magnitude of the conditioned reflexes. The rule of the relationship of the magnitude of the effect and the intensity of excitation becomes abruptly changed; now both strong and weak stimuli are comparable in their effects, or, which happens even more often, strong stimuli produce a smaller effect than the weak ones (the equating and paradoxical phases), the strong stimuli decreasing and the weak ones increasing their effects (equating and paradoxical phases on a high level). Excitable dogs with strong cortical cells show an increase in their response to strong stimuli under indicated conditions, but the increase of the response to weak stimuli is considerably greater so that, eventually, we reach both the equating (more often) and paradoxical phases.

Let us now take a reverse case. Let us decrease the excitability to food. In general, the result appears to be the same, i.e., the same equating and paradoxical phases; the effect of strong stimuli again becomes equal to that of the weak ones or even becomes smaller. There appears, however, an essential difference. This time, the effect of weak stimuli either remains unchanged or decreases towards the end of the experiment after the application of strong stimuli (equating and paradoxical phases on the low level). The results reached are such that the dog under strong stimulation refuses to take food, and takes it only under a weak stimulus. Moreover, with excitable dogs, a state of restlessness may be observed; the dog whines, moves to and fro in the stand. This state, on the whole, resembles the approach of an hypnotic state (a struggle between excitation and inhibition).

How are we to understand the described facts? Since in both cases inhibition gets hold of the strong stimuli and since the aroused inhibition irradiates and may for the second time influence weak stimuli—which could be observed in the experiments, especially with a lowered excitability to food—it was decided to carry out the same experiments with the exclusion of strong stimuli. A strict rule was thus manifested: the effect of weak stimuli runs parallel with the increase or decrease of the excitability to food, i.e., increases with the increase of that excitability and drops with its decrease. In this manner, the whole phenomenon was simply explained as the spreading of that excitability from the subcortical mass to the cortex.

But what happens when we use strong stimuli? Let us begin with the first case. When the excitability to food is increased, the effect of strong stimuli is either slightly increased, as compared with the increase in the effect produced by the weak stimuli, or, which happens more often, is decreased, while this decrease becomes very abrupt through repeated application of these stimuli during the experiment. It becomes quite clear that with the increase of the excitability of the cortical cells—which is indicated by the increase of the effect due to weak stimuli—the formerly strong stimuli become maximal, if they were not already such, whereas the formerly maximal stimuli become super-maximal. An inhibition develops then against the latter, which become dangerous in the sense of a functional overstrain of the cell, according to the rule of the limit of the intensity of excitation. This is exactly similar to what happens in ordinary experiments when excessively strong stimuli do not give a greater but a smaller effect in comparison with strong stimuli, which are below the limit of intensity. What in the latter case becomes an absolute intensity of the stimuli, takes place in the former case at the expense of an increase of instability (lability) of the cell. That all this is interpreted correctly may be proved also by the fact that, with a further increase of excitability to food, the formerly weak stimuli reach a limit, become super-maximal, and then provoke an inhibition.

Yet how are we to understand the case of inhibition of strong stimuli when the excitability to food is lowered? Where from and why does inhibition now arise? Obviously, we are dealing here with a more complicated fact. Yet, it seems to me, it can be satisfactorily understood if we connect it with the following well-known facts.

However variegated is life, in general, yet every one of us, as well as the animal, must have a large number of stimuli which are always the same, i.e., those which fall always upon the same elements of the cortex. These elements then, sooner or later, must reach a state of inhibition, overtaking the mass of the hemispheres and leading to a state of hypnosis and sleep. We see this constantly in our own life as well as in our experiments with dogs, especially when they are isolated from a variety of stimuli. For this reason, we often have to struggle with a handicap coming from a developing hypnosis. The chief counteraction to this hypnotization comes, of course, from unconditioned stimuli applied by us in our experiments, mostly from periodical partial feeding. Therefore, by decreasing the excitability to food, we give the upper hand to hypnotizing excitations and should obtain a state of hypnosis, which actually takes place, as was shown above.

This is not all. We must still explain why, during the hypnosis, the strong stimuli are among the first to be subjected to inhibition, and why the equating and paradoxical phases take place. In this case, we may take advantage of the following observations, in which the mechanism of the phenomena is more or less clear. In our experiments, we became acquainted long ago with the fact that at the beginning of hypnosis there is a divergence between the secretory and the motor components of the food reflex. Under the artificial conditioned stimulus as well as under a natural excitation (seeing and smelling food), the saliva runs freely, yet the dog does not touch the food, i.e., the inhibition developing in the hemispheres somehow gets hold first of all of the motor area. Why? We thought, because this part of the hemispheres worked most during the experiments, since the dog had to maintain a state of complete wakefulness. This supposition received earnest support from further observations. At the very first sign of hypnotization, the dog under a conditioned stimulus turns in the direction of the food. When the food container is offered, the dog follows it by movements of its head when the container is raised or lowered or moved from side to side, but it cannot take any food and merely opens the mouth a little, whereas the tongue very often hangs motionless from the mouth as though it were paralyzed. And only after continued excitation through the offered food do the movements of the mouth become broader, and eventually the animal takes some food into its mouth, but even then the chewing act is interrupted by comical halts of a few seconds, until finally begins an energetic, greedy act of eating. (Dr. M. C. Petrova).

When hypnotization is further developed, the animal merely follows the food by moving its head, but does not even open its mouth. A little later, it merely turns with its whole body in the direction of the food, and finally there is no other motor reaction whatsoever.

There is an obvious sequence in the inhibition of various parts of the motor area of the cortex, according to their work in these experiments. During the experiment with food reflexes, most work is being done by the masticating muscles and the tongue, then by the muscles of the neck, and finally by the body. It is in this order that they are overtaken by the inhibitory process. Therefore, the part that worked most is first subjected to the effect of the spreading inhibition. There is a complete coincidence in that the exhaustion in a cortical cell consistently leads to the appearance in it of an inhibitory process. Thus, inhibition, irradiating from cells continually excited by the conditions of the experiment, is summated with the inhibitions proper of the working cell, and here it reaches its maximal intensity.

Such an interpretation of phenomena may be rightfully carried over to the case, analyzed by us, of the decrease in the excitability to food. The hypnotizing effect of the environment, which acquires a greater weight when the excitability to food is lowered, naturally is felt first in the cells of the conditioned excitors, which worked most energetically under the influence of stronger stimuli.

Therefore, subcortical centers, in a greater or less measure, determine the active state of the hemispheres and so change, in a multiform manner, the relation of the organism to the external world.

There are also some of our experiments (the most recent one being somewhat artificial in form, it is true) which corroborate the important significance of subcortical centers in the activity of the cortex.

Given below are Dr. D. I. Soloveychik's experiments on the influence of the ligation of the seminal duct and the grafting of a small piece of a seminal gland from a young animal (this was done simultaneously) upon conditioned-reflex behavior.

The experiments were first performed upon a dog known for a long time (five to six years) to have a very weak cortical tissue. After the collision of the excitatory with the inhibitory process, the dog showed symptoms of neurosis, which lasted five weeks. At first, all the conditioned reflexes disappeared; then they gradually reappeared, but showed a distorted relationship between the intensity of excitation and the corresponding effect; and only gradually, through a series of phases, was the normal activity of the cortex re-established. Later on, the conditioned-reflex behavior of this dog became considerably weaker. The effects of the conditioned stimuli became smaller and smaller. It became necessary to increase by various methods the excitability to food. The formerly strongest stimulus now took the last rank from the point of view of its effectiveness. All stimuli sharply declined in effect after a single repetition. A change in the habitual order of conditioned stimuli was followed by the disappearance of all conditioned reflexes for several days.

Two or three weeks after the operation, the situation was radically changed. All the reflexes increased considerably in magnitude. The normal relationship between the intensity of the stimulus and that of the response was re-established. Through repetition, the reflex no longer decreased, nor did a change in the order of stimuli have any negative effect. Even a collision of the excitatory and the inhibitory processes, repeated more than once, remained now without the slightest effect upon the activity of the cortex.

This condition of the dog lasted for two or three months, and then it rapidly returned to the state in which it was before the operation. A similar operation performed upon the second seminal gland of the same dog was accompanied by a similar result. The same phenomena occurred also with another dog.

Thus, the processes which took place in the seminal gland, both nervous and chemical, manifested themselves very vividly in the activity of the cortex. However, to such questions as: in what manner? directly or by the intermediary of subcortical centers? by a nervous path or a chemical method, or by a method of summation?—no precise answer can be given until further analysis. Of course, similar questions, relating to the effect upon the cortex of the excitability to food, are as legitimate. However, taking into consideration the effect of both external and internal unconditioned stimuli of subcortical centers, obviously directed towards them, and judging from the considerable duration of their action (which would be impossible for cortical cells) and also turning our attention to the extraordinary intensity of the activity of these centers after the control over them by the hemispheres had been lowered, or eliminated, we may consider that very probably the above-described modifications in the activity of the cortex are secondary, for the greater part, at least, and not primary, i.e., they take place under the influence of modifications in the excitability of the subcortical centers.

Finally, I shall also describe Dr. G. P. Conradi's experiments, which are related to the same question. By the use of three tones of the same musical instrument, three conditioned reflexes were formed in a dog reacting to three unconditioned stimuli: to acid with the low tone, to food with the medium tone, and to a strong electric current, applied to the skin of the shin, with the high tone. When these were fully established, the following interesting phenomena could be observed. First, with the low and medium tones a defensive reaction could be observed at the beginning of their action, and only after continuation of the excitation did it change into either the acid or the food reflex. Secondly, intermediate tones, which were also tried, were found to be related mostly to a defensive reaction. The regions of generalized "acid" and "food" tones were very limited. The whole diapason of tones, both beyond the limits of our extreme tones and in the interval between the low and medium tones, provoked a defensive reaction. Since the relative physical strength of conditionally acting tones could not determine such differences between them, these must be attributed to differences of intensity in the excitation of the subcortical centers.

In conclusion, it may be said that our experiments, as related above, are, of course, only the first tentative experimental approach of one of the most important physiological questions of the interaction of the cortex and the nearest subcortical centers.

CHAPTER 12

BEKHTEREV'S REFLEXOLOGICAL SCHOOL

Alexander L. Schniermann

*Bekhterev's Reflexological State Institute for Brain Researches,
Leningrad*

I. Introduction

At the very outset of my task—the exposition of Bekhterev's teaching
and of the works of his school—I am confronted with many difficulties.
The first of these is due to the fact that this teaching is the result of about
fifty years of work of a scientist of exceptional fecundity and wide conception. Bekhterev has written not less than six hundred scientific works in
the fields of anatomy and physiology of the nervous system, psychology,
pedology, pedagogy, psychotechnics, defectology, neuropathology, psychopathology, and clinical neuropsychiatry. Furthermore you will see that
Bekhterev's reflexology was an attempt to generalize his colossal experience. Its significance lies not only in its being a new method of research
but also in its presenting a very broad synthesis of all Bekhterev's knowledge of human personality and of its correlation with nature and society,
Bekhterev's reflexology being almost a world-conception.

The other difficulty in expounding Bekhterev's teaching is caused by its
extremely dynamic nature. Like all great scientists, Bekhterev could
never stop at a once accepted principle; he was always aspiring to new
ways, always moving forward. From the old speculative psychology to
experimental psychology, from experimental psychology to objective psychology, and from the latter to reflexology—such was his way. Yet even
reflexology could not remain at a standstill, permanently standardized,
being subjected to an evolutionary process both during Bekhterev's life
and after his death.

These facts induce me to pay special attention to the history of reflexology and to the perspectives of its further development. Bearing this in
mind, I begin my paper with a brief historical review of the development
of reflexology. This being done, I shall pass on to the exposition of the
fundamental features of Bekhterev's teaching and of the present state of
reflexology. I shall conclude this article by giving an account of the
relation existing between reflexology and other tendencies of behavior
teaching.

II. Brief History of Reflexology

V. M. Bekhterev began his scientific work in the last quarter of the past
century when all the work in the field of psychoneurology, which is divided
nowadays into a series of separate branches, was confined to the clinics of

mental and nervous diseases.[1] It is interesting to note that Bekhterev's early works dealt mostly with the problems of the anatomy and physiology of the nervous system. Being Flexig's pupil, he published a great number of works concerning the structure and conduction paths of the brain, etc. As a result of these researches there appeared in 1888, the first edition of *Conduction Paths of the Brain and Spinal Cord* (4). This book passed through many editions, was extended to two volumes, and became a manual for neuropathologists and psychiatrists. Bekhterev centered his investigations on the study of the structure of the brain and of its functions. In 1883, in a work of his, Bekhterev revealed for the first time the functions of the thalamus opticus (2). Later on, there followed a series of other researches, among which, of first interest, was a work concerning the physiology of the cerebral cortex motor sphere (3). This work proved that an extirpation of the cerebral cortex in dogs causes the disappearance of trained movements (giving of paw), whereas the innate movements remain intact. From Bekhterev's numerous physiological investigations, which I am unable to cite here, there resulted a voluminous book in seven parts, *Bases of the Teaching Concerning the Functions of the Brain* (8).

All these strictly objective investigations formed the basis upon which Bekhterev tried to build up his clinical work. Moreover, he searched for these objective methods even in the actual clinical work itself, which work at those times was performed mostly by means of subjective methods.

Space does not allow me to discuss here the important rôle that Bekhterev played in the history of psychoneurology in Russia. I shall mention only some aspects of his activity which I consider as very important for the development of reflexology.

Beginning with 1897 a series of works appeared in which were stated, for the first time, the objective indexes of neuroses, hysteria (6, 7), hypnotic states, suggestion in hypnosis, etc. (31). This objective tendency could not but have its influence upon Bekhterev's psychological conception. Indeed, we find in him one of the pioneers of experimental psychology in Russia. Yet, later, Bekhterev outgrew even experimental psychology, which he thought was not objective enough. His inclination to submit psychical processes to an objective account made it quite indispensable to discover the materialistic bases of these processes. This obliged Bekhterev to oppose the then prevailing idealism in psychology and philosophy. However, the old naïve mechanical materialism could not, of course, meet his claims, and therefore he opposed both tendencies by his energy principle. In 1896 he expounded, for the first time, his teaching concerning the provoking of nervous conductivity by the detention of nervous energy and concerning the receptor organs, which he declares are transformers of the outer energies (8). This standpoint concerning energy reached its full development in his classical work, *Psychic Activity and Life* (10). The psychical processes are viewed here as the result of an accumulation of the nervous-current energy in the cerebral cortex.

---

[1]The division of the two clinics took place at the St. Petersburg Military Medical Academy after the beginning of the twentieth century.

In 1904 Bekhterev already had in mind the plan of an *Objective Psychology* (9) which was to be substituted for the old subjective one, the subject of this new science consisting of all the objective correlations existing between personality and the inorganic, the organic, as well as the social environment. Later on, this sum of correlations was characterized by Bekhterev's term, *correlated activity*. Yet the organization of this new science required not only fundamental statements but also new methods of investigation. As seen above, Bekhterev searched for these objective methods both in his experimental and clinical work. Certainly in studying the already formed reactions, he could make use of the methods of experimental psychology, adopting the objective results and excluding all subjective interpretation. But it was also necessary to find a method of studying human reactions in the very process of their formation (*in statu nascendi*).

In 1905 Boldyrev's report appeared (from Pavlov's physiological school) on the method of training the "conditioned" ("psychical") salivary reflexes in dogs (35). Yet this method, necessitating operation, was unadaptable to individuals.[2] There are numerous other reasons, of which I will speak later, why this method could not satisfy Bekhterev. In 1907 Bekhterev reported his experiments performed in collaboration with Spirtov, which experiments aimed at forming in dogs an "artificially associated respiratory motor reflex" (11). Somewhat later Anfimov formed the same reflex in persons (13).

In 1908 Protopopov worked out in dogs the artificially associated motor reflex on the basis of the defensive paw movement provoked by electrical stimulation of the skin (49), and in 1910 Molotkov obtained, by means of the same method, in individuals the associated motor reflex of the sole (41). This method appeared to Bekhterev more advantageous than Pavlov's method of the salivary conditioned reflex. Besides the impossibility of extending Pavlov's method to people,[3] it also could not answer the purpose of a diverse study of human correlated activity, as it dealt only with those functions which were not submitted to the so-called "active effectiveness" of the personality. It must be realized that Bekhterev was interested in the study not only of purely physiological laws but also of all reactions forming human correlated activity. From that standpoint the motor sphere promised richer material than the sphere of secretion. Thus the method of associated motor reflexes became one of the fundamental methods of investigation in Bekhterev's school, whereas the method of conditioned secretory reflexes remains the principal method of Pavlov's. The term *associated reflex* was adopted by Bekhterev's school instead of Pavlov's *conditioned reflex* as determining in a more precise way those conditions under which this reflex is formed (the association of two stimulations).

---

[2]Krasnogorski tried to study the conditioned food reflex in children by recording the movements of the epiglottis (1907), but the recording of the salivation did not then prove feasible.

[3]Only after the invention of Lashley's funnel did experiments on people prove possible. And they were performed for the first time by Watson in the United States and some years later in Russia by Krasnogorski and Yushchenko.

The subject and method of objective psychology (17) being determined, Bekhterev initiated its organization and from 1907-10 published two large volumes of his new teaching (12). As an objective biosocial teaching of correlated activity, *Objective Psychology* already contained the chief features of reflexology. The term *reflexology* appeared for the first time in 1912 (22).

Bekhterev's objective biosociological principle expounded in *Objective Psychology* left its mark upon all the work of his school at this period. Then also those researches were commenced which brought in the genetic method, this method becoming later one of the most characteristic and indefeasible parts of Bekhterev's reflexology. I mention here the first observations on the development of the neuropsychic activity of infants, performed at the Pedological Institute founded by Bekhterev in St. Petersburg (16-19). With these observations, a systematic study of the ontogenesis of correlated activity began. At the same time Bekhterev manifested a great interest in the phylogenesis of behavior. In this way that side of Bekhterev's teaching developed which later was transformed into *Genetic Reflexology* (32).

On the other hand, a great many sociological problems confronted Bekhterev, and we see him performing a series of investigations in the fields of social education (20), social psychology (21), etc. These investigations formed the basis of the future *Collective Reflexology* (25).

This objective biosociological tendency could not but have its influence upon Bekhterev's clinical work. In 1910 he introduced his method of the associated motor reflex into clinical psychiatry (18). Furthermore, in 1912 he put the problems of psychiatry, in the field of the prophylaxis of mental diseases, into direct connection with social problems (23). During the last fifteen or twenty years of his life, Bekhterev worked on the creation of *Pathological Reflexology* (26), which, unfortunately, remained unfinished.

In 1918 the first edition of *General Bases of Human Reflexology* (24) appeared—the result of many years of Bekhterev's work and also the plan of work for more than one generation. We find here a definitive presentation of the conception of human personality as a product of the biological and social environment and we also see that quite a distinct line is drawn between psychology, of all tendencies and schools,[4] and reflexology, the only strictly objective scientific discipline which studies human personality in its outer manifestations in objective correlations with its environment.

During Bekhterev's life, *General Bases of Human Reflexology* passed through three editions, each new edition increasing in size and experimental material, which proves the extent of the work of Bekhterev's school. The accumulated empirical material found its precise place in the system of reflexology, at the same time developing, altering, and improving the system itself.

---

[4]Including even those psychologists calling themselves "objectivists," who utilize objective methods but who deal with "consciousness" and other subjective phenomena.

During the last years of his life, Bekhterev revised, many times, his teaching in connection with other scientific tendencies, explaining and defining these correlations. In a short brochure, *Psychology, Reflexology, and Marxism* (27) published in 1925, Bekhterev revealed very successfully the crisis of present-day psychology and its insolvency in dealing with behavior problems. And here also he elucidated and defined the philosophic premises of his teaching, especially his energy standpoint expounded in 1904. Even then, at the basis of all nervous phenomena as well as of all world-phenomena, Bekhterev put the process of a constant transformation of energy; confirming it later, he stated the materialistic character of the process (in the philosophic but not the physical sense of the word). He considered it expedient to strengthen the ties between reflexology and dialectic materialism; it seems that, in the latter, Bekhterev found a satisfactory world-conception, which afforded him a solid materialistic basis, without the necessity to adopt the simplified schematization of the mechanists. Bekhterev believed reflexology to be in no contradiction with dialectic materialism; furthermore, he thought that only reflexology as a strictly objective teaching of human personality, under the standpoint of psychophysical monism, can answer to the claims of the dialectic method. The union of Marxism with reflexology (not with social psychology) promises to reveal the laws of social phenomena, in the sense of the genetic development of the new powers of production, of the new forms of labor and industrial relations, etc. Bekhterev, perceiving the sociological side of reflexology, also acknowledged its biological significance, due to the phylogenesis of human personality; and in connection with dialectic materialism, he understood reflexology as a biosociological discipline, of quite an independent significance. "Reflexology," said Bekhterev, "stands with one foot on biology and with the other on sociology, and must therefore be an independent scientific discipline, establishing the ties between biological and sociological knowledge, but not to be confounded with either of them."

III. PRINCIPAL STATEMENTS OF BEKHTEREV'S TEACHING

General Bases of Human Reflexology is a book of a somewhat unfamiliar structure. On one hand, it offers rather rich empiric material gathered together during several decades of work; on the other hand, much attention is paid here to theoretical statements, to the elucidation of the subjects and methods of the teaching, and to the setting forth of its biological principles, etc. As you will see below, the empiric material is also presented in a most unusual form. In fact, a reader inexperienced in reflexological history might receive the impression of heavy accumulation and of disproportion. Sometimes it is even difficult to decide whether the theoretical part proves to be too voluminous or whether there is too much empiric material which should form only the basis of the theoretical part of the new discipline.

Nevertheless, I hope that if you know the history of reflexology the unfamiliarity of this form will not perplex you. You see here the development of a new teaching which is, as yet, not quite accomplished. This teaching was founded on rich empiric material, though partly acquired by means of old methods. In this book the author aspires to formulate the methodological settlement of the new discipline and, at the same time, to place it into its relationship with all the rich empiric data, correlating the whole with the facts of physics, chemistry, and biology. If you will take into consideration the colossal erudition of the author, which could not, of course, but have its influence on his arguments, I suppose, this book will not give the impression either of heavy accumulation or of disproportion.

The size and the concentration of the contents of *General Bases of Reflexology* compel me to give up the attempt of presenting it in a more or less exhaustive way. I shall reduce my task to a general elucidation of the biological premises of reflexology, to the determination of the contents of correlated activity, to the formulation of the problems and methods of reflexology, and also to the shortest possible summary of the empiric material.

A

In order to penetrate into the meaning of Bekhterev's teaching, it is necessary, first of all, to realize that this teaching is based upon a strictly objective biological scientific conception.

"Put yourself," says Bekhterev, "in the place of a creature from another world, of another nature, which came, for example, from another planet. This creature arrived on the earth and is supposed to meet with people; it begins to study these beings, which produce incomprehensible sounds. Now I should ask you: what must be the method this creature has to use when observing human life in all its complicated manifestations? This creature of another planet, of a different nature, ignoring human language, has it to use the method of a subjective analysis when studying the various forms of human activity and of the stimuli which provoke it, attributing therewith to persons unnatural emotions, emotions of another planet, or has it to study human life and its various manifestations in a strictly objective way, trying to reveal the diverse correlations existing between persons and the environing world, as we do ourselves when studying the life of microbes and other protozoa?

"I think there can be no hesitation in the answer. It is quite evident that a creature of a superior nature can study all manifestations of human personality only from a strictly objective standpoint, never applying a subjective analysis of the supposed inner emotions and never presenting any interpretations by analogy with himself, as, of course, such an analogy cannot exist.

"This is the way we must study the various activity of persons, i.e., their actions, speech, mimicry, gestures, and the so-called instinctive or (to be more exact) the hereditary organic manifestations. Our standpoint must be a strictly objective one, and, being connected with the outward and inward influences, free from any subjective analysis and analogy with ourselves. At the same time we must, of course, follow the line of the naturalistic scientific study of the object in its social environment, elucidating the correlations existing between actions of behavior as well as other manifestations of human individuals and the outer stimuli which provoke them; this we must do as for the present so for the past, in order to find the laws to which these manifestations are submitted and to determine the correlations arising between persons and the physical, biological, and, especially, the social environment."

As a biological scientific teaching, reflexology aspires to discover the genesis of the fundamental properties of human correlated activity, issuing from the general properties of living matter. Hence a series of chapters of *General Bases of Reflexology* are allotted to the teaching of the origin and evolution of correlated activity in the phylogenetic scale.

The principal property of living matter is its capacity for reproductive activity. Under the latter, Bekhterev understands the capacity of living matter to reproduce those changes which occur in it under the influence of outer conditions, these reproductions being made possible by the presence of even a slight stimulus of the same nature. It seems as if, under the influence of reflexes, there occur some fine modifications within the minute structure of living matter, as if there appear some traced paths—paths of the least resistance. Thus the experience of the past does not remain traceless. The reflex is a creative factor of individuality. The capacity of reproductive activity lies in the very nature of living matter and may be observed even in organisms which have no nervous system. With the appearance of the latter, only the improvement of the correlations of the organism with the environment takes place, and at the same time it becomes possible to perform coordinated reactions in diverse parts of the body in response to outer stimuli. The uniqueness of the body reactions is a direct consequence of the reproductive activity of the living organism; every reaction alters the physiological state of the organism, and therefore the following reaction in answer to the same stimulus can be altered. Every reaction is the resultant of two factors, one being the specific stimulus of the environment, and the other, the inner conditions which consist of the sum of the characteristics of the given individual; these characteristics are due not only to hereditary laws but also to the whole of the precedent experience. Thus the individual experience appears as a factor of the individual evolution.

Yet, what are the principal actions of the individuals subjected to evolution in the process of phylogenesis? Such are the actions of attack and defense.[5] We observe these actions of defense and attack even in protozoa in the form of extension or contraction of their cellular surface. With plants these acts are manifested mostly in their morphogenesis and in some cases in direct motor reactions of attack (*Drosera rotundifolia*) or defense (*Mimosa pudica*).

In animals we see the development of special differentiated organs of

---

[5]All kinds of reflexive actions which are connected not only with self-preservation but also with nutrition, reproduction, etc., are attributed to these principal groups of defense and attack.

attack and defense and also the formation of a complicated coordination of motor actions which answer to the same purpose. We meet here not only the direct attack and defense reflexes but also the orientation reflexes, consisting of the adaptation of the highly differentiated receptor organs to the stimulus. The chief rôle is played here by the nervous system with its coordinated activity. We see, on a par with the excitement of one group of the body-apparatus, the inhibition of others. Thus a possibility is given for the development of such complicated coordinated actions as the concentration reflex or alertness reflex, i.e., the maximal preparation of the organism for attack or defense (with an outward display of inhibition).

As you see, the complication and improvement of the defensive and aggressive actions depend closely upon the amount of experience of the individual or species. In so far as both of these depend, to a large extent, upon the environment, the process of evolution of correlated activity in the phylogenetic scale is directly connected with the changes of the conditions under which occurs the evolution of the vegetative and animal world. For example, the fixation of plants to one place limits the extent of their experience and hence the possibilities for the development of their correlated activity, whereas animals, which are more or less unlimited in their movements, possess greater possibilities. The conditions for the development of the correlated activity of animals living in the ground (worms) or even in water (fish) are less advantageous than those of animals living above the ground, etc. Thus the modification of the environing conditions plays an important rôle in the development of the correlated activity. Of quite as great an importance are the differentiating organs of movements when facilitating the use of the changing conditions of the environment to the profit of the organism. Finally, the development of correlated human activity is due to the milieu of mutual effectiveness of individuals—the social environment (the "superorganic world").

These are the principal statements of the biogenesis of correlated human activity presented in an extremely short and general exposition.

B

In the process of phylogenesis, correlated activity is subjected to evolution and complication. At every given state of evolution it consists, on one hand, of the sum of innate (inherited) reflexes and, on the other, of reflexes which were trained during the process of individual experience. To the former should be attributed those reflexes which, being the acquisition of the species, are revealed in a ready form, without precedent individual experience either from the very moment of birth or somewhat later. They are divided into exogenous reflexes (stimulated by exterior stimuli) and endogenous reflexes (stimulated by interior or organic stimuli.) Exogenous as well as endogenous (inherited) reflexes lie at the base of the superior or correlated (acquired) reflexes, the accompanying stimuli acquiring the properties of the fundamental reflexogenous stimuli. For instance, on the basis of the simple (innate) defensive reflex provoked by a burn or prick on the hand, there arises an associated reflex of a defensive character at the sight of every hot object or sharp instrument. Among the associated (acquired) reflexes a special group of reflexes appears, reflexes which were trained under natural conditions. They are very constant and homogeneous and remind us by these characteristics of the simple (inherited) reflexes. They disappear only under the condition of frequent reproduction, if they are not reinforced by the fundamental reflexogenous stimulus, revealing, in that way, their associative origin. These reflexes are called "natural associated reflexes" (for example, blinking in response to menacing hand movements). Another special group is formed by complicated organic reflexes (known in literature as "instincts"). There lies at the basis of these reflexes an inherited biological tendency, guaranteeing the life of the individual and species (reflexes of nutrition, reproduction, social reflexes, etc.). Yet one may suppose that the manifestation of these reflexes in many cases (especially in the superior stages of development) takes place under the guidance of the precedent individual experience. In other words, the instinctive actions are due not only to the innate but partly also to the acquired reflexes.

As to the morphological substratum of different reflexive actions, Bekhterev believes that the inherited reflexes are effected by means of the spinal cord and of subcortical nodes, whereas the associated reflexes are formed by means of the cerebral cortex with a probable participation of the subcortical nodes. The complicated organic reflexes are manifested by means of the subcortical nodes and partly by means of the cerebral cortex, as with associated reflexes. They differ from other reflexes in that they have as fundamental stimuli those stimulations which arise from the interior organs and tissues and are transferred to the cerebral cortex partly through the vegetative nervous system and partly through the blood directly.

The nature of the nervous process which forms the basis of all reflexive actions is deduced by Bekhterev from the general cosmic process of energy-transformation. The energy of the outer stimuli, when affecting our receptor organs (mechanical, termal, chemical energies), is transformed by these organs into molecular energy of the colloidal formation of the nervous tissue—the so-called nervous current. The latter, being transferred by means of centripetal fibers to the centers, can be directly transferred to the centrifugal fibers, which conduct the current to the periphery—to muscles and glands. Here takes place the transformation of this energy into the molecular energy of muscles and glands, which again passes over to mechanical, thermal, and chemical energies. In some other cases the nervous energy can accumulate in the centers, though remaining in its nature the same nervous current. Yet the responding part of the reflex arc will remain inhibited. Such an accumulation of nervous energy in the centers of the cerebral cortex is accompanied by subjective emotions. Later on, the motor part of the reflex is released, the accumulated energy discharges, and we say that perception (or thought) has passed over to action.

As seen above, the scheme of reflex accounts for all the phenomena of behavior, not excepting even the so-called "psychical" processes. The associated reflexes which lie at the basis of the latter can be of different characters: for instance, in "perception" the orientative reflexes of the receptor organs are of great importance; in those cases when we think by the agèncy of words, we deal with inhibited speech reflexes.

Owing to limited space, I cannot give a detailed analysis of the different complicated "psychical" processes, the associated-reflex nature of which Bekhterev establishes in the last chapter of his book. Yet from the examples already cited we can conclude that from Bekhterev's standpoint all acts of behavior answer to the scheme of reflex. *Thus reflexology extends its objective study to the whole of human behavior.*

C

What are the ways and methods of the reflexological investigation of correlated activity?

In order to study the outward human hereditary and complicated organic reactions as well as the acquired reactions which develop under the influence of outer and inner stimulations of the present or of the past, reflexology can attain its object by the following ways:

1) By means of an objective biosociological study of all outer manifestations of personality, by the revealing of the correlation of these manifestations with the outer and inner, present or past stimuli, and also by a study of the successive development of the correlated and in particular of the associated-reflex activity of infants from birth.

2) By investigating the laws of the development of associated-reflex activity, occurring under different conditions. Here both experimentation and observation must be used.

3) In studying the mechanism of correlation of the given reflexes with diverse stimuli—present or past, outer or inner. The knowledge of this mechanism in animals can be acquired by destroying their brain; in people, by observing pathological cases.

4) In a study of the onto- and phylogenesis of correlated and especially of associated-reflex activity in relation to the histogenetic development of the cerebral-hemispheres.

5) In a study of the correlations of the objective processes of associated-reflex activity with the verbal report of experienced emotions.

The principal experimental method of reflexology consists, as already stated, in educating the associated motor reflexes on the basis of the defensive reflex, caused by means of electrical stimulation of the skin. It differs from the above-mentioned method (41) in that the reflex is formed of the hand but not of the foot. Yet reflexology made and makes use also of other methods of experimental training of the associated reflexes on the basis of simple (innate) reflexes[6] as well as on the basis of other associated reflexes.[7] In his early investigations (3) Bekhterev also used the method of training (*Dressurmethode*), which he thought expedient even later,

---

[6]Associated respiratory reflex (Anfimov), associated circulatory reflex (Chaly), associated knee reflex (Schevalev), etc.

[7]Associated reflexes on the basis of those reflexes which are provoked by means of a verbal stimulus in the form of instruction (Dobrotvorskaya) or of command (Ivanov-Smolensky), etc.

though under the condition of a strictly objective interpretation of the results.

In line with these methods which enable us to study the very process of formation of reaction, reflexology can also utilize those methods which are adopted in case of an established reaction. Here we can cite the methods used in experimental psychology yet under the condition of a strictly objective experimental performance and of a complete refusal of any subjective psychological interpretation of the results. On a par with experimentation, observation is also of great importance in reflexology. But observation in reflexology must bear the marks of a strict objectivity both during the process of accumulation of the material and during its elaboration and interpretation. The method of observation is of special significance when studying the development of correlated activity in infants, from their very birth. The results of these observations expounded in *General Bases of Reflexology* reveal the laws of the ontogenesis of correlated activity and elucidate therewith its mechanisms. There is also a special plan for observing children of school age. These observations, completed by natural experiments, aim at revealing the correlations of different reactions of the studied persons with the outer stimuli. By revealing the progressive and regressive reflex-complexes, this observation presents rich pedagogical material and shows which of the children's reactions has to be stimulated or inhibited. When speaking of the practical significance of the reflexological methods, it is of interest to note that Bekhterev utilized these with diagnostical purposes also; for instance, the method of revealing simulated deafness by means of training associated reflexes on the basis of sound stimuli. This method received a premium at the hygienical exhibition at Dresden in 1911.

D

As shown above, *General Bases of Reflexology,* forming a basis for a reflexological conception and revealing its methods, presents too rich an empiric material, which occupies more than half of this book. This material consists mostly of the works of Bekhterev's school performed during the first decades of our century and, consequently, by new methods of investigation. We find here some data of former investigations which are closely related to reflexology. The greatest part of this empiric material is connected with those laws which are revealed in artificially associated reflexes.

The exposition of this material is interesting, as Bekhterev applies the laws revealed by him or by his pupils to the everyday facts of human behavior. On the other hand, he correlates these laws with cosmic validity.

"The cosmic process," says Bekhterev, "which in an objective study represents an uninterrupted chain of more and more complicated correlations of matter, finds its realization according to the same fundamental principles. Independent of this fact, this realization will be manifested in the form of the planetary movement or planetary process or in the form of a process taking place in inorganic and living matter, in particular in the form of life-phenomena of human beings or of human society—the so-called superorganic world with all the complications of its outer relations."

The fundamental principles which Bekhterev reveals in the laws of associated-reflex activity are, indeed, very generalized. These are the principles of energy-saving, of constant variability, of mutual effectiveness, the principles of cycles, of economy, of adaptation, of differentiation, of synthesis, of function, the principles of inertia, of compensation, of evolution, of selection, of relativity, etc.

At first sight such a classification can appear very artificial and roughly mechanistic; as a matter of fact, it represents only a general scheme, *genetically* connecting reflexological laws with general laws, though not identifying them. Under the generalized title of this scheme—the reflexological laws find a full development of their qualitative precision and specificity.

In his analysis of reflexological laws, Bekhterev leans partly upon the data of the general physiological investigations (especially upon the works of Vedenski's physiological school—the parabiosis teaching and the dominance-teaching of Ukhtomski).

Being unable to give here a detailed exposition of the laws revealed by Bekhterev in the works of his school concerning the study of associated-reflex activity, I shall refer to some of them when speaking of the current problems of reflexology.

IV. PRESENT-DAY PROBLEMS OF REFLEXOLOGY

The center of Bekhterev's school is located at the Reflexological Institute for Brain Researches in Leningrad. This Institute was founded by Bekhterev in 1917.[8] The reflexological work performed here is divided into a series of branches and forms the subject of study of several divisions, guided by Bekhterev's pupils. The principal fields of the reflexological work in the Institute are as follows: general reflexology (Schniermann); individual reflexology (Myasishchev); age-reflexology (Osipova); collective reflexology (Lange); genetic reflexology (Shchelovanov). There are also performed, on a par with these purely reflexological investigations and in close correlation with them, scientific works in the field of the general physiology of the nervous system (Vasiliev) and of brain-morphology (Pines).

A series of laboratories of other establishments which study reflexological problems are working in contact with the Institute. These are the laboratories of medical colleges, clinics, hospitals, and children's institutions, etc., both in Leningrad and in other towns of the U.S.S.R. As I am unable to elucidate here the whole reflexological work already performed, I shall give only a brief description of those problems which I think, for the present moment, of first importance.

General Reflexology. The work in the field of general reflexology aims at establishing the general laws of the correlated activity of individuals

---

[8]Now directed by V. P. Osipova.

and to reveal its general mechanisms. The analysis of results is almost physiological. The present period of this work may be characterized as the period of a detailed qualitative analysis of correlated activity. In line with the study of the relatively elementary mechanisms of associated-reflex formation on the basis of a simple reflex (or of another associated reflex), we come to the study of more complicated mechanisms of correlated activity. The work here develops in the line of analysis (the analytical study of the significance of the receptor and effector functions in the elementary working process (1) as well as in the line of synthesis—the study of mechanisms of mutual effectiveness in synthetic reactions (53). There are performed on the pathological material in psychiatric clinics parallel investigations of the latter type (52). The study of the mechanisms of mutual effectiveness, which I consider as one of the fundamental problems of general reflexology (51), permits us to undertake an investigation of these qualitative characteristics which differentiate the more complicated phenomena of correlated activity from their prototypes—the associated reflexes of the first order. In going deeper into the qualitative analysis of correlated activity, we do not renounce the first principle of reflexology— submitting all manifestation of correlated activity, in accordance with their genesis, to the scheme of a reflex—but, when stating the objective qualitative properties of the complicated manifestations, of correlated activity, we deduce them by means of analysis and synthesis from the primitive reflex mechanisms.

The study of the mechanisms of mutual effectiveness allows us also to go deeper into the physiological analysis of that mechanism lying at the base of the correlated reflex, which at first sight seems to be quite primitive. A new elucidation of the formation, disappearance, and differentiation of associated reflexes is received when studying them from the standpoint of the complicated mutual effectiveness of the central processes. This effectiveness finds its physiological explication in the dominance-teaching of Ukhtomski.

In particular two problems are set forth: inner inhibition as coherent inhibition (50) and the rôle played by effector apparatus in the differentiating activity of the central nervous system (54).

As you will see, these problems are connected not only with experimental investigations in the field of general reflexology but also (and even more so) with observations on the development of associated reflexes of infants. Here is one of the points of divergency of Bekhterev's and Pavlov's physiological conceptions. The latter, as is well-known, localizes the analytic functions of outer stimulations in the receptor part of the reflex arc. These divergencies are to be referred to the difference in the methods of investigation. It must be supposed that the mechanisms of mutual effectiveness in the motor sphere are more accentuated than those of the secretory one.

A comparative study was recently performed of the secretory and motor methods; investigations have also been started with the aim of revealing the mutual effectiveness of motor and respiratory reflexes. Parallel investigations on animals are also being performed.

Among the reflexological investigations of practical significance, it is expedient to mention the attempt to treat alcoholics by training defensive reflexes in response to stimuli connected with alcohol. This method was put into practice in a psychiatric hospital by Kantorovich (38).

Individual Reflexology. Individual reflexology aims at studying the individual variations of correlated reflex activity (42) and at establishing the relation of these variations to the constitutional data and to the behavior characteristics; it aspires also to build up, on the basis of all these data, reflexological typology. The performance of this work necessitates many human subjects. The program of the work in this field requires the application of various methods of investigation: the reflexological laboratory method must be accepted as well as clinical observation, anthropometry, and biochemical investigation. The very method of reflexological experimentation used here must take into account the possibility of a maximum account of the different reactions which can serve as indexes of the associated-reflex process. From all the original methods which were worked out in this field, it is of interest to mention the method of training the cerebral pulse associated reflex in innate cases of the unclosed fontanel of the cranium as well as in cases depending upon some operative defect (30) and also the method of formation of the associated neurogalvanic reflex (44). The study of the animal (motor) and vegetative (respiratory and galvanic) reactions and their mutual effectiveness in the process of formation and differentiation of the associative reflexes (43) offers fundamental material for the description of reflexological types. One must note that in the field of individual reflexology as well as in the field of general reflexology the study of the mutual effectiveness of reflexes is viewed as one of the fundamental problems.

The characteristics stated by diverse reflexological experiments are correlated with the data of constitution and heredity, with behavior characteristics, with conditions of social environment. On the basis of the investigations already performed, a series of fundamental reflexological types was stated; plastic, torpid, excitable, inhibitable. Intermediate and mixed types are also described (30, 44).

When studying the typical variations of associated-reflex activity the investigator meets with extreme variations lying on the borderline of pathology. Therefore, in order to get a more complete elucidation of these variations, work with pathological material is performed parallel with fundamental investigations. When stating the types of correlated reflex activity and correlating them with the data of the biological (heredity, constitution) and social factors (environment), individual reflexology elucidates also the biogenesis and sociogenesis of these typical variations.

Age Reflexology. The problem of age reflexology is a very voluminous one; it embraces the questions of the general mechanisms of correlated reflex activity in their development, as well as the questions of children's reflexological typology. As subjects, age reflexology uses normal children of school age. Parallel investigations are performed on physically defective children (blind, deaf, and dumb). Researches in this branch of reflexology embrace hundreds of children. One ought to mention, among the total number of investigations connected with the study of the general mechanisms of children's associated-reflex activity, the work concerning the study of formation of associated reflexes at school age (47), the study of their differentiation and of their synthetic reactions (48). One must note that age reflexology, too, centers its researches, in line with the study of the isolated reactions, on the study of the synthetic results of their mutual effectiveness.

As to the work in the field of children's typology, this kind of investigation is rather widely extended (46, 56, 57) and embraces not only normal but also pathological material. Here, as well as in individual reflexology, the data of the reflexological experiment are correlated with the data of heredity, constitution, behavior, and social conditions. Thus the significance is revealed of the biological and social factors in forming children's reflexological types.

One must cite also the investigations concerning the elaboration of the method of associated-reflex therapy, when applied to children's pathological habits.

Collective Reflexology. Collective reflexology centralizes its work on revealing the sociogenetic elements of behavior. It aims at studying the mechanisms of mutual effectiveness of individuals in a collective. The changes in the reactions of separate individuals during their mutual influence in the collective (28), the difference between individual work and work in collaboration, the influence of the collective on the individual and of the individual on the collective (29)—these are the principal problems of collective reflexology. Here are studied the rather simple actions— associated reflexes trained on the basis of electrical stimulation of the skin or a verbal command (45)—as well as more complicated actions— speech reactions in the form of judgments (28), and actions undergoing alterations as a result of the mutual influence revealed in collectives. It proved possible by means of these investigations, which were performed on several collectives, to state various forms of mutual effectiveness between individuals and collectives. The type of reaction of a given individual when in a collective depends not only upon the individual himself but also upon the structure of the collective. The same person who appeared as socially excitable in one collective can appear as socially inhibited in another. The mechanisms of mutual effectiveness in a collective depend on one hand upon the sex and age of the individuals and on the other upon their social characteristics (their vocational index, social class, etc.).

In connection with the above-mentioned, there arises the problem of studying the mechanisms of mutual effectiveness in collectives of different biosocial groups. This task is commenced by studying three biosocial groups of children:(1) normal children (school-children and pupils of children's homes); (2) retarded children (pupils of special schools for retarded children); and (3) problem children brought up in special institutions. These groups were subjected to an extremely wide and varied biosocial study, the following factors being taken into consideration: heredity, constitution, endocrinology, nervous system (animal and vegetative), data of a pedagogical observation, of social environment, of personal reflexological investigations, and, finally, data of the collective experiment (40). The whole of this large theme forms at present one of the central points of collective reflexology researches.

Genetic Reflexology. The study of the development of correlated activity in the process of ontogenesis and phylogenesis forms one of the most important branches of reflexology. This task is performed in a special division of the Reflexological Institute for Brain Researches and in the Clinic of Infant Pedology and Neuropathology which is attached to the Institute.

The Genetic Division of the Institute studies the development of human and animal sucklings—behavior parallel with brain histogenesis. Besides this work, special investigations are performed revealing the influence of extirpation of different parts of the brain and of different organs (especially of the endocrine glands) upon the development of correlated activity. It is of interest to mention that the Genetic Division succeeded in bringing up puppies deprived of one brain hemisphere; no difference was noted between these and normal puppies in reflex formation and differentiation (39, 33). The comparative study of the development of different animal sucklings reveals the progressive significance of experience and acquired reactions in connection with the complication of the organization and behavior; on the contrary, the quantity of inhibited mechanisms which are ready at the moment of birth diminishes with the complication of organization. Hence those reactions which appear in animals of a lower organization as innate, in animals of a higher organization appear only as the result of experience. Thanks to this fact, the reactions of the latter species reveal a higher adaptation to the environing conditions (55).

As to the study of the ontogenesis of correlated activity, one must first mention the work revealing the interesting interdependence existing between the development of the first associated reflexes of an infant and the functional reaction. It appears that the formation of the correlated reactions to light and sound is possible only from that moment (the third month of life) when the stimulations transferred from eyes and ears begin to provoke functionally dominant reactions, i.e., orientative reactions during the performance of which all other movements are inhibited. I must refer also to the already mentioned researches in the field of genetic reflexology which revealed the significance of the mutual effectiveness of the effector apparatus in the analysis of the outer stimulations (36).

The work connected with the study of the development of sleep in infants and dogs (34) must also be cited. These investigations state that sleep is formed during that life-period when the cerebral cortex does not yet function and reveal that the mechanism of sleep depends, to a large extent, upon those sections of the nervous system which lie below the cortex, whereas the cortex serves only as the point of departure from which the sleep mechanism is set at work. These data contradict the conception of

Pavlov's school, which reduces the mechanism of sleep to a diffused inhibition extended over the cerebral cortex. One can say that the work in the field of genetic reflexology in revealing the development of correlated activity casts light upon many of its mechanisms which we find already formed in adults.

Besides its theoretical interest, the task of genetic reflexology is also of practical importance. It is to the investigations in this field that we owe the first diagnostic scheme of the development of infants. This scheme enables us to discover the earliest divergencies of pathological cases from normal development (37). Researches in infant pedagogy have also been started.

These are the principal problems of Bekhterev's reflexological school presented briefly.

V. Reflexology and Related Disciplines

Recently, in line with a series of problems in the field of the direct investigative work, reflexology was confronted with a series of methodological problems. A special methodological section was organized in the Reflexological Institute. This section aims at the systematic elaboration of the general methodological statements of reflexology and the correlation of reflexology with other tendencies of behavior study, and also at the elaboration of all the concrete systematic problems of reflexology from the standpoint of dialectic materialism.

The work performed by this section stated that Bekhterev's reflexological school, in accordance with the last aspirations of its creator, stands firmly on the basis of dialectic materialism. How is reflexological teaching built on this basis? Reflexology studies correlated activity in its historical development, in its evolution from one form to another. Genetically deducing the superior manifestations of correlated activity from the inferior ones, reflexology by no means reduces the former to the latter and neglects neither its objective nor its subjective qualities. It pays special attention to those new qualities which appear as the result of the mutual effectiveness of reflexes. Reflexology does not deny the subjective qualitative characteristics of correlated activity (consciousness), but explains behavior in its causal connections, deduced from objective reality. Otherwise, reflexology would enter the line of idealism, which deduces existence from consciousness.

Since reflexology lies at the crossroads of biology and sociology, it has to lean upon them when explaining its laws. The "qualitatively determining" type of validity in reflexology is presented by biological laws when studying correlated activity in animals, and by sociological laws when studying human behavior. In that sense, biology and sociology form the "methods of knowledge" in reflexology.

Thus Bekhterev's reflexology is a strictly objective teaching of human correlated activity, built upon the basis of materialistic dialectics and utilizing biological and sociological methods of knowledge. This fact determines the relation of reflexology to other Russian tendencies in behavior study.

I shall refer to this question very briefly.

1) The teaching of Pavlov's school (the teaching of conditioned reflexes) forms a branch of the physiology of the nervous system. It has as its subject not the whole system of correlations between personality and environment but only its nervous mechanisms, it being a physiological teaching in the narrow sense of this word. It could be a biological teaching of a wider significance, if it utilized sufficiently the evolutionary genetic conception. Sociology as a method of knowledge takes no part in the teaching of conditioned reflexes. Thus the teaching of conditioned reflexes is not as broad as reflexology.

In building its independent biosociological teaching, reflexology leans partly upon the teaching of conditioned reflexes, in so far as the latter studies the physiological mechanisms which lie at the basis of the actions of correlated activity.

2) Subjective psychology, in its classic form, differs so distinctly from reflexology both in its subject ("soul," "consciousness") and in its method (introspection) that I shall not discuss it. I shall merely remark that for psychology, working with the method of introspection, the evolutionary genetic method is cut off forever.

3) It is more difficult to differentiate reflexology from the psychology of behavior or objective psychology (I have in view those Russian psychologists who call themselves "objectivists" and who consider human behavior to be their subject), as this teaching has adopted the subject and the investigation methods of reflexologists. It seems to me that the difference between such a "hybrid" psychology and reflexology (as well as the insolvency of this psychology) can be best revealed by referring to its methods of knowledge. Though almost all psychologists pretend to lean upon biology and sociology, the psychology of behavior uses, in fact, an "autistic" method of knowledge (i.e., it becomes its own method, deducing the behavior laws from subjective emotions, instead of deducing them from objective biosocial relations). The various tendencies of objective psychology suffer with "methodological autism" of different stages, but, in fact, each one bears elements of idealism. The evolutionary genetic method in this tendency remains at the stage of good intentions.

4) Dialectic materialism in psychology (Kornilov's school) stands nearest to reflexology, as it endeavors to base its teaching upon the principles of dialectic materialism. Yet, in spite of the great evolution which this school has undergone on its way to objectivism, it could not definitely break away from the old psychological autism, as it also proved unable to reject the very title "psychology." The traces of methodological autism, and hence of idealism, are to be found in this school even now. The evolutionary genetic method here also remains unadopted.

5) Comparative psychology or biopsychology (Wagner's school), standing on the basis of the evolutionary genetic study of behavior, could be expected to possess all the characteristics which would make it possible to utilize the evolutionary genetic method for an objective study of behavior. Yet this teaching differentiates so much the separate stages of behavior

development and elucidates them in such a subjective way that it bears, even more than other tendencies of objective psychology, elements of idealism. Reflexology has little in common with the foreign tendencies in psychology leaning upon subjective conceptions. American behaviorism (antroponomy) stands nearer to Bekhterev's reflexology, aiming at a strictly objective study of behavior and also utilizing the evolutionary genetic method, though differences in the very "method of knowledge" still remain. I think that in the future the methodological work in the field of each tendency of human behavior teaching will contribute not only to productive work within the tendencies themselves but also to the possibility of establishing a common language for all the teachings.

At the end of this short review of Bekhterev's reflexological teaching I am compelled to emphasize, once more, that the real meaning of this extremely dynamic teaching can be revealed only by the study of its ways and perspectives. That is why I thought it necessary to pay so much attention to the history of reflexology and to the present lines of its development. At the same time, the limited space of this paper obliged me to be most compact, even *schematic,* in my exposition. I should consider my task accomplished if this short review would excite the reader's desire to gain an insight into the original reflexological investigations in order to get a more complete conception of Bekhterev's reflexology.

REFERENCES*

1. ABRAMOVICH, Z. A., ILINA, O. S., & LYCHINA, E. T. Concerning the method of analytic study of the receptor and effector functions in selective reaction. *Novoe v refleksologii i fiziologii nervnoi sistemy,* 1930, No. 3.

2. BEKHTEREV, V. M. Die Functionen der Sehhügel (Thalami optici): experimentelle Untersuchung. *Neur. Zentbl.,* 1883, No. 4.

3. ————. Physiology of the cerebral cortex motor sphere. *Arch. psikhiartrii,* 1886-87.

4. ————. Conduction paths of the brain and spinal cord. St. Petersburg, 1888. (2nd ed., 2 vols., 1898.)
   Die Leitungsbahnen im Gehirn und Rückenmark. Berlin.
   Les voies de conduction. Lyons, 1900.

5. ————. The contact theory and the teaching concerning the provoking of nervous conductivity by the detention of nervous energy. *Obozrenie psikhiatrii,* 1896.

6. ————. Objective indexes of neuroses and hysteria. *Obozrenie psikhiatrii,* 1897.

7. ————. Objective indexes of local hyperaesthesia and anaesthesia in traumatic neuroses and hysteria. *Obozrenie psikhiatrii,* 1899-1900.
   Ueber objective Symptome lokaler Hyperaesthesie und Anaesthesie bei den sogenannten traumatischen Neurosen und bei Hysterie. *Neur. Zentbl.,* 1900, No. 5.

8. ————. Bases of the teaching concerning the functions of the brain. (7 vols.) St. Petersburg, 1903-07.
   Die Functionen der Nervencentra (3 vols.) Jena.

*This list contains only those works of Bekhterev's school to which I refer in this paper. They are of first interest for the study of the history and current development of reflexology.

9. —————. Objective psychology and its subject. *Vestnik psicologii*, 1904. *Rev. scient.*, 1906.

10. —————. Psychic activity and life. St. Petersburg, 1904. L'activité psychique et la vie. Paris, 1907. Psyche und Leben. Wiesbaden, 1909.

11. —————. On the method of associated motor reflexes. *Proc. Soc. Clin-Nerv. & Ment. Dis. Milit. Med. Acad. St. Petersburg*, 1907.

12. —————. Objective psychology. (3 vols.) 1907-12. Objective Psychologie oder Reflexologie. Berlin, Leipzig, 1913. La psychologie objective. Paris, 1913.

13. —————. Objective researches of nervous and psychic activity. *Obozrenie psikhiatrii*, 1908.

14. —————. On the reproductive and associated reaction in movements. *Obozrenie psikhiatrii*, 1908. Ueber die reproductive und associative Reaction bei Bewegungen. *Zsch. f. Therap.*, 1909, 1, No. 1.

15. —————. The significance of motor-sphere researches for the objective study of human nervous and psychic activity. *Russky vratch*, Nos. 33, 35, & 36. *Folia neurobiol.*, 1910, 4.

16. —————. Objective study of the neuropsychic sphere of infants. *Vestnik psicologii*, 1909.

17. —————. Problems and method of objective psychology. *Novoe slovo*, 1909. Die objective Psychologie und ihre Begründung. *J. f. Psychol. u. Neur.*, 1909, 14.

18. —————. On the application of associated motor reflexes as objective methods of research in the clinic of nervous and mental diseases. *Obozrenie psikhiatrii*, 1910. Ueber die Anwendung der associativ-motorischen Reflexe als objective Untersuchungsmethode in der klinischen Neuropathologie und Psychiatrie. *Zsch. f. d. ges. Neur. & Psychiat.*, 1911, 5, No. 3.

19. —————. Individual development of the neuropsychic sphere according to the data of objective psychology. *Vestnik psicologii*, 1910.

20. —————. Problems of social education. *Pedagogicheskii vestnik*, 1910.

21. —————. Subject and problems of social psychology as an objective discipline. *Vestnik ananiya*, 1911.

22. —————. Fundamental principles of the so-called objective or psycho-reflexology. *Obozrenie psikhiatrii*, 1912. Was ist Psycho-Reflexologie? *Dtsch. med. Woch.*, 1912. Qu'est-ce que la psycho-reflexologie? *Arch. neur.*, 1913.

23. —————. Principal problems of psychiatry as an objective discipline. *Russky vratch*, 1912, No. 6.

24. —————. General bases of human reflexology. Leningrad: 1st ed., 1918; 2nd ed., 1923; 3rd ed., 1926.

25. —————. Collective reflexology. (2 vols.) Petrograd, 1921.

26. —————. Personality diseases from the standpoint of reflexology. (Bases of pathological reflexology.) *Voprosy izucheniya i vospitaniya lichnosti*, 1921.

27. —————. Psychology, reflexology, and Marxism. Leningrad, 1925.

28. BEKHTEREV, V. M., & LANGE, M. V. Data on experiments in collective reflexology. *Novoe v refleksologii i fiziologii nervnoi sistemy*, 1925, No. 1.

29. —————. The influence of the collective on the individual. *Pedologia i vospitaniya*, 1928.

30. BEKHTEREV, V. M., & MYASISHCHEV, V. N. Associated-reflex alterations of the cerebral pulse. Trudy Gosudarstvennyi Institut Meditsinskikh Znanii. Leningrad, 1929.

31. BEKHTEREV, V. M., & NARBUT, V. M. Objective indexes of suggestion in hypnosis. Obozrenie psikhiatrii, 1902, Nos. 1 & 2. Les signes objectives de la suggestion pendant le sommeil hypnotique. Arch. de Psychol., 1905 (Oct.).

32. BEKHTEREV, V. M., & SHCHELOVANOV, N. M. Concerning genetic reflexology. Novoe v refleksologii i fiziologii nervnoi sistemy, 1925, No. 1.

33. BLAGOVESHCHENSKAYA, V. P. Development of associated reflexes in puppies deprived of one hemisphere during the early days of their life. Novoe v refleksologii i fiziologii nervnoi sistemy, 1929, No. 3.

34. BLAGOVESHCHENSKAYA, V. P., BELOVA, L. A., KANICHEVA, R. A., & FEDOROVA,— (under the direction of N. M. Shchelovanov). On the development of the sleep and waking of dogs. Novoe v refleksologii i fiziologii nervnoi sistemy, 1926, No. 2.

35. BOLDYREV, —. Formation .of the artificially conditioned (psychical) reflexes and their properties. Proc. Soc. Russ. Physicians St. Petersburg, 1905-06.

36. FIGURIN, N. L., & DENISOVA, M. P. Further material on the problem concerning the differentiation of associated reflexes of infants. Trudy II Siezda Fiziologov. Leningrad, 1926.

37. —————. A short diagnostic scheme of the development of infants. Novoe v refleksologii i fiziologii nervnoi sistemy, 1926, No. 2.

38. KANTOROVICH, N. V. An essay on the associated-reflex therapy of alcoholism. Novoe v refleksologii i fiziologii nervnoi sistemy, 1929, No. 3.

39. KLOSOVSKI, B. N. The technique of the operation and the morphological and several functional results of the extirpation of one brain hemisphere of a puppy. Novoe v refleksologii i fiziologii nervnoi sistemy, 1929, No. 3.

40. LANGE, M. V., & LUKINA, A. M. Ashner's reflex, the nervous system and behavior of children. Novoe v refleksologii i fiziologii nervnoi sistemy, 1926, No. 2.

41. MOLOTKOV, A. G. The formation of associated motor reflexes to light stimulations in individuals. St. Petersburg, 1911.

42. MYASISHCHEV, V. N. On the typic variations of the associated motor reflexes of individuals. Novoe v refleksologii i fiziologii nervnoi sistemy, 1925, No. 1.

43. —————. On the correlation of the inner and outer reaction. Novoe v refleksologii i fiziologii nervnoi sistemy, 1926, No. 2.

44. —————. On the associated neurogalvanic reflex. Sbornik Gosudarstvennyi Institut Meditsinskikh Znanii posvyashenyi pamyati Bekhtereva. Leningrad, 1929.

45. OPARINA, N. V. An essay on training associated reflexes of collectives of children of school age. Novoe v refleksologii i fiziologii nervnoi sistemy, 1926, No. 2.

46. OSIPOVA, V. N. On the associated-excitable and associated-inhibitable types in children. Voprosy izucheniya i vospitaniya lichnosti, 1926.

47. —————. Rapidity of the formation of associated motor reflexes of children of school age. Novoe v refleksologii i fiziologii nervnoi sistemy, 1926, No. 2.

48. —————. On the problems of speech command and group variations in the activity of the central nervous system of children. Novoe v refleksologii i fiziologii nervnoi sistemy, 1929, No. 3.

49. PROTOPOPOV, V. P. On the associated motor reaction to sound stimulations. St. Petersburg, 1909.

50. Schniermann, A. L. Associated reflex and dominance. *Novoe v refleksologii i fiziologii nervnoi sistemy,* 1926, No. 2.

51. ——————. The mechanisms of mutual effectiveness as the principal problem of associated-reflex teaching. *Voprosy izucheniya i vospitaniya lichnosti,* 1929, Nos. 3 & 4.

52. ——————. The mutual effectiveness of the associated reflexes of narrowminded persons. *Novoe v refleksologii i fiziologii nervnoi sistemy,* 1929, No. 3.

53. ——————. On the mutual effectiveness of the synergetic and antagonistic associated reflexes of the upper extremities in individuals. *Novoe v refleksologii i fiziologii nervnoi sistemy,* 1929, No. 3.

54. Schniermann, A. L., & Oparina, N. V. Material on the problem concerning the rôle played by effector apparatus in the differentiating activity of the central nervous system. *Novoe v refleksologii i fiziologii nervnoi sistemy,* 1929, No. 3.

55. Shchelovanov, N. M. On the specific particularities of the development of human nervous activity in comparison with animals. Trudy II Siezda' Fiziologov. Leningrad, 1926.

56. Sorokhtin, G. N. Reflexological types in children. Leningrad, 1928.

57. ——————. The inhibitive type. *Novoe v refleksologii i fiziologii nervnoi sistemy,* 1929, No. 3.

CHAPTER 13

PSYCHOLOGY IN THE LIGHT OF DIALECTIC MATERIALISM

K. N. KORNILOV

Moscow State University

THE METHODOLOGICAL PREMISES OF PSYCHOLOGY

1) In order to understand exactly what constitutes psychology from the standpoint of dialectic materialism, or, in short, Marxian psychology, it is necessary to examine those methodological premises which lie at the foundations of the teaching of Marx, Engels, Plekhanov, Lenin, and upon which Marxian psychology is built.

What, then, are these methodological premises?

It must be understood that in this article it is not possible to dwell on the social and economic sides of the question in detail, although they occupy such a tremendously important place in Marxism. I must confine myself for the most part to the methodological, philosophic bases of Marxism, which are universally known by the name of dialectic materialism and which have a direct relation to the problem under discussion.

As is well known, the philosophic point of view of the founders of Marxism, Karl Marx and Friedrich Engels, came into being at the time when a deadly war was being waged between the idealistic and the materialistic wings of the students of Hegelian philosophy. In this war Marx and Engels joined the materialistic side headed by Ludwig Feurbach, who, contrary to Hegel, admitted the primacy of matter, nature in relation to thought. Marx and Engels, however, did not entirely become followers of Feurbach who, having broken with the Hegelian philosophy, failed to perceive its extremely valuable dialectic method.

The historical merit of Marx and Engels lies in their employment of the dialectics of Hegel, which in their hands became a thoroughly materialistic conception and formed the basis of dialectic materialism. In fact, as is well known, the starting-point of the whole philosophic system of Hegel is the belief in the absolute spirit, which, in its self-development, subject to definite dialectic laws, realizes itself in material nature, which thus becomes something secondary and derivative. It follows, therefore, that the dialectic process of development of existing phenomena is, according to Hegel, of a thoroughly idealistic nature in so far as the process is the process of the self-development of the spirit. Marx substituted for the Hegelian absolute spirit, material nature as something original and primordial, and in this way brought up the question of dialectic laws of the development of actual reality, that is, nature, human society, and thought.

Marx himself formulated in the following lines his divergence from the philosophy of Hegel in the preface to the second edition of the first volume of *Das Kapital* (16):

"My dialectic method is not only different from the Hegelian, but is directly opposed to it. The life-process of the human brain, i.e., the process of thinking, Hegel transforms under the name of 'the Idea' into the independent subject in the demiurgos of the real world, and the real world is only the external phenomenal form of 'the Idea.' With me, on the contrary, the ideal world is nothing else than the material world reflected by the human mind. With him (Hegel) it (dialectic) is standing on its head. It must be turned right side up again, if you would discover the rational kernel within the mystical shell."

Marx did this by actually applying materialistic dialectics to the solution of social and economic problems. These were brought to light in his main work *Das Kapital*.

Engels, who studied the question of dialectics and of its concrete application to the field of science, has expressed the results of the study in his chief works, *Anti-Dühring* (7), *Ludwig Feurbach* (8), and in particular in a recently published book of his *Dialectics of Nature* (9).

The disciples of Marx and Engels developed and supplemented the inheritance of the founders. Thus was created the system, which, according to Marx, should not only explain the world, as previous philosophers have done but should also help with its theoretical explanations to change and rebuild it on new and more rational lines.

Such in its main features is the historical position of the teaching of Marx and Engels with regard to the development of philosophy.

2) We will pass now to the systematic exposition of the main methodological principles of dialectic materialism, which we will require later on in proving our psychological theory. At this point, however, the question arises of whether these philosophic and methodological premises are necessary at all in psychology or in any other branch of concrete positive science. Does not this traditional philosophic basis act only as a brake to the strictly scientific development of psychology as one sometimes hears from certain psychologists? This sceptical attitude toward philosophy would be perfectly justified if in psychology, as in other sciences, the main task was to collect facts without attempting to understand and explain them in the light of theory.

Since pure empiricism does not satisfy any one of the sciences, and sooner or later it becomes necessary to turn to theoretical generalizations, the philosophic analysis of fundamental conceptions on which the given science works becomes a matter of necessity. Engels makes fun of the scientific writers who endeavored in their writings to avoid any form of philosophy, and therefore were obliged in their theoretical influences to make use of the worst possible philosophy. Engels says: "Scientists imagine that they have freed themselves from philosophy, when they either ignore it or blame it. But since they cannot move a step without thought, and for thought it is necessary to have logical definitions, and these definitions they borrow carelessly either from the current theoretical stock-in-trade of so-called "educated" people, who retain the last shreds of worn-out philosophic systems, or from the crumbs of a compulsory university course in philosophy. The latter tends to give a fragmentary point of view, and leads to the confusion of the opinions of people belonging to entirely different and for the most part worse schools. Or these definitions are derived from the uncritical and unsystematic reading of all kinds of philosophical writings—so that in the end the scientists find themselves bound fast to philosophy, but unfortunately, in the majority of cases, to the worst kind of philosophy. Those who blamed philosophy most heartily become most often slaves of the vulgarized remains of the worst philosophic systems" (9, p. 37).

Thus from the point of view of Marxism, methodological and philosophic proofs are indispensable for all sciences, including psychology.

At this point, however, a question arises, disclosing the reason for the sceptical attitudes of many scientists with regard to philosophy: What must that philosophy be in order to really act as a methodological help and not as a brake on science? As a reply to this question, Marxism declares war against idealism and the idealistic philosophic system in all their shades and variations, beginning from the most consistent and complete system— Hegel's—and concluding with the mongrel, incoherent, and sometimes almost radical systems of the pseudo-materialistic order, such as the empiriocriticism of Avenarius, Mach, and so on.

All these idealistic systems stand in direct contradiction to science and scientific facts, and this explains the scepticism of many scientists with regard to philosophy since these scientists do not know any other philosophy except idealistic philosophy. Therefore dialectic materialism objects to regarding philosophy to be what idealistic systems usually say it is, that is, a superstructure and a complement to the facts of all sciences, because this is just what made philosophy metaphysical through and through and, in this way, inimical to positive science.

From the Marxian standpoint philosophy should be a *methodology of science* and consist of *logic* and *dialectics* only. Therefore Engels said: "Dialectic materialism—this is, generally speaking, not philosophy but simply a *Weltanschauung,* which is expressed and proved not in one particular system but in all actual science. . . Consequently, philosophy is in this case abolished, that is to say, it is at one and the same time 'surpassed and preserved.' It is expelled in its entire form but preserved in its actual content" (7).

Dialectic materialism is a philosophy of this kind, that is, a methodology of science. Since it cannot possibly contradict the facts of positive science, it is sometimes called "within-science philosophy."

It is on such an order of methodology of science that we want to base the Marxian psychology.

3) What then are the principal conceptions of scientific methodology

with which dialectic materialism deals? We must first of all discuss the conception of *matter,* the basis both of philosophy and of positive science. What, from the point of view of dialectic materialism, is matter? That which we call matter is, from the point of view of dialectic materialism, nothing but nature, the external world, and the objective actuality which exists independently of our consciousness. Or, in the words of Lenin: "Matter is the philosophic category which is given to a man in his sensations, which is copied, photographed, and reflected in our sensations, although existing independently of them" (13, Vol. X). Therefore matter is not the combination of sensations, nor the product of consciousness, nor is it something secondary, as idealists affirm. Matter, that is, nature, the external world, is the primary object, existing independently of our consciousness, and giving, as we shall see later on, the contents of our consciousness.

What proofs have we relating to the existence of matter as objective reality? Idealism endeavors to decide this question by means of pure theory, but this is a vain effort. Only one proof exists, and that is collective human experience which, realizing itself for thousands of years through men's labor, corroborates unreservedly the fact that the object of these activities, nature or the external world in general, exists as objective reality, independent of our consciousness. "Putting the question outside human experience, of whether objective reality corresponds to human thought, makes it a purely scholastic question," says Marx. "The question—is human thought capable of knowing objects in their actual form? —is not a theoretical but a practical question. Experience should prove to man the truth of his thought" (17).

Engels speaks from the same standpoint when he says: "The real unity of the world consists in its materiality, and the latter has been proved not by clever phrases—which are just so much smoke—but by facts accumulated during the long and gradual process of development of philosophy and scientific knowledge" (7, p. 35).

Matter, therefore, is the starting-point for all further discussion. But, is not matter substance, in some way absolute, unchanging, and permanent? Does not dialectic materialism, *ipso facto,* fall into metaphysics? No, it does not, and here is the reason.

Assuming matter as the foundation of existence, dialectic materialism differs from the so-called metaphysical materialism of the eighteenth century in that it does not recognize matter as something absolute, unchanging, and of uniform quality. Engels develops his views of this question in detail, and in his *Dialectics of Nature* declares that matter, as such, is purely a creation of the mind and an abstraction because, when we reduce all objects to matter, we are diverted from all their qualitative characteristics. Therefore matter, as such, as distinguished from definitely existing matter, is not only anything sensuously existing. Therefore science, striving to discover matter as such, attempting to bring the qualitative differences up to the purely quantitative differences between combinations of identical small particles, does exactly what it would have done if, instead of cherries, pears, or apples, it had sought fruit as such—if, instead of cats, dogs, and sheep, etc., it had sought mammals as such. This is a one-sided mathematical point of view, according to which matter is determinable only quantitatively, while qualitatively it is fundamentally the same.

In fact, matter has different shapes and forms which are known only in movement, because movement is the principal form of existence. "There is nothing to be said of bodies which do not move," said Engels. Therefore movement, in the general meaning of the word, that is, as a means of the existence of matter, as an inherent attribute of matter, covers all changes and processes going on in the universe, beginning from elementary movement and ending with thought. In this way the movement of matter cannot be reduced to merely mechanical movement, to elementary transposition; the movement of matter is also light and heat, electrical and magnetic currents, chemical combinations and transformations, life and consciousness. Movement, consequently, is not only transposition but also a qualitative change. Such is the dialectic interpretation of matter in Marxism, quite foreign to the former substantive metaphysical interpretation of matter.

4) The next question which arises is: What constitutes, from the standpoint of dialectic materialism, human *consciousness?* If, as we have stated above, nature or the external world in general is original and primordial, then it will be clear that being primordial it should precede consciousness. This consciousness appears only when the organization of matter and the qualitative nature of its motion reach a definite and fairly high degree. In this respect, primary and loosely organized matter is characterized only by physical and chemical reactions, which are, in fact, the properties of matter in motion. As the composition of matter becomes more complicated, and as it adopts a specific cellular structure along with physical and chemical reactions, there appear also those reactions which we call organic. In living creatures with highly organized nervous systems, we find the clear expression of those internal reactions of the activities of the brain which are called consciousness, thought, psyche. Lenin in this question takes sides whole-heartedly with Marx and Engels, and gives the following definition of consciousness: "Matter, acting on our senses, produces sensations. The sensations depend on the brain, nerves, and retina, etc., on matter organized in a definite way. The existence of matter is independent of sensation. Matter is primordial. Sensation, thought and consciousness are the highest products of a special form of organized matter. This is the view taken by materialists in general and by Marx and Engels in particular" (12, p. 38).

Thus, that which we call consciousness or psyche from this point of view is indistinguishable in its nature from matter, as idealists teach, and is not more than *one of the properties of most highly organized matter.* In the living organism, then, there is nothing except matter, and living matter is nothing more than the highest form of organized matter.

Where and how does this property called psyche or consciousness show itself? It shows itself in the fact that the various physiological processes taking place in the living organism, apart from finding their external objective expression in motion, also find a subjective expression in thought, feeling, desire, etc., or, as Feurbach rightly says: "That which for me subjectively is a purely spiritual, immaterial, unsensual act is in itself objectively a material sensual act. Here neither side of the antinomy is removed, and here the true unity of both sides is disclosed" (10, Vol. X). Plekhanov expresses this idea of Feurbach's as follows: "Every psychological state is only one side of the process, of which a physiological phenomenon composes the other side" (19). Or, as Bukharin still more concisely puts it: "Psyche is the introspective expression of physiological processes" (4).

5) Having given the interpretation of matter and consciousness we will pass now to the examination of the question of the relation between consciousness and existence, between our perceptions and the external world. From the point of view of dialectic materialism, this relation is understood as the *reflection* in our consciousness of objects of existence. Lenin described this in the following words: "Our senses reflect objective reality—that which exists independently of humanity and of human senses" (12).

Thus it is not consciousness which gives its contents to existence, as idealists assert, but, on the contrary, consciousness borrows its contents from the outside world which it reflects, or, more exactly, from those concrete conditions which surround the man. This has been well expressed by Marx: *"My relationship to my environment—this is my consciousness."* This methodological principle of dialectic materialism Marx afterwards proved in his social and economic writings, in spite of the purely idealistic point of view reigning at that time—that the social relations of people are determined by the degree of development of the consciousness of people or of their social, political, ethical, and other opinions. Marx, as is well known, supported the directly opposite idea. This was that social relations are determined in the first place not by people's consciousness but by the economic structure of society, by its economic or technical level, by the state of development of productive form of nature, and arising from its relations in productions, which in the end determine people's consciousness and ideology. Upon this is based Marx's well-known formula: *"It is not consciousness that determines existence, but, on the contrary, social existence that determines consciousness."*

It is impossible in this article to examine in detail a number of problems directly connected with or arising from the afore-mentioned principles of dialectic materialism. We will say only briefly that, since objective reality exists independently of our consciousness, here follows the doctrine of dialetic materialism with regard to time, space, and also causality, which is not a form of human contemplation, as idealists think, but exists outside of human consciousness and is a form of the being of the material existence, reflected only in our consciousness. Lenin says: "The world is the motion of matter conformable to laws, and our knowledge, being the highest product of matter, is in a condition only to reflect these laws"

(12, p. 137). At this point the question arises: Can our consciousness reflect with exactitude the existing realities which are independent of it? Are not those Kantian and other philosophers right when they affirm that penetration into the reality existing independently of our consciousness is impossible, because this reality as a world of "things in themselves" is inaccessible by its very nature to our knowledge. For the latter the "world of phenomena" alone is accessible.

Dialectic materialism must emphatically object to such a method of treating the problem, since it leads to agnosticism and through this to metaphysics. From the standpoint of dialectic materialism, the objects of the external world perceived by us contain that which is already known and that which is as yet unknown to science. There is no impassable boundary between these two spheres of the existence of material things, and the process of knowledge of the external world is just that ignorance gradually gives way to knowledge, which finds its fullest and most exact reflection in the gradual perfection of scientific knowledge. Or, in the words of Lenin: "In the theory of knowledge, as in all other fields of science, it is necessary to think dialectically, that is, not to assume that consciousness is something rigid and unalterable, but to analyze through what medium knowledge arises out of ignorance, and by what means incomplete, inaccurate knowledge becomes fuller and more accurate" (12, p. 80). That is why Engels says that "materialism, like idealism, went through various stages of development. It must take a new form with every great new discovery, constituting an epoch in science" (8, p. 36).

Thus, from the standpoint of dialectic materialism, the state of scientific knowledge at a definite historical epoch, though it may not be the absolutely true reflection of the world and can give only a relatively true picture of that historical epoch, is, nevertheless, a successive growth of scientific knowledge, and each new achievement in science is a step on the road to the most accurate reflection of objective reality. The history of the development of science and the practice of the life of mankind confirms this.

These are the conclusions springing directly from the main principles of dialectic materialism and connected with the problems of matter, consciousness, and their relations. We have seen that all these problems can be comprehended and solved only under one indispensable condition, that is, by approaching them from a dialectic point of view. We will now turn to the question of what is dialectic method, and what part it plays in philosophy and science in general and in psychology in particular.

6) We have already seen that the founders of materialistic dialectics were Karl Marx and Friedrich Engels since they have supplanted the idealistic dialectics of Hegel, which are concerned with the main principles of the development of absolute spirit through the study of the principal laws of the development of material reality, that is, nature, human society, and thought. Engels therefore defined the dialectic method as "the general and therefore widely effective and important law of the development of nature, history, and thought." Herein lies the main difference be-

tween dialectic materialism and the materialism of former epochs, and especially of the French materialism of the eighteenth century. Dialectic materialism holds that the world is a combination of processes, eternally changing and developing, whereas, in the words of Engels, "The specific limitation of French materialism consists in its inability to conceive the world as a process, as matter which is in a state of continuous development. This idea corresponded to the contemporary state of scientific knowledge and to metaphysical, that is, to the anti-dialectic method of philosophic thought" (8, p. 37).

Dialectic materialism, therefore, regards inorganic nature, organic nature, and human society as no more than stages of the consecutive development of matter. We have already seen how Engels, speaking of matter, always takes matter in motion since motion is the basic form of every kind of existence, so that of bodies which do not move there is nothing to be said. On considering the question of matter, we observed that Engels constantly emphasizes the fact that movement is not only simple mechanical transposition of particles of matter but also a change in the quality of matter. From this arises a system of different shapes and forms in the motion of matter; the most primitive form of matter may be reduced to simple mechanical motion of uniform particles of matter, which belongs to the study of mechanics. The mechanics of the molecules, which is the study of physics, have their own distinct qualitative form. A still more complicated form is the physics of atoms, which belongs to the field of chemistry; it becomes more and more complicated until we reach albumen in the study of biology; biological forms, as they become more complicated, give a new qualitative characteristic to the behavior of living creatures, which we call psyche or consciousness. This, entering as it does into the conception of man, serves as the subject of the study of psychology. Finally the behavior of people under the conditions of social life acquires new qualitative peculiarities and regularities, and this serves as the subject of the study of sociology.

Each of these qualitative forms of motion conditions specific laws, inherent to this particular domain. From the more complicated forms of motion arise "higher laws," and, according to Engels, "the lower laws, although they continue to act, are relegated to the background." That is why the higher laws cannot unreservedly be reduced to the lower; this will lead only to the uncritical simplification of subtle forms of reality, and by no means to their strictly scientific explanation. Let us take one of these "higher laws," for instance, Darwin's law of the struggle for existence. No one will dispute the fact that this law exists among living creatures. At the basis of their activities there lie, of course, the laws of mechanics, but to say that the struggle for existence is only the mechanical motion of matter would be to give no explanation at all. So it would be, as Engels says, "pure childishness to reduce all the various historical developments and complications of life to the one-sided and meagre formula of the struggle for existence. To say this is to say nothing or even less than nothing" (9, p. 63).

There, in the manner of approaching the question of complex phenomena of nature, of reducing or not reducing them to the simpler mechanical laws, lies one of the main differences between dialectic materialism and mechanical materialism. "The materialism of the eighteenth century," says Engels, "was for the most part mechanical. The exclusive application of standards borrowed from mechanics to chemical phenomena, that is, to such phenomena where mechanical laws naturally apply but are relegated to the background by other higher laws, is the first specific and unavoidable characteristic of the limitation to which classic French materialism was subject" (9, p. 27).

This is why Engels condemned those scientists who "regarded motion always as mechanical, as transposition. This misunderstanding led to an insane desire to reduce everything to mechanical motion, which tended to disguise the specific nature of other forms of motion. Chemical reactions are impossible without thermal and electrical changes, organic life is impossible without mechanical, molecular, chemical, thermal, electrical, and other changes. But the existence of such subsidiary forms does not exhaust the essence of the main form in each case. There is no doubt that some time we shall be able through experiments to reduce thought to molecular and chemical motion in the brain, but would this exhaust the essence of thought?" (9, p. 27).

At this point a question arises having a direct relation to psychology: Is it possible to *reduce* psychic life, the thinking processes of man, to the simple mechanical motion of matter, and would this, in the words of Engels, exhaust the essence of thought? Dialectic materialists say that to identify psychic life and mechanical motion is not correct. One of the greatest Marxians in Russia, Plekhanov, expresses himself on the subject as follows: "Materialism does not try to reduce all psychological phenomena to the motion of matter, as its antagonists declare. For the materialist, sensation, thought, and consciousness are the internal states of matter in motion. None of the materialists who have made their mark in the history of philosophic thought reduced consciousness to motion or explained one by the other. If the materialists have asserted that in order to explain psychological phenomena there is no necessity to invent a special substance—the soul, if they asserted that matter is capable of 'thinking and feeling,' then this ability of matter appeared to them to be as basic and therefore as inexplicable a property of matter as motion" (8).

In another place Plekhanov says, no less definitely, "It always seems to the antagonists of materialism, who generally have the most vague, absurd ideas about it, that Engels did not define correctly the substance of materialism and that in fact materialism reduces psychological phenomena to material ones" (8, pp. 9-10). Lenin is no less emphatic on this point when he says: "In Diderot we have the real point of view of the materialist. This does not consist in deducing sensation from the movement of matter or reducing it to the movement of matter, but in the view that sensation is one of the properties of matter in motion. Engels supports Diderot in this view" (12, p. 39). Thus we see that, although dialectic materialism admits thought as a process taking place within matter, still it does not follow that thought is the motion of matter. And even if thought could be reduced to the motion of matter, in any case the qualitative peculiarity of thought would not be exhausted.

Such are the main points of difference between dialectic materialism and mechanical materialism.

7) At this point we shall pass to the examination of the main principles of the dialectic method.

The main principles of dialectics were, as is well known, established, formulated, and proved in the first instance by Hegel. As we have already said, with Hegel these principles had a wholly idealistic character, in so far as they were applied to the development of the universal spirit, and were therefore understood as the logical laws of thought. Marx and Engels transferred these dialectic principles from the domain of logic into the province of actual processes of development of the material world, that is, nature and history. That is why Engels reproaches Hegel with the fact that his dialectic laws were not drawn from nature and history but were imposed on them as laws of the mind.

Engels regards three of these laws as fundamental: *the law of the transformation of quantity into quality, and vice versa, the mutual penetration of opposites, and the law of the negation of negation.*

Let us pause for a moment to examine each of these and their significance for science in general and for psychology in particular.

Of the law of transformation of quantity into quality, Engels speaks as follows: "In nature qualitative changes may take place in a strictly definite way for each separate case only by means of quantitative gains or of quantitative losses of matter or motion (so-called energy)" (9, p. 21).

What is here understood by "qualitative changes" which follow as a result of quantitative changes? By the former are understood those stages in the development of any phenomenon when it acquires new properties and becomes subject to new laws which formerly did not belong to it. The best examples of these "qualitative changes" are those forms of the motion of matter of which Engels spoke. Beginning with simple mechanical transposition and ending with the more complex forms of the motion of matter, which belong to the domains of physics, chemistry, biology, and so on, these forms of the motion of matter, although they are one connected process of the development of matter, differ widely from one another in their specific properties and in the law to which they are subject.

According to the law, the qualitative changes do not come about gradually, but immediately, suddenly, with a definite *leap.* That is why this law is sometimes called the law of *leaping development.*

But it would be wrong to think only that quantity changes into quality and that the reverse process does not take place. This would not be a dialectic point of view but a mechanical one because, as Engels says: "The mechanical conception leads to the explanation of all changes by change of place, a qualitative difference by quantitative, and ignores the fact that quantity and quality interact, that quality may change into quantity, just as quantity changes into quality, that here we have mutual re-action." Engels emphasizes the fact that often "a multitude of changes in quality can be observed, as to which it is not yet proved that they are called out by quantitative changes" (9, p. 5).

Therefore all quantitative processes have at the bottom definite quantitative relations, since quality and quantity are simply two sides of one and the same process.

What are the concrete scientific facts proving the effectiveness of this law?

We will follow this up, beginning with inorganic nature and ending with the phenomena of social order. We know that in physics for every substance there is a maximum temperature under which matter assumes a new qualitative form.

Take an example from Engels: if water is heated to a temperature of 100° C. it turns into steam, but if it is cooled to a temperature of 0° it becomes ice. The qualitative transformation is accomplished not by degrees but all at once, by a sudden leap. This we see also in chemistry, where new qualitative formations appear only when elements taking part in the reaction have a definite quantitative relation to each other.

We can observe this dialectic process in biology. The Dutch botanist, De Vries, was able to demonstrate that formations of new species took place not through evolution, that is, by the gradual accumulation of changes, but suddenly, by mutation. Finally, we observe this process also in social life, where an old, worn-out social and economic epoch is replaced by a new, qualitatively different one, not as a result of an evolutionary but of a revolutionary process.

With regard to psychology, this law of the process of leaping development, accompanied by the transformation of quantity into quality, and vice versa, finds its most obvious and fruitful application in experimental psychology, which deals with the very quantitative definitions embraced in this principle.

In fact the entire perception of external influence by our senses and a number of facts proved in an experimental way show us this. Such, for instance, is the qualitative distinction of the principal spectral colors.

As is well known, at the basis of this distinction lies the excitation of our nervous system, corresponding to the quantitative distinction in the number of vibrations of ether waves. Thus, 729 billion vibrations give us violet; in the gradual but insignificant quantitative reduction in the number of these vibrations we do not notice any qualitative change of color, and only when the vibrations are reduced quantitatively to 621 billion do we feel the qualitative distinction from violet to blue; further, 599 billion vibrations give green; then there is a sudden change to yellow with 521 billion vibrations, etc. We see that the quantitative reduction or increase of nervous stimulus causes a qualitative distinction in the colors perceived on the retina, and that this is entirely subject to the principle of leaping development.

We notice the same thing with regard to hearing. The quantitative increase of nervous stimulus under the influence of the vibrations of sound waves gives a qualitative distinction in the tones and half-tones received by our ears, and proceeds at the same "leaping" pace. Thus, within the limits of the first gamut for 261 vibrations we get "do," for 293 vibrations "re," and for 329 vibrations "mi," and so on.

This principle of "leaping" development is brought out still more when we examine the minimal and differential limits of stimulation. We begin to receive qualitatively all kinds of stimuli when these stimuli reach a definite quantitative limit: for instance, a weight of not less than 0.002 gram is necessary for the skin to experience the slightest pressure; the temperature must be increased to $1/8°$ C. before the slightest increase of heat can be felt; to hear the faintest sound, a cork ball, weighing 0.001 gram must be dropped from a height of 0.001 meter on a glass plate, at a distance of 0.001 meter from the ear. The increase in the differential limit of stimulation is subject to the same principle. In order to render the weight resting on the hand noticeably heavier, it would be necessary to increase this weight by not less than $1/17$ of its former weight; in order to make a room, lit by 1000 candles a very little lighter, it would be necessary to add not less than 1% of the candles already lit; in order that an orchestra of, let us suppose, 70 musicians, should sound a very little louder, it would be necessary to increase the number of musicians by 10, i.e., by $1/7$.

We are taught this also by the theory of contrasts: the qualitative distinctions of contrasts are noticeable only when the qualitative changes in the contrasting components reach a definite stage.

Undoubtedly, the development and growth of the more complicated psychophysiological processes, fatigue, practice, memory and forgetting, etc., are subject to the same principle. Experiments confirm this at every step. Thus the forgetting of shades of gray, according to Lehmann, does not increase in proportion to the time elapsing from the moment of reception, but increases in leaps, and if, five seconds after remembrance, all reproductions are true, then after 30 seconds tone reproduction remains at 83%, but after 120 seconds becomes only 50%. This happens also in the case of memory; here there is also no direct proportion between the quantity of acquired material and the qualitative effect of memory. If, according to Meumann, we take a line composed of 8 syllables to be learned, it will be necessary to repeat it 5 times, while a line twice as long must be repeated 17 times, and a line of 24 syllables must be repeated 30 times. Leaping development is very easily seen in memory. The same can be observed with regard to the increase of fatigue, practice, and so on.

It would be only just to presume that the emotional sphere is also subject to the principle of leaping development, although it would be difficult to apply here the dependence of qualitative changes on quantitative increases. We can, however, establish here those "junctures," as Hegel called them, which condition the leaping development. It is well known that each emotion of definite quality, when it reaches a certain limit of development, enters a new qualitative stage. This is obvious in the elementary sensations of satisfaction and dissatisfaction, which, when they are prolonged over a certain length of time and reach a certain pitch of intensity, pass into the directly opposite condition. Even if we take more complicated forms of behavior, we see that a feeling of self-respect, on reaching a certain point, becomes pride, economy becomes meanness, boldness becomes insolence, and so on, that is, they pass into a state which, although belonging to the same species, is qualitatively distinct from the previous state.

Leaving for a moment these particularities, let us take the behavior of man as a whole. Much of this behavior will become comprehensible to us if it is examined from a dialectic point of view, that is, according to the principle of leaping development.

Why is it that important facts often pass without leaving any trace, while some scrap of casual conversation, a fleeting encounter, or a passing remark calls out a sharp reaction, changing our behavior entirely? This is determined to a considerable extent by the weakness of man at the definite " juncture," where only the slightest additional weight is necessary, in order to get an effect out of all proportion to the external influence, qualitatively changing entirely the behavior of man.

It may be here pointed out that the law of mutual dependence of quality and quantity recently received its fullest and most fruitful development in the field of psychology through the school of Gestalt psychology. That which we called above "quality," the "qualitative changes" out of which arose new properties and laws are those *Gestalten* which, by virtue of their structure, determine the elements and parts belonging to them. This principle—methodologically extremely fertile and thoroughly dialectic—attacks at the roots that mechanical attitude which until lately reigned supreme in psychology, both subjective and objective. It regarded human personality merely as the sum of experience, or reflexes. From the dialectic point of veiw, human personality is, naturally, a definite, qualitative, structural unity, the separate parts of which can be understood only in connection with the properties and laws of the whole. The experimental work of the representatives of Gestalt psychology has proved this brilliantly.

Such are the concrete facts drawn from various fields of scientific knowledge, which prove that the dialectic law has general methodological significance for science, and is an essential element of the theory of scientific knowledge.

8) It is necessary now to study the second law of dialectics, *the law of the mutual penetration of opposites.*

The best definition of this law was given by Lenin, who said: "The bifurcation of unity and the knowledge of its contradictory parts is the main point, one of the essentials, one of the chief—if not the principal—peculiarities or features of dialectics. This is how Hegel viewed the question. The identity of opposites (or nature, their "units") is the recognition of contradictory, mutually excluding, opposite tendencies in all the phenomena and processes of nature, spirit, and society." Thus we see that the most characteristic point of this law, as its name tells us, is that it reflects the presence in actual reality of contradictory agents and tendencies, which interact and in this way influence the process of development of real activity.

Therefore the development of any phenomenon or system is always *self-development,* to be explained only through the interacting opposites inherent in the phenomenon or system, the contact and struggle of the opposites effect the leaping transition from one qualitative form to the other of which the first dialectic law speaks.

It is clear from Engels' examples that actual reality, which begins with mechanics and ends with the complicated phenomena of social life, is saturated with mutual penetration of opposites. In magnetism and electricity the mutual penetration of polarities may already be observed. All chemistry is based on the phenomena of attraction and repulsion.

As to organic life, the cleverest proofs of the second law of dialectics are the phenomena of life and death. "The negation of life," says Engels, "is, by its very nature, founded in life itself so that life is always thought about in relation to its unavoidable result, included in it from the embryo—death. The dialectic comprehension of life is just this—to live means to die" (9, p. 15). Other examples referred to by Engels in that field are the "unity of movement and equilibrium" and the "struggle of heredity and adaptation."

As regards the phenomena of social and economic life, the classic examples of the presence of the mutual penetration of opposites are those facts analyzed by Marx in *Das Kapital*: the growth of production and exchange of goods in capitalistic society preconditions all the contradictions of contemporary class society, the division of society into two main antagonistic classes, the competition among capitalists, imperialistic wars between separate countries, and so on.

The dialectic laws mentioned above find their reflection in psychology also. That side of the law which says that actuality is not the mechanical union of separate things and processes, but a most complicated structural unity, the separate parts of which are influenced by both the whole and the interaction with other parts—this side of the law finds its full justification in psychology. It must be clear to us at this point that the personality of a man and his behavior are a particular but, at the same time, an individual and complicated unity, and not merely a mechanical association of separate facts of this behavior—reaction, reflexes, psychological phenomena, or whatever name we may choose to call them. And because the personality of man is a structural if particular unity, we regard this personality and its behavior from one standpoint, as conditioned by social and biological causes, and from another, as conditioning in its turn separate acts of behavior of this personality. In this consists the extraordinary difficulty of the study of psychology—that the personality of man and his behavior are conditioned by the extremely complex system of interactivity, causes, and conditions, to give a comprehensive analysis of which would be tremendously difficult.

The dialectic law we have examined, however, says not only that each definite material system is a structural unity of interacting causes and conditions but also that the main tendency of these mutual relations is the struggle between opposites, and that this struggle conditions the development of this unity. The question arises: What kind of struggle between opposites conditions the unity and the development of human personality and its behavior, and in what form does this struggle express itself?

Here it is necessary, first of all, to indicate the main starting-point for all psychology, which sets as its task the study of the behavior of a whole, living, and concrete human personality—the starting-point lies in its interaction with environment. This interaction may be reduced to the struggle of two opposing tendencies, which in their unity form what we call the behavior of the living organism. This act of struggling leads, on one hand, to the adaptation of the living organism to its environment, while, on the other hand (and especially in the case of man), it leads at the same time to the adaptation of the environment of the demands of the man. "Acting upon nature, man changes his own nature," says Marx. This is the continuous life-conflict of man or, in other terms, the establishment of equilibrium and the disturbance of the balance between the individual and his surroundings. In this consists the process of behavior of the living organism. Engels rightly expresses the essentially dialectic nature of this process when he says: "In the living organism we observe a permanent equilibrium of the whole organism, which is always present in motion; we observe here the living unity of nature and equilibrium. Every equilibrium is relative and temporary" (9, p. 23).

Thus the fact of the equilibrium of the individual with his environment and the upsetting of this equilibrium—are two antagonistic tendencies dialectically joined in unity of behavior,—constitute the main psychological fact, which is reflected in the second dialectic law.

The second equally essential law, confirming the mutual penetration of opposites in the field of psychology concerns the very structure of human personality. Here also we find the presence of two antagonistic tendencies—the innate or hereditary reactions, on one hand, and the acquired reactions or habits, on the other.

In fact, if the former, that is, the innate reactions are the products of the hereditary experience of the previous generations, the second, acquired reactions must be the product of the personal experience of the individual; if the first appear ready, the second, on the contrary, demand for their formation considerable effort and exercise. If the first are conventional, the second, on the contrary, possess a most original and creative character in spite of this antinomy; one form of reaction organically passes over into the other, forming in the personality of man an organically blended unity. This is why an endless argument goes on about instincts. Those who hold the anti-dialectic, the metaphysical point of view, regard these instincts as static, as a special process, inherent from birth in the living organism, while others, approaching the question dialectically, regard them as dynamic, that is, as a transient form of behavior, afterwards organically wedging them into the formation of habits of man.

The structural unity of human personality together with its development consists of this mutual penetration of innate and acquired forms of behavior.

Along with this it is possible to indicate in the personality of a man and his behavior a number of other antagonistic tendencies, such, for instance, as the interaction between the conscious and the unconscious. These, if understood from an anti-dialectic point of view, lead to a metaphysical explanation of those states, as is the case with Freud, for instance, who interpreted "the unconscious" as a special sphere veiled in a kind of a mystic shroud, secluded and nested in the personality of man. From the dialectic point of view, what are called "conscious" and "unconscious" are no more than the transitory and interacting factors in behavior, the qualitative differences of which are determined by nothing else but by differences in physiological mechanisms, that is to say, by the work of the cortical and subcortical centers of the brain.

Corresponding fully to the law of interpenetration of opposites are also those forms of behavior of man which are characterized by inhibition and excitation, irradiation and concentration, strain and relaxation, and so on.

Thus all the above facts taken from psychological reality prove the second dialectic law to be true.

9) The third dialectic law is *the law of negation of negation.* According to this law, the separate processes of material reality (*thesis*) change in their dialectic development into factors of their direct negation (*anti-thesis*), the negation of which, in their turn, lead to the confirmation of the primary situation of the thesis but at a higher stage (*synthesis*).

In order to understand the meaning of this law it is necessary first of all to analyze carefully what is meant by "negation." It may be pointed out here that the term "negation" should in no case be viewed from the point of view of formal logic, where negation between "*a*" and "*not a*" always excludes the mutual relation and transition of these objects into each other, because formal logic is concerned with objects in a static condition. Dialectic logic gives quite another meaning to "negation." Dialectic logic takes material activity in movement, in its dynamic development, where the inter-negation and contradiction existing between actual processes never exclude, although they may limit, each other. This is why Engels says: "Negation in dialectics does not mean simply "no" and is not a declaration of the non-existence of something or its arbitrary destruction. The character of negation is determined here, first, by the general and, secondly, by the special nature of the process. I must not only negate but also remove the negation. I must consequently construct the first negation so that a second negation remains or becomes possible. How is this done? It depends upon the nature of every separate case. If I crush a barley seed or an insect, I commit the act of the first negation but make the second impossible. For each series of things there is a peculiar species of negation which makes development possible. This applies also to each species of representations and ideas" (7, p. 128).

Among the examples taken from various fields of knowledge and prov-

ing the importance of this law, we will take the following, beginning with
the examples to which Engels refers. Here is an instance of the law of
negation which Engels takes from mathematics. Let us take any algebraic quantity and call it "a." The negation of it brings forward "$-a$."
Should we negate this second quantity, by multiplying $-a$ by $-a$ we get
a^2, i.e., the original positive quantity but a stage higher.

The transformation of a seed also serves as an example. Through negation a seed is transformed into a plant and then, by a second negation,
into a number of seeds. A larva, a primitive living creature, is transformed first into a chrysalis, and then into a more perfect creature—a
butterfly. Engels takes an example from social life, community of land
ownership, as is found among all primitive people. With the development
of culture, community ownership of land changes to private ownership,
which in its turn gives place, in a socialist state, to public ownership. An
analogous example is found in Marx's theory, proved in detail by him in
his *Das Kapital*. In its main lines his theory shows that "the capitalistic
method of production and appropriation and the capitalistic private
ownership arising from it constitute the first negation of individual private ownership based on personal labor. The negation of capitalistic production imposes itself with the necessity of the natural law. This is the
negation of negation."

Engels gives examples of the importance of the law of negation in
ideology and particularly in philosophy. Ancient philosophy was naïvely
materialistic. It was replaced by idealism, that is, the negation of materialism. Idealism in its turn was negated by contemporary dialectic
materialism.

In psychology this law may be fully proved. As an illustration we
shall indicate the following facts, which supplement those already observed when we examined the second law of dialectics. We then saw that
the equilibrium attained by the organism and its surroundings negates itself after the subsequent restoration of this equilibrium, but at a higher
stage; it is enriched by the experience of preceding reactions. We saw
also that unconscious hereditary forms of behavior, such as instinctive reactions, afterwards change into conscious forms of behavior habits, which
by exercise continuing up to a definite limit again lose their character of
conscious activity and become automatic. Analogous examples are the
acts of remembering, of subsequent forgetting, and of new reproduction
in a richer and often creative form. This triad can be observed in the
process of scientific synthetic perception and description. These change
into the stage of deepened experimental analysis in order to reach their
climax in theoretical synthetic inferences and generalizations, etc.

Such is the importance of the third important law of dialectics.

10) In conclusion an essential question arises. What are these laws
of dialectics? What is their actual meaning and significance for science
in general and for psychology in particular?

As to their origin, Engels gives the following exhaustive reply: "How
does the mind acquire these principles? Does it find them in itself? No

—we deal with the form of existence, with the form of the external world, and these forms thought can in no case draw from itself, but only from the outside world. Principles prove to be not starting-points, but are abstracted from them. It is not nature and human life which are guided by principles, but the principles themselves are right only in so far as they agree with nature and history. This is the only materialistic interpretation of this question" (7, p. 27). That is why Engels reproaches Hegel with the fact that his dialectic laws are not taken from nature and history, but are imposed on the latter as laws of the mind.

The laws of materialistic dialectics, then, constitute the widest theoretical generalization drawn from experience, from actuality. And since this actuality does not constitute anything static, but is in constant motion and development, therefore the laws of materialistic dialectic are the laws of every kind of motion and development both in nature and in human society and thought. Laws of dialectics are distinguished in this way from the analogous and well-known laws of formal logic—the logic of identity, the law of contradictions, and the law of the exclusion of the third. The last-named law applies to things and processes in their complete form, as if they were in a state of repose. But it is hardly worth while to say much about this—to say that nothing in the world is in absolute repose and that the very conception of repose has a relation and conditional meaning, being only a particular and temporary part of motion. Therefore, when the law of identity says that everything is identical with itself, this law assumes significance only for those people who hold a dialectic point of view, when things are taken in repose, since in motion things change all the time and cannot be identical with themselves. From the point of view of dialectic materialism the laws of formal logic are only particular instances of the laws of dialectic logic. In spite of the relations of the laws indicated, we see that, while the laws of formal logic constitute the common inheritance of science and are known to all, the laws of dialectics are far from being so widely known, although they are much more important for science.

But if, as we have already said, the laws of dialectics are the laws for all changes and development, have not these laws much in common with those established by the supporters of the theory of evolution? We can find a complete answer by Lenin. He says: "Hegelian dialectics, as the most comprehensive, the richest in content, and the most profound as regards the study of development, were regarded by Marx and Engels as the greatest achievement in classic German philosophy. All other formulae of the principles of development they counted one-sided and poor in content, distorting and maiming the true course of development. In our time, the idea of development, of evolution, penetrated almost completely the social consciousness but by other routes, not through Hegel's philosophy. This idea, however, in the formula based on Hegel which Marx and Engels gave to it, is much more comprehensive and richer in content than the current idea of evolution. Development, as if repeating the stages already passed through, repeating them in another way, on a higher level ('negation of negation')—development, so to speak, in spiral form and not in a straight line, leaping development, catastropic, revolutionary; 'breaks in gradualness,' transformation of quantity into quality, internal impulses to development produced from within by contradictions, the collision of different forces and tendencies acting on a given body or within the limits of a given phenomenon or within a given creature; the interdependence and the closest intimate connection of all sides of each phenomenon (more and more new sides are being discovered by history, which brings forward a whole universal process of motion subjected to definite laws—these are a few features of dialectics showing that they are much fuller than the usual theory of development."

Thus we see that the laws of dialectics differ radically from the laws of formal logic and from the general principles of evolutionary theory. We shall turn now to the question: In what lies the concrete significance of dialectics in science? We think that the importance of such general theoretical laws in science is twofold: first, such laws are *explanatory principles*, in so far as they help in the analysis of the complicated facts of actuality, and, secondly, they are the guiding principles in scientific research; in other words, they could be employed *as a method of research.*

Let us examine both propositions, beginning with dialectics as an explanatory principle. What does dialectic give us from this point of view?

Dialectic teaches us to take each phenomenon, including human personality, not in its static but in its dynamic aspect, in its development. Only such a dynamic attitude towards the personality of man can give us the right interpretation of such factors in behavior as natural and acquired reactions, instincts, habits, temperament, character, etc. These, dialectically interpreted as interpenetrating opposites of one process of development, shed their metaphysical husk of some static force inherent in the nature of man. But this is not all. Dialectic laws teach us that a dynamic attitude towards the interpretation of human personality is not sufficient, if the development of the personality is supposed to be a gradual and uninterrupted process. The latter is not an unbroken thread from the unravelled skein of life, as one usually hears it spoken of. Human personality and behavior resembles rather the skein itself, in which the thread of life is entangled in a contradictory and, it would seem, in a willful way. Dialectic helps us to understand and disentangle these contradictions, in so far as it speaks of breaks in gradualness of the transformation of quantity into quality, of the collision of various forces and tendencies contradictory to each other, which are internal impulses to the development of the personality and behavior of man.

None of these, however, would explain the behavior of man if dialectic had not brought forward the principle that no phenomenon can be understood and explained without a comprehensive consideration of all reasons and conditions connected with it, of all relations existing between the separate factors determining the given phenomenon.

These are the dialectic laws, the result of theoretical generalizations derived from the actual study of natural phenomena and human society.

From these laws we know that in the study of the behavior of man it is necessary to pay attention to the dynamic elements in his behavior, the integral nature of its structure, and the legitimate transition of one form of behavior into another in direct opposition to it and negating it. It is necessary also to understand the complicated nature of the conditions governing the phenomena under observation. Only by taking all these into consideration can we arrive at an exact description as a reflection of actuality in human behavior, and at an exact explanation as an establishment of those interacting connections and dependences which govern behavior.

It is necessary to understand that from the knowledge of merely general laws of dialectics the legitimate course of the phenomenon cannot be established, because as we have seen, the laws of dialectics should be drawn from actuality and not imposed upon it. There is no doubt, however, that a knowledge of the laws of dialectics is extremely valuable when it is necessary to analyze complicated reality, to understand it, to analyze and find out its main moving tendencies and causes. Here lies the importance of dialectic as an explanatory principle.

Dialectic is not only an explanatory principle but at the same time a guiding principle, *a method of scientific research.*

From the point of view of Marxian methodology, the chief aim of all scientific work is not only the theoretic study of a given phenomenon but the practical mastery of it for the purposes of social utilization. Marx and Engels persistently emphasized the point that their teaching was not dogma but guidance to action. Therefore it is necessary not merely to *know, but to know so as to be able to do*—this is the principal task of scientific knowledge from the point of view of Marxian methodology, and from this derives its definition of the method as a means of knowing and mastering some phenomenon of nature or society.

In order to master some phenomena, its advent must be *foreseen.* Only from the point of view of *prevision* and, through this, of *mastery* and *regulation* of the phenomena studied can we make an estimate of the relative significance of the several methods of scientific research. It is at this point that dialectic begins to play a tremendous part as a method of research, of prevision of the advent of a phenomenon studied, and of its changes.

All scientists are aware that during the process of work, even when their research work on some problem is going well and it seems possible to conduct it to a definite result, one always meets with individual facts or observes tendencies which do not fit into the plan of research and are even in contradiction to it. Such experiments are usually called "accidental" and do not therefore receive attention, particularly since, after statistical treatment they are lost view of, and do not exercise any noticeable influence on the final result. As a matter of fact, to scientists of dialectic turn of mind, such experiments should appear extremely symptomatic, since, while nothing "accidental," that is without cause, exists for dialectics, every single "accidental fact" can, on the basis of dialectic principles, become the source of a rising tendency, which if carried out to a definite limit, might bring out, in a "leap," new qualitative characteristics and in this way lead to new and unexpected results.

Such is the meaning of dialectics—as general methodology of scientific knowledge, as an explanatory principle, and as a method of research.

At this point we will conclude our account of the methodological premises of dialectic materialism in their relation to psychology, and pass on to the direct examination of what constitutes the study of psychology.

MARXIAN PSYCHOLOGY, ITS SCOPE, AIMS, AND METHODS

1) To obtain a clear idea of what constitutes psychology from the point of view of dialectic materialism, it must be understood from the first that we refute the traditional conception of psychology as a science treating of the mind, consciousness, emotions, psychical processes, and so on. These definitions belong to the various schools of *subjective psychology*. The methodological premises examined above prompt us to refute these definitions of psychology. Apart from the fact that our definitions are fundamentally opposed to the assumptions of the subjective school of psychology, which always end in idealism, we cannot hold with them from a purely empirical point of view. As a matter of fact, the abstract analysis of the mind, artificially cut off from a number of other vital functions of the organism, the usual underestimation of the material bases of the mind, which condition *the formal side* of behavior and make psychology an explanatory discipline and not a purely descriptive one, and finally the entire neglect of the social agents determining *the contents of the consciousness of man* in his general behavior—none of these harmonizes with the thoroughly social teachings of Marxism, which, as we have seen, aims not only at the theoretical explanation of the phenomena of nature and society but at actual mastery of them for social purposes. These assumptions also do not agree with the purely materialistic conception of man, whose psyche may be regarded as merely the introspective expression of physiological processes. We are unable for these reasons to admit the soundness of the position of subjective psychology in the general interpretation of its scope.

On the other hand, we are not at all inclined to associate ourselves with the adherents of the extreme *objective school of psychology,* which either flatly denies the existence of the human consciousness or identifies it with the mechanical movement of matter. We regard this attitude as wrong, since its methodology is founded on what is for us unacceptable—mechanical materialism with its usual simplification instead of explanation of the complex phenomena of actuality. It has been already noted that dialectic materialism is not inclined to deny the existence of psychical phenomena in man. It takes these phenomena only as the subjective expression of physical and physiological processes taking place in the organism and having their objective external expression in movements.

We regard psychical phenomena as one, but not identical with the physiological processes conditioning them. It is, not without reason, therefore, that the school of dialectics regards psychical phenomena not as something supernatural or superimposed but simply as *the other side of physiological processes showing peculiar qualitative features* (4, pp. 137, 147). These "peculiar qualitative features" of consciousness must not be forgotten, since without it the individual is incomplete.

The reason for our disagreement with both the extreme objective and the subjective schools of psychology lies in the fact that neither of them actually studies the individual as a united whole, in which objective and subjective manifestations are fused organically. It has been the custom for centuries to divide man into two parts, the body and the soul. The followers of this tradition assert that these two parts differ entirely from each other in nature and, in fact, exclude each other. This tradition of the duality of man has left an ineffaceable stamp on each of the above-mentioned schools, where the individual is studied either from the subjective or the objective side. It is obvious, therefore, that in dividing the individual into two parts each of these schools studies human behavior in part only. The objectivists focus their attention on the study of reflexes or reactions, which they regard as merely the external manifestations, actions, and behavior of the individual, ignoring their subjective expression, the consciousness. On the other hand, the subjectivists aim at the study of the consciousness, underestimating its objective mechanisms and expressions. It need hardly be pointed out that in neither case is the individual as a whole dealt with, since the study of the individual apart from his consciousness, or the study of the consciousness isolated from its material bases can give only a defective representation of the integral, living, concrete individual.

On account of the general unsatisfactoriness of the methodological premises of the above schools, the problem arises of finding a conception of psychology which would provide an organic synthesis of the objective and subjective in human behavior, in so far as the living, integral, and concrete individual constitutes exactly such an organic synthesis. As Ludwig Feurbach says: "Physiology and psychology are not reality, only anthropology is reality, only the point of view of sensuousness and contemplation is reality, since only this point of view gives me *integrality* and *individuality*. It is not the soul that thinks and feels, because the soul is only an embodied hypostatized function or phenomenon of thinking, feeling, or volition thrown into a particular entity. It is not the brain that thinks or feels, because the brain is physiological abstraction, an organ removed from integrality, from the cranium, from the head, and from the body in general, and regarded as something independent. The brain acts as an organ of thought only when connected with the human head and body" (10, Vol. I, p. 157).

It follows then that psychology should be a unity of the subjective and objective, a *theory of the behavior of a living, integral, concrete individual in concrete social conditions*.

2) What then is the personality of man, and what is the structure of personality? The methodological premises mentioned above predetermine the answer to this fundamental question of psychology.

First of all, if materialism teaches us that the individual is an organic unity, an organic synthesis of the objective and subjective (this subjectivity being understood merely as a property giving certain qualitative characteristics to objectivity), dialectics show that the individual—like all other phenomena—is not constant and immutable, but on the contrary is mutable and dynamic and can be understood only in its dynamics, development, and behavior. We can therefore define psychology as the science of *behavior,* and in this way of the *development,* of the individual. This is the first point necessary for the understanding of the structure of personality.

The dialectic approach to the study of the individual induces us to admit a second point, that the individual is a *qualitative unity* possessing inherent qualities and laws peculiar to him alone which cannot be mechanically reduced *only* to physical and chemical or physiological laws. We must not forget the profound truth of Engels' words: "We shall no doubt reduce thinking by means of experiments to material processes taking place in the brain, but is the substance of thinking completely explained by this?" It is obvious that more could still be said on this point since thinking has its own special laws—*the laws of logic.* It would, of course, be a fruitless task to explain, for example, the law of identity or any other logical law by some chemical formula.

The specific quality of the properties inherent in the individual as a definite qualitative unity does not permit us to consider the structure of this individual as the simple sum of the elements composing this structure. We say that the whole is greater than the parts of it taken together, and the representatives of the German Gestalt psychology rightly extend this formula when they say that "whatever takes place in any part of the whole is determined by the internal nature of the structure of this whole." This methodological point prompts us to refute the purely mechanical conception of the structure of the personality of man as the simple sum of "emotions," "reflexes," or "reactions." The subjectivists and objectivists are both very frequently guilty of such conception. This patchwork understanding of the structure of the individual is radically anti-dialectical and must therefore be discarded. This is the second important point necessary for the correct understanding of the structure of the individual.

Further, in studying the structure of the individual we must take into consideration the antagonistic tendencies in the development and behavior of the individual, interpenetrating and negating each other and determining the process of development of the individual.

We have already described this process in some detail when speaking of the methodological premises of psychology. Finally, while recognizing that the qualitative unity and integrality of the individual are specific, we cannot consider the individual as a self-sufficing entity, from which all the explanatory principles of its existence could be drawn. We have seen that in reality each separate element is determined by a complex system of interacting collections, and no phenomenon can therefore be examined apart from the elements and causes by which it is determined.

It is regrettable that in the study of the individual what would be thought the generally admitted claim of science has been grossly violated. Some psychologists, mainly those of the subjective school, have sought and are still seeking the explanatory reasons for these specific properties and rules in the psyche itself (psychic causality, apperception, determining tendency, and so on); others, mostly of the objective school, look for these explanations in anatomical and physiological mechanisms, again within the narrow limit of the individual. Neither of these schools, however, speaks —or, if so, only in a general way—of the so-called "environment," i.e., of social conditions and their influence on behavior.

Therefore, the different points of view on psychology become clear: on the one hand, it is regarded as a science of the abstract "soul," and, on the other, as a branch of natural science in no way connected with this soul. In the latter case no importance is attached to man's consciousness, since man is here studied apart from his social relations; and, without consideration, the consciousness obviously loses all its significance.

Marxian psychology, along with the biological elements, attaches still greater importance to social agencies and to their influence on man's behavior, since the individual is no more than the product and at the same time the sum of social relations. As a matter of fact, from the Marxian standpoint man became a man, the social animal with the most highly developed psychophysiological system, with the gift of speech and thought, only because he began during the process of adaptation to his environment *to prepare* tools for production. Labor and the processes of labor—these are the sources from which sprang the biological changes in the structure of the human organism. Thus labor turned man into a social animal connected with others by complex social ties.

Articulate speech grew out of these social relations of labor, and together with this its subjective expression, thinking in words, an indispensable medium for any ideological work.

Thus, everything that is human, everything that distinguishes man from the beasts, is, historically speaking, only the product of labor and, in this way, of social relations.

Bukharin, a noted Russian Marxian, describes in the following way this dependence of man on his social conditions. He says: "If we examine separate individuals in the process of development, we observe that essentially they are packed with the influences of their environment to the same extent that a sausage is filled with meat. A man is bred in his family, in the street, in school. He speaks the language that is the product of social development, thinks with the conceptions worked out by a number of previous generations, sees around him other people with all their ways of life, sees before him the whole order of life, which influences him every second. Like a sponge, he continually absorbs new impressions. On this material he forms himself as an individual. Every individual therefore is social in his core. Every individual is a conglomeration of social influences, tied in a small knot."

It is not only in their historical development that people are products of social conditions; they are governed by them still more in their present-day behavior. What, in fact, is this behavior in our present-day conditions? It is, first of all, *working behavior,* the mainspring of man's existence.

What is present-day society from the point of view of work? It is the combination of definite *classes,* differing entirely as to the part taken in the productive working processes. At this point it becomes possible to understand the tremendous differences in people's behavior, which are determined by the class to which they belong. Therefore we presume that one of the essential branches of psychology should be *class psychology.* This would aim at the study of the behavior of definite social groups, in relation to the position held by them in the system of production. For this reason, in our work on differential psychology, we give first place to the social anamnesis of the people tested, since we consider there is not and cannot be any individual psychology isolated from class psychology. Marxian differential psychology is above all a class psychology, because only on the foundation of the study of moving social forces can the psychology of single individuals become comprehensible to us.

When the influence of social conditions on man's behavior is taken into consideration, dialectic materialism gives it rightful place to the *consciousness* of man. In the social process consciousness plays an essential part. One of the greatest Russian Marxians, Plekhanov, defines the social rôle of consciousness as follows: "Though it is not consciousness which determines existence, but existence which determines consciousness, it does not follow that consciousness has no place in the historical progress of mankind. Being determined by existence, consciousness in its turn influences the further development of existence" (18, Vol. XII, p. 259). Plekhanov also points out the definite place occupied by consciousness among other agents determining the social process.

"All historical research must begin with the study of the system of production and the economic relations of the given country. But research must not stop at this; it should show how the dry bones of economics are covered with the living flesh of social and political forms, and then (and this is the most interesting and attractive side of the work) with human ideas, feelings, efforts, and ideals" (18, Vol. VII, p. 233).

Consciousness is not an unnecessary supplement to, but an adaptive function in the behavior of man. Marx has expressed this very well in the following words: "The spider performs an operation, akin to weaving, and the bee constructs its waxen cells in a manner which might well put to shame certain people—architects, for instance. But the worst architect is distinguished from the finest bee in that, previous to constructing the cells in wax, he has first constructed them in his head. The results of the process of labor were already present before this process began, in the imagination of the worker. He not only changes the form of what was bestowed by nature, but he realizes in this his conscious aim, which, like a law, determines the medium and character of his action, and to which he submits his will" (16, Vol. I, Pt. 3).

That is why we cannot deny the adaptative part played by the consciousness of man, nor agree with the position of those philosophers and scholars who, at the Sixth International Congress of Philosophy, held at Harvard University in 1926, made the following statement: "The soul or consciousness, which played the leading part in the past, now is of very little importance; in any case both are deprived of their main functions and glory to such an extent that only the names remain. Behaviorism sang their funeral dirge while materialism—the smiling heir—arranges a suitable funeral for them" (20, p. 642). With regard to this we must say that, whereas naïve materialism is in fact organizing "a suitable funeral" for consciousness, dialectic materialism, on the other hand, is restoring that pseudo-corpse to life, considering that although consciousness will not take the "leading rôle," still something more than the "mere name" remains. As a matter of fact, what remains is a limited but, at the same time, important rôle, which we have indicated above. To ignore this in the process of studying the behavior of man would undoubtedly be a mistake.

3) It would here be noted that the synthetic view of the structure of personality by no means excludes an analytical treatment in the study of separate elements of the behavior of this personality. We regard *reactions* as the responses of the living organism to the stimuli of its surroundings. Therefore from an analytical point of view we call psychology "reactology," that is, the science of the reactions of the individual.

Reactions are a *biosociological* conception, under which it is possible to group all the phenomena of the living organism, from the simplest to the more complicated forms of human behavior in the conditions of social life. The reactions of man in connection with his social relations acquire a social significance. In this we observe the main distinction between psychology and physiology. The latter also studies the reactions of man, but studies them without any reference to his social relations, while in psychology these relations constitute the principal content of the reactions studied. This is why we regard psychology as a social science rather than as a branch of natural science.

We regard the conception of reactions as the basis of the analytical study of psychology, and we prefer it to the purely physiological conception, deprived of every subjective content, of *reflexes,* with which only extreme reflexologists and objectivists operate, and to the narrow psychological (separated from all objective mechanism) conception of *emotions,* on which the subjectivists work. The conception of reactions seems to us more acceptable since it includes, with the biological and formal quantitative elements inherent to the reflex, the whole wealth of qualitative ideological content, foreign to the conception of the reflex.

The three following elements may be regarded as formal quantitative facts in reaction: first, the *rate* at which the reaction takes place, from the moment when the stimulus appears to the moment when it is met by a responsive movement; secondly, the *intensity* of the reaction, that is to say, that force with which the responsive movement proceeds on being stimulated; and thirdly, *the form of the reaction*—which may be understood as the *way traversed* by the stimulated organ, *the rate of movement* of this organ, and the *total period of time* covered during its movement.

The elements enumerated, however, do not exhaust the contents of the reaction. Besides the formal quantitative elements inherent to reaction there are also *interior contents*—its *social significance*—which are expressed, for instance, when a person writes a letter to inform someone of his coming, or of the death of a relative or friend. From this we may conclude that the *behavior of a person taken as a whole, as well as every separate reaction of a person, represents unity of form and content of qualitative and quantitative elements and of biological and social significance.*

4) The methodological premises examined above determine entirely the methods employed by us in the study of reactions. We look upon method not only as a means of *knowing* some particular phenomenon but also as a means of *securing control* over this phenomenon. In order to control this phenomenon it is necessary to *foresee* its advent. From this point of view of *foreseeing*, we estimate the value of different methods of scientific research. We presume that the first and most elementary stage of human knowledge in the sense of prevision is the *method of simple objective observation.*

What does this give us? Applied alone, the most that it does, is that it helps us to *establish* a fact and *describe* it comprehensively. We speak of its application to single cases since the multiple application of observation becomes the statistical method, the importance of which we will refer to later. In any case the method of observation of complex phenomena gives only the minimum possibility of prevision of the advent and results of the further development of the phenomena under observation. Only when dealing with very monotonous, mechanically recurring phenomena, as, for instance, in astronomy and a few other sciences, can we, by this method, foresee and foretell the development of the object observed.

Much more important, in the sense of prevision, is the *statistical method* of research. In this case objective observation of definite analogous phenomena is multiple and then is submitted to a quantitative calculation. This method makes it possible to establish *the degree of probability* of the advent of the particular phenomenon. There is no authentic prevision in this case, except those rare cases when the statistics obtained show 100% of probability, that is, full authenticity. The statistical method does not give authentic prevision for the same reason that objective observation does not give it. In this case we deal only with the description of facts, without explaining them, without establishing the reasons, just as in the statistical calculation we establish only the presence of a prevailing *tendency* without disclosing the reason for the recurrence of the given phenomenon a particular number of times or for its reaching a particular degree. And the more complex the phenomenon, the more likely it is to be the result of many causes and the clearer becomes the narrowness of the limits and the powerlessness of the statistical method.

The third and more perfect stage of scientific knowledge in the sense of prevision is *the experimental method.* Here we are enabled to disclose the principal *cause* of a particular phenomenon and, in this way, not only to describe but also to explain it, thus giving fully authentic results, on the basis of which we can foresee the approach of the given phenomena and control them.

Let us now consider the *test method*. This we regard as *simple deduction*, as a conclusion drawn from general principles, established by means of inductions, that is, on the basis of objective observation, statistical and experimental methods, applied to individual cases. Therefore, the importance of this or that system of tests is wholly determined by those of the above-mentioned inductive methods the tests are influenced by.

Passing now to the description of psychological experiment, it should be remarked that this differs from ordinary scientific experiment in so far as the results, in the case of psychology, usually show two features: on one hand, the objective quantitative evidence of reaction given by the apparatus applied, and, on the other hand, a corresponding qualitative evidence given by the person tested.

Since, however, all scientifically-conducted experiments should exclude conflicting elements and be uniform in character, it follows that psychological experiments should not form an exception in this respect. Their objective and subjective elements should be carried to an unconditional unity, and in this uniting of qualitatively various elements in one whole lies, perhaps, the greatest difficulty of conducting psychological experiments, as compared to both scientific experiments and to pure introspection, where we deal only with homogeneous elements. But whenever the slightest dissonance occurs between the subjective and objective data, not to speak of open conflict, there can be no doubt that since the data of self-observation are prone to be mistaken, they should always take a subordinate position in relation to the objective side of the experiment. The task of the psychologist in this case is almost analogous to that of a doctor diagnosing a disease. The physician also tries to bring into agreement and connection the subjective evidence of the patient and the objective signs of the disease, keeping, however, the center of gravity on the objective evidence and only under its control establishing the diagnosis of the disease. Similarly, in experimental psychological research it is necessary to bring into agreement the evidence of self-observation with that of objective valuations, controlling the first by means of the last.

From all this we can make our final conclusion, *that only the objective side of an experiment is a sufficient guarantee of its authenticity. As regards the subjective side, that is, the data of self-observation, these possess significance only in so far as they are corroborated by the objective facts.*

5) Here the question arises: What are the problems treated in our Institute, and how are they solved in accordance with our methodology? In reply we must point to the fact that only five years have passed since we first began to study psychological problems in the light of dialectic materialism. During this time our attention has been occupied mainly with the working out of our methodological principles and the search for concrete means by which to direct our experimental work. This search was conducted by two main paths: first, the study of so-called *class and*

collective psychology and, secondly, the study of the *structure and mechanism* of separate concrete forms of the behavior of men and animals.

In the first section of the work on class and collective psychology, we group under the head of class psychology the study of individuals as representatives of a definite, social, productive group. From our standpoint, class psychology is a branch of comparative psychology, setting us the task of distinguishing between the behavior of representatives of different classes. It is scarcely necessary to explain why class psychology is now the center of attention in Marxian psychology. The point is that in the study of behavior we cannot operate with man taken in the abstract, man in general, since from the Marxian standpoint man is a combination and product of definite social relations, and, first of all, of those connected with production, that is to say, class relations. It is obvious, therefore, that the behavior of man must bear the stamp of the class to which he belongs. In fact, if we take the constitutional peculiarities of people, the sphere of their instincts and emotions, the nature of their perceptions, the formation of their habits, everything, including their manner of thinking and speaking, we see that all these forms of behavior in different classes and sub-classes (the bourgeoisie, the proletariat of the towns and villages, the intelligentsia, etc.) possess their own specific features and distinction, very little studied up to the present.

Along with the study of class psychology the problems of collective psychology also claim our attention. By the latter we understand the study of those characteristic peculiarities in behavior, arising under the influence of the mutual relations of people. The importance of the study of the collective behavior of people for Marxian psychology can hardly be enlarged upon here since, if the latter aims not only at the theoretical explanation of this behavior but also at its control for the purpose of its social rationalization, then the best way to achieve this purpose is to study collective and, particularly, class psychology.

That is why this year our Institute is undertaking extensive psychological research in class and collective psychology in one of the important manufacturing enterprises in Moscow. It is too early, of course, to speak of any concrete results of our researches in that field.

6) With regard to another cross-section of our research, that is, the study of the structure and mechanisms of separate forms of the behavior of human beings and animals—we have a series of complete experimental works already published. It is necessary to pause here for a description of those which are more or less connected with our methodology.

We shall begin with an outline of those works in general psychology which have been carried out by the so-called *reactological method,* set out in detail in my book, *The Study of Human Reactions* ("reactology"). By this method it is possible to obtain at one time the quantitative and qualitative characteristics of the phenomena of reactions.

As mentioned above, the quantitative and qualitative elements of the phenomena of reactions are: first, *the rate at which the reaction takes place;* secondly, its *intensity;* thirdly, the *form of movements in reaction;* and, fourthly, its *contents or social significance.* In order to study the rate at which the reaction takes place, we used a method generally known in psychology as the *chronometric method,* using a Hipp chronoscope. In measuring the intensity of reactions, we used the *dynamometric method,* employing an instrument specially designed by me for this purpose, the *dynamoscope.*

The latter shows in milligrams and millimeters the work done during the reaction. For the quantitative calculation of the form of movement of the reaction we employ *the motor-graphic method,* and, with the assistance of the dynamoscope, obtain the triple expression indicated above: first, *the size, or the way traversed* by the stimulated organ; secondly, the *rate of movement* of the organ; and, thirdly, *the period of time* during which the organ moves.

The dynamoscope is so constructed that it can be attached to the chronoscope, and therefore it is possible to obtain at one and the same time all the three types of reactions, the speed rate, intensity, and form of movement.

The contents of reactions, however, are subject to qualitative measurements as supplied by self-observation, the significance of which we accept only under one condition, that is, if they are controlled by the objective data.

Since all the various reactions of man can be reduced to a few principal forms, beginning with the simplest and ending with the most complicated, research work was carried out chiefly on those main forms. There are seven main forms of reaction. Taken together they constitute what we call the *gamut* of man's reactions, on account of their gradually increasing complexity. These seven main forms of reaction are as follows:

The first and most elementary is the so-called *natural* reaction, during which a person remains in a more or less natural stąte, executes his tasks without any particular strain as far as it is compatible with his nature, and distributes his energy more or less equally between the objects of his work and his movements. As a rule the natural type of reaction under the condition of everyday life is inherent to that type of work which requires neither intense mental activity nor intense muscular exercise. Under laboratory conditions, the simplest prototype of this kind of reaction is the quiet and free reacting of the persons undergoing the tests to simple stimuli of seeing, hearing, feeling, etc.

The second form is *muscular reaction.* In this case a person strains his energy intensely, concentrating it mostly in his movement. Under this head should be grouped such reactions as in the case of a wood-cutter hewing wood or a laborer working on the soil. In the laboratory experiments this type of reaction was obtained by various kinds of stimuli while the whole of the energy of the subject was concentrated on the movement of one of his arms.

The third form is the *sensory reaction,* during which almost all energy is concentrated on the object of work, and distracted, more or less, from movement, as, for instance, in the case of a turner, a watchmaker, etc. In the laboratory experiments the attention of the subjects had to be concentrated entirely on the perception of the stimuli.

The fourth form is the *discriminatory reaction*. In this case it is necessary to react to more than one stimulus, and to distinguish from among those already known a certain new stimulus. A typical example of this kind of reaction is that of composition in printing. In the laboratory environment similar reactions are obtained by the producing of one of two or four or an even greater number of previously conditioned stimuli, to which the subject must react.

The fifth is an even more complicated reaction—the *selective reaction*. In this case the subject not only distinguishes the stimuli but also combines each of them with some movement or with the refusal to make such a movement. Such, for instance, is the reaction of a tram-driver, a chauffeur, etc. In the laboratory the prototype of this is the reaction of the subject to various stimuli with previously conditioned movements or his refusal to make these movements in response to each of these stimuli.

The sixth form is the *reaction of recognition*. Here the person reacts to stimuli previously unknown to him. In everyday life, these conditions are obtained when a person visits a museum or exhibition with which he was formerly unacquainted. In the laboratory these reactions are caused by the presentation to the subject of various objects of printed matter with which he was formerly unacquainted.

Under the last and most complex form are included the reactions *of logical order*. In this case the subject reacts to stimuli demanding sometimes very complicated logical operations. The best illustration of these reactions in daily life is constituted by the processes of the mind of the representatives of liberal professions when they accomplish various logical operations after the perception and conscious recognition of the material presented. In the laboratory these were reactions beginning with simple primitive association of words and concluding with the most complex forms of influence, calculations, etc.

7) By the juxtaposition of the data of all the subjects, in the analysis of the data of natural reactions, the typological side of the research work emerges with extreme clearness. It appears that all the people tested showed a marked tendency to one of the four following types of reaction: one type of reaction, which was quick and strong, has been called by us *the muscular active;* another, which was slow but strong, *the sensorial active* type; a third type was quick but of low intensity—*the muscular passive;* and the fourth was slow and of low intensity—*the sensorial passive* type.

It should be here pointed out that, in the correlation of dynamic and motor-graphic sides of reactions, a complete parallelism is present. With the increase of the intensity of reaction there is also an increase in the route covered and the average rate of movement of the reacting organ, with, however, but slight change in the period of time of the movement.

In the transition to muscular reaction of all the persons tested a different law was discovered. During the concentrations of energy on the reacting organ the reaction reached its greatest speed and intensity, with a parallel increase in the route covered and the rate of movement of the reacting

organ.   In the case of the sensorial method of reacting a contrary effect
was produced. During the concentration of all the energy on the stimulus
the reaction slowed down noticeably, and its intensity fell, while the route
covered and the rate of movement of the reacting organ decreased.

By the juxtaposition of the data of these three types of reaction we saw
clearly the tendency of each of the subjects to one or another method of
reacting with regard to speed, intensity, and form of movement of the
reactions. At this point the necessity arose of finding out if it was possible,
and if so how far possible, to achieve the transition of persons from one
manner of reaction to another.   For this purpose, persons exhibiting a
tendency to a definite type of reaction were made to react in an entirely
different way.

The results were as follows: First, persons of the *sensorial passive type,*
that is, subject to slow reactions of low intensity, pass over easiest of all to
the directly opposite manner of reaction, i.e., the quick, strong reaction.
Secondly, persons of a *sensorial active* type, that is, reacting slowly but
strongly, very easily increase the rate of their reactions, but with difficulty
lower their intensity. Thirdly, persons of a *muscular passive* type, that is,
with quick reactions but of low intensity, increase the force of the reactions
easily, but slow them down with difficulty.   Fourthly, persons of a muscu-
lar-active type, that is, with a tendency to quick and intense reactions,
find it most difficult of all to pass to the opposite manner of reacting, i.e.,
to the slow and weak reactions.

It must be noted, in particular, that experiments carried out at the same
time on the measurement on the dynamoscope of energy expended at the
instant of reaction and the measurement on the ergograph of energy expended during protracted work did not show a strict correlation. The
expenditure of a tremendous amount of energy in separate reactions is absolutely no guarantee that during prolonged work a person may expend a
correspondingly larger amount of energy. Very frequently intense reactions require a very small amount of energy when the work is prolonged,
and, on the contrary, weak reactions at each separate instant are sometimes
combined with a considerable amount of energy expended during prolonged work.

It is interesting here to note that the sex of the persons tested does not
play any part in the intensity of the reactions.   Extensively conducted tests
made on more than fifty persons of both sexes failed to show any appreciable difference due to sex.   In both cases there were men as well as women
who expended either tremendously much or surprisingly little energy in
the process of reactions.

With regard to research work on the more complex forms of reaction,
that is to say, discrimination, selection, recognition, and the logical type of
reaction, the results of all these researches proved only one point.   That
is: the greater the task in the sense of quantity and complexity of
stimuli presented and of their combination with movements or logical
operations, the slower was the reaction, together with a great reduction in
the amount of energy expended in movement and in the figures showing
the form of the movement.

Thus all the research work conducted on different kinds of reactions is clearly marked with the stamp of a definite regularity existing between the quantitative and qualitative sides of reaction, between the transitory, dynamic, and motor elements on one hand, and the complexity of the central process of the reaction on the other. We see, in fact, that in muscular reaction, where, as is well known, the central process is of an elementary nature (leading many psychologists to identify this reaction with simple reflexive movement), the external release of energy in the movements of the reacting organ reaches its maximum in the minimum period of time of the reaction. Then, in the sensorial reaction, where we are faced with a more complex central process, the intensity of the peripheral expenditure of energy falls, together with the general slowing-down of the time of the process of the reaction. Finally, during the further complication of the central process in the reactions of discrimination, selection, recognition, etc., we observe anew the same gradual decline of both the peripheral expenditure of energy and of the figures characterizing the form of movement, together with the consequent slowing-down of the time of the reaction. Thus, it appears that with the complications of the central process of the reaction, a slowing down takes place in the time of the reaction, with a reduction in the expenditure of energy on the movement of the reacting organ, as well as in the route and rate of this movement. The central and the peripheral expenditures of energy prove to be two polarities mutually negating each other in the process of reaction.

I have called this point *the principle of the monopolar expenditure of energy,* in an attempt to express the distinction between the two contradictory elements in the process of reaction—the central and the peripheral—in which the complication and strengthening of one is invariably accompanied by the fall of the other.

The facts of life, apparently, entirely corroborated the truth of this principle. It is impossible, for instance, to be engaged in some complicated mental work, demanding great central expenditure of energy, and at the same time expend a great deal of energy on external movements of the organism, and vice versa. This can be seen in the external position of the body during profound mental activity. There is neither gesticulation nor movement; only a face expressing deep concentration, staring its fixed gaze on a single point, tells us that the organism is striving to reduce its expenditure of energy to the minimum, even to the movement of the eyeballs. Facts disclosed about the physiological nervous system and the neuro- and psychopathology of the regulating activity of the central mechanism, which are governed by laws that when violated cause a sharp increase in the reflexive activity of the organism, clearly demonstrate the principle of monopolarity in the behavior of man.

Starting from this principle of monopolar expenditure of energy, I have drawn some conclusions in reactology which could be applied by teachers and psychotechnicians since the central expenditure of energy is usually termed mental labor and the peripheral expenditure as physical labor. I have, therefore, drawn the conclusion that the present intensive striving after the synthesis of mental and manual labor in the Soviet Union might be achieved, both in theory and practice, not by their simultaneous fusion but by a regular consistent transition from one form of labor to another. With regard to this, experimental facts show that the transition from peripheral expenditure of energy to central takes place with greater difficulty than the opposite process. This is tantamount to saying that the transition from mental labor to physical is always easier than the opposite process. In practice this means that to transform a mental worker into a manual worker is much easier than to change a manual worker into a mental worker.

8) It will not do, however, to overestimate this principle and regard it as universal, particularly in such a dynamically developing process as human behavior. Like all principles, it has its definite limits of application, beyond which, according to the laws of dialectics, it turns into its own opposite. This finds its confirmation with particular clearness in my latest experimental researches. In the course of research on the more complicated reactions, especially those demanding logical operations, one meets very frequently with single experiments found to be in opposition to the prevailing monopolaric tendency of reactions. It has occurred to me that perhaps we are finding here an embryo of another tendency which is dialectically in direct opposition to the principle of the monopolaric expenditure of energy. Great efforts were required to establish these tendencies as permanent and stable. For this I was obliged to complicate still further, quantitatively, the system of stimuli and observe the qualitative changes in reactions. To put it exactly, instead of the complicated operations with logical reasoning, I passed to immeasurably more complex stimuli in the form of mathematical problems, to which any subject would react after the process of having solved them. On the ground of the previously established principle of monopolaric expenditure of energy, it would appear that I should have achieved a still greater reduction in the size of the reaction, while, as a matter of fact, I achieved the direct opposite; the intensity of the reaction under the influence of too complex stimuli, instead of falling, rose sharply and acquired an explosive nature. I therefore called these reactions *explosive* and the principle causing their appearance the *principle of explosiveness.*

It is clear, then, that the transition from monopolarity to explosiveness is entirely subject to the dialectic principle of leaping transition from quantity to quality. The quantitatively small increase in complexity of the central element of the reaction leads to the slowing-down of its effective part and, in this way, to the confirmation of the principle of monopolarity. The qualitatively great complication of the central elements of reaction, on the contrary, leads to sharp, explosive, speeding-up of the motor side of the reaction.

On their application to the concrete behavior of man both these principles show that, if his intellectual activities are the consequences of an intense central expenditure of energy with a slowed-down periphery, then the affective activity of man forms the opposite case. This would be the explosive speeding-up of the periphery with the slowing-down of the central expenditure of energy, that is, with the lowering of intellectual activity. Reactions such as outbursts of rage, laughter, impetuous admiration, utmost bewilderment—all these are the best examples of these kinds of explosive reactions. Unfortunately, the mechanism of all such reactions is as yet very little known. According to Lipps, the mechanism of these reactions implies the presence of so-called "physical dams," slowing down the reactions. Kuno Fischer regards this mechanism as the "contrast of motions," Freud as the process of "elimination of internal obstacles," and Hamann as the "leap from loaded state to discharge," etc.

It is hardly necessary here to say that such formulae of the mechanism of explosive reactions are too general, undifferentiating, and in some cases incorrect. No more can be expected, however, from research of a purely theoretical nature.

Our experimental researches, disclosing the mechanism of explosive reactions, make these formulae more exact, give them a definite content. As we have seen above, they show that by no means all transitions from slowing down to speeding up, nor all "leaps from loaded state to discharge" lead to explosive reaction.

For this it would be necessary to have stimuli which would be sufficiently complex to cause a sufficient central straining followed by a consequent sudden release; such is the content of the principle of explosion.

Unfortunately, within the limits of this article it is quite impossible to dwell on other theoretical conclusions, described in detail in *The Study of Human Reactions*. I must say, however, that the reactological method has been found to be practical, and is the subject of several important monographs written by our colleagues.

9) I have dwelt in my book on the practical side of reactology for psychotechnicians and teachers. A research worker of this Institute, A. R. Luria, has concentrated his attention on *the forms of movement* in reaction. He has studied the affective sphere of behavior, of criminals, in particular, and has published a series of essays on the subject.

Another member of the Institute, Z. I. Chuchmarev, in his published work, "The subcortical psycho-physiology," has applied the reactological method in the field of neuropathology, studying *the intensity* and *form of movement* in the reactions of persons suffering from encephalitis.

Other experimental works published by members of the staff of the Institute are listed at the end of this chapter (14, 15, 5, 21, 6, 1, 2, 3).

This, in its main features, is the nature of our work on the structure and mechanism of the behavior of man and animals.

10) In conclusion, I must remark that we are fully conscious of the deficiencies in our work. It would indeed be strange if there were none, when we consider that it is only five years since we started along our way. We are, however, firmly convinced that only along this way may be reached the true and fundamental solution of such problems of behavior, which like those of class psychology have been scarcely touched in psychological literature up to the present time. We have set ourselves the task of filling

this gap and of making our contribution to the international work of those psychologists who, in a strictly scientific way, are studying the problem of the behavior of man.

REFERENCES

1. ARTEMOV, V. A. Reproductive processes. *Proc. Moscow Instit. Exper. Psychol.*, 1928, **3**.
2. BOROVSKI, V. M. Experimentelle Untersuchungen über den Lernprozess: III. Labyrinthstudien an weissen Ratten. *Zsch. f. vergl. Physiol.*, 1927, **6**, 489-529.
3. —————. Experimentelle Untersuchungen über den Lernprozess: III. *Zsch. f. vergl. Physiol.*, 1928, **7**, No. 2.
4. BUKHARIN, —. Attack. (In Russian.)
5. CHUCHMAREV, Z. I. Subcortical psychophysiology. Kharkov, 1928.
6. DOBRYNIN, N. F. The subject of attention. *Proc. Moscow Instit. Exper. Psychol.*, 1928, **3**.
7. ENGELS, F. Anti-Dühring.
8. —————. Ludwig Feurbach. (Preface by Plekhanov.)
9. —————. Dialectics of nature. (In Russian.)
10. FEURBACH, L. Collected works.
11. KORNILOV, K. N. The study of human reactions.
12. LENIN, —. Materialism and empiriocriticism.
13. —————. Collected works. (In Russian.)
14. LURIA, A. R. The conjunctive motor method and its application to research in affective reaction. *Proc. Moscow Instit. Exper. Psychol.*, 1928, **3**.
15. —————. Die Methode der abbildenden Motor bei Kommunikation der Systeme und ihre Anwendung auf die Affektpsychologie. *Psychol. Forsch.*, 1929, **12**, Nos. 2 and 3.
16. MARX, K. Das Kapital.
17. —————. Theses on Feurbach.
18. PLEKHANOV, —. Collected works. (In Russian.)
19. —————. Cowardly idealism.
20. TILLY, F. Contemporary American philosophy. *Proc. 6th Int. Cong. Phil.*, 1926.
21. VYGOTSKI, L. S. The problem of dominant reactions. *Proc. Moscow Instit. Exper. Psychol.*, **2**.

PART VII

BEHAVIORISM

CHAPTER 14

ANTHROPONOMY AND PSYCHOLOGY

WALTER S. HUNTER

Clark University

Anthroponomy is a science of human behavior. It is not a system of psychology. An exposition of a science ordinarily calls for a presentation of methods and results,[1] but in the present chapter we are given the task of comparing anthroponomy and psychology with reference to the major aspects of the two fields of endeavor. The discussion will therefore be concerned primarily with such general issues as the following:

1) What are the subject-matters of the two sciences?
2) What are the chief methods employed?
3) What kinds of results are secured in the two fields?

Let us first comment upon the two terms, anthroponomy and psychology. More and more in America the term psychology fails to designate adequately the character of the scientific study of human nature. Psychology, if the word means anything, means a study of psychic factors, processes, or states. To the extent that psychology is defined as the study of immediate experience, this immediate experience is regarded as something mental. It is true that from the beginning of the science most psychologists have included in their treatises and papers material on human behavior and on the anatomical structures associated with that behavior; but this material, which at the point of its inclusion is not regarded as mental but as physical, does not make the science psychological. It rather detracts from the claim that the study of mental processes is a science, since this material is introduced for purposes of explanation and in order to give practicality to the studies made. Psychologists have more or less frankly adopted a dualistic metaphysical position which assumes the reality of mind and matter, although they would apparently be equally at home, as psychologists, with a mental monism. However, as the years pass, more and more psychologists become convinced that even such general metaphysical positions have no vital connection with scientific experiments. As a philosopher, if one denied the validity of the dualistic position, one would necessarily uphold some alternative view; as a scientist this is not necessary. In science one may study human behavior, rocks, or chemical processes without even raising the question of their ultimate mental or physical nature. Certain parts or aspects of the world are chosen for analysis. Experiments are made, and on the basis of these experiments the characteristics and laws of the phenomena are derived. Psychology as such, however, cannot exist without the assumption that some of the world at least is mental.

---

[1] I have elsewhere given such a presentation (11), and the reader is referred to that book for a survey of the factual material of anthroponomy.

Only that which can be observed or experimentally tested comes within the domain of science. Purpose, vitalistic principles, and entelechies have been practically eliminated from all science, except from some biology and psychology, not because science needs a materialistic philosophy but because purpose, vitalistic principles, and entelechies do not lend themselves either to observation or to experimental testing. They remain but words marking the present but not the future limits of explanation through the medium of experimentation.

I have chosen the term anthroponomy to designate the science of human behavior in preference to the term behaviorism. This latter term, although popular, suggests a system rather than a science; and it is, in addition, too broad a term since much behavior is properly and historically outside of the field of this particular science. Anthroponomy is derived from the Greek *anthropos* meaning *man* and *nomus* meaning *law,* a derivation sanctioned by such words as *astronomy* and *agronomy,* words which were also probably distracting when they were first introduced.[2] Anthroponomy, as a term, contains no implication of a psychic or mental process.

Before we embark directly upon the discussion of the three major topics above listed, one broad difference in method between psychology and anthoponomy should be indicated. The psychologist believes that one part or characteristic of man is his mind, his consciousness, his experience. The study of this phase of human nature is the fundamental task of the science. If we ask a contemporary psychologist what he means by the term consciousness, or experience, he will reply by enumerating such things as sweet, red, and kinaesthetic strain almost exactly as the Scottish philosopher Reid did, or he will reply by enumerating such things as roses, books, configurations, and melodies almost exactly as did the philosophers Berkeley and Hume. (A few psychologists, usually non-experimentalists, will also reply that consciousness is an agency active in adjusting the organism to its environment.) I shall have occasion to comment further upon this in a following paragraph. At the present moment, I wish to point out that

---

[2] In connection with our suggestion of a new term for the science of human behavior, it may interest the reader to be referred to the history of two other terms, consciousness and psychology, neither of which established itself quickly. The term consciousness does not seem to have been used in its psychological meaning until the time of Descartes (about 1637), and even one hundred and fifty years later it could still be treated by eminent men as a term designating a separate power of the mind. Psychology as a term seems to have first been used between 1575 and 1594 by continental Europeans (Freigius, Goclenius, and Casmann) in various Latin works; but it was almost one hundred and fifty years more before Wolff's rational and empirical psychology (in Latin) gave vogue to the term. The term did not appear in English writing and discussion until early in the nineteenth century, and in the middle of that century Sir William Hamilton still found it necessary to marshal detailed arguments in favor of the new term as a designation for the philosophy of mind. The first book in England to be called psychology seems to have been Spencer's *Principles of Psychology* (1855). The term was not well established there, however, until Sully wrote the *Outlines of Psychology* in 1884 and until Ward published his article on psychology in the *Encyclopaedia Britannica* in 1886. This was the year of the appearance of Dewey's *Psychology,* the first important American book to be so called.

consciousness or experience for the psychologist is merely a name which he applies to what other people call the environment of man. I urge even the mature psychologist to read again in Locke, Berkeley, Hume, and Reid. These great modern champions of the mind nowhere prove that mental phenomena exist. They merely assert that fact. The present-day psychologist likes to stress the argument that such things as red and middle C are mental because they are different from light or sound waves. Water, however, is different from hydrogen and oxygen. Is water therefore mental? Where any two phenomena in nature differ, is one to be called mental? If so, which one shall be mental, and what good comes of calling it such a name?

The psychologist seeks to understand human nature by calling the external and internal environments mental and then by proceeding to the study and analysis of these environments. The only time that success has attended his efforts is when the environment has been used merely as a stimulus for the subject, with the mental hypothesis either forgotten or in the background. It has been in this fashion that the work on sensory processes has been done and such theories as those of vision, audition, and depth discrimination elaborated. The psychological method of studying man is thus an indirect one in the sense that the conclusions concerning human nature are drawn from an ostensible study of human environments. Such a method was theoretically worthy of a trial fifty years ago. Its failure as a method for the analyzing of human nature gave rise to anthroponomy.

The general method of anthroponomy is a method of direct observation and experiment using organic human behavior as its subject-matter. It is unnecessary to label either man or the environment as mental, psychical, or physical. The whole universe may be composed of ideas in the minds of man and God, as Berkeley said, but such a hypothesis cannot affect experimental work save as it leads the psychologist to study reds, greens, movements, and extensions on the supposition that he is thereby studying mental phenomena! The aspects of human behavior which are most peculiarly the concern of anthroponomy are language behavior, learning, interstimulation and response, and the prediction of behavior on the basis of sample performances. These phenomena are subjected to as direct analysis and experiment as are the phenomena studied in chemistry, physics, or biology. Anthroponomy also interests itself in many other phases of human behavior. It studies the genetic aspects of human behavior through the medium of animal and child behavior. And it is seriously concerned with abnormal behavior and with sense-organ function. In these problems it receives the cooperation of other sciences to such a degree that the problems can hardly be said to be predominantly its own.

The first of the three problems which we listed for discussion was that of the subject-matter of the two sciences. Both psychology and anthroponomy take as their goal the understanding of some aspect of the human individual, leaving other aspects to such sciences as anatomy, physiology, and biochemistry. The aspect of man which the psychologist studies is that which is termed mental, or psychical, or experiential. (That all psychologists include more or less behavioristic material in their work does not invalidate the statement, because it is the psychic material and not the behavioristic material which characterizes the science.) In order that it may not be said that I misrepresent the psychologist's position, let me quote from Bentley. With variations, the quotations might be taken from the writings of almost any psychologist. Bentley says (1, p. 15) that psychology "seeks to describe and to understand experience and the activities of the total organism in which experience plays an essential part." And again he says (1, p. 19) with reference to psychosomatic functions, "Always mental resources and always bodily resources of the organism are called into use for carrying out these functional performances. That is why the psychologist calls them 'psychosomatic' functions, thus distinguishing them from the purely bodily or 'somatic' functions, such as the growth of bone and the operations of enzymes and ferments." One cannot, of course, fail to see the implication in this latter statement that the somatic processes which have no accompanying psychic aspect lie beyond the domain of the psychologist.

If we now ask what experience is we are confronted by the psychologist's distinction between an experience and a physical object or between the science of psychology and the science of physics. This distinction is stated by Wundt, Titchener, and Bentley as that between an object which exists independently of human experience and an object which exists only as experienced. Let us again consult Bentley on this point. "The objects and events of physics and of the rest are regarded *as if they outlasted the experiencing of them and continued as independent of the act of apprehension.* Animals, the earth's strata, the ocean's substance, the planet's course, and the electron's oscillations are one and all regarded as if ordered, arranged, and preserved in existence wholly apart from the experiencing organism which discerns them. But what shall we say of the objects and the operations of the psychologist? We shall say of these that they *are* only when they are-in-experience" (1, pp. 31-32). In psychology, "When we proceed to the examination of our tones and noises, ... ; of our lights, colors, colds, warmths, sweets, sours, and the like, we must take care that we do not slip from *experiencing* to the things *experienced,* to noisy cities, to tuneful voices, to sunlight and shadows, to the chill of the night, the warmth of the noon, and so on to the other *independent objects*" (1, p. 35). "And when I say that I listened last night to an orchestra composed of violins, 'cellos, double basses, wood-winds, brasses, and the rest, it is obvious that I am attempting a rough analytic description of the orchestra and not of anything connected with my organism. It scarcely seems possible that such things as books and violins should be mistaken for the furnishings of the mind; but this is precisely the first error that the beginner drops into in his quest for component qualities" (1, p. 36).

Let me give one more quotation from Bentley with reference to "images" and to "sensations" from within the organism: ". . . . a moment's reflection will make it obvious to the reader that 'myself imagined as walking' or 'myself remembered as walking' is just as much an object of the physical order as 'myself now perceived as walking' . . . We all do say in the vernacular that an object which we remember or think about is only a 'mental object'; but there we only mean that the object is not at the moment present to the senses. It is no more 'mental' than the book now in your hand is 'mental' " (1, p. 38). "Many persons think that, when they announce such an interesting fact as palpitation and trembling in sudden fear or the dryness of the throat in continued thirst, they have observed and reported psychologically. They are mistaken. This is one of the nine hundred and ninety-nine *wrong* ways of analysis!.... But although they may come to be known through processes of experience (a group of pressures of alternating intensities, in the one case; a complex of warmth and dull massive pressure, in the other), the palpitation and the dryness are no more mental than' the heart and the throat themselves are mental" (1, pp. 38-39).

Psychologists may be divided roughly into two camps on the basis of their treatment of meaning. One camp, represented by the Wundtian tradition, excludes meaning from observable mental phenomena. The other camp, represented by such diverse tendencies as are present in the imageless thought psychologists, the functionalists, the purposivists, and the Gestalt psychologists, includes meaning. The result is that the Wundtians, speaking through Bentley, would say that the meaning-users are describing physical objects; and the meaning-users would retort that the Wundtians are dealing with non-existent artifacts. I almost agree with both schools! I think nothing could be more barren than the Wundt-Titchener-Bentley psychology. It does not describe concrete things seen, heard, or felt as these exist in the inner, i.e., the sub-cutaneous, or in the outer environment. Nor does it give us a description of something mental which actually exists. And, if I agree that the Wundtian psychology is barren, I also agree that the other psychologists are not describing conscious processes, experience, when they describe books, pains, hungers, tastes, colors, and melodies. Perhaps these phenomena are more properly labeled physical, but in any case they are the constituents of the inner and outer environments as viewed by common sense. Both groups of psychologists are seeking to understand a phase of human nature by the indirect route of environment. Bentley and the other Wundtians abstract qualities, intensities, durations, and clearnesses (sometimes adding other attributes, sometimes dropping one or more) from the environment and call the material selected experience. The users of meaning take concrete objects from the environment and call these experience. If this is the path followed by the psychologists in attempting to throw light upon the nature of man, what is to be said of that followed by the students of behavior, the anthroponomists?

The anthroponomist does not deny the existence of the common-sense environment. He refuses, however, to be diverted from the direct study of man into the recording of environmental peculiarities. If you were to ask an anthroponomist to describe a certain room in the Clark laboratory, he would respond as follows: "The walls of the room are pale blue, the ceiling is white, and the floors are brown. A large gray-toned rug is upon the floor. The furniture is of a golden color; it is heavy and hard. Upon entering this room in the morning, a stale odor is easily detected, and one is at times disgusted by this odor." It must not be assumed that I am the only student of behavior who would admit the existence of such an internal and external environment as I have just described. Would anyone venture to suggest that Weiss would deny hearing the tuning forks with which he has worked, or that Lashley would refuse to say that he had seen and touched the brains of white rats? If you will turn to an article written by Carr (3, pp. 60-61) in 1912, you will find that Watson is definitely on record as having seen environmental objects of the after-image type. Let me quote some extracts from Carr's account: "After serving as a subject in a test involving considerable eye fatigue, Professor Watson was engaged in carefully and steadily observing one of the writer's eyes throughout several periods of five to six minutes duration each. The room was pitch dark with the exception that the observed eye was illumined by a minature electric flashlight. . . .

"After one of these observations, the flashlight was turned off for a period of rest. Shortly afterwards there developed in the darkness an extremely vivid and realistic positive after-image of the eye.... All of the minor details of coloring and marking came out distinctly.... Just before the lights were turned on, an added tinge of reality was produced" when the phantom eye actually winked.

"Professor Watson has had considerable practice in the observation of after-images and is, apparently, more than ordinarily sensitive to the phenomenon."

If these statements are not sufficient, a brief inspection of the writings of any behaviorist will convince the reader that the behaviorist is neither blind, deaf, anosmic, ageusic, nor anaesthetic. He lives, and admits quite frankly that he lives, in the same world of objects and events which the psychologist and the layman alike acknowledge. Let us, therefore, hear no more from the psychologist that his opponent denies the existence of these things. What the behaviorist does deny is that any of the objects or events in the world have been shown to be mental or psychic.

One of the objects in the environment which the anthoponomist sees, hears, feels, and smells is called *homo sapiens, man.* The various members of this species differ in height, weight, color, cleanliness, race, religion, etc., just as rocks differ in size, weight, density, chemical constitution, age, location, and commercial value. The anthroponomist takes man as his experimental material just as the other scientists select other objects in the environment for their experimental material. Bentley says that the rocks and the men which I see are physical objects. The meaning-users say these objects are experiences and therefore mental. But neither of the terms mental and physical is really an answer to the question. They are merely names used in order to include or exclude certain phenomena from the science. One must never forget that, when the psychologists accuse the behaviorists of denying the existence of a part of the world, the psychologists ignore certain facts: (*a*) that the anthroponomist only denies that any one has shown the psychic, mental, character of the environment; (*b*) that the anthroponomist denies that consciousness exists as an agency working for the environmental adjustment of the organism for the sole reason that observation and experiment do not justify such a conclusion; and (c) that the anthroponomist himself has offered at least three hypotheses concerning the probable nature of the environment. These three hypotheses are as follows: first, the electron-proton hypothesis of Weiss (18). Weiss accepts the most recent advances in physics and chemistry which go to show that objects in our environment are electron-proton aggregations. Stones, tables, books, storms, silver, and gold are ultimately electric charges. And so likewise are the human animals and the aggregations of human animals which make up society. If the phenomenon of a storage battery is a matter of electrons and protons, so is the phenomenon of family life—unless the physicists are all wrong, or unless there is something in family life which is not an object in the external or internal environment. Personally, I think that Weiss is undoubtedly correct. I see no immediate way or need, however, to apply this principle to *change* our experimentation. All of our anthroponomical experimentation is in harmony with this theory. This, furthermore, is exactly the case in physics. Many problems in that science are attacked and solved without involving in any specific way the electron-proton conception of the nature of the universe. Even in physics it is still permissible to speak of steel and carbon and to make studies upon these substances without directly involving the question of the nature of the atom. The psychologist should, therefore, not reproach Weiss if the latter continues speaking of biosocial responses instead of attempting to state the molecular activities which make up these responses.

The second hypothesis concerning the nature of the environment is that of Lashley (12). Lashley speaks of the environment as consciousness, conscious content, or quality, following an old tradition of the psychologist, and consciousness for him is "a complex integration and succession of bodily activities which are closely related to or involve the verbal and gestural mechanisms and hence most frequently come to social expression." Lashley also stresses the ultimate physicochemical nature of these bodily integrations.

The third hypothesis concerning the nature of environmental objects is my own (7, 8, 9). In a series of articles, I have elaborated the hypothesis that red, sweet, salt, emotion, books, trees, and storms are all cases of a particular stimulus-response relationship. This particular bit of behavior is the irreversible *SP-LR* relationship. (The letters stand for sensory process and language response.) The present chapter is hardly the place to offer a résumé of these papers. It will perhaps be worth our while, however, to give a brief explanation of the hypothesis inasmuch as it bears specifically upon our present problem, the subject-matter of the science of psychology and anthroponomy, as well as upon the problem of the nature of the methods used in these disciplines.

Let us apply our hypothesis to the case where new environmental objects make their appearance as this occurs when hitherto undifferentiated overtones of a clang are "reported" by the subject. "The beginner in the psychology laboratory does not hear these overtones, although physics can demonstrate that correlated vibrations exist in the stimulus. The subject is not 'conscious' of the tones,—at least he makes no verbal report of their presence and for scientific purposes he is said to be unaware of them. The experimenter now presents the vibration frequency of the first overtone (*SP*) by itself. This stimulus elicits response *LR*. *SP* is then presented as a part of a complex stimulus in order to see whether or not the same response, *LR*, will now appear. If it does not, the training is continued. *Just as soon as the verbal response, LR, is made to the complex stimulus, just so soon does the subjectivist say that the 'consciousness of the overtone' is present* . . . . . Why do we not say that *LR* is the subjectivist's 'consciousness' and not merely a criterion.of its presence? Because *LR*, if it is to be rated as 'conscious,' must in its turn have a language response conditioned to it and so be the beginning part of [an *SP-LR*] situation. Only in the irreversible situation do we have 'consciousness.' ɣ It now becomes a fertile field of experimentation to determine what stimulus aspects may be determiners of language responses and not merely of non-language responses. The irreversible relationships between these stimulus aspects and the language responses will be the 'states of consciousness.'

"We have chosen the two cases of the lower limen of sensitivity and the discrimination of component aspects of a complex situation, as the most vital aspects of adult human nature upon which to base our formation, for a very definite reason. If it were possible we should follow the truly genetic method in the establishment of our thesis as well as in its application. There are, however, no well established facts concerning the 'consciousness' of infants and children, so that we must of necessity test our conception upon adults. When, however, we examine that situation at this age level, it is found that the phenomenon termed 'consciousness,' although very generally conceded to exist, is very complex and has a long history in the individual's lifetime. We must therefore select for analysis the most definite, least ambiguous, and most experimentally inviting of the instances where 'consciousness' is extended or where new 'consciousness' arises. Having arrived at our formulation upon this basis, its adequacy— and, therefore, its truth—can be tested by examining its harmony with certain accepted data gathered from adults, children, and infra-human animals and by observing the extent and vitality of the experimental implications of the conception.

"In the two fundamental cases of conscious limen with which we have dealt, nothing has been found which does not come under our formulation. These cases, while convincing, may nevertheless not be thought crucial. If so, then the critical case for the formulation is the following: Can a receptor which does not normally condition 'consciousness' be made to do so? Stated from our point of view as a matter for scientific verification: Can activity in a receptor which does not normally condition a language response be made to do so by training? To be sure we have almost shown that this is possible to a limited degree, for the so-called subliminal receptor activities do not normally condition language activities. Perhaps the really crucial case comes with receptors all of whose activities psychology now treats as permanently subliminal to 'consciousness.' Can the receptors in the viscera which do not condition 'sensation' be made to do so by training? Only positive results can be crucial, *for the everyday training of the subject may have resulted in connecting with language responses all of the different kinds of receptors which it is possible to connect.* All that training may be able to do may be of the order discussed above. This, however, is a matter for experiment and not for theory to decide" (7, pp. 15-17).

Such are the anthroponomists' hypotheses concerning the nature of environmental objects, hypotheses which are mutually supporting and not antagonistic one to the other. Let us turn now to a consideration of the subject-matter of the science as this problem concerns the classification of the sciences of psychology and anthroponomy, on the one hand, and the sciences of physics, chemistry, mathematics, and biology, on the other hand.

I have said that the environmental object selected for study by the anthroponomist is man. And yet the anthroponomist does not attempt to study all phases of man. Anthroponomy is the science of the behavior of the human organism as a whole. The problems of this science necessarily cover a wide range. Some are shared with the related sciences of anthropology, sociology, physiology, neurology, physics, chemistry, and mathematics, while other problems are studied little if at all outside of anthroponomy. Anthroponomy thus takes its place among the sciences which study *specific* objects in the environment. Here also belong such disciplines as botany, which studies plants, geology, which specializes upon the inorganic structure of the earth, and physiology, where the functional activities of the various structures of the body become the subject-matter for investigation. In contrast to this group of sciences, which is characterized by the study of *specific* environmental objects, stands the group specializing upon those fundamental and *general* characteristics which are thought to be essential to all environmental objects. Here belong at present only mathematics, physics, and chemistry. Chemistry and physics analyze, synthesize, weigh, and measure men, rats, rocks, gases, light, and other objects in search of the fundamental general properties of nature. Mathematics seeks to write formulae for all processes whether they occur in the rat or in light. The science of anthroponomy, we have said, belongs in the group with geology, botany, and the other specific sciences. Man's learned behavior, his language responses, and his social activities are events in nature, in the environment, and as such they are partially illuminated by the general laws of mathematics, physics, and chemistry. This illumination, to be sure, is less than is desirable, but this is true in the relation of each science of organic processes to the group of general sciences.

I think we can now see the purport of those hypotheses concerning the nature of the environment which the students of human behavior have offered. Weiss's statement that such objects as white rats, red cows, tones, pains, and marital behavior are electron-proton combinations is merely the recognition that, if the contemporary general sciences of mathematics, physics, and chemistry are correct, we may ultimately write the results of anthroponomy in terms of mathematical formulae. Lashley's hypothesis and my own deal less with the future and more with the present. They, therefore, seek to state environmental happenings in relation to man's action system when this latter is viewed as another object in the common-sense environment.

Let us now return to the subject of psychology and see where its adherents would place it in relation to the other sciences. Titchener says that psychology and physics deal with the same world of experience, but from two very different points of view. Psychology studies the world with man left in it, i.e., it studies experience as dependent upon the nervous system, whereas physics studies experience as though existing independently of the nervous system. Psychology should, therefore, be classified with the general sciences as a discipline laying bare the general traits of mind, where mind is defined as "the sum-total of human experience considered as dependent upon a nervous system" (13, p. 16). *The reasonable aspect of this statement seems to me to come from the tacit recognition of the stimulus-response relationship which exists between the total environment and the human organism.* If we substitute the term environment for experience, the statement then reads: psychology studies the total environment viewed as existing only at the moment when it affects the (human) nervous system, whereas physics studies the total environment viewed as existing beyond the moment when it affects the (human) nervous system. Such a revised statement is less philosophical than Titchener's, but it is still unacceptable because of the implication that human nature should be studied not directly but indirectly through an analysis of the environment. What Titchener means, however, by "dependent upon the nervous system" is something quite subtle and not at all the crude fact that practically all relations between man and his environment ("experience") are mediated by a nervous system. This is where the concept of "conscious" processes slips into his psychology. "Experience viewed as dependent upon a nervous system" means, in fact, for him experience as observed and as conscious. As Titchener says: "We assume that everybody knows, at first hand, what human experience is, and we then seek to mark off the two aspects of this experience which are dealt with respectively by physics and psychology. Any further definition of the subject-matter of psychology is impossible. Unless one knows, by experience itself, what experience is, one can no more give a meaning to the term 'mind' than a stone can give a meaning to the term 'matter' " (13, p. 9).

Let us turn now to the second problem which we are to consider: What are the chief methods employed by the two sciences? Psychology has two methods of gathering data. One is individualistic, and the other is social. One is held to be less, and the other more scientifically fruitful. The first, or individualistic, method is utilized whenever one person undertakes to observe experience and build a science upon these observations. This method has given rise to the old armchair variety of psychology, and yet the method has never been repudiated. In speaking of the method, Calkins writes: "The method has obvious advantages. It makes no especial conditions of time and place; it requires no mechanical adjunct; it demands no difficult search for suitable material; at any moment, in all surroundings, with no external outfit, one may study the rich material provided by every imaginable experience. In an extreme sense, all is grist that comes to the psychologist's mill." *That the method has not been repudiated is due to*

the fact that the data gathered by it form the basis for the interpretation of
the results secured by the social method.

The individual method in psychology is usually introspection. Although all psychologists use introspection in the psychological part of their work, very few have attempted to explain in detail what it is and what its limitations are. For a psychological discussion of the problem the reader is referred to papers by Dunlap (5), Dodge (4), and Titchener (14, 15, 16). In these papers, as elsewhere, it is perfectly evident that the term introspection has no valid meaning except as a designation for a method of studying, analyzing, and describing conscious processes, or what is called immediate experience. If there are no mental states, if the world of reds, greens, pains, and hungers is not mental, then the term introspection has no meaning that the term observation does not have. When I reject both consciousness and introspection, as Washburn (17, p. 89) says the behaviorist does, I do so because no one has ever proved, or given me clear reasons why I should believe, that the inner and outer environments of man are mental.

Washburn urges the behaviorist to utilize the basic stimulus-response mechanism involved in what the psychologist has called introspection. And I (9) have also given an analysis indicating how one student of behavior takes what seems valid in the psychologist's method and relates it to the larger phenomenon of the subject's report. Psychologists still say, however, that the student of behavior implicitly assumes and uses consciousness whenever he makes an observation. To watch a rat run a maze, it is said, requires consciousness on the part of the one doing the watching. My answer to the psychologist is as follows: (a) No one has ever shown that the rat, its whiteness, or its movement is in any way mental. Therefore when I observe the rat in the maze, I am not observing a mental state or a mental experience. (b) The only relationships which exist between the observer and the rat are relationships of stimulus and response. The rat in running the maze stimulates the observer who makes such response as counting errors, recording time, or speaking words. When the experimenter-observer behaves in any of these ways by giving the responses which are conventional in the laboratory (or in any other situation that might be involved), he is observing. No mental, psychic processes have ever been demonstrated in this situation, although their existence has often been asserted. If a second observer observes the first observer, again the only relationship between the two is one of stimulus and response. We may extend the series of observers infinitely without finding a reasonable excuse for introducing a mental factor. Each observer is confronted by certain stimuli and responds to these stimuli. This stimulus-response situation is the phenomenon of observation. So if a baby follows a moving light with its eyes, it is said to observe the light. If a dog pricks up his ears when a sound occurs, the dog is said to observe the sound. However, the term scientific observation is applied not to all responses made to stimuli but only to certain highly conventional verbal and manual responses which can leave a permanent record or which have a value in the interstimulation and response of discussion among scientific men.

Hollingworth (6, p. 96) has suggested that the difference between anthroponomy and psychology is due to the sensuous bias of the adherents of the two sciences. The psychologists are chiefly interoceptive, and the anthroponomists, chiefly exteroceptive. Hollingworth says that contrasted with the bias of the psychologist "is that of the exteroceptist. He is more commonly called a behaviorist, and his passion is all for vision. According to this school, as I understand it, the only objects comprising the world are visual in nature. Hence visual observation, direct or indirect, is the only method to be utilized in science. If other than visual objects do perhaps exist, they are at least to be studied only through their visual manifestations or through correlated visual phenomena. Only with reluctance is occasional permission given to take advantage of auditory observation, as in the noting of cries on the part of lower animals, or the speech reports of man. But the account of all objects in the lower sensory modes is rigorously excluded from psychology." This statement, it seems to me, misconceives the anthroponomist's problem, which is the study of behavior and not the description of the remaining world of objects. Physics, chemistry, and other sciences are quite competent to describe that world. The anthroponomist in no sense limits the stimuli which he gives his subjects to those of vision. He studies the responses of animals to all kinds and combinations of stimuli. However, the anthroponomist in observing his subjects during an experiment does depend very largely upon his own eyes, although he may verify by audition or olfaction the presence of an auditory or an olfactory stimulus if one of these is being applied to his subject. This dependence of the anthroponomist upon vision during his observations corresponds to what is found in all sciences and arises from the excellence of visual stimuli in determining that type of response which is called scientific description. There is no a priori reason why the anthroponomist should not attempt to record, for example, maze errors or times on the basis of auditory stimuli received from the subject who is in the maze. The experimenter's olfactory receptor might even be used as a determiner of this observational response. There is, however, no reason why he should be forced to develop such a technique when a perfectly satisfactory one is already available in terms of the visually determined habits which the experimenter has already developed in common with other scientific men. If the subject, whose behavior is being studied, produces sounds, odors, or temperatures by his behavior, the experimenter may have his observational behavior aroused by those stimuli, although the results would probably be more accurately recorded by some mechanical device which could be affected by the stimuli in question. In this case the observational behavior of the experimenter would be released directly by stimuli, probably visual, from the recording device.

The second, or social, method of psychology is utilized wherever an experimenter utilizes subjects other than himself. Let me illustrate this method in a simple way. First, I take one blue paper disc and one black paper disc. These I mount upon the spindle of a rotating wheel in the proportion of three blue to one black. The wheel is set in rapid rotation, and my subjects are called in one at a time. I point to the discs and say, "What color quality is that?" Each subject responds in turn. "A dark, poorly saturated blue." If I change the proportion of blue and black, my subjects respond differently. These are the observable facts upon which both psychologists and anthroponomists can agree, and yet notice how different are the interpretations placed upon these facts. The anthroponomist says in a very matter-of-fact way, "It looks as though the behavior of your subjects was controlled by a change in the visual stimulus, when your instructions remained constant. This suggests to me that man reacts to blue light of various intensities. It might now be well to state the visual stimulus in physical terms of wave-length and energy in order that we may know more exactly just what the visual stimulus is and thereby help some one else in his efforts to repeat our observation." The psychologist interprets the experiment as follows: "Each subject has an immediate experience of color quality, intensity, and saturation. This inference is justified because we are all men and because I know that under the same conditions I have these experiences and use the same words to describe them. Let us by all means get the physical measurements suggested in order that later observers may be certain to get this experience." This interpretation by the psychologist makes us more certain than ever that the task which he has undertaken is that of describing the total environment as it appears to man and not that of describing some fundamental aspect of man himself.

The science of psychology is built upon inferences concerning the environment. These inferences are drawn from the observable facts gathered by the social method of that science. Against this method, and, therefore, against this science, I raise these objections: (a) An *unnecessary* and an *impossible* task is undertaken in attempting to reconstruct the environment as it appears to adult man, to children, and to animals. (b) The genetic point of approach, which has already proved valuable in understanding nature, requires that our investigation of man begin with the simpler stimulus-response problems and extend to the more complex ones later when we have mastered our technique. (c) The psychologist, as psychologist, limits himself to observing the language responses of his subjects because this behavior is bound up so closely with the discriminable aspects of the environment. These language responses are admittedly late in appearance in the animal world, and yet the psychologist utilizes the language responses of adult members of European cultures in his hypothetical reconstruction of the environment not only of man but of all animals. By thus limiting himself to the language situation, the psychologist omits much that is valuable in understanding both man and the environment. (d) The psychologist persistently violates one of the great canons of science when *he fails to harmonize his problem to be investigated with the methods to be employed.*

This last point I consider of the very greatest importance. I must, therefore, comment upon it at some length. Let us revert, first, to the experiment with the blue and the black discs. The psychological problem is this: How does the *experience* of blueness change with the alteration of the relative proportions of blue and black on the color wheel? The experimental method involves *stimulating* the subject auditorily with instructions and visually with the colored discs. The subject's behavior, called in this case his report, is then recorded. The psychologist draws his conclusions in terms of *experience,* whereas I submit that the only conclusion justified is that the subject behaves in a certain manner when stimulated in a certain way.

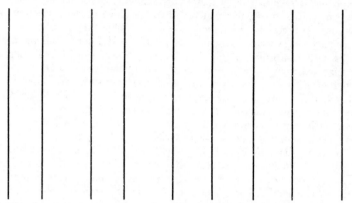

FIGURE 1

We may again illustrate the criticism by an experiment as conducted by the Gestalt psychologists. The problem is: How does the subject see the lines of Figure 1? The method of solving this apparently simple problem is as before. The subject is brought into the room. His eyes are stimulated with the lines of Figure 1, and he is given auditory instructions. As a result the subject says, "I see four groups of two lines each. At one moment the line on the right stands alone, and at another moment the line on the left is without a partner." The Gestalt psychologist now concludes that the subject has an experience of groups, or of figure and ground. The behaviorist would say that, when stimulated in this manner, the subject responds in at least two different ways. [In my *Human Behavior* (11, Pt. II, Chap. 4, and also pp. 318-322) I have presented the treatment given by anthroponomy to problems of this type.] In neither of these experiments, however, would the behaviorist rest content with formulating his problem merely in such a manner that the method available would bear upon the problem formulated. In each case he would further insist upon checking up his results using some other form of behavior than the verbal response of the subject.

Suppose we turn now from the external to the internal environment. Let the psychologist again state his problem. This time it will be as follows: What is the influence of the simple affective processes upon the knee-jerk? (2). (Or the problem might have been, how many affective qualities are there? In this case, the method would differ from what we are about to describe, but the same type of criticism would be applicable.)

The method selected involves the use of an apparatus for eliciting the knee-jerk and of certain "indifferent, pleasant, and unpleasant" words. When the subject's eyes are stimulated by the words and when he is stimulated auditorily in the proper way, he says, "Pleasant." We now proceed to apply the visual stimuli simultaneously with the tap on the patellar tendon. The results recorded indicate the magnitude of the knee-jerk under the several conditions. The psychologist thereupon concludes that pleasantness and unpleasantness did or did not affect the response in question.

Had a student of behavior used this method, the problem would have been formulated directly in terms of the method as follows: What is the influence of visual word-stimuli upon the patellar tendon reflex under such and such conditions? The fundamental error in the psychologist's procedure is that the problems formulated and the conclusions drawn can have no real bearing upon the methods employed and the results secured, since the psychologist takes as his general problem the reconstruction of his subject's environment and not the study of his behavior. When problems are formulated in terms of available methods, the scientist is much less prone to spend his energies in the fruitless effort to solve problems which at the present moment lie far beyond the best available technique. The student of behavior is not altogether guiltless here, for occasionally he also formulates problems which are quite unrelated to the methods employed in their solution. The difference between such a mistake on the part of an anthroponomist and a simliar mistake made by a psychologist lies in the fact that, by the definition of the subject-matter and goal of his science, the *psychologist is forever committed to this error,* while in the case of the anthroponomist only a momentary lapse from rigid scientific method has occurred.

In the description and criticism of the psychologist's methods, we have by implication given many of the characteristics of the methods used by the anthroponomist. It is only fitting and proper, however, that we should describe certain characteristics of these methods more in detail. As in psychology, so in anthroponomy, chief reliance is placed upon the social method as a method of gathering data. The anthroponomist will at times work upon himself as subject, but he appreciates the great difficulty of controlling and checking many factors which influence behavior where the subject and the experimenter are one, and *he absolutely refuses to use this individualistic method as the basis for interpreting the results of his scientific labors.* The methods of the anthroponomist always involve the presentation of stimuli and the consequent arousal of behavior in the subject. Sometimes one stimulus is emphasized in the experimental situation so that this stimulus finally may be said to control the behavior. Sometimes the subject is merely placed in a general environmental situation and his behavior observed. So far as is practical, the specific stimuli which determine the behavior are recorded, and the experimenter notes what seem to him to be the important aspects of the response. Where the conclusion is drawn that the red stimulus, in a red-green discrimination experiment, e.g., controls the behavior, there is no implication that the red stimulus is effective *by itself.* Many other stimuli are cooperating, particularly stimuli from the stomach of the hungry subject and stimuli from the muscles and skin. The conclusion, in reality, is that, under these experimental conditions where the stimuli from the skin, muscles, viscera, ears, etc., are kept *constant,* the *deciding* factor in controlling the response is the wave-length difference between the two visual stimuli. To be sure, there are configurations of stimuli at work and the organism does act as a whole, but under the conditions of the experiment described, the most significant conclusion to be drawn refers to the stimulus which plays the deciding rôle. Wherever it can be shown that the subject's behavior is controlled by a particular grouping of stimuli, that conclusion should be drawn. Any other use of the Gestalt concept seems unnecessary.

This brief discussion of the stimulus-response nature of behavioristic experiments leads me to state three further points: (*a*) The psychologist conducts exactly similar experiments, but he is so engrossed in his effort to reconstruct the subject's environment and so hypnotized by the significance of language behavior that he slurs over the essential character of the observed facts in his desire to attain the goal which he has set himself. If Burtt and Tuttle, for example, had realized that, in dealing with their so-called affective processes, they were dealing with a bit of behavior, the first step that would have been taken would have been to assure themselves that this particular bit of (visceral?) behavior was present. Having shown its presence as a result of the word stimuli, they could then have studied the facilitory and inhibitory relations between this behavior and the knee-jerk. (*b*) Some psychologists have said that the behaviorist, when he uses the stimulus-response concept, ignores the contribution which the organism makes to the nature of the behavior. This seems to me to be a remarkably uncalled-for accusation. Has not the behaviorist always appealed to the results of heredity and previous training as factors which cooperate with present stimuli in determining behavior? Was there ever a behaviorist who explained maze behavior without calling upon the retained effects of a previous training for a part of his explanation, or a behaviorist who ignored childhood peculiarities in accounting for adult behavior? (*c*) The third point concerns the psychologist's criticism of the behaviorist's use of the stimulus-response category. By what right, so the criticism goes, does the anthroponomist say, "I used a red light as the stimulus," or "I trained the subject using a cube and a sphere as stimuli." Since the behaviorist accepts the theories of physics and chemistry as adequate for the explanation of nature, it is said that all stimuli should be stated by him in terms of these sciences. This criticism ignores the fact that the behaviorist, like the physicist, accepts a common-sense view of the environment as the milieu for his experimentation. This we have been at great pains to point out earlier in the present chapter. The anthroponomist has no more hesitancy in saying that he gave water to his chicks in order to see whether they would drink than a chemist has in saying that he has completed the analysis of water into H_2O. The chemist does not find it necessary to drop the word water and substitute for it some electron-proton term. Wherever the situation demands that the wave-lengths of light, the vibration frequencies of sound, and the chemical constituents of odorous substances be stated, the anthroponomist meets the demand, but not otherwise. As anthroponomy advances to ever more and more rigorous experimentation, it is to be expected that such specifications of the stimuli and of the organic conditions will occur more and more frequently. Until that time, let us proceed in a matter-of-fact way, suiting our specifications to the practical needs of the moment.

We shall limit ourselves in the remainder of our discussion to a brief statement concerning the third problem formulated above, "What are the results of the science?" With reference to anthroponomy it need only be said that the results secured bear directly upon the fundamentals of human behavior. The anthroponomist himself specializes more upon language behavior, learned responses, and the facts of interstimulation and response than any other scientist, and in addition he cooperates with others in the study of various additional aspects of man in so far as these affect organic behavior. *All of these results are possible without omitting from the resulting picture of human nature any observable and verifiable datum.* The anthroponomist even goes further and offers various hypotheses concerning the nature of the inner and outer environments as these are reported by his subjects. Nowhere is it necessary to introduce the concept of consciousness, or experience, conceived as another mode of existence, or as another aspect of the physical world. Nowhere does the anthroponomist study the subject's environment except as a possible source of stimuli for the subject's behavior.

The psychologist thinks that he secures two types of results, one he assumes concerns consciousness, or experience, and the other we all agree is behavior. The behavioristic results of the Wundtians have been deplorably slight in amount when one considers that most of their experiments have involved stimulus-response situations in a subject other than the experimenter. The adherents of biological functionalism have been more fortunate in their results in spite of their theory that mind is an instrument of adjustment in the struggle for existence. This outcome of their work has been possible because their systematic point of view has encouraged the direct study of man. It is only to be regretted that they have mixed up experience and behavior so thoroughly that the conclusions which they have drawn from their experimental work must in many cases be rejected, and in many cases the work must be repeated with the problems reformulated in harmony with the accumulated results of anthroponomy. No combination of "experience" and behavior is necessary or possible in the accurate portrayal of human nature. If we consider the results secured by the most consistent and logical students of (so-called) consciousness, the followers of the Wundtian tradition, we see that these results (so far as they concern psychology and not behavior) consist of a vast array of least discriminable aspects of experience, blueness, tonality, contact, pain, sweet, noisiness, intensity, clearness, duration, and others.

When we turn to the work of Gestalt psychologists, we find that experimental results are stated in terms of unique configurations and not in terms of the abstract and highly artificial products of the Wundtian school. This is an advantage to the extent that new aspects of the environment are discovered, an advantage, i.e., if we think that the way to understand man is through a study of the environment. As yet the Gestalt movement has not worked far enough into the problems of systematic psychology to reveal just how it will treat these problems of general theory. The movement so far has been limited largely to the field of "perception" and to an elaboration of the concept of the organism as a whole. Sooner or later, however, it must face the many other problems of classical psychology, as these appear in such questions as the natures and interrelations of "perception," "imagination," "affection," "attention," and "thinking." I can see no evidence as yet which would lead me to believe that Gestalt psychology as a science of "experience" will escape many of the culs-de-sac into which the psychology of discriminable aspects of experience has fallen. After all, a Gestalt is merely another unique but more complex aspect of the environment. And it will be just as difficult for the adherents of that point of view to classify and synthesize unique Gestalten as for their opponents to synthesize unique elements or unique least discriminable aspects of the universe.

It is sometimes said by Gestalt psychologists that the chief result to be obtained by their method of approach to psychology is an insight into the neural processes of man and that the study of Gestalten is merely a means to this end. Köhler in particular has emphasized this, and he has in addition sought in a brilliant way to apply the principles of physics to the problems of neural processes. There is much, therefore, in Köhler's psychology which is in harmony with Loeb's tradition in biology and with Weiss's theories in anthroponomy. And yet, in spite of this, I cannot react optimistically toward such a program for two reasons: (a) Ever since the days of Wundt's physiological psychology, the students of psychology have sought neural correlates for complex as well as for simple experiences with little or no success. On what grounds, therefore, are we to expect better success from the attempt when made by the Gestalt psychologists? To be sure they will propose theoretical neural functions different from the ones proposed by the Wundtians. So much is certain, because the Gestalt psychologists are seeking neural correlates for Gestalten and not for the least discriminable aspects of experience. (b) My second reason for pessimism with reference to the attempt to dissect neural functions by means of environmental studies is the same as my reason for rejecting a science which studies human nature by means of analyses of the environment. Why all this indirectness? If one wishes to study neural functions, why not study them directly? Why not begin where the physiologist has left off and carry on from that point? The work of Lashley and Coghill will throw more light on neural functions than fifty years of speculation by the Gestalt psychologists added to the fifty past years of Wundtian speculation, because Lashley and Coghill are attacking their problems directly and in the light of the present status of the sciences dealing with that problem. *If the Gestalt psychologists are able to formulate a hypothesis which will be valuable in the understanding of neural function, it will be a result of the stimulus-response data which they will*

*inevitably accumulate in their studies and not a result of the experiential
hypothesis with which they, like the Wundtians, burden their use of the
social method of investigation.*

Here at the close of our discussion the reader, particularly if he is not
an anthroponomist, may wonder why it is not possible, or practical, to
have both the science of psychology and that of anthroponomy, and he
may wonder why the adherents of the two sciences find it necessary to dispute so much with each other. Physiologists are not carrying on controversies either with psychologists or with anthroponomists, and it may seem
strange that each of the latter two groups cannot go its way in peace.[3]
There is no prospect that the anthroponomist will ever accept the psychologist's viewpoint. No compromise is possible, however much it may
be desired, because (a) the admission of a little mentalism is as erroneous
as the admission of all of mentalism; and (b) a little psychology and a
little anthroponomy when added together no more make a science than does
the addition of, let us say, a little ethics and a little geology.

I think there are three important reasons for these controversies, and
the last reason is fundamental. (a) The first reason is social in character.
Both groups of scientists are classified academically as psychologists. Both
belong to the same learned societies. Both teach the same research students. There is thus no practical way to avoid a constant clash in the
scientific, not the personal, field. (b) The second reason concerns the
problems studied. Many of these problems are purely behavioristic in
nature and are investigated by men in both sciences. Such problems are
those of learning, work, interstimulation and response, sensory function,
language responses, and abnormal human behavior. This great overlapping of the work carried on by men in the two fields constantly throws
into relief the fundamental differences in interpretation which exist between psychologists and anthroponomists. (c) The third reason concerns philosophy. Psychology, *as psychology,* has no subject-matter for
study except as the assumption is made that certain objects or aspects of
objects in the world are mental, psychic, or except as the assumption is
made that the world contains psychic agencies which play a rôle in nature.
Psychology, *as psychology,* thus owes its existence and the delimitation of
its field to the acceptance of a philosophy of mental monism or of mental-
physical dualism. If mental experiences and psychic agencies are not matters of assumption but of observation, it is strange that the anthroponomist
is neither able to observe them nor to find in his experimental results any
evidence of their presence. Anthroponomy, in contrast with psychology,
does not have the limitations of its field set by philosophy. I would go
further and insist that anthroponomy is based upon no philosophical point
of view. It is true that when behaviorists indulge in metaphysics they
usually champion the view of materialistic monism, but they might as well
defend mental monism, since in a monism there is no essential difference
between the two. An experimentalist could hardly champion a mental-

---

[3]It should be noted that the psychologist, at least the experimental psychologist,
is not at peace even with himself, for he too sees the inevitable conflict between
his proper mentalistic work and his added behavioristic work!

physical dualism unless he were prepared to show in his experiments the reality of such a dualism. This demonstration has never been made. *The fundamental position of the anthroponomist is that everything that can be shown to be present in or to influence human behavior will be dealt with by his science* or by some other science of the organism if the behavior, for example, digestion, lies outside the field of anthroponomy. If the professional or the amateur philosopher wishes to take the results of anthroponomical experimentation and talk about their philosophical significance, no one can stop him. Indeed some good for philosophy might result. I confess to a reasonably intimate acquaintance with philosophy and with the historical outgrowth of psychology from philosophy, and I feel no hesitancy in asserting that anthroponomy has no more contact with philosophy than has chemistry or geology.

REFERENCES

1. BENTLEY, M. The field of psychology. New York: Appleton, 1924. Pp. xvi +545.

2. BURTT, H. E., & TUTTLE, W. W. The patellar tendon reflex and affective tone. *Amer. J. Psychol.*, 1925, **36**, 553-561.

3. CARR, H. A. Some novel experiences. *Psychol. Rev.*, 1912, **19**, 60-65.

4. DODGE, R. The theory and limits of introspection. *Amer. J. Psychol.*, 1912, **23**, 214-229.

5. DUNLAP, K. The case against introspection. *Psychol. Rev.*, 1912, **19**, 404-413.

6. HOLLINGWORTH, H. L. Sensuous determinants of psychological attitude. *Psychol. Rev.*, 1928, **35**, 93-117.

7. HUNTER, W. S. The problem of consciousness. *Psychol. Rev.*, 1924, **31**, 1-31.

8. ————. The symbolic process. *Psychol. Rev.*, 1924, **31**, 478-497.

9. ————. The subject's report. *Psychol. Rev.*, 1925, **32**, 153-170.

10. ————. General anthroponomy and its systematic problems. *Amer. J. Psychol.*, 1925, **36**, 286-302.

11. ————. Human behavior. Chicago: Univ. Chicago Press, 1928. Pp. x+355.

12. LASHLEY, K. S. The behavioristic interpretation of consciousness. I & II. *Psychol. Rev.*, 1923, **30**, 237-272; 329-353.

13. TITCHENER, E. B. A textbook of psychology. New York: Macmillan, 1910. Pp. vii+565.

14. ————. Description vs. statement of meaning. *Amer. J. Psychol.*, 1912, **23**, 165-182.

15. ————. Prolegomena to a study of introspection. *Amer. J. Psychol.*, 1912, **23**, 427-448.

16. ————. Schema of introspection. *Amer. J. Psychol.*, 1912, **23**, 485-508.

17. WASHBURN, M. F. Introspection as an objective method. *Psychol. Rev.*, 1922, **29**, 89-112.

18. WEISS, A. P. A theoretical basis of behavior. (2nd ed.) Columbus, Ohio: R. G. Adams, 1929. Pp. 479.

CHAPTER 15

THE BIOSOCIAL STANDPOINT IN PSYCHOLOGY

ALBERT P. WEISS

Ohio State University

Definition. Simply stated, psychology studies how the behavior of the newborn infant becomes the behavior of the mature adult. More specifically, psychology is the science which studies the changes in the sensorimotor and environmental conditions by which the newborn infant (regarded as a biological organism) becomes the mature adult who participates in those activities which make up human civilization.[1]

THE NEWBORN INFANT

The properties of the newborn infant are those given by the biological sciences to the extent that they are descriptions of morphological and functional properties based on anatomy, physiology, biochemistry, biophysics, chemistry, physics.

This specifically excludes a superphysical or "vital" principle, and it implies that the only forces that are operative in changing infantile behavior to adult behavior are inheritance, the physical and social environment, and the bodily changes that are the progressive effects of sensorimotor function.

ELEMENTS IN HUMAN BEHAVIOR

The mature adult is an organism that has acquired those movements which make up the personal, domestic, public, vocational, and recreational activities of the community of which he is a member.

The observation and study of human behavior is reduced to a description of (*a*) biophysical stimuli, (*b*) biophysical reactions, (*c*) biosocial stimuli, (*d*) biosocial responses. It is assumed that any action which the individual performs is adequately explained when the genetic and phylogenetic interrelationships of these elements are described. A mental factor is excluded because there is no justification for assuming that during the change from infancy to maturity any other forces are operative than those described by the natural sciences.

The Biophysical Stimulus. This is any form of energy which produces function in a sense-organ or receptive tissue. Description and measurement are in the units of the physicist, chemist, or physiologist. The classes of

---

[1] The more detailed development of this point of view is given in the writer's book: A theoretical basis of human behavior. (2nd ed.) Columbia, Ohio: R. G. Adams, 1929.

biophysical stimuli are visual, auditory, tactual, temperature, pain, gustatory, olfactory, kinaesthetic, organic, static (vestibular), vibratory. These classes represent a historical classification which is useful but which can be further reduced to physical and chemical properties.

The biophysical stimulus ends when a chemical or physical change occurs in a sense-organ or receptive tissue, and this in turn is transformed into a nervous excitation or a nervous process which is the beginning of the biophysical reaction. The distinction (between stimulus and reaction) is purely arbitrary.

The Biophysical Reaction. This begins when the physical or chemical changes in the sensory tissue are transformed into the nervous excitation which is propagated through a network of sensory, connecting, and motor neurons and ends in muscular contractions or glandular secretions of some sort. These contractions and secretions may in turn produce other biophysical stimuli which act on kinaesthetic or organic receptors within the body. The excitations from these may lead to movements which adjust the body and its parts for manipulating and handling the object and regulating the visceral reactions so that an appropriate energy supply is available for the muscles that are used in the manipulation.

A biophysical reaction is called a subreaction when it is so weak that neither an outside observer nor the subject himself can describe the contractile components. Sometimes the individual himself may be unable to localize the effectors directly, but he may have acquired substitute reactions through which he indicates to himself and others the nature of the original stimulating conditions. These sub- and substitute reactions are classified under the various subjective categories like sensations, imagery, feeling, etc.

Even the simplest biophysical reaction, such as discriminating the taste of an orange, is complicated with social stimuli that have already interacted with the stimuli which act on the gustatory receptors so that it is impossible for the adult to report how he learned to discriminate the taste. For such discriminations as those of awareness, consciousness, memory, perception, emotion, etc., the sensorimotor conditions are still more obscure. The biophysical reactions in the adult represent the interactions of many preceding stimulus conditions which the individual is unable to describe in such a manner as to reveal the genesis of the subjective categories.

The biophysical reaction ends with the contraction of muscles or the secretion of glands, and a complete description of any biophysical reaction would be one which enumerated every muscle contraction. Practically, this is impossible, but in describing human behavior names have already been developed for grouping together many of the contractile and secretory effects into such categories as reaching, peeling, chewing, walking, inspecting, speech, etc.

The Biosocial Stimulus. This is a biophysical stimulus which has become a socialized substitute for other forms of stimulation. Its most characteristic form is represented by language. Biosocial stimuli may be names for objects, names for the relations between objects, names for particular groupings as in generalization or abstraction. Any object or event which is socially important is given a name which becomes a substitute stimulus for the objects or the events. In its origin the name of an object is acquired as is any handling or manipulating reaction. It is only one more reaction to a given set of stimuli. However, its biophysical character is relatively unimportant, and any biosocial stimulus usually has a number of different forms, oral, written, printed, different languages, etc. The biosocial stimulus is independent of the objects and events for which it is the symbol, is relatively permanent, and may be produced at any time.

Through grammar and syntax a very complex method (classification) has been developed by which the reactions to many objects and many relations are brought together into stimulus combinations which are based on social equivalences rather than upon physical resemblances. The limit of this grouping is reached in mathematics where symbols are substituted for relationships and through a special syntax (algebra) quantitative stimuli are derived which are substitutes for conditions which have not yet appeared (prediction) or which indicate relationships (generalizations) which are not obvious from the mere inspection of objects and events.

The range of a biosocial stimulus is given when all linguistic combinations into which a word may enter are described. An approach to this limit would be a comprehensive treatise on the subject for which the biosocial stimulus is the name. Such a treatise would give the different "meanings" of the biosocial stimulus.

The Biosocial Response. Biosocial responses fall into two classes:

1) The biophysical reactions which produce a biosocial stimulus (speech in all of its forms).

2) The biophysical reactions which produce the stimuli from which the social status of the individual may be derived.

All biosocial responses are biophysical reactions, but the responses are not classified according to the contractile effects (as in the biophysical reactions) but according to the responses in other individuals. The biosocial response is acquired first as a supplementary reaction (as a verbomotor name), which is added to the manipulating and handling reactions that are acquired at the same time. Through social interaction this name becomes a response which is uniform for many individuals, however variable their manipulating reactions may become.

HUMAN BEHAVIOR

Human behavior is the totality of the biosocial response systems which establish the individual's social status in the community of which he is a member. In the order of complexity the actions of individuals pass through simple movements, biophysical reactions, biosocial responses, temporary response series (for various ages and conditions of life), permanent response series (the career), the behavior life-history.

For scientific analysis and investigation, the behavior life-history of the individual may be divided into five major categories: personal, domestic, public, vocational, and recreational behavior.

Personal Behavior. In this class is placed the behavior which differentiates one person from another. Personal habits in eating, dress, manner of working, conversation; personal responses to other individuals as affable, loyal, emotional, optimistic, stolid, intelligent, cooperative, neurotic, melancholy, and what in general may be called the "personality" of the individual.

Domestic Behavior. This includes the responses which form part of the activities in the family and intimate group life: protection against the weather, preservation of health, treatment in sickness, preparation for food and family recreation, training others or being trained for the participation in the wider activities of adult social life. In general, domestic behavior includes those responses which are made by the individual in his status as father, mother, son, daughter, grandfather, grandmother, uncle, aunt, and a gradually widening circle of relations.

Public Behavior. This class includes those responses through which the social organization is maintained; it includes those activities which form an ever-widening interaction between the individuals of the group, state, or federation, such as learning and obeying civic regulations, participating in customs which characterize the community, paying rent, taxes, voting, and those activities which maintain the political stability of the social organization.

Vocational Behavior. This type of activity includes the responses through which society as a whole maintains its industrial and economic stability. Vocational behavior includes the trades, professions, and those responses which form the basis of exchange with other individuals in maintaining a specialization of labor that is directed toward increasing the commodities and activities available for the individual, with a minimum expenditure of time and energy.

Recreational Behavior. These responses represent the play activities through which the individual develops variety in his behavior. Games, sports, travel, amateur activities of all kinds, theater, concert, and the many forms of expressing sociability.

These five classes are not mutually exclusive. What is vocational behavior for one individual may be recreational for another. However, in any specific case it is not difficult to describe the actual conditions, and this is all that is necessary. The behavior life-history of the individual is a continuous series of responses which are constantly changing. Any given adult activity is the terminal of two series of antecedents: (*a*) an ontogenetic series which traces backward to some infantile form of movement; (*b*) a phylogenetic series which traces backward through the social or institutional modifications to some primitive social form.

Human behavior as differentiated from animal behavior has the effect of removing some of the limitations of disease and death; extending the sensory range and enlarging the environment; compensating for faulty inheritance through education; reducing the time and energy required for food, shelter, and protection; extending the available energy and skill in movement by mechanical power and machinery; using cooperative efforts to limit competition and exploitation; increasing the variability in behavior in the direction of invention, and new forms of physical and social control. Through the development of biosocial stimuli and biosocial responses human behavior has become organized into social institutions concerned with the production of food, clothing, shelter, medicine, storage, transportation, distribution, communication, the principles of personal, communal, and international exchange, invention, education, utilization of natural resources, mechanical power, machinery, protection, pensions, insurance, vocational organization, etc.

LANGUAGE

The language responses seem to be the essential differentia between human and infrahuman behavior. Speech is an acquired modification of the sensorimotor mechanism of the same type as any other handling or manipulating reaction. The fact that it originated as an oral form of behavior involving the sensorimotor elements of the speech mechanism is largely due to the fact that the vocal mechanism possesses superior stimulating properties and a relative independence from other reactions.

Language is made up of the contractile effects of the muscles which produce the sounds, signals, written or printed stimuli to which the individual responds (within certain limits) in the same way as to the original objects and events for which the speech stimuli are substitutes. By this process for each object and relation between objects, old or new, past or present, there is available a substitute stimulus which may be stored in books and libraries and made available to any individual. In effect this gives human beings a double universe. The totality of the language responses and the language records approach a unit correlation between the linguistic achievements of a group and all the changes in objects and relations between objects which have occurred, are occurring, and (as prediction) are likely to occur in the future.

BIOPHYSICAL VERSUS BIOSOCIAL EQUIVALENCE

Language responses developed before anything was known of the sensorimotor organization of the individual and before it was known that all of human behavior was the product of sensorimotor function. As a result the categories of human behavior are linguistically classified more on the basis of individual and social survival than upon their relation to sensorimotor function. However, many different sensorimotor functions may be equivalent from the standpoint of survival. Thus the individual may manifest benevolence in many ways, each of which is different as a sensorimotor condition. "A kind word" may be used in one instance, the giving of money in another, taking care of dependent members in another; even actual punishment under some conditions may be an act of benevolence. From the sensorimotor standpoint these actions are all different, but because they have the same biosocial effect they may be classified as having the type of equivalence which is indicated by the term benevolence.

In investigating human behavior both the individual sensorimotor and the social categories must be considered. In building up new habits the sensorimotor components are the more important; in establishing the social status of the individual the social component is the more important.

SENSORIMOTOR INTERCHANGEABILITY

Sensorimotor interchangeability is a relationship in which the sense-organs or muscles of one individual are used by another. This relation approaches a limit in which all individuals (dead or alive) are united into a single sensorimotor system. Through language responses a functional continuity is established from one individual to another, from one generation to the next, and between communities separated by great distances. A form of cooperative behavior arises which approaches a condition in which the natural resources (organic and inorganic) of the earth, the specific inheritance and specific abilities of any one individual, are at the disposal of all other individuals. Through sensorimotor interchangeability there is developed the specifically human achievement called civilization.

BIOSOCIAL VERSUS MENTALISTIC PSYCHOLOGY

The difference between the mentalistic and the biosocial point of view is that mentalism assumes that human achievement may be studied as the product of some uniform entity such as mind. It has been assumed that the properties of the mind were the key to the control and the modification of human behavior. The problem is not so simple. Even when mind is defined in a relatively clear manner, as the totality of the sensations, images, feelings, perceptions, conations, meanings, thoughts, experiences, consciousness, etc., which an individual may have, an experimental analysis of these categories seems to represent only a small fraction of the whole set of conditions through which the individual becomes a participating unit in a social organization. This fraction is an important one because through its investigation we learn more about sensorimotor function, which after all is the basis of social interaction. However, the traditional psychological experiment was not based upon the assumption that it was investigating sensorimotor function but that it was investigating the properties of a hypothetical mind.

In the biosocial point of view the so-called mental categories are absorbed in the ontogenetic and phylogenetic analysis of biophysical reactions and biosocial responses. The biosocial point of view calls for a direct investigation of those conditions which are already classified by the natural and social sciences as essential conditions for human behavior. Every action is a sensorimotor function. To affirm that it is also a mental function does not seem to help in initiating that type of experimental program which leads to more effective methods in the control of individual and social behavior.

PART VIII
REACTION PSYCHOLOGY

CHAPTER 16

RESPONSE PSYCHOLOGY

KNIGHT DUNLAP

The Johns Hopkins University

In rereading the presentation of modern psychology from the "response" point of view, or what I prefer to call "scientific psychology," embodied in my contribution to the *Psychologies of 1925*—and rereading it with as critical an attitude as it is possible for a parent to take towards his own child—I am impressed with three things. First, that however prophetic the presentation may have been at the time of its writing, it today represents in a distinct way the actual situation in American psychology, particularly as regards those psychologists most directly involved in experimental research. Secondly, the arguments which the purposivists, the mechanists, the behaviorists, and the Gestalters make against each other are in the main merely arguments for scientific psychology. Thirdly, the presentation I made five years ago still seems an adequate one, still highly useful for the student of some initial training; and I am unable to better it, except by a few further developments, partly in explication, partly in the presentation of further hypotheses which may possibly contribute to still further progress in the next decade. I may therefore save valuable printing space and economize the reader's time, by re-endorsing and recommending what I have said in my first two lectures (7, 8), in the *Psychologies of 1925* [the third lecture (9) was designedly less fundamental], and, proceeding from that point on, I can also avoid some needless repetition by referring the reader to my *Elements of Scientific Psychology* (2) for details, although on certain points I have been able to make great improvement since the printing of the first edition (shortly to be revised), especially in regard to the topics of instinct and habit. What I have to present below are certain advances over the formulations previously made.

I

The term "conscious" and "consciousness" are subject to great misunderstanding, and my earlier method of employment of these terms is partly at fault. The reader may receive the impression that, in spite of disclaimers, scientific psychology assumes some mystic stuff, process, or state, similar to the consciousness of James, Wundt, and Titchener. Let us proceed, therefore, to the clarification of this conception by the method which I have been in the habit of using in my classes.

I hold up a pencil, and inquire of the class whether they can see it or not. The unanimous response is, "Yes." I hold the pencil behind my back, and inquire whether they now see it, and the unanimous reply is, "No." I then call their attention to the fact that persons blindfolded, or devoid

of eyes, could not see the pencil and ask them whether, in their understanding of the verb "to see," I am employing the word correctly, and
again the response is unanimous. I then announce to them that the meaning of the verb "to see," as we have used it in these instances, is the meaning in which we use the term in psychology, and the only meaning we employ. I then ask them if they agree to the proposition that *seeing* really occurs, and is an important event in life, in spite of the admitted fact that there
are persons who are incapable of seeing. Again there is complete unanimity.
I then announce that I should be glad to hear at any time of any person who
either in the present or past doubts or has doubted that proposition.

I next call attention to the fact that there are a multitude of questions
and problems concerning seeing—as to the biological mechanism, the physical conditions, and the psychological conditions (some of which are controversial), but that we have not so far attempted to answer any of these
or to take any stand in regard to them. We have merely agreed as to
what we mean by the term, as an indispensable preliminary to the discussion of the problem.

I proceed in a similar way to elicit the fact that there is a complete
agreement as to the fundamental meaning of the verbs "to hear," "to
taste," and "to smell." Next, I point out the usefulness of adjectives and
nouns, both concrete and abstract, in the discussion of events and processes.
I call attention, for example, to the verb "to work," as a general term
under which are subsumed the more particular verbs "to plow," "to saw,"
"to typewrite," "to cook," etc. Also to the general substantive "labor"
and the adjective "laborious," and the abstract noun "laboriousness." I
then point out that there is a need for a generic verb under which to subsume "to see," "to hear," "to taste," "to smell," and any other verbs we
may subsequently find which obviously need to be subsumed under the same
class of verbs. I point out next that we do not need to invent such a verb,
as there is one already in common use, namely, the verb "to sense-perceive,"
which we may shorten to "to perceive." I explain also that there may be
other and confusing usages of this verb "to perceive," and that alternatives,
such as "to sense" and "to intuit," are possible.

The next step is to ask the students whether or not they can individually
remember what they had for breakfast on a certain day, ten days preceding.
To this question several answers are received, chiefly "yes," "no," and
"not certainly." By further discussion, agreement as to the use of the
term "to remember" is reached. The verbs "to imagine" and "to anticipate" are then brought up in the same detailed way, and agreement reached
upon them. It is then pointed out that these verbs are not, by the conventions of the English language, subsumed under the verb "to perceive"
(in the usage of "to sense," at least), but are conventionally subsumed
under "to think." Various phrases in common use are brought in here to
enforce this point, and the term "to think" is accepted as defined solely in
terms of "to imagine," "to remember," and "to anticipate," with the warning that we may, or may not, find still other verbs meriting or demanding
subsumption under "to think" along with these.

The common usage of "to feel" is next brought out by reference to the usages "to feel tired," "to feel sorry," "to feel hungry," "to feel angry," etc. The three terms "to perceive," "to think," and "to feel" are then brought together, and it is pointed out that it is theoretically possible that there may be still other terms on the same level, such as "to will," but that it is not necessary to consider that point at present.

The correlated adjective and substantive terms, such as "vision," "visual," "auditory," etc., are indicated as defined solely with reference to the verbs. The question is then raised as to the possibility of a still higher generic term which will include "to perceive," "to think," and "to feel," and it is pointed out that we have in common everyday use such a term, namely, the term "to be conscious." The usage is emphasized by pointing out that if a person is assumed to see, or otherwise "to perceive," or to image or otherwise think, to feel in any way, he is unanimously said to be *conscious;* that if he does none of these things he is said to be *not conscious.*

The final procedure is to the more abstract terms. The significance of abstract terms is indicated by reference to goodness, loquacity, triangularity, etc., and attention is then called to the fact that we have the term consciousness in common use in a way exactly parallel to these other abstract terms.

It is not difficult to make clear to the student that in the procedure outlined there have been no explanations of any of the items designated nor have any theories been introduced, beyond the basal theory of the significance of agreement and disagreement which is accepted whenever two persons talk together, whether these persons hold this or that philosophical theory. The whole procedure is readily understood as the pointing-out of facts concerning which there is no disagreement as to their actuality and the convention of assigning names to them. What does need repeated emphasis over a long period of weeks or months, especially to the student who has absorbed confused theories of behavioristic, psychoanalytic, or other loose types of thought, is that psychology attaches no other meanings to these terms than the ones which have been thus detailed, and that whatever theories or explanations may be considered later must always be brought down to application to what is really meant by the terms, and that no other meanings shall be covertly or illicitly introduced. Even the students sophisticated by the isms admit that no one has ever denied consciousness in the sense in which it is used in scientific psychology for the simple reason that no one has seriously or will seriously deny that seeing and hearing, etc., occur, in spite of the admitted fact that there are many who are sightless and many totally deaf.

II

Scientific psychology, as may be readily seen by referring to my lectures in the *Psychologies of 1925*, steers clear of both mechanism and purposivism, as these isms are preached by their zealous propagandists. No one denies that there is a system and a corporeal object through which the mental life proceeds. The most obstinate purposivist spends much time in explaining this mechanism and in showing that his purposive factors—instincts or whatever they are—are an important part of it. The most devout mechanist admits that human beings actually have purposes, and that the purposes are not unconnected with persons' actions. It is only in their philosophical explanations that these isms differ; and the scientific psychologist has no philosophical interpretations. We are interested in determining experimentally how the mechanism works and what part purposes play. It is perhaps the absolute determinism and the crude materialism of the mechanist to which the purposivist objects, and it is the supernatural element which the purposivist insists is expressed in purposes which excites the ire of the mechanist. The scientific psychologist rejects both. He sees no profit in assumptions which do not lead to experimental test; and materialistic, supernatural, deterministic, and libertarian assumptions are in this category.

In the working-out of the mechanism through which the mental processes are developed, scientific psychology has discarded the old stimulus-response viewpoint and recognizes integration as the cardinal process. When, in the simple reaction-time measurement, a reactor is instructed to respond to a flash of light by a finger movement, we may still call the limited areal light patch "the stimulus" and the finger movement "the response." But we insist that these terms are abstractly used and that the real stimulus is a *pattern* involving vast areas of receptors, and the real "response" is also a widely distributed pattern in which the muscle actions which depress the finger are only a detail. In these terms, the problems of learning (including the conditional reflexes) become much more intelligible, and are soluble in a systematic way.

Extensions which I have urged recently in this conception are really but the carrying-out of features which are implicit in it. Perceptual patterns cannot be considered separately. In the reaction-time measurement, the instructions which have preceded the stimulus are an admitted part of the stimulus pattern, along with the total results of the preceding reactions to "the same stimulus." We have even admitted that the visceral patterns of feeling (emotion) are important parts of the total patterns involved, not only in separately specified "responses" but also in the integrative process of learning. Ideas, also, have been admitted as parts of the stimulus pattern, as may be demonstrated by comparing the reactions of reactors who have had the same incomplete instructions, but who have thought, one that he was expected to do this, the other that he was expected to do that.

III

What I have suggested in my heretical hypothesis of learning and unlearning (10) is that the total effects of the different parts of patterns is not to be understood in a simple additive way, especially as concerns the ideational parts, but that certain factors may work in what may be loosely called a subtractive way. This leads naturally to the conception that in the integrative process of learning, repetition, which has in the past been given an absolute value, may be merely a negative condition; that the "fixing" of an integrative condition established in a given "reaction" is entirely due to the nature of the stimulus pattern, and that it has in itself nothing to do with the probability of recurrence of the response type. Or, put in looser metaphor, the repetitions, whether few or many, are the carriers of the actual factors in learning or unlearning (both being the establishment of new integration relations) so that by repetition the probability of recurrence may be increased or may be lessened.

This brings us to the vital point in learning. The total pattern established in learning is never the pattern which is expected to produce the response later, but always includes both fewer and more factors. We expect a certain part of the pattern involved in learning to produce a certain part of the reaction pattern when combined with varying other stimulation patterns or parts. In the conditions determining this dominance of parts of stimulus patterns and the practical methods of securing dominance lies the great problems of learning.

IV

In the hypotheses as to the general determining factors in integration, the brain and the cerebrum in particular have long occupied the throne. The phrenologists, in assigning mental functions to cortical areas, merely followed a conception which had already been developed, and which they made more explicit. The later physiologists, with their theories of "centers," continued the phrenological conceptions while rearranging the "faculties." Popularly, "brain" differences are supposed to be extremely important for mental life, and the inheritance of mental characteristics is assumed to be bound up directly with the inheritance of brain characteristics.

Psychology in America has discarded the phrenological conception rather thoroughly, a result for which I think we have largely to thank Shepherd Ivory Franz. Scientific psychology has been driven by the logic of the situation to the conclusion that there is no differentiation of *kind* between the functions of one brain-cell and any other brain-cell in the normal brain at any time, although there may be a differentiation in the intensity of action of the different neurons. The specific function of the brain from this point of view is integrative solely, and in that integration the specificity involved is a specificity of connection. Neuron A, for example, when stimulated "passes on" the irritation to this cell and not to that, because it is connected with this cell and not with that; conversely, neuron A can be stimulated by neuron B (which perhaps is in the lead-in chain from the retina), and cannot be stimulated directly by neuron C (which perhaps is in the afferent chain from the cochlea). Neuron M, whose cell-body lies in the geniculate body, is connected directly with only a few cells in the cortex; neuron W, lying entirely in the cortex, may be connected directly with many other neurons. These differences are topographical, not qualitative. On the other hand, certain other cells in the periphery, the receptors, may have a different *kind* of function from those in the cortex or cord. This is the logical result of the response point of view, in consequence of the failure of evidence for qualitative differences in the cortex, the ease with which one neuron apparently takes over the function of another, if connections are established, and the fact that so far as can be seen no qualitative differences are needed to explain the integrative facts.

I now desire to extend this hypothesis still further, adding a consideration which seems to me of vital importance, and which is the logical termination of the progression away from phrenology. This may be expressed in the statement that for practical purposes any healthy human brain is potentially equal to any other healthy human brain so far as mental processes are concerned. This hypothesis excludes from consideration pathological brains, whether microcephalic, syphilitic, or otherwise degenerated or undeveloped. It involves the assumption that it is futile to look to inherent brain capacities or potentialities for the explanation of individual mental differences and, of course, for racial mental differences. It places the responsibility for mental heredity entirely outside the brain. It does not, however, deny the possible importance of inherent differential characteristics of the brain for certain functions of the type which would commonly be classed as physical (such as muscular strength and endurance).

Popularly, size of brain, as well as other characteristic differences of structure of "normal" brains is supposed to be important in the human being. The relatively greater weight of the female brain, for example, is considered to have some direct bearing on male and female mental differences. Psychologists generally have abandoned this conception, although recognizing the phylogenetic importance of relative brain weight. There is an anomaly here, which the suggested hypothesis may resolve. The striking fact that the brain, relatively, is enormously greater in the foetus and infant than in the adult may also be of significance in relation to the features of phylogenetic development.

If we suppose that the brain at birth, or just before, has in every case a potentiality far greater than it will ever be called upon to actualize, we shall be prepared to expect the differences in potentiality which may exist to be of no practical importance in view of the low level of performance which will be required. If (to resort to analogy) one automobile has a 60-horsepower engine, another a 90-horsepower, but if both are restricted to a speed of 10 miles per hour over a level course, the difference in horsepower is negligible. The difference in gearing, adjustment of carburetor, accelerator, etc., may be important, but one engine is equal to the other engine.

The analogy is defective, however, because the brain is subject to training. It is not assumed by the hypothesis advanced that two given human brains are actually equal in their performances. The brains commence to be trained from birth, or from a period antedating birth.

The training is given by means of the transit patterns impressed upon the brain, and may be considered as the systematic adaptation of the brain to the demands made upon it by the organism. We may say, in fact, that the brain seems to be the only part of the organism which can be trained; which is but a little stronger than the more conventional statement that habit formation is the outstanding function of the brain. The limits, as well as the details of the training are set, not by brain limitations nor by the environment alone, but by the environmental action as mediated or transformed by the peripheral organs and tissues.

In different environments, the same organism would respond in different ways, and would therefore receive different training. This principle is universally accepted. In the same environment, two organisms with different peripheral mechanism would give different training to two brains which might initially be alike. Perhaps this principle also might be generally accepted. We come then to the final question as to the difference which would result when different brains, with equivalent peripheral mechanisms, were subjected to the same environment; and the new hypothesis is that there would be no difference.

In order to illustrate this proposition, let us make a supposition. Let us suppose that a thousand infants from the Wolof tribe of Africa were exchanged at birth for a thousand new-born babies from Dublin, and that for the next twenty-one years the thousand Wolofs were subjected to the Irish environment in which the Dublin infants would have been brought up, and the infants of Irish extraction were similarly "brought up Wolof." We should expect to find that the transplanted groups, on the average, differed less from their foster folks than the two groups of foster folks differ from each other. In other words, two groups of different stock, brought up under the same environmental influence, would differ less than if brought up in different environments. The approximation might perhaps be greatest in the "mental" characteristics, but we might expect to find some even in the "physical" characteristics.

We should expect to find, however (although behaviorists might dissent), that very considerable differences would remain between the foster children and their foster folks. Skin color, texture and color of hair, facial characteristics, skull form, limb proportion, leg musculature, and certain other details would obviously be modified but little from the parental types. We have every reason to expect that mental characteristics also would show stock tendencies still (although we do not as yet know what the basal stock characteristics are), and we may admit that the mental differences between regular Wolofs and neo-Wolofs (i. e., Wolofs-by-adoption) would be far less than the differences between regular Wolofs and the regular Irish; and the neo-Irish (i. e., the Irish-by-adoption) likewise would be mentally much more like the Irish than were their parents; but there would still be mental differences between the regular breeds and the changelings they harbored.

But now, let us suppose that instead of the babies being interchanged only their brains were swapped, assuming for the sake of the argument that a successful surgical operation of this kind could be performed. According to our hypothesis, as the infants grew up, the Irish-brained Wolofs would not differ in any way from the entire Wolofs and the Wolof-brained Irish would not differ from the regular Irish.

The hypothesis, in short, assigns the source and basis of mental differences (and most physical differences as well) to the periphery, instead of to the brain. It is the demand made upon the brain by the periphery which determines its development; and any healthy human brain is capable of responding to the maximal demands which any human organism is capable of making.

The presence of embryonic nerve-cells in adult brains is evidence that brains are provided with many more cells than will be needed. The relative unimportance of parts of the frontal lobes has long been suspected. The re-establishment of peripheral connections with the brain after the usual "centers" have atrophied is a sign of far more than "functional" education. The brain has no difficulty in handling adequately afferent currents due to stimulations as far apart in frequency as those of light and sound. Is there any reason to doubt that if receptors were developed capable of responding to the intermediate ranges, and connected with the cortex in early infancy, the cortex could effectively integrate the afferent current from these into the general pattern?

What details of the periphery determine the brain development and ultimately the response characteristics? First of all, the receptors. The deaf and the color-blind do not suffer from cerebral defects, but from receptorial. Color-blindness does not make a great difference to the mentality of the civilized person; but how about the savage? The deaf child is strikingly like the feeble-minded, until by lip-reading he compensates for the defect. In civilized groups, we find strains that are anosmic—another defect that civilization makes less vital, since we no longer depend on smell for protection against poisons, or as sex stimulations. These compensations, however, are made by the brain. I do not suppose that mental differences between breeds are to be accounted for in any important degree by receptorial differences. Yet there is a distinct field for investigation into the individual mental differences correlated with receptorial differences. Musculature is probably a more important source of mental variation. The Wolof is known to differ from the white man in the development of his musculature. Does it not affect his "mind"? Muscle patterns are important factors in the restimulation of the brain. A slight effect on the brain modifies it, and thereby contributes anew to further modification of transit patterns, so that the ultimate effects of slight deviations *may* be enormous.

I should like to know more about the sole plate interposed between efferent neuron and muscle. It can be paralyzed, so that with nerve and muscle unimpaired in functional capacity no action occurs because neuron cannot excite muscle. Is the permeability or non-permeability of the sole plate an all-or-none affair, or are there gradations? What an enormous effect on muscle patterns would be made by even a slight change in the transmission of the sole plate! This is something worth considering.

Glandular differences have long been considered as possible sources of mental difference. In spite of the vast claims that have been made, we really know little about glandular effects and their variations. But it is not wise to rule out important possibilities because of absurdities that have been perpetrated by enthusiasts. We do know that certain of the skin glands of negroes differ from the white man's type. But what of his liver and pancreas? What of his salivary glands and his kidneys? What of his ductless glands? Unfortunately, we know little about the glands of any breed, although we do know that the internal secretions of the sex glands have mental affects of a profound kind. Ancient peoples have believed that the development and type of sex organs, aside from the glands, were somehow correlated with mental characteristics. Perhaps the ancients were on the right track here, as they were in so many other instances.

The course of development of modern psychology for some years has been towards the periphery as the place to search for the control of mental processes, and away from the brain as a *deus ex machina*. The brain is more and more conceived as having but one function, namely, integration expressed as transmission and habit formation. More and more we are convinced that all brain neurons have one and the same kind of function qualitatively. More and more we have become interested in muscle-patterns and glandular activity. The hypothesis I urge is but the logical conclusion of our progressive reconstructions.

If the hypothesis is taken seriously, it will at least have a beneficial effect —we shall be spurred to more detailed and more extensive investigation of peripheral differences. A really great field for psychology is anthropometry—not the dull measurement of skulls, but the measurement of sensory acuity and stimulability, the determination of glandular characteristics, the detailed study of musculature. I should even go so far as to say that psychologists should begin to take a belated interest in the study of heredity of hair texture and color and of skin characteristics, as well as in skeletal and muscular details. Not that these are immediate determinants of response type, but the whole periphery hangs together.

VI

The abandoning of the old doctrine of instincts was a necessary step in the application of scientific methods to psychology. With this has gone the reformation of the general doctrine of heredity; but scientific psychology by no means overlooks the actual importance of heredity. The net result is that we no longer attempt to classify details of either structure or function as "inherited" on the one hand and acquired on the other, but recognize the cooperative effects of heredity and environment throughout (5, pp. 155-159, and 11). Artificial problems are frequently much simpler than actual ones (which is perhaps the reason for the artificial creations), and in this case the problems of heredity have become much more difficult to understand because they are nearer to the knotty facts. Hence there will be a rather slow movement of psychologists and biologists to the newer and more scientific formulations. Many will continue to force vital phenomena into the old categories of "nature" and "nurture."

There is, however, a necessary reform closely connected with the abolition of discrete "instincts," which I have been a little late in urging (3, pp. 89-90), but which is an essential part of the progress of scientific psychology. This is in the description of the emotions. Psychologists still speak of the emotions as if they were discrete entities. Even some of the would-be radicals, who belatedly followed the scientific movement in regard to instinct, still base their theories on the assumption of discrete entities. "Fear," "love," etc., are described, and made explanatory factors as if they were as unique and different as so many islands in a placid sea.

This is, of course, an anachronistic point of view. The emotions constitute a polydimensional continuum, in which we arbitrarily and for convenience designate certain ranges by certain names, and ignore the remaining ranges. "Fear," for example, is a qualitatively variable emotion. The "fear" which I have in one connection is vastly different from the "fear" in another contingency. Certain "fears" are qualitatively more closely allied to certain angers than those angers are to certain other angers, or those fears to certain other fears. The complexes we call fear grade off into sex feeling in one direction, into anger in another, into hatred in another, into depression in another, into mere anticipatory feeling in another, into mere tenseness in another, into horror in another, and so on. The limitations of language are probably responsible for the considerations of the more common names as if they designated unique emotional elements.

There may be emotional elements. I suspect there are, and have elsewhere (2, pp. 315-316) given an indication of the types we may expect to find. But if so, the specifically named emotions are varying combinations of these, and are no more unique or fundamental than are the great ranges of emotional "states" which are not as specifically named. The fear that is obviously close to "anger" is just as unique, just as fundamental, as the "fear" that is not so close to "anger"; and none of the different "fears" is more fundamental than the others.

That the fundamental terms applied to qualitatively graded continuities do not necessarily indicate basic qualities we have long known in the field of color. The early color names are originally applied from practical considerations—some to dyes or pigments, some to ranges of hues conspicuously presented by sky or plant life or some other aspect of nature. But the fundamental "green" and "red" of color theory are not the hues to which the names are commonly applied.

Just so, the name "fear" has been applied to a range of emotion which arises in certain typical situations, regardless of the wide variation in both internal states and external behavior. From the point of view of the situation, a threatened injury which may result in withdrawal in one case, or complete inhibition in another, may be said to arouse "fear" in both cases. From the point of view of behavior, the withdrawal and the inhibition are radically different and the internal states may be vastly different even when the external behavior is of the same type.

In short, the popular classification of emotion, as adopted by the older psychology (including behaviorism), is a classification based in the main on causal situations, and very little on behavior, visceral states, or any other psychological facts.[1]

Scientific psychology, therefore, must begin to use the stock emotion names with full recognition of the fact that they are really the names of typical stimulus patterns, and not names of typical emotional "expression" nor names of typical emotions. We must look deeper for the psychological analysis of the emotional life. This reform completes the cycle which commenced with the rejection of images and sensations, and proceeded through the rejection of "instincts."

It is no wonder that attempts at further analysis based on this assumption that the emotional response is the same where the emotional stimulus is the same, regardless of the organism, and ignoring its actual differences in behavior, have always resulted in finding exactly what the analyzer set out to find.

VII

The topic of desire is increasingly important in scientific psychology. When I first made the list of nine desires (5, pp. 15-16, and 2, p. 324), I had no notion that it was more than an illustration of the type of list that must eventually be drawn up, nor did I consider it important to decide whether these desires were actually different modes or tissue states, or merely classifications. In further study of the function of desires in racial psychology, political psychology, and the psychology of religion, I have been astonished at the degree of completion which the list actually has, and have found a steadily increasing value in the consideration of the various problems in the light of these desires. It is apparent now that the applicability to psychopathology and criminal psychology is just as great. Within the last year it has become evident that an enormous advance is possible in all these lines by the use of these guiding threads, and I can confidently predict that five more years will see a revolution wrought in these branches of psychology.

For adequate results, however, this work must be accompanied by serious attempts to determine the organic seats of the several "desires." Many persons have supposed that the list of desires is merely a list of instincts under a new terminology, overlooking the important differences I have elsewhere emphasized (4).[2] This misunderstanding has been facilitated, of course, by my own lack of preciseness of terminology, since I applied the term "desire" to the affective elements involved, as well as to the desire proper, which is a common practice due to the lack of a distinctive term for the "affective" basis of a desire. Appetence, or appetency, is, of course, an abstract term, and has been commonly used as synonymous with desire. "Drive" has acquired a special theoretical significance. "Appetite" strictly applies only to certain so-called "physical" desires. Various other terms

---

[1]This is just the opposite of the classification of activities into instinct which is based on teleological factors.

[2]Also, as concerns feelings—including desires—(2, pp. 312-313).

are ambiguous in their meaning. I have hesitated to introduce a new term, but shall hesitate no longer. I shall use *appet* as the concrete term to designate an actual affective basis of a desire. I shall use *appetence* as the abstract term referring to appets. It should be noted that I am not introducing a new conception, since everyone who has carefully discussed desire has assumed this appetent factor. Theories as to the nature and exact functions of appets vary. It has apparently been held by certain divisions of the psychoanalytic school that there is but one appet, and that a mysterious force called the libido. I would understand McDougall to contend that there are a number of appets, and that they are psychic forces. I understand that Woodworth calls the appets "drives," and attaches a certain interpretation which I do not clearly understand. I have rejected all these interpretations, and have made a distinct hypothesis concerning the appets; namely, that there are *probably* several appets, qualitatively different; that they are experiencible facts, just as colors, sounds, and other sentienda are experiencible; and that their being experienced depends on the excitation of certain visceral receptors, just as the experience of colors depends on the excitation of visual receptors. I have brought appets out into the periphery.

Quite aside from my hypothesis as to the nature of appets, it is to be at once admitted that a desire, in the complete sense, includes analytically: (*a*) an anticipatory idea of some condition not yet attained, and (*b*) the appetence of the ideated condition. An appet not associated with a definitely ideated object is not a desire (I suppose it would be called an "unconscious desire" by certain psychoanalysts; to which I should object that it is not necessarily "unconscious" at all, and that calling it a desire is the very confusion we should avoid). On the other hand, a mere anticipatory idea is by common consent not a desire. Now, the factor in desire for which an organic seat is to be sought is the appet, not the anticipatory idea. When earlier I attributed the food desire to the stomach, it was the appet only that I so allocated.

The importance of my desire hypothesis, therefore, lies in the following detailed assumptions:

1) The appets are peripheral, and not "central."

2) They are not mere categories or class names, under which activities are teleologically arranged.

3) They are experiencible facts, not mysterious forces.

The desires, and the instincts, are therefore not to be confused, although the desires, as a matter of fact, may be real explanatory factors which the instincts confusedly represent.

The investigation of desires in the problem of racial and political psychology is to be based on recognition of the fact that the desires are conditioned both by organic conditions and by thought. If different breeds of men have certain characteristic tissue conditions, then desire will, under similar environmental conditions, be different. On the other hand, the desires can be modified by modification of thought habits, and also by modifications of tissue conditions where such modification is possible. The desire for food, for example, can be temporarily abolished either by changing the stomachic conditions or by preventing the thought of food from arising. Modification of the type of stomachic condition, or modification of the thought habits concerning food, through whatever causes, may modify in a more or less permanent way the type of food desire. Similar conditions apply to the sex desires and to all the other desires.

VIII

There has been evident an increasing tendency among psychologists to use the term "unconscious" in the loose explanatory way which was introduced by the Freudians, a tendency against which scientific psychology must resolutely set itself if it is to avoid the quagmire of merely verbal explanations which is fatal to further progress. I have elsewhere (6, 1) pointed out in detail the vicious effects resulting from the confused conceptions of the Freudians, and shall merely summarize here.

In the first place, there is no objection to the term "unconscious" when used with strict reference to the meaning of "conscious" as that term is employed in everyday life and by scientific psychology. At certain times, an individual may perhaps correctly be said to be unconscious, as under the influence of ether, or in an exceptionally sound, dreamless sleep. Even when he is "conscious" (of certain contents) he is necessarily unconscious of everything else in the universe.

There is, on the other hand, nothing but confusion in the use of the term for conditions for which psychology has long had other and precisely significant terms.

1) Retention. For responses once actualized, there may be established a "permanent possibility" of reactualization. Having once had a certain desire, I may have it again. If I have once thought John Smith was a crook, the probability that I will sometime later think the same thing about him may be increased. If I have once achieved a certain shot at billiards, the probability of making it again under proper stimulation may be increased. (We must not overlook, however, the possibilities of decreasing the probabilities.) To say that in the intervals between the responses, I am continuously but "unconsciously" desiring the condition, continuously but "unconsciously" thinking that Smith is dishonest, continuously but "unconsciously" shooting billiards, is as stupidly confusing as it would be to say that in the intervals between glancing at the face of my watch I am continuously but "unconsciously" seeing it. Such usages merely make it possible (and probable) for the confused psychologist to deceive himself into the conviction that he can "explain" anything whatever by merely referring it to the verbal concept of the "unconscious," for this term becomes actually the designation of "that which needs explanation, but which we are unable or unwilling to explain."

2) The modification of response, that is to say, learning or habit formation. This is, of course, another aspect of the problem of retention. Every response modifies the responding organism. What I have done, perceived, thought, felt, in preceding days and years, of course, has entered

into the determination of what I do, perceive, think, and feel now. This is no Freudian discovery, but a fundamental postulate of psychology for many years. The Freudian discovery (analogous to someone's going out and discovering the moon) was that in some cases, in responding consciously, we are not conscious of the vast stretches of past life which have contributed to the present response. The real joke in the situation is that psychology has long recognized that not only in these apparently peculiar cases but *in all cases except certain special ones* one is unconscious, during a specific response, of the antecedent conditions: The exceptions are those thought responses in which one thinks of the past, and these occur relatively seldom. Further, psychology has long recognized that in certain cases, the antecedent conditions can be "recalled" by appropriate stimulations, and that what cannot be recalled at one time or under one set of circumstances may be recalled at another time in other circumstances; and further, that certain antecedents cannot be recalled by any technique available. It is necessary to go even further in scientific psychology, and point out that *in no response* is there consciousness of the response itself but always of something else, and that, for consciousness of the end-part of any response (the muscle pattern), a *second response,* stimulated by the muscle pattern itself, is necessary. This is of course implied in the James-Lange theory of the emotions.

3) The greatest confusion, however, is due to the use of the term "unconscious" to designate factors which, in the common usage of the term, psychology designates as *conscious.* The looser literature is full of statements to the effect that one "unconsciously put out his hand," etc., when the meaning is not that the individual was unconscious of putting out his hand but that he had not a *purpose* to put out his hand. In all these loose usages (and they are legion) the references are to performances that are as "conscious" as any act the individual performs; and the meaning the writer would have, if he could think clearly at all, is merely that the individual was unconscious of certain things, but not necessarily of the things which are implied by the loose statement.

In all these confusions there is perhaps a basis of confusion in our common usage of the adjective term "conscious" in two different ways. We speak of a man as "conscious" when he is conscious of something, and we speak of a response as "conscious" when through it one is conscious of something. On the other hand, we apply the term to the content which the individual is conscious of, as when we say a movement of the hand or some other member was "conscious." The second usage is, of course, a derivative one, and need not interfere with precise analysis; but great confusion is introduced when we discuss the thought procedures, if we forget that fact. A "conscious thought" means literally that one is thinking of something. This is all it means in common speech and in psychology. But it is easy, by analogy with the references to "conscious movements," to assume that a "thought" is some entity which "consciousness" surrounds like an aura, or from which it emanates like an effluvium; in which case it is easy (and utterly misleading) to assume that there may be entities devoid of this aura. The fundamental trouble with the dealers in the Freudian unconscious is that they have totally forgotten what the word "conscious" means.

REFERENCES

1. DUNLAP, K. Mysticism, Freudianism, and scientific psychology. St. Louis: Mosby, 1920. Pp. 173.

2. ——————. Elements of scientific psychology. St. Louis: Mosby, 1922. Pp. 368.

3. ——————. The identity of instinct and habit. *J. Phil.*, 1923, **19**, 85-94.

4. ——————. Instincts and desires. *J. Abn. & Soc. Psychol.*, 1925, **20**, 170-173.

5. ——————. Social psychology. Baltimore: Williams & Wilkins, 1925. Pp. 261.

6. ——————. The subconscious, the unconscious, and the co-conscious. Studies in honor of Morton Prince. New York: Harcourt, Brace, 1925. Pp. 245-253.

7. ——————. The theoretical aspect of psychology. Chap. 14 in Psychologies of 1925. Worcester, Mass.: Clark Univ. Press, 1926. Pp. 309-329.

8. ——————. The experimental methods of psychology. Chap. 15 in Psychologies of 1925. Worcester, Mass.: Clark Univ. Press, 1926. Pp. 331-351.

9. ——————. The application of psychology to social problems. Chap. 16 in Psychologies of 1925. Worcester, Mass.: Clark Univ. Press, 1926. Pp. 353-379.

10. ——————. A revision of the fundamental laws of habit formation. *Science*, 1928, **67**, 360-362.

11. JENNINGS, H. S. Prometheus. New York: Dutton, 1925. Pp. 86.

PART IX
DYNAMIC PSYCHOLOGY

CHAPTER 17

DYNAMIC PSYCHOLOGY

Robert S. Woodworth
Columbia University

There is a curious contrast in present-day psychology between the mutual hostility of the several schools, on the one hand, and the solidarity of the group of psychologists, on the other. From the insistence of each school on the futile and reprehensible tendencies of the others, you would scarcely expect to find them meeting in associations and congresses on a footing of mutual respect and interest, nor to see them laboring together on abstract journals and the like; yet this cooperation is just what you find. They must have more in common than would at first appear, and this curious cleavage into schools, a phenomenon almost peculiar to psychology among the sciences of the day and probably to be regarded as a symptom of adolescence, must be less fundamental than it seems.

"Dynamic psychology," as I have used the words for twenty years, does not aspire to be a school. That is the very thing it does not wish to be. Personally, I have always balked on being told, as we have been told at intervals for as long as I can remember, what our marching orders are—what as psychologists we ought to be doing, and what in the divine order of the sciences psychology must be doing. Instead of bringing down the tables of the law, it has seemed to me a more important and really more ambitious undertaking to approximate a definition of psychology by proceeding from below upwards, in the hope of reaching a definition that would cover the scientific work of all psychologists. There must be something substantial underlying the solidarity of the psychological group, and the phrase, dynamic psychology, if broadly conceived, suggests the common trend, so far as I have been able to grasp it.

Any system of psychology which starts with the assumption that most students of the subject are on the wrong track has little chance of being adequate, however stimulating it may be for the moment. One might better start with such premises as these:

1) The presumption is that all sincere and able investigators are doing something worthy of being included in the system.

2) This presumption holds rather of the actual research of psychologists than of their attempts to formulate systems. In the latter effort, they are exposed to the danger of spinning out theories that have only a tenuous connection with their actual findings, and to the further danger of seeking to exalt themselves by the familiar process of trampling on the prostrate forms of their fellows.

3) The total psychological group is presumably wiser than its individual members, when the question is one of aim and trend.

It will probably be agreed by all that psychology studies the individual organism. The individual is studied, to be sure, in relation to the environment, but everything centers in the individual, from the psychologist's point of view. It is clear also that psychology is concerned with the activities rather than with the structure of the individual—that it is closer to physiology than to anatomy. The distinction from physiology is not perfectly easy to draw, but there would be wide agreement with the formula that psychology considers the individual as a whole, leaving to physiology the activities of the various cells and organs and their mutual relations.

It does not appear to me that such a definition commits us to "act psychology" or to "self psychology." Certainly consciousness of activity or of the self is not to be included in our general definition, though there may be real psychological problems expressed in these words. The "subject" in psychology is the organism, not the self, and the activity is any process which depends upon the life of the organism and which can be viewed as dependent upon the organism as a whole.

Now in describing activities or processes, psychology is sure to make use of the notions of cause and effect, and so to be a study in dynamics. At this point, however, if not before, objections begin to arise. We are urged to keep our skirts clear of those old-fashioned notions of cause and effect. Our attention is called to the fact that critical modern science dispenses with causation and explanation, and limits itself to description. Psychology, accordingly, would take a step backwards if it stressed such ideas more than it has been wont to do. It should rather seek to follow the older sciences by eradicating them.

But it is curious to find physics and astronomy still making abundant use of cause and effect. The question is raised as to the origin of the solar system, and elaborate computations are made to determine whether this or that explanation is adequate. The best explanation is perhaps that the near approach of another star to our sun was the cause of the splitting-off of matter from the sun, which later condensed into the planets. It would seem from such discussions that astronomy, though one of the oldest and best developed sciences, had not yet fully reached the status of a critical science.

Physics is no better. Does not physics include dynamics, the study of the "motion of bodies as affected by the forces which act upon them"? Here we meet that old word, "force," supposed to be banished from modern scientific theory. To be sure, as we read on we find that force is defined as the product of mass and acceleration, or as that which generates a certain momentum by acting for a given time, and that, for the purposes of dynamics, all we need to know about a force is the momentum which it generates in unit time. If force is thus defined in terms of the motion it produces, it seems at first thought a superfluous concept, or at best a convenient symbol which adds nothing to the description of the motion which force is said to produce. Such and such a motion, so it would seem, is simply said to be the effect of that which causes it. But when we look a little further, we find that the force acting upon a certain system is not defined in terms of the changes which it produces in that system, but in terms of its effects on other systems, previously studied. The force is, for example, gravity, already well known, and the question is raised as to the effect of this force upon any system whose motions are to be described or predicted. With respect to any given system, a force is something acting upon that system from outside. No doubt in a complete description of an all-inclusive system the notions of force, causation, and explanation would all be dissolved. But science is very far from attempting to compass all the motions in the universe within a single description. It always deals with systems that are subject to outside influences, i.e., to forces; and, thus, however critical it may be, and however hypercritical in its use of terms, it has frequent use for the ideas embodied in such words as force and cause.

The system which psychology attempts to describe, the organism, is anything but a complete or closed system, and therefore psychology is bound to make much use of the notion of causes or forces, whether frankly so-called or referred to as conditions, stimuli, influences, situations, or what-not. Not only are there external factors that affect the individual's activity, but we know that the organism never acts absolutely as a whole, however convenient we may find the expression, "activity of the organism as a whole," in our definition of psychology. A person is engaged in difficult reading, and meanwhile another, metabolic process is going on within him, with the result that suddenly hunger pangs break in upon his reading and very likely interrupt it. Such being the state of the matter, any psychology which became so critical as to exclude altogether the notion of cause and effect, and limited itself to describing experience as just a stream of happenings, would, in my opinion, be no science at all. But there is no such psychology in the laboratory, or anywhere outside of a theoretical definition. Always stimuli, conditions of the experiment, instructions to the subject, and attitudes of the subject are brought into the description. Therefore I conclude that even introspective psychology, however "existential" it may set itself to be, is really dynamic at heart.

Existential psychology, as represented by Titchener (5) and by Weld (7), professes to read all meaning and value out of the field of its observations, and to do so in obedience to a general canon of critical science. Let us see. The physicist is making an observation. His eye is fixed upon a dial, and he records the position of the pointer at a certain time. He does not record his mere sensory experience; he records the reading in terms of degrees of temperature, or volts, or whatever he knows the reading to mean. Moreover, if you asked him what he had observed, you might be much surprised at the length to which he would go in assigning meaning to this simple sensory experience. If you asked him why he made no record of the candlepower of the light illuminating his dial, he would say that that fact was entirely irrelevant and valueless for the matter in hand. Certainly his observations are not free from meanings and values in any absolute sense. The meanings and values that have to be read out in order to get purely existential data are preconceptions, hasty inferences, fear of consequences, or concern for practical utility—in short, meanings not belonging in the system which one is endeavoring to observe and describe. But a psychologist, examining the phenomena manifested by an individual, may find meanings, purposes, desires, valuations as existent processes appertaining to that individual. If psychology is to describe so much of the existential world as is manifested by the individual, it must, sooner or later, take account of such meanings and values, and must not allow itself to be frightened off by the mere sound of those words.

Let us grant that psychology ought to be existential, i.e., that it should be tough-minded in its insistence on definitely factual data. There is nothing in that requirement that limits psychology to the study of sensations, or that limits it to the study of the individual as an experiencer. There is nothing that prevents it from studying the individual's motor behavior. It is admitted that biology can study the individual organism in all sorts of ways, and still remain perfectly existential and critical. To discover the reason for excluding behavior study from the strict boundaries of psychology, one has to go back into history. Psychology started, and long continued, as an enterprise of isolated individuals. There were no laboratories, no special facilities for studying other persons. Each isolated student, when he approached psychological questions, took his own experience as his source of information, and thus psychology centered in the psychologist himself and consisted in a study of one's own experience. With the advent of laboratories and groups of psychologists, the subject of an experiment became typically someone other than the investigator himself, and psychology became in practice the "psychology of the other one," to use a pregnant phrase of Max Meyer. But if we are studying the "other one," there is no excuse for limiting the study to his "experiences"; we should study his behavior as well, if only to round out our study and to see things in their relations. It will scarcely be satisfactory to regard behavior study merely as a related discipline, for neither behavior study nor experience study is anything but a fragment when taken alone.

At one time in its history, psychology was defined as the science of inner experience, and so distinguished from the physical sciences, which were based on outer experience. But it was impossible to distinguish sharply between inner and outer experience, and, besides, psychology, to be complete, had to consider outer experience as well as inner. Wundt attempted to draw the distinction as between mediate and immediate experience, psychology taking the immediate, and physics the mediate. But as far as the experience of the scientific observer is concerned, it is as immediate in physics as in psychology. Then Mach and Avenarius concluded that experience was the same, whether utilized by physics or by psychology, and that the difference lay entirely in the point of view. Physics took its observed facts as related to each other, but as independent of the observer, while psychology considered its facts as related to the individual who happened to be the observer. The field of psychology included all experience, considered in its relation to, or in its dependence upon, the experiencing individual. Such a definition seems at first sight to allow psychology all the room it could possibly desire. But it is not true in a literal sense that psychology covers all experience. As a science, it covers only experience that has been scientifically observed. Further, the data obtained by the physicist in his scientific observations are seldom of any use to psychology, not being made from the psychological point of view, nor under conditions arranged to bring out their relation to the observer. Psychology, according to this definition, is limited to the experience of psychological observers as dependent upon those observers. Psychology is limited, then, to the study of certain types of observation. If it is further true—which I do not believe—that all the existential material that can be got from a study of observation consists in sensations, without meanings of any sort, psychology is restricted to the study of sensory processes, and its field is decidedly narrowed. Moreover, the beautiful symmetry of the formula, all experience to physics when examined from its point of view, all experience to psychology when examined from its different point of view, has disappeared, and we are left without any aesthetic ground for adhering to that particular definition. It is best to keep so much of it as points to the individual as the focus of psychological study, and to say that psychology is the study of the experience and behavior of the individual, both terms being used in the broadest possible sense consistent with existential data. Then, since experience is really not passive, but depends on the life and energy of the individual, we can combine experience and behavior under the inclusive term, "activity," and say that psychology is the study of the activities of the individual as an individual.

Such a definition can claim some symmetry for itself at that. Within the broad field of biological science, it contrasts our science with physiology, the study of the activities of parts of the organism, and with sociology, the study of groups of individuals.

The proposed definition approximates definitions given by behaviorists as well as by introspectionists, and evidently covers all the positive findings of both wings. What it disregards consists of tabus set up by the different schools against certain positive findings of other schools. It removes, for example, the behaviorist's tabu against all the findings of introspection. Apparently the behaviorist started from the old and outgrown conception of introspection as revealing an inner world, separate from the natural world, and he conceived that the only way to rid psychology of supernaturalism was to banish introspection. On the positive side, the behaviorist started with fruitful studies of the behavior of animals, and wished to extend this line of study to the human subject. He wished to study the facts of human and animal behavior as they appear to the scientific observer rather than as they appear to the performing individual. Now, since the observable activities of other persons are executed by muscles and glands, the behaviorist thought himself forced to the conclusion that all behavior data consisted in muscular and glandular activity.

In reality, since behavior is constantly affected by stimuli to the sense organs, and since the organization of motor and glandular activities is an affair of the nervous system, the behavior which is observed is no more muscular and glandular than it is sensory and cerebral. But, taking as his premise the statement that all behavior is muscular and glandular, and then finding in common usage, as well as in the "traditional" psychology, such terms as thinking and emotion, conscious and unconscious, the behaviorist felt that, if his psychology were not to be too meager, he would have to formulate some conception of these processes in muscular and glandular terms. So thinking became subvocal speech, and emotion visceral behavior; the conscious was the verbalized and the unconscious the unverbalized (6, p. 346). If you accept these conceptions, you are in the way of being scientific, but otherwise you are back in the dark ages of myth and religion.

Two things are clear regarding these behavioristic conceptions. In the first place, their only reason for existence is to explain phenomena which the individual experiences in himself. They were not suggested by an unprejudiced study of the viscera and the speech organs. There is nothing in the known activity of the speech organs to lead to the notion of their "implicit" activity or to the notion of thinking; and there is little in the known activity of the viscera to suggest the idea of emotion. Why do not the behaviorists inaugurate a straightforward study of visceral activities, beginning, one would expect, with the more obvious activities of digestion and peristalsis, instead of making so much of the obscure movements which they call emotion? Why, except that emotion is otherwise known to them, and because, from the *experience* of individuals, it is known to be a matter of great interest? So I say that the behaviorist is logically bound to admit experience, as well as behavior, as a characteristic of the individual.

In the second place, these particular conceptions of the behaviorists are evidently hypotheses, and therefore should not be used to define psychology. They belong in the superstructure of the science and not in its foundations. Instead of being regarded as dogmas, they should be promoted to the more honorable status of respectable scientific hypotheses. Even if they should be disproved, as is the fate to be expected of all rough-and-ready hypotheses, they may have served well as stimulators of research. But their failure would not shake the foundations of the dynamic psychology which accepts them as hypotheses, though it would undermine a behaviorism which regarded them as essential to the definition of psychology. A definition of the science should not rest upon hypotheses.

The greatest deficiency of behaviorism is that it minimizes the receptive phase of the organism's activity, the processes ordinarily called sensation and perception. Behaviorism has either to regard these as motor processes, or else to exclude them altogether from the list of the organism's activities. Regarding them as motor performances is cumbersome at the best, and not stimulating to research. Regarding them as "environmental" leads to the proposal that they should be left to other sciences whose concern is with the environment (2, p. 36). If colors are purely environmental, why should the psychologist study them? When, however, we find a color-blind individual, we have simply to say that his environment is peculiar, unless we are willing to recognize color vision as an activity of the organism, and so as a proper study for psychology (and physiology). Light is not simply an environmental fact, a stimulus to the organism, for all radiation is not luminous and the distinction between the luminous and the non-luminous can be made only by try-out upon the organism. The illuminating engineer cannot measure light by purely physical means, but needs the organism as a registering instrument in his photometry. In the same way, the telephone engineer cannot content himself with the physics of sound, but has to try out the audibility of different sounds and combinations of sounds upon the organism as a registering instrument having certain limitations and peculiarities. It is interesting to find that these engineers even make practical use of the notion of "sensation units," derived from Fechner. We also find them making many of the important contributions of the present day to the psychology of sensation. So it is far from true, as behaviorists have sometimes said, that the notions of sensation and perception are simply a hang-over from primitive conceptions of the soul, or purely visionary in some way. On the contrary, they belong to one of the most scientific—as well as practical—parts of psychology, and the behaviorist's tabu against them, so far as it is heeded by psychologists, prevents them from doing part of their proper work, and keeps them out of touch with workers in the physical sciences. Just as the existential psychology, as defined, would hamstring psychology on the one side, so behaviorism would hamstring it on the other. Dynamic psychology refuses to be a party to any such mutilation.

As far as its positive contributions are concerned, however, behaviorism belongs squarely within the pale of a dynamic psychology, defined in the general terms we have used. And the same is obviously true of another very important modern school, the Gestalt psychology. So much is clear at once from the insistence of this group of psychologists upon the study of the *conditions* under which any perception or learning occurs. To study the dependence of an event upon conditions is to study dynamics. The concept of Gestalt itself is a dynamic concept, and the critiques which these psychologists direct against sensory analysis, the conditioned reflex, and learning by trial and error, all belong within the field of dynamic discussions in a psychological sense and quite apart from the particular physical dynamics which the authors seek to apply to the organism. But I would not grant that Gestalt psychology included all scientific psychology, until this school shows how it can take up into its system the positive findings of sensory analysis, motor analysis, and the analysis of learning. So long as the Gestalt attitude towards these lines of psychological investigation remains purely negative, I am forced back upon the premises with which I started this paper. Here we have able investigators—Helmholtz, Sherrington, Pavlov, Thorndike, to mention just a few—and we have findings repeatedly verified and bearing all the earmarks of scientific results. The results may be in need of reinterpretation, but as results they certainly stand. But the Gestalt psychologists give the impression of believing that this whole analytic style of investigation is fundamentally unsound. Dynamic psychology cannot define its aim in such a way as to exclude any line of investigation that has proved fruitful, or that might prove fruitful, and would regard the distinction between the Gestalt psychology and other scientific psychology as not fundamental. In short, the Gestalt idea, though highly important and fruitful, belongs in the superstructure of psychology, and not at its foundations.

In another paper, I have sought to show how dynamic psychology, using the concepts of stimulus and response, and using in particular the notion of a total sensorimotor reaction as consisting of a series of responses, has room both for sensory analysis and for the Gestalt findings on perception. Gestalt psychology, as it still seems to me, goes too far in telescoping this series of responses into a single continuous dynamic process. But I am willing to admit that I may still be misreading the Gestalt position, as I did in the article just referred to, when I said of the Gestalt psychologists: "Finding configuration to exist outside the organism, they suggest that it passes by some continuous flux into the organism, so that there need be no unfigured stage in the organism's response" (8, pp. 67-68). Köhler has very courteously pointed out (4, p. 174) that I have here entirely misunderstood the Gestalt position, and is curious to know how such a misunderstanding arose. Diligent search in the *Physische Gestalten* (3) and elsewhere has failed to show me any passage that would give any warrant for the statement quoted, and I can only suppose that it arose as a hasty rationalization of the importance assigned by Köhler to the notion of physical Gestalt.

The various hormic psychologists, exemplified by McDougall and Freud, certainly operate with dynamic concepts, striving, wish-fulfilment, conflict, repression, transference, and a host of others. The difficulty is to bring these concepts down to earth, so as to let them work along with stimulus and response, set, association, conditioning, learning, and forgetting. Dynamic psychology would certainly not need to include in its constitution the statement that purpose or striving is ultimate, and outside of the realm of cause and effect, nor to take any stand on the biological question of mechanism versus vitalism. Nor would dynamic psychology postulate that all causes in the psychological realm consist of wishes or purposes. When Freud says that no act is accidental, he means that every act has a motive. "We have solved the riddle of errors with relatively little trouble! They are not accidents, but valid psychic acts. They have their meaning; they arise through the collaboration—or better, the mutual interference—of two different intentions." "This meaning of errors will unavoidably become of the greatest interest to us and will, with justice, force all other points of view into the background. We could then ignore all physiological and psychophysiological conditions and devote ourselves to the purely psychological investigations of the sense, that is, the meaning, the purpose of these errors" (1, pp. 26, 19).

There are, then, two objections to taking our cue from psychoanalysis when we are seeking a general definition of our science. The psychoanalysts furnish anything but a model of scientific method, and they treat with indifference the simpler and probably more fundamental problems of dynamics, so that if we followed their definition we should mutilate psychology beyond the hope of recovery. Purpose enters dynamic psychology as a cause among causes, but it cannot be permitted to crowd the others out.

Psychology is admittedly not the only way of studying the organism dynamically. Physiology so far is the same, and the distinction between them is not easy to draw so as to coincide with all the labors of physiologists and psychologists. The distinction which assigns the activities of the organism as a whole to psychology, and the activities of the organs and cells to physiology, is at least a good approximation to the facts. I like it also because it seems to take care of the mind-body problem sufficiently for the purposes of science. There is no mind-body problem in everyday life, but the problem emerges when the two sciences study the organism with their different techniques. The parallelism is not a parallelism between physiological and mental activities, but only a parallelism between two different descriptions of the same activity. Where the psychologist speaks of eating one's dinner, the physiologist, more analytically, speaks of the contraction of certain muscles under the excitation of certain nerves, etc., but he is describing the same identical process as the psychologist. When the psychologist speaks of seeing the color blue, the physiologist speaks of processes in the retina, the optic nerve and its brain connections. There is no doubt, to my mind, that seeing blue is identically the same process as that which the physiologist describes. If he were able to give a much more complete analytical description than is possible today, he would not, to be sure, ever find the color blue as an experience, just because that experience is the total process which he is breaking up into parts. Sensory experience, from this point of view, belongs as fully in the stream of natural events as does muscular contraction. Every activity of the individual is susceptible of physiological analysis, and no doubt of chemical and physical analysis. But the possibility of such analysis does not destroy the activities of the individual which are to be analyzed. Psychology, then, is free to deal with the facts of sensation, feeling, and purpose as well as with motor activities, without any fear of getting outside of the field of natural science.

REFERENCES

1. FREUD, S. A general introduction to psychoanalysis. (Trans. by G. S. Hall.) New York: Boni & Liveright, 1920. Pp. x+406.
2. HUNTER, W. S. Human behavior. Chicago: Univ. Chicago Press, 1928. Pp. x+355.
3. KÖHLER, W. Die physischen Gestalten in Ruhe und im stationären Zustand. Erlangen: Weltkreisverlag, 1920.

4 ——————. Gestalt psychology. New York: Liveright, 1929. Pp. xii+403.

5. TITCHENER, E. B. Systematic psychology: prolegomena. New York: Macmillan, 1929. Pp. xii+278.

6. WATSON, J. B. Psychology from the standpoint of a behaviorist. (2nd ed.) Philadelphia: Lippincott, 1924. Pp. ix+429.

7. WELD, H. P. Psychology as science. New York: Holt, 1928. Pp. vii+297.

8. WOODWORTH, R. S. Gestalt psychology and the concept of reaction stages. Amer. J. Psychol., 1927, 39, 62-69.

PART X

"FACTOR" SCHOOL OF PSYCHOLOGY

CHAPTER 18

"G" AND AFTER—A SCHOOL TO END SCHOOLS

C. SPEARMAN

University of London

I. THE PRESENT HAPPY CONJUNCTURE

Of all the rival schools of psychology today, surely this one of *g* has been the very Cinderella. Encountering as it did the strongest vested interests, it has had to suffer from the three greatest unkindnesses, which are ignorement, misrepresentation, and even, it must regretfully be added, not a little plagiarism. Still out of this long-suffering it has developed a great virtue of patience and tolerance. Whilst the other schools have flaunted abroad in brilliant attire, it has only drudged on in the seclusion of research. And whereas others have been essentially destructive, it has remained almost wholly constructive. Its followers do not, like the behaviorists, tell us to abolish introspection; nor, like the Berlin gestaltists, try to make us renounce analysis; nor, like the structuralists, bid us postpone indefinitely the problems of function; nor, like the functionalists, have us pay little heed to structure. Instead of such negations the factorists find good in everything, even in the other "ists." They only want a place in the sun for everyone—including themselves. They seek for the widest measure of reconciliation.

But, before trying to bring about such happy relations, all around, they had first to set their own house in order. And this they seem now at last happily able to do. For many years they have drawn a line between the so-called "general theory" of two factors on the one hand and the "subtheories" on the other. The former proves and locates the factors, the latter attempt to explain them. Thus the former lays the indispensable scientific foundation, whereas the latter serve rather as a roof or crown, and can even—at the price of unwieldy thinking—be left out of account. The good fortune of the present moment consists in the fact that—contrary to common opinion—the general theory appears to be no longer seriously disputed by any psychologist of authority. This assertion we shall proceed to examine and verify, taking each main item of the general theory in turn.

But first a word may be said about another common misconception of the theory of factors, namely, that it can concern only those psychologists who are profound mathematicians. Truly enough, the theory does raise certain points whose adequate treatment requires all the mathematical study and training that are available—and perhaps more! But these are not points that everyone is obliged to settle for himself. On the contrary, they can quite well be left to those who specialize in this line. The conclusion reached by such experts must, so far as they go, be taken by others simply on faith. But this is no serious drawback; much the same seems to occur in almost all other sciences, even physics itself. For the purposes of ordinary work, the mathematics required by the psychologist who would need only to understand and utilize the chief findings of the theory of factors are no more than should be possessed by every normal child long before he or she leaves school. Most assuredly they are such as should be mastered by everyone who ventures to express any scientific opinion of his own. And they will scarcely be found missing in any person who studies the present volume.

II. The General Theory of Two Factors

After this preamble, let us, as promised, consider the "general theory" point by point. It arose as a rebound from the doctrine of faculties. These had constituted the foundation of classical psychology from the earliest days. The most ancient and cardinal of them had been Sense, Intellect, Memory, and Imagination. Little behind in antiquity and dignity had come Attention, Language, and Movement. Innumerable others had been proposed; and, indeed, continue to be so in greater profusion than ever. For although nowadays all psychologists join heartily enough in condemning the faculties, most are but renouncing the old name whilst retaining the old thing. Under some such title as Power, Capacity, Ability, Type, and so forth, they flourish more and more. Instances are the alleged "censorship," "foresight," "capacity to notice resemblances," "power to break up a complex and properly evaluate its parts," "ability to rearrange a bit of mental content in any new and prescribed way," the "extroverted type which apprehends and elaborates outer stimuli," or "introverted type which concerns itself with the subjective perception released by the objective stimulus."

Now what, if anything, has really been wrong with all these faculties, whether so named or otherwise? Nothing was fundamentally amiss, in my opinion, so long as the faculty was only taken to indicate a *class* of mental operations put together because they had some resemblance (as indicated by the class-name). But things became very wrong indeed so soon as the modern experimentalist proceeded to *measure* such a faculty, assuming for this purpose that one member of the class could represent all the rest. Thereby the members were treated as not only having a class resemblance to each other but also as being perfectly correlated together. For certes, nothing can serve as a measure of anything else except just in so far as two are intercorrelated. When the physicist measures a degree of temperature by the height of a thermometer, he obviously assumes that the two go perfectly hand in hand. Similarly, when a psychologist measures the power of attending to any vocational duties by the test of attending to printed numbers, he is assuming that the one sort of attending is perfectly correlated with the other sort. From a protest against this assumption sprang, then, the whole theory of factors. Any such assumption, it was now urged, stands at least in need of supporting evidence; otherwise the pretended

tests of mental ability are in danger of doing the testees grave injustice.[1]
Despite this protest, unfortunately, such unwarranted measurements are
still allowed to make or mar the careers of innumerable men, women, and
children all over the civilized world. To this doctrine of some half a
dozen faculties, there would seem to have been only one serious rival. The
faculties had been based on differences in the *form* of mental operation. An
obvious amendment was to take also into account the differences in *content*.
But so doing rendered the abilities that must be considered different infinitely numerous; every idea provided an independent one of its own. It
was the doctrine of the Herbartians, and of gloomy scientific outlook. For
such an enormous number of abilities must needs render any adequate
measurement of a person's mental make-up a sheer impossibility. But, in
truth, here again was a view for which no definite evidence had been
brought forward; the mutual independence of these abilities, limited each to
a single idea, had only been assumed, not in any wise proved.

Seeing that the trouble had lain in assuming without evidence either that
the different abilities were perfectly correlated together or else that they
were perfectly uncorrelated, the natural remedy was to devise and employ
some method by which correlation could be definitely measured. Accordingly, about a quarter of a century ago, the present writer proceeded to
construct what are now commonly called correlation coefficients. These
are numbers which become unity when the two compared abilities (or
other variables) go perfectly together; they drop to zero when the two are
quite independent. Later, indeed, I found that such coefficients had already been devised elsewhere, and had even in one instance been applied to
psychological purposes. But this application had been nullified by a defect
that still impaired the correlational method (disturbance by "attenuation").[2] So there yet remained an almost virgin field to be explored by
means of these coefficients, when once they had been amended. In this way,
such coefficients became the first great pillar for all theories of factors. The
legitimacy of their usage, once hotly contested, is now admitted by everybody.

The immediate result of using them was to show that the correlations
between the abilities on trial were neither perfect (as demanded by the
doctrine of faculties) nor zero (as demanded by Herbartianism), but had
instead values varying freely between these two extremes. For science
this result seemed to be as disastrous as Herbartianism itself. Any account
of mental make-up appeared to require an infinite number of correlational
coefficients. This would obviously pass the bounds of what is humanly
comprehensible. Psychology seemed to arrive at a deadlock.

At this point a fortunate discovery was made. Although the correlations

---

[1]For this and many later points, reference must be made to *The Abilities of
Man* by the present author (22), which contains the most comprehensive account
of the work of the numerous investigators belonging to this school. About the
"faculties" in particular, see Chap. III.

[2]For the original discovery of this "attenuation," see (20, pp. 89-90). For the
most complete account, see Kelley (11, Section 57).

between the different abilities had completely failed to satisfy either the doctrine of the classical faculties or that of the Herbartian ideas, they did convey a surprising impression of regularity. The exact nature of this has been described in various ways. First as "hierarchy"; then as "equi-proportionality"; now, usually, in terms of "tetrad differences."[3] But all these amount in substance to exactly the same thing; the regularity discovered is that which, if perfect, would make everyone of the tetrad differences exactly equal to zero. However, no such exactness was ever observed, or could reasonably be expected. For there was bound to occur at least some disturbance by what are called the errors of sampling; and to make allowance for these just by looking at the table of coefficients was, to say the least of it, hazardous. So this procedure of trusting to one's general impression from the table was as soon as possible abandoned. The theory of two factors came to rest instead upon the two following procedures. The first was mathematical. If the true values of the tetrad differences were exactly zero, then the actually observed values would, owing to the sampling errors, certainly not be so. Instead, they would tend to deviate therefrom by small but appreciable amounts, whose usual magnitude should admit of calculation by means of the theory of probability. Such a calculation was achieved. It is at present being largely employed, and all serious dispute about its validity has at last died away (almost the only point still at issue is the minor one as to the best approximation formula to be used when the complete one becomes inconveniently laborious).

After thus calculating theoretically these small deviations of the tetrad differences from zero, which were to be expected when the real ones were zero exactly, the next step was to see how far these theoretical values agreed with those actually observed. The upshot of the comparison was to show that the two were usually an extremely close match. The fact of this being so, in a great number of cases at any rate, is now corroborated all around. On making deductions for the sampling errors, then, the residual or true tetrad differences must be taken to come right down to zero.

The next pillar was again mathematical; it brings the "factors" on the scene. It consists in the theorem that, when all the true tetrad differences tend to be zero, *then and only then* the score obtained by each person in each test tends to be resolvable into two parts of the following kinds. One part depends on an element or factor which remains always the same in all the abilities of the same individual. The other part depends on a second factor which, even for the same individual, differs freely from one ability to another. The former factor has been named "general intelligence" or "general ability." Any such thing as this, admitting as it does of definite measurement, seems to have been an entirely new idea in the world. In

---

[3]If a, b, c, and d denote any four abilities, a tetrad difference is the correlation between a and b multiplied by that between c and d minus the correlation between a and e multiplied by that between b and d: or in the usual symbols,

$$r_{ab} \cdot r_{cd} - r_{ac} \cdot r_{bd}$$

particular, it was violently opposed to the reigning doctrine of faculties. However, both these names for it (especially the "intelligence") soon appeared to go beyond the evidence so far available. For this evidence had only located the factor statistically and had not yet defined it psychologically. For all that had been shown so far it might turn out to be the merest stunt. Hence, prudence recommended that the names of "general intelligence" or "general ability" should be replaced by the non-committal letter of the alphabet g. A further reason for preferring the bare letter is that the terms "general intelligence" or "general ability" are apt to suggest some separate mental power capable of existing on its own account, whereas in truth no such "general ability" has ever been found apart from some "special ability," which constitutes the other factor and has been denoted by s. The two factors are, for the general theory at any rate, nothing more than two values derived from one and the same real thing; this itself is the whole score obtained by any individual for the whole of some concrete mental operation. To pass from either abstract value, g or s, to any underlying separate entity is the task, not of the general theory, but at most of the explanatory sub-theories. However, in whatever way we name them, the theorem that two such factors as g and s ensue when, and only when, the tetrad differences are zero is no longer disputed by anyone.

What may be called another pillar of the general theory is the method which has been devised for comparing g and s with respect to their comparative influences or "weights" in any ability. The result of using this method has been to show that these comparative "weights" differ from one ability to another very largely; sometimes g is prepotent, sometimes s. This, too, is a matter that can no longer be contested.

There remains a sixth and last pillar. So far as the preceding account has gone, division of a person's test score into the said two parts has only been shown to be theoretically possible. But a method was also invented to carry out the division even in actual practice. The process suggested was, in fact, an extremely simple one. It consisted in testing very numerous different abilities which may even be selected at random, and then taking a mean of all the results. Throughout such a hotch-potch of tests the person's g, being always the same, will continue to exercise its influence undisturbed; thus, if it be larger than that of another person, it will reinforce this advantage with every different ability taken into account; whereas the s's, since these change in magnitude freely from one ability to another, will on an average have much the same size for him as for anyone else. In the long run, then, a person's score will be dominated by, and therefore afford a measure of, his g alone. The principle is the same as that of composite portraiture; here many photographs are taken of different individuals from the same point of view. Then the printing is done on the same paper from each negative in turn (from each very briefly). The total effect is to bring into prominence whatever characters the persons have in common, and to leave only a trace of whatever varies from one individual to another.

Between one or two years after the present writer had proposed this hotch-potch procedure of measuring g, it was adopted in actual practice by Binet. For he threw together very numerous tests in an unsystematic fashion (22, pp. 24, 68), calling the whole collection a "scale." His usage of these tests amounted, in substance, to taking their mean result, which he called the person's "intellectual level." His only fundamental addition to the proceeding work on the theory of factors—but an addition of great value—was his standardization of this "level" for age. His scale and others on the same hotch-potch principle (even without standardization for age and with no pretense at any psychological system) had quick and immense success. During the quarter of a century that has since flowed by, hundreds of thousands of persons have been tested in such a manner. Even the name of "general ability" with its supplement of "special ability" have become household words. And if the testers have not recognized whence these concepts originated, if they have overlooked that this hotch-potch procedure—otherwise arbitrary, meaningless, and even ridiculous—was really, though tacitly, borrowed from the theory of g, these past omissions on their part do not alter the present fact that g is still the only thing that their procedure can rationally be shown to measure, even approximately.

We see, then, that the concept of g has the characteristic of springing essentially out of the results of actual testing; in this sense it may be called internal or autochthonous to them. Consequently, I would urge with greatest emphasis that it should not be confused with any concept of "intelligence" derived from external considerations, be these psychological, philosophical, educational, biological, or otherwise. The g may or may not eventually turn out to conform to any such concept; but certainly cannot be assumed to do so without evidence. This point may become of vital importance even for immediate practical purposes. For instance, when considering whether a test is a good one or not. Good for what? For measuring scholastic educability? Or adaptibility to new situations? Or the power to break up a complex and properly evaluate its parts? Or simply to measure g? The replies to all such different questions are by no means bound to be always the same.

Such, then, is the *general* theory of two factors with its six foundation pillars: correlation coefficients; calculated deviations of tetrad differences from zero; observation of these deviations; proof of the two factors; their relative weights in abilities; and their actual measurements in individuals. None of these six is in the least assumptive; every one of them is a matter of rigorous demonstration. And not one of them appears at the present day to be seriously challenged by any psychologist of competence. Those who still seem to oppose them do so only by mixing them up with the "sub-theories" which seek to explain them,—and which, no doubt, do introduce controversial matter.

Still, if I am here mistaken, and some psychologist does still challenge any of these six pillars of the general theory, may these words of mine stimulate him to come frankly forward and state his case!

III. Explanations of g and s

From the general theory of g and s, let us now turn to the sub-theories which attempt to explain them. Of these only three have hitherto received sufficient advocacy to make their consideration here worth while.

The first of them consists in taking g as measuring some *quality* which characterizes the whole nervous system of any individual in a manner or to an extent peculiar to himself. This was the original view of the present writer, the proposed quality being described as the comparative "plasticity" of each nervous system (13). A similar view seems still to be held by many authorities, though without any attempt that I can find to indicate in a more definite manner what sort of quality is intended. Possibly Freeman (6) would rank himself here.

The first objection to this view is its vagueness. Some opponents of it have gone so far as to declare that in speaking of the "plasticity" of the nervous system the problem of g is not solved, but only stated. Further, this view leads on to the difficulty of imagining any quality of the brain—or mind, for that matter—which could reasonably be supposed to constitute the general individual difference. Of any such general quality nothing would appear to be known in either physiology or anatomy. The microscopic structure of the brain shows wide differences from one region to another region; but it has not revealed any characteristic qualitative difference from the whole brain of one individual to the whole brain of another.

The second main explanation—and the one now preferred by the present writer—is that the brain (or a large portion of it) possesses some total quantitative characteristic, which works *as if* there were a constant output of energy, distributed to different constituents of the brain in varying proportions.

To enter into the merits and demerits of this energic explanation would carry us far beyond the scope of the present work; especially, as the chief arguments for it do not derive from individual psychology (which we are discussing now) but come rather from general psychology. As for the contrary arguments, these also have come mainly from another field, physiology. We may, however, note in passing that this last or physiological evidence has just undergone almost a revolution. From being the strongest opponent of the energic explanation it has suddenly—under the inspiration of Lashley (14)—becomes its strongest supporter. Furthermore, some physiological results have very recently been published by Travis (29), which, if verified, will be epoch-making. And his explanation—as he himself writes explicitly—falls quite within the scope of the energic view in the broad sense in which this is favored by the present writer. But when once an "energy" has to be granted for any reason, it must needs be supplemented by some sort or description of "engines." This, so far as the brain is concerned, would naturally be supplied by its different parts or constituents that have special functions. In terms of the two-factor theory, these engines would inevitably constitute, or form part of, the s's.

The third main explanation is closely akin to the view of Herbart.

For it takes the brain to be divisible functionally into a very large number of elements whose total effect is the sum of the elemental effects. But the elements are clearly no longer the Herbartian ideas. As to what they are intended to be instead, very little appears to have been even suggested. Sometimes, however, a hint seems to be made at the cerebral neurons, whose number is, of course, prodigious. At other times, as in some writings of Thorndike, the favored elements appear to be the points of junction between one neuron and another; these points, of course, are far more numerous still. Yet a third and particularly interesting suggestion is that of Thomson, according to which the required elements may be found in the "genes" which are commonly held responsible for mental and physical heredity.

Now, the observed regularity in correlation coefficients (that is to say, the tendency to zero tetrad differences) would certainly be satisfied well enough by such a summative effect of extremely numerous hypothetical elements, each individually being of very minute size. In this case, the g of an individual by no means ceases to exist; it simply represents the mean value of the elements falling to his lot. But this explanation of the zero tetrad differences—unlike that supplied by the theory of energy and engines—involves some *further assumptions*. The main one is that each individual should be endowed with a very large random sample of the elements. Now we know from statistics that the means of all large random samples tend to equal one another; so that, on the preceding assumption, all persons would be about equally "intelligent." This conclusion not only is revolting to common sense, but seems to be definitely disproved by such work as that of Thurstone (28).

Be this as it may, the wisest course at present is not to set these rival explanations by the ears, but rather to see how far and with what advantage they admit of mutual reconciliation.

To begin with, none of them could hope to satisfy the criterion of zero tetrad differences *quite* exactly. Even the mere calculation of correlational coefficients involves some approximations for which allowance would be needed. Yet more disturbing are the approximations involved in calculating the sampling errors of the tetrad differences. But most serious of all is the possibility—in fact, almost certainty—that our representation of every test score by such an extremely simple function of g and s, as described above, is itself merely a first approximation to the truth (in accordance with Taylor's theorem). Among the numerous reasons for believing this to be the case, an obvious one is that test scores, like examination marks, are almost always obtained by some more or less artificial device. This is sure to complicate matters. The test scored will not be a simple but a complex function of any such underlying factors as g and s; hence, the present simple formulation must needs be more or less inexact. If so, the same will probably be true of the zero tetrad differences criterion, which led to this simple formula.

Besides this margin of inexactitude for all the explanations alike, another reason for not pressing their rival claims too jealously is that they are not even mutually exclusive. The two proposed characters, uniform qualitative and total quantitative, respectively, may perhaps run parallel with one another; whilst either or both may possibly be served by large random samples of minute elements. Quite unfounded is, then, the common view that the three rival explanations of the factors are to be held pistol-like at the heads of psychologists, demanding an instant and final choice between them. Before choosing any, we should at least proceed to examine all the procurable evidence.

Nevertheless, no such hesitation is needed, or even feasible, as regards the factors themselves. These, as we have seen, are adequately proved already. And it is they, as we are going to see, that *give access to all the further information required;* information not only helpful towards explaining the factors, but even towards measuring them more correctly than is done at present; and above all, towards discovering and measuring all the other main constituents in a person's mental make-up.

IV. QUALITATIVE LAWS OF NOEGENESIS

So far we have been considering two very different things: on the one hand, the "general theory," which leads to the factors g and s; on the other, the "sub-theories," which try to explain them. We have noted that, contrary to the common belief, the general theory taken apart from the sub-theories is no longer really in dispute. But have we not here fallen from Scylla into Charybdis? Are not g and s, thus divorced from their explanation, left devoid of scientific significance?

Some such view finds frequent expression; the g is declared to be something that cannot be described; and this reproach would indeed be valid enough, if what we have so far seen constituted the whole of the business. But really, between the general theory and the sub-theories there intervenes a very large *middle stage*. This uses the general theory with its almost meaningless factors as a tool, whilst it takes the sub-theories with their hypotheses as its goal; itself, it is neither meaningless nor hypothetical, but consists essentially of actual *observations*. By means of these observations, then, the meaning of the factors is gradually but surely determined. And the farther this determination goes, the smaller and less dangerous becomes the eventual jump in the dark when the final stage does arrive of explanatory hypothesis.

This progress through the three stages constitutes in fact the very essence of all investigation by means of factors. To begin with, these factors are hardly at all defined psychologically, but only proved and located statistically. There is not, as in the older and still current psychology, first an ability conceived and then its measurement sought. Instead, there is first a measurement made and then the appropriate ability conceived. All this is what has been meant by calling the method of factors a Copernican revolution. If anyone is shocked at it, he may perhaps be heartened by remembering that, after all, the physical sciences are in no better plight. The original discovery of electricity, for instance, consisted in nothing more than observing that certain attractions and repulsions of amber, paper, and so forth, occur in such a manner as to suggest one uniform cause. This cause the investigators proceeded to call "electricity"; such a name had no whit more definitely meaning than our g at the stage of the general theory. Soon, however, electrical explanations did begin to be proposed; for example, the hypothesis of two fluids, positive and negative; such hypotheses are quite comparable with ours of energy, or even of samples. But besides trying such guesses at the inward nature of electricity, investigators devoted themselves to finding out the conditions under which it makes its appearance. And the knowledge of these conditions is what really constitutes the main portion of electrical science. The "electricity," originally nothing but a denotative word, has served as a body upon which subsequently more and more meaning has crystallized. And just such a development of knowledge of actual facts has been the main work about g for the last score of years.

Now, the prime condition for the appearance of g in any ability might naturally be expected to lie in the quality of the cognitive processes which it involves. What, then, is the general qualitative character of the mental performances wherein the criterion of tetrad differences has been satisfied, so that g must be present?

How remote is this question from the older one which perplexed symposium after symposium of the leading psychologists! Here in this new question is no inquiry as to the nature of some "intelligence" without ever agreeing first as to what this name is intended to denote! Instead, there is an investigation of something which, if not described, has at any rate been definitely located. Nor is here the reply one derived from perhaps genial, but certainly incommunicable, "intuition," psychological or biological. Instead it is a plain answer to be founded upon the most complete qualitative and quantitative observations, which anyone else can verify in detail for himself.

This plain answer, so far as present knowledge goes, is that g occurs only when the abilities concerned are what has been called "noegenetic"; this word being the collective name for the following three laws, which are at the same time processes.[4]

The first may be formulated by saying that *a person has more or less power to observe what goes on in his own mind.* He not only feels, but knows that he feels; he not only strives, but knows that he strives; he not only knows, but knows that he knows.

Turning to the second law—this states that, *when a person has in mind any two or more ideas* (using this word to embrace any items of mental con-

---

[4]For the fullest account of these three laws, see (21). For a much briefer and simpler exposition, see (22, pp. 164-167).

The title of "noegenetic" is given to all processes that possess two virtues connected respectively with the words "noetic" and "genetic." By "noetic" is here meant all knowing (perception or thought) immediately based upon adequate grounds. "Genetic" covers all knowing in so far as it generates any content originally (that is to say, exclusive of mere reproduction). Evidence has been given that—almost reversely to the usual opinion—these two virtues are strictly concomitant; every noetic process is genetic and vice versa.

tent, whether perceived or thought of), *he has more or less power to bring to mind any relations that essentially hold between them.*

Proceeding to the third and last of the laws—this enounces that, *when a person has in mind any idea together with a relation, he has more or less power to bring up to mind the correlative idea.*

Proof that these three laws suffice to measure the actual scope of g has been given in detail elsewhere (22, Chap. XI). But some indication to this effect may readily be obtained by examining any of those tests of "general intelligence" or "general ability" which are in most common usage. Conspicuous here, for instance, is the test where two words are given and the testee has to say whether their meanings are the same or different. Obviously, success in the test depends on cognizing the relations of sameness and difference. It is a clear case of our second noegenetic law. Or again, if anyone were asked to mention some other test employed very often, the choice would probably fall upon that in which a word is given and the testee has to respond with the word which means just the opposite —an obvious case of our third noegenetic law. On demand for yet another very frequent test, it would as likely as not be that of "analogies." Here the question put to the testee might, for instance, be: "A glove is to a hand as a boot is to what?" To answer it, he has first to see how a glove is related to a hand, and then he has to apply this relation to a boot and so arrive at the idea of foot. The first part of the test involves the educing of a relation; the second part, that of a correlate. Among the next most common tests is the understanding of paragraphs. Here all the words are usually intelligible enough when taken singly; the crux lies in understanding them in their mutual relations. Much the same may be said for the old, but still admirable, completion test of Ebbinghaus. Again, the much prized test of vocabulary obviously appeals to the testee's store of concepts; and the formation of these depends almost entirely upon cognizing relations.[5]

With these precisely defined noegenetic processes may be contrasted the high-flying definitions of intelligence a priori, as, for instance, the ability of the individual "to adapt himself adequately to relatively new situations in life," or "to inhibit or re-define instinctive adjustments in the light of imaginally experienced trial or error." What particular connection have *these* with the ability to see that good is the opposite to bad?

Nevertheless, we are still only at the beginning of our inquiries. After seeing that g falls within the domain of noegenesis, we must go on to the far more searching question as to whether it extends throughout this domain. And in point of fact, as the reader will have noticed, the examples

---

[5]So I cannot but think that Thorndike, like Homer, nodded when he singled out the understanding of paragraphs and the extent of vocabulary as being tests into which "the use of relations" does *not* enter! Note also that the noegenetic laws do not talk vaguely about "using" relations, but indicate precisely the two manners— and sole two—in which their usage is possible. And such a precise understanding of these two manners would seem indispensable for treating the relations effectively.

quoted are always from the second and third laws, never from the first. This seems to represent fairly enough the general state of present knowledge. Up to now, no method seems to have been devised whereby the ability indicated by the first law can be tested at all. As yet, then, the evidence speaks neither for nor against this law involving g. We can cope with the question only in so far as it concerns the second and third noegenetic laws. Do these manifest g throughout their respective domains? To answer this, we need some way of submitting these domains to a general survey; we must be able to divide them up into regions and sub-regions, searching for the presence of g in each.

Now, the theory of noegenesis—alone, I believe, among all the current doctrines of psychology—does afford such an exact and comprehensive survey of the whole cognitive area. To begin with, the cases both of the second law and of the third admit of being divided up according to the nature of the relation involved. Of these relations three are "ideal," being those of resemblance, evidence, and conjunction. Seven are "real": those of space, time, objectivity, identity, attribution, causation, and constitution. Evidence has been brought that g is manifested by *every one* of these ten classes (22, Chap. XI). We may note, in particular, that it is by no means confined to what many authorities have adopted as the peculiar sphere of the "intellect," namely, the operations of "reasoning," which involve essentially the relation of "evidence." The latter does indeed often occur among tests, as shown in the following example:

> "All Russians travelled with Danes, some Danes travelled with Dutch, all Dutch travelled with Spaniards. Can you conclude as to whether Russians travelled with Dutch?"

But on the other hand, the test of opposites, for instance, involves no relation of evidence; only that of likeness. For an example where relations mainly involved are neither of these two, reasoning or likeness, we may take the following:

> "Warmth is to stove as sharp is to what? cut? knife? pain?"

Obviously, warmth is an attribute of stove, as sharp is of knife; the relation in either case, then, is that of "attribution."

Having thus mapped out the whole area of noegenesis into divisions according to different classes of relations involved, we can now go on to make cross-divisions, according to the different classes of mental content related (the "fundaments" of the relations). About each such cross-division we can ask whether it manifests g. Here we reach a point on which mental testers do seem to have expressed their views definitely enough. Basing their theories on difference of mental content, they have divided up ability into separate "levels" or otherwise named water-tight compartments. The most frequent and important of these tendencies has been to make a separate compartment for an "intellectual" or "abstractive" or "verbal" kind of ability as contrasted with the perceptual kind. This intellectual ability has been taken to be the peculiar and sole province of the test of "general intelligence," that is, g. But for such a delimitation the authors appear to present no definite evidence. They do not employ the means supplied by the method of factors, and no other means of procuring definite evidence would appear to be known. When we do proceed to utilize this method, which alone is effective, all these divisions of cognitive ability into different levels and compartments prove to be illusory. In particular, the self-same g has been discovered in sensory perception as in "intellectual" thought. Indeed these two have been found to correlate up to the high value of .9.[6] The present author is even inclined to think the sensory perception, when properly handled, will eventually make the best of all tests for g. Here again, then, the presence of g appears to characterize eductive processes universally.

If the preceding question was searching, still more so is the following one. We no longer ask simply *whether* g is present, but *in what degree it is so.* Nevertheless here again the factor method appears able to supply the information required. For this method actually gives the correlation between any ability on the one hand, and pure g on the other. In this correlation we have a precise measurement of how far the ability and g coincide. It thus indicates that which has been called the "saturation" of the ability with g.

The very exactitude of this method quickly revealed that such saturation involves many complications, for which careful allowance must be made. Among these are the following: the manner of selecting the group of subjects for investigation; the suitability of the tests in respect to difficulty; accidents in the procedure; and variation in the "breadth" of the ability at issue (22, Chap. XII). But none of these obstacles has been found insuperable. And investigations along such lines have indicated some theorems of exceptional importance, though doubtless still in need of much verification and even rectification.

One is that all the different classes of relations involve g to about the *same extent;* not only do they all introduce g but they do so in about equal degrees.

Another of these theorems is that the influences diminishing the saturation with g fall mainly into three categories. The first consists in dependence of the tests on the testee's *sensory organs* (receptors or cerebral tracts). For example, a test would tend to have only a small correlation with g if it were given orally in a very low tone of voice, so that the success of the test would appreciably depend on the testee's acuteness of hearing. The second diminishing influence is dependence on the subject's *motor organs* (effectors or cerebral tracts). A test becomes the less diagnostic of g the more the success depends on muscular strength, speed, or even dexterity. The third kind of diminishing influence was less expected. It consists in dependence of the test on the person's powers of retentivity. One might easily imagine that the ability to retain, no less than the ability to educe, must largely depend on general psychophysiological health, so that the power of retention and that of eduction should be highly correlated; but at present the experimental results, so far as they go, indicate nothing of the sort. Here, incidentally, we have evidence

[6] See a very important work shortly to be published by W. Line.

of how gravely misleading is the common definition of what is measured by the tests as being "the capacity to learn." For learning as defined in any dictionary would certainly seem to include retentiveness.

Yet another fundamental theorem, which at the present stage of research, however, can hardly claim to be more than a venturesome suggestion, is that after elimination of the said sensory, motor, and retentive influences—as also, of course, all merely accidental disturbances—the correlation of every eductive ability with pure g approaches to being perfect. The corollary would be that all localized function of the brain, cerebrum, or cortex—in a word, all "engines" (22, p. 133)—deal solely with sensation, movement, and retention. Herewith, we find ourselves inveigled into some of the greatest difficulties of physiological psychology. The evidence gleaned by our method is so far undeniably weak. But it has the advantage of being obtained along new lines.

Anyway, we have perhaps seen enough to show that the study of human abilities has been—and in the most fundamental matters—advanced by two things; the general theory of two factors, and the doctrine of noegenesis. These two have cooperated as the right leg with the left. It would be deplorable, then, if the use of these two aids to research were confined to any particular psychological school. That this still happens would appear to be largely the effect of the great fallacy mentioned above—the supposition that either the general theory of two factors or that of noegenesis depends on anything assumptive, hypothetical, or otherwise fundamentally controversial. Both these "theories" deserve this name only in its original Greek meaning of actual observation; they represent nothing fictitious at all, but only the result of observing systematically and comprehensively.

V. Quantitative Laws

Evidently enough, however, the noegenetic laws we have so far been considering can represent only one-half of any complete scheme of cognition. They are purely *qualitative* and indicate what kind of noegenetic processes *may* occur. As their indispensable supplement, then, they required further and *quantitative* laws to say under what conditions these processes *do* occur.

At once the problem faces us: What do we mean by cognitive "quantity?" To this, the theory of noegenesis has replied that such quantity has two dimensions, clearness and speed (21, Chap. XI). And this pair fits in well enough with the actual practice of measurement. For here also we find two dimensions, which are the goodness of the performance and the speed with which it is done. To bring the theory and the practice together, we need only assume that the inward virtue of clear cognition can be inferred from the outward virtue of the good performance; here in mental science, as in physical, measurement has to be effected vicariously.

Having thus arrived at showing how mental tests come to have not one but two measurements of success, namely, goodness and speed, we may go on to ask in which of the two it is that g manifests itself. Assertions on this point have been, and still are, abundant enough. The most usual trend of them is that, whereas the true intelligence manifests itself in the goodness of a performance, the intelligence of g as tested is mainly a matter of speed. Now, as regards the a priori concepts of "true" intelligence, these appear too multifarious and equivocal for scientific handling at all. But as regards the tested g, here the method of factors does supply definite and detailed observations. The upshot has been to show that g has *both* dimensions, goodness and speed. The two virtues appear, in fact, to be alternative manifestations of one and the same underlying functional unity. In general, a test can be so framed and conducted as to direct the testee's g predominantly into either channel at the expense of the other one [the comparative advantages of these two procedures belong to the topic of practical technique, which does not concern us here (27, Chap. XIV)].

From this general concept of cognitive quantity and from the problems which it raises, let us pass on to the general laws which prescribe the conditions by which this quantity is regulated. Of these there are six, the first being as follows:

> "Every mind tends to keep its simultaneous output constant in quantity, however varying in quality" (22, Chap. XV).

The classical case—noted already by Nemesius—is that of looking at a dozen or so marbles lying together on the floor. Any four or five can be seen distinctly at the same time, but never more than about this number. Much greater exactitude was introduced into such experiments by Lehmann (15). And outstanding at the present day is the corroborative work of Wirth (34).

What is the connection between this quantity of output and the previously discussed clearness of cognition? The two seem to be at bottom the same. The quantity of output is, in essence, nothing else than the quantity of clearness. But now we may note further that within the dimensions of clearness itself there are two subdivisions; these are the same as those of physical energy; they consist, that is to say, of intensity and extensity. Taking the case of the marbles again—it is quite possible to perceive simultaneously not merely five, but dozens, and even hundreds. Then, however, these will be perceived in an extremely vague manner (much too vague to allow of being counted); the great extensity will have been purchased at the price of little intensity. If, reversing matters, extreme clearness be demanded, then the number of marbles attaining to this will not even be five but only one. Altogether, then, cognitive quanity may be said to have three dimensions: intensity, extensity, and speed. (Even here, it would be easy to show that physical science is analogous.)

All these facts supplied by the law of output raise corresponding problems about cognitive ability. In particular, is g manifested in the extensity or in the intensity? Observation again seems to answer readily, *both*. For either an extensive or an intensive eduction may be effective in measuring g; there is little difference between the two (22, Chap. XV).

After the law of output comes that of retentivity. But this law has itself been shown to divide up into two that have little connection with one another. The first of them, termed the law of dispositions, runs as follows:

"Cognitive events by occurring establish dispositions which facilitate their recurrence" (9, p. 115).

Especially important among such dispositions are those by which any mental events, through accompanying each other on one occasion, acquire a tendency to do so again later on; in a word, they form "associations," or "bonds." For example, when the sight of lightning has been frequently followed by the sound of thunder, thereafter such a sight, even if not actually followed by such a sound, tends to reproduce the idea of it.

How, then, is this law of dispositions related to g and s? We have here two kinds of problems, dynamic and static. The former include the momentous question as to whether a person's g or his s can be increased by the virtue of retentivity; or, what comes to nearly the same thing, by means of practice. This is almost equivalent to the old crux as to the relative influences of nature and nurture. In spite of its difficulty, this problem would seem to be obtaining some light from the theory of two factors. There has been a large amount of evidence to the effect that the practice or retentivity can largely improve s but cannot in general cause any increase of g (22, Chap. XV).

Turning to the static problems—does the person with the greatest amount of g tend to have the greatest retentivity? As we have already seen, the answer so far gleaned from the theory of two factors has been unexpectedly in the negative. The two endowments, amount of g and retentivity of dispositions, would appear to vary almost independently. Unanimous on this point have been the experimental results of Hamid (9), McCrae (17), Perera (19), Strasheim (24), and Walters (30), not to mention others.

The second division of retentivity is that belonging to the law of inertia or persistence. It runs as follows:

"Cognitive processes always begin and cease more gradually than their (apparent) causes" (22, Chap. XVII).

A simple but drastic instance is when, after some painful experience, one cannot for a long time afterwards, as it is said, "get it out of one's head."

Dynamically, the influence of this law has shown itself in disturbing cognitive activities when these are immediately preceded by others in some way incompatible with them. Statically, the inertia and the g would appear to be nearly or quite independent; that is to say, a high degree of inertia may with almost equal probability be found in a person having a large or a small degree of g. Once more, it is surprising to find that two such general characteristics of the brain have so little interdependence. But the evidence is still far from conclusive.

Acting in the reverse direction to the law of retentivity is that of fatigue. Its formulation runs:

"The occurrence of any cognitive event produces a tendency opposed to its occurrence afterwards" (22, Chap. XVIII).

Examples are abundant on every side, whether in work or in play, in industry or in education. After continuing a strenuous performance long enough, we tend to do it more slowly and less well. Dynamically, fatigue appears to influence both g and s. Any hard work lowers subsequent ability not only for that particular kind of work but also for every other kind; so that to this extent g is reduced. But when the subsequent work is of the same kind, it is affected in higher degree, so that to this extent there is also a reduction of s. As regards the static problems, however, we again find—but the evidence is still weak—a surprising independence between g and fatiguability. The correlations so far obtained have been near to zero (22, Chap. XVIII).

The next law has been expressed in the following formula:

"The intensity of cognition is controlled by conation" (22, Chap. XX).

Here again we are assailed by numerous questions both dynamic and static. How far does the measure obtained for the person's g depend on the effort he puts forth? And similarly, about his s's? Again, does his superiority depend on being favorably disposed towards the testing situation? Or upon strength of the instincts which the tests call into action? Or upon mere power to attend? And possibly connected with such questions is the further one as to why, if g is always one and the same thing, we are continually being obliged to differentiate one sort of intelligence from another; such as the "quick" from the "profound" kind, or "originality" from "common sense"? On all these matters, more or less information has already been gleaned by the theory of two factors. With respect to the first of them, for instance, there have recently been several investigations as to how far a high score for g depends on the intensity of the effort made. The result has been unexpectedly in the negative. Of course, *some* effort is needed to get a good score (or perhaps to cognize at all); but no more is required, it would appear, than is readily exerted by any normal person. High degrees of it seem to result principally in increasing the speed of the performance at the expense of its quality (32, 33).

There remains yet another quantitative law, which in a sense lies deeper than all the others. It may run as follows:

"Every manifestation of the preceding four quantitative laws is superposed upon, as its ultimate basis, certain purely physiological influences" (22, Chap. XXV-XXIII).

Suppose a person's activity on any occasion—say, when reading some poetry—to be most favorably conditioned in respect of all the other quantitative laws; that of output is satisfied because no distraction is affecting him; that of dispositions, because he has read the poem often previously; that of inertia, because he has read it only a few seconds before; that of fatigue, because he has been as far as possible resting himself; that of conation, because he is now exerting himself to the utmost. In spite of all these advantages he may still make poor headway with the poem, because he is too young, or very ill, or half asleep, or congenitally a moron. Here, in age, health, heredity, and so on, we encounter influences where pure psychology reaches its last limits. If any causal explanation is to be supplied, this can come only from psychophysiology. The facts themselves to be explained, however, can be observed and studied on their own account, that is to say, psychologically. And very numerous, accordingly, are the investigations of this kind which have been carried out in respect to s. To enter into details, however, would far exceed our present scope.

Looking back over this summary review of the quantitative laws of noegenesis, we may venture to raise again claims similar to those for the laws of quality. Once more, the doctrine of noegenesis in most intimate combination with the general theory of two factors has produced definite information about human ability. And this information has not been confined to matters of mere detail (these we have had to leave unmentioned, for want of space). It has managed to cover, more or less effectively, the *most fundamental problems*.

VI. Broad Factors

Not yet by a long way, however, have we come to the end of our "middle stage"; that which intervenes between the general theory of g and s, on the one hand, and the hypothetical explanation of these, on the other. So far, we have only taken into consideration the cases where the criterion of the two factors is perfectly satisfied (within the limits of the experimental error). What about the exceptional cases where it is *not* satisfied?

To start with, a word may be said on the not uncommon practice of putting up such exceptional cases as an argument against the theory of two factors. This practice is quite unjustifiable. If the criterion is really sometimes satisfied and sometimes not, then such a discrepancy should only spur us on to discover what are the conditions to which it is due. In general, the onus of accounting for these exceptional cases should rest upon those who allege them to exist.

Now, a few of the exceptional cases were discovered at the very beginning of the whole concern with factors. They arose from the four following correlations: that between Latin grammar and Latin translation; between French prose and French dictation; between counting letters one at a time and three at a time; and between two nearly identical tests of cancelling the letters of the alphabet. A conspicuous feature which did not, and could not, escape notice in every one of these four pairs was that the two abilities in it were extremely akin; they could be said to be partly the same, or to "overlap." And obviously enough, such overlapping supplied good and sufficient reason for the criterion of tetrad differences not being satisfied.[7]

---

[7] To see this, imagine first any two abilities to satisfy the criterion, so that they have the same g but quite different s's; the likeness between them will derive solely from the g they have. If now, without altering the g, we make the s's overlap, this will obviously increase the correlation between these two abilities without altering any of the other correlations. Hence the criterion is bound to fail, just as it has been found to do.

That constituent in respect to which (over and above g) any group of abilities overlap each other has been called a "group factor;" it invests the group with more or less functional unity. But in order really to have scientific significance the group or overlapping must not be confined to such an extremely narrow range as the counting of dots, or as the cancelling of letters; it must extend over, and thus confer some functional unity on, a range broad enough to be important.

In this way we are brought back to the "faculties" again, which are still playing a large part in educational, medical, and industrial psychology. For each of these faculties, as we saw, has been tacitly taken to constitute just such a functional unity; and here the overlapping factor, if it really existed, would certainly embrace a range of very great breadth and importance. But such overlap had been only an assumption. No evidence had been obtained, or even appeared to be obtainable. This deficiency was now, however, made good by the theory of two factors. The long missing link was at last supplied, and it showed that in the immense majority of cases such unifying broad factors did *not* exist. This negative result has again and again been pushed amazingly far. Take, for example, the formboards of Goddard and of Dearborn, respectively. The former test required each of a large number of blocks to be fitted by the subject as fast as possible into an aperture made to corresponding dimensions. The other test differs from the foregoing solely in that two or more blocks had to be fitted *together* into the same aperture. This seemingly slight difference between the two tests turned out to make them wholly independent of one another (except in so far as each of them involved a certain amount of g); of any group factors there appeared to be no trace (22, p. 228).

Still, among all such negative results there do "stick fiery off" some rare but brilliant exceptions. Pre-eminent among these has been the already mentioned law of inertia. For although this law extends over all mental operations whatsoever, nevertheless a common factor (not g) has been found to run throughout (22, Chap. XVII). This common factor has shown itself, moreover, to be unitary, in that it satisfies the criterion of tetrad differences. On such grounds, this factor seems to be legitimately called a second "general" one. It in no way clashes with g—nor even, as has been said, mars its theoretical beauty—for it is of a fundamentally different kind. The two only supplement each other. Inertia does not, as g does, express any ability to educe new mental content; nor does it even, like reproduction, involve ability to reproduce old mental content; it is not usually measurable by any single performance at all, but solely by the disturbance that the lag in one performance causes in the start of another one.

This second general factor has been denoted by the letter p, to indicate that it appears provisionally to be corrected with what has generally been called the "type" of "perseveration," or "secondary function," or "introversion." Still, too much credit should not be assigned to any such earlier doctrine. For these "types" have in truth been based on no better evidence than all the "faculties," which turned out to be so illusory. That the functional unity of the perseveration or introversion was formerly a mere unsupported guess is shown by the fact that the domain then assigned to it has now been proved to be altogether erroneous (22, Chap. XVII). The method of factors alone has really supplied all the solid evidence for both the existence and the domain of the functional unity; and in doing so it has picked out this inertia in extraordinary contrast to all the other alleged types or faculties, which it has uncompromisingly rejected.

To explain this second general factor, the suggestion has been made of connecting it with the first one, by attributing both to the same psychophysiological energy, but to different aspects or dimensions of this. The g would thus represent the degree of energy available for use in any of the engines; p, its inertia on transfer from one engine to another. This double use of the concept of energy leaves it, of course, no less hypothetical than before. But as a working hypothesis, it acquires additional credit by being able to deal with both the general factors simultaneously and harmoniously.

Besides these two general factors, there has been found evidence for one, and only one, more; chiefly through the researches of Flugel (5). As is well known, the amount of mental output of any person, although tending to keep a constant level on the whole, is continually oscillating about this level. And this oscillation has been shown not to be wholly due to changes in the difficulty of the work; there remains a large residue which can be explained only by changes in the efficiency of the worker. To this discovery, in itself of little moment, the theory of two factors has made a vital addition; namely, that, although the oscillations appear to cover the whole range of cognitive activity, still throughout them there runs something common and unitary. The evidence is the same as that for g and p. In this way we are led to the third general factor; to it has been given the name of o (22, Chap. XIX). Its practical importance remains as yet chiefly a matter of surmise. As regards explaining it, here once more the concept of energy has been found usable. As g denotes its amount and p its inertia, so may o denote the unsteadiness of its supply. Probably, it is some manifestation of fatigue.

Another peculiarly interesting case—involving the possibility, not indeed of further quite general factors, but at any rate of one or more very broad ones—is that of verbal ability. For although we have already seen that this by no means covers the whole area of g, still it may possibly have a broad area of its own which g does not cover. The answer afforded by experiment seems to depend largely upon the sort of persons tested. If these have all received approximately the same education, then no such extremely broad factors have any considerable influence. But if, on the contrary, the education of the persons has differed widely—say, some have come from much better schools than others, or some have done much reading at home, or some speak a second language at home—then such broad factors, according to our results, do attain to degrees of much importance

(3, 23). On the other or perceptual side, it may be added, we have found nothing of the sort: contrary to the common assertion, there has been manifested *no* very wide non-g factor in perceptual ability.

Herewith we reach the end of the cases to be here mentioned where the criterion of zero tetrad differences is *not* found to be satisfied. This limitation, however, is only that prescribed by our available space; we have had to confine ourselves to the cases of greatest magnitude. Naturally, these do stand quite isolated. Investigation has revealed several further ones of more or less inferior importance, chiefly among them being afforded by the curious observations about "mechanical ability." For an account of these further non-conforming cases, as also of their theoretical significance, reference must be made elsewhere (22, Chaps. X-XX).

As after the section on the qualitative laws and after that on the quantitative ones, so here once more after consideration of broad factors, we seem entitled to claim that definite information of the most fundamental sort has been gained by the general theory of two factors in conjunction with the doctrine of noegenesis. And the information has been gained without the support of any assumption or hypothesis. Accordingly, it can be, and ought to be, verified, corrected, and utilized by psychologists whatever may be the school to which they profess to belong: energists, samplists, or what-not.

VII. OREXIS

Naturally enough, the fruitfulness of the general theory of two factors for the investigation of cognitive abilities suggested that its services might be turned to the other great side of mental make-up which comprises feeling, striving, and the like. Or, in a word, "orexis," as it has been named by one of those who has done most to increase our knowledge of it, Aveling.

This extension of the method was accordingly attempted in a very large investigation made by Webb, and with a success which even surpassed our expectance. The correlations between different traits of character were discovered to display a regularity of just the same sort as that already found between abilities; so that here also, some general factor was proved to exist. Further observation, still on lines similar to those used for investigating the nature of g, indicated that this new factor was provisionally describable as "consistency of action, resulting from volition or will." But to maintain an open mind on this matter pending further inquiry, it was—like g, p, and o—denoted only by a noncommittal letter of the alphabet. Still, in order to give at least a hint of its apparent connection with will, the letter chosen was w (31).

Now, to uphold such a factor as "will" seemed at that time to be a strange anachronism. On few things had modern psychologists been pluming themselves more than on having emancipated themselves from just this effete superstition, as they regarded it. The dozen years or so, however, which have lapsed since w was discovered would appear to have brought only more and more confirmatory evidence. Especially the study of mental pathology and of "difficult" children seems to have rendered the admission of some such factor indispensable. Modern writers seem here once more to have fallen into the pit of oversimplification. The orectic mechanism, after all, does not consist simply of a number of instincts each fighting for its own hand. It includes some additional agency to control and coordinate these.

Superficially seen, such a march of science might look like a retreat, a going-back to the original Charioteer of Plato. But really the movement has more resembled the ascent of spiral stairs to a place which, though corresponding with the starting-point, lies on a higher level. The older view had been little more than a vague surmise, glorified indeed by poetry, but incapable of further progress. Whereas the newer view was founded on positive observation; it admitted of exact verification, and it promised unlimited further extension.

Accordingly, unlike Plato's Charioteer, the knowledge about Webb's w was soon carried to a more advanced stage. Garnett, in particular, made a great step forward on the mathematical side. He showed how to deal not only with one general factor but with several of them simultaneously. He thus moved forward from the theory of "two factors" to that of functional analysis in general (7, 8). And this mathematical extension has since received many further developments such as those contributed by G. H. Thomson (26), J. R. Thompson (25), Wishart (35), Dodd (4), Black (1), Mackie (16), Daniell (2), and especially Kelley (12) and Holzinger (10, p. 91, and elsewhere).

The immediate use to which Garnett put his new statistical tool was to prove that—on taking more of Webb's data into consideration than the latter had done himself—there was evidence not only of g and w but also of yet another factor, which he called c. Subsequent research, however, would seem to indicate that this c was, after all, only the obverse side to p, or in other words non-perseveration.

And indeed the four general factors, g, p, o, and w, would appear sufficient to achieve mental analysis over a very wide region. Among the results obtained by their means is the explanation of the already mentioned problem, as to why and how intelligence has been so often and so emphatically declared to be of various kinds. Evidence has been found that when people observed in others what they called "profound" intelligence, this could be resolved into a combination of a large g with a large w. Just the same analysis, but with less g and more w, was discovered for "common sense." In order to account for what has been called "quick" intelligence the p had to be made small; and just the same analysis was obtained for "originality" (22, Chap. XX).

Still, all such services rendered to orexis already are no more than a pledge, it is hoped, of much more to be done in the future. An instance of where the theory of two factors might lead to great advance is in enumerating the human "springs of action," or "instincts" as they are now more often called. At present, every psychologist seems to think he ought to make out a new list for himself; and this independent procedure, unfruitful though it may be for science, is at any rate easily done. For such lists are really nothing more than classifications; and these can be made from an unlimited diversity of standpoints. But trouble comes over the scene when most of the authors tacitly assume that their lists signify much more than mere classes, and handle them as if they represented functional unities. In fact, we have here once more the old fallacy of "faculties" and "types"— these and the instincts are all tarred with the same brush. And the remedy, too, would in all cases seem to be the same. What the instincts need is to be no longer merely classified, but to be expressed in terms of unitary functions.

Even this case of the instincts is not the end of the difficulties which may perhaps be solved along kindred lines. Think of all the mental traits which are habitually used to describe human character. A partial list of them has been given by Partridge (18), and runs into thousands! It begins with:

"Abandoned, abject, abnormal, abrupt, absorbed . . ."

and ends with:

". . . Wide-awake, wishy-washy, worthless, wretched, witless, woebegone, worrying, worthy and zealous."

A survey of such a list indicates the gross inadequacy of the current device whereby some half a dozen traits are picked out more or less arbitrarily to constitute the whole "profile" of an individual. Profiles of the sort can be constructed in literally millions; and without any definite grounds for preferring one to another. What we really need is a unique list of a few ultimate functional unities, so as to set forth the profile of *these*. Insight into this situation appears to be rapidly gaining ground. During the last few months the present writer has himself received numerous letters, inquiring as to how tables of orectic correlations—normal or pathological—can be brought to manageable simplicity by means of expression in terms of functional unities.

VIII. Looking Backwards and Forwards

Summarizing the theory of factors, we may note first the common error that the usage of these necessarily presupposes an advanced knowledge of mathematics. To probe the foundations of this theory, doubtless, or to develop it along novel lines, may need mathematical aptitude and training of high order. But just the same may be said of the ordinary measurement of limens; and yet, whoever could not actually measure them would nowadays hardly be recognized as a psychologist at all. Of the two, calculation of a limen and calculation of tetrad differences, the latter is not the harder task, but the easier. Such a state of affairs seems to be shared by all sciences, even physics itself. To dig the mathematical foundations of this is left to a comparatively small body of specialists, but the simpler formulae derived from these specialized researches are used in actual practice by every physicist.

No less erroneous have we found the common belief which takes the general theory of two factors to be founded upon some dubious assumptions or hypotheses. Fundamentally, it is built on nothing assumptive or hypothetical, but on undisputed mathematical theorems and actual observations. The admixture of assumption and hypothesis does not appear on the scene until an attempt is made to render the observations more intelligible—to "explain" them. Such an attempt need never be made at all; many writers prefer to muddle along without. Furthermore, even when the explanations offered differ widely from one another, it does not at all follow that they are mutually inconsistent. Thus it is quite conceivable that g should be explained *either* by the hypothesis of energy, *or* by that of sampling, *or* by both hypotheses simultaneously. The theory of factors, in fact, is essentially such as to waive the matters that are most controversial; it affords means of pushing on with positive observations, each verifiable on its own account. Its real trend is not to kindle, but to quench, the warring between the different schools.

This leads us to yet a third popular fallacy about the theory of factors, and perhaps the gravest of them all. This is to the effect that the factors, until they do receive some assumptive or hypothetical explanation, possess little or no positive content; they are thought to remain something indescribable, or even meaningless. This view overlooks that the method of factors involves three stages. The initial one is, by means of actual observations and some simple formulae, to discover that the factors exist and where they do so. Such location (unlike the customary psychological definitions) serves to determine the factors unequivocably. But it does leave their psychological significance remarkably scant. Before the final stage of explanatory hypothesis, however, there intervenes the indefinitely long middle stage; here the factors, despite their poverty of significance, can still be utilized to obtain a limitless harvest of further observations. And then these observations proceed to repay their debt; although originated by the help of factors that are almost meaningless, they proceed, in their turn to invest these factors with richer and richer meaning.

Already the results obtained in this way appear to have been extraordinarily abundant. Here we have had space to chronicle summarily only the most fundamental of them, each of which deserves—and no doubt will some day receive—many volumes on its own account. As a pre-eminent instance may be quoted the evidence which has linked up the factor g with the processes of noegenesis; processes which, like the factors, are free from assumption or hypothesis and have been actually observed. In particular g has shown itself to be co-extensive with the two noegenetic processes called the educing of relations and that of correlates. This result has been gained from an immense amount of qualitative and quantitative observations made by very numerous investigators. As a general fundamental fact— making due reservation for all the inevitable additions and corrections to befall eventually—this identifying of g with eduction promises to serve as a polar star to guide our further advances throughout the region of individual psychology.

But this hopeful glance at the future suggests yet another one. If individual psychology can get such benefit from the factors, what about the other region of psychology called "general"? Is this also to become a beneficiary?

Our answer may confidently be, Yes! General psychology to a large extent consists in classification by resemblance; but this usually admits of being done in a diversity of ways. And such option of procedure leads to grave confusion, which is largely responsible for psychological controversy. Great relief is felt and progress made whenever some or other of the classifications gains any distinct advantage over the rest. This advantage is sometimes afforded by reference to a bodily organ. For example, the division of visual sensations into chromatic and achromatic has become much more stable in psychology since the former were shown to characterize a particular kind of nerve-ending in the retina. For contrast, look at the classifications of the chromatic sensations among themselves; this still remains in endless dispute, because here the proposed different classes do not possess any known separate organs.

Now, just as potent as the advantage conferred upon any proposed class by a separate bodily organ may be that which comes from unity of function. And any class which, owing to this unity of function, secures for itself dominance in the sphere of individual psychology, is almost certain to extend its influence sooner or later over to the other or general sphere. For example, since individual psychology has managed to evolve out of the chameleonic "intelligence" the stable and functionally unified g, and has sharply delimited this by the noegenetic processes, we may reasonably expect that both the g and the noegenesis will eventually establish themselves in general psychology also; whilst the other concepts of "intelligence," not being so advantaged, will gradually fade away into the background.

Visions of the future may even allow themselves a still more distant range. This year physicists have been impressively proclaiming what marvellous offspring are born to their science from wedding the experimental method to mathematical analysis. But such a marriage is just what is being commenced by the functional analysis considered here. Some day, maybe, psychologists too will bring forth their quantums and their relativities.

But how in all this, it may be asked, is any of the promised help afforded towards softening the warfare between schools? Something in this direction, it may be replied, has already been exemplified by the unending and unprogressive controversy about "intelligence." So long as any such concept continues to represent only a class, it must almost necessarily remain equivocal and vacillating; for the simple reason that classification can be done in an unlimited variety of fashions. But so soon as the merely classifying concepts in psychology are replaced by definitely located functional unities as recommended here, then this prime source of discord between schools will automatically come to an end.

But there is yet another road by which a remedy may be sought against this deadly canker of psychology, the splitting up into discordant schools. It consists in our general policy, as embodied in the preceding pages, which may be formulated as that of advancing along the line of best evidence;

otherwise expressed, as that of proceeding from the better to the less well known—from what is more likely to gain general assent to what is less likely. By virtue of this principle it is that our own march has been divided into three stages. First has come—free from complication with all else—the basis of actual observations and mathematical demonstrations. In the second stage, we are still busy with observations, but now mingled with more or less precarious inferences. Last to arrive are the mere assumptions and hypotheses. Put these first, and the whole band of investigators is at once violently split up into warring forces. Put them last, and the rage of controversy soon dies down into the amenities of postprandial speculation.

But this policy does not stop at its applications to our own procedure; it bears no less on that of others. Take for instance the school of behaviorism. This seem to have two main roots, metaphysical and methodological. The first of these consists in an attempt to found psychology on the doctrine of materialism. How could one for a moment suppose that any metaphysical doctrine whatever—much less this peculiarly contentious one— could fail to arouse forthwith a bitterly hostile opposing school! Now, with our policy of admitting evidence in due order, such monstrous attempts to bluff psychology—by tacitly assuming just that which cannot possibly be proved—will be relegated to the limbo of things lost. Turning to the second or methodological root of behaviorism—this consists in a belief that the observation of behavior supplies psychology with its most certain and reliable data. So far, excellent. We can, no doubt, cognize much more certainly whether a man's risorial muscles are being contracted than whether his thoughts are turned to villainy. But why, when we have observed the former fact securely, should the behaviorist forbid our going on further and attempting to establish the second fact also? Here again is a pernicious bone of contention that might have been escaped by our policy of taking the evidence, in due order indeed, but nevertheless completely.

As another instance, take the Berlin school of Gestalt, or better—as Aveling has proposed—"formalism." Here the start is made by casting out the associationist foundation of psychology in elementary "sensations," replacing these by the perception of whole things, as we find it to occur in ordinary life. Again excellent, up to a point. Undeniably, the whole percepts are the data best known to us. But after thus beginning here rightly enough, why does this school order us to stop here, forbidding us to go further by way of analysis and inference? What but horrid war could possibly be excited by such an arbitrary attempt at mutilation and sterilization of procedure? And how simply would this trouble be dissolved away, if these formalists, instead of wilfully stopping short at the phenomena of whole percepts, were then to give fair hearing to the further evidence also!

What has just been remarked about two of the present belligerent schools of psychology could easily be extended *mutatis mutandis* to all the others. In every case, it seems to me, much of the modern disastrous clash of psychologies might similarly be transformed into mutually tolerant cooperation. Such, then, is the policy of the school of functional analysis and of noegenesis. Its main desire is to abolish schools, in the sense of parties who are not cooperative. It pleads in general that different species of evidence should be given hearing in the order of their security. It urges in particular that all observations should be examined on their own merits, and not mixed up with—therefore perturbed by—inferences and hypotheses that are less certain and hence more controversial. It comes, then, not as a further combatant in the psychological arena, but as an apostle of peace.

REFERENCES

1. BLACK, T. P. Proc. Roy. Soc. Edinburgh, 1929, **49**, 72-77.

2. DANIELL, P. J. Boundary conditions for correlation coefficients. Brit. J. Psychol., 1929, **20**, 190-194.

3. DAVEY, C. A comparison of group verbal and pictorial tests of intelligence. Brit. J. Psychol., 1926, **17**, 27-48.

4. DODD, S. C. On criteria for factorising correlated variables. Biometrika, 1927, **19**, 45-52.

5. FLUGEL, J. C. Practice, fatigue and oscillation. Brit. J. Psychol., Monog. Suppl., 1928, **4**, No. 13. Pp. 92.

6. FREEMAN, F. N. Mental tests. Boston: Houghton Mifflin, 1926. Pp. ix+503.

7. GARNETT, J. C. M. On certain independent factors in mental measurements. Proc. Roy. Soc. London (A), 1919, **96**, 91-111.

8. ———. General ability, cleverness and purpose. Brit. J. Psychol., 1919, **9**, 345-366.

9. HAMID, S. A. Some factors of effectiveness in mental ("intelligence") tests. Brit. J. Psychol., 1925, **16**, 100-115.

10. HOLZINGER, K. J. On tetrad differences with overlapping variables. J. Educ. Psychol., 1929, **20**, 91-97.

11. KELLEY, T. L. Statistical method. New York: Macmillan, 1924. Pp. xii+390.

12. ———. Crossroads in the mind of man: a study of differentiable mental abilities. Stanford University: Stanford Univ. Press, 1928. Pp. 245.

13. KRUEGER, F., & SPEARMAN, C. Die Korrelation zwischen verschiedenen geistigen Leistungsfähigkeiten. Zsch. f. Psychol., 1906, **44**, 50-114.

14. LASHLEY, K. S. Basic neural mechanisms in behavior. Psychol. Rev., 1930, **37**, 1-24.

15. LEHMANN, A. Die körperlichen Aeusserungen psychischer Zustände. II. Die physischen Aequivalente der Bewusstseinserscheinungen. Leipzig: O. R. Reisland, 1901. Pp. viii+327.

16. MACKIE, J. The probable value of the tetrad difference on the sampling theory. Brit. J. Psychol., 1928, **19**, 65-76.

17. McCRAE, C. Thesis in Library of University of London.

18. PARTRIDGE, G. E. On outline of individual study. New York: Sturgis & Walton, 1910. Pp. v+240.

19. PERERA, H. S. Thesis in Library of University of London.

20. SPEARMAN, C. The proof and measurement of association between two things. Amer. J. Psychol., 1904, **15**, 72-101.

21. ———. The nature of "intelligence" and the principles of cognition. (2nd ed.) London, New York: Macmillan, 1927. Pp. viii+358.

22. ———. The abilities of man: their nature and measurement. London, New York: Macmillan, 1927. Pp. xxiii+415.

23. STEPHENSON, —. Thesis in Library of University of London.

24. STRASHEIM, J. J. A new method of mental testing. Baltimore: Warwick & York, 1926. Pp. 158.

25. THOMPSON, J. R. Boundry conditions for correlation coefficients between three and four variables. *Brit. J. Psychol.*, 1928, **19**, 77-94.

26. THOMSON, G. H. On the formation of structure diagrams between four correlated variables. *J. Educ. Psychol.*, 1927, **18**, 145-158.

27. THORNDIKE, E. L., *et al.* The measurement of intelligence. New York: Teach. Coll. Bur. Publ., 1926. Pp. xxvi+616.

28. THURSTONE, L. L. A method of scaling psychological and educational tests. *J. Educ. Psychol.*, 1925, **16**, 433-451.

29. TRAVIS, L. E., & HUNTER, T. A. The relation between "intelligence" and reflex conduction rate. *J. Exper. Psychol.*, 1928, **11**, 342-354.

30. WALTERS, —. To be published shortly.

31. WEBB, E. Character and intelligence. *Brit. J. Psychol., Monog. Suppl.*, 1915, **1**, No. 3. Pp. ix+99.

32. WILD, E. H. Influences of conation on cognition. *Brit. J. Psychol.*, 1917, **18**, 147-167.

33. —————. Influences of conation on cognition. Part II. *Brit. J. Psychol.*, 1928, **18**, 332-355.

34. WIRTH, W. Paper read at International Congress of Psychology, 1929.

35. WISHART, J. Sampling errors in the theory of two factors. *Brit. J. Psychol.*, 1928, **19**, 180-187.

PART XI
ANALYTICAL PSYCHOLOGIES

CHAPTER 19

L'ANALYSE PSYCHOLOGIQUE

PIERRE JANET
College of France

The science of physiology studies the general laws of digestion or circulation in all the individuals of the same species, in an effort to find the functions of the average individual of the group. Practical medicine requires something more than this; knowledge of the various modifications of this function in certain definite individuals is necessary in order to determine in what way it differs from the normal and in order to attempt to re-establish the functioning necessary for the prolongation of life.

The same is true in the field of psychology; psychology determines with more or less precision the great psychological functions as they are and as they ought to be in the average man. However, when attempting to become practical and render service to jurisprudence, pedagogy, and mental therapy, psychology is obliged to become more concerned with concrete cases and to determine to what degree a particular individual is removed from the normal. A magistrate, in order to prevent a second offense, must know the modifications of conduct which have played an important rôle in the accomplishment of this act and which have prepared for its repetition. A teacher, directing the education of a particular child, cannot limit himself to the application of a general education suitable to the average child but not necessarily suitable to this individual. He must know exactly to what extent this child differs from the others, and in what way it is necessary to modify the general methods of teaching for him. The doctor who is especially interested in neuropathy and insanity considers abnormal individuals exceptional by definition and cannot treat them with precision if he does not know what constitutes their irregularity, what distinguishes them from others. Psychology of the individual is the necessary consequence of practical psychology which departs from generalities to render service to individuals.

L'analyse psychologique is the indispensable method of psychology of the individual, which has for its object the search for those characteristic behavior traits which distinguish an individual from others. If this is true, it is impossible to indicate in a general way the rules and methods of an *analyse psychologique*. This analysis will vary according to one's proposed aim; it cannot be the same when it is a question of reforming a criminal, educating a child, or curing a neurotic. Above all, this analysis will continue to vary with the progress of science itself as it discovers new functions and new methods for determining the state of each particular function. Today the measurement of basal metabolism enters into the physiological analysis of a patient, whereas several years

Submitted in French and translated for the Clark University Press by Dorothy Olson.

ago it was never considered. *L'analyse psychologique* changes every day, and I can survey only very rapidly a few examples to show the high points of a useful analysis today.

The first individual analyses seem to have been made by means of *scholastic examinations* in which young persons were subjected to a series of questions on the elements of the various sciences or the history of their country in order to determine the extent of their intellectual acquisitions. These examinations, which are still universally applied especially in the field of vocational guidance, are not without value and are of great assistance in discovering particular aptitudes. However, these examinations may well be reproached for their narrowness since they stress only the acquisitions of the memory. It is well known that a good verbal memory capable of reproducing whole courses is no proof of the value of an individual and that failures of this verbal memory do not necessarily indicate great psychological gaps.

A long time ago—for life passes rapidly—I thought that another memory, closely associated with the preceding one but not identical with it, was of more importance from the psychiatric point of view. Memory of the events of one's own life play a part in the development of personality, and more or less distinct and easily evoked memories of certain emotional situations in one's life are of great importance in certain psychological disorders. In my works published between the years 1886 and 1892, I have shown by numerous illustrations that memories of certain dramatic circumstances to which the subject had not succeeded in adapting himself presented themselves to the mind in the form of unsolved problems, reproduced in a pathological form the original emotion, and by means of various mechanisms gave rise to neurotic symptoms; this I called *traumatic memory of an unassimilated event*. The search for these memories, though difficult, might in some cases give rise to a very useful psychological analysis. I very often resort to this method, which obtains some interesting cures through the modification of this traumatic memory.

However, is it necessary to conclude that this search for traumatic memory constitutes all *l'analyse psychologique* even in the case of a neurotic? Alas! a lengthy experience with patients has disillusioned me on this point. It is often a great mistake to attribute to this or that memory of the patient, even though it be an emotional one, such considerable influence on présent disorders. Present exhaustion does not always bear any relation to the more or less conscious persistence of certain memories of this sort. In many cases, the emotional event and its memory have at the start played an important part for a certain period. The disorder to which they have led, the bad thought habits, and the subsequent exhaustion have become independent of the memory itself, and the modifications of the memory do not act upon them. Infectious diseases often terminate in disorders which persist indefinitely even after the disappearance of the microbe, and no tardy and useless disinfection will effect a cure of these remaining disorders. In other cases, constantly repeated slight emotions, which have been quickly forgotten, have made important modifications of the psychological functions.

Maladjusted reactions to social situations, so ably pointed out by Adolf Meyer, in speaking of the origin of dementia praecox, faulty education, and many other circumstances, may be more important than this or that memory. Finally, one must not forget hereditary constitutions, and those little understood diseases such as colic-bacillary infections so common among neurotics. The psychiatrist must be a well-informed psychologist, but he must also be a doctor. To insist upon pursuing indefinitely an analysis of memories is to misunderstand many other elements which play an important part in mental disorders.

The mind consists of a group of functions which has evolved through the centuries and through the life of the individual as well, and moral equilibrium demands the presence of all these functions. They do not all function at once, but they should be ready to function when circumstances demand. It is always necessary to discover whether some important function or group of functions has been destroyed and whether their failure to function is not the cause of the present disorder. If an individual complains of not being able to read, it is not necessary to search for traumatic memories relative to improper reading, when it would suffice to say that he has a disorder of the eyes.

In fact, phylogenetically older psychological functions have definite organs; those which are less ancient, however, have definite centers in the nervous system. In both these cases, alterations of functions are in accord with discernible modifications of function. L'analyse psychologique must understand these studies made upon organs, and upon modifications of reflexes manifesting organic alterations. To limit analysis to non-organic psychological disorders is to raise in vain all kinds of metaphysical problems and to misunderstand the importance of organic difficulties even in a psychosis. L'analyse psychologique applies equally well to hemiplegia, aphasia, and delirium. Discovery of a change in function naturally becomes more difficult when it is a question of recent operations whose difficulties do not manifest themselves by means of readily perceptible organic modifications. Above all, it is necessary to guide one's self by the study of the functioning of psychological habits. The method of examination by means of tests is still in its infancy; its great difficulty lies in the fact that it cannot yet indicate to which function of the mind the correct execution of a particular test corresponds. However, it is making progress, and in the future will be of great importance in the distinction between functions which remain intact and those which have undergone modification.

An important characteristic of psychological functions is that they are not all of the same value. They present varying degrees of complexity and efficiency and seem to have been acquired gradually in a certain order. They may be arranged in a hierarchy in which the higher functions rule and interfere with the lower ones, thus giving to acts a greater efficiency in both time and space. In the brutal destruction of organs, lesions may by chance destroy functions irregularly. For example, a man may lose the elementary function of vision and still retain the superior function of reflection. This is one of the important characteristics of these so-called organic lesions.

In most cases, it is a case of a general disorder striking all functions, suppressing the superior ones first and descending downward on the psychological hierarchy. The importance of disorders of the higher functions, especially in the field of belief, is shown in various deliria in which lower functions such as assertive belief continue to exist. Determination of the degree to which the disorder has attained is important in the appreciation of the degree of *psychological tension*. *L'analyse psychologique* which is not limited to the notation of ideas and memories acquired by the individual, but which seeks to penetrate more profoundly into the constitution of the mind, should strive to determine the degree of lowering of psychological tension.

Unfortunately, this study is not yet sufficient. It is not alone sufficient to have numerous perfected mechanisms but it is also necessary that these mechanisms function properly under all circumstances. When an automobile stops, it does not necessarily mean that some part is broken; it may simply lack oil. One can sum up briefly by means of the expression *psychological force* those modifications of conduct which are still difficult to measure such as power of movement, number of actions, their undisturbed duration, their rapidity, etc., always keeping in mind their hierarchical values. In fact, it seems that the more elevated an act is in the hierarchy, the more energy it requires.

Diminution of force and modification of the important relationship between tension and psychological force are becoming elements of vast importance to psychological analysis. This diminution of energy is most apparent in certain feelings and deliria. The feeling of pressure, in which effort plays a predominant rôle, indicates a diminution of the functioning of those tendencies for which psychological activity of the whole personality seeks to substitute. Feelings attached to morose inactivity and to melancholy indicate with greater precision a certain general weakness. However, one must suspect these measures of energy as a result of certain feelings and delirium; the latter are regular reactions which may be modified by all sorts of influences and which may easily be mistaken. One of the most important studies of *l'analyse psychologique* will be the appreciation of the degree of psychic energy of an individual and the extent of his weakness; we know nothing of the nature of this psychic energy, but we must study its manifestations and succeed in measuring it as the physicist measures an electric current without understanding the nature of it.[1]

Briefly, *l'analyse psychologique* does not insist upon a pre-established system of study, but consists in the application to definite individuals of all psychological and physiological knowledge; incomplete and difficult, it will doubtless make progress, thanks to the development of psychology proper.

---

[1]See my earlier works (1, 2).

REFERENCES

1. JANET, P. Obsessions et psychasténie. (2 vols.) Paris: Alcan, 1903, 1908. Pp. 600.

2. —————. De l'angoisse à l'extase. (2 vols.) Paris: Alcan, 1926, 1928. Pp. 527; 697.

3. —————. La faiblesse et la force psychologique. Paris: Chahine, 1930.

CHAPTER 20

PSYCHOANALYSIS
ITS STATUS AND PROMISE

J. C. FLUGEL
University of London

All readers of this volume who have already a pretty extensive knowledge of contemporary mental science will probably agree that psychoanalysis and behaviorism are the two most original and startling of all the psychologies that hold the field today. Both involve striking changes in method and outlook and represent definite departures from the main trend of psychological development; and (in spite of the very considerable degree of acceptance which behaviorism has met with in America—as distinct from other parts of the world) it may still be said that both are looked at with suspicion by the great body of the world's psychologists. But, if they are alike in these respects, psychoanalysis and behaviorism differ in nearly all other directions. Indeed, in certain ways they represent the two extreme tendencies in present psychology. Introspective observation of consciousness and explanation in terms of conscious thoughts and motives constitute the classical method of psychology. This method has however, always been supplemented by the observation of (objective) behavior—if only in order that there may be something for introspection to explain. Behaviorism, inspired by the progress of modern physical, and above all of physiological, science bids us give up both the practice of introspection and the attempt to explain conduct in terms of consciousness. Psychoanalysis, while in no way minimizing the value of objective observation and indeed making considerable use of it, has endeavored to extend the method of explanation in terms of consciousness by employing the already familiar concept of the unconscious much more consistently and frequently than has been done by any previous school. Instead of abandoning such explanation as soon as introspection fails to reveal the presence of adequate motives, it makes a bold attempt to see how far light can be thrown upon the obscurer phemonena of thought, feeling, and behavior by the assumption that these, too, are determined by psychological motives, but motives of an unconscious and therefore unintrospectable kind. In so doing, it does not in any way assert the impossibility of physiological explanations, such as are usually sought by other schools of psychology in these circumstances; indeed it hopes that adequate physiological correlations will one day be forthcoming. But it refuses to abandon the search for psychological causes just because introspection does not reveal them, and, by adopting and extending the concept of the unconscious, it seriously postulates for the first time in the history of psychology a thorough psychological determinism, according to which every psychological event is regarded as having a psychological cause. It is probably true that such an assumption is logically implied in every theory of psychophysical parallelism; but the school of psychoanalysis is the first to have the courage to convert this philosophical assumption into a true working hypothesis, thereby putting psychology in the same category as the physical sciences, so far as concerns the fundamental methodological postulate of an unbroken chain of causality.

These two concepts—of the unconscious and of psychical determinism—are fundamental in psychoanalysis. If we refuse to accept these concepts, psychoanalysis can have little meaning for us. There are, of course, psychologists who will not allow that such concepts are justifiable; they explicitly deny the former concept and implicitly deny the latter (by invariably turning to physiology where introspection fails). But, in considering the position of psychoanalysis as a school of psychology, it is well to point out that of its two most fundamental doctrines, one, that of the unconscious, has already been held by many psychologists and philosophers of different schools, while the other, that of psychical determinism, would seem to be logically implied in the most popular modern solution of the age-old problem of the relation between mind and body.

But if there is nothing very unorthodox about its basic postulates, it must be admitted that in many respects—its history, its methods, its ways of thought, its terminology, its personnel—psychoanalysis lies uniquely apart from the main body of psychological science. This is well illustrated by the fact that there was no section on psychoanalysis in *Psychologies of 1925;* doubtless, because of its peculiar position at the moment, it did not appear to be a "psychology" within the meaning of the term that was adopted. The inclusion of such a section in the present volume shows, however, that the barrier between psychoanalysis and other psychological systems is being slowly broken down—a circumstance that will surely be welcomed by all who consider that psychoanalysis has some real contribution to make to the study of the mind. And yet this circumstance must not blind us to the existence of the important differences that separate psychoanalysis from other schools of psychology. The editorial welcome that has now been accorded to psychoanalysis seems, rather, to afford a suitable occasion for an attempt to review the status of psychoanalysis as a branch of psychology, with reference both to its present position as a science and its promise for the future.

Historically, psychoanalysis owes much of its relative isolation to the facts (*a*) that it was originated not by a pure psychologist but by a physician; (*b*) that, to an extent almost if not quite unique in the history of science, its main features were developed by its founder before it attracted any appreciable notice from the scientific world at all. These historical reasons were strongly reinforced subsequently—as soon as Freud's views came to be at all widely known—by a psychological reason: the fact that the discoveries of psychoanalysis aroused incredulity and displeasure. They seemed at once so surprising and so repellent that there appeared to the ordinary psychologist to be but little inducement to forsake his own safer, more orthodox, and more comfortable line of work for a method that had only produced results that were deemed unlikely to be true, and, even if true, would be decidedly unwelcome. The obvious course was to remain aloof and either neglect the claims of psychoanalysis, leaving it to psychoanalysts themselves to prove their points if they could do so, or else to meet them critically with an endeavor to show that the methods of psychoanalysis were faulty and its conclusions consequently unsound. Most psychologists adopted the former course; a few decided on the latter, and with their arguments we shall have to deal. Still some few others, however, having conquered their first incredulity, saw the apparent reasonableness and possible great significance of psychoanalytic findings, and proceeded to fit them into their own psychological systems wherever they were able. Of this latter group, some became again more critical upon a closer acquaintance, while others have continued to hold in the main a favorable opinion of psychoanalysis, though, partly because the workers in this class have been so few and partly because the task itself is difficult, they have so far achieved only a small degree of amalgamation between psychoanalytic results and those achieved by other methods. Meanwhile, the psychoanalysts on their side have made very few attempts at a *rapprochement,* and from Freud himself downwards have built up such theories as they needed with but little reference to those of "academic" psychology. Indeed they have, paradoxically enough at first sight, established a far firmer contact with the other sciences of human life, notably with anthropology, than with mental science proper, chiefly because they found in many of these other sciences, concerned as they are with fundamental and archaic human institutions, more data germane to those which they themselves encountered in their own study of the deeper layers of the mind.

The term "psychoanalysis" itself threatened at one time, largely through the indiscretions of journalists and publishers, to become so wide as to lose all significance. But recently there has been a healthy tendency to restrict its application to the work of Freud and his school, and such a restricted meaning seems to be now adopted in all psychological and medical circles. As used in this way, the term still denotes four things, which can be at least theoretically distinguished. The first of these is a method— the peculiar feature of which is that it serves at one and the same time as a means of psychological investigation and as a therapeutic instrument. The second meaning of the term refers to the facts discovered by this method. In the third meaning the term is extended to cover the conclusions that are drawn from these facts and the theories that are founded on them. In the fourth place the term is used to designate the study of further facts (obtained otherwise than by the psychoanalytic method and often taken from very varied fields) in the light of the facts and theories already mentioned.

The attitude of the analyst towards these wider data is, in general, similar to that which he adopts towards the data presented by an individual patient. In both cases he endeavors to direct an impartial, evenly distributed attention to the material as it presents itself, quietly noting resemblances and differences, until certain connections force themselves upon him, leading to provisional conclusions, which are in turn accepted, rejected, or modified in the light of further data. Hence, although the fields are, in many ways, very different, the procedure itself is fundamentally the same as that in the case of what, for the sake of convenience, we have here distinguished as the psychoanalytic method proper.

Such a distinction of the various (legitimate) meanings of the term "psychoanalysis" is useful because the chief difficulties that have been raised about the scientific status of psychoanalysis are to a great extent concerned with the relations between these different meanings. More particularly is this the case with regard to the distinction between the second and third meanings. The chief controversy here concerns what can be regarded as observed fact and what is mere hypothesis. But this question in its turn leads back to the distinction between psychoanalysis as a method and psychoanalysis as a body of discovered facts, for it has been thought that the method itself is liable to distort the facts it is desired to study—that the so-called facts are indeed artifacts. As regards the fourth meaning, the chief problem at issue is whether the interpretations made by the psychoanalytic writers can be regarded as independent confirmations of results obtained more directly by the psychoanalytic method, or whether there is here a vicious circle in which the distorted facts and interpretations obtained by this method are illegitimately read into the anthropological, aesthetic, or biographical data under consideration, which data are then erroneously regarded as affording corroboration of the original conclusions.

The problems connected with the first three meanings are closely interconnected and depend in the last resort upon questions connected with the psychoanalytic method. We must therefore start our critical considerations by dealing with the method. As is well known, this method was originally developed as a substitute for the evocation of memories under hypnosis, and in its essential features has been unchanged for many years, though auxiliary measures which aim at bringing about more favorable circumstances for the working of these essential features have been the subject of considerable experimentation and discussion. The most fundamental of the features in question is the process of *free association*. The subject of the analysis is asked to abandon the usual conscious control of thought, to cease thinking for any particular purpose or about any particular theme. Having adopted this attitude, he is then to say (but naturally not to do!)·everything that comes into his head—even though much of what occurs to him may appear senseless, disjointed, painful, intimate, or impolite. The method involves the fullest confidence in psychical determinism, the assumption being that, just in so far as conscious direction is abandoned, the flow of thoughts will be determined by unconscious factors, the nature of which will become more clearly apparent than when conscious direction is maintained.

The instruction given to the subject, though it sounds so simple, is far

from easy of fulfilment. Indeed, when the attempt is made, it soon becomes apparent that the free flow of thought is constantly impeded and
that the subject's mind becomes the seat of conflicts, which prevent an
easy, uninterrupted sequence of ideas. The causes of interruption themselves seem to belong to various levels. At the one extreme the subject
may be clearly conscious of certain ideas, but (from shame, embarrassment,
or other motives) may hesitate to say them out aloud in the presence of
the analyst. At the other extreme the subject may find that for appreciable periods his mind becomes little better than a blank, containing at most
some faint and vague impressions of his actual environment—and this in
spite of his utmost conscious efforts to overcome the stoppage. In this
latter case it seems clear that some inner but unknown force is impeding
the associations, that there is an unconscious resistance to the appearance
of certain ideas in consciousness, just as in the other case there is a conscious disinclination to communicate such ideas as are already there.

It is evident that this method of free association has some features
which differentiate it from other methods of psychological observation
and experimentation. In particular, the determination to say everything and to put no check on either thought or expression, if it is
honestly persisted in, soon leads the subject into intimate topics which
neither his own feelings nor our ordinary social and ethical conventions
will allow him to discuss except under conditions which insure confidence and privacy. Indeed in many cases he would refuse to discuss
them at all, had he not a strong motive for doing so, this motive being supplied, in the case of the neurotic patient, by the suffering that
his neurosis entails. In other cases it has to be supplied by professional
or scientific considerations or by the deeper lying "compulsion to confession" which, according to some psychoanalytic writers, is a fundamental characteristic of the human mind. Here at once we encounter a
great difficulty of the method from the strictly scientific point of view
—the fact that this need for confidence and privacy makes it difficult or
impossible for others to obtain full information as to what takes place
during the process of analysis. For a third person to be actually present
would fatally disturb the privacy. For the words of the analysand to
be taken down in full (either by a concealed shorthand writer or by
a dictaphone) would be to betray the confidence which he has placed
in the analyst. Even subsequently published abbreviated accounts have
often to be curtailed, or certain details of the reports have to be modified,
though in psychoanalysis details are often of supreme importance for
conveying understanding and conviction.

But these disadvantages, formidable as they may seem, are not really
so significant in practice as might at first appear, for the reason that,
even if the conditions of privacy and confidence did not exist, there
would still remain almost impossible obstacles in the way of presenting
a permanent and complete record of any individual analysis. There
are two such obstacles. In the first place, the analyst's conclusions and
convictions are based, not only on the mere words utttered by his patient,

but also on the emotional expression that goes with their utterance—their varying intonation, loudness, and tempo, the pauses which are made between them, and the gestures, and other bodily movements that accompany them—all of which cannot be reproduced on any written report. We are here face to face, not so much with a peculiar difficulty of the psychoanalytic method, as with a general deficiency of written (as distinct from spoken) language. While written language is tolerably adequate for the conveyance of the cognitive contents of our minds, it is much less suitable than spoken language for indicating the presence and nature of affective states. Suppose that in conversation we make a given announcement to two people, A and B; both may, for reasons of convention or politeness, reply in the same formal terms; and yet we may be quite clear from the way in which the words are spoken, from involuntary bodily manifestations, etc., that our announcement is pleasing to A and displeasing to B. But now suppose, further, that we wish to convey in writing to a third person, C, the result of our announcement to A and B. If C is for any reason unwilling to believe our account of the opposite feelings aroused in A and B, we shall find it extraordinarily difficult to convince him, since the spoken words were the same in both cases, and language is incapable of conveying adequately the subtleties of emotional expression upon which we based our judgment. The psychoanalyst is in a very similar position if he tries to carry conviction to a sceptical outsider. It is impossible for him to prepare any written report that shall provide another person with all the data from which he himself draws his conclusions, since many of these data are not communicable by means of written language. Indeed the "talkie" seems the only medium through which these data could be made generally available.[1]

And yet, even if this most recent invention of physical science could help us to surmount this difficulty, another difficulty lies in wait, namely, the impossibility of conveying adequately the great mass of material that goes to an analysis in a way that could be apprehended by a fellow-scientist with ordinary powers of patience and endurance. A complete psychoanalysis is—as is now well known—a very lengthy business, extending over months and years of daily work. A "talkie" of corresponding length—of anything from three hundred hours upwards—would be unendurable, and even a condensed written report containing anything in the nature of an attempt to convey the full material of three hundred sittings would in the majority of cases remain unread; probably for this reason no such full report seems as yet to have been made. We

---

[1]The day after I wrote this sentence, I learned from the newspaper that the "talkie" had been employed experimentally in Philadelphia in the process of obtaining a confession from a suspected murderer, so that the full facts concerning his confession should be subsequently available for study and evaluation. There is, of course, a certain parallelism between the need for subsequent evaluation of legal evidence of this kind and the need for evaluating psychoanalytic evidence.

have here a particularly crass example of a difficulty that is liable to beset all scientific records that cannot be reduced to quantitative form. The naturalist, for instance, describing the habits of some little-known animal can make only a relatively brief summary of his actual (perhaps very numerous) observations, illustrated by complete description of a few typical examples of concrete behavior on the part of the animal, either by means of word pictures or with the help of photograph or film. For the rest he can only invite his colleagues to give themselves the trouble of making fresh observations of their own. And this is what the psychoanalysts have done. They have given summarized reports of their general conclusions drawn from long protracted analyses, illustrated them by fuller accounts of the analysis of concrete items of material (e.g., of dreams, of phantasies, and of instances of parapraxia[2]), and have invited others to undertake similar analytic studies on their own account. Their procedure has not in reality been different from that of other scientists in a similar predicament.

The invitation to repeat the observations under like conditions seems to be an adequate (perhaps indeed the only possible) reply to those who doubt the correctness of the psychoanalyst's descriptions of the facts observed, and of the conclusions he has drawn from these facts. This—combined with a reference to the history of psychoanalysis, which has shown a frequent remolding of theory to suit newly gathered data —should be sufficient to deal with those earlier critics of psychoanalysis who considered that analysts worked with preconceived theories and chose their facts to fit these theories. It is still perhaps the only possible reply to those more modern critics who insist that the psychoanalytic method, as practiced, necessarily distorts the facts to be observed—though the reply is in this case obviously less satisfactory. Such critics maintain that corroboration of the facts by fresh observers working by the same method is scientifically valueless, since, by adopting the method proposed by psychoanalysts, the new workers render themselves liable to the same distortion of judgment that affected the original observers.

To explain this objection we have to take account of a complication which, for the sake of simplicity, we have hitherto omitted from our considerations of the psychoanalytic method. The process of free association, which we have described as the most essential feature of this method, does not in itself demand an activity on the part of the analyst beyond that of an attentive listener; nor does it, strictly speaking, demand the presence of an analyst at all, for auto-analysis is theoretically at least a possible procedure and is in practice often resorted to in minor matters. Nevertheless, although by general admission psychoanalysis demands a much greater passivity on the part of the physician than do other forms of psychotherapy, it is, of course, true that the analyst is not entirely passive. A psychoanalytic interview is not a monologue with an audience

---

[2]This term has been adopted by psychoanalysts as a general designation of the minor errors and forgettings included by Freud under the name of "the psychopathology of everyday life."

of one, but a conversation between two people in which the patient plays the leading part. Now, in so far as the analyst participates in the conversation, the method undergoes a complication; the essential process of free association is interrupted and supplemented. A complicating factor of this kind obviously adds greatly to the difficulties of psychoanalysis as a method of pure science—however much it may add to its therapeutic efficiency. The analyst starts his work with certain expectations and presuppositions gained from his own experience and his general knowledge of the subject. It is clear that these presuppositions are liable to bias his interpretation of the material with which his patient presents him and that this interpretation may in turn exercise a suggestive influence upon the patient. This latter influence, furthermore, seems likely to be all the greater in view of the admitted occurrence of the transference—an affective *rapport* of a peculiar kind between patient and analyst, which always occurs in a successful analysis, and which is held by psychoanalysts themselves to have certain features in common with that which occurs in hypnosis. What is more natural to suppose, therefore, than that the patient accepts the interpretations of the analyst in virtue of a heightened suggestibility induced by this *rapport?* The very process of being analyzed is, then, it would seem, calculated to distort the analysand's judgment in favor of psychoanalytic theories, and, as this process is regarded by analysts as one of the most important prerequisites for forming a sound judgment as to the correctness of psychoanalytic views, it would seem as though they had skilfully succeeded in entrenching themselves in a position in which they are effectually isolated from all criticism.

The case against psychoanalysis from this point of view looks very black indeed. To many opponents the case seems closed. But to show that there are reasons which appear to render the conclusions of the psychoanalyst unlikely does not in itself prove them to be untrue. What methods of supporting his conclusions are open to the analyst? In the main, two. In the first place, he can attempt to meet the charges directly, by bringing evidence to the effect that suggestion does not in fact play the rôle in psychoanalytic practice with which it has been credited. In the second place, he can endeavor to support the correctness of psychoanalytic conclusions indirectly, by showing that they are in harmony with facts which can be observed quite independently of the psychoanalytic method. In following this second course he necessarily makes use of the last of the four above-mentioned meanings of the term psychoanalysis, extending the term so as to include the study from the psychoanalytic point of view of data gathered from numerous and varied fields, in themselves quite unconnected with psychoanalysis.

We shall deal first with the direct method of defense. The arguments that have been, or may be, brought forward under this head are fairly numerous:

1) It has been pointed out that psychoanalysts—and this applies especially to the pioneers of the method—should themselves be in a good

position to judge how far the influence of suggestion is at work, since many of them (including of course, Freud himself) had enjoyed long practice with suggestive therapeutics before they adopted psychoanalysis. Indeed, having had experience with both methods, they should, other things equal, be in a better position than their critics to understand the points of resemblance and of difference between the two procedures.

2) An analysis carried out with the help of an already trained analyst (hetero-analysis), though strongly recommended, is not always regarded as essential; auto-analysis is a possible substitute for hetero-analysis, at least in some cases, and this was, of course, the only method available to certain pioneers, again including Freud himself. Some of the earliest and most original members of the psychoanalytic school were therefore immune to the influence of suggestion, in that form at least which is here in question.

3) It is maintained that the development of psychoanalytic doctrine shows that this doctrine, far from being constructed a priori, was a matter of gradual growth, as new and often unsuspected facts were discovered. Freud himself has frequently modified his views as his knowledge and experience increased. Some of the modifications that were due to him were certainly not of the kind that would have been made had his object been to safeguard or clarify pre-existing theories. On the contrary, they show unmistakable signs of having been forced upon him by experience. The best known of these modifications is that which concerns the nature of sexual traumata in childhood; whereas he at first believed that these traumata were always in the nature of real occurrences and that the impressions which came to light during the analysis of certain cases were, as they appeared to be, genuine memories, he later found that such impressions were in many cases mere phantasies, though this did not prevent them from exerting a traumatic influence. A no less striking instance was the introduction of the concept of narcissism which, though it has proved amply justified by its usefulness in practice, has undoubtedly rendered his theoretical conceptions more complex and difficult, since it spoiled the attractive simplicity of the theory of opposing sexual trends and ego trends, and, by extending the sphere of the sexual trends into the self, rendered the function of the ego trends much more obscure than they had been at first. Such a complication of hitherto existing views—a complication which, while it solves some problems, necessitates a revision of theory in other directions—is of frequent occurrence in empirical science, but is seldom if ever found in a priori speculation, which always aims at relatively simple, wide, and clear-cut concepts. We may bear in mind too, in this connection, that, right up to the present time—more than three decades after the enunciation of the first principles—psychoanalytic doctrine shows no signs of becoming fixed or crystallized; on the contrary, it exhibits every indication of healthy growth, important and far-reaching additions having been made within the last few years.

General considerations of this kind appear therefore to confirm the assertions of Freud and other psychoanalysts that the development of psychoanalytic theory has followed and been built on fact, rather than vice versa.

The ultimate verdict in this particular matter must lie with the historian of science. Meanwhile we may safely say that no serious attempt has as yet been made by the critics of psychoanalysis to show *in detail* the supposed influence of preconceived ideas upon the historical development of psychoanalytic theory.

4) In conformity with the contention that psychoanalytic doctrine as a whole has always been based upon discovered fact, it is also claimed that in individual analysis the analyst is frequently unable to foretell the precise significance of any particular symptom or other manifestation, but is on the contrary often surprised to find its meaning quite other than that which he might have anticipated on the basis of his existing knowledge and presuppositions. Owing to the relative inaccessibility (for reasons we have already dealt with) of the full facts concerning individual analyses, the value of this claim is much more difficult to assess than the corresponding claim concerning the development of psychoanalytic doctrine as a whole. Those who hold that "suggestion" (in the last resort both of analyst and analysand) is chiefly responsible for the alleged "discoveries" of psychoanalysis will doubtless discount the statement of analysts as to the frequent non-fulfilment of their expectations. It is certainly worth noting, however, that this statement concerning individual analyses is in full harmony with their (more easily verifiable) contentions as to the development of general psychoanalytic theory.

5) The counter arguments hitherto dealt with aim at showing that certain features of psychoanalytic history and procedure make it impossible to believe that suggestion can have exercised the influence which is ascribed to it by certain critics of psychoanalysis. These arguments are concerned principally with the mind of the analyst. Another line of defense is to consider the mind of the analysand and to show that his attitude is such as to preclude the influence of suggestion on the imagined scale. It is pointed out that the transference situation, which determines the attitude of the analysand to the analyst, is based upon a repetition or re-living, not only of the love, respect, and admiration that has been felt by the analysand towards important persons in his earlier life, but also of the hate, jealousy, and envy that he has felt towards the same or other persons. Although the first-named elements of the transference undoubtedly favor a receptive attitude (and indeed according to psychoanalytic views are essential for the operation of suggestion under any circumstances), the more hostile elements which compose the "negative" aspects of the transference lead, on the contrary, to an attitude of obstinacy and suspicion, which predisposes the patient to discount or disbelieve what is said by the analyst. Indeed many patients are far more acutely critical of psychoanalysis than are any theoretical opponents. Since these hostile elements inevitably dominate the situation for a great part (in many cases the major part) of the analysis, the picture of the

docile patient gladly accepting the interpretations of the analyst is in reality very far removed indeed from the truth.

It *is* true, however, that no analysis is possible in the face of complete and permanent hostility; the positive elements of the transference do undoubtedly play an essential, though by no means an exclusive, part in the analysis. Here, it may be said, is after all a means by which suggestion becomes effective in the end. The psychoanalytic reply to this renewed charge is that in psychoanalysis, as distinct from all other psychotherapeutic methods, the transference itself is analyzed. The aim of the analyst, when faced with a positive transference is the same as that when he is faced with a negative transference; in both cases he endeavors to trace the affective attitude of the patient to its source in earlier emotional relationships, and, in so far as he is successful, the patient is ultimately freed from any abnormal dependence on, or any unreasonable love or hate towards, the analyst. The fact that the positive transference supplies an important driving force for the whole work of analysis does not alter the analytic procedure with regard to it; like a scaffolding that is essential for the construction of a building, it is removed when the construction itself is finished. Indeed its removal is essential for the final stages of the work, and the process of removal is recognized by psychoanalysts as one of the most difficult and delicate portions of their task; an over-strong positive transference, which makes a patient unwilling to break with the analyst, is one of the severest obstacles that is liable to be encountered, impeding as it does both psychological exploration and therapeutic effect (although in initial stages it may have helped in both these directions).

Summing up, therefore, under this head, it is maintained that the positive transference cannot account for the great suggestive influence that is sometimes credited to it, and this for three reasons:

a)   It is more than counterbalanced by the negative transference.

b)   It is apt to hinder rather than to help the analysis itself (except perhaps in the earliest stages).

c)   It is itself analyzed and dissolved in successfully completed analyses.

6)   The arguments against the view that psychoanalytic findings are due to suggestibility in the patient are strongly reinforced by the fact that similar findings have been made in the case of psychotic patients (e.g., paranoids, manic depressives, schizophrenics—who are notoriously not amenable to suggestion).

There is here a question of simple observation and report of the spontaneous utterances and interpretations of the patients themselves rather than of interpretation by the analyst. Indeed most of the observations made on insanity do not require the psychoanalytic method at all, and thus should, strictly speaking, be classed under the (second) heading of independent corroborative evidence.

7)   The last two arguments lead on naturally to certain wider considerations, which, in the view of psychoanalysts themselves, have probably

more weight than all the other replies to criticisms with which we have dealt. What is true of the mind of the analysand is, psychoanalysts would maintain, true of the human mind in general. The power of suggestion can be overrated as regards both the process of analysis and human life as a whole. Indeed it may be said that the fear of suggestion may easily, and often does, take on a neurotic quality. The discovery of "suggestion" by psychology has been followed by something in the nature of a phobia, in which one important part of this discovery, viz., that suggestion depends upon an inner subjective process and not upon an external power, is apt to be forgotten or discounted. Psychoanalysis itself has greatly added to this aspect of our psychological knowledge by showing that the subjective process in question consists in exteriorizing or "projecting" certain inner mental forces (connected ultimately with the parent *imagines* and embodied in the "superego"). It is only in virtue of such a projection on to another person that this person can acquire anything resembling that formidable and dangerous power which those who fear suggestion have in mind. The supposed danger of exposing oneself to suggestion at the hands of the psychoanalyst is largely due, therefore, to a fear of our own unconscious as thus projected. This supposed danger can take different forms in different individuals. The plain man thinks it is his mental or moral health that is in jeopardy. The psychologist (by a process of rationalization) thinks it is his power of scientific judgment.

With this argument the psychoanalyst definitely carries the war into his opponent's territory, by asserting that the alarm which certain psychologists have displayed as regards the influence of suggestion is a psychological reaction to the threat of exposure of their unconscious forces —a threat which, of course, the very existence of psychoanalysis entails. In so far as there is truth in this view, it is likely to prove ultimately of much greater avail than all the other lines of defense that we have examined. It makes it possible to show that the objections are themselves in the nature of neurotic manifestations of a phobia, whereas, if we once accept the objections at their face value, detailed refutation of them, however logically compelling, is likely to meet with no more success than is elsewhere encountered by attempts to combat a neurotic fear by conscious reasonings.

So much for the first method of defense, which endeavors to clear the process of analysis itself from the charges of being vitiated by suggestive influences. The second method of defense is wider and less specific in its range and purpose. It consists of the attempt to show that psychoanalytic conclusions can be verified by independent evidence. We may perhaps distinguish two main varieties of this method, according to whether the endeavor is to show (*a*) that actual data obtained by the psychoanalytic method can be objectively tested, or (*b*) that the general conclusions arrived at by the employment of the psychoanalytic method are in harmony with facts that are available quite independently of this method and that cannot possibly be affected by psychoanalytic views.

1) In the first variety there fall such procedures as the verification
of infantile memories recovered during analysis, the detection of complexes or character qualities in unknown persons who have submitted to
an analyst a written report of certain of their dreams, the foretelling of
events (e.g., a divorce) in the history of individuals on the basis of their
symptoms or their writings, or—more generally—the foretelling of future
social tendencies (e.g., the desire to return to the gold standard after the
war) on the basis of psychoanalytic insight into the unconscious meaning of these tendencies. Under this heading may also be included such
control experiments as the attempted analysis of artificial dreams composed by selecting words at random from a dictionary—an experiment
which, by the reported failure of the analysis, provided evidence in favor
of the genuineness of the analytic results in other cases.

On the whole, the work done along these lines, though occasionally
impressive, has been small in quantity and unsystematic in character.
The only serious attempt at such objective verification on a larger scale
has been by means of Jung's word-association experiment, which clearly
shows the existence of affective tendencies that can in some cases be discovered only by the psychoanalytic method itself. But the full possibilities of even this experiment do not seem to have been exhausted; it
is usually employed as a means of preliminary orientation for analysis
rather than as a means of control, such as it might have afforded if it
had been used by a second analyst who drew from it such conclusions as
were possible and then compared these conclusions with those of a col-
league in charge of the psychoanalysis itself.

In the paucity of attempts at objective control along these lines we
may perhaps see a regrettable consequence of the dissociation between
psychoanalysis and experimental psychology. Most psychoanalysts, being
primarily therapeutists, were little interested in the niceties of experimental control which are here in question. It is greatly to be hoped
that a *rapprochement* between analysts and experimentalists will, in the
near future, lead to a fruitful cooperation in this field.

2) Incomparably more work has been done along the second line.
Some of this work lies in fields that are not far removed from that of
the psychoanalytic method itself, fields that are connected primarily
with the psychological examination of the individual mind. Another
part of the work, as already indicated, has been concerned with matters
that are remote from the regions of therapeutics or of individual psychology, employing for the most part data provided by anthropology,
mythology, history, and aesthetics.

As an example of the first kind we may cite the work on parapraxia
("the psychopathology of everyday life") and on wit. Freud originally
showed—and many others have corroborated him—that human behavior
within these fields exhibits much the same processes as those revealed
by the psychoanalytic method in neurosis and in dreams, and, in particular,
that such behavior is largely determined by unconscious motivations and
by intra-psychic conflict. The great advantage of these fields for demon-

strations of psychoanalytic conclusions is that the mechanisms involved are, as a rule, much simpler than those of neurotic symptoms or of dreams (at least of adults' dreams) and that it is easy to point out that in many cases the psychoanalytic interpretation is spontaneously adopted by those who know nothing whatever of psychoanalysis. Thus we all tend to take offense if our name is misspoken or misspelled, or if anothr name is substituted for it; we are likewise hurt when a rendezvous is cut, and the plea that it was forgotten does not mollify our feelings. In fact we feel and behave just as if the mistakes and forgettings were psychically determined, just as if a person *wished* to show that we are not sufficiently important to make it worth his while to remember our name or the appointment he has made with us. Indeed such "mistakes" may be deliberately produced (as when in a play one character persistently addresses the other by the wrong name) and are always understood in the psychoanalytic sense (in this case as a sign of contempt). It would be possible, starting from such simple and universally understood examples, to construct a series of instances of gradually increasing complexity, ending with cases which require elaborate treatment by the psychoanalytic method before their meaning is revealed. The argument from continuity here speaks powerfully in favor of the psychoanalytic interpretation in the latter cases.

Not only the general fact of unconscious motivation but many of the detailed mechanisms through which it manifests itself—condensation, allusion, symbolization, etc.—are illustrated in humor and parapraxia. Thus, whole classes of wit depend upon that simple form of condensation which is employed in the pun. The pun itself, however, often indicates some sexual or hostile tendency as well as pure pleasure in the play of words, and there is again a continuous transition from the pun or *double entendre* to the distortion of a word in order to express some hidden tendency (as when I myself in a lecture once had the misfortune to refer to Schrötter—a writer who had, to my annoyance, anticipated some observations of my own—as Störer [i.e., "disturber"]). Similarly with symbolism. In France I once witnessed a "curtain raiser" where the scene took place in a dentist's consulting room. The dentist who carried out a variety of operations on the teeth of a female patient, continually described these operations in terms which left no doubt that they were veiled allusions to various sexual procedures, and the whole effect of the play depended upon an appreciation of this symbolism—which indeed appeared to be understood by everyone. There was here a complete parallelism between the indirect expressions employed for the purposes of humor and the symbolism so frequently found in dreams ("displacement from below upwards," in this case from vulva to mouth). Conversely, dreams sometimes employ expressions which could easily be used for purposes of *double entendre* or other forms of humor, as when in a dream the idea of semen is depicted by a group of sailors ("seamen"), or when the contrasted ideas of freedom to roam abroad and the necessity of remaining in a cramped and crowded home environment are symbolized by two individuals called respectively "Mr. Percy Porty" (= passport) and "the Sardine" (from the phrase "packed like sardines").

Coming now to wider fields that are remote from direct psychoanalytical considerations, an essential feature of the psychoanalytic application along these lines is that the data themselves were not collected by psychoanalysts, but are common property, having been given to the world by the labors of artists, anthropologists, mythologists, historians, and literary men, or in other cases having been handed down and well known for many generations. In dealing with this material we entirely obviate the disadvantage that inevitably appertains to data gathered by the psychoanalytic method proper, namely, that it is almost impossible to present to others the full material as it was available to the analyst himself. On the contrary, the same data now confront both the psychoanalyst and his critic. The question is: How far are these data in harmony with psychoanalytical conclusions drawn from clinical material? If the agreement is striking, it does not prove the correctness of psychoanalytical deductions in any given case or from any given patient, but it does raise a strong presumption in favor of the general validity of these conclusions.

Now, actually of course, psychoanalysts have appealed to parallels of very different degrees of cogency, or at least of obviousness. In some instances the parallel is beyond all dispute. If psychoanalysts have found that men in their unconscious minds have wished to kill or castrate their fathers, to cohabit with their mothers, or to eat their children, it cannot be denied that these unseemly desires are portrayed as actual occurrences in myth; where, for instance, Oedipus (albeit unknowingly—corresponding to a repression of the wish) marries his mother after murdering his father, where Cronos castrates his father and is in turn castrated by his son, having in the interval developed a cannibalistic taste for the flesh of his own children. The only conceivable way to deny the validity of the parallel would be to take a weapon resembling that of the psychoanalyst himself and to say that these myths are themselves only symbolic, that they do not mean what they appear to mean, but are indirect representations of (say) the sunrise, the sunset, or the change of seasons. But this would be to revive a line of thought which (though it admittedly contains some truth) no longer finds much favor with mythologists. It leaves us, too, with the awkward problem as to why the indirect representations in question should have taken such repulsive forms (for even if we regard the ancient myth-makers as merely nasty-minded forerunners of the modern psychoanalyst, it is scarcely possible to account for the persistence of their myths for countless generations except on the assumption that they made a very general appeal).

In other cases the myths themselves are not *clear* portrayals of the tendencies that analysts profess to find in the unconscious of their patients, but are themselves, it is maintained, *symbolic* of these tendencies—the symbolism, however, being much the same as that which is found within the individual mind. Here the value of the corroborative evidence, if any, is more difficult to weigh. The fact that conclusions drawn from a study of the individual mind can be applied to products of the group mind (such as myths) adds to the *interest* and *importance* of these conclusions if they are correct, but it does not in itself prove their *correctness*; it may indicate merely that the analyst is committing the same mistake in both cases, and to maintain that we have "proved" a piece of dream symbolism by applying our interpretation to a piece of mythology and then triumphantly pointing to the correspondence, is to argue in a circle. But if there are circumstances in the myth itself which, *independently* of clinical experience, point to the correctness of the interpretation, then we have really obtained an objective corroboration of the general possibility of such symbolism's occurring in the human mind. Such would be the case, for instance, if historical evidence concerning the development of the myth showed that it had gradually acquired the symbolic form and had originally represented the psychoanalytic interpretation in an undisguised way. Only slightly less convincing would be the discovery of an undisguised variant of the myth among the same or neighboring people. Actually, of course, such attempted verification has most often taken the form of collecting more or less numerous variants, each of which seems to support the interpretation in one way or another. In the course of this work psychoanalysts have found themselves involved in a fierce anthropological controversy between the modern followers of Bastian and his *Elementargedanken* upon the one hand and the new historical or diffusionist school upon the other. The psychoanalyst in the search for anthropological parallels for the facts which he believes himself to have discovered by his own methods tends to be more interested in the point of view of the former school. As a psychologist, too, dealing with apparently fundamental and deep-lying processes (processes, too, which exhibit in their general characteristics a most striking resemblance from one patient to another), he is likely to expect an essential similarity in the products of the human mind, even though obscured by superficial differences of time and place and culture. Indeed his work seems to provide a very striking corroboration of the fundamental idea underlying the theory of Bastian, inasmuch as it reveals a surprising constancy in the nature of the more important symbolical relationships, which appear to remain largely influenced by conscious contacts. But there is no necessary antagonism between the work of the psychoanalysts and that of the diffusionists—and this in spite of the violent attacks that have been made on psychoanalytical interpretations by members of the latter school. To trace the history and diffusion of human culture through its various migrations is a useful and important undertaking, but to show historically how a given belief or practice has migrated does not absolve us in the least from the task of considering its psychological significance, any more than a complete account of the life of a historical person from the cradle to the grave should lead us to suppose that that person was a robot devoid of thoughts or plans or wishes.

Nevertheless it remains true, of course, that the attempt to obtain corroborative evidence for psychoanalytic findings from anthropological material must pay due regard to historical evidence and, failing this, historical likelihood. It is for psychoanalytic purposes less convincing, for instance, to compare two apparent variants for the same myth if they come from two very different parts of the world (and may therefore have had very different histories) than if they are found in allied peoples and neighboring localities, and are therefore almost certainly variations of the same theme; while, on the other hand, mere difference of locality does not guarantee the separate and spontaneous employment of the same symbolic expression, unless it can be clearly shown that there is no possibility of the myth's having been passed from one locality to the other by means of culture contact. But, when all due precautions of this kind are taken, the psychoanalyst is still able to point to so many cases in which a number of variants of the same myth, so to speak, interpret each other (by providing a series of steps from undisguised wish-fulfilment to highly distorted and symbolic expressions of a corresponding wish) that he may justly claim to have established in this way an independent corroboration of many of his clinical discoveries; in the sense that, even if these clinical discoveries had never been made, it would still be theoretically possible to draw the same conclusions from a study of the myths alone.

What we have here said with regard to myths holds good also, *mutatis mutandis,* to other anthropological material (e.g., comparative theology and ritual) and to the data obtainable from history, biography, and art. In view of the undoubted difficulties that attend the proof of conclusions drawn solely from material gathered by the psychoanalytic method, such independent verification from sources that are open to the fullest investigation by all would seem to be of the highest importance from the scientific point of view.

In so far as we admit that psychoanalysts have, along the various lines we have considered, given satisfactory proof of the essential correctness of their main contentions, we must admit also that psychoanalysis has opened up new vistas of the utmost promise and importance, not only for psychology but for all the sciences—both pure and applied—that deal with human behavior and human institutions. If, as psychoanalysts maintain, human conduct is largely determined by mental tendencies that are normally unconscious, and if psychoanalysis provides us with a means of bringing these tendencies to consciousness and thus making them accessible to understanding and control, then it would seem that a most important step has been taken towards the overcoming of what is by universal admission the greatest menace to our present culture—man's ignorance, and consequent imperfect mastery, of himself, an ignorance which, so long as it persists, renders the advances of physical science at least as dangerous as they are beneficial. The inner conflicts revealed by psychoanalysis within the individual's mind, conflicts which entail an immeasurable quantity of suffering and inefficiency, are paralleled by social, national, and racial conflicts, which, at the lowest estimate, cause a vast amount of waste and friction, and, in the opinion of many able judges, threaten the very existence of human culture. At present, owing to these conflicts, man can make but little intelligent use of his intellectual powers or scientific knowledge, because both are liable to be employed in the service of unconscious motives, of the nature and goals of which he has but little understanding. If psychoanalysis can increase that understanding, new and dazzling possibilities are opened up for human evolution guided by conscious and intelligent desire.

It would seem, in fact, no exaggeration to say that psychoanalysis has it in its power definitely to increase the importance of the biological rôle of consciousness (with its uniquely delicate powers of reasoning and discrimination), since it can extend the range of biological processes that are capable of entering the field of consciousness. The significance of psychology will be correspondingly extended; indeed it is likely to become the most important of all the sciences, as far as human welfare is concerned, and will probably be regarded as fundamental to all the applied sciences of human life (politics, law, economics, etc.), in much the same way as chemistry and physics are fundamental to all the arts of manipulating our physical environment. The great contribution that psychoanalysis is destined to make in this extension of psychology is already very clear. In the present chapter we have only been concerned with the applications of psychoanalysis to wider fields, in so far as these applications help us to estimate the general validity of psychoanalysis itself. If we grant this validity, however, it at once becomes apparent that not only do these applications of a psychological viewpoint to other fields enrich psychology itself (psychoanalysis has for the first time created a true comparative psychology of human life, in which illuminating comparisons can be made between the *individual* mental products of childhood and maturity, health and disease, and the products of *group* life as manifested in myth, belief, and institution), but that they immensely deepen our outlook on these other fields, by enabling us to contemplate social phenomena in the light of the fundamental motives that produce them.

As in the case of individual analyses, a conscious realization of the motives underlying social conduct tends to make possible a rationally controlled modification or readjustment of these motives and of our attitude towards them. It is pretty clear that in certain ways psychoanalysis is already producing such a modification of our social life, as the result of the diffusion of some of the more general results of psychoanalytic inquiry and of a more widespread realization of the importance and value of the psychological standpoint in studying conduct—social and individual.

This is particularly marked in the field of sex, where an increased freedom of thought and discussion—largely due to the filtration of the simpler psychoanalytic concepts into literature and journalism—is tending slowly to replace the intolerance and hypocrisy of the last century. Through psychoanalysis the idea is gradually gaining ground that suppression and dogmatic adherence to ancient codes is not necessarily the only—or indeed the best—method of dealing with the sexual difficulties of our time. In this field psychoanalysis has not only increased our scientific knowledge of a most important part of psychological and sociological reality, but has increased the general ability to contemplate this portion of reality without shame or panic.

Great as this social achievement is, it seems likely to be overshadowed sooner or later by an even greater one. The psychoanalytic researches of the last few years into the structure of the ego have resulted in discoveries about the nature and development of human morality, which, when in turn they begin to become part of general knowledge, cannot but produce a far-reaching critical discussion of our most fundamental ethical conceptions. These recent researches have shown, in the words of Freud, that "the normal man is not only far more immoral than he believes, but is also far more moral than he has any idea of." The morality that is here in question (the "super-ego" in psychoanalytic terminology) is, however, the morality of the unconscious, and partakes of many of the characteristics of the unconscious that have already become familiar through the earlier psychoanalytic investigations of the libido. It is, for instance, archaic and infantile in its origin and pattern, it is modified only slowly, if at all, by the experiences of later life, it lacks all delicate discrimination, and is but little in touch with outer reality. Owing to these attributes, it is often incompatible with conscious moral standards, which, in persons of intellect and education, are, in our present society, apt to be greatly modified by reflection, teaching, and experience, as life proceeds. Our unconscious morality is therefore liable to condemn much that consciously we should approve or at least regard as harmless. This relative inaccessibility of our unconscious morality to "real" considerations leads to one particularly important differentiating feature: an inability to distinguish adequately between immoral desires on the one hand and immoral actions on the other, the former being treated as harshly as the latter. Harshness indeed is another general characteristic of the super-ego. One of the most startling of the revelations of psychoanalysis concerns the human capacity for unconscious self-punishment in response to an unconscious sense of guilt. This irrational "need for punishment" is the cause of an incalculable amount of human misery and loss of efficiency, which may be removed in so far as it proves possible to bring our unconscious morality into closer relation with our conscious apprehension of reality. The possibilities in this direction for the emancipation of the human mind and of human culture are themselves immense. But even this is not the whole story. One of the most surprising features of our unconscious morality is what one brilliant investigator has illuminatingly called its "corruptibility." In spite of its severity, it is often willing to permit a certain license to immoral and anti-social tendencies, on one condition, viz., that compensatory suffering be endured. This suffering may be relatively independent of the gratification of the tendencies in question (indeed it may be projected and thus become vicarious!) or—at the other extreme—it may be so intimately fused with this gratification as to take the form of sadistic self-punishment. But, in whatever way it manifests itself, this "corruptibility," leading as it does to an unnatural alliance between opposing tendencies in the mind rather than to a genuine solution of conflict,[3] is in the long run prejudicial to true morality. Indeed there is ample reason to believe not only that it may lead to a pernicious connivance at anti-social conduct, but that a large proportion of existing criminality is actually thus brought about.

Meanwhile, returning in conclusion to the more immediate problems that confront us as students of the mind, the most urgent need from the point of view of pure science would seem to be the establishment of closer relations between the psychoanalyst and the "academic" psychologist.

In this matter, questions of method are of supreme importance. Experimental psychology has worked out methods that are in many ways more scientifically exact than those of psychoanalysis, but at the expense of neglecting some of the most important aspects of the mind. It is nearly thirty years since Titchener wrote that our ignorance of the affective processes was "something of a scandal to experimental psychology." The scandal still to a considerable extent remains, but in the meantime psychoanalysis has achieved far more in this direction than all other schools of psychology together. Its methods are, however, still highly cumbersome and inconvenient; it has, in fact, not yet reached the experimental stage. So far as clinical observation is concerned, psychoanalysts have not as yet been able to sit down and study by their methods this or that abstracted problem, as the experimentalists have done. They have simply studied the human mind as a whole, and, as their experience has widened, their attention has been drawn first to this and then to that aspect of the mind. Such specially directed research as there has been is concerned almost entirely with the wider applications of psychoanalysis (psychoanalysis in our fourth sense). At the present moment, if a graduate student in psychology expresses the desire to do research on psychoanalysis, it is only along this line, if at all, that he can safely be advised to proceed. If he were to start to work by direct clinical methods (psychoanalysis in our first sense), he would first have to submit to a prolonged analysis of himself, and then, only after several further years of work, could he hope, by good fortune and acute observation, to make definite discoveries of his own. This circumstance seems necessarily to limit very greatly the direct psychological value of the psychoanalytic method in the hands of pure psychologists, for (short of endowments on a great scale) very few would undertake such work, unless they were assured of adequate remuneration. Such remuneration will, as a rule, come only from the use of psychoanalysis for therapeutic purposes, and here, too, its use is apt to be limited by the high cost of the lengthy treatment. Eventually, however, funds may be forthcoming, which (as in the case of other forms of therapy) may make it possible to apply an expensive form of treatment to a large number of patients at small cost to themselves. Indeed there are already a number

---

[3]If one seeks for a social parallel, one is reminded of the cooperation of the churches and of the boot-leggers towards the maintenance of prohibition.

of psychoanalytic clinics where work of this kind is carried out. An extension of this work will open up greater possibilities for the collection of psychoanalytic data on a large scale and will make it worth while for promising students of psychology to specialize in this direction.

Lastly, it has still to be seen how far the obvious difficulties in applying true experimental methods to psychoanalysis are really insuperable. It may be that a body of psychologists fully trained both in experimental psychology and in psychoanalysis (at present there are scarcely any such) may find means of overcoming many of these difficulties. It would seem, for instance, that such subjects as dreams, wit, symbolism, failures of memory, word association (here, of course, some work has already been done), moral concepts and feelings, inhibitions occurring during mental work, spontaneously occurring *Einfälle* (such as numbers)—these might serve as starting-points for analysis by strictly controlled experimental methods. Such fragmentary experiments on real and artificial dreams as have for instance been described by Bleuler (a friendly critic) and Wohlgemuth (a hostile one) might be systematically repeated and extended. Even the questionnaire method is capable of bringing in useful corroborative results (as Conklin's questionnaire on the foster-child phantasy has shown). What eventual success such methods may achieve it is, of course, impossible to say at present. In view of the vast benefits that psychology would be likely to derive, if psychoanalysis could be made amenable to experimental technique, the attempt seems emphatically to be worth the making.

CHAPTER 21

INDIVIDUAL PSYCHOLOGY*

ALFRED ADLER
Vienna

The point of departure upon this line of research seems to me to be given in a work entitled "Die Aggressionstrieb im Leben und in der Neurose," published in 1906 in a collective volume, *Heilen und Bilden* (1). Even at that time I was engaged in a lively controversy with the Freudian school, and in opposition to them, I devoted my attention in that paper to the *relation* of the child and the adult to the demands of the external world. I tried to present, howbeit in a very inadequate fashion, the multifarious forms of attack and defense, of modification of the self and of the environment, effected by the human mind, and launched on the momentous departure of repudiating the sexual aetiology of mental phenomena as fallacious. In a vague way I saw even then that the impulsive life of man suffers variations and contortions, curtailments and exaggerations, *relative to the kind and degree of its aggressive power.* In accordance with the present outlook of individual psychology, I should rather say: relative to the way the power of cooperation has developed in childhood. The Freudian school, which at that time was purely sexual psychology, has accepted this primitive-impulse theory without any reservations, as some of its adherents readily admit.

I myself was too deeply interested in the problem of what determined the various forms of attack upon the outer world. From my own observations, and supported by those of older authors, also perhaps guided by the concept of a *locus minoris resistentiae,* I arrived at the notion that inferior organs might be responsible for the feeling of psychic inferiority, and in the year 1907 recorded my studies concerning this subject in a volume entitled *Studie über Minderwertigkeit der Organe und die seelische Kompensation* (2). The purpose of the work was to show that children born with hereditary organic weaknesses exhibit not only a physical necessity to compensate for the defect, and tend to overcompensate, but that the entire nervous system, too, may take part in this compensation; especially the mind, as a factor of life, may suffer a striking exaggeration in the direction of the defective function (breathing, eating, seeing, hearing, talking, moving, feeling, or even thinking), so that this overemphasized function may become the mainspring of life, in so far as a *"successful* compensation" occurs. This compensatory increase, which, as I showed in the above-mentioned book, has originated and continued the development of a human race blessed with inferior organs, may in favorable cases affect also the endocrine glands, as I have pointed out, and is regularly reflected in the condition of the sexual glands, their inferiority and their compensa-

---

*Submitted in German and translated into English for the Clark University Press by Susanne Langer.

tion—a fact which seemed to me to suggest some connection between individual traits and physical heredity. The link between organic inferiority and psychic effects, which to this day cannot be explained in any other way, but merely assumed, was evident to me in the mind's experience of the inferior organ, by which the former is plunged into a *constant feeling of inferiority*. Thus I could introduce the body and its degree of excellence as a factor in mental development.

Experts will certainly not fail to see that the whole of our psychiatry has tended in this direction, both in part before that time and quite definitely thereafter. The works of Kretschmer, Jaensch, and many others rest upon the same basis. But they are content to regard the psychic minus quantities as congenital epiphenomena of the physical organic inferiority, without taking account of the fact that it is the *immediate* experience of physical disability which is the key to the failures of performance, as soon as the demands of the outer world and the creative power of the child lead it into "wrong" alleys and force upon it a one-sided interest. What I treated there as failure appeared to me later as a premature curtailment of the cooperative faculty, the social impulse, and a greatly heightened interest for the self.

This work also furnished a test for organic inferiority. As proofs of inferiority it mentions insufficient development of physical form, of reflexes, of functions, or retardation of the latter. Defective development of the nerves in connection with the organ and of the brain-centers involved was also considered. But the sort of compensation which would under favorable circumstances occur in any one of these parts was always insisted upon as a decisive factor. A valuable by-product of this study, and one which has not yet been sufficiently appreciated, was the discovery of the significance of the birthmark for the fact that the embryonic development at that point or in that segment had not been quite successful. Schmidt, Eppinger, and others have found this insight correct in many respects. I feel confident that in the study of cancer, too, as I suggested in this connection, the segmental naevus will someday furnish a clue to the aetiology of carcinoma.

In trying thus to bridge the chasm between physical and mental developments by a theory that vindicated in some measure the doctrine of heredity, I did not fail to remark explicitly somewhere that the stresses engendered by the relation between the congenitally inferior organ and the demands of the external world, though, of course, they were greater than those which related to approximately normal organs, were none the less mitigated, to some degree, by the variability of the world's demands; so that one really had to regard them as merely relative. I repudiated the notion of the hereditary character of psychological traits, in that I referred their origin to the various intensities of organic functions in each individual. Afterwards I added to this the fact that children, in cases of abnormal development, are without any guidance, so that their activity (aggression) may develop in unaccountable ways. The inferior organs offer a temptation but by no means a neccessity for neuroses or other mental miscarriages. Herewith I established the problem of the education of such children, with prophylaxis as its aim, on a perfectly sound footing. Thus the family history, with all its plus and minus factors, became an index to the serious difficulties which might be expected and combatted in early childhood. As I said at that time, a hostile attitude toward the world might be the result of excessive stresses which must express themselves somehow in specific characteristics.

In this way I was confronted with the problem of character. There had been a good deal of nebulous speculations on this subject. Character was almost universally regarded as a congenital entity. My conviction that the doctrine of congenital mental traits was erroneous helped me considerably. I came to realize that characters were guiding threads, *ready attitudes* for the solution of the problems of life. The idea of an "arrangement" of all psychical activities became more and more convincing. Therewith I had reached the ground which to this day has been the foundation of individual psychology, the belief that *all psychical phenomena originate in the particular creative force of the individual, and are expressions of his personality.*

But who is this driving force behind the personality? And why do we find mostly individuals whose psychological upbuilding was not successful? Might it be that, after all, certain congenitally defective impulses, i.e., congenital weaknesses, decided the fate of our mental development, as almost all psychiatrists supposed? Is it due to a divine origin that an individual, that the human race may progress at all?

But I had realized the fact that children who were born with defective organs or afflicted by injuries early in life go wrong in the misery of their existence, constantly deprecate themselves, and, usually, to make good this deficiency, behave differently all their lives from what might be expected of normal people. I took another step, and discovered that children may be artificially placed in the same straits as if their organs were defective. If we make their work in very early life so hard that even their relatively normal organs are not equal to it, then they are in the same distress as those with defective physique, and from the same unbearable condition of stress they will give wrong answers as soon as life puts their preparation to any test. Thus I found two further categories of children who are apt to develop an abnormal sense of inferiority—*pampered children and hated children.*

To this period of my complete defection from Freud's point of view, and absolute independence of thought, date such works as *Die seelische Wirzel der Trigeminusneuralgie* (3), in which I attempted to show how, besides cases of organic origin, there were also certain ones in which excessive partial increase of blood-pressure, caused by emotions such as rage, may under the influence of severe inferiority feelings give rise to physical changes. This was followed by a study, decisive for the development of individual psychology, entitled *Das Problem der Distanz,* wherein I demonstrated that every individual, by reason of his degree of inferiority feeling, hesitated before the solution of one of the three great problems of life, stops or circumvents, and preserves his attitude in a state of exaggerated tension through psychological symptoms. As the three great problems of life, to which everyone must somehow answer by his attitude, I named: (*a*) society, (*b*) vocation, (*c*) love. Next came a work on *Das Unbewusste,* wherein I tried to prove that upon deeper inspection there appears no contrast between the conscious and the unconscious, that both cooperate for a higher purpose, that our thoughts and feelings become conscious as soon as we are faced with a difficulty, and unconscious as soon as our personality-value requires it. At the same time I tried to set forth the fact that that which other authors had used for their explanations under the name of *conflict, sense of guilt,* or *ambivalence* was to be regarded as symptomatic of a *hesitant attitude,* for the purpose of evading the solution of one of the problems of life. Ambivalence and polarity of emotional or moral traits present themselves as an attempt at a multiple solution or rejection of a problem.

This and some other works dating from the time of the self-emancipation of individual psychology have been published in a volume bearing the title *Praxis und Theorie der Individualpsychologie* (6). This was also the time when our great Stanley Hall turned away from Freud and ranged himself with the supporters of individual psychology, together with many other American scholars who popularized the "inferiority and superiority complexes" throughout their whole country.

I have never failed to call attention to the fact that the whole human race is blessed with deficient organs, deficient for coping with nature; that consequently the whole race is constrained ever to seek the way which will bring it into some sort of harmony with the exigencies of life; and that we make mistakes along the way, very much like those we can observe in pampered or neglected children. I have quoted one case especially, where the errors of our civilization may influence the development of an individual, and that is the case of the underestimation of women in our society. From the sense of female inferiority, which most people, men and women alike, possess, both sexes have derived an overstrained desire for masculinity, a superiority complex which is often extremely harmful, a will to conquer all difficulties of life in the masculine fashion, which I have called the *masculine protest.*

Now I began to see clearly in every psychical phenomenon the *striving for superiority.* It runs parallel to physical growth. It is an intrinsic necessity of life itself. It lies at the root of all solutions of life's problems, and is manifested in the way in which we meet these problems. All our functions follow its direction; rightly or wrongly they strive for conquest, surety, increase. The impetus from minus to plus is never-ending. The urge from "below" to "above" never ceases. Whatever premises all our philosophers and psychologists dream of—self-preservation, pleasure principle, equalization—all these are but vague representations, attempts to express the great upward drive. The history of the human race points in the same direction. Willing, thinking, talking, seeking after rest, after pleasure, learning, understanding, work and love, betoken the essence of this eternal melody. Whether one thinks or acts more wisely or less, one always moves along the lines of that upward tendency. In our right and wrong conceptions of life and its problems, in the successful or the unsuccessful solution of any question, this striving for perfection is uninterruptedly at work. And even where foolishness and imbecility, inexperience, seem to belie the fact of any striving to conquer some defect, or tend to depreciate it, yet the will to conquer is really operative. From this net-work which in the last analysis is simply given with the relationship "man–cosmos," no one may hope to escape. For even if anyone wanted to escape, yes, even if he *could* escape, he would still find himself in the general system, striving "upward," from "below." This does not only fix a fundamental category of thought, the structure of our reason, but what is more, it yields *the fundamental fact of our life.*

The origin of humanity and the ever repeated beginning of infant life rubs it in with every psychic act: "Achieve! Arise! Conquer!" This feeling is never absent, this longing for the abrogation of every imperfection. In the search for relief, in Faustian wrestling against the forces of nature, rings always the basis chord: "I relinquish thee not, thou bless me withal." The unreluctant search for truth, the ever unsatisfied longing for solution of the problems of life, belongs to this hankering after perfection of some sort.

This, now, appeared to me as the fundamental law of all spiritual expression: that the total melody is to be found again in every one of its parts, as a greatest common measure—in every individual craving for power, for victory over the difficulties of life.

And therewith I recognized a further premise of my scientific proceeding, one which agreed with the formulations of older philosophers, but conflicted with the standpoint of modern psychology: *the unity of the personality.* This, however, was not merely a premise, but could to a certain extent be demonstrated. As Kant has said, we can never understand a person if we do not presuppose his unity. Individual psychology can now add to that: this unity, which we must presuppose, is the work of the individual, which must always continue in the way it once found toward victory.

These were the considerations which led me to the conviction that early in life, in the first four or five years, a *goal* is set for the need and drive of psychical development, a goal toward which all its currents flow. Such a goal has not only the function of determining a direction, of promising security, power, perfection, but it is also of its essence and of the essence of the mind that this portentous goal should awaken feelings and emotions through that which it promises them. Thus the individual mitigates its sense of weakness in the anticipation of its redemption.

Here again we see the meaninglessness of congenital psychic traits. Not that we could deny them. We have no possible way of getting at them. Whoever would draw conclusions from the results is making matters too simple. He overlooks the thousand and one influences after birth, and fails to see the power that lies in the necessity of acquiring a goal.

The staking of a goal compels the unity of the personality in that it draws the stream of all spiritual activity into its definite direction. Itself a product of the common, fundamental sense of inferiority—a sense derived from genuine weakness, not from any comparison with others—the goal of victory in turn forces the direction of all powers and possibilities toward itself. Thus every phase of psychical activity can be seen within one frame, as though it were the end of some earlier phase and the beginning of a succeeding one. This was a further contribution of individual psychology to modern psychology in general—that it insisted absolutely on the indispensability of *finalism* for the understanding of all psychological phenomena. No longer could causes, powers, instincts, impulses, and the like serve as explanatory principles, but the final goal alone. Experiences, traumata, sexual-development mechanisms could not yield us an explanation, but the perspective in which these had been regarded, the individual way of seeing them, which subordinates all life to the ultimate goal.

This final aim, abstract in its purpose of assuring superiority, fictitious in its task of conquering all the difficulties of life, must now appear in concrete form in order to meet its task in actuality. Deity in its widest sense, it is apperceived by the childish imagination, and under the exigencies of hard reality, as victory over men, over difficult enterprises, over social or natural limitations. It appears in one's attitude toward others, toward one's vocation, toward the opposite sex. Thus we find concrete single purposes, such as: to operate as a member of the community or to dominate it, to attain security and triumph in one's chosen career, to approch the other sex or to avoid it. We may always trace in these special purposes *what sort of meaning the individual has found in his existence,* and how he proposes to realize that meaning.

If, then, the final goal established in early childhood exerts such an influence for better or worse upon the development of the given psychical forces, our next question must be: What are the sources of the individuality which we find in final aims? Could we not quite properly introduce another causal factor here? What brings about the differences of individual attitudes, if one and the same aim of superiority actuates everyone?

Speaking of this last question, let me point out that our human language is incapable of rendering all the qualities within a superiority goal and of expressing its innumerable differences. Certainty, power, perfection, deification, superiority, victory, etc., are but poor attempts to illumine its endless variants. Only after we have comprehended the partial expressions which the final goal effects, are we in any position to determine specific differences.

If there is any causal factor in the psychical mechanism, it is the common and often excessive sense of inferiority. But this continuous mood is only activating, a drive, and does not reveal the way to compensation and overcompensation. Under the pressure of the first years of life there is no kind of philosophical reflection. There are only impressions, feelings, and a desire to renew the pleasurable ones and exclude those which are painful. For this purpose all energies are mustered, until motion of some sort results. Here, however, training or motion of any sort forces the establishment of an end. There is no motion without an end. And so, in this way, a final goal becomes fixed which promises satisfaction. Perhaps, if one wanted to produce hypotheses, one might add: Just as the body approximates to an ideal form which is posited with the germ-plasm, so does the mind, as a part of the total life. Certainly it is perfectly obvious that the soul (mind—*das seelische Organ*) exhibits some systematic definite tendency.

From the time of these formulations of individual psychology dates my book, *Ueber den nervösen Charakter* (7), which introduced *finalism* into psychology with especial emphasis. At the same time I continued to trace the connection between organic inferiority and its psychological consequences, in trying to show how in such cases the goal of life is to be found in the type of overcompensation and consequent errors. As one of these errors I mentioned particularly the *masculine protest,* developed under the pressure of a civilization which has not yet freed itself from its overestimation of the masculine principle nor from an abuse of antithetic points of view. The imperfection of childish modes of realizing the fictitious ideal was also mentioned here as the chief cause for the differences in style of living—the unpredictable character of childish expression, which always moves in the uncontrollable *realm of error.*

By this time, the system of individual psychology was well enough established to be applied to certain special problems. *Zum Problem der Homosexualität* (8) exhibited that perversion as a neurotic construct erroneously made out of early childhood impressions, and recorded researches and findings which are published at greater length in the *Handbuch der normalen und pathologischen Physiologie* (9). Uncertainty in the sexual rôle, overestimation of the opposite sex, fear of the latter, and a craving for easy, irresponsible successes proved to be the inclining but by no means constraining factors. Uncertainty in the solution of the erotic problem and fear of failure in this direction lead to wrong or abnormal functioning.

More and more clearly I now beheld the way in which the varieties of failure could be understood. In all human failure, in the waywardness of children, in neurosis and neuropsychosis, in crime, suicide, alcoholism, morphinism, cocainism, in sexual perversion, in fact in all nervous symptoms, we may read lack of the proper degree of *social feeling.* In all my former work I had employed the idea of the individual's attitude toward society as the main consideration. The demands of society, not as of a stable institution but as of a living, striving, victory-seeking mass, were always present in my thoughts. The total accord of this striving and the influence it must exert on each individual had always been one of my main themes. Now I attained somewhat more clarity in the matter. However we may judge people, whatever we try to understand about them, what we aim at when we educate, heal, improve, condemn—we base it always on the same principle: social feeling! cooperation! Anything that we estimate as valuable, good, right, and normal, we estimate simply in so far as it is "virtue" from the point of view of an ideal society. The individual, ranged in a community which can preserve itself only through cooperation as a human society, becomes a part of this great whole through socially enforced division of labor, through association with a member of the opposite sex, and finds his task prescribed by this society. And not only his task, but also his preparation and ability to perform it.

The unequivocally given fact of our organic inferiority on the face of this earth necessitates social solidarity. The need of protection of women during pregnancy and confinement, the prolonged helplessness of childhood, gains the aid of others. The preparation of the child for a complicated, but protective and therefore necessary civilization and labor requires the cooperation of society. The need of security in our personal existence leads automatically to a cultural modification of our impulses and emotions and of our individual attitude of friendship, social intercourse, and love. The social life of man emanates inevitably from the man-cosmos relation, and makes every person a creature and a creator of society.

It is a gratuitous burden to science to ask whether the social instinct is congenital or acquired, as gratuitous as the question of congenital instincts of any sort. We can see only the results of an evolution. And if we are to be permitted a question at all concerning the beginnings of that evolution, it is only this—whether anything can be evolved at all for which no possibilities are in any way given before birth. This possibility exists, as we may see through the results of development, in the case of human beings. The fact that our sense-organs behave the way they do, that through them we may acquire *impressions* of the outer world, may combine these physically and mentally in ourselves, shows our connection with the cosmos. That trait we have in common with all living creatures. What distinguishes man from other organisms, however, is the fact that he must conceive his superiority goal in the social sense as a part of a total achievement. The reasons for this certainly lie in the greater need of the human individual and in the consequent greater mobility of his body and mind, which forces him to find a firm vantage-point in the chaos of life, a δος που σίω!

But because of this enforced sociability, our life presents only such problems which require *ability to cooperate* for their solution. To hear, see, or speak "correctly," means to lose one's self completely in another or in a situation, to become *identified* with him or with it. The capacity for identification, which alone makes us capable of friendship, humane love, pity, vocation, and love, is the basis of the social sense and can be practiced and exercised only in conjunction with others. In this intended assimilation of another person or of a situation not immediately given, lies the whole meaning of comprehension. And in the course of this identification we are able to conjure up all sorts of feelings, emotions, and affects, such as we experience not only in dreams but also in waking life, in neurosis and psychosis. It is always the fixed style of life, the ultimate ideals, that dominates and selects. The style of life is what makes our experiences reasons for our attitude, that calls up these feelings and determines conclusions in accordance with its own purposes. Our very identification with the ultimate ideal makes us optimistic, pessimistic, hesitant, bold, selfish, or altruistic.

The tasks which are presented to an individual, as well as the means of their performance, are conceived and formulated within the framework of society. No one, unless he is deprived of his mental capacities, can escape from this frame. *Only within this framework is psychology pos-*

sible at all. Even if we add for our own time the aids of civilization and the socially determined pattern of our examples, we still find ourselves confronted with the same unescapable conditions. From this point of vantage we may look back. As far as we can reasonably determine, it appears that after the fourth or fifth year of life the style of life has been fashioned as a prototype, with its particular way of seizing upon life, its strategy for conquering it, its degree of ability to cooperate. These foundations of every individual development do not alter, unless perchance some harmful errors of construction are recognized by the subject and corrected. Whoever has not acquired in childhood the necessary degree of social sense, will not have it later in life, except under the above-mentioned special conditions. No amount of bitter experience can change his style of life, *as long as he has not gained understanding.* The whole work of education, cure, and human progress can be furthered only along lines of better comprehension.

There remains only one question: What influences are harmful and what beneficial in determining differences in the style of life, i.e., in the capacity for cooperation?

Here, in short, we touch upon the matter of preparation for cooperation. It is evident, of course, that deficiencies of the latter become most clearly visible when the individual's capacity to cooperate is put to the test. As I have shown above, life does not spare us these tests and preliminary trials. We are always on trial, in the development of our sense-organs, in our attitude toward others, our understanding of others, in our morals, our philosophy of life, our political position, our attitude toward the welfare of others, toward love and marriage, in our aesthetic judgments, in our whole behavior. As long as one is not put to any test, as long as one is without any trials or problems, one may doubt one's own status as a fellow of the community. But as soon as a person is beset by any problem of existence, which, as I have demonstrated, always involves cooperative ability, then it will unfailingly become apparent—as in a geographical examination—how far his preparation for cooperation extends.

The first social situation that confronts a child is its relation to its mother, from the very first day. By her educational skill the child's interest in another person is first awakened. If she understands how to train this interest in the direction of cooperation, all the congenital and acquired capacities of the child will converge in the direction of social sense. If she binds the child to herself exclusively, life will bear for it the meaning that all other persons are to be excluded as much as possible. Its position in the world is thereby rendered difficult, as difficult as that of defective or neglected children. All these grow up in a hostile world and develop a low degree of cooperative sense. Often in such cases there results utter failure to adjust to the father, brothers and sisters, or more distant persons. If the father fails to penetrate the circle of the child's interest, or if by reason of exaggerated rivalry the brothers and sisters are excluded, or if because of some social short-coming or prejudice the remoter environment is ruled out of its sphere, then the child will encounter serious trouble in acquiring a healthy social sense. In all cases of failure later in life it will be quite observable that they are rooted in this early period of infancy. The question of responsibility will naturally have to be waived there, since the debtor is unable to pay what is required of him.

Our findings in regard to these errors and erroneous deductions of early childhood, which have been gathered from a contemplation of this relation complex which individual psychology reveals, are exceedingly full. They are recorded in many articles in the *Internationalen Zeitschrift für Individualpsychologie,* in my *Understanding Human Nature* (10), in *Individualpsychologie in der Schule* (11), and in *Science of Living* (12). These works deal with problems of waywardness, neurosis and psychosis, criminality, suicide, drunkenness, and sexual perversion. Problems of society, vocation, and love have been included in the scope of these studies. In *Die Technik der Individualpsychologie* (13) I have published a detailed account of a case of fear and compulsion neurosis.

Individual psychology considers the essence of therapy to lie in making the patient aware of his lack of cooperative power, and to convince him of the origin of this lack in early childhood maladjustments. What passes during this process is no small matter; his power of cooperation is enhanced by collaboration with the doctor. His "inferiority complex" is revealed as erroneous. Courage and optimism are awakened. And the "meaning of life" dawns upon him as the fact that proper meaning must be given to life.

This sort of treatment may be begun at any point in the spiritual life. The following three points of departure have recommended themselves to me, among others: (*a*) to infer some of the patient's situation from his place in the order of births, since each successive child usually has a somewhat different position from the others; (*b*) to infer from his earliest childhood recollections some dominant interest of the individual, since the creative tendency of the imagination always produces fragments of the life ideal (*Lebensstyl*); (*c*) to apply the individualistic interpretation to the dream-life of the patient, through which one may discover in what particular way the patient, guided by the style-of-life ideal, conjures up emotions and sensations contrary to common sense, in order to be able to carry out his style of life more successfully.

If one seems to have discovered the guiding thread of the patient's life, it remains to test this discovery through a great number of expressive gestures on his part. Only a perfect coincidence of the whole and all the parts gives one the right to say: I understand. And then the examiner himself will always have the feeling that, if he had grown up under the same misapprehensions, if he had harbored the same ideal, had the same notions concerning the meaning of life, if he had acquired an equally low degree of social sense, he would have acted and lived in an "almost" similar manner.

REFERENCES

1. ADLER, A. Der aggressionstrieb im Leben und in der Neurose. In Heilen und Bilden. (3rd ed.) Munich: Bergmann, 1906.

2. ———. Studie über Minderwertigkeit der Organe und die seelische Kompensation. (2nd ed.) Munich: Bergmann, 1907. Pp. vii+92.

3. —————. Die seelische Wirzel der Trigeminusneuralgie.

4. —————. Das Problem der Distanz.

5. —————. Das Unbewusste.

6. —————. Praxis und Theorie der Individualpsychologie. (2nd ed.) Munich: Bergmann, 1924. Pp. v+527.
The practice and theory of individual psychology. New York: Harcourt, Brace, 1924.

7. —————. Ueber den nervösen Charakter: Grundzüge einer vergleichenden Individualpsychologie und Psychotherapie. Wiesbaden: Bergmann, 1912. Pp. vii+196.
The neurotic constitution: outlines of a comparative individualistic psychology and psychotherapy. (Trans. by B. Glueck & J. E. Lind.) New York: Moffat, Yard, 1917. Pp. xxiii+456.

8. —————. Zum Problem der Homosexualität. Munich: Reinhardt, 1917. (Out of print.)

9. —————. Handbuch der normalen und pathologischen Physiologie. Berlin: Springer.

10. —————. Menschenkenntnis. (2nd ed.) Leipzig: Hirzel, 1928. Pp. vii+230.
Understanding human nature. (Trans. by W. B. Wolfe.) New York: Greenberg, 1927. Pp. xiii+286.

11. —————. Individualpsychologie in der Schule. Leipzig: Hirzel.

12. —————. Science of living. New York: Greenberg, 1929.

13. —————. Die Technik der Individualpsychologie. I. Die Kuntz, eine Lebens- und Krankengeschichte zu lesen. Munich: Bergmann, 1928. Pp. iv+146.
The case of Miss R. New York: Greenberg, 1929.

14. —————. Problems of neurosis. London: Kegan Paul, 1929.

PART XII

SOME OF THE PROBLEMS FUNDAMENTAL
TO ALL PSYCHOLOGY

CHAPTER 22

CONDUCT AND EXPERIENCE

JOHN DEWEY
Columbia University

I venture to discuss this topic in its psychological bearings because the problem as defined for me by the editor is "a *logical* analysis of behavior and of experience" as these terms figure in current discussion, controversy, and psychological inquiry. "Conduct," as it appears in the title, obviously links itself with the position taken by behaviorists; "experience," with that of the introspectionists. If the result of the analysis herein undertaken turns out to involve a revision of the meaning of both concepts, it will probably signify that my conclusions will not be satisfactory to either school; they may be regarded by members of both as a sterile hybrid rather than a useful mediation. However, there are many subdivisions in each school, and there are competent psychologists who decline to enroll in either, while the very existence of controversy is an invitation to reconsideration of fundamental terms, even if the outcome is not wholly satisfactory.

Before we enter upon the theme, two general introductory remarks may be made. One is that the subject is so highly complex and has so many ramifications that it is impossible to deal with it adequately. The difficulty is increased by the fact that these ramifications extend to a historical, intellectual background in which large issues of philosophy and epistemology are involved, a background so pervasive that even those who have no interest in, or use for, philosophy would find, if they took the trouble to investigate, that the words they use—the words we all must use—are deeply saturated with the results of these earlier discussions. These have escaped from philosophy and made their way into common thought and speech.

The other remark is that I have no intention of delimiting or bounding the field of actual inquiry in psychology by introducing methodological considerations. On the contrary, I am a firm believer in a variety of points of approach and diversity of investigations, especially in a subject as new as psychology is. To a considerable extent, the existence of different schools is at present an asset rather than a liability, for psychology will ultimately be whatever it is made to be by investigators in the field. To a certain extent, a variety of points of view serves the purpose that is met in all the sciences by the principle of multiple hypotheses. While there is immediate confusion, it may turn out that the variety will, in the end, secure a greater fullness of exploration than would otherwise have been the case.

The discussion, because of its great complexity, may be introduced by reference to the controversy, so active about thirty years ago, between structuralists and functionalists. The introspectionists are more lineal descendants of the structuralists than are the behaviorists of the functionalists, and I do not mean to equate the terms. A brief review, couched linguistically in dogmatic terms, will be used as an introduction. The basic error of the structuralists was, it seems to me, the assumption that the phenomena they dealt with had a structure which direct inspection could disclose. Admitting, for the moment, that there are such things as conscious processes which constitute "experience" and which are capable of direct inspection, it still involves an immense leap of logic to infer that direct inspection can disclose their structures. One might go so far as to say that, supposing that there are such things, they are just the sort of things that are, in their immediate occurrence, structureless. Or, to put it in a more exact way, if they have any structure, this is not carried in their immediate presence but in facts that are external to them and which cannot be disclosed by the method of direct inspection.

Take, for example, the classification of some of the immediate qualities as sensations, others as perception, and the sub-classification of sensations into auditory, visual, tactile, etc. As a classification, it involves an interpretation, and every interpretation goes outside of what is directly observed. I can attach no meaning to the statement that any immediately present quality announces, "I am sensory, and of the visual mode." It is called visual because it is referred to the optical apparatus, and this reference depends upon facts that are wholly external to the quality's own presence: upon observation of the eyes and anatomical dissection of bodily organs. The distinction between qualities to which the names "sensation" and "perception" are given involves a still more extensive operation of analytic interpretation, depending upon further considerations objective to what is immediately present and inspected.

The difficulty cannot be met by saying that a "sensory" quality is immediately given as simple, while a perceptual one is a complex of simples, for this distinction is itself precisely the result of an analytic interpretation and not an immediately given datum. Many "percepts" present themselves originally as total and undifferentiated, or immediately simple, and the least discriminable simple quality termed a sensation is itself arrived at as the end-term of a prolonged research, and is known as an end-term and as simple only because of extraneous reference to bodily organs, which is itself made possible by external apparatus.

A simple example is found in the fact that sensorimotor schematism of some sort is now a commonplace in most psychological literature. If it could be detected by direct inspection of immediate qualities, it would always have been a commonplace. In fact, it is a product of an independent investigation of the morphology and physiology of the nervous system. If we generalize from such an instance, we shall be led to say that the structure of so-called mental process or conscious process, namely, of those immediate qualities to which the name "experience" was given, is furnished by the human organism, especially its nervous system. This object is known just as any other natural object is known, and not by any immediate act called introspection.

We cannot stop at this point, however. No organism is so isolated that it can be understood apart from the environment in which it lives. Sensory receptors and muscular effectors, the eye and the hand, have their existence as well as their meaning because of connections with an outer environment. The moment the acts made possible by organic structure cease to have relevancy to the milieu, the organism no longer exists; it perishes. The organisms that manifest a minimum of structure within themselves must have enough structure to enable them to prehend and assimilate food from their surroundings. The *structure* of the immediate qualities that have sometimes been called "consciousness," or "experience" as a synonym for consciousness, is so much external to them that it must be ascertained by non-introspective methods.

If the implication of the last two paragraphs was made explicit, it would read: The structure of whatever is had by way of immediate qualitative presences is found in the recurrent modes of interaction taking place between what we term organism, on one side, and environment, on the other. This interaction is the primary fact, and it constitutes a trans-action. Only by analysis and selective abstraction can we differentiate the actual occurrence into two factors, one called organism and the other, environment. This fact militates strongly against any form of behaviorism that defines behavior in terms of the nervous system or body alone. For present purposes, we are concerned with the fact as indicating that the structure of consciousness lies in a highly complex field outside of "consciousness" itself, one that requires the help of objective sciences and apparatus to determine.

We have not finished with the topic of the extent of this objective structure. It includes within itself a temporal spread. The interactions of which we have just spoken are not isolated but form a temporal continuity. One kind of behaviorism is simply a generalized inference from what takes place in laboratory experimentation plus a virtual denial of the fact that laboratory data have meaning only with reference to behavior having a before and after—a from which and an into which. In the laboratory a situation is arranged. Instructions being given to the subject, he reacts to them and to some, say, visual stimulus. He accompanies this response with a language response or record of some sort. This is all which is immediately relevant to the laboratory procedure. Why, then, speak of sensations and perceptions as conscious processes? Why not stick to what actually happens, and speak of behavioristic response to stimuli? It is no derogation to the originality of those who began the behaviorist movement to say that a behavioristic theory was bound, logically, to emerge from laboratory procedure. Conscious processes drop out as irrelevant accretions.

There is something in the *context* of the experiment which goes beyond the stimuli and responses directly found within it. There is, for example, the *problem* which the experimenter has set and his *deliberate* arrangement of apparatus and selection of conditions with a view to disclosure of facts that bear upon it. There is also an *intent* on the part of the subject. Now I am not making this reference to "problem," "selective arrangement," and "intent" or purpose in order to drag in by the heels something mental over and beyond the behavior. The object is rather to call attention to a definite characteristic of behavior, namely, that it is not exhausted in the immediate stimuli-response features of the experimentation. From the standpoint of behavior itself, the traits in question take us beyond the isolated act of the subject into a content that has a temporal spread. The acts in question came out of something and move into something else. Their whole scientific point is lost unless they are placed as one phase in this contextual behavior.

It is hardly possible, I think, to exaggerate the significance of this fact for the concept of behavior. Behavior is serial, not mere succession. It can be resolved—it must be—into discrete acts, but no act can be understood apart from the series to which it belongs. While the word "behavior" implies com-portment, as well as de-portment, the word "conduct" brings out the aspect of seriality better than does "behavior," for it clearly involves the facts both of direction (or a vector property) and of conveying or conducing. It includes the fact of passing through and passing along.

I do not mean to suggest that behaviorists of the type that treats behavior as a succession rather than as serial exclude the influence of temporal factors. The contrary is the case.[1] But I am concerned to point out the difference made in the concept of behavior according as one merely appeals to the *effects* of prior acts in order to account for some trait of a present act, or as one realizes that *behavior* itself is serial in nature. The first position is consistent with regarding behavior as consisting of acts which merely succeed one another so that each can be understood in terms of what is actually found in any one act taken by itself, provided one includes the *effects* of prior acts as part of the conditions involved in it. The second position, while, of course, it recognizes this factor, goes further. In introducing into behavior the concept of series, the idea of ordinal position connected with a principle which binds the successive acts together is emphasized.[2]

The import of the formulation just made may be more definitely gathered from a consideration of the stimulus-response concept. That every portion

---

[1]For example, Hunter says: "Has not the behaviorist always appealed to the results of heredity and previous training as factors which cooperate with present stimuli in determining behavior? Was there ever a behaviorist who explained maze training without calling upon the retained effects of previous training for a part of his explanation, or a behaviorist who ignored childhood peculiarities in accounting for adult behavior?" (2, p. 103).

[2]It is not meant, of course, to carry over in a rigid way the mathematical concept of series, but the idea underlying this concept, namely, that of sequential continuity, is employed. It is meant that even the instances in which abrupt succession is most marked, i.e., jumping at a noise when engaged in deep study, have to be treated as limiting cases of the serial principle and not as typical cases from which to derive the standard notion of behavior-acts.

of behavior may be stated as an instance of stimulus-response, I do not doubt, any more than that any physical occurrence may be stated as an instance of the cause-effect relation. I am very sceptical about the value of the result reached, until that which serves as stimulus and as response in a given case has been carefully analyzed. It may be that, when the concept of cause-effect first dawned, some persons got satisfaction by stringing gross phenomena together as causes and effects. But, as physical science advanced, the general relation was forgotten by being absorbed into a definite analytic statement of the particular conditions to which the terms "cause" and "effect" are assigned. It seems to me that there is considerable behavioristic and semi-behavioristic theory in psychology at present that is content merely to subsume the phenomena in question under the rubric of *S-R* as if they were ready-made and self-evident things.

When we turn to the consideration of *what* is a stimulus, we obtain a result which is fatal to the idea that isolated acts, typified by a reflex, can be used to determine the meaning of stimulus. That which is, or operates as, a stimulus turns out to be a function, in a mathematical sense, of behavior in its serial character. Something, not yet a stimulus, breaks in upon an activity already going on and *becomes* a stimulus in virtue of the relations it sustains to what is going on in this continuing activity. As Woodworth has said: "Very seldom does a stimulus find the organism in a completely resting, neutral and unpreoccupied status" (4, p. 124). The remark has to be developed, moreover, by noting two additions. The first repeats what has just been said. No external change is a stimulus in and of itself. It *becomes* the stimulus in virtue of what the organism is already preoccupied with. To call it, to think of it, as a stimulus without taking into account the behavior that is already going on is so arbitrary as to be nonsensical. Even in the case of abrupt changes, such as a clap of thunder when one is engrossed in reading, the *particular* force of that noise, its property as stimulus, is determined by what the organism is already doing in interaction with a particular environment. One and the same environmental change becomes, under different conditions of ongoing or serial behavior, a thousand different actual stimuli—a consideration which is fatal to the supposition that we can analyze behavior into a succession of independent stimuli and responses.

The difficulty cannot be overcome by merely referring to the operation a prior response in determining what operates as stimulus, for exactly the same thing holds of that situation. Nor can it be overcome by vague reference to the "organism as a whole." While this reference is pertinent and necessary, the *state* of the whole organism is one of *action* which is continuous, so that reference to the organism as a whole merely puts before us the situation just described: that environment change *becomes* a stimulus in virtue of a continuous course of behavior. These considerations lead us to the second remark. A stimulus is always a *change* in the environment which is connected with a *change* in activity. No stimulus is a stimulus to action as such but only to a change in the direction or intensity of action. A response is not action or behavior but marks a change in behavior. It is the new ordinal position in a series, and the series is the behavior. The ordinary S-R statement is seductive merely because it takes for granted this fact, while if it were explicitly stated it would transform the meaning of the S-R formula.

The discussion thus far has been so general that it may seem to have evaded the concrete questions that alone are important. What has all this to do with the familiar rubrics of analytic psychology, sensation, perception, memory, thinking, etc., or, more generally speaking, with psychology itself? Taking the last question, our conclusion as to the serial character of behavior and the necessity of placing and determining actual stimuli and responses within its course seems to point to a definite subject-matter characteristic of psychology. This subject-matter is the behavior of the organism so far as that is characterized by changes taking place in an activity that is serial and continuous in reference to changes in an environment that is continuous, while changing in detail.

So far, the position taken gives the primacy to conduct and relates psychology to a study of conduct rather than to "experience." It is, however, definitely in opposition to theories of behavior that begin by taking anything like a reflex as the type and standard of a behavior-act, and that regard it as possible to isolate and describe stimulus and response as ultimates that constitute behavior, for they themselves must be discovered and discriminated as specifiable determinations within the course of behavior. More definitely the position taken points, as it seems to me, to the conception of psychology recently advanced by Dr. Percy Hughes (1), namely, that psychology is concerned with the life-career of individualized activities.[3] Here we have something which marks off a definite field of subject-matter and so calls for a distinctive intellectual method and treatment and thus defines a possible science.

The burning questions, however, remain. What meaning, if any, can be attached to sensation, memory, conceiving, etc., on the basis of conduct or behavior as a developing temporal continuum marked off into specific act-situations? In general, the mode of answer is clear, whatever the difficulties in carrying it out into detail. They designate modes of behavior having their own discernible qualities, meaning by "qualities" traits that enable one to discriminate and identify them as special modes of behavior.

Two considerations are pertinent in this connection, of which the second can best be discussed later along with a discussion of what has been so far passed over: psychology as an account of "experience." The first consideration may be introduced by pointing out that hearing, seeing, perceiving in general, remembering, imagining, thinking, judging,

---

[3]It is not germane to my subject to go into detail, but I cannot refrain from calling attention to what Dr. Hughes points out, that behaviorism in one of its narrower senses,—the behavior of the nervous system,—takes its place as a necessary included factor, namely, a study of *conditions* involved in a study of life-careers, while whatever is verifiable in the findings of psychoanalysts, etc., also takes its place in the study of individual life-careers.

reasoning, are not inventions of the psychologist. Taken as designations of acts performed by every normal human being, they are everyday common-sense distinctions. What some psychologists have done is to shove a soul or consciousness under these acts as their author or locus. It seems to me fair to say that the Wundtian tradition, while it developed in the direction of denying or ignoring the soul and, in many cases, of denying "consciousness" as a unitary power or locus, in its conception of least-discriminable qualities as identical with ultimate simple "conscious processes" took a position which did not come from the facts but from an older tradition.

What we are here concerned with, however, is the fact that the ordinary man, apart from any philosophic or scientific interpretation, takes for granted the existence of acts of this type, which are different from acts of locomotion and digestion. Such acts, in a purely denotative way apart from conceptual connotation, constitute the meaning of the word "mental" in distinction from the physical and purely physiological. Is the use of "mental" as a designative term of certain modes of behavior found in every human life-career tabu to one who starts from the standpoint of behavior in the sense mentioned above?

The issue turns, of course, about the introduction of the idea of distinctive and discernible qualities that mark off some kinds of behavior and that supply a ground for calling them mental. To many strict behaviorists any reference to qualities seems a reversion to the slough of old introspectionism and an attempt to smuggle its methods in a covert way into behaviorism. Let us see, then, what happens when the position is analyzed. We can hardly do better than to start from the fact that the physicist observes, recalls, thinks. We must note the fact that the things with which he ends, protons-electrons in their complex interrelations of space-time and motions, are things with which he *ends* conclusions. He reaches them as results of thinking about observed things when his inferences and calculations are confirmed by further observations. What he starts with are things having *qualities,* things qualitatively discriminated from one another and recurrently identifiable in virtue of their qualitative distinctions.

Dr. Hunter, in justifying the use of ordinary objects, whether of the environment or the organism in connection with *S-R* behavior, instead of trying to formulate everything in terms of protons-electrons, remarks: "Even in physics it is still permissible to speak of steel and carbon and to make studies upon these substances without directly involving the question of the nature of the atom" (2, p. 91; cf. p. 104). To this may be added that it is not only permissible but necessary. The physicist must refer to such things to get any point of departure and any point of application for his special findings. That water is H_2O would reduce to the meaningless tautology H_2O is H_2O unless it were identified by means of the thing known to perception and use as water. Now these common-sense things from which science starts and in which it terminates are qualitative things, qualitatively differentiated from one another.

There can be no more objection, then, to the psychologist's recognizing objects qualitatively marked out than there is for the physicist and chemist. It is simply a question of fact, not of theory, whether there are modes of behavior qualitatively characterized that can be discriminated as acts of sensation, perception, recollection, etc., and just what their qualitative traits are. Like other matters of fact, it is to be decided by observation. I share, however, the feeling against the use of the word "introspection." For that reason, I employed earlier the word "inspection." "Introspection" is too heavily charged with meanings derived from the animistic tradition. Otherwise, it might be fitly used to designate the common act of observation when directed toward a special kind of subject-matter, that of the behavior of organisms where behavior is what it is because it is a phase of a particular life-career of serial activity.

Of course, these general conceptions remain empty until the acts of sensation, perception, recalling, thinking, etc., with those of fear, love, admiration, etc., are definitely determined as occurring in specified and distinctive junctures or crises of a life-career. Such a task is undoubtedly difficult; but so is any other scientific inquiry. The chief objection, it seems to me, to the narrower forms of behaviorism is that their obsession against the mental, because of previous false theories about it, shuts the door to even entering upon the inquiry. It should even be possible to give the more general term "awareness" or "consciousness" a meaning on this basis, though it would not be that of an underlying substance, cause, or source. It would be discerned as a specifiable quality of some forms of behavior. There is a difference between "consciousness" as a noun, and "conscious" as an adjective of some acts.

Behaviorists have, some of them at least, implicitly admitted the principle for which I have been arguing. They have said that the psychologist uses perception, thought, consciousness, just as any other scientist does. To admit this and then not go on to say (and act upon the saying) that, while they form no part of the subject-matter of physicist and physiologist, they do form a large part of the subject-matter that sets the problems of the psychologist seems strange to me—so strange as to suggest an emotional complex.

Personally I have no doubt that language in its general sense, or symbols, is connected with all mental operations that are intellectual in import and with the emotions associated with them, but to substitute linguistic behavior for the quality of acts that renders them "mental" is an evasion. A man says, "I feel hot." We are told that the whole affair can be resolved into a sensory process as stimulus and linguistic response. But what *is* the *sensory* process? Is it something *exclusively* capable of visual detection in the nervous system under favorable conditions, or is it something having an immediate quality which is noted without knowing about the sensory process as physiological? When a man sees and reports the latter, is there no immediately experienced quality by which he recognizes that he is looking at neuronic structures and not, say, at a balloon? Is it all a matter of another physiological process and linguistic response?

The exposition has brought us to the threshold of the "experience" psychology. Indeed, it will probably seem to some readers that we have crossed the threshold and entered a domain foreign to any legitimate behavioristic psychology. Let me begin, then, by saying that the logic of the above account does not imply that *all* experience is the psychologist's province, to say nothing of its not implying that all experience is psychic in character. "Experience" as James pointed out long ago is a double-barrelled word. The psychologist is concerned exclusively with experiencing, with detection, analysis, and description of its different modes. Experienc*ing* has no existence apart from subject-matter experienced; we perceive objects, veridical or illusory, not percepts; we remember events and not memories; we think topics and subjects, not thoughts; we love persons, not loves; and so on, although the person loved may by metonymy be called a "love." Experiencing is not itself an immediate subject-matter; it is not experienced as a complete and self-sufficient event. But everything experienced is in part made what it is because there enters into it a way of experiencing something; not a way of experiencing *it,* which would be self-contradictory, but a way of experiencing something other than itself. No complete account of what is experienced, then, can be given until we know *how* it is experienced or the mode of experiencing that entered into its formation.

Need of understanding and controlling things experienced must have called attention very early in the history of man to selection from the total object of the way it is made what it is by the manner in which it is experienced. I heard it, saw it, touched it, are among the first, as they are among the most familiar of these discriminations. "I remember seeing it" would, in some cases at least, be regarded as better evidence for belief than "I remember dreaming it." Such discriminations are not themselves psychology, but, as already stated, they form its raw material just as common-sense determinations of the difference between oil and water, iron and tin, form the original subject-matter of physics and chemistry. There is no more reason for denying the reality of one than of the other, while to deny the reality of either leaves the science in question without any concrete subject-matter.

The discrimination of various modes of experiencing is enormously increased by the need of human beings for instruction and for direction of conduct. It is possible, for example, that a person would never differentiate the fact of getting angry from an experienced obnoxious subject-matter, if others did not call his attention to the rôle of his own attitude in the creation of the particular hateful situation. Control of the conduct of others is a constant function of life, and it can be secured only by singling out various modes of experiencing. Thus, when I say that such selected experiencings or modes of individual behavior supply primary raw material but are not psychological in themselves, I mean that they are primarily treated as having moral significance as matters of a character to be formed or corrected. They are selected and designated not for any scientific reason but in the exigencies, real or supposed, of social intercourse and in the process of social control termed education. The word "moral" hardly conveys in its usual sense the full idea. A child is told to look where he is going and to listen to what he is told, to attend to instructions given him. Indeed, it is rather foolish to cite instances, so much of our contact with others consists in having attention called to attitudes, dispositions, and acts that are referred to ourselves.

Hence, the statement only raises the question of what takes place when these acts and attitudes, abstracted from the total experience, become definitely psychological subject-matter. The answer is, in general, that they set problems for investigation, just as other qualitative objects, fire, air, water, stars, set problems to other investigations. What is seeing, hearing, touching, recalling, dreaming, thinking? Now inspection of these acts to determine their qualities is as necessary as is observation of physical objects and behaviors to determine their qualities. But just as no amount of direct observation of water could ever yield a scientific account of water, so no amount of direct inspection of these individual attitudes and ways of experiencing could yield a science of psychology. Observation helps determine the nature of the subject-matter to be studied and accounted for; it does not carry us beyond suggestions of possible hypotheses when it comes to dealing scientifically with the subject-matter.

It is at this point that the significance of objective material and methods comes in, that derived from physiology, biology, and the other sciences. Identifying modes of individual experiencing with modes of behavior identified objectively and objectively analyzable makes a science of psychology possible. Such a statement cuts two ways. It gives due recognition, or so it seems to me, to the importance of methods that have nothing to do with the immediate quality of the ways of experiencing, as these are revealed in direct inspection, or, if you please, introspection. But it also indicates that the subject-matter which sets the problems is found in material exposed to direct observation. This is no different from what happens in the physical sciences, although *what* is observed is different, and the observation is conducted from a different, because personal and social, standpoint.

At a certain period, for example, religionists and moralists were deeply concerned about the nature and fate of human characters. They made many shrewd and penetrating observations on human dispositions and acts on ways of experiencing the world. Or, if this illustration does not appeal, substitute modern novelists and dramatists. But aside from an earlier tendency to interpret and classify such observations in terms of the animistic tradition, and later by a logical misconception of Aristotle's potentialities (transformed into "faculties"), these observations did not form a psychology. They do not become truly psychological until they can be attacked by methods and materials drawn from objective sciences. Yet apart from such observations, psychology has no subject-matter with which to deal in any distinctive way in contrast to the physiologist and physicist, on the one hand, and the social student, on the other.

The position here taken differs, then, in two important respects from that of the introspectionist school. The latter assumes that something called "consciousness" is an originally separate and directly given subject-matter and that it is also the organ of its own immediate disclosure of all its own secrets. If the term "experience" is used instead of consciousness, it assumes that the latter, as it concerns the psychologist, is open to direct inspection, provided the proper precautions are taken and proper measures used. A philosopher by profession who does not know much psychology knows the historic origin of these ideas in Descartes, Locke, and their successors in dealing with epistemological problems. He has even better ground than the professed psychologist for suspecting that they are not indigenous to psychological subject-matter but have been foisted upon psychology from without.

The special matter in point here, however, is not historical origin but the doctrine that direct observation, under the title of introspection, can provide principles of analysis, interpretation, and explanation, revealing laws that bind the observed phenomena together. Without repeating what was said at the outset to the effect that the structure of immediately observed phenomena can be discovered only by going outside of the subject-matter inspected, I refer to it here as indicating one difference between the position here taken and that of the introspectionists. It is a difference between subject-matter that constitutes a *problem* and subject-matter that is supposed to resolve the problem. To discriminate and recognize cases of audition, vision, perception, generally, merely exposes a problem. No persistence in the method which yields them can throw any scientific light upon them.

The other difference is even more fundamental. Psychologists of the school in question have assumed that they are dealing with "experience" instead of with a selected phase of it, here termed experiencing.) I do not, for example, see anything psychological at all in the determination of all the least-discriminable qualities of "experience." The result may yield something more or less curious and interesting about the world in which we live; the conclusions may be of some use in aesthetics or in morals for aught I know. But all that is strictly psychological in the endeavor consists in whatever it may incidentally teach about the *act* of sensing and the *act* of discrimination. These are modes of experiencing things or ways of behaving toward things, and as such have psychological relevancy. It may be doubted whether more would have not been found out if they had been approached directly as acts and not under the guise of finding out all the qualities which can enter into experience. It is not, in short, the qualities of things experienced but the qualities that differentiate certain acts of the individual that concern the psychologist. They concern him not as ultimates and as solutions but, as has been said, as supplying him with data for investigation by objective methods.

The fallacy contained in the doctrine that psychology is concerned with experience instead of with experiencing may be brought out by considering a style of vocabulary dear to the heart of the introspectionist.

When he speaks of sensation, he does not mean an act but a peculiar content.[4] A color or a sound is to him a sensation; an orange, stone, or table is a percept. Now, from the point of view here taken, a color or sound may be an object of an act termed sensing, and a tree or orange may be an object of the act of perceiving, but *they* are not sensations or perceptions, except by a figure of speech. The act of shooting is sometimes called fowling, because fowl are shot at. Speech even reverses the figure of speech and speaks of the birds killed as forming so many good shots. But, in the latter case, no one dreams of taking the figure literally, ascribing to the dead birds the properties characterizing the shooting. To call a tree a percept is merely a short way of saying a tree is perceived. It tells us nothing about the tree but something about a new relation into which the tree has entered. Instead of cancelling or submerging the tree, it tells of an additive property now taken on by the tree, as much so as if we had said the tree was watered by rain or fertilized.

I hope the aptness of the illustration to the matter of confusion of experiencing with experience is reasonably clear. The tree, when it is perceived, is experienced in one way; when remembered, reflected upon, or admired for its beauty, it is experienced in other ways. By a certain figure of speech we may call it an experience, meaning that it is experienced, but we cannot by any figure of speech call it an experiencing. Nevertheless, the tree *as* experienced lends itself to a different type of analysis than that which is appropriate to the tree as a botanical object. We can first discriminate various ways of experiencing it, namely, perceptually, reflectively, emotionally, practically—as a lumberman might look at it—and then we can attempt to analyze scientifically the structure and mechanism of the various acts involved. No other discipline does this. Some study must deal with the problem. Whether the study is called psychology or by some other name is of slight importance compared with that fact that the problem needs scientific study by methods adapted to its solution.

The results of the analysis, if successful, undoubtedly tell us more about the tree as an experienced object. We may be better able to distinguish a veridical tree from an illusory one when we know the conditions of vision. We may be better able to appreciate its aesthetic qualities when we know more about the conditions of an emotional attitude towards it. These are consequences, however, of psychological knowledge rather than a part of psychology. They give no ground for supposing that psychology is a doctrine regarding experience in the sense of things experienced. They are on all fours with the use of the fact of personal equations by an astronomer. The discovery and measurement of personal equation in respect to the time assigned to a perceived event is a psychological matter, because it relates to a way of seeing happenings, but the use of it by an astronomer to correct his time-reading is not a matter of

---

[4] I have alluded to Locke as a part author of the introspectionist tradition. He always, however, refers to sensation as an act. Even his "idea" is an object of mind in knowledge, not a state or constituent of mind taking the place of the scholastic species as true object of knowing.

psychology. Much less does it make the star a psychological fact. It concerns not the star but the way the star enters into experience as far as that is connected with the behavior of an experiencing organism.

Returning to the question raised earlier—it now appears that, if the acts of sensing, perceiving, loving, admiring, etc., are termed mental, it is not because they are intrinsically psychic processes but because of something characteristic which they effect, something different from that produced by acts of locomotion or digestion. The question whether they do have distinctive consequences is a question of fact, not of theory. An a priori theoretical objection to such terms as conscious, mental, etc., should not stand in the way of a fair examination of facts. No amount of careful examination of the nervous system can decide the issue. It is possible that the nervous system and its behavior are *conditions* of acts that have such characteristic effects that we need a name to differentiate them from the behavior of other things, even of the nervous system *taken by itself.*

The above is written schematically with omission of many important points, as well as somewhat over-positively, in order to save time and space. The account may be reviewed by reference to the historical background to which allusion has been made. Modern psychology developed and formed its terminology—always a very important matter because of the rôle of symbols in directing thought—under the influence of certain discussions regarding the possibility and extent of knowledge. In this particular context, *acts* were either ignored or were converted into contents. That is, the function, the peculiar consequences of certain acts, that renders them fit to be called mental was made into a peculiar form of existence called mental or psychic. Then these contents were inserted, under the influence of the theory of knowledge, as intermediaries between the mind and things. Sensations, percepts, treated as mental contents, intervened between the mind and objects and formed the means of knowing the latter. Physics dealt with the things as they were in themselves; psychology, with the things as they were experienced or represented in mental states and processes. In this way, the doctrine arose that psychology is the science of all experience *qua* experience; a view later modified, under the influence of physiological discovery, to the position that it is the science of all experience as far as it is dependent upon the nervous system.

The tendency was reinforced by another historical fact. The special formulations of physics were made in disregard, as far as their own content was concerned, of qualities. Qualities ejected from physics found a home in mind, or consciousness. There was supposed to be the authority of physics for taking them to be mental and psychic in nature. The convergence of these two historic streams created the intellectual background of the beginnings of modern psychology and impregnated its terminology. Behaviorism is a reaction against the confusion created by this mixture. In its reaction it has, in some of its forms, failed to note that some behavior has distinctive qualities which, in virtue of the distinctive properties of the consequences of these acts, are to be termed mental and conscious.

Consequently, it took a study of the organic conditions of these acts to constitute all there is to behavior, overlooking in the operation two fundamental considerations. One of these is that the distinctive functions of the nervous system cannot be determined except in reference to directly observable qualities of the acts of sensing, perceiving, remembering, imagining, etc., they serve. The other is precisely the fact that their behavior is the behavior of *organs* of a larger macroscopic behavior and not at all the whole of behavior. If it were not for knowledge of behavior gained by observation of something else than the nervous system, our knowledge of the latter would consist merely of heaping up of details highly curious and intricate but of no significance for any account of behavior.

Since this discussion intends to be for the most part a logical analysis, I can hardly do better than close by citing a recent statement from a distinguished logician. Speaking of the reflective and analytic method of philosophy, Mr. C. I. Lewis says: "If, for example, the extreme behaviorists in psychology deny the existence of consciousness on the ground that analysis of the 'mental' must always eventually be in terms of bodily behavior, then it is the business of philosophy to correct their error, because it consists simply in a fallacy of logical analysis. The analysis of any immediately presented X must always interpret this X in terms of its relations to other things—to Y and Z. Such end-terms of analysis—Y and Z—will not in general be temporal or spatial constituents of X but may be anything which bears a constant correlation with it . . . . . In general terms, if such analysis concludes by stating X is a certain kind of Y-Z complex, hence X does not exist as a distinct 'reality,' the error consists in overlooking a general characteristic of logical analysis—that is does not discover the 'substance' or cosmic constituents of the phenomenon whose nature is analyzed but only the constant context of experience in which it will be found" (3, p. 5).

REFERENCES

1. HUGHES, P. In introduction to psychology: from the standpoint of life-career. Bethlehem, Pa.: Lehigh Univ. Supply Bureau, 1928.
2. HUNTER, W. S. Psychology and anthroponomy. Chap. 4 in Psychologies of 1925. Worcester, Mass.: Clark Univ. Press, 1926. Pp. 83-107.
3. LEWIS, C. I. Mind and the world-order. New York: Scribner's, 1929. Pp. 446.
4. WOODWORTH, R. S. Dynamic psychology. Chap. 5 in Psychologies of 1925. Worcester, Mass.: Clark Univ. Press, 1926. Pp. 111-126.

CHAPTER 23

THE INHERITANCE OF MENTAL TRAITS

TRUMAN L. KELLEY

Stanford University

We may believe that for some considerable time in the evolution of the human species the existence of a problem of biological inheritance was unsuspected by mankind. It seems quite certain that long before any thought was given to the control of inheritance of mental traits, rules were drawn up for the transmission of social distinctions and property rights. There has thus become established the idea of the hereditary transmission of the foibles and card houses of one generation to the neglect of thought about the permanent and living protoplasm of succession.

A child might be expected to see a bottle floating down a stream, claim it for his own, shunt it into a stagnant pool peacefully supporting such things, and, having done so, to think of the stream in terms of its flotsam and jetsam, but the adult who fails to see the stream as a living thing, content or boisterous, confined or rampant, but moving ever onward from an untraced source above to an unknown terminus below, is not living in the world of continuity but of childhood or of make-believe.

It is presumably true that in the human lifetime more is picked up, mastered, and incorporated into the daily and intimate structure of living than is the case with any sub-human form of life. The foal is born fully equipped for life except for a short period in which it receives maternal milk and protection. The human child has a long period of infancy and immature youth and picks up a language, a religion, a vocation, likes and dislikes, a process—sometimes weird—for reaching conclusions, a more or less distorted awareness of sex, and a belief in the transmission of acquired properties.

Now surely this richness of accretion is definitely human—it is one important thing that differentiates man from animal and it is not to be belittled. Of the various human values of social inheritance, one in particular affecting genetic inheritance is so non-bestial as to be nearly superhuman, though undoubtedly it is but a rising human charactertistic. The highest of our social arts, that is, of our somatic modifications, leads ever more indubitably to a knowledge and mastery of our racial past, of our genetic origins, and of our future possibilities. If that which is added after birth leads to an understanding of the antecedents of birth and to their consequences not only upon the present but also upon future generations, then it is an acquired trait having (or which may have) genetic consequences. Its justification, its value, is thus rooted in a deeper stratum of life than one affecting merely the social inheritance of man, for we then have the genetic transmission of an acquired trait, or, more

[423]

exactly, modification of genetic transmission by an acquired trait. This is a possibility, just as it is possible that the flotsam of the river can be made to serve in the construction of plummets, seines, dams, etc., for the knowledge and control of the river itself.

What more complete and self-contained a social life can there be than one in which the somatic structures of one generation are so full of wisdom (for it is the cerebrum, utilizing social heritage, not sex glands, that mediate knowledge) that they determine the choice of the germ-cells of the generation to be and see to it that that generation is germinally as well as somatically in step with social evolution. We may make the observation that the most consciously progressive of all mental traits, inherited or acquired, is that one that aims to assure that the inherited traits of the next generation shall be good from the racial standpoint.

Though the present chapter is entitled "The Inheritance of Mental Traits," and not "Eugenics," the two subjects are indissoluble, for who desires to know the laws of mental heredity except because of the promise of such knowledge for the improvement of the future, and who desires to improve inheritance without being driven thereby to a study of the laws of heredity? We may well then consider the importance of the inheritance of mental traits from the standpoint of eugenics.

It is difficult to draw a line between social and biological inheritance when dealing with mankind and with racial as distinct from individual growth or evolution. Consider the five following hypothetical situations, each involving changes from one generation to the next. In each instance the first generation is composed of 50 per cent pure (homozygous) feeble-minded and 50 per cent pure geniuses.

a) *Omnipotent and benevolent education:*
Mating at random and all unions are fertile. By social edict all children not geniuses pursue a special training with the result that the entire second generation react like geniuses, i. e., they are geniuses. They give appearance of breeding true under the conditions of special training only.

b) *Benevolent non-fertility:*
Mating at random, but f. m. *vs.* f. m. and f. m. *vs.* g. unions prove non-fertile under environmental conditions prevailing during period of the first generation. Second generation is of geniuses and they breed true.

c) *Benevolent social edict:*
By social edict the geniuses alone breed, with the result that the second generation is of geniuses and they breed true.

d) *Social utilization of benevolent hormones:*
Mating at random but by social edict preceding mating all f. m. act or are so treated as to release hormones which react upon their germ-cells, making them the same as those of the geniuses. The second generation is composed of geniuses and they breed true.

e) *Benevolent instincts and non-fertility:*
No imposed restrictions upon marriage, but the original natures are such that f. m. always choose f. m. mates and g. always choose g. mates. The f. m. matings prove sterile. Second generation composed of geniuses and they breed true.

In which of these five situations is there transmission of acquired characters? In (a), (c), and (d) the intelligence of the body politic has been instrumental in creating the genius second generation, because the coordinated intelligence which has led to selective breeding or special training is at least in part an acquired trait. The biological geneticist would probably say that there was no transmission of an acquired trait in situation (c), involving a benevolent social edict. However, the first generation acquired something—that represented by the edict established —dependent upon language, social contacts, cooperation, not possessed by an earlier generation which radically modifies the germinal structure of all subsequent generations. If this is not, in the profoundest of meanings, a genetic modification due to an acquired trait, I am at a loss to characterize it.

In this situation the race has acquired something (the belief that only *g. vs. g.* matings should be consummated) that affects subsequent generations in the most fundamental manner conceivable. I shall hold, therefore, that the possibility of a racial transmission of acquired characteristics exists and I am certain geneticists will subscribe to this, though if they choose to say the same thing in other words I shall see no occasion to object. The social scientists have no need to differ with biologists as to what constitutes inheritance. Let each group attempt to understand the other, but, of course, let each define his terms as best meets the needs of his own problems.

Commonly the geneticist leaps from germ-cell of one generation to that of the next (from gamete to gamete), concerning himself with the body structure under standardized conditions of nurture (somatic phenomena) only for the purpose of inferring germ-cell structure. In the words of Babcock and Clausen: "Heredity is concerned with germinal materials rather than with somatic characters; . . . heredity is genetic continuity of germinal material between parents and offspring" (1). The problem of inheritance to the geneticist is that of inferring the germ-cell structure of the offspring from the inferred germ-cell structure of the parents, which is inferred from somatic phenomena. The growth of the soma, due to nurture and to nature, and its limits are to him disconcerting phenomena to be eliminated so far as possible by study of the experimental animals under invariable conditions of nurture and at invariable ages. On the other hand, the educator and psychologist are intrinsically interested in the phenomena of growth and their relation to inherited traits. The foci of interest are not the gametes of successive generations, but the soma, including the relationship between the mature soma of parent to the maturing soma of offspring.

There is a crudeness, or directness, in the study of inheritance by the social scientist which eliminates a substantial amount of theory—that which brings in germ-cell structure and its combinations. These are not necessary parts of a study of inheritance. When it is remembered that one's concept of the germ-cell as it concerns specific characters is an inference from observable phenomena in parents and offspring, or progenitors and descendants, it becomes clear that the observable phenomena constitute the basic point of approach. Innumerable theories, elaborate or primitive, may be called upon to explain the observed facts—the more elaborate the richer in suggestion of issues to be investigated and tested, and the more primitive the more certain that hypothesis will not lead astray. If one supposes that inheritance of mentality is according to a specific pattern based upon the latest knowledge of linkage of factors, segregation, and independent assortment, then tests galore of the hypothesis are suggested, in fact so many and so exacting that it is impossible to make them. If one merely supposes that there is biological inheritance of mentality, then the proof called for requires the devising and the utilizing of a test of mentality for a heterogeneous population of adults and for their offspring, an allowance for nurture differences throughout, and the securing of a measure of the net correlation remaining between mentality of parent and that of offspring. Even in this case the test is so fraught with difficulties that it has not been carried through in any very satisfactory manner to date. Surely, until we can test this simplest of hypotheses it is futile to attempt tests of much more complicated ones.

The geneticist differentiates his "characters" by color, presence or absence, or some other qualitative spatial (i.e., body location) difference. If upon close examination the difference is seen to be quantitative and not qualitative, so that there is somatic overlapping of the groups supposed to possess and not to possess some character, he chucks it aside as inappropriate for his study. He is entitled to do this, but where would the student of mental inheritance be if he did the same? The mental traits of the psychologist (i. e., characters of the geneticist) are not seen or counted. Not only is the problem of somatic overlapping always present but, far more serious, there is not a single mental trait as yet positively known to be discrete from others in the sense that "eyeless" and "spineless" are in *Drosophila*. The process of the geneticist in inferring germinal structure of offspring from the germinal structure of parents as inferred from direct observation of characters sensorially discrete is hazardous enough. When such observation is impossible, so that the existence and discreteness of the traits (characters) are themselves matters of inference the task is futile, at least until this inference last mentioned can be made with an assurance now entirely lacking.

The Mendelian geneticist will surely understand that this is not a criticism of his work. It is merely a statement that there exists a field of biological transmission, that of mental inheritance, which cannot now be investigated by such of his methods as apply to much more elemental structures than man. The physical chemist can today describe the interior structure of the hydrogen atom with remarkable detail and he can use this knowledge in prophesying the behavior of this atom. That he cannot do the same with lead does not prevent him from ascertaining many remarkable things that lead will do.

In a personal conversation with the writer a certain eminent biologist advised the immediate junking of all biometrical studies of the inheritance of mental traits and concentration upon studies of the *Drosophila* type with a view, first, that the nature of the mechanism of inheritance be ascertained, secondly, that mental characters in man be found following this mechanism, and, thirdly, that then and only then could a practical control of mental inheritance be considered a possibility.

Even were this procedure to promise success within a reasonable length of time, which it does not, it would not seem desirable to the writer, but rather both cumbersome and logically unsound. If careful and sufficient observation of the relationship between offspring and ancestors enable a serviceable description of offspring, knowing the traits of ancestors, then a description of the mechanism whereby the offspring attain their traits is a gratuity. It holds exactly the same place as any hypothesis in a scientific study. The hypothesis must explain the facts, and not the reverse. What we need first are facts of mental inheritance in man, based upon careful and extensive observations.

It seems to the writer that the attempt to picture the inheritance of feeble-mindedness—known by every careful tester of intelligence not to be a single trait or sharply differentiated from normal intelligence—as that of a unit recessive Mendelian character is an illustration of an attempt to fit facts to a hypothesis. Even to test the hypothesis in this case it would be necessary to have a criterion of "unitness" in the mental field and none such is known to be available. Secondly, a criterion of "recessiveness." This is not a necessary part of a modern Mendelian concept of inheritance, and it is certainly a puzzling idea as regards intelligence. The more tractable concept of allelomorphs is more fundamental in the neo-Mendelian picture. To my knowledge no criteria for the determination of recessiveness, or of allelomorphs, in the mental field has been proposed. Thirdly, a criterion of the specific Mendelian mechanism active, for there are many widely different phenomena which can fall under the neo-Mendelian scheme. Finally, there is implied a knowledge of the genetic structure of the parents of the feeble-minded and of the non–feeble-minded studied for comparative purposes. The means of ascertaining this knowledge in controlled cultures has thus far baffled geneticists—one needs but mention the skeleton in their closet, the possibility that *Drosophila melanogaster* is a hybrid. The difficulty of doing so in connection with the ancestors of the feeble-minded can well be imagined. In fact, the problem has been made quite insoluble by tying it up at this stage of our knowledge with a hypothesis as to the mechanism of inheritance. There is neither need nor present benefit in doing so.

In no field of science does history reveal that observation waited upon hypothesis. The typical procedure is observation, hypothesis, new observation to test hypothesis, new hypothesis, etc. At each step it is essential that the hypothesis be adequate to explain the facts then available and that it immediately be subjected to rigid experimental or observational tests. The steps which seem to have been followed by those who place mental inheritance, as known by present facts, under a specific Mendelian pattern are as follows: (*a*) observation of facts suggesting mental inheritance; (*b*) postulating a mechanism in harmony with certain known facts about peas, fowls, and fruit flies; (*c*) no testing of the hypothesis upon mental data. The hypothesis did not grow out of the original facts of mental inheritance, nor was it subjected to a penetrating examination involving the original data as well as new mental data collected for the purpose. The method is open to criticism, and the conclusions from it should not be considered scientific.

The conviction that the mental traits of offspring are more similar to those of parents than to people in general is much better grounded than that mental inheritance is according to a dominant-recessive pattern. A hypothesis incorporating the first idea and not the second is to be preferred at this stage of our knowledge. It is sufficient, for it is not so exacting as to violate known facts nor does it impose limitations the reasonableness of which is beyond our present means of testing.

When one considers the great variety possible under Mendelian inheritance it is not probable that a subsuming of facts now known about mental traits and their inheritance, and of facts likely to be discovered soon, under the Mendelian scheme, would offer any difficulty. The typical scatter diagram showing the relationship between a mental trait in parent and in child is such as to suggest blended inheritance, not alternative. Two, and perhaps more, Mendelian patterns can be invoked to "explain" this situation: one is that the character is a strict blend of single factors in the parents, plus a variability factor (such as is a grey wing color in *Drosophila*); and the other is that several, perhaps a large number, of factors combine to create, with an unmeasured variability factor, the observed character. The differentiation between these two, and perhaps more, hypotheses calls for a detail quite beyond us. The point is that the failure to specify the particular genetic pattern operating does not imply a disagreement with the versatile general Mendelian hypothesis. In the matter of blends there is no ground for alarm (as many would view it) lest the mental facts fall outside of Mendelian boundaries. Should they in truth so fall, we would not expect it to be provable for many generations, any more than we expect to be able to prove the opposite.

In the matter of variability there is more occasion to think that the Mendelian view is inadequate, but here it seems to be inadequate to explain its own most ideal phenomena. Seemingly a prevalent view of the geneticists today is that variability in culture accounts for a part only of such variability in character of homozygous individuals as is found. The remaining variability is admittedly an as yet unsolved riddle. The psychologists can well refrain from drawing Mendelian analogies and follow wherever the mental data alone lead.

The chromosome basis of germinal matter suggests 24 linkage groups in man. As every chromosome is represented in every cell, including, of course, nerve-cells, there is a genetic richness which makes such present psychological discussions as that pertaining to Spearman's hypothesis of a single general mental function fall into an entirely different class. In mental life we have yet to clearly distinguish between a half dozen or so mental traits. The genetic structure is so much more than ample for our psychological needs that it does not restrict our thought a particle.

The following observation by Crew should be taken to heart by students of mental inheritance: "In man, as has been stated, there are 24 pairs of homologous chromosomes. If that which applies to *Drosophila* holds also in the case of the human, and there is every reason to postulate that it does, then in man there are 24 groups of linked characters and there are infinitely greater opportunities for crossing-over between the chromosomes. It is not likely, therefore, that linkage (save sex-linkage) will be quickly or readily recognized and it can be expected that man will exhibit an exceedingly great variety in his characterisation. The map of the chromosomes of man will not be made yet awhile, if ever."(3). At present all that biology can do in this connection is to support the idea that linkage groups exist. For data as to independent mental traits (linkage groups?) one may be referred to Spearman's *Abilities of Man*, (13), or the present writer's *Crossroads in the Mind of Man: a Study of Differentiable Mental Abilities* (9). The linkage groups in *Drosophila* are four in number and of different "lengths," as measured. The number of chromosomes is four and their directly observed lengths are quite closely proportional to the "lengths" of the linkage groups. Thus the chromosome as the origin of the linkage group is strongly indicated. Thomas Hunt Morgan and others state that there is one important requirement of the chromosome view: "It was obvious from the beginning, however, that there was one essential requirement of the chromosome view, namely, that all the factors carried by the *same* chromosome should tend to remain together. Therefore, since the number of inheritable characters may be large in comparison with the number of pairs of chromosomes, we should expect to find not only the independent behavior of pairs, but also cases in which characters are linked together in groups in their inheritance. Even in species where a limited number of Mendelian units are known, we should still expect to find some of them in groups" (11). Though there seems to be no conflict between the idea of linkage and the dependence of certain mental functions, it would be unsound to say that the study of differentiable mental abilities supports the linkage theory, for genetic linkage is defined in terms of an entirely different technique and different phenomena, both being impossible at present in dealing with human mental phenomena.

Mendelian doctrine is neither in conflict with accumulated psychological data, nor does it shed new light upon the psychological issues. At best only questionable analogies can be drawn. Psychologists should reaffirm, if challenged, their independent status and vigorously pursue the study of mental inheritance, taking their cues from the fascinating and abundant facts of mental life. They should determine mental traits unitary in a psychological sense and relate them to hereditary, environmental, and age co-variants. It will then be time to interpret, if possible, in the light of cytological evidence and controlled breeding experiments made upon lower organisms. Whether this be possible is not of prime importance, for the psychological study will yield its own adequate social values. Galton has led the way in this endeavor and though the volume of his conclusions as to heredity is small, such as it is, it stands unquestioned. Galton's point of view, unattached to a specific mechanism of inheritance, was nevertheless forward-looking and constructive.

What does the biologically trained geneticist know of mental measurement, of independence in mental traits, of modifications due to differences in nurture, of changes with growth, and of racial mental differences? Without profound knowledge of these things he is not equipped to contribute to the problem of mental inheritance though his knowledge of controlled genetic investigation be exceptional. The first demands of this difficult problem are a thorough psychological, statistical, and measurement background.

The logic of the philosopher and the vision of the seer proclaim the problem worthy of untold effort and devotion. Thorndike discusses the interdependence of nature and nurture and then states that the *"most fundamental question for human education* asks that we assign separate shares in the causation of human behavior to man's original nature on the one hand, and his environmental or nurture on the other" (15, p. 3). In connection with racial betterment he writes: "Until the last removable impediment in man's own nature dies childless, human reason will not rest" (16 p. 342). The immutable imminence of the issue has been caught by Bergson, who writes: "[The occasional fleeting vision] shows us each generation leaning over the generation that shall follow. It allows us in a moment of insight to perceive that the living being is above all a thoroughfare, and that the essence of life is in the movement by which life is transmitted" (12).

The importance of knowing the parts heredity and environment play in the life of a man and of his progeny can hardly be overstated, but just what form this knowledge should take depends upon one's philosophy or his mental mold into which he fits or tries to fit the facts of life. The following statement is made by Thorndike: "Any man possesses at the very start of his life . . . numerous well defined tendencies to future behavior. Between the situations which he will meet and the responses he will make to them, preformed bonds exist . . . What a man is and does throughout life is a result of whatever constitution he has at the start and of all the forces that act upon it before and after birth." After pointing out the dependence of each factor upon the other Thorndike states that the "most fundamental question for human education asks that we assign separate shares in the causation of human behavior to man's original nature on the one hand and his environment or nurture on the other. In this . . . we neglect, or take for granted, the cooperating action of one of the two . . . in order to think more successfully and conveniently of the action of the other" (15 pp. 1-3).

This suggests to me a picture, which may, or may not, be the same as that of Thorndike, of the individual at some age sufficiently after birth that nurture shall have played a part as follows:

$$\left.\begin{array}{l}\text{Individual at age } k, \\ \text{independent of nurture}\end{array}\right\} = x_o + y_{a\ldots k} + y_{b\ldots k} + \ldots + y_k \quad [1]$$

wherein x_o is original nature at time of birth (or better at the union of the germ-cells), $y_a \ldots k$, $y_b \ldots k$, $\ldots y_k$ maturation factors of x_o first appearing at successive stages $a, b \ldots k$. Now if environment affects these factors by various amounts respectively $e_a \ldots k$, $e_b \ldots k$, $\ldots e_k$, the individual at age k may be represented by

$$x_k = x_o + y_a \ldots k + e_a \ldots k + y_b \ldots k + e_b \ldots k + \ldots + y_k + e_k \quad [2]$$

After a certain age, say age a, the traits of an individual become measurable, and if they were measured perfectly our measure of the individual in some designated trait would be

$$y_b \ldots k + e_b \ldots k + \ldots + y_k + e_k \quad [3]$$

which, if we are skilful enough could be divided into an original nature component $y_b \ldots k + \ldots + y_k$ and a nurture component $e_b \ldots k + \ldots + e_k$. Whether I have given Thorndike's meaning or not, I do believe that a concept substantially as here expressed in symbols has lain at the root of most of the psychological and educational attempts to differentiate between nature and nurture influences. We have sought to express the total ability of the individual along a given line as equal to the sum of two parts, one nature and one nurture.

Let us consider another symbolic statement, based upon the idea that the individual at each and every moment is changing due to an inner urge and an outer mold. We will designate his status at birth in some trait by the symbol x_o. Then $x_o + \Delta_o$ is his status at the end of the next moment after Δ_o growth due to inner impulse has taken place. There can, however, be no growth except as nurture (food, geography lessons, etc.) permits it, so the Δ_o must be multiplied by a quantity e_o which ordinarily must be in the neighborhood of 1.00. Thus the status of the individual at the end of the first moment is $x_o + \Delta_o e_o$, which we will designate x_a. Similarly, at the end of the second moment we have

$$x_b = x_a + \Delta_a e_a = x_o + \Delta_o e_o + \Delta_a e_a \quad [4]$$

One should note that in this statement x_a (and a fortiori x_b) is not pure original nature and that Δ_a is not pure original tendency to grow, but only tendency to grow in the light of both hereditary and environmental antecedents.

At age k the individual is represented by

$$x_k = x_j + \Delta_j e_j = x_i + \Delta_i e_i + \Delta_j e_j = \ldots = x_o + \Delta_o e_o + \ldots + \Delta_j e_j \quad [5]$$

From equation [5] we may express the ratio of status at age k to immediately preceding age j thus:

$$\frac{x_k}{x_j} = 1 + \frac{\Delta_j}{x_j} e_j \quad [6]$$

Now clearly if this second statement is fairly adequate in showing how x_k, the status of the individual at age k, comes about, there is no means of differentiating between the sum of the environmental factors and the original nature impetuses, for the final attainment is not the sum of independent parts but the sum of products. Whereas in [2] the factors contributory to the final outcome segregate readily, in [5] they do not. Following the lead of [6] the important and perhaps solvable problem is that of determining the parts played by past attainment on the one hand and present environment on the other in bringing about an immediate change. Theoretically this immediate change is that of a fraction of a second. However, for functions in which the momentary environmental factor, e, differs but slightly from 1 (as in the case of height [see p. 437]) a much longer period than the "moment" can be used for the elementary time interval—perhaps a year would be satisfactory.

Referring to [6], we see that if our measures were accurate it would be relatively simple to differentiate between Δ_j/x_j and e_j by a controlled experiment involving different e_j factors. This is of fundamental importance to the teacher, and if [5] is correct it is a necessary step in the real solution of the problem of inheritance. Equation [6] suggests that what we need is a careful study of short-interval changes in capacity as related to changes in environment and to differences in initial abilities.

The relationship covered by the equation, $x_b = x_a + \Delta_a e_a$, has to do with some single mental function. Thus, if x_b is a person's musical ability at age b, it is set equal to x_a, his musical ability at a shortly preceding age a, plus $\Delta_a e_a$, his tendency to grow in this short interval as affected by the environmental influence of the interval. *Pari passu* the individual is developing in other respects. He is like an army having several units advancing upon a broad front, all fed from a common base, but meeting different obstacles on their way. These various units have a sort of independence of movement, particularly when all goes well, but an ever increasing system of communication is built up as they progress, leading to a dependence in functioning. Where it is possible to tap the resources of neighboring units or to circumambulate serious obstacles a disentanglement of the parts played, by the drive of the unit and by the difficulty to be overcome, as progress takes place, is a problem of great complexity. How much simpler the issue if but a single unit pushed across known and unavoidable obstacles. The disentanglement of the parts played by the drive of human nature and the aids and obstacles of nurture does, at best, offer serious difficulties.

In the case of the advancing army it would be simpler to judge correctly the credit to be given for progress made by each of two branches of the service, such as air and infantry, than of two mutually dependent units such as one infantry company and its neighboring company. Just so in studying human nature it will be simpler to appraise properly the factors conditioning progress in two quite discrete mental functions than in two which are interdependent. For example, we may expect a differential study of development of the nature and nurture factors in musical development and of those in geometric ability to be possible while the child is developing, whereas a study of the unique development of literary appreciation and of written composition, each separately, might be quite impossible because of the mutual dependence of the two.

It seems therefore that an important prerequisite to environment and heredity studies that extend beyond single features is a determination of what constitutes the most independent factors of mental life. These are the things whose changes should be related to heritable and environmental causes.

The approach mentioned, looking upon growth as a product of inner urge and outer opportunity, is not the usual approach; so when referring to the extensive work already done I must revert to the summation picture provided by equation [2].

No attempt will be made to review the literature upon this subject, but merely to comment upon a few recent outstanding findings which have been reported. Many of these are found in the *27th Yearbook of the National Society for the Study of Education, Nature and Nurture,* Parts I and II. Thorndike (17) investigated the resemblance of siblings in intelligence, allowed for differences in age, corrected for attenuation, and made a certain allowance for the fact that his pairs consisted only of siblings found within a limited grade range, and reached a correlation value of .60. Upon comparing this with .52, found by Pearson for the resemblance of siblings in eye color, hair color, and cephalic index, he infers "that the influence upon intelligence of such similarity in environment as is caused by being siblings two to four years apart in age in an American family today is to raise the correlation from .52 to .60." Let us interpret this in other terms. If we express influences in an additive manner we may say that the variance (= the standard deviation squared) in intelligence of American children of a certain age is equal to the variance due to (a) inheritance (biological, not social) plus that due to (b) the environment likewise experienced by one's sib, plus that due to (c) other environment, plus that due to (d) other causes (including chance), if any. If the total variance is called one, the magnitude of the second factor (b) as drawn from Thorndike's inference is $.60^2 - .52^2$, or .09. A 9–per-cent influence upon a total outcome is very material. The sibs have the same parents and home and some of the same playmates and teachers. They have different environments due to one being the older and the other the younger, one sometimes a boy and the other a girl, some of their playmates different, and in part different teachers. It may well be that this non-common environment is more important in its effect upon intelligence than is the common environment. Estimating it as about the same we have about 20 per cent of the total variance in intelligence due to environment and the rest to heredity, chance, or what-not. This result is for ages in the neighborhood of 16.

Though a substantial environmental influence is found, I am inclined to consider the 9 per cent an underestimate, because I think the influence upon correlation of the selective nature of Thorndike's sample is greater than he estimated, leading to a correlation of perhaps .70 between siblings instead of .60. To make the issue clear consider the following:

Let x and y represent true scores of sibs, after due allowance for age, as deviations from the mean of the sample investigated.

Let X and Y represent the same as deviations from the mean of the universe, i.e., of an unselected population.

The correlation, as ordinarily determined, is

$$r_{xy} = \frac{\Sigma xy}{N\sigma_x\sigma_y} = \frac{\Sigma xy}{N\sigma^2_x} = 1 - \frac{\Sigma (x\text{-}y)^2}{N2\sigma^2_x} = 1 - \frac{V (x\text{-}y)}{2Vx} \qquad [7]$$

In this statement $\sigma_x = \sigma_y$, for the scatter diagram is a double-entry table, the score for the younger sib being entered along one axis and for the older along the other and then for the same pair entry is made in the reverse manner. We define Vx by equation [8] and $V (x\text{-}y)$ in a similar manner.

$$\sigma_x\sigma_y = \sigma^2_x = \sigma^2_y = Vx \text{ (read the ``variance of the } x\text{'s'')} = Vy \qquad [8]$$

If we deal with deviations of scores of the selected sample from the mean of the unselected population, we can have a function similar in form to that of r_{xy} which will not be, according to definition, a product moment coefficient of correlation, but which will nevertheless be a truer representation of the correlation in the unselected population because deviations are taken from the mean of this unselected population. This is the function Thorndike computes, leading to his value .60:

$$r_{XY} = 1 - \frac{V(X\text{-}Y)}{2VX} \qquad [9]$$

The value that we are searching for is that of an unselected population, which I will represent by attaching primes, thus:

$$r'_{XY} = 1 - \frac{V'(X\text{-}Y)}{2V'X} \qquad [10]$$

Dr. Thorndike has used r_{XY} as a fair measure of r'_{YX}. Let us look into this more closely. If, considering age, X is low (low intelligence for one sib) then, as pointed out by Thorndike for the sample dealt with, there is likelihood that Y will be lower than would be the case in the unselected population. As the freedom of Y is partially limited, $X\text{-}Y$ for low values of X will tend to be smaller than in the unselected population. A similar situation holds where X is high. Only in the middle range, where there is no selection, will the observed differences tend to be of the same size as in the unselected population. Accordingly $V(X\text{-}Y)$ is less than $V'(X\text{-}Y)$. If this were the only issue, we could immediately say that r_{XY} is greater than r'_{XY}. Let us examine the denominator terms. Is VX, the variance of the scores in the selected sample, equal to $V'X$, the variance in the unselected population? Clearly VX can be greater or less than $V'X$ depending upon the nature of the selection. For selection of the sort described we are not at this point certain that r_{XY} is smaller or larger than r'_{XY}. The problem cannot be solved without utilizing facts covering the specific nature of the selection. Now Thorndike most happily provides his detailed scatter diagram. From a study of this I judge regressions to be linear and the selection to be of the sort shown in Figure 1: O is the mean of the unselected population, T of the skewed sample, and u the estimated point where there is least selection in the sample. Approximately sibs having a score X_j, or x_j, will have their full complement of brothers and sisters represented. Accordingly the regression of y upon x for the particular value x_j will be the true regression, i.e., y estimated from x_j in the selected sample will give the same point as Y estimated from X_j in the unselected population. We may now refer to Figure 2 where this principle has been employed to obtain the regression lines, and accordingly the correlation coefficient, for the unselected population. OA and OB are the axes for the unselected population. OI and OH, shown for comparison only, are regression lines having the slope .60 corresponding to Thorndike's value for r_{XY}. GF and GE regression lines having the slope .40 corresponding to an r_{xy} of .40 estimated from the correlation of Thorndike's Table 6 corrected for attenuation. $\bar{y}$ is y estimated for x_j, but as mentioned this is also a point on OQ the line giving the regression of Y upon X in the unselected population. Therefore OQ is drawn so that it passes through the point N. If we now measure the slope of OQ we obtain .70 as the correlation r'_{XY} sought for.

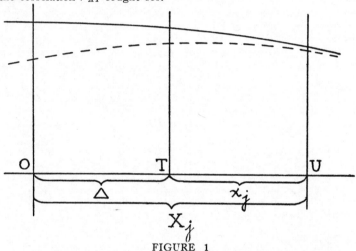

FIGURE 1

PORTIONS OF UNSELECTED (FULL LINE) AND SELECTED (DASH LINE) DISTRIBUTIONS AS ESTIMATED

If my estimate of a correlation in intelligence of .70 between siblings in an unselected population of American sixteen-year-olds is near the mark, and if Pearson's figure of .52 is correct for physical traits, and if the biological laws of inheritance are the same in the case of mental and physical traits, then we find the variance of that part of the nurture factor that is common to two siblings in the neighborhood of 16 years of age and about two years apart in age to equal .22 — as given by $.70^2 - .52^2$. Further, if we estimate that one half of a child's milieu is similar to that of his sib and one half different, then the rest of nurture is as important as the part mentioned, so that 44 per cent of the total variance is due to the variability in nurture and 56 per cent to the variability in inheritance, or other (if any) cause.

It is pertinent to call attention here to Willoughby's (18, pp. 58-59) determination, based upon mental tests of parents and children of average age about 13, of the variance due to all environment, following R. A. Fisher's coefficient of environment technique (4). The argument which Fisher makes leading to his coefficient of environment, though circuitous, has been very carefully thought out. It is true that there are in Willoughby's mental-test data important hazards not present in Fisher's physical data, but even so there is probably some significance in the results yielded by Fisher's technique. Dr. Willoughby found the variance due to environment to equal .46. Unfortunately neither in the case of the 44 per cent mentioned above nor of the 46 per cent derived by Willoughby do we

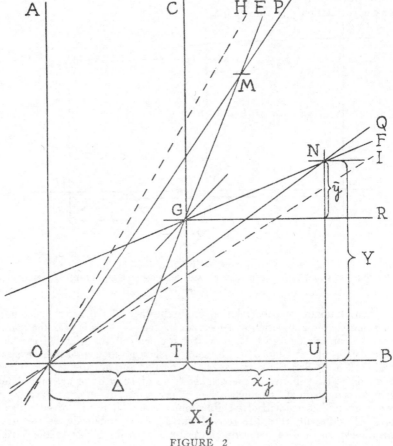

FIGURE 2

REGRESSION LINES OF UPPER RIGHT QUADRANT OF SCATTER DIAGRAM, AS ESTIMATED have even approximate probable errors, not to mention systematic errors which may be more serious. I would imagine them to be large in both instances. The closeness of the two figures should be considered a coincidence and not an experimentally established agreement.

In passing, it is interesting to note that Fisher, using Pearson and Lee's data upon stature, span, and forearm, found no environmental influence. He states: "An examination of the best available figures for human measurements shows that there is little or no indication of non genetic causes" (4, p. 433). He also finds that: "In general, the hypothesis of cumulative Mendelian factors seems to fit the facts very accurately."

The interesting findings reported by Freeman and others (5) indicate a rather high correlation between intelligence and environment, though I would judge but little higher than that suggested by Thorndike's or Willoughby's data. Their results are difficult to interpret in the variance terms just used because raw coefficients of correlation rather than those corrected for attenuation are reported and because allowance, when dealing with correlations, for the selective nature of the sample dealt with has not been attempted. Several of their results support the argument earlier made that specific Mendelian mechanisms should not, at this stage of our knowledge, be assumed. To quote one finding bearing upon this: "In the case of 26 children studied, both parents were rated as feeble-minded. If intelligence were inherited according to the Mendelian law, all of these children would be feeble-minded. It was found, however, that only four had an $I.Q.$ below 70 and these only slightly below. The average $I.Q.$ of 81 for these 26 children is higher than would be expected according to the Mendelian law, but is considerably below that of the entire group of children studied."

In addition to making a study of foster children Freeman[1] and Holzinger (6) have studied twins. For their purposes the twins were divided into identical and fraternal types by Professor H. H. Newman, an authority upon twinning. Various measures were available to Dr. Newman and he considered all of them in making his division, but the exact recording in print of the steps followed so that another could verify or repeat his classification has not as yet been made. From the standpoint of further research this is clearly of greater importance than any or all of the specific findings reported upon the 102 pairs (50 classified as identical and 52 as fraternal) studied. To build up a structure and draw important deductions, upon premises not subjected to the scrutiny of fellow-workers, is not assuring. Perhaps time and publication opportunity have not as yet permitted Dr. Newman's report to appear, in which case these remarks are out of place as applying to the study under discussion, but they are not out of place as applying to several identical twin studies which have long been in print and not here discussed because of a failure to publish the exact criteria used in the selection of subjects.

---

[1]Notes kindly supplied to the writer by Dr. Freeman upon an address delivered by him before the *American Association for the Advancement of Science,* December, 1929.

Upon the assumption that twins differ in the closeness of their inherited similarity in a graded manner from most similar to the similarity of unlike sibs and not in a sharply bimodal manner, which assumption is, so far as we know, as congruent with the facts of mental life as any other, many of the results reported by Freeman and Holzinger can be accounted for if, when classification was made, (a) most reliance was placed upon number of finger ridges, (b) some reliance was placed upon height, and (c) still less upon cephalic index. This would account for the otherwise strange figures reported by Dr. Freeman, following Holzinger's t^2 technique (6, pp. 246-247), indicating the nurture is about one-fourth responsible for cephalic index and has practically nothing whatever to do with finger ridges. It is obvious that if twins had been classified as identical provided they had the same cephalic indices the t^2 technique would have indicated nurture to be of zero importance in determining cephalic index and of much importance in determining the number of finger ridges. Since it is not cephalic index but number of finger ridges that appears solely (very nearly) a matter of heredity, the inference is that number of finger ridges was the trait considered of greatest importance and that accordingly this result is a mere trick of the means employed in making the selection of the two types of twins.

Though one holds a reservation as to the classification, it still is interesting to look at the consequent results, for one may well believe that the hereditary similarity of the twins classified as "identical" is much closer than that of those classified as "fraternal." Dr. Holzinger has devised the following formula:

$$t^2 = \frac{\text{variance of differences between fraternals caused by nature}}{\text{variance of differences between fraternals caused by nurture}} = \frac{_ir - _fr}{1 - _ir} \qquad [11]$$

in which $_ir$ is the correlation between identical twins and $_fr$ that between fraternal twins. Two important assumptions underlying this formula may be mentioned: (a) that the identical twins as classified have identical inheritance and (b) that errors in the instruments of measurement may be considered negligible or in other words represented by the probable error of t^2, a formula for which is given by Holzinger. Assumption (a) has been discussed. Let us here, with Holzinger, assume that it is valid and look further. A formula not involving assumption (b) can readily be derived. Using τ^2 in which the systematic effect of chance errors is allowed for in place of t^2 in which it is not, and representing the reliability coefficient of the measure in question by r_{11}, the formula is,

$$\tau^2 = \frac{_ir - _fr}{r_{11} - _ir} \qquad [12]$$

It seems to me that it is this latter formula that is demanded. I have not attempted to determine the probable error of τ^2, but estimating reliability coefficients for Holzinger's data as in column "r_{11}" of Table 1 we get τ^2

values, as recorded, which for mental traits are very different from Holzinger's t^2 values. The τ^2 values may be in considerable error due to faulty values of reliability coefficients. Any who have carefully studied the Stanford-Binet and the various Stanford Achievement tests will know that the reliabilities estimated cannot be serious underestimations. We also have the interesting ratio a^2, defined and given by [13],

$$a^2 = \frac{\text{variance of difference between fraternals caused by nature}}{\text{total true variance of difference between fraternals}} = \frac{{}_ir - {}_fr}{r_{11} - {}_fr} \quad [13]$$

The nurture factor is, of course, $1 - a^2$.

TABLE I

CORRELATIONS BETWEEN TWINS (CORRECTED FOR AGE) AND VALUES OF t^2 FROM HOLZINGER, AND RELIABILITY COEFFICIENTS (ESTIMATED) AND VALUES OF τ^2 AND a^2 BY KELLEY

Variable	Correlation Identical	Correlation Fraternal	r_{11}	t^2	τ^2	a^2
Standing height	.93	.65	1.00	4.0	4.0	.80
Weight	.92	.63	1.00	3.6	3.6	.78
Head length	.91	.58	1.00	3.7	3.7	.79
Head breadth*	.89	.55	1.00	3.1	3.1	.76
Cephalic index*	.90	.58	1.00	3.2	3.2	.76
Total finger ridges	.97	.46	1.00	17.0	17.0	.94
Binet $M.A.$	.86	.60	.9	1.9	6.5	.87
Binet $I.Q.$	.88	.63	.9	2.0	12.5	.93
Word meaning	.86	.56	.9	2.1	7.5	.88
Arithmetic	.73	.69	.7	.2	imag.	imag.
Nature study	.77	.65	.8	.5	4.0	.80
History and literature	.82	.67	.85	.8	5.0	.83
Spelling	.87	.73	.85	1.1	imag.	imag.
Educational age	.89	.70	.95	1.7	3.2	.76

*Correlation and t^2 values given by Freeman at A. A. A. S., 1929, meeting.

An examination of Table 1 enables some interesting comparisons. That variance in standing height is, under prevailing conditions, but .80 due to nature, and cephalic index but .76 is, to say the least, surprising. These, coupled with the high value for number of finger ridges, cannot but cast doubt upon (a) the assumption of a sharp dichotomy in the types of twins, or (b) the means employed in making the selection of the types, or (c) both. According to the calculation, two of the τ^2 values are negative, that is, they have no real meaning. If the reliability coefficients should in truth be slightly larger than estimated, these τ^2 values would become real but large, and the corresponding a^2 values would be slightly less than 1.00 and not at all of the order yielded by the raw data. For example, for arithmetic, using Holzinger's value of t^2, which is .2, the corresponding value for a^2 is .13, while the correct value reached by allowing for the unreliability of the test must be in the neighborhood of 1.00. The value .13, though perhaps in harmony with a view which attributed practically all of arithmetic ability to nurture is not warranted by the data, for the test is known to have a reliability much less than one. If we allow for unreliability and obtain a value of, say, .98, it is hardly consistent with ordinary experience, which would indicate that arithmetic is one of the most "taught" subjects within the experience of the child, and therefore, relative to, say, a Stanford-Binet or educational age, is more a matter of nurture. The t^2 technique is indefensible upon logical grounds, and the τ^2 (or a^2) technique gives results which are unreasonable, judged by common experience. We seem, therefore, forced to the conviction that the basic assumption of a sharp dichotomy of the mental similarity of the two groups of twins as selected is unwarranted.

Dr. Freeman has studied three pairs of twins classified as identical, the members of the pairs having been reared apart since infancy. Of these fascinating subjects two pairs showed very similar intelligence quotients and the third pair indubitably different quotients. One such pair, if the classification can be trusted, is sufficient to nullify a belief in the all-sufficiency of nature.

It must be apparent to one examining such detailed studies of heredity and environment in the human species as those of Burks (2, pp. 319-321) Holzinger, Freeman, and others that a statement of the relative importance of nature and nurture in the abstract is impossible, when dealing with mental traits, for, on the one hand, the more varied the environments under which children grow up the greater relatively is the importance of environment and, on the other hand, the more varied the genetic structure of parents the more important relatively is heredity. Notwithstanding the important study of May and Hartshorne (10) indicating that the evidence for the heritability of "deceit" is equally strong as that for "intelligence," we must anticipate in harmony with the varying results in Holzinger's data that further study will show that environment does ordinarily affect certain traits, relative to inheritance, more than others. Furthermore a general statement as to the relative importance of these two factors can hardly be equally sound as descriptive of children at different ages. Table 2 may fairly represent the situation and if so it largely reconciles the seeming differences in the findings of Burks, Holzinger, Freeman, and others.

TABLE 2 (*hypothetical*)

HEREDITARY AND ENVIRONMENTAL CONTRIBUTIONS TO THE VARIANCE IN INTELLIGENCE OF A HOMOGENOUS GROUP COMPOSED OF WHITE CHILDREN ATTENDING THE PUBLIC SCHOOLS OF AMERICA

Age	Variance due to differences in environment		Variance due to differences in heredity		Total variance
	Gross	Percentage	Gross	Percentage	
0	.00	0	1.00	100	1.00
4	.10	9	1.00	91	1.10
8	.20	17	1.00	83	1.20
12	.50	33	1.00	67	1.50
16	.80	44	1.00	56	1.80
Middle age	1.00	50	1.00	50	2.00

If it is persistently kept in mind that it is not environment, but only differences in environment that are significant, it is not unreasonable to think that the stimulus of dull parents to make a child say "mamma," "papa," "hunguy," "go-go," is quite on a par with that of bright parents content with the same words and the same ideas. To do these simple things at an early age constitutes intelligence as measured by our tests. If one runs over the exercises of the Stanford-Binet, he can quite easily classify the abilities called for into three classes: (a) those equally demanded by "poor" or "good" environments [sample: *Tie a shoestring into a bowknot as per sample shown*]; (b) those ordinarily demanded by neither [sample: *Counting backwards*]; and (c) those more likely to be called for by good environments than by poor [sample: *What's the thing for you to do if a playmate hits you without meaning to do it?*]. The (c) type are found late in the scale. Below average parents are fully possessed of (a) type abilities and may, due to the lack of (c) type thoughts, actually constitute a more potent stimulus for these abilities than superior parents. The figures of Table 2 seem to the writer reasonable from a priori considerations. They are in harmony with a principle early made use of by Thorndike (14) that the longer nurture acts the greater its effects, which principle has been used by the present writer (7) with seemingly very reasonable results.

Let us see if they are in harmony with the findings of Burks, Freeman, and others, Holzinger, Thorndike, and Willoughby. For a group of average age 8.2, Burks concludes that "home environment contributes about 17 per cent of the variance in I.Q." Table 2 has 17 recorded for total environment at age 8. There is no great discrepancy here. For a group of average age about 11.0, Freeman and others find an environmental contribution which, if expressed in terms of variance (which the writer is unable to do with any satisfactory precision) might amount to 50 per cent. The table records 33. The "home" group of Freeman and others is presumably exceptionally heterogeneous in nurture for 8 1/2 per cent were negroes, and the average Taussig scale difference between real fathers and foster fathers is very large, being approximately two points. The Taussig scale is as follows: 1, *professional;* 2, *semi-professional and business;* 3, *skilled labor;* 4, *semi-skilled;* 5, *labor.* With so large an environmental difference there is obviously more than usual opportunity for environment to show its effect. Also, as suggested by Dr. Burks, there may have been a tendency for the brighter parents to select brighter foster children. All things considered, there is no clear discrepancy between the findings of Freeman and others and the estimate of Table 2.

Dr. Willoughby's subjects averaged about 13.0 years of age, so his figure, 46, is somewhat higher than would be found for this age in Table 2.

Dr. Holzinger's data upon twins of mean age 13.4 would indicate, if the classification into types could be trusted, a very small nurture variance, in fact one smaller for mental traits than for physical traits. The apparently small importance of nurture is out of harmony with Freeman and Holzinger's earlier findings in the case of foster children and is not in harmony with the figures of Table 2.

Dr. Thorndike's subjects averaged about 16 years of age, and the figure which I have estimated from his data, 44, agrees with that of Table 2. Table 2 is merely a deduction from such data as here discussed, but that the results of such widely different investigations so nearly fit into a single scheme suggests that the picture is a somewhat reasonable approximation to the truth.

In conclusion I would enumerate the important steps called for, as I see them, in the study of mental inheritance: first, a determination of psychologically independent mental traits; secondly, a recasting of the picture of nature and nurture in such terms that they are not looked upon as being independently additive in producing a final outcome; thirdly, a definition of the problem in terms of somatic phenomena and so broadly as to permit concomitant variations in heredity, environment, and maturity; fourthly, a study of long-time development split up into short intervals, each yielding its own important contribution; fifthly, a definition of mental elements and the facts of their relationship in their own terms not ignorant of, but independent of, the elements and mechanisms of the student of primitive forms of life. Finally, out of this should come a serious endeavor to alter present and future generations in harmony with social advance and genetic progress.

REFERENCES

1. BABCOCK, E. B., & CLAUSEN, R. E. Genetics in relation to agriculture. (2nd ed.) New York: McGraw, Hill, 1927. Pp. 673.

2. BURKS, B. S. Comments on the Chicago and Stanford studies of foster children. 27th Yrbk. Nat. Soc. Stud. Educ., Part I, 1928, 317-321.

3. CREW, F. A. E. Organic inheritance in' man. Edinburgh: Oliver & Boyd, 1927. Pp. 242.

4. FISHER, R. A. The correlation between relatives on the supposition of Mendelian inheritance. Trans. Roy. Soc. Edinburgh, 1918, 52, 399-446.

5. FREEMAN, F. N., HOLZINGER, K. J., & MITCHELL, B. C. The influence of environment on the intelligence, school achievement, and conduct of foster children. 27th Yrbk. Nat. Soc. Stud. Educ., Part I, 1928, 103-217.

6. HOLZINGER, K. J. The relative effect of nature and nurture influence on twin differences. J. Educ. Psychol., 1929, 20, 241-248.

7. KELLEY, T. L. The influence of nurture upon native differences. New York: Macmillan, 1926. Pp. vii+49.

8. ——————. Interpretation of educational measurements. Yonkers, N. Y.: World Book Co., 1927. Pp. xiii+363.

9. ——————. Crossroads in the mind of man: a study of differentiable mental abilities. Stanford University: Stanford Univ. Press, 1928. Pp. vii+238.

10. MAY, M. A., & HARTSHORNE, H. Sibling resemblance in deception. 27th Yrbk. Nat. Soc. Stud. Educ., Part II, 1928, 161-178.

11. MORGAN, T. H., STURTEVANT, A. H., MULLER, H. J., & BRIDGES, C. B. The mechanism of Mendelian heredity. New York: Holt, 1915. Pp. xiii+262. (Rev. Ed., 1922.)

12. SALEEBY, C. W. Progress of eugenics. (Foreword by H. Bergson.) London: Cassell, 1914. Pp. 259.

13. SPEARMAN, C. The abilities of man: their nature and measurement. London, New York: Macmillan, 1927. Pp. xxiii+415.

14. THORNDIKE, E. L. Measurements of twins. *J. Phil., Psychol., & Sci. Meth.,* 1905, **2**, 547-553.

15. ——————. Educational psychology. Vol. I: The original nature of man. New York: Teach. Coll., 1913. Pp. xi+277.

16. ——————. Eugenics: with special reference to intellect and character. In Eugenics: twelve university lectures. (Foreword by L. F. Barker.) New York: Dodd, Mead, 1914. Pp. 319-442.

17. ——————. The resemblance of siblings in intelligence. *27th Yrbk. Nat. Soc. Stud. Educ.,* Part I, 1928, 41-53.

18. WILLOUGHBY, R. R. Family similarities in mental-test abilities. *27th Yrbk. Nat. Soc. Stud. Educ.,* Part I, 1928, 55-59.

CHAPTER 24

NORMALITY

C. SPEARMAN

University of London

I. NATURE OF NORMS

Few words are more common in psychology than "norms," "normal," and especially "abnormal." But not often are they submitted to the scrutiny they deserve. For in them, or in other words more or less synonymous, would appear to lie the key to many a psychological problem.

Consulting our good friend the dictionary, we find that a "norm" is "a rule or an authoritative standard." Quite accordingly, the "normal" is said to be that which "conforms to the standard or rule claimed to prevail in nature"; whilst the "abnormal" is that which "deviates from the natural structure, conditions, or course."

But after all *what* is the "natural structure, conditions, or course"? And who set up an authoritative standard? What nature of standard? And by what authority?

II. ABNORMALITY AND ANOMALY

Such questions are not a little alarming. We seem in danger of slipping overboard into the unfathomable seas of epistemology and metaphysics. For does not *everything* that occurs belong to the natural structure, conditions, or course? Does not the essential mission of science consist in showing that nature *always* conforms to rules? But in that case any deviation from structure or any non-conformity to rule is impossible. The abnormal does not exist. There can at most be some illusion of it.

Still even in such an illusion, in the seeming abnormality—or, as it has been more usually called, "anomaly"—there appears to lie one of the most dangerous pitfalls for experimental psychologists. These are apt to approach their researches with views already formed and fixed as to what the structure and rules of nature really are, with the result that all observations which deviate from such expectancies are consciously or subconsciously dismissed as erroneous.

There is another danger which is similar but more subtle. Here the investigator does maintain a more or less open mind as to what shall be the experimental result of his work, but he still has a strong bias in favor of getting *some* result. Whatever seems to interfere with this consummation is apt to be welcomed coldly. At best it is statistically "smoothed" away. This is indeed a ground upon which to tread delicately. To smoothing must be thanked a large proportion of the greatest results in science. Even an average—or, for that matter, a correlation coefficient

—is at bottom only an instance of it. And yet, on the other hand, what grievous sins may not be laid at its door! One warning at least may be ventured. In his seemingly anomalous results the scientist is sometimes entertaining an angel unawares. The deviation he finds from the normal course of the world which he knows may really be the peeping-out of another and unknown world from behind it. And so the researcher who keeps loyal to truth may come into great good fortune. In astronomy, the failure of the observations of Uranus to comply exactly with the known "structure of nature" led to enriching this nature by the discovery of Neptune. Still more wonderful results followed from noting that the observations of the bending of light failed to follow exactly the rules laid down by the authority of Newton.

For the other side of the picture, where the anomaly was indeed noticed but only to be dismissed as troublesome, we may look to psychology and Hume. He wrote that if any person had become acquainted with all shades of blue from the darkest to the lightest with the exception of one particular shade, then he would undeniably be able to imagine this shade also. But since such a result conspicuously failed to agree with the structure of nature as depicted in his doctrine of associationism, he lightly turned away, with the remark that: "The instance is so particular and singular, that 'tis scarce worth our observing." In truth this form of mental process, far from being "particular and singular" is now known to pervade the whole universe of cognition; it is one of the three fundamental processes of "noegenesis" (1, 2,). By so dismissing what seemed to be an anomaly, he unwittingly stayed the march of psychology for nearly two hundred years.

III. The Unusual as Abnormal

Although the preceding kind of "norm" would appear to be that which most simply and directly corresponds both with the historical derivation of the word and with its present definition, yet it is by no means the most common in actual linguistic practice. Much more frequently the norm at issue does not consist in any definite "rule" claimed to prevail in nature, but rather in that vaguely indicated complex of events that we look on as the "usual run of things."

An outstanding instance is that of abnormalities in the structure of the human body. Thus a perennial interest is taken in dwarfs; we marvel at Philetus of Cos, who was so small that he kept weights in his pockets to keep himself from being blown away. But no less of our curious attention is devoted to giants, from old Og, the king of Bashan, to the modern Chinaman, Chang. So, too, pennies are readily forthcoming at a fair to peep at a Seurat, the "living skeleton"; or at a Daniel Lambert, who weighs some seven hundred pounds; or at a Trovilloo, who has a large horn growing out of his forehead. As high show-prices could have been demanded, no doubt, by men "whose heads do grow beneath their shoulders."

On the mental side, however, the course of nature—or the imagination of the chroniclers—has been less prolific of such wide departures from what is usual. A large proportion of them has consisted only in appetite for unusual foods and drinks, as for pebbles (Battalia), live coals (Richardson), knives (Cummings), and even corrosive sublimate (Soliman)—or, on the contrary, in unusual abstinence, as the case of Miss Fleiger, who is said to have lived entirely on the smell of flowers. Another large section of cases have concerned the spending of money; most often, there was an unusual aversion to so doing, as with Elwes and Dancer; or even the reverse, as with the painter Morland. More cases than enough have been recorded of unusual cruelty, such as that which the notorious Mrs. Brownrigg meted out to her luckless apprentices. And sometimes a person is so abnormal as to do brutal deeds upon himself; we hear of self-castration, and even of self-crucifixion (Lovat).

An interesting point about these abnormalities of the body or of conduct is the attitude with which they are received by society. This has almost always been one of dislike and contempt (though not to the extent of preventing Buchinger, a dwarf without hands, feet, legs, or thighs, from wooing and winning four wives!). And such hostility to the abnormal person has been nearly independent of his or her real merits. Indeed, if a man did only such a harmless thing as put his legs into his coat sleeves and his arms into his trousers, he would be lucky if he got home without being seriously molested.

Nor is the reason far to seek. The "usual" is closely allied to the *moral*. Originally, the latter word simply meant what is usual. The fact is that most of the disturbances between men terminate in these settling down to some tolerable way of living together. The subsequent maintenance of such behavior is at bottom the observance of a treaty (none the less so for being tacit). By accumulation and concatenation of such peace-preserving use and wont, society becomes very sensitive to anything novel. No one can predict how far the disturbances may eventually spread; the fall of one of a set of ninepins may entail that of all the rest; a single person taking his bath before his habitual hour may upset the day's work of the whole household.

IV. THE EXTREME AS ABNORMAL

Closely akin to, but nevertheless distinguishable from, the preceding case of unusualness is that of extremeness. The great distinction consists in that the latter character is solely quantitative, whereas the former one implies something qualitative also. In consequence, only the unusual cases, not the merely extreme ones, form a definite group with its own peculiar origin and its own special requirements.

Take, for instance, the children in a school who have the lowest "intelligence quotients." If these children are regarded as constituting an unusual group, they are straightway taken to have something amiss with them; they are branded with the name of mentally defectives; they belong to the undesirables; they ought—by better breeding or otherwise—to have been debarred from ever coming into existence; or, in a more optimistic mood, they ought at least to have their endocrine glands examined. All this is quite otherwise if our children are simply regarded as occupying the extreme position at the bottom of the school. From such a viewpoint there is no cause for worry. *Some* of the children *must* be at the bottom. Little grounds are apparent for special breeding, and none for medical treatment. Indeed, one would be at a loss to know where to begin, as there is no manifest limit. We might take the bottom 1% or the 10% or the 25%, and so on quite arbitrarily.

All that we have been saying about the children of very low standing might be repeated about those who stand very high. If these represent only extreme cases, there is not much more to say about them. But if they constitute an unusual group, we break out into panegyrics on their "genius," or, reversely, we misdoubt that—by way of compensation—they must somehow be more or less unsound.

V. THE MYSTERIOUS AS ABNORMAL

Common as may be, in ordinary literature, however, the application of the term "abnormal" to the unusual and even to the merely extreme, something more is needed for a person or event to be admitted into that section of psychology which is expressly designated as abnormal. Especially helpful for gaining entry would appear to be some degree of mysteriousness.

On this ground, probably, it is that every treatise on abnormal psychology brings within its purview the topic of *dreams*. For these are certainly nothing unusual. Nor do they well come under any category of extremeness. And we have not even any good ground for referring back to our first section, where the abnormal meant that which escapes from the reign of law. For whether we agree with the ancients who believed that dreams foretell the future, or with the moderns who hold that they mirror the past; whether we attribute them in greater degree to sensory stimuli coming from without or to thoughts arising within; whether we with Freud ascribe them to the urgings of sex, or with Adler to the desire of power, or with Janet to fear, or with Stekel to hate, or with many of the ancients to blind mechanism; by all accredited theories alike, the course of dreaming is really no less subject to law than that of waking. Indeed, perhaps even more so; if, as many believe, the dreaming life is alone exempt from the influence of that sole lawbreaker, "free will."

But of mysteries, of bafflings to search after knowledge, on the other hand, dreams are full to overflowing. For it is they that constitute the great rock upon which has foundered the very science of knowledge; on them has broken up the seeming bulwark of certitude, which consists in the evidence of our own senses. Vaingloriously the "plain man" declares that he will only "believe what he sees." And to no purpose does the more cautious materialist pin his faith rather to that which he can touch. Such confidence, already shaken by occasional illusions and hallucinations, is quite destroyed by the regular visitation of dreams, wherein we see, touch, and have all the other sensory perceptions of both things and persons, and yet are irresistibly convinced by subsequent experience that these very things and persons were at the time elsewhere. That which we perceive in ordinary life may or may not be really existent; but at any rate the bare fact of perceiving them with our senses can no longer be taken as sufficient proof. If not really, at least perceptually, "we are such stuff as dreams are made on."

In even heightened measure, perhaps, the same may be said of hypnosis, trances, somnambulism, and so forth. These, too, never fail to gain a place in any account of abnormal psychology. And for them also, the right of entry would seem to be largely due to their mysteriousness. Once more we see and touch what really does not exist. And these experiences are all the more wonderful because of their rarity, their strange origin, the ethical and social disturbances to which they may give rise, and above all, perhaps, the extraordinary mental powers with which their subjects are apt to be credited, powers that can overjump space and time.

Penetrating deeper into this region of the mysterious-abnormal, we arrive at the frankly "occult" or, as it has been more pompously entitled, "parapsychology." Not yet for most critics beyond the bounds of scientific credibility is the phenomenon of thought-reading with the aid of bodily contact. Darker, but yet found believable by many, lies "telepathic" communication. For those of still stronger faith, there is the sphere of "telekinesis," wherein material objects can be moved without material means, a well-known instance being "levitation." And even sturdier believing powers are needed for acceptance of "materialization," which consists in material objects being actually created by mental means. Beyond this again lies finally the limitless domain of sheer superstition, magic, witchcraft, demonology, and the rest of it.

VI. THE SEXUAL AS ABNORMAL

Not so easy to account for is the fact that a place in abnormal psychology is often assigned to sexual life. What is there mysterious about *this?* Surely, we need not be surprised that the male and female should experience—on occasion, at any rate—an ardent desire to consummate those bodily acts by which fertilization is brought about; or even that in the consummation they should find an intense pleasure. These are but very natural and suitable incentives to do what is indispensable for the survival of the race. And as much can even be said of the fact that this instinct to bodily fertilization may be accompanied by the emotion of "love"—a spiritual going-out of each mate to the other—which not only protects both partners to the transaction, but at the same time confers alike on giver and taker what is probably the greatest bliss in human experience.

Nor can the giving of the name abnormal to sexual life be explained on the ground of these often lending themselves to disturbances, deformities, and even monstrosities. For this would refer to it only in its aberrations, not in its healthy course.

More to the point perhaps is the interesting inclination that exists to "draw a veil" over sex life though at its healthiest; a tendency, however, which displays large variations, even in civilized Europe—for instance, from the rigor of the early Victorian middle classes to the license of the modern bank-holiday excursionists. One might even speak of a supernormal and subnormal pudicity. But to settle where and why such boundaries should be laid down belongs rather to the "normative disciplines" (see Section XV).

VII. The Pathological as Abnormal

The preceding topic has led us to the confines of another one which also plays a part, and perhaps the largest of all, in the psychological literature of the abnormal; we arrive at mental *pathology*. So closely have been linked these two concepts, of the abnormal and the pathological, that often they are taken as synonymous.

What, then, constitutes a "pathological" state of mind? By what criterion is it to be adjudged as such? Here is a question which has not only been answered in widely different manners, but also has involved points of great personal and even social importance.

Certainly, at any rate, no reliable criterion can be derived from the state of the brain. For a large proportion of admittedly insane persons have shown no perceptible brain lesion. Conversely, many have been found to suffer from injury to the brain without appreciable insanity.

Compelled, then, to place our criterion in the mental processes themselves, shall we say that insanity consists in a general deficiency of reasoning power? Assuredly, no such statement will be made by anyone who has had even a passing acquaintance with, say, a typical paranoiac. Nor can anyone, instead, take insanity to lie in defective reasoning about some particular subject. For on this showing, it is hard to see who would be left to count as sane. Shall we, then, go beyond defects of reasoning and say that the insane are those whose mental processes are weak all around? Many cases are fitted this way well enough; all their mental activities do become slower and less intense; they may even fall into a stupor lasting for years. At least as often, however, insane persons seem to display not less but rather more intense activities than sane ones, more continuous and lively movements, more elaborate phantasies, more frequent and violent emotions, more powerful instinctive urges, especially the two primary ones of egoism and sex.

Naturally enough, then, this "norm" by which to judge insanity is nowadays at any rate not taken to be established by any absolute characters, but by relative ones; the insane person is not to be known by the degree, nor even by the quality of his mental activities in themselves, but rather by their failing to adapt themselves to his biological situations. Here is ground enough for condemning his illusions and obsessions, irrelevant or incoherent discourses, defects of memory, needlessly distressing emotions, unmotivated acts of violence both on other people and often on himself. But even such a biological norm as this seems not too easy to sustain throughout. For would it not depict as pathological all those who are inclined to endanger their own lives, and would not this bring into the ranks of the insane most of the military heroes throughout history! Or, if we took a broader view, calling those sane who do good, if not necessarily to themselves, at any rate to society as a whole, we might be hard pressed not to count as lunatics many eminent statesmen, and even theologians.

The problem is further complicated by the fact that for most practical purposes the crux does not lie in settling whether a person is mentally pathological or not; but whether he is *too much so to be tolerated*. And hereupon the scene is at once invaded by a terrible swarm of politico-ethical theorems; justice for all, liberty to the individual, the greatest good of the greatest number; and of such, many more. But at this point the psychologist diffidently cedes place to the majesty of law and the wisdom of philosophy.

VIII. The Criminal as Abnormal

The remaining chief topic for which a section is generally reserved in abnormal psychology is that which deals with criminals.

Here, evidently, is something closely akin to what we have just been considering. For, as before, the persons are those whose behavior has been found by others intolerable. But if so, then why should not these two classes, in common fairness, be treated similarly?

And this indeed raises one of the greatest questions of the day. How are criminals to be treated? Many enthusiastic criminologists urge that they ought no longer to be looked on as wicked, but only as mentally ill. And this viewpoint, it is claimed, should abolish all punishment. Instead of this barbarous custom of former ages, this gratifying of the savage lust for revenge, as the would-be reformers regard it, we ought to substitute the milder measures of mental medicine. One answer to such a claim would be to make a general comparison between the denizens of the jail and those of mental hospitals. For although no single formal definition may serve as a norm to distinguish them adequately, and although certain individual cases might equally well be assigned to either residence, yet on the whole the two classes stand out distinctly enough. If any man really could not tell which class he had got among, we might safely prophesy to which of them *he* was heading!

Nevertheless, even granting that the two classes are, on the whole, distinguishable, this fact by itself is no certain proof that criminals ought to be punished. There still remains the much pleaded argument that punishment does not make them any better. But surely no one ever thought it did! The aim of punishment from time immemorial has been rather to *deter others*.

From this standpoint there appears to derive rather a new norm for deciding whether criminals should be treated as such or not. Punishment becomes useless in those cases which are too unlike the ordinary run of events to act as a precedent for these. For instance, if a man were to be pardoned after committing a murder during a fit of epilepsy, this exoneration, under such exceptional conditions, would not do much to encourage other persons to murder in ordinary circumstances. But if, on the other hand, a murderer were to be let off on the ground that his parents had not in his childhood analyzed out his complexes, such a judgment might hearten would-be murderers in considerable number.

IX. CENTRAL NORMS

In all the preceding sections the stress has been laid on "abnormality." Such "norms" as do find mention have little interest save as means to delimit the abnormal. And even this task they have performed in a singularly ineffective manner. They have almost always been very indefinite, and often they have been quite arbitrary. But now we come to the conditions where almost all this is reversed. The "norm" itself is of primary importance, whilst the term "abnormal" slides into desuetude. Further, the norm does not, in general, consist in a limiting value, but in a central one. And it is in itself, usually at any rate, perfectly definite.

Such a central value admits of being found for any group of cases— any "population," as it has been called technically—in respect to any character that has degrees, either quantitative or even qualitative. If the characters can supply a unit—as is done by time, space, and frequency— the usual central value is the arithmetical average. Thus, there might be established the average reaction-time of the children in some school-class—or again, the average error of localization made by a single person; here, the "cases" constituting the "population" are not individual people, but individual acts of localizing. Examples of frequency furnishing units are given by the average "span" of a person for counting dots seen tachistoscopically, or the average number of repetitions required for memorizing a series of nonsense syllables. When the character measured presents only quantity and no unit—as might happen, for instance, in estimations of selfishness—then the average value of the character cannot possibly be calculated. But this can be replaced by its median value, that is to say, by the character of the central case. In the preceding example, the children could be ranked in order of selfishness and then the central or "median" child could be taken as the standard of normality. A further device serving the same purpose is to pick out that degree of the character which is possessed by the largest number of cases. Such a degree—sometimes called the "mode" of the frequency distribution—generally approximates the aforesaid central values. But not necessarily so; it can, upon occasion, be one of the extreme values. For instance, if a mental test is excessively difficult, the score made by the largest number of testees may have the extreme value of zero.

Having somehow or other got your central value (or mode), what can you do with it? Here lies the rub! Usually, this single value is made to stand as representative of the whole population. Can it really perform this function? For some purposes, it certainly can; but the trouble is that many psychologists take it to serve other, and indeed all, purposes. For them the idea of the whole population is simply replaced by that of some single central value. As an example may be quoted a document recently circularized to several people asking for their opinion as to whether the negro is or is not inferior to the white man. And behind this circular lay evidently the gravest interests at stake; nothing less, it would seem, than the whole political future of such countries as the United States and South Africa. Now to begin with, we may well be shocked at the equivocality of the term "inferior." Inferior in *what?* Intelligence? Memory? Morality? Self-control? Waiving this point, however, as foreign to our present topic, what are *"the* negro" and *"the* white man"* really intended to mean? The most natural way of interpreting them seems to be as men of average excellence in the negro and the white populations, respectively. But then the question only ceases to be obscure by becoming pointless. For, as every statistician knows, *all* populations—if measured finely enough—have different averages.

Possibly, indeed, the circular might be interpreted in quite another way; it might be taken to inquire whether *every* negro is inferior to *every* white man. But to ask this would be stranger still. Such a case of total superiority of one large population over another one is hardly to be found anywhere; in the present racial question, to think of it would be absurd.

Here as often elsewhere, then, the central value of a character is quite insufficient for the purposes of science. Although it is undeniably the most important of all single norms to be derived from a population, it frequently stands in urgent need of further and subsidiary ones.

X. LATERAL NORMS

In order to supplement the central value of a population, it is natural to seek out other values which lie to either side. And the general plan is remarkably simple. Having found the central value which divides the whole population into two halves, we apply the same procedure to each half by itself; for each half we calculate the average (or the median).

But the chief interest of this value lies not so much in itself as in its difference from the average of the whole population. Such a difference affords a measure of what is called the "dispersion" or "scatter" of the whole. To serve this purpose, however, a less obvious way is commonly adopted. First, the distance is noted between the average value for the whole population and the value for each single case in it; then each of these distances is squared, and all the squares are added together; finally, the total is divided by the number of cases. The result of all this is entitled the "variance" and written as σ^2. The root of this, or $\pm\sigma$, is often called the "standard deviation."

The preceding norms—those of central position and of dispersion— carry us a long way in statistics. But they are far from being all that is possible or even—for some problems—indispensable. Instead of only three values, one in the center and one on either flank, there may be required a long series of them at regular intervals. Let us take as example the results obtained by Dr. Davey for some pictorial tests applied to boys and girls. The frequency was counted of all the scores amounting to 1 or 2, 3, or 4, 5 or 6, and so on, through the cases, but for each sex separately. All these frequencies represented side by side constitute for each sex a "frequency distribution." The actual results are given in Figure 1.

FIGURE 1

——————— Girls

‒ ‒ ‒ ‒ ‒ ‒ ‒ Boys

Now, two such sets of norms as *these* really would supply at any rate a preliminary basis on which to institute a scientific comparison between the negro and the white man.

XI. SAMPLES AND PROBABLE ERRORS AS NORMS

But this brings us up to the fateful theme of "sampling." Every actual investigation is necessarily limited to some definite number of cases; these may amount to, say, twenty, or a hundred, or, in rare instances, a thousand. In our example there were 99 boys and 106 girls. But for most scientific purposes we are obliged to generalize; the results gained, if they are to be of any real service, must be taken to hold for cases existing in other places and at other times. We are, therefore, reduced to the device of regarding the cases which we do examine as constituting a representative sample of the whole population which we have in view ultimately. Though measured only in a sample of cases, the norms are taken to hold for the whole population.

Now, for this transference to be valid, the cases in the sample must at least satisfy two conditions: they must be selected sufficiently at random, and they must be sufficiently numerous. Much the harder of these two conditions is the first. For almost always the cases to which the investigator has access present some character peculiar to themselves, and to this extent are by no means representative of the whole population. Thus, in our preceding example, it would be folly to take the norms as being those for boys and girls of any kind. It would be rash even to assume that the cases of boys and those of girls are really comparable with one another.

Severe enough, however, is even the second condition, namely, that the cases should be sufficiently numerous. And almost worse than simply braving this danger is the not uncommon device of, ostrich-like, shutting one's eyes to it. Thus many psychologists, when trying to show that some two variables are intercorrelated, refrain from actually calculating the correlation and its probable error on the ground that the number of cases is too small; they trust instead to their general impression. In truth, such limiting one's self to a general impression does not remove the danger, but only excludes it out of one's view. The correlation and the probable error would not create, but only reveal, the inadequacy of the number of cases.

This "probable error" is itself a norm which may produce the gravest fallacies, even in the hands of some of the leading psychological statisticians. Suppose, for example, x to be any value that is actually observed whilst x' is the value to be expected from some theoretically conceived situation. And suppose further that the probable error of x is just about equal to the difference between x and x'. What can we conclude as to whether the theory holds good or not? The said statisticians pronounce the chances for and against the theory to be about equal.

Now, in truth, the probable error is that value which an observation has equal chances of attaining or not attaining *when the theory does hold good*. This fact teaches us next to nothing as to the chances of the theory *not* holding good.

The whole affair is as if a bag contained originally 50 white balls and 50 black, to which were then added an unknown number of other balls that might be either black or white. Suppose we now draw a white ball. Is it not absurd to claim knowledge that the chances are even as to whether this ball belonged to the original ones or to those added afterwards? Obviously, all depends on how many balls were added and what was the proportion of white to black in these.

But suppose, next, that the discrepancy of x and x' was not equal to, but three times as large as, the probable error. Such a value, statistics teaches us, would be attained only about once in a hundred times when the theory holds. We can then reflect that an event which occurs in so small a proportion of times is unlikely to occur just when we happened to make our observation; the coincidence would be at least strange. We conclude that the evidence is very adverse to the theory. From this example it is easy to infer that a single observation can rarely, if ever, prove a theoretical situation to exist, though it may easily bring strong evidence *against* its existence. Theory achieves most of its triumphs, not so much by direct proof, as rather by continued default of disproof.

But so far we have considered only the occurrence of a single observation at a time. Suppose that instead, as often happens, the observations obtained at any time are very numerous. We may take a well-known experiment which supplied six thousand observed "tetrad differences." Shall we again say that, if the discrepancy of any of these from its theoretical value is three times as large as its probable error, the evidence

about the theory is very adverse? On the contrary, over sixty (6000÷
100) such discrepancies ought to be *expected* from the theoretical situation.
Indeed, a few discrepancies ought to be expected as much as five times
the probable error.

Matters may be much more complicated still. Instead of only one
specified theoretical situation, there may be several competing with each
other.

Seeing how difficult it really is to derive and employ norms, including
probable errors, with reasonable scientific certainty, one cannot but wonder
at the prevalent optimism on the matter. As, for instance, when the
behaviorist studies the emotional behavior of five or six babies, and from
the results thinks to establish norms of general human nature.

Far too often the investigator contents himself with the smallest and
therefore most inadequate sample possible, that is, one case only. Usually
himself! Among the most pernicious instances is the tendency of every
psychologist to take his own experience as a general norm in respect to
"images." That this should have befallen Titchener, for example, seems
to have been calamitous for this whole psychological generation. And
the following is a suggestive personal anecdote of an even greater man.
He had been expressing himself warmly to the present writer on this
very point; the tendency of psychologists to judge all persons by themselves. Not ten minutes later, he himself charged Zola and others with
talking about olfactory images; the most careful introspection, he said,
has shown him that the sense of smell does not supply "images" at all!

XII. Undefined and Shifting Norms

We have just been considering the difficulties introduced into the use
of norms owing to the need of replacing the "populations" really in view
by mere samples of these. But there are further troubles which afflict
populations and samples alike. One of these derives from what is called
the "heterogeneity" of the cases included. That is to say, the individuals
differ in respect to age, or sex, or social status, or racial origin. By reducing the number or degree of such variations, the problems become less
complicated, less subject to fallacies, and therefore more readily amenable to correct solution.

Often, however, the current attacks on heterogeneity go far beyond
this. They depict it as a sprite capable of any malignant trick, such as
conjuring up will-o'-the-wisp correlations where none really exists. Some
of these statisticians demand that heterogeneity should be eliminated altogether. But this is impossible; for, in last resort, *every* two or more
individuals are more or less heterogeneous to one another. Others content themselves with only denouncing heterogeneity of a few particular
kinds, but give no definite ground for picking out just these rather than
others. And their choice seems to the present writer often blind and
arbitrary. If any heterogeneities are to be specially discredited, the
objections to them should be explicitly stated. And then it will frequently
be found that the very same heterogeneity which is fatal for one purpose
may be harmless for another, and, of course, vice versa.

Another great trouble derives from the difficulty in providing the populations or samples with definite boundaries. Consider again our example of scores at pictorial tests. Obviously, it would be absurd to put forward these values as norms without any regard to what ages we had in view. For adults might have very different norms from children; and again, the older of these from the younger. But it might be worse than absurd—because more likely to mislead—if we were to take no heed of what social classes we intended to include; a norm correct enough for one class might be quite inapplicable to another.

We may note, too, that this last-mentioned evil of ill-defined boundaries will not be removed by the measures taken against the preceding evil of heterogeneity. Boundaries are not rendered sharper by being made to include a less extensive and varied area. The range of age from 12 to 13 years is no better delimited than that from 6 to 16. If instead of comprehending all the adults of a nation, the investigator limited himself, say, to the professional classes, the boundary line would become not more but less definite. And if he went on to restrict himself still further, as to the theatrical profession, he might become still worse off. This difficulty became very noticeable when the report of the testing of the American Army assigned to the theatrical profession the bottom place of all. One wonders whether it was made to include the supers and call-boys!

The danger of indefiniteness with its consequent equivocality is augmented by the fact that even if the population (as also any samples drawn from it) is well defined at any one time, it may be rendered indefinite by varying from one time to another. For example, the present writer, when endeavoring to find some population capable of supplying norms, thought about the totality of schools under the London County Council. This totality was not only as large as could be desired, but also in itself quite definite. But it could be utilized only by way of the results of the annual scholarships. And the standard of these, unfortunately, appeared to be far from stable.

In all such difficulty of procuring definite norms, there is one last resource. It consists in renouncing the attempt to get a population delimited on any rational system, and adopting instead one which has only an empirical and therefore more or less arbitrary basis, but which on the other hand possesses some exceptional importance. An outstanding example is the testing of the American Army. Here the results were not in the least indefinite; they were simple facts; but they were obtained on such a gigantic scale and under such interesting conditions, that they could claim universal notice. Something of the sort may be said of the Stanford-Binet scale, despite this having been derived from only about two thousand cases. For subsequently the application of this scale—thanks, no doubt, to Terman's wonderful skill in modifying the work of Binet—has spread over most of the civilized world.

XIII. Pseudo-Norms

So far, we have been considering the difficulties that beset the establishment of norms for a population of individuals in respect to a single character. Let us now go on to norms for a population of characters in respect to a single individual. The pre-eminent instance is the attempt to derive from all the different abilities of any individual some single norm indicating his "general level" of intelligence.

Now, an attempt of this kind encounters all the same difficulties as the other kind. In particular, there is still the need that the population of abilities should have definite limits. It is astounding to see how psychologists still go on complacently applying their tests of "general intelligence" without ever settling what this is intended to comprise; not even whether or not it is to include most of the chief classes of mental operation, such as memory, imagination, and sensory perception.

But this fault in their procedure, though not yet actually remedied, might conceivably be so; the limits of such "general intelligence" might possibly be laid down with tolerable definiteness by some international conclave, whereas another and new difficulty now arises which would appear to be essentially insuperable. Statistical "norms," as we have seen, can be derived only from some population of comparable single cases. Individual persons, reactions, repetitions, and so forth, do obviously supply these, each person, reaction, or repetition constituting a separate case. But abilities do *not* supply any such comparable cases. Thus some psychologists might take "judgment" to constitute one case of ability and "memory," ten; whilst others might reverse these numbers. Either procedure is just as arbitrary as the other.

Still, this impossibility of finding comparable single cases in ability as we actually observe it does not preclude us from *inventing* such cases and assuming them *hypothetically*. Thus there is nothing to stop us from assuming a single element in ability to be supplied by each cortical neuron. And then conceivably we might be able to demonstrate that such elements, did they exist, would produce results consistent with what we now actually observe. But at least the hypothetical nature of these elements should be openly admitted, and the demonstration should be explicitly formulated. In default of doing either of these things, the alleged "general level" of intelligence or ability is no real "norm" at all, but only a pseudo-norm.

XIV. Some Special Kinds of Norms

A few words may be appended on certain kinds of norms which are rather special in their nature, but nevertheless have considerable interest for psychology. One such is presented by a "limen" or "threshold." Thus, a person's limen for discriminating tones may be set at 3 d. v., although actually he may sometimes have discriminated rightly between tones differing by much less than this, and, conversely, he may often have responded wrongly when the difference was much greater. For theoretical purposes three distinct theoretical standpoints have been adopted. One is to assume hypothetically that the person's discrimination power is all the time constant in itself, but is more or less affected by accidental disturbances. And these disturbances are then taken to be eliminated adequately by the operation of averaging. The second standpoint again leads to the procedure of averaging, but it discards the hypothesis; it contents itself with calculating the average value of the person's responses, and stops at that; it is behavioristic. The third standpoint is still less rigorous. It does not bother itself to obtain even the average value of the responses. Instead it takes as norm any more or less central value that convenience or caprice may suggest; such as, for instance, 70% right answers.

Another special kind of norm is that supplied by correlation coefficients. If the cases in any population vary in any two respects—say, persons vary in respect to two kinds of memory—then a large value for one of the variables may go with either a large or small one of the other. The coefficient measures the average tendency to congruence between the two. Students sometimes, on finding this coefficient small, urge that nevertheless some individuals are large in both (or small in both), so that for these individuals the correlation is high. Statistically, however, this viewpoint is improper. The congruence of the two variables for any individual is only coincidence, not correlation; the latter has no existence until the whole population is considered.

Another kind of "norm," and one that engenders far more confusion, is conveyed by the word "type." This plays a large part in current individual psychology. We hear a great deal of "sensory type," "memory type," "types of attention," and so forth, without end. Now, according to the dictionary, a type is some fundamental structure characterizing a whole group; as, for instance, the erect posture is typical of man. It is widely different from an average, which may not belong to any member of the group at all; thus, the average number of wives for a group of men would probably be a fraction of a wife. Psychologists, however, pay little heed to this strict meaning of the word "type." They employ it rather as a maid-of-all-work. Sometimes they take it to denote extreme cases, which serve as reference points for the remainder; thus, a person is said to be "typically" visual-minded, when vision with him completely dominates all the other senses. At other times it is used to denote each of the two peaks produced in a frequency distribution by mixing together two very unlike classes, say, the motor dexterity of boys and girls. Most often—and most misleadingly—it is, like "faculty," used to denote any individual difference, but with an assumption that this difference constitutes a unitary function; thus, a person is said to belong to the concentrative "type" of attention, assuming that a person who can concentrate on one sort of object can also concentrate on other sorts.

As a further instance of these special kinds of norms may be mentioned the well-known "normal frequency distribution." From the geometrical point of view, these are represented by the familiar bell-shaped figures.

As for their interpretation, this has been derived from at least four quite different assumptions. But perhaps the most significant of these is that whereby the observed values are taken to be sums of extremely numerous independent elements, each of these elements having a very small magnitude. The distribution of such values may be regarded as a "normal" one because here, humanly speaking, all explanation comes to an end; the elements, owing to their minute size, elude all investigation; we label them collectively as "chance." Conversely, the possibility of explaining arises for such influences as are not so minute, but instead are large enough to be individually appreciable; that is to say, explanation begins to be feasible where there are *deviations* from the normal distributions. Partly for this reason (however obscurely realized); and partly also because such distributions, although never occurring exactly, do very often with rough approximation; and partly, again, because this kind of distribution is peculiarly amenable to mathematical development; for such reasons, the great majority of statistical formulae were originally based on assuming this normal distribution, and in strictness are not valid for any other. Recently, however, this gap has to a large extent been filled up; many statistical formulae have been extended to a variety of frequency distributions, and even to complete generality. This last has been achieved, for instance—contrary to the statement of some statisticians who should know better—in the proof of the main formulae of the theory of "two factors."

To conclude this section, it may be mentioned that not infrequently the term "normal" has been applied in a broader sense than any of those indicated above. It has been taken to cover not only standards by which observations are oriented but also those by which they are judged. In this latter case, however, a more usual term is "criterion." Thus, in the theory of "two factors," the zero value of the tetrad differences is commonly called a criterion rather than a norm.

XV. Normative Disciplines

Before closing this sketch, an allusion may be made to certain branches of knowledge which, by their very essence, may lay down norms. There is logic, which lays down truth, as the norm for thinking. There is ethics, which expounds the good, as the norm for willing. And there is aesthetics, which indicates the beautiful, as a norm for the fine arts. Indeed such a normative character has often been taken to afford the boundary line between the philosophic and the natural sciences. The latter simply aim at describing phenomena. The former make rulings as to their worth.

Here in these normative sciences it is that norms and criteria become especially hard to separate from one another. But usually the latter may be distinguished by being more superficial. Thus a "criterion" of beauty is furnished by any principle that anyone may choose in order to appreciate the facts more effectively, whereas a "norm" of beauty controls the objective facts themselves, and thus supplies content to what has to be appreciated. However, here we must stop, on pain of transcending all bounds of psychology.

REFERENCES

1. SPEARMAN, C. The nature of "intelligence" and the principles of cognition. London, New York: Macmillan, 1923. Pp. viii+358.

2. ————. The abilities of man: their nature and measurement. London, New York: Macmillan, 1927. Pp. xxiii+415.

CHAPTER 25

MOTIVATIONAL PSYCHOLOGY

LEONARD T. TROLAND

Harvard University

I. STATEMENT OF THE PROBLEM

The term motivation has come into vogue to signify certain demonstrable or supposed processes which determine conscious action. Narrowly and popularly conceived, motivational psychology would be concerned primarily with "motives," but broadly and scientifically considered, it deals with all of the determinative functions and dynamics of mind (cf. 32). Problems in motivation start us upon a quest for "explanations" as to why individuals behave or desire in particular ways. Such explanations can scarcely be complete and satisfactory unless they deal not only with fundamental forces but also with the specific structure of the action personality which is involved. Thus, the study of motivation should lead to the formulation of a system which is nearly as broad as the whole field of psychology, although the details of this field will be viewed from a special standpoint.

Although modern psychology comprises many divergent schools of thought, the problems of motivation can be formulated in terms appropriate to each of them. The popular and legal conceptions of a motive are more harmonious with the standpoint of introspective psychology than they are with the points of view of behaviorism or of psychoanalysis. However, it appears, paradoxically, that the newer and more radical movements in psychology have concerned themselves more with motivational problems than have the traditional schools. Indeed, this fact constitutes one of the principal aspersions upon the latter. In the present discussion, I shall endeavor to formulate the motivational problem and some aspects of its solution in terms which are significant for each of the outstanding psychologies of the day.

For common-sense thought, the search for a motive involves seeking the causation of some act or aspect of behavior. It is in harmony with popular ways of thinking that this motive should be conceived as a mental or conscious, rather than as a physiological, entity. However, if we adopt a strictly behavioristic point of view, the motivational agencies must, of course, fall in the latter category. We must state the entire problem and its solution in "objective" terms. I have suggested (30, Chap. 3) that, on this plane of investigation, we define the problem of motivation as that of discovering the foundations of any given *response specificity*. By response specificity is meant the exact relationship which exists between a given stimulus and the motor reaction which it sets off. In terms first clearly presented by Holt (7, pp. 153-171), the reaction is a mathematical function of the stimulus or of the external situation. Motivational analysis from the behavioristic point of view must reveal the physiological mechanism and developmental origin of any given function of this sort. We are, therefore, led to a study of neuromuscular mechanics and their sources in heredity and in the influence of environment.

However, just as the behavioristic standpoint itself is blindly one-sided, so a purely objective study of motivation must fail to deal with all of the problems which are initially before us. Not only is it popularly supposed that motives are conscious, but problems in motivation can be formulated exclusively from the introspective angle, without any reference at all to behavior. Introspectively, we have to deal with the phenomena of desire, purpose, and emotion, together with other aspects of *affective* life, which are intrinsically more interesting than any of their so-called overt expressions. The motivational phenomena of consciousness, or of direct experience, comprise the life of desire or striving (16, Chaps. 9 and 11). Such appetitional processes may be either positive or negative, directed towards the attainment or the avoidance of certain so-called "ends." These "ends" are particular forms of consciousness, towards which the other phases of the experience move.

When we endeavor to give a systematic account or "explanation" of appetitional experiences, we ordinarily find difficulty in locating adequate causes for the observed effects. The experiences in question appear to be causally fragmentary. For this reason, among others, the *psychoanalytic* thinkers (21) have postulated the existence of a *subconscious* mental realm, within which are to be found the fundamental motivating forces. The Freudian theory of the libido (5) and of repressed complexes provides a very intriguing explanation for many normal as well as abnormal mental events. The extensions and modifications of the theory, introduced by other psychoanalysts—such as Jung (9, 10, 11) and Adler (1) (and we should probably include McDougall [18])—make possible the presentation of a rather complete motivational doctrine in terms of subconscious or unconscious agencies. In spite of their hypothetical character, views of this sort cannot properly be neglected in any systematic treatment of motivational problems.

Psychoanalytical explanations are, of course, not restricted to an exclusively mental subject-matter, but can be applied also to facts of behavior. However, in such applications, they involve a *motivational psychophysiology,* wherein bodily expressions are accounted for in terms of subjective forces. Neurologists customarily reverse this relationship, and explain the psychical phenomena on the basis of organic conditions. Such ways of thinking lead to the quest for a comprehensive psychophysiology of motivation, which will unite the objective data with those of introspection and of psychoanalytic theory, omitting none of the relevant and interesting ideas. In another publication (30), I have endeavored to develop such an explanation as this in considerable detail, and in the present article I shall confine myself primarily to an outline of the views which I have thus previously advocated.

I may say, in condonation of this plan, that I consider the merits of my system to consist almost exclusively in the manner in which it synthesizes the teachings of most of my contemporaries and predecessors in this field.

II. The Mechanism of Response

General Principles. Since the clearest formulation of the motivational problem can be made in terms of physiological concepts, it is most profitable to approach the question from the behavioristic point of view.[1] For the behaviorist, psychological facts consist primarily in a relationship between stimuli (or stimulus situations) and effector reactions. Given a certain set of circumstances, *S,* a definite set of movements or postures, *M,* supervenes. Each such association of *S*-factors with *M*-factors constitutes a specific response configuration. A man sees an enemy and flees; he meets a friend and says, "Hello." From a strictly behavioristic standpoint, the problem of motivation consists in systematizing and, perhaps, "explaining" such response specificities.

The thoroughness of explanation which is demanded will determine the nature of the required theorizing. A superficial analysis may involve little more than a classification of responses according to types. Thus, we may distinguish between simple reflexes, instincts, conditioned reflexes, voluntary action, and so forth. A more profound study, however, must lead to a consideration of the neuromuscular mechanism through which the stimulus situation controls the reaction. Since I feel that mere classification and the formulation of response properties from a strictly external point of view can hardly be regarded as explanation, I shall direct attention at the outset to the neuromuscular apparatus.

Regarded from a physical standpoint, excluding all reference to consciousness, response consists in a series of events, displaced successively in space and in time, but bound together to form a propagation of influence.[2] This series may be considered as beginning with an object, or a set of objects in the environment of the organism. The objects act, via the stimulus (some special form of energy or force, such as light), upon the sense-organ, where they excite definite receptor processes. The propagation continues, along afferent nerve channels, through numerous nerve-centers, into the efferent neural paths to find its way to the musculature. Here, various postures or movements are determined and adjust the relation of the organism to its surroundings. It is evident that, if we are to explain any given response specificity, we must present an intelligible account of the manner in which the response propagation operates in the given instance. This account must be expressed in strictly physiological or physical terms, without inclusion of psychical concepts.

Fortunately, the present status of nerve physiology is such as to permit a reasonably satisfactory formulation of the principles which must be involved in the response process (2, 6). The receptors, such as the rods and cones of the retina, offer sensitive surfaces which register the kind, inten-

---

[1] For a discussion of behaviorism, see (22).

[2] For a more detailed analysis of response along these lines, see (31, pp. 156-160).

sity, and space-time pattern of various environmental energies. These characteristics are represented intraneurally by variations in the forms of the nerve-currents which pass along the afferent conductors. The physical nature of the nerve-currents themselves, with their quantitative properties, is quite well understood. At the nerve-centers, where afferent and efferent conductors are brought into conjunction, specific afferent currents liberate equally definite but configurationally different efferent disturbances. The latter, in conjunction with the mechanical properties of the skeletomuscular apparatus, determine the character of the reaction. It is therefore evident that the determinants of response specificity must reside in the nerve-centers, since it is here that particular types of linkage between environmental influence and motor expression are established.

Neural Conductance. Now, although the neuromuscular mechanism has many peculiar properties of its own, its action follows the general principles which apply to any propagational device. In electrical conducting systems, the direction, the intensity, and even the quality of the process depends upon the *distribution of conductances*: the flow follows the line of "least resistance" or of greatest conductance. This line is determined, in the first instance, by the architecture of the conducting medium; in the nervous system, by the anatomical structure. Nerve-currents, like electrical ones, are confined to the material paths of the conducting units. There can be not the least doubt that many forms of response specificity rest mainly upon such anatomical foundations. The types of response which we call "reflex" are outstanding examples. However, even in the case of the simplest reflexes, something more may be involved than a mere conjunction of neurons. There must, at least, be a central mechanism of discharge which governs the pattern of the motor reaction.

The gross architecture of the neuromuscular system is laid down almost wholly by ontogenetic forces, so that the historical basis of reflex, and similar response specificities must be adjudged as hereditary. The more complex forms of response, however, appear to be determined in large measure by the special life-history of the individual. Hence, they require particular consideration of factors in addition to the crude anatomical juxtaposition of neural elements. Juxtaposition is, of course, an indispensable prerequisite in any case, but, in responses of an advanced type, it seems to play a general and not a specific determining rôle. The types of response which interest us the most in human life appear to be mediated by that vast conjunction field of afferent and efferent conductors which is known as the *cerebral cortex* (27). In this field, almost any receptor can be connected, in almost any way, with almost any effector. The gross anatomy of the cortex provides us with practically no basis upon which to predict the motor reaction from a knowledge of the stimulus. We are therefore compelled to consider the part that may be played by conductances which are represented in a manner more subtle than by anatomical structure. We must be prepared, moreover, to find that such conductances are determined by environmental forces rather than by hereditary factors.

Thinking along these lines, we note that, from the anatomical standpoint, there appear to be numerous alternative paths of conduction leading from any given afferent channel, through the cortex, to a wide variety of efferent channels. Each of these paths involves a distinctive group of *synapses,* or neural contact points. The path of conduction which is actually followed, in any given instance, must be that which presents the *highest synaptic conductance,* or the lowest synaptic resistance to the given disturbances.

Now, it is evident that a thoroughgoing doctrine of motivation, from the physiological standpoint, must deal with the conductional mechanisms of both cortical and subcortical responses and must explain how those conductance values which are not hereditary can be laid down by "experience." In other words, we must establish a comprehensive reflexology, combined with a theory of cortical learning.

Reflexes and Instincts. It would not be appropriate, in the present brief survey, to enumerate the various reflexes which operate in the human or other animal economies. These subcortical mechanisms are adequately considered in textbooks of physiology (e.g., 25), and their underlying principles have been handled in masterly fashion by such writers as Sherrington (24) and Fulton (6). Reflexes may be classified as circulatory, respiratory, alimentary, excretory, reproductive, and so on. They are characterized by a substantial independence of volition, and by uniformity throughout the members of a given species. However, we should not fail to realize that reflex processes are intimately associated with the more complex forms of response. Cortical and subcortical adjustments frequently occur in parallel, sometimes in alliance and sometimes in interference. The reflex activities which are aroused by sexual and by algesic stimulation sustain especially close relationships with cortically regulated activities. The pain reflexes include those functions of the sympathetic sector of the nervous system which have been so fruitfully studied by Cannon (3) and his collaborators. They mediate a set of bodily adjustments which prepare the organism for mortal combat.

Complex reflex reactions, like those which are associated with the sympathetic system, shade over into so-called *instincts* (28). Viewed out of relation to their conscious accompaniments, instincts partake of the nature of reflexes in that they appear to have hereditary foundations which are common to all members of a given species. However, in general, "instincts" are conceived to possess a greater modifiability than are reflexes, and seem to be capable of extensive elaboration through learning. Recent investigations have shown that the "instincts" of fear and rage are quite definitely reflex in character, in the sense that they have reliable subcortical mechanisms (3). From the physiological standpoint, fear is characterized by the sympathetic reactions which we have considered above, while rage adds to these a group of movements of the voluntary muscles, released through a definite hypothalamic nerve-center. The so-called sexual instinct seems also to be composed in large measure of a constellation of reproductive reflexes.

The concept of instinct has played a major rôle in modern discussions of motivation. A wide variety of opinions have been expressed concerning the existence and nature of instincts. Some writers, such as McDougall (17), endeavor to ground the doctrine of motivation almost exclusively in instincts, whereas other writers, like Kuo (12), deny the existence of instincts altogether. One purpose which I have had in mind in formulating my own views concerning motivation has been to arrive at a resolution of this uncertainty and conflict regarding instincts.

III. THE PHYSIOLOGICAL MECHANISM OF LEARNING

Fundamental Laws. Aspects of response which involve primary reflexes alone can be explained in purely physiological terms, on the basis of anatomical conduction mechanisms which have been laid down by heredity. The pressing problems of motivation have to do with those developments which depend upon the life-history of the individual in relation to his environment. In an endeavor to understand the neural mechanism of such developments, we may have recourse to three general principles, all of which can be stated in terms of neural conductance. These principles are (*a*) the law of use (26, p. 244)—with its correlative, the law of "disuse"; (*b*) Pavlov's law (20); and (*c*) the law of effect (26, p. 244).

Now, if we had to deal with an action system consisting exclusively of alternative reflexes, we might hope to find some learning effects which could be attributed to the law of use alone. The frequency of stimulation of any particular reflex mechanism would be determined by the environmental incidence of its peculiar stimuli, and such frequency might be reflected in an increase in the liability that the reflex in question would be set off. Thus, the constellation of reflex conductances in one individual might come to differ from that in another individual. However, an empirical study of the facts does not confirm the notion that such a scheme of differentiation is of much importance. Reflexes seem to be born well exercised and to gain comparatively little in facility through use.

The first important appeal, in an attempt to understand learning, must therefore be to Pavlov's law, or to *the principle of conditioning.* This principle comprises an aspect of the old law of association by contiguity, stated in physiological terms. It assumes a reflex and hereditary response connection between S and M, and states that simultaneity of a second stimulus, T, with this combination will establish an effective degree of connection between T and M. This amounts to saying that the T-M conductance is raised from substantially zero to some finite value by the given temporal contiguity. We must suppose that the anatomical channels which connect all afferent with all efferent paths are especially susceptible to conductance increases along energized neural patterns. The afferent paths for S and T are innervated by the environment, while the efferent path for M is actuated by the hereditarily established S-M relationship.

However, it will be appreciated immediately that Pavlov's principle, by itself, cannot lead to new forms of motor innervation. It can only establish new ways of setting off the innervations which are provided by heredity. Since, in nearly all animal species, behavior is modifiable on the motor, as well as on the sensory, side, we must appeal to an additional principle. This appears in the so-called "law of effect," which has been formulated and interpreted in many different ways. The law of effect characteristically involves three postulates: (a) the existence of random responses, (b) possible facilitation of such responses through the medium of their environmental effects, and (c) possible inhibition on a similar basis.

The postulate of random response assumes that the pressure of stimulus-generated afferent nerve-currents can break through the central synapses to yield non-reflex motor consequences which, unaided, would be strictly ephemeral in nature.[3] The synaptic locus of such connections must be sought for in the cerebral cortex, with its multitudinous potential connections. The variety which characterizes these random activities must be supposed to rest upon "accidental variations" that occur, from time to time, in the relative conductances of these junctions.

The principle of use can undoubtedly play a part in rendering such connections permanent, but is ordinarily inadequate to overcome the principle of fluctuation. Furthermore, the establishment of given random responses by use alone would be no guarantee of their biological utility. We must therefore introduce a mechanism by which random responses can be reinforced or suppressed, as the case may be, on the basis of their environmental effects. Observation of human and of animal behavior shows that such a mechanism is provided by certain receptoral or afferent systems, with their associated central processes. Thus, stimulation of the gustatory-olfactory receptors with good food leads to the facilitation and "stamping in" of concomitant random responses, while excitation of the so-called "pain" nerve-endings of the body has an opposite effect.

Beneception and Nociception. It is comparatively easy to divide all of the receptive systems into three classes,[4] as follows: (a) beneceptors, which are tuned to stimuli indicative of a beneficial action of the environment upon the organism or species; (b) nociceptors, aroused characteristically by stimuli that are associated with injurious conditions; and (c) neutroceptors, having neither of these characteristic connections. The principal neutroceptive systems are those of vision, audition, mechanical touch, and kinaesthesis. Nearly àll other receptor species possess definite beneceptive or nociceptive relationships. However, it must be appreciated that the functions of beneception and of nociception, respectively, are dependent not only upon the anatomical identity of the given afferent channel, but upon the intensity of stimulation and the state of adaptation of the latter. The most potent beneceptive apparatus is undoubtedly that of erotic sensibility, although those gustatory and olfactory paths which are aroused by good food form a close second. The saccharoceptive system of the mouth is of prime beneceptive importance. The afferent channels which respond to

---

[3]For a more detailed consideration of the neural mechanics of random response see (30, pp. 173-176).

[4]I have discussed the classification of receptive systems, along these lines, in (30, Chap. 12).

moderate saltiness and to warmth are beneceptive, but their functions become nociceptive at higher intensities of stimulation. The outstanding nociceptive systems, however, are those of "pain," of which there are many varieties. The afferent processes corresponding to unpleasant odors, and to bitter and sour (in all except very low intensities) are also nociceptive, as are the sensory mechanisms that are aroused by an empty stomach, a full bladder, or a distended large intestine. Low intensity erotic excitation may also be classed as nociceptive.

It should be noted that the grouping of receptive system as bene- and nociceptive is logically independent of any correlated pleasantness or unpleasantness; the classification is based entirely upon objective biological considerations. However, it is desirable to have a somewhat definite notion as to the nature of the physiological processes which accompany beneception and nociception, respectively. Observation upon the behavior of men and animals shows that forms of specific response which are concomitant with, or are closely followed by, beneceptive excitation may be facilitated at the time, and always show an increased tendency to recur later. Those which come into similar relationships with nociceptive processes suffer an opposite change. These observations can be translated at once into the statement that beneception ordinarily conditions an increase in the conductances of those cortically controlled specific responses which are relatively concurrent with it, while nociception conditions a reverse effect. Succinctly expressed, if we symbolize the degree of beneception-nociception by B (a variable having positive and negative values) and the cortical conductances under consideration by C, then:

$$\frac{dC}{dt} = kB \qquad [1]$$

where k is a constant. It follows from this formulation that the conductances increase in proportion to B when the latter is positive and that they decrease in proportion to it when it is negative.

Retroflex Action. I have proposed the term *retroflex action* (30, pp. 215-216) to describe this process by which beneceptive or nociceptive stimulation stamps in or out concurrent, or semi-concurrent, responses. It is, of course, to be understood that, in the human being, such responses are primarily cortical in their synaptic determination, and that the majority of them are initiated through the mechanism of random activity, already discussed above. However, the conditioning of reflexes, in accordance with Pavlov's principle, may also be facilitated or discouraged in a retroflex way. Indeed, it seems doubtful whether reflex conditioning is ever very effective without assistance of this kind.

Moreover, the facts in the case lead us to conclude that retroflex processes *themselves* are subject to conditioning. This means that the central mechanisms which increase or decrease the conductances may be set off by secondary and non-hereditary stimuli. Thus, e.g., the inhibitory action of "pain" can be transferred to a visual or to an auditory excitation, such transfer being referable to a primary contiguity between pain and the particular neutroceptive pattern which is involved. It is to be presumed that the retroflex sense-channels are connected with special subcortical nerve-centers which engineer the conductance changes that we are discussing. Evidence from anatomy and pathology indicates that the centers in question are located in the thalamus. Conditioned or secondary retroflex action must involve an arousal of these thalamic mechanisms by virtue of association, and through sensory channels different from those with which they are congenitally connected.

It is evident that the primary (unconditional) retroflex mechanisms must constitute one of the most important motivational systems to be found within the organism. The various forms of retroflex action in any species are hereditarily established, but can be elaborated through conditioning in many different ways, according to "experience." Retroflexes, primary, secondary, tertiary, and so on, mold the behavior system of the individual. They form the *hereditary basis of learning by experience,* without which such learning could not be guided with reference to biological needs.

The theory of retroflexes furnishes us with a basis for explaining many forms of so-called *instinctive* behavior. As we have already noted, a great deal of what passes for instinct can be classed physiologically as complicated reflex action. However, instinctive behavior is usually conceived to possess a degree of adaptive flexibility which surpasses the capabilities of any simple reflex. Instinct consists not so much in doing the right thing at the right time as in seeking experimentally for an indefinitely foreseen goal, which is nevertheless definitely accepted when found. That this aspect of unrest or of striving can be formulated satisfactorily in objective terms, has been shown by the work of Craig (4) and of Tolman (28).

It is possible to explain the process neurologically on the basis of negative, or nociceptive, retroflex action. This later process naturally operates so as to repress any concurrent form of cortically adjusted response, but since the living organism is always responding, the suppressed behavior must be replaced by something different. Consequently, there must be a ceaseless variation of response, which continues until the nociceptive stimulus is removed. As examples, we may consider the influence of hunger or of pain upon behavior. It is obvious that the form of response which accompanies the removal of the nociceptive stimulus will be inhibited, in the long run, less than other concurrent forms will be, and hence that it will eventually become dominant over them. Positive, or beneceptive retroflex action also plays a part in the development of so-called instinctive response, but, instead of leading to unrest, it reinforces the activities which initially make its excitation possible. In food-getting, the removal of hunger excitation is accompanied by beneceptive taste and smell processes, which reinforce the food-bringing responses. Erotic gratification habituates the individual in those lines of conduct which yield maximal erotic stimulation.

It should be evident that the potentialities of the retroflex scheme are adequate to enable it to account for highly diverse individual action systems, such as we find among human beings. Explanations along these lines could be developed exclusively in physiological or behavioristic terms, but it is in the interests of brevity, at this point, to introduce the psychical side of the equation, so that we can present a balanced psychophysiological account of the more advanced motivational processes.

IV. THE RÔLE OF AFFECTION IN MOTIVATION

General Psychological Principles. As we have seen in our introductory discussion, motivational questions ordinarily involve psychical or conscious factors, in addition to considerations of behavior. We have also noted that motivational problems can sometimes be stated in subjective terms alone. Clearness is attained by a separation of the physiological and the psychological concepts, but it is neither appropriate to the problem nor humanly expedient to neglect the latter.

When we consider the psychical side of the motivational equation, we find that we have to deal with a group of so-called "subjective phenomena." These constitute the facts of *direct experience,*[5] for any given individual, and fall under such captions as "sensation," "perception," "affection," and "volition." What the individual can observe or know directly about his own motivation, apart from scientific speculation, comprises a set of facts for us to study. These facts can be considered in and for themselves, by purely introspective methods or, on the other hand, they can be studied in relationship to physiological factors such as those which we have already discussed above.

Numerous attempts have been made to construct comprehensive theories of motivation in purely psychical terms. The two most interesting and successful theories of this type are the hedonistic and the psychoanalytic doctrines. These two kinds of hypotheses have much in common with each other, but are distinguished by the fact that the psychical terms of the psychoanalytic theory are largely additions to the data of direct experience, while the older hedonistic doctrines looked to experience, as given, to reveal the sources of motivation.

The philosophical status of the hedonistic doctrine is somewhat paradoxical. A considerable number of radical thinkers, such as Epicurus, Bentham, and Mackaye (15), have advocated the doctrine in universal terms and without reservation, and the majority of unsophisticated, common-sense individuals seem to be convinced practically of its truth. The ends which we seek seem to be characterized generally by their pleasantness or by relief from unpleasantness. Yet most psychologists and philosophers, both ancient and modern, have shunned the hedonistic view as if it were an infectious disease. Some modern psychologists (e.g. 19), even express scepticism or disbelief in the very existence of pleasantness and unpleasantness (affection), or assign to it a position of vanishing importance in the mental economy. After a protracted and careful study of this situation, I cannot but feel that both sides of the argument have been influenced by passion and prejudice more than by the facts or by the logical

---

[5]For a detailed discussion of what is meant by "experience," see (31, Part I).

possibilities which are involved. The facts are entirely consistent with a thoroughgoing hedonistic view, as I shall attempt to show.

First, however, we must establish certain general principles and concepts having to do with the subjective realm. I shall use the term *consciousness* to stand for a momentary cross-section of any individual experience. Such an experience consists of phenomenally given data alone, exclusive of all inferences concerning the causes of the data. The facts of psychophysiology indicate almost conclusively that the totality of any given individual experience is determined in its nature and changes by physiological variables located in a restricted portion of a corresponding cerebral cortex. The most likely position for this area is in the frontal lobes, where we may suppose the contemporary afferent nerve currents to converge into a sort of focalizing activity which releases the related efferent innervations. *Direct* psychophysical correlations or functions must therefore be established between consciousness and these cortical factors. Relations between psychical variables and afferent or efferent processes are of an *indirect* type, involving physiological intermediaries.

When we consider consciousness or experience in the light of motivational questions, we are concerned to know how the psychical system is related to action or response. We wish to learn what particular features of consciousness are involved in the determination of behavior. A comprehensive answer to this question must state that experience or consciousness in its totality has "action significance." If experience as a whole is correlated with the focal process in the cortex, then all parts of this experience must be related to the response flux which is constantly passing through the given cortical domain. There are undoubtedly many forms of response—reflexes, instincts, and the like—which can occur *independently* of such cortical factors, but there can be no portion of direct experience which is irrelevant to the response which actually does operate through the "region of determination of consciousness" in the cerebrum. Nevertheless, it may be possible to single out certain aspects of consciousness which are more significant than are others with respect to *changes* in the form of response. In the waking, or even in the sleeping, state, response is constantly present; so-called "will" or "volition" is concerned, not with the initiation of action in general, but with its change from one form to another.

Psychical Nature of Affection. Now, consciousness consists of a configuration of qualitatively different constituents. The configurations are largely spatial, but they change in time, throughout the course of the given experience. The qualitative constituents can be classified, and can even be arranged into serial systems, showing dimensions of qualitative variation. Complex experiential configurations can also be treated in a similar manner and the various dimensions of such systems give rise to the concept of an *attribute*. Some attributes are specific to restricted classes of psychical constituents (e.g., saturation, as an attribute of color), whereas other attributes may attach to total consciousnesses or experiences. Among the latter is to be counted pleasantness-unpleasantness or *affection*.

Many different views have been expressed regarding the psychological nature of affection. According to my observation, it is a universal property of consciousness in any form. It is not an "element," in the sense that it can be regarded as divorceable from the context in which it is found, but it is an irreducible attribute or dimension of the psychical system. In this status, it manifests variations in algebraic degree between the polar opposites of maximal pleasantness and maximal unpleasantness, with a zero or indifference point somewhere between them. This linear dimensionality can be treated quantitatively by means of algebraic symbolism, so that what we may call the *affective intensity* of any consciousness is represented by a. When a is equal to zero, we have the indifferent condition; when its values are negative, there is a corresponding unpleasantness; whereas positive values indicate the degree of pleasantness.

Since affective intensity, a, is regarded as an instantaneous property of any consciousness, it can be plotted as a function of time, $a = f(t)$, and this function can be integrated, in accordance with the equation,

$$A = \int a \, dt \qquad [2]$$

between any two different instants, t_0 and t_1. A may be described as the total amount of elapsed affection, and may be regarded as the technical equivalent of what is commonly called *happiness*. It is clear that the values of A may be positive, negative, or nil.

Psychological Theory of Affection. In order to develop an intelligible account of the part played by affection in motivation, we must first establish a psychophysical theory of affection. Many different hypotheses have been advanced to deal with the relationship in question, but I have found that one of the following form is the most successful in handling the facts (29). Let c stand for the average conductance value of the cortical synapses which are operative at the instant, t, in the "region of determination of consciousness" which we have considered above. Then, we hypothecate that

$$a_t = k \frac{dc}{dt}. \qquad [3]$$

This equation implies that the affective intensity is algebraically proportional to the rate of change of the cortical conductances in question, being positive when and in proportion as the latter are increasing and being negative when and in proportion as they are decreasing. If there is no change in the conductance at the given instant, the affection will be indifferent.

By a process of simple integration, we can determine a relationship between A, for any interval t_0 to t_1 and the cortical conductance at the end of the interval in question. From equations [2] and [3],

$$A = \int a \, dt$$
$$= k \int \frac{dc}{dt} \, dt$$
$$= k \int dc$$
$$= kc + k_0 \qquad [4]$$

where k_0 is the "constant of integration." In other words, the total integrated amount of affection in the given time interval is proportional to the "net change" (algebraically expressed, as in the usual stock-market terminology) in conductance during the same interval.

It should be clear at once that this hypothesis regarding the psychophysiology of affection establishes a paramount significance for the latter in the theory of motivation, for the determination of response specificity. Conductance values, such as c, are symbols for the probability that the corresponding concatenation between afferent and efferent patterns will be operative under appropriate stimulus conditions. In so far as the pattern of response is regulated via the focal region in the cortex, which is directly related to consciousness, the affective history will determine the form of response which becomes dominant.

V. Conditions and Consequences of Affective Experience

Peripheral Conditions for Affection. It is clear that if the hypothesis which we have developed above is a complete representation of the cortical conditions for affective experience, we can derive its more peripheral conditions by ascertaining the relations between peripheral factors and changes in the cortical conductances. The more important of these relationships have already been indicated in our discussion of the laws of use, conditioning, and of effect. By combining the various postulates which we have already laid down, we can reach the following conclusions: (*a*) Other things equal, the upbuilding of specific responses, through use, should be accompanied by pleasantness, and their lapse, through disuse, by unpleasantness. (*b*) Repetition of any given form of response will yield diminishing returns of pleasantness, as the cortical conductances approach an asymptotic limit. (*c*) Stimulation of beneceptors will result in pleasantness, and of nociceptors, in unpleasantness. (*d*) Conditioned retroflex action will be accompanied by positive or negative affection, according to the identity of the conditioned processes. (*e*) Conflicts or interferences between competing response tendencies will be unpleasantly represented in consciousness, whereas alliances will have pleasant concomitants.

The above conclusions provide us with a general basis for explaining nearly all types of affective experience in terms of their afferent conditions. Conclusions (*a*) and (*b*) apply particularly to the pleasures of novelty and to the displeasures of monotony. Conclusion (*c*) accounts for nearly all purely sensory pleasures and displeasures. Conclusion (*d*) covers affections of the associative type, including those attached to "sentiments" and "complexes." Conclusion (*e*) deals with the affective accompaniments of the complex interactions between primary, secondary, and more advanced response developments.

Action Consequences of Affection. Of even greater interest for our present theme, however, are conclusions which emphasize efferent rather than afferent factors. It is clear that, while affective intensity, a, merely indicates the *direction* in which response tendencies are being altered at a given instant, integrated affection, A, summarizes the actual changes which have been established during a given time interval. We must not forget, of course, that this significance of A is confined to those types of response which have had conscious representation during the interval in question. Alterations in the properties of subcortical pathways, or in cortical pathways which lie outside of the synergic focus which determines consciousness, will not be directly represented. However, we have reason to believe that, in the human being, such sub-focal alterations are of minor importance. In so far as we are dealing with "voluntary" behavior, we evidently have to do with responses operating through the cortical focus. Thinking along these lines, we can see that the types of behavior which bring pleasure will be "stamped in," while those which bring unpleasantness will be "stamped out," in proportion to the integrated affections which attach respectively to them, throughout their histories.

It should be noted how this doctrine embodies the teachings of more primitive hedonistic theories, and at the same time accommodates itself to the actual difficulties which these theories have encountered. Earlier hedonisms have laid emphasis either upon anticipated (future) or present happiness, as the determinant of action; the present theory puts the whole burden of determination upon past affection. The instantaneous present affectivity is merely an index of an effect which is being integrated in time. The choice of alternatives cannot be predicted accurately, on the basis of anticipated or presently experienced affectivity, although these factors will establish significant probabilities. The direction of anticipation is controlled by past experience, while the latter is the record of a continuous succession of one-time "nows." But, in many special cases, the affective integral throughout the past may be entirely opposed to present and to anticipated events. The environment situation is all-important in determining the actual state of affairs in any given instance. Hence, quite frequently, a man's past pleasures may induce him to make actually unpleasant and prospectively unfruitful decisions, in the present; without violation of a hedonistic doctrine of the type which we are here advocating. This kind of explanation applies as well to Joan of Arc as to Edgar Allan Poe. It should be noted, moreover, that a "hedonism of the past," such as ours, places the motivational determinants where they causally belong. Effects should be temporarily subsequent to their conditions, and "final causes" have no proper place in a scientific theory, although we can explain them as final effects in terms of our hypotheses.

VI. DEVELOPMENTS AND APPLICATIONS OF THE THEORY

General Considerations. The concepts and principles which have been established above provide us with a means for dealing effectively with the majority of contemporary teachings regarding motivation. Fortunately, most of these propositions fit into or become corollaries of the doctrine which we are advocating, rather than inviting rejection as contradictory to it. The teachings in question have to do mainly with (a) the part played by reflexes in behavior, (b) the processes of learning, (c) the nature and operation of instincts, (d) the nature and operation of sentiments and complexes, (e) the nature of emotion and its relation to instincts and complexes, and (f) the structure of human personality.

Our discussion, thus far, indicates a rather sharp division between responses occurring through a focal region in the cerebral cortex and other types of response which are largely subcortical in their determination. In the human being the latter are mainly of a reflex character, and do not involve learning.[6] However, it should not be inferred that the higher and lower types of response ordinarily go on without interaction. The fact is that, from a biological point of view, the cortical and subcortical responses usually form a well-integrated system.

A partial basis for such integration may be found in the fact that a single afferent process can simultaneously evoke reflex and cortical activities. Thus, cold may produce "goose flesh" accompanied by elaborate protective reactions; certain odors excite salivation simultaneously with voluntary movements directed towards food-getting. As a rule, the reflex and the cortically controlled responses are mutually helpful, although this is not always the case. A further aspect of such alliance between higher and lower processes appears in the fact that each retroflex mechanism has an associated set of reflex expressions. Thus, pain excitations bring about innervation of the sympathetic nervous system, at the same time that they inhibit concurrent cortical responses. Furthermore, when conditioned retroflexes are established, the corresponding conditioned reflexes are also likely to be formed. This means that, at a later time, the conditioning stimulus will set off the appropriate reflex reactions while facilitating or inhibiting the cortical activities, as the case may be. For example, erotic fixation' upon a particular person of the opposite sex may cause the later perception of this person to arouse sexual reflexes while at the same time facilitating concurrent cortical conduction.

Considerations of this sort lead us to pictures of response activity which seem adequate to explain most of the so-called phenomena of "instinct." These phenomena involve a complicated integration of reflex processes with cortically mediated and reflexly governed behavior. More or less appropriate reflexes are set off through subcortical channels, while cortical adjustments contribute the more elaborate responses which are required for success in the given situation. Although the reflex factors are essentially unmodifiable, the total mechanism possesses a high degree of flexibility; the reflexes and retroflexes can be conditioned and reconditioned, while the corresponding cortical adjustments can be molded under the dictates of the retroflex processes, ad libitum. Such changes constitute learning in accordance with the laws of Pavlov and of effect.

Instincts and Emotions. The majority of psychologists have treated emotion as an essentially subjective phenomenon and have endeavored to identify its physiological correlates. James (8, pp. 442-485) considered that the substance of an emotion consists of the organic sensations which follow

---

[6] In certain lower animals, such as the rat, there is undoubtedly less differentiation in kind between cortically and (say) thalamically controlled responses (14).

from reflex, instinctive, or other impulsive action. Lange (13) looked for the physiological basis of the emotional experience in vasomotor changes, while McDougall (16, p. 324) has established a very significant correlation between lists of emotions and of instincts. This same general plan of attack can be pursued consistently with the views which are expressed in the present article, if we associate particular emotions with specific types of retroflex process. Thus, fear is evidently closely related to pain processes, while love is correlated with reproductive retroflexes.

Now, a detailed study of bene- and nociceptive channels, together with the retroflex activities which we have assumed to be associated with them, shows that there are a sufficient number of such channels to account for the major species of emotion. However, it is a fact of common experience that emotions exist in almost infinite variety, and such variations must be accounted for in terms of different kinds and patterns of retroflex conditioning. The majority of writers on emotion have endeavored to identify some characteristic simple content of the emotional *consciousness*. It has seemed to me, however, to be preferable to treat the emotions as complicated *experiences* (30, Chap. 19). An emotion, in other words, cannot be characterized satisfactorily in terms of any instantaneous psychical structure, but must be regarded as following a typical course in time. It starts with sensation or perception, develops impulse, feeling, and kinaesthesis, and ends in satisfaction or disappointment. Various temporal phases of such emotional sequences can be distinguished rather clearly, and are sometimes regarded as being complete emotions. Such is the case, for example, with joy, despair, and sorrow. We can hardly hope that a scientific definition of emotion will correspond in all instances to popular usage.

Although emotions, regarded as psychical phenomena, are intrinsically complicated, their physiological conditions may be capable of simple formulation. Thus, it has seemed to me satisfactory to say that *emotions are concurrent with retroflex excitations for which the organism is not adequately prepared.* This means that emotions accompany initial, or relatively initial, processes by which useful reactions are learned under the influence of bene- or nociceptive stimulation, or of corresponding *conditioned* retroflex excitations. When the appropriate responses have been established, there will still be pleasantness and unpleasantness, but the intricate emotional experience will have given way to simpler and more direct action experiences. In the case of nociceptive excitations, successful learning will tend to protect the organism against further similar stimuli. In the case of beneceptive processes, there will be immediate recourse to adjustments which conserve these processes and bring them to a maximum. It is evident that such an interpretation demands that emotional experiences should be strongly affective and, also, that they should be characteristically kinaesthetic.

Cannon (3, Chap. 19) has recently advocated the view that the essential physiological condition of emotional experience consists in participation by thalamic processes, rather than by general or specific proprioceptive activities, as implied by James. Perhaps I may be pardoned for pointing out that this aspect of the emotional process is definitely incorporated in a detailed treatment of the subject which I had previously given (30, esp. Section 119). The evidence upon which I based my opinions in this connection appears to be essentially the same as that cited by Cannon, and it is noteworthy that we have arrived independently at the same conclusions.

Unfortunately, the scope of the present article will not permit us to discuss the properties of specific emotions, but I have dealt with some of these elsewhere.

Complexes and Sentiments. In early childhood, primarily stimulation of the retroflex mechanisms through beneceptive or nociceptive channels furnishes the principal basis of learning by experience. In adult life, however, the molding of behavior is largely under the control of *conditioned* retroflex processes. Each established conditioning of a retroflex comprises a control mechanism for further learning, as well as the psychophysiological basis of a specific affective sensibility. It is therefore evident that particular retroflex conditionings correspond closely with what the psychoanalysts call "complexes," or with what McDougall and Shand (23) call "sentiments." Sentiments and complexes are ordinarily conceived in psychical terms, and are frequently assumed to reside in a hypothetical subconscious realm. However, they are always characterized by a semi-permanent association between an originally neutral stimulus pattern and an affective or emotional process. Thus the philatelist has a stamp-possession complex or sentiment, while another man may experience extreme displeasure in society. Neither of them was born in this condition, but their particular interests or aversions are constantly regulating their behavior and leading to the formation of new subsidiary habits.

The retroflex explanation of sentiments and complexes differs from that of most of the psychoanalysts in that it provides *a wide variety of affective foundations.* We are not restricted to eroticism or to the ego, but can base our explanations upon any primary beneceptive or nociceptive mechanism. In order to differentiate between a sentiment and a complex, I have suggested (30, pp. 370-371) that the former term be limited to associative groupings which involve only one unitary retroflex system; complexes may then be defined as *complex sentiments,* or conditioned retroflex assemblies embracing more than one fundamental affective process. Many such complex constellations are to be found in the constitution of human personality. Undoubtedly the most important of them is the so-called *ego complex,* which may involve all of the retroflex mechanisms in one integrated system.

Purpose and Desire. The concept of purpose would appear to be a very important one in the theory of motivation, but it has been a stumbling-block for most philosophical and psychological thinkers. The doctrine of retroflexes, like psychoanalytic doctrines in general, provides a very ready way of dealing with purposes. From the purely introspective angle, any purpose can be identified with an image which represents the desideratum or "end" of a given line of action. The desiderative aspect of the accompanying experience may be identified with its *affective trend,* and the latter is closely correlated with the fortunes of the purpose which is involved. If the purpose is being fulfilled or realized perceptually, the affective intensity progresses from algebraically lower to algebraically higher values. However, if the fortunes of the purpose are opposite to this, the affective progression takes the opposite direction.

These subjective phenomena can be explained psychophysically, if we suppose that purposes are correlated with specific retroflexes. Typically, the latter will be conditioned rather than primary, since the concept of purpose ordinarily implies a definite configuration and not a simple sensory quality. Primary retroflexes may be regarded as underlying relatively undifferentiated *desires,* which give rise to more and more complicated purposes through "experience." It should be clear that our general theory makes retroflexes, of any kind, regulators of action and molders of character; and purposes stand in a similar relationship to the facts on the psychical side of the equation. Purposes are not "ends," but beginnings.

The Structures of Action Personalities. It should be evident that the theory above outlined allows for the development of a wide variety of response systems, the natures of which will be determined by the stimulus environment of the given individuals. Since no two organisms will have the same stimulus environment, the action systems which are developed under the guidance of identical retroflex mechanisms must be different. However, although the general retroflex endowment of all individuals of the same species is presumably the same, quantitative variations are to be expected. Some individuals are more "strongly sexed" than are others, meaning that their erotic retroflexes are more powerful, and such variations must have an important bearing upon the systems of response which they develop. On the other hand, it is to be supposed that individuals of the same species, when placed in a generally similar environment, will be led to generally similar forms of response; and these forms will cluster about the more important retroflex schemes, such as those of alimentation, reproduction, and self-protection. Generic systems of behavior, thus determined, take on the aspect of instincts, because (*a*) they have evident biological functions, (*b*) they are comparatively constant throughout a given species, and (*c*) they are closely bound up with particular reflexes or groups of reflexes. As a matter of fact, however, if our theory is correct, they are largely products of *learning.* A radically different environment would produce unrecognizably different results.

The limits of the present article will not permit a study of the various typical complexes and affective-action systems which characterize contemporary human beings. I have dealt elsewhere (30, Chaps. 22 and 23) with what I consider to be the essential features of the "ego complex" and of the erotic sentiments which seem to be the dominant factors in human personality. The mechanisms of sexual motivation are relatively simple in comparison with those of the ego. As we have noted, the latter appears to incorporate all of the retroflex-affective units in a complicated mosaic, comprising what the individual has learned concerning the types of response which are necessary for his own preservation. Although the ego complex is frequently in conflict with erotic tendencies, it nevertheless incorporates sexual factors. Many other minor and subsidiary complexes can also be adequately treated in terms of the retroflex theory.

It should be pointed out that this theory not only leads us to expect the formation of a comparatively rigid set of habits in the individual, but also a constant remodelling of these habits to meet changing environmental conditions. Retroflexes, either primary or conditioned, are always operating to steer the organism along lines of conduct which are biologically useful. It should be noted, furthermore, that the concept of response intrinsically involves a specific stimulus in all cases, so that the mere ingraining of a habit does not necessarily guarantee its repetition. The appropriate stimulus must first be given. Hence elaborate and profound systems of response may lapse entirely when the environmental situation is radically altered.

VII. CONCLUSION

It is a corollary of the complete psychophysical theory of motivation which I have advocated in the present article that all action tendencies which are established through the medium of integrated cortical conduction should be functions of corresponding affective histories. The strength of any such action tendency will, in fact, be proportional to the time integral of the affective intensities which have been correlated with the given form of response during the total life-history of the individual. It follows that the choice of alternative lines of conduct in the face of a given stimulus will be determined by *the greatest past affection,* which is proportional (according to our hypothesis) to the greatest present conductance. The doctrine, as a whole, is therefore *hedonistic* in character, but comprises a "hedonism of the past" rather than of the present or the future. It is also evident, of course, that in so far as responses are reflex, hereditarily established, or via channels which are not directly correlated with consciousness, this affective correlation cannot hold.

However, we may imagine that the subcortical levels of nervous adjustment carry with them their own *subconscious* psychical systems, with respect to which the affective laws may still hold. It should be obvious that only a minute portion of the total structure of the cerebral cortex can be represented in consciousness at any instant. Hence, the greater part of what has been learned in the past must be sub-focal and subconscious. Yet this comparatively inactive part of the action system will not of necessity be entirely without bearing upon the conduction choices of the moment. Such considerations evidently pave the way for a physiological explanation of many Freudian concepts and phenomena.

As a final comment, I should like to re-emphasize a point very frequently made but seldom effectively pursued, that the psychological theory of motivation provides a basis for developing a theory of *correct conduct.*

If we can ascertain the general basis of all actual human behavior, we shall most certainly be faced by the principles which must guide us in properly planning such behavior in advance. In my more elaborate discussion of motivational problems (30, Chap. 28)—to which I have already referred the reader with undue frequency—I have outlined a "substitute for ethics" which I hope may eventually bring forth some comment from thinkers in the field of morals.

REFERENCES

1. ADLER, A. A study of organ inferiority and its psychical compensation. (Trans. by S. E. Jelliffe.) New York: Nerv. & Ment. Dis. Publ. Co., 1917. Pp. x+86.

2. ADRIAN, E. D. The basis of sensation. New York: Norton, 1928. Pp. 122.

3. CANNON, W. B. Bodily changes in pain, hunger, fear and rage. (2nd ed.) New York: Appleton, 1929. Pp. xvi+404.

4. CRAIG, W. Appetites and aversions as constituents of instincts. Biol. Bull., 1918, **34**, 91-119.

5. FREUD, S. A general introduction to psychoanalysis. (Trans. by G. S. Hall.) New York: Boni & Liveright, 1920. Pp. x+406.

6. FULTON, J. F. Muscular contraction and the reflex control of movement. Baltimore: Williams & Wilkins, 1926.

7. HOLT, E. B. The Freudian wish and its place in ethics. New York: Holt, 1915. Pp. vii+212.

8. JAMES, W. The principles of psychology. Vol. II. New York: Holt, 1910. Pp. vi+704.

9. JUNG, C. G. Collected papers on analytical psychology. (Trans. by C. E. Long.) London: Baillière, Tindall & Cox, 1916. Pp. 410.

10. ————. Psychology of the unconscious. (Trans. by B. M. Hinkle.) New York: Moffat, Yard, 1916. Pp. iv+566.

11. ————. Psychological types. (Trans. by H. G. Baynes.) New York: Harcourt, Brace, 1926. Pp. xxii+654.

12. KUO, Z. Y. Giving up instincts in psychology. J. Phil., 1921, **18**, 645-666.

13. LANGE, C. Ueber Gemüthsbewegungen. (Trans. by H. Kurella.) Leipzig, 1887.

14. LASHLEY, K. S. Brain mechanisms and intelligence Chicago: Univ. Chicago Press, 1929. Pp. xiv+186+11 plates.

15. MACKAYE, J. The economy of happiness. Boston: Little, Brown, 1906. Pp. 533.

16. McDOUGALL, W. Outline of psychology. New York: Scribner's, 1923. Pp. xvi+456.

17. ————. An introduction to social psychology. (20th ed.) London: Methuen, 1926.

18. ————. Outline of abnormal psychology. New York: Scribner's, 1926. Pp. xiii+566.

19 NAFE, J. P. An experimental study of the affective qualities. Amer. J. Psychol., 1924, **35**, 507-544.

20. PAVLOV, I. P. Lectures on conditioned reflexes. (Trans. by W. H. Gantt.) New York: International Publishers, 1928. Pp. 414.

21. PFISTER, O. The psychoanalytic method. (Trans. by C. R. Payne.) New York: Moffat, Yard, 1917. Pp. 588.

22. ROBACK, A. A. Behaviorism and psychology. Cambridge, Mass.: Sci-Art, 1923. Pp. 284.

23. SHAND, A. F. The foundations of character. London: Macmillan, 1914. Pp. xxxi+532.

24. SHERRINGTON, C. S. The integrative action of the nervous system. New York: Scribner's, 1911. Pp. 411.

25. STARLING, E. H. Principles of human physiology. (4th ed.) London: Churchill, 1926. Pp. 1088.

26. THORNDIKE, E. L. Animal intelligence: experimental studies. New York: Macmillan, 1911. Pp. viii+297.

27. TILNEY, F., & RILEY, H. A. The form and functions of the central nervous system. (2nd ed.) New York: Hoeber, 1923. Pp. 1020.

28. TOLMAN, E. C. The nature of instinct. *Psychol. Bull.*, 1923, 20, 200-216.

29. TROLAND, L. T. A system for explaining affective phenomena. *J. Abn. Psychol.*, 1920, 14, 376-387.

30. ————. The fundamentals of human motivation. New York: Van Nostrand, 1928. Pp. xiv+521.

31. ————. The principles of psychophysiology. Vol. I. New York: Van Nostrand, 1929. Pp. xx+430.

32. WOODWORTH, R. S. Dynamic psychology. New York: Columbia Univ. Press, 1918. Pp. 210.

NAME INDEX

SUBJECT INDEX

CLASSICS IN PSYCHOLOGY

AN ARNO PRESS COLLECTION

Angell, James Rowland. **Psychology: On Introductory Study of the Structure and Function of Human Consciousness.** 4th edition. 1908

Bain, Alexander. **Mental Science.** 1868

Baldwin, James Mark. **Social and Ethical Interpretations in Mental Development.** 2nd edition. 1899

Bechterev, Vladimir Michailovitch. **General Principles of Human Reflexology.** [1932]

Binet, Alfred and Th[éodore] Simon. **The Development of Intelligence in Children.** 1916

Bogardus, Emory S. **Fundamentals of Social Psychology.** 1924

Buytendijk, F. J. J. **The Mind of the Dog.** 1936

Ebbinghaus, Hermann. **Psychology: An Elementary Text-Book.** 1908

Goddard, Henry Herbert. **The Kallikak Family.** 1931

Hobhouse, L[eonard] T. **Mind in Evolution.** 1915

Holt, Edwin B. **The Concept of Consciousness.** 1914

Külpe, Oswald. **Outlines of Psychology.** 1895

Ladd-Franklin, Christine. **Colour and Colour Theories.** 1929

Lectures Delivered at the 20th Anniversary Celebration of Clark University. (Reprinted from *The American Journal of Psychology*, Vol. 21, Nos. 2 and 3). 1910

Lipps, Theodor. **Psychological Studies.** 2nd edition. 1926

Loeb, Jacques. **Comparative Physiology of the Brain and Comparative Psychology.** 1900

Lotze, Hermann. **Outlines of Psychology.** [1885]

McDougall, William. **The Group Mind.** 2nd edition. 1920

Meier, Norman C., editor. **Studies in the Psychology of Art: Volume III.** 1939

Morgan, C. Lloyd. **Habit and Instinct.** 1896

Münsterberg, Hugo. **Psychology and Industrial Efficiency.** 1913

Murchison, Carl, editor. **Psychologies of 1930.** 1930

Piéron, Henri. **Thought and the Brain.** 1927

Pillsbury, W[alter] B[owers]. **Attention.** 1908

[Poffenberger, A. T., editor]. **James McKeen Cattell: Man of Science.** 1947

Preyer, W[illiam] **The Mind of the Child: Parts I and II.** 1890/1889

The Psychology of Skill: Three Studies. 1973

Reymert, Martin L., editor. **Feelings and Emotions: The Wittenberg Symposium.** 1928

Ribot, Th[éodule Armand]. **Essay on the Creative Imagination.** 1906

Roback, A[braham] A[aron]. **The Psychology of Character.** 1927

I. M. Sechenov: Biographical Sketch and Essays. (Reprinted from *Selected Works* by I. Sechenov). 1935

Sherrington, Charles. **The Integrative Action of the Nervous System.** 2nd edition. 1947

Spearman, C[harles]. **The Nature of 'Intelligence' and the Principles of Cognition.** 1923

Thorndike, Edward L. **Education: A First Book.** 1912

Thorndike, Edward L., E. O. Bregman, M. V. Cobb, et al. **The Measurement of Intelligence.** [1927]

Titchener, Edward Bradford. **Lectures on the Elementary Psychology of Feeling and Attention.** 1908

Titchener, Edward Bradford. **Lectures on the Experimental Psychology of the Thought-Processes.** 1909

Washburn, Margaret Floy. **Movement and Mental Imagery.** 1916

Whipple, Guy Montrose. **Manual of Mental and Physical Tests: Parts I and II.** 2nd edition. 1914/1915

Woodworth, Robert Sessions. **Dynamic Psychology.** 1918

Wundt, Wilhelm. **An Introduction to Psychology.** 1912

Yerkes, Robert M. **The Dancing Mouse** and **The Mind of a Gorilla.** 1907/1926

CLASSICS IN PSYCHOLOGY

CLASSICS IN PSYCHOLOGY

Advisory Editors
HOWARD GARDNER
AND
JUDITH KRIEGER GARDNER

Editorial Board
Wayne Dennis
Paul A. Kolers
Sheldon H. White

A NOTE ABOUT THE AUTHOR

CARL MURCHISON was born in Hickory, North Carolina, in 1887. After attending Wake Forest College, he received a Ph. D. in psychology from Johns Hopkins University. In 1923 he succeeded G. Stanley Hall as Professor of Psychology and Director of the Department of Psychology at Clark University. He remained there until 1936, at which point he left Clark to found the Journal Press, which he directed until his death in 1961.

Murchison was primarily an editor. He assembled several widely-used handbooks and directed the important project which assembled autobiographies of major psychologists. A representative example of Murchison's editorial sagacity, and an important summary of the state of psychology at its mid-century mark, is the collection *Psychologies of 1930*.